YALE UNIVERSITY PUBLICATIONS
IN ANTHROPOLOGY

NUMBER 40

CULTURE AND ETHOS OF KASKA SOCIETY

JOHN J. HONIGMANN

NEW HAVEN

PUBLISHED FOR THE

DEPARTMENT OF ANTHROPOLOGY, YALE UNIVERSITY

BY THE

YALE UNIVERSITY PRESS

London: Geoffrey Cumberlege, Oxford University Press

1949

WENDELL C. BENNETT

Editor

PRINTED IN THE UNITED STATES OF AMERICA

PREFACE

IN the summer of 1943 I had my first experience with Northern Athapaskan Indians at Fort Nelson, British Columbia.[1] At that time it had already been pointed out to me by Professor Cornelius Osgood that certain marked personality features distinguished Athapaskan people which might make it difficult to approach them in interpersonal relations. This observation was corroborated by my own field work. After my return in the fall of 1943, my discussions and reading developed a strong interest in the problem of ethos. At that time the concept denoted little more to me than the notion of the "spirit" of a people. Analysis of the principal works dealing with this and related approaches revealed no clearly formulated methodology for studying the phenomenon, and I became interested in filling this gap. It also seemed that the Northern Athapaskan area would be a suitable place for the study of ethos since in that region communities were small enough to permit extensive participation without too far sacrificing the value of intensive research. Furthermore, the people were manifestly characterized by a distinctive "spirit." It was also hoped that the development of a clearly defined methodology would be useful for studies of national character, which, in connection with the war, were then assuming considerable prominence.

During the summer of 1944 some time was spared from an historical reconstruction of aboriginal Kaska culture to make observations of the emotional behavior of a few informants and to record some of their emotional attitudes. Little was done with this material, although several important emotional trends in the society's behavior were apparent. The experience convinced me that I still lacked the primary requisite for making any satisfactory headway in the study of ethos. I needed a more precise method which would guide the interpretation of data. During the winter of 1944–1945 I was able to work out a method and, through the cooperation of Professor Osgood and the Department of Anthropology at Yale University, test its utility in a study of some aspects of Chinese ethos as reflected in two individuals. The experience convinced me that, with minor changes, the method would serve as an instrument for the exploration of the emotional aspects of motivation and behavior in the field. With this accumulated knowledge, I returned to Lower Post, British Columbia, Canada, on June 9, 1945 to study both the contemporary culture and the ethos of Kaska society. Somewhat over two months were spent in Lower Post, observing and participating in native activities and collecting personality materials. In the middle of August my family and I left the trading post with members of the Upper Liard River tribe, who were returning to their winter settlements. Following two weeks of camping with these people at a point in Yukon Territory where the Alaska Highway crosses the Liard River, twentythree miles northwest of Lower Post, we began a leisurely trip upriver, stopping briefly at each family's winter settlement. The next three months were spent in one of the largest family settlements. In December, following the freezeup of the river and the arrival of suitable conditions for overland travel, we walked back to Lower Post, again visiting winter settlements, renewing acquaintances, and catching up with local news. Christmas was spent

---

[1] Honigmann, *Ethnography and Acculturation of the Fort Nelson Slave* (1946).

3

in Lower Post, and on December 26th we boarded the bus for the railhead at Dawson Creek. Analysis of the material was begun toward the end of my stay in the field and completed in New Haven. A description of Kaska culture and ethos, containing a large part of the material in the present monograph, was submitted in 1946 to the Graduate School of Yale University in partial fulfillment of the requirements for the degree of Doctor of Philosophy. The preparation of this final report was generously aided by a University Fellowship.

Acknowledgment is made to the Department of Anthropology and to the Peabody Museum of Yale University for funds enabling me to carry out two seasons of field work among the Kaska Indians. To the faculty of the Department of Anthropology I am indebted for unceasing stimulation, criticism, and encouragement. I must particularly mention the intellectual inspiration received from Professor Cornelius Osgood during my graduate years at Yale, and the help provided by Professor Clellan S. Ford in formulating a description of the analytical method which I followed in this study of Kaska culture and ethos. Professors George P. Murdock, Wendell C. Bennett, and Irving Rouse also read portions of the manuscript and made important suggestions. To my colleagues, the students in the department, I wish to express appreciation for their patience and interest in listening to the many expositions of the successive stages of this research project. I am also deeply obliged to my wife who, despite natural misgivings, ventured to try the northern winter and, by her presence and cooperation, greatly facilitated my work. Her interest, aid, and penetrating criticism were particularly valuable during the analysis and description of the data. David and Karen also contributed, their company in the field serving to throw light on many aspects of native child and adult behavior. A number of people, by their friendship and hospitality, promoted our comfort in the North. Among these I must refer to the resident Catholic missionaries, members of the Oblates of the Immaculate Conception, Father Pierre A. Poullet, who generously placed his home at our disposal when we returned to Watson Lake Airport in December, and Father Bernard Arsenault. I can also not forget to mention Hans Anderson, Clarence Millspaugh, and Bill Strong, traders; and the trappers, Leo Cormier, Fred Herbert, Knute Hillgren, Nick Prosnick, Llewellyn Phillips, Ben Malanson, and others, who, by their many kindnesses, facilitated and enlivened our stay in Lower Post.

Finally there are my friends among the Upper Liard Indians. Without their generosity in providing us with shelter, guidance, meat, fish, and, when our food stores ran low, lending us "grub," I would not have been able to finish this work adequately. Since I was taken completely into the confidence of some of these people, and because the data contain highly personal and intimate material, it is necessary to preserve the anonymity of the members of this group. Therefore fictitious names have been employed for all my informants.

New Haven, 1946.   JOHN J. HONIGMANN

CONTENTS

ILLUSTRATIONS

PLATES

TEXT FIGURES

TABLES

INTRODUCTION

THE introductory material consists of four parts. First the concept of ethos is treated from the historical as well as definitive points of view. Attention is given to the methodological aspects of those studies in the field of "culture and personality" which immediately influenced the writer's thinking particularly since his initial field work.[1] Following a definition of ethos, a theory is briefly presented on the manner in which the ethological characteristics of a society become established in the early socialization of children. A statement of methodology follows which points out the conditions which must be known in order to repeat the field work and analysis upon which the descriptions of Kaska culture and ethos are based or to duplicate the work in another society. In other words, the "conditions of the experiment" are presented with some of the thoroughness that has recently been solicited from anthropologists.[2] The introduction concludes with an alphabetical "directory" of the principal informants arranged with cross-references to parents and other relatives whenever possible and other useful information.

PREVIOUS STUDIES OF ETHOS

Over centuries men have noted differences in the emotional aspects of behavior manifested in different societies. From the time of the Greeks travelers have reported their impressionistic pictures of the emotional character of the behavior which they have encountered in groups they visited.[3] It is to be expected that when the task of studying preliterate societies became one of the principal tasks of the anthropologist he should have been aware of the earlier attempts to characterize emotionally the behavior of exotic peoples. The reports of early field workers are frequently marked by paragraphs referring to the "temperament" or the "moral and intellectual characteristics" of the societies which were under observation. Other ethnographers sought to rectify travelers' prejudiced views of preliterate societies as, on the one hand, idealized havens of human welfare and, on the other, barbarous survivals of an original state of savagery. Beyond these steps, however, anthropologists were slow to proceed in the qualitative characterization of the emotional aspects of the phenomena which they were studying.

An explanation can be ventured for the apparent unwillingness of anthropologists to follow travelers in the emotional characterization of social life. The field worker, no matter how keenly he might appreciate the unique qualities of the behavior which he encountered, was impressed by scientific values that demanded great reliability and rigor in his reporting. As a scientist the anthropologist realized that generalized and impressionistic characterization had to be replaced by more systematic and verifiable methods of observation and interpretation.

[1] Honigmann, *Ethnography and Acculturation of the Fort Nelson Slave* (1946).

[2] Kluckhohn, *The Personal Document in Anthropological Science* (1945), 152.

[3] The unscientific study of national character, as we have recently been reminded, is very old indeed and has perennially been injected with fresh vigor by partisan interest. See Hertz, *Nationality in History and Politics* (1944); Huxley and Haddon, *We Europeans* (1935), 61–67.

9

The inductive approach. The scientific tradition of the early part of the twentieth century was strongly inductive in its methods.[4] It is against this inductive emphasis in early social science that we find one of the earliest definitions of the characteristic emotional quality of the behavior of a given social group. For Sumner the ethos was "the totality of characteristic traits by which a group is individualized and differentiated from others."[5] He also pointed out that the folklore, riddles, poetry, drama, and literary fiction of a society were useful to discover an ethos because they revealed facts about the mores as well as the longings of a people.[6] He indicated the learned nature of ethos by warning that "Modern scholars have made the mistake of attributing to *race* much which belongs to the ethos, with a resulting controversy as to the relative importance of nature and nurture."[7] In briefly applying his concept to cultural materials, Sumner characterized the ethos of the Chinese as "industrial and materialistic" in contrast to that of the Japanese, which he saw as "militant."

Sumner's definition of ethos as the totality of a group's characteristic traits continues to have an influence with sociologists and anthropologists. It is, for example, found in the conception of ethos as "*Die Gesamtheit der menschlichen Einstellungen, Willens- und Bildungsrichtungen.*"[8] It influenced Young's view of ethos as "societal character" derived from "Those patterns of culture of a particular society which most distinguishes it from other societies,"[9] and is found in Gorer's definition: "The sum of the varied behaviors, ideas, and aims of a social group."[10]

The configuration approach. Other students of social life, in their search for an approach to the study of the emotional aspects distinguishing the behavior of different societies, proceeded from a relatively more deductive point of view, which appeared as the century progressed. Notably Sapir and Benedict followed the leads of German historical philosophers like Dilthey and Spengler, who had already approached conceptualizations of similar phenomena in their *Weltanschauung* and *Zeitgeist* studies.[11] As early as 1918 Spengler had sought to synthesize the spirits of two periods of western civlization in single terms which would refer to the souls from which the behavior characterizing those societies originated.[12]

In 1924 Sapir wrote: "We may perhaps come nearest the mark by saying that the culture

---

[4] In regard to the application of psychological techniques to the study of societies, inductive values were related to the lack of a satisfactory deductive theory for guiding observation and interpretation. Such theories could, in turn, develop only after sufficient data had been accumulated. The beginnings in France of a deductive point of view in psychological studies of society may be discerned in the questionnaire devised by Van Loon and Thurnwald. (See Van Loon and Thurnwald, *Un questionnaire psycho-physio-morphologique pour l'étude de la psychologie des races* [1930].) That serious interest in such studies never developed in France is perhaps due to the traditional French emphasis on induction.

[5] Sumner, *Folkways* (1906), 70.

[6] Sumner, *Folkways* (1906), 561.

[7] Sumner, *Folkways* (1906), 74.

[8] *Die Wandlung des Ethos* (1925), 4.

[9] Young, *An Introductory Sociology* (1934), 26.

[10] Gorer, *Society as Viewed by the Anthropologist* (1940), 25.

[11] Spengler, *Decline of the West* (1926), 74.

[12] It is interesting to note that the inductive tradition dominating social science in the early part of the twentieth century led Sumner to reject attempts to describe the "soul of the people" as duplicating for groups "processes which are now abandoned for individuals." Sumner, *Folkways* (1906), 74.

conception which we are now trying to grasp aims to embrace in a single term those general attitudes, views of life, and specific manifestations of civilization that give a particular people its distinctive place in the world. Emphasis is put not so much on what is done and believed by a people as on how what is done and believed acts on the whole life of that people, what significance it has for them. The very same element of civilization may be a vital strand in the culture of one people, a well nigh negligible factor in the culture of another."[13] Sapir called this conception, "spirit" or "genius."

Ruth Benedict credits Dilthey and Spengler with recognizing "the importance of integration and configuration" in cultures or civilizations.[14] Her statement that "Cultures . . . are more than the sum of their traits" marks the growth of an integrative approach to ethos. She develops the view that "A culture, like an individual, is a more or less consistent pattern of thought and action. Within each culture there come into being characteristic purposes not necessarily shared by other types of society." Cultures are unique "configurations" of forces that condition "the thoughts and emotions of the individuals who participate in those cultures."[15] Boas' words: "Dr. Benedict calls the genius of culture its configuration,"[16] clearly relates her approach to the work of other anthropologists and sociologists.

Kluckhohn has developed Benedict's point of view in speaking of a plurality of "cultural configurations" or "implicit or suppressed premises that tend to be characteristic of a certain group." In some cases, he believes, these premises may be combined in "a single dominant master configuration . . . 'the integrating principle of the culture' or . . . 'the ethos of the society.' "[17] This more particularized notion is shared by M. E. Opler in speaking of a "theme" of a culture as "a postulate or position declared or implied, and usually controlling behavior or stimulating activity which is tacitly approved or openly promoted in a society."[18]

A significant feature of Kluckhohn's and Opler's definitions is their departure from conceiving of the emotional aspects of behavior as lying in a single overall term or "monistic urge."[19] In focusing on specific configurations, "premises," or "postulates," these writers suggest an important contribution to a methodology aiming toward greater precision in the interpretation of ethos. It will be noted, however, that Sapir and Benedict have directed attention from behavior to the underlying ideas on which behavior may be assumed to rest or from which it emanates. Methodologically this turning to a psychological explanation for the characteristic emotional aspects of the behavior of a social group is quite significant.

The psychological approach. One shortcoming in the work produced by those anthropologists whom we have classified with the *Weltanschauung* philosophers is the lack of specific methods which can be used to duplicate the operations by which the final statement of ethos, genius, or configuration was obtained. One solution to the need for principles that would better guide deduction and analysis was suggested by the developing science of

[13] Sapir, *Culture, Genuine and Spurious* (1925), 168.

[14] Benedict, *Patterns of Culture* (1934), 47.

[15] Benedict, *Patterns of Culture* (1934), 42–50.

[16] In Benedict, *Patterns of Culture* (1934), xvii.

[17] Kluckhohn, *Covert Culture and Administrative Problems* (1943), 218.

[18] Opler, M. E. *Themes as Dynamic Forces in Culture* (1945), 198.

[19] Kroeber has referred to Spengler's "monistic urge to conceive every major culture as a harmonious whole, expressing one set of attitudes at every point and without remainder." Kroeber, *Configurations of Culture Growth* (1944), 832.

personality psychology. One of the keynotes of this psychology was an interest in attitudes and values as key forces in determining social behavior. Margaret Mead applied the principles of this branch of science to the study of social behavior. Her reference to the values which "a culture . . . embodies . . . in its structure, in its politics and religious systems, in its art and literature" and by which "each new generation is shaped firmly and definitely to [these] dominant trends,"[20] may be considered an attempt to understand the emotional aspects of behavior by inferring the society's dominant attitudes or goals.

In 1939 Bateson also approached the problem of ethos with the tools of personality psychology. "Ethos," he says, "is the system of emotional attitudes which govern what value a community shall set upon the various satisfactions or dissatisfactions which the contexts of life may offer."[21] In another place he speaks of the ethos as expressed in a "tone of appropriate behavior" or in "a definite set of sentiments towards the rest of the world, a definite attitude toward reality."[22] It is apparent that for Bateson the ethos is primarily a covert phenomenon which can be derived by means of an analysis of verbalized attitudes and other behavior.

Bateson's conception of ethos contains additional suggestions for deriving ethos through systematic observation plus controlled inference. It is not yet completely satisfactory, as Bateson himself points out, because it lacks a scientific vocabulary by which the ethos can be explicitly defined. "The best we can do," he says, "is to sketch an ethos or a personality in a diffuse journalistic or artistic style and then sum up that sketch in a few words whose significance is fixed by that sketch."[23] The study of ethos, therefore, was still somewhat in the stage of travelers' impressions.

According to Bateson and Mead, in their earlier work with ethos "no precise scientific vocabulary was available, the ordinary English words were used, with all their weight of culturally limited connotations, in an attempt to describe the way in which the emotional life of these various South Sea peoples was organized in culturally standardized forms. This method . . . transgressed the canons of precise and operational scientific exposition proper to science; it was far too dependent upon idiosyncratic factors of style and literary skill; it was difficult to duplicate and it was difficult to evaluate."[24]

To overcome these shortcomings the authors attempted the photographic method "of stating the intangible relationships among different types of culturally standardized behavior by placing side by side mutually relevant behaviors" even though these were spatially and contextually separated. The pictures were selected for "the same emotional thread" running through them.[25] They represented a variety of social situations in which "the Balinese character is revealed."

Although this method of photographic analysis presents obvious advantages, it is not sufficient without some literary description. Bateson and Mead's work is methodologically significant mainly as an attempt to demonstrate by relatively objective reporting the

[20] Mead, *Sex and Temperament* (1939), vi.

[21] Bateson, *Naven* (1936), 220.

[22] Bateson, *Naven* (1936), 119.

[23] Bateson, *Naven* (1936), 268.

[24] Bateson and Mead, *Balinese Character* (1942), xi.

[25] Bateson and Mead, *Balinese Character* (1942), xii.

emotional aspects of behavior (i.e., behavior from which emotion can be inferred). Unlike Bateson's earlier point of view, that ethos "is the system of emotional attitudes," and therefore covert, *Balinese Character* suggests that ethos is the expression of a socially conditioned character structure in social behavior.

The influence of psychoanalysis. During the last two decades psychoanalysis has exerted a constantly increasing influence in psychiatric, psychological, and anthropological theory. One of the products of this cross-fertilization has been the revival of studies in character structure applied to both contemporary nations and to exotic groups. The influence of psychoanalysis is most marked in the studies of basic personality undertaken by Kardiner, Linton, and DuBois. Both the character structure and the basic personality approaches are interested in relatively similar phenomena and both are related to the study of ethos. This has been demonstrated with reference to character studies in the work of Bateson and Mead but the studies of Erikson and Fromm should also be mentioned.[26] Kardiner's definition of "basic personality type" as "that personality configuration which is shared by the bulk of the society's members as a result of the early experiences which they have in common" and which "may be reflected in many different forms of behavior and may enter into many different total personality configurations"[27] bears an operational resemblance to Bateson's definition of ethos as "the system of emotional attitudes which govern what value a community shall set upon the various satisfactions and dissatisfactions which life may offer."

Linton has pointed to the value of the basic personality concept for anthropologists in stating that the term "suggests a type of integration, within a culture, based upon the common experiences of a society's members and the personality characteristics which these experiences might be expected to engender . . . . By employing the concept of a societal personality structure it becomes possible to place the focal point of culture integration in the denominator of the personalities of the individuals who participate in a culture."[28] Linton also points out that not every culture may reveal an "*idée fixe*" on which Benedict's configurational analysis depends. "The outstanding contribution which the *basic personality structure* approach makes to integrational studies is that it provides a logical place for cultures which are not" so dominated.[29]

Definition. The present paper has been especially influenced by the method developed by Kardiner and Linton as well as the work of Bateson and Mead. It tries to meet the lack of an adequate operational approach to ethos by offering an explicit statement of methodology and utilizing some of the concepts of psychoanalytic psychiatry and those branches of psychology which have been influenced by psychoanalysis.[30]

Our survey has indicated that definitions of ethos have varied according to the interests

[26] Erikson, *Observations on Sioux Education* (1939); Erikson, *Observations on the Yurok: Childhood and World Image* (1943); Fromm, *Escape from Freedom* (1941).

[27] Kardiner, *The Psychological Frontiers of Society* (1945), vi.

[28] In Kardiner, *The Individual and His Society* (1939), viii–ix.

[29] In Kardiner, *The Individual and His Society* (1939), ix.

[30] LaBarre's recent study seen when the major portion of the present paper was completed has also utilized psychiatric concepts in describing Japanese character structure. His definitions of ethos as "temperament" or "psychological nationality" are close to Bateson's and Mead's conception of this phenomenon. LaBarre, *Some Observations on Character Structure in the Orient. The Japanese* (1945), 321. See also Leighton's treatment of the concept of sentiments. Leighton, *The Governing of Men* (1945), 384.

of the workers in this field. In some cases ethos has been implicitly or explicitly regarded as primarily a covert phenomenon underlying the emotional aspects of social behavior, while in other cases the ethos was taken to mean principally the emotional quality of behavior itself.[31] For present purposes it will be assumed that the understanding of an ethos requires cognizance of both the emotional aspects of behavior and of the motivational sources from which those aspects arise. Ethos will be defined as the socially patterned dominant motivations of personality and their expression in motivated behavior and the material results of, or material aids to, such behavior. The dominant motivations constitute a dynamically interrelated system of meanings, goals, or values by which the individual views himself and the external world.[32] This configuration corresponds to Sapir's "world of meanings."[33]

PATTERNING OF DOMINANT MOTIVATIONS

We have referred to the dominant motivations as socially patterned, by which we mean that they are learned or inculcated through the behavior of other members of the society of which the individual is a member. It is now proposed to examine briefly the manner in which this learning is accomplished.

Patterning is secured through socialization. Every individual must be raised in a society and most of his attitudes, ideas, and behaviors are influenced by the expectations of that group. In the socialization process each individual interprets and reacts to those expectations in a characteristic fashion, but respond to them he must. As Mead has pointed out, this process leaves no room for the development of complete social deviants. She has questioned the implication that the deviant behaves "in a personal or individual manner as if he were in some way distinct from the culture" and has emphasized that all individuals are, to some extent, conditioned by the social group in which they were born.[34]

Anthropological interest in socialization is dual. First there is an interest in the principles governing the acquisition of those forms of behavior which the individual superimposes on inherent capacities like hunger and aggression and which guide the manner in which those potentialities will be expressed.[35] The second is an interest in the principles governing the acquisition of the dominant motivations.[36] The approach rests on the assumption that in the early years of life it is not so much *what* is learned as *how* learning takes place that is important in patterning the world and self-views. Furthermore it is assumed that formal

[31] For brief definitions of these various notions of ethos and related concepts see Appendix B.

[32] The concepts of world view and self-view offered here partly overlap with the syndromes which Maslow has referred to as the security and self-esteem systems and also reflect the thinking of Adler. See Maslow, *A Theory of Human Motivation* (1946); Maslow, *Dynamics of Personality Organization* (1943); Maslow and Mittelmann, *Principles of Abnormal Psychology* (1941), 131–153; and Adler, *Understanding Human Nature* (1927).

[33] Sapir, *Cultural Anthropology and Psychiatry* (1932), 236.

[34] Mead, *Cultural Approach to Personality* (1943), 95–96. See also Mead, *Educative Effects of Social Environments* (1942), 51–53.

[35] See for example Miller and Dollard, *Social Learning and Imitation* (1941); Whiting, *Becoming a Kwoma* (1941); Ford, *Society, Culture and the Human Organism* (1939); Ford, *A Comparative Study of Human Reproduction* (1945).

[36] This approach to socialization is represented in such works as Kardiner, *The Individual and His Society* (1939); Kardiner, *The Psychological Frontiers of Society* (1945), and Mead, *And Keep Your Powder Dry* (1942).

learning techniques, whether based on reward and punishment or imitation, have an effect beyond the acquisition of socially approved behavior. This effect can be summed up as the influence of social pressures imposed by parents and parent surrogates on the malleable personality of the young child. For example, as these pressures enhance the view of the self and lead to feelings of friendliness in a congenial environment, or as they undermine the feelings of adequacy and lead to expectations of failure in, or hostility from, the world, these social influences pattern the basic motivational system.

Kardiner suggests that "there is a limit to the sort of culture content which can be transmitted by direct learning process."[37] Murdock adds to this that "whereas behaviorists look primarily to the inherited mechanisms of learning for the interpretation of behavior, Freudians look to the conditions of learning, and in particular to the structure of the family relationships under which the earliest human learning occurs in all societies."[38]

A generally held thesis is that the socially prescribed methods for responding to the early capacities and needs of the child vary considerably in different societies. For example, the time at which these responses come in relation to the development of the child's abilities, the intensity with which the responses make their impact, the relative gratification and frustration which they engender, and the characteristic behaviors with which the child replies to these responses, all vary between different social groups. Observations of such differences may be correlated to differences in the basic personalities which influence adult behavior, leading to the conclusion that in each society the process of socialization may pattern a distinctive system of world and self-views.

The dynamics of patterning. In the broadest terms the dominant motivations may be understood as originating from the interaction of certain inherent predispositions of the organism with the expectations of the social group into which the human being is born. At the earliest level of socialization, in the first few weeks of life, the infant literally fails to distinguish between himself and the environment. These early days, however, see the beginning of the structuring of the world and self-views. Early gratifications which remove the inherent dislike of hunger and cold are apprehended as pleasurable, while non-gratification in these areas is unpleasant. Such pleasurable emotional experiences as hunger satiation, warmth, and comfort are the earliest forms of what later comes to be more clearly perceived as a feeling of adequacy, mastery, or security. Conversely non-gratification of such tensions becomes the forerunner of feelings of failure, anxiety, and insecurity. There can be little question but that these and other early experiences play a fundamental role in determining the dominant ideas with which the individual will continue to respond to the world and to himself.[39]

As the organism grows and differentiation of tensions and satisfactions begins to develop, the child comes to distinguish specific emotional meanings for these states as well as for the persons who become associated with them. Where originally the tensions and satis-

[37] Kardiner, *The Concept of Basic Personality Structure as an Operational Tool in the Social Sciences* (1945), 109.
[38] Murdock, *The Common Denominator of Cultures* (1945), 141.
[39] See Ribble, *The Rights of Infants* (1943); Maslow and Mittelmann, *Principles of Abnormal Psychology* (1941), pp. 268–269.

TABLE I. SOME EARLY EXPERIENCES IMPORTANT IN PATTERNING
EMOTIONAL ASPECTS OF PERSONALITY[40]

Experience	Emotional Significance
Feeding (including sucking, nursing, regularity of feeding, nutritional aspects of food)	Earliest sense of security and adequacy is derived from the satisfaction of the alimentary needs; persistent non-gratification interferes with the development of a sense of mastery, leading to pessimistic attitudes toward the world and the devaluation of the self. Unconscious equivalences with feeding may be set up which result in exaggerating the importance of oral and alimentary regions.
Weaning (abrupt, early, delayed, etc.)	Abrupt and early weaning may be traumatic; delayed weaning may become associated with emotional passivity. Unconscious equivalences with the mother as a frustrating object may appear in connection with abrupt or early weaning.
Sphincter training and attitudes toward sphincter processes	Severe sphincter training may influence the development of compulsive and rigid attitudes toward many life situations. Unconscious equivalences may become associated with buttocks, anus, or feces.
Attitudes toward autoerotic gratification	Early sexual restrictions have a large function in determining the sexual attitudes of later life; childhood masturbation also may aid in the development of feeling of mastery.
Attitudes toward aggression	Aggression in children is a result of frustration consequent to the child's imperfect ability to master situations rationally. Its encouragement may develop reliance on crude forms of control; its suppression may become associated with submissiveness and passivity (probably because such suppression is usually strongest in societies emphasizing the authority of parents toward children).
Induction of affectivity (including contact and handling, rejection, over-protection, quarreling between parents, parental dishonesty, and parental insecurity)	The induction of affectivity through affectional stimulation by adults is important in determining the child's later ability to love other objects as well as the self. An absence of early warm human relations may lead to emotional isolation, affect hunger, emotional rigidity, etc.
Relations with authority (including domination by parents and others, over-severe discipline, apportioning of praise and appreciation)	The independence and spontaneity of the child is developed in a social setting demanding rational attitudes toward authority; a too authoritarian setting may lead to submissiveness, frustration, hostility, rebelliousness, and self-devaluation. Strong parental authority may assist in developing a tyrannical superego.
Character of early disciplines (including chronic frustration, humiliation, cruelty, as well as the severity of the ideals demanded)	Disciplines which demean and humiliate the child or demand over-severe ideals lower the feeling of self-worth and influence the development of superego attitudes; inconsistent disciplines may cause anxiety and insecurity. Forms of discipline may arouse unconscious equivalences involving the role of the buttocks, the role of women as sadistic, etc.

[40] No attempt has been made to cite the literature from which this table has been compiled because it largely represents the synthesis of a great amount of reading. I am indebted to Professor A. H. Maslow for suggesting several points to include.

TABLE 1—(*Continued*)

Character of the learning process	A learning process in which direction is wholly in command of parents may destroy ability for initiative and develop passivity and dependence; certain types of learning are probably correlated with the later attitudes toward authority.
Early responsibility	The inculcation of a sense of responsibility in childhood probably helps to maintain a responsible character in later life. Absence of demands for responsibility may lead to dependence and a lower evaluation of the self.
Relations with siblings (including favoritism and sibling rivalry)	Among the earliest interpersonal relations, relations with siblings pattern expectations and attitudes in later social relations.
Relations with parents	All of the early experiences involve relations with parents. Such relations pattern future interpersonal relations.

factions which brought the child into interaction with the social environment were few, the growing capacities of the child now open the way for many more gratifications and frustrations at the hands of its socializers. All of these experiences add their marks to the initial conceptions of the world and the self.

Extensive psychiatric observation in western society (and, in recent years, in a few non-European groups) has made clear the importance of the early years of childhood for the development of dominant motivational trends and leads us to be able to point to certain categories of childhood experience as of greatest importance in patterning a basic world of meanings.[41] The most important of these experiences are arranged in Table 1 with a brief statement of their assumed significance for the organization of basic personality. The absence of any large body of adequately validated universal data regarding the manner in which any one experience becomes correlated with specific aspects of motivation makes any *a priori* interpretation of its influence impossible. The present paper may itself be regarded as a further attempt to secure such validation. There is therefore no intent to imply types of experiences to which personality types in every society can be directly correlated. Rather we would emphatically maintain that the effect of any one of these experiences is always influenced by the *totality* of early life experiences to which the child is exposed. Obviously submission to authority would not have the same dynamics in a group which also patterns a deeply loving relationship of parents to children as submission would have in a society that tends to reject children. The items in Table 1, then, are merely a few universal childhood experiences which, when taken together, are, from what we know, probably among the most significant of those determining the patterning of personality.

Some evidence is available for assuming that the system of dominant motivations derived from the gratifications and frustrations of these early experiences does not readily

[41] See especially DuBois, *The People of Alor* (1944); Kardiner, *The Psychological Frontiers of Society* (1945); Bateson and Mead, *Balinese Character* (1945); Erikson, *Observations of Sioux Education* (1939); Ritchie, *African as Suckling and Child* (1945), and Hallowell, *Aggression in Saulteaux Society* (1940).

disappear or change, but rather persists.[42] That is, the personality configuration created in this fashion tends to maintain itself and to resist casual efforts of reeducation.

All early experiences are closely related to the relationship of the child to his parents, parental surrogates, or parental extensions.[43] We will refer to the child's earliest meaningful interpersonal relationship with parents or parental surrogates as the *oedipal situation*. Often we find societies in which the father is singled out as the disciplinarian. Toward him the child, especially the boy, must be compliant and reserved. As a result of these socially patterned expectations, considerable fear is manifested toward that parent, and this attitude is often accompanied by a disproportionate affect invested in the mother. This is the classical oedipal pattern of western society.[44] From such a complex are derived conscious and unconscious expectations that will later be extended to many other social relationships and will also be expressed in the relationship of the individual to the supernatural. These expectations tend to persist through life. Where security in childhood lies in placating a strong and harsh parent in order to keep in his good graces, security in later life may tend to be sought in submission and passivity in human relations. Aggression or assertiveness becomes revolt in this pattern. The world view in such instances may, for example, regard men in dominant positions as threatening and potentially dangerous, while the self-view will motivate reserve, hesitancy, and timidity.

METHOD

The method followed in investigating Kaska culture and ethos may be considered under three aspects: first, the author's preparation for field work; second, the techniques adopted for the collection of data, and, finally, the procedure followed in the analysis of the data.

Preparation. At the time when work was undertaken in 1945 the author had already spent three months in the field working with Kaska Indians. He was, therefore, familiar with the people whom he now proposed to study more intimately. A didactic psychoanalysis lasting several months had succeeded in clarifying much of psychoanalytic theory and practice. Training as well as wide reading in the fields of psychology and psychiatry gave further background for handling personal data. Several months spent as a research assistant, obtaining and analyzing life histories of alcoholics in urban American society, furnished important practical experience in interviewing and making judgments of adjustment in a semi-psychiatric situation.

Field techniques. The ethnographer presented himself as a friend of the Indians. He was always sympathetic to any complaints addressed to him, whether these were directed

---

[42] Maslow, *Dynamics of Personality Organization* (1943), 532–534; Nadel, *Review of Naven* (1938); Nadel, *The Typological Approach to Culture* (1936–1937), 278–279.

[43] The term parent extensions is used to designate relatives, such as the mother's brother, the mother's sister, grandparents, and others who, in some societies, may be in frequent interaction with the child and so effect the diffusion of some of the affect which, in western culture, is typically bound up in the parent-child relationship. See Mead, *The Family and the Future* (1942); Malinowski, *Sex and Repression in Savage Society* (1927).

[44] It also appears to be the pattern in Chinese society. See Dai, *Divided Loyalty in War* (1944); Yang, *A Chinese Village* (1945), 128–130.

against the government, white men, or other Indians with whom the ethnographer was also friendly. Above all the ethnographer (as well as his wife) sought to adopt a permissive attitude toward the people. Censoriousness was definitely shunned and it was only after a high degree of familiarity and confidence had been attained that any attempt was made to enforce elementary hygiene by stopping indiscriminate spitting in the tent or floorless cabin. At about the same time some attitude had to be taken with reference to the problem of alcohol. In one or two episodes alcohol released so much aggression and nuisance in two men (aggression which tended to manifest itself toward the ethnographer), that drinking began to pose a serious problem. The ethnographer, therefore, informed his host that as far as he, the ethnographer, was concerned he would not join any more drinking parties that fall or winter. The host, Old Man, was somewhat chagrined and regretful for what had occurred but no further brewing was done for several weeks. It may be pointed out that this episode, except for instituting a brief period of strain, did not seriously impair rapport where this relationship had previously been established with individuals.

All field work was conducted in English and no interpreters were employed. The author, together with his wife and family of two children, ages two and four, lived first in Lower Post, the summer residence of the Kaska Indians, and then traveled with one group to its winter trapping area. Three months were spent in a winter settlement containing four Indian families.

Field procedure, as much as possible, followed the method of participant-observation. During the summer the author and his wife attended Indian dances and participated in many other cultural activities, including two potlatches, several gambling games, and a meat packing trip. In addition Indian camps were frequently visited and people were made welcome whenever they chose to visit the home of the ethnographer, which was located close to the hub of the trading post. In the winter, visiting was greatly increased because of the fact that all life was centered in a small settlement where interpersonal contacts were frequent. During this latter period the writer accompanied Indians hunting, fishing, and traveling. He also assisted them in a number of other cultural undertakings, like house building, toboggan construction, and trapping. Participant-observation obviously involved making notes of all ethnographically significant details which came to the writer's attention. Where observation presented problems, questions were noted and their answers sought by means of direct questioning.

Behavior manifested in the social interaction between the ethnographer, or the members of his family, and Indians was also carefully observed. Upon analysis these relationships proved to be revealing in instances of both positive and negative transferences noted in informants. An effort was also made to remain conscious of transferences established on the part of the ethnographer. To guard against bias these had to be taken into account when analyzing data derived from the objects of such relationships.

A "personality data sheet" (hereafter referred to as P-data sheet) was kept for those individuals with whom the ethnographer came into close and frequent interaction. The sheets consisted simply of dated verbatim or abstracted transcripts of remarks and conversations expressing attitudes, wishes, and complaints. Folktales brought out in casual conversation were also entered as well as certain behaviors which, at the time they were observed, seemed of small value as ethnographic data. A specimen portion of a P-data sheet is shown below.

P-DATA SHEET—OLD MAN

9:27:45 (Old Man's Place). Discussing River Joe's loneliness this first winter of his widowhood and his plans for finding a new wife, Old Man said: "He calls himself Taku Injun. Why don't he go to his own people to get wife?"

9:29:45. "I got nobody to cry to when I'm small kid. I try to make toboggan myself, small one. I burn it lots of times. I put it too close to fire. When I'm little kid I'm shy. I got no really mother. I got nobody make me anything."

According to Old Man, Harry Lang advised Hans to stay with Old Man a couple of years. "'If you do that,' he tell him, 'you're gonna have everything, little thing.'" Traveling around at Frances Lake, Hans had nothing. Trapping in a different country every winter, he would leave his traps in one place and then be without them in the next season. Now he is beginning to accumulate goods, said Old Man. "I don't think that man talk to his wife. I just hear his wife talking."

Old Man said maybe Peter Tom was not going to return to Louis Maza's place for the winter because Maza was too "mean" to Peter. Old Man pointed out that Peter got all the meat, ran Louis' trap line, and cut the wood. Louis only visited the line in November.

"First I keep my old lady we had trouble always. She want to wear sweaters at night too." His wife told Old Man that he could quit her if he didn't like her ways. He told her she should learn. "'Don't cook straight meat; what we gonna do with this grub? No use keep it all winter.' Sometimes she start to cry. Now this time she's all right."

9:29:45 (Evening). "I dream Irene Wiley grow more small. She go down a high hill. She start to pack water for my old woman down a high hill. Summer trail down there. My wife standing there. I left my gun there too. I go down too. Irene go down hill; she get smaller. Big kettle she packing around. She go down in the mud. Sqš, sqš you hear. Gee, I laugh. 'Irene,' I say, 'you grow small.' She say, 'Uncle, you wait. Airplane fly around. That's why I so scared I grow small.' I pack water up again. I don't want her to pack. She too small. I lost my pack. Lots of meat on top of the hill. That's why I figger I go to mountain. Lots of bunch. We come back quick. I don't know Mrs. Harry [Lang]. She feel bad. I don't think they move."

[What does it mean, Irene growing small?] "I figger maybe when she go down to Liard maybe she got sick."

The dream came to Old Man's mind after he had been talking about Irene Wiley going to Lower Post with a white man. Old man said that while Irene was with him last winter she set traps but did not visit them again.

A daily journal was also kept in order to record the temporal sequence of events for future study as well as note their immediate impression on the ethnographer.

To increase the amount of verbalization by informants, with the aim of securing information about a wider range of behavior, a series of one hour interviews were conducted with a limited number of subjects willing to cooperate. Nine such subjects were secured but many of these could not be prevailed upon to continue the procedure after two or three hours. With one person interviews were conducted throughout the summer and early fall for a total of over fourteen accumulated hours. During the first interviews the person was invited to tell the story of his or her life. It was quickly evident that most of the Indians did not have the historical sense necessary to give a chronological record of this type. As interviews continued and some subjects became more accustomed to talking in the ethnographer's presence, a number of "expressive interviews,"[45] were devised. These followed both active and passive techniques. In the passive interviews an attempt was made to duplicate as much as possible the psychoanalytic situation in which a subject is invited to speak freely whatever comes to his mind. In most cases where active participation of the ethnographer occurred in such interviews, the latter's question or direction was noted so that this influence could later be evaluated in analyzing the flow of communication. It was observed that strong or persistent questioning tended to produce confusion and arouse discomfort in many people. This made active interviewing extremely difficult. On the other hand if subjects were left alone with the invitation for spontaneous communication, they often said nothing. All of these behavioral reactions were regarded as important data for subsequent analysis. Another form of behavior was noted in two or three people. They manifested a rapid flow of more or less chronological detail which contained little in the way of personal attitudes or reactions to life experiences. This was a difficulty that could not be overcome. Each interview opened with a request for dreams. If any dreams were submitted, an attempt was made to secure associations. Only once or twice were dreams interpreted to subjects. Interviews were paid for at the conclusion of each hour and were, for the most part, recorded verbatim but in "long hand." They were always conducted in privacy, some in the ethnographer's home during the absence of his family, others on a log in the brush some distance from camp. Most interviews with men, however, were conducted in a small camp which the ethnographer had erected in a secluded area in Lower Post.

Finally, the Rorschach technique was used to secure verbal responses and additional behavioral data. Like interviews, Rorschach protocols were attached to the P-data sheets which, in some cases, soon expanded into files.

During the time that informants were being interviewed, tested, or engaged in conversation, they were freely treated to cigarettes or cigarette tobacco. In a few cases interviews were followed by lunch or supper at the ethnographer's home.

Analysis. Up to this point discussion of method has been largely limited to the preparation for field work and the techniques followed in the observation and recording of behavior (including verbalization in the word "behavior"). When the collection of data was completed, two types of material could be distinguished, ethnographic data, which had been classified into categories specified in the *Outline of Cultural Materials,*[46] and personality data, consisting of interviews, Rorschach records, and the P-data sheets.

Analysis was first employed to construct a cultural background for the study of Kaska ethos. This was done primarily with the ethnographic data, although in some instances attitudes and experiences recorded on the P-data sheets were also utilized when these added knowledge that had not otherwise been observed or reported. The construction of the cultural background may be schematically described as follows:[47]

[45] Kluckhohn, *The Personal Document in Anthropological Science* (1945), 106–109.

[46] Murdock, *et al., Outline of Cultural Materials* (1945).

[47] Nothing in the following outlines should be taken to deny that observation is not always compounded of some degree of inference or that perception is not always largely selective.

PROCEDURE	EXAMPLE
1. Observation of behavior, material products of behavior, and material aids to behavior. (The important assumption underlying observation was that most of the behavior observed by the anthropologist is socially patterned.)	The manufacture of a toboggan by Hans Donnelly.
2. The psychological results of behavior inferred from (1). (By psychological results of behavior is meant the knowledge, attitudes, and values which are acquired from the individual's "interaction with his environment and consequent learning."[48])	Satisfaction with a job getting done tempered with frustration at being forced to work with poor materials and inadequate tools. Increasing awareness that native manufactures rarely approximate commercially derived products in quality. Increasing regard for commercial as over against native manufactures.
3. Attitudes and ideas inferred from (1) and (2), or communicated through verbal behavior, which consciously or unconsciously underlie the behavior in (1)	Ideas specifying the appropriate materials, their treatment and assembly, necessary in order to complete a useful toboggan. The desire to build a toboggan which would enable Hans to transport food, shelter, and clothing to the trap line in winter and on which to bring back fur. A useful toboggan seemed to be far more important than a fully finished vehicle and no ideas of perfectionism were inferred from either behavior or object.
4. Classification of (1), (2), and (3) according to the categories of the *Outline of Cultural Materials.* (Historical and acculturation data were conventionally excluded from the cultural background and reserved for inclusion elsewhere in the monograph.)	Most of the data could be classified under "travel and transportation—land transportation." The ideas regarding native products versus commercial products were classified under "Acculturation."

It will be understood that part of this process of inference occurred almost simultaneously with, or shortly after, the act of observation. Inference, however, may continue to occur at any time after observation as, for example, when observed and inferred data are reexamined in the light of subsequent observed behavior or additional experience (e.g., reading) on the part of the ethnographer.

The next step, after the process of analysis was felt to be sufficiently completed, was to describe the observed and inferred data. In the description of Kaska culture the *Outline of Cultural Materials,* according to which the data had been provisionally classified, was departed from in several respects. At this point a reexamination of the data was undertaken to discover whether the observed behaviors served primarily adaptive or adjustive goals—

[48] Linton, *The Cultural Background of Personality* (1945), 33.

that is, whether they were directed toward maintaining life in, or processing resources of, the physical environment (technical culture) or whether they were oriented toward securing the adjustment of individuals in the social environment (social culture).[49] When this had been done a third division, ideational culture, was devised to contain primarily *reported* ideas and attitudes directed toward the supernatural, natural, and social environments. Besides serving adaptive and socially adjustive goals, these ideas may also be regarded as assisting in securing the adjustment of the individual to himself. Each of the first two major divisions of Kaska culture was then reanalyzed to determine how well they were fulfilling their adaptive and adjustive functions. The evaluation of personal adjustment was largely reserved for consideration in connection with Kaska ethos. The results of the reanalysis were written up in sections labeled "Conclusions" which were appended to the three main divisions.

The second aim of analysis was to formulate a picture of Kaska ethos. Schematically this may be represented as follows:

PROCEDURE   EXAMPLE

Situation A

1. Observation of behavior (and, in some cases, the material products of behavior).
(The underlying assumption, that most behavior observed by the anthropologist is learned, has already been stated.)

Men delay their return to the trap line.

2. The emotional aspects of behavior (and, in some instances, of the material products of behavior) inferred from (1).
(By the emotional aspects of behavior is meant those features of behavior from which motivation can be derived deductively. Similarly, working with material products, attention is directed toward the features from which motives can be inferred.)[50]

Delay and procrastination.

3. The emotional aspects of the psychological results of behavior inferred from (1) and (2).

A reduction of the anxiety aroused by the task of being faced with going to the trap line.
Anxiety engendered as the result of delaying an important task and thereby imperiling subsistence.[51]
Delaying the return to the trap line results in a

---

[49] The notion of presenting behavior from its adaptive and adjustive aspects is derived from Kluckhohn and Stagner. See, Kluckhohn, *Navaho Witchcraft* (1944), 46; Stagner, *Psychology of Personality* (1937), 6–8.

[50] Interesting comments on the role of intuition in the inference of emotion will be found in Hebb, *Emotion in Man and Animals: An Anlaysis of the Intuitive Processes of Recognition* (1946).

[51] This inference is important as an index of the relative weakness of the defense chosen to relieve the anxiety engendered by the task to be done.

sense of being relieved from an arduous and unpleasant necessity whose uncertain rewards and required effort engender a sense of anxiety and doubt.

Situation B

1. Observation of behavior.

People fail to keep their promises to cooperate in making a parka.

2. The emotional aspects of behavior inferred from (1).

Temporizing, vaccilation, procrastination.

3. The emotional aspects of the psychological results of behavior inferred from (1) and (2)

A reduction of the anxiety aroused by the task of making a parka in accordance with a promise. Anxiety engendered as the result of risking friendship by refusing cooperation.
Failure to keep a promise results in a sense of being relieved of an unpleasant duty.
People would rather promise cooperation and then fail to keep the promise than refuse co-operation straightforwardly.

Situation n

4. The dominant motivations inferred from the emotional aspects of n situations.
(The dominant motivations correspond, as already been pointed out, to a socially conditioned world of meanings. These meanings determine the conscious and unconscious emotional significance of the internal and external situations which the individual encounters. Such significance, it is assumed, is expressed in motivated behavior or in the products of behavior called forth in that situation.)

Flexibility, operating to define situations that threaten the resources of the ego.
Deference, operating to define situations that threaten to imperil human relations.

5. Classification of n situations under the dominant motivations by which they are defined.

Procrastination is an aspect of flexibility.
The reluctance to make outright refusals and the tendency to promise without fulfilling the promise are aspects of deference.

The inferential process presented above, especially as it yields dominant motivations, involves many psychiatric and psychological assumptions. Although some of the inferences may be hard to follow by those not too familiar with work in psychiatry and psychoanalysis, one does not, it seems, have to agree with Kardiner that, "In each instance the derivation of basic personality was an exercise in psychopathology, and as the matter now stands no one without an expert knowledge of psychodynamics can make any contribution to the technique."[52]

Following the completion of the analysis, the next step was to describe the dominant

---

[52] Kardiner, *The Psychological Frontiers of Society* (1945), xvii.

motivations of the Kaska Indians and to illustrate their operation with selected and inferred data.

The process by which the ethos was analyzed will now be considered in greater detail. Circumstances permitted an opportunity to develop the major outlines of this theory in the field, leaving sufficient time to verify many conclusions in subsequent and directed observation and interrogation. Insights into the ethos were first derived by what may be described as empathy into, or psychological penetration of, the attitudes and values of the group. Such an empathic relationship may, of course, be deliberate as well as unconscious. Several times the writer sought purposefully to put himself in the place of the people in order better to gauge the basis of their emotions.[53] At other times he felt himself becoming blunted in the analysis of emotional nuances of behavior because he had unconsciously developed too great a readiness to accept the cultural milieu. Here empathy was unconsciously achieved. Such unconscious identification was regarded as dangerous because it resulted in failure to analyze certain emotional expressions as different from those found in our own society. Recognition of this fact quickly led to conscious readjustment. It cannot be denied that deliberate conscious empathy into an exotic group is an important mechanism for providing a foundation on which to predict behavior.[54]

One of the first steps in analysis was to verify the fact that the Kaska nation as a whole possessed a reasonable degree of homogeneity. This was accomplished in the field by establishing that the behaviors and products of members of different Kaska tribes were similar, and by an inspection of the Rorschach protocols collected.[55] With this homogeneity established, it seemed likely that further analysis based on the observation of a few tribes could be applied to the Kaska as a whole. This does not deny that the picture of the ethos presented is merely one which was derived from the people studied. Further investigation of additional subjects may lead to some modifications in the final theory.

Two principal steps may be distinguished in the analytical process: first, the inference of socially patterned dominant motivations from ethnographic data and, second, the inference of this system from the personality data, including interviews, Rorschach records, dreams, folk-tales, and the casual bits of conversation and items of behavior noted on the P-data sheets. Both of these steps are combined in the schematic outline presented above.

In the first step, the analysis of the ethnographic data, a series of behaviors and a few material products of behavior were inspected in order to infer recurrent forms of emotional (i.e., motivated) expression, that were assumed to be related to the world of meanings.[56]

[53] Psychological penetration of individuals is an established part of psychiatry. See Kardiner, *The Psychological Frontiers of Society* (1945), 219. See also Krige and Krige, *The Realm of a Rain-Queen* (1943), 109–110.

[54] It is probably to such an experience that Hoebel alludes when he says that the "feel" for a culture includes "the observer's sense of what is . . . *probable* and *fitting* . . . " in that culture (italics ours). Hoebel, *Discussion* (1943), 228.

[55] Hallowell has suggested the utility of the Rorschach Test for determining the homogeneity of social groups. Hallowell, *The Rorschach Technique in the Study of Personality and Culture* (1945), 207–208.

[56] It is appreciated that emotion is a product of many other factors, including nutrition as well as endocrine and constitutional processes, and is also dynamically related with the intellectual elements of perception. The physiological aspects of emotion are not included in the present study because of the fact that adequate methods were not available for studying their influence and because, in some cases, there is as yet too little evidence concerning the extent to which such influences are subject to social conditioning.

Simultaneously the second step was carried out, the analysis of the personality data. Dreams were interpreted in accordance with the recognized principles of dream interpretation and their emotional aspects noted.[57] Rorschach records were scored and mean scores computed for adults and children.[58] In the analysis of these means closer attention was paid to adults' than to children's protocols. This was done for the reason that the bulk of the ethnographic data had been derived from observation of adult behavior and most of the personality material, like dreams and interviews, was also received from the mature section of the society. It was therefore thought that, in inferring dominant motivations, adult data from these sources could not be validly equated with the records of children's behavior in the Rorschach situations, because children were still in the process of having their basic motivations shaped by the society.

Analysis of folktales was undertaken on the assumption that these traditions retain an emotional significance beyond their obvious themes because they reflect emotionally impressive childhood situations of paramount significance to the individual or because they contain, in symbolic form, wishful solutions of important problems of interpersonal relationships, like the relationship of the sexes. Folktales were not sought for, nor were published sources of Kaska tales consulted. The usefulness of folktales was related to the fact that they were spontaneously offered and a careful record was kept of the conditions under which such material was produced. In analyzing the tales, the emotional significance of the situations in which they were told, as well as of the narratives themselves, was inferred.

As this process went on we accumulated inferences of motivation from two sources—ethnographic data and personality data. We also accumulated inferences of motivation from both consciously and unconsciously directed behavior. All of these inferences were now brought together and studied for consistencies and contradictions. If contradictions were found, they were examined by reference to psychoanalytic processes like repression and reaction formation.

When the various data had been studied to infer motivation and consistencies or contradictions had been noted, it was found possible to isolate ten basic motivations for Kaska personality. By combining some of these to reduce overlappage, six dominant motivations were finally arrived at as underlying the emotional aspects of Kaska behavior.

Once these categories were accepted, the ethnographic and personality data were again studied with the aim of formulating explicit definitions of these basic motivations *applicable only to the Kaska*. The motivations now became principles by which the data could be classified.

[57] Some of the literature utilized includes Freud, *The Interpretation of Dreams* (1938); Stekel, *The Interpretation of Dreams* (1943); Sharpe, *Dream Analysis* (1937); Gutheil, *The Language of the Dream* (1939); and Lowy, *Psychological and Biological Foundations of Dream-Interpretation* (1942).

Symbols for dreams recognized in European and American society were not regarded as valid for interpreting Kaska dreams unless, in the opinion of the ethnographer, associations or other data, confirmed that meaning. Native ideas of dream interpretation were taken into consideration wherever possible.

[58] Among works utilized are Klopfer and Kelley, *The Rorschach Technique* (1942); Beck, *Rorschach's Test: I Basic Processes* (1944); Beck, *Rorschach's Test: II A Variety of Personality Pictures* (1945); Maslow, *Rorschach Psychology* (1945); and Bochner and Halpern, *The Clinical Application of the Rorschach Test* (1945). A few additional references will be cited in the text.

When the process of analysis was completed, there came the task of describing the operation of the world of meanings by selecting behavioral examples of its operation. In thus describing the emotional characteristics of Kaska behavior as demonstrating the operation of the world and self-views, we were occupied in describing Kaska ethos.

One more problem was set at this point—the analysis of the development of Kaska ethos. This analysis was particularly concerned with intensifying one aspect of the study of the ethnographic data. That is, we were here concerned with inferring the dominant motivations as psychological results of socialization situations. However, as Kardiner also discovered, we found it impossible to derive with any adequate validity the basic motivations from only the analysis of this portion of the life cycle.[59] Instead it was necessary for the analysis to include knowledge of motivation which had already been inferred from a wide variety of adult activities. When this was done it was found possible to match certain psychological results of socialization with dominant motivations inferred from adult activities.

A description, called "Development of the Ethos," was then written of the relationship of the psychological results of socialization to adults' dominant motivations.

INFORMANTS

The principal individuals who will be referred to in the following pages, the informants and subjects of the study, are listed below for ready identification. Heads of families have been numbered and brought out to the margin while their children, if unmarried and still living, are indented thereunder. The only exceptions to this procedure have been made in the case of adults (like John Kean and the Wiley sisters) who, even though currently unmarried, maintain their own homes for at least part of the year. All these persons were previously married and are now divorced or widowed. Ages, in some cases given in years and months, are indicated in parentheses. The bracketed numbers, following the ages of a few family heads, refer to parents still alive at the time when field work was begun. Moiety membership (expressed as Wolf or Crow) is indicated where such affiliation is generally recognized; children belong to the mother's moiety.

1. Ardo, Eva (20). A Dease River Indian who is orphaned and lives with various brothers and sisters. Eva was married shortly before we left Lower Post in August 1945. Several years previously she had given birth to an illegitimate child which had died. Wolf.
2. Barre, Billy (56). A Dease River Indian living with his second wife. Wolf.
   a. ———, Daisy (43). A Nelson Indian and a half-sister of Nick, Peter, and Xavier Lang but full sister of Mildred Lang. She has been married many times.
   June (14), Willy (8), Helen (3)
3. Cross, Edward (45). A Nelson Indian.
   a. ———, Mrs. (41). Crow.
   James (13), Dan (12), Mary (9), Jack (6), Eddie (4)
4. Cross, Harvey (28). A Nelson Indian.
   a. ———, Beatrice (18) [2a].
   Baby (2)

[59] Kardiner, The Psychological Frontiers of Society (1945), 102.

5. Day, Richard (17). A *métis* who early in life, lost his mother and was raised by his white father. He traps with his mother's brother, Edward Prince. Wolf.

6. Dickson, Mrs. (c. 55). The widow of a white man, she lives with her daughters and a son-in-law some distance from Lower Post. Little intensive contact was had with this family.

7. Donnelly, Hans (30) [27]. Unlike his mother, he is known by his father's name. Born at Frances Lake, he joined the Liard River Indians following his marriage. Crow.

  a. ————, Paulette (22) [18]. A previous infant was lost to this quarter Cree woman. Wolf.
  Terese (1)

8. Joe, River (63). A part Tlingit and part Liard River Indian who was widowed in the fall of 1944. He was married to one of Skipper's sister's daughters, a *métise*, and hence all of his children are one quarter white. Many of his children have died. Crow.
  Bud (c. 35), who is in a mental hospital; Ted (20), Flower (17)

9. Kean, John (32) [11]. He lost one wife through a miscarriage and was later separated from her sister. Both women were daughters of Old Man and were John's maternal cross-cousins. Crow.

10. Kean, Nitla (26) [11]. He spent most of his life around Frances Lake where he was raised by Old Metša following the death of his mother immediately after childbirth. His life and personality are presented in Appendix A.[60] Crow.

  a. ————, Adele (22). Although her father now traps at Frances Lake, she was born a Lower Pelly River Indian. She married Nitla after having had an illegitimate son who is now living with her father. A third child was lost to her at birth. Wolf.
  Anne (2)

11. Kean, Old (74). Originally he came from the Mackenzie slope many years ago. He married one of Old Man's sisters and is now designated an Upper Liard Indian. One other son, Louis, lives at Frances Lake. Classified Wolf.

12. Lang, Harry (31) [2a]. Originally a Nelson Indian, he was educated in boarding school and then joined the Upper Liard Indians following his marriage. His life and personality are presented in Appendix A.[61] Classified Crow.

  a. ————, Anna (21) [18]. Formerly married to John Kean, she is one quarter Cree. Wolf.
  Roger (5), Lenny (1.3)

13. Lang, Mildred (45). She is married to a white man and has adopted Stella Wiley's daughter, Anne, being childless herself. A half sister of Nick, Peter, and Xavier Lang, she is the maternal aunt of Harry Lang.

14. Lang, Nick (37). A Nelson Indian who has been twice widowed and is raising two sons. His two wives were daughters of Skipper.
  Mack (8), Boxer (7)

15. Lang, Peter (41). A Nelson Indian. He was also twice married and lost both women through death. His two wives were daughters of the current Mrs. Man.
  Elsie (11), who was adopted by Mrs. Man; Marie (4)

16. Lang, Xavier (47). A Nelson Indian.

  a. ————, Josephine (43) [11]. Her child is by a former marriage. Crow.
  Jack Kean (12), who spends most of his time with his maternal grandfather, Old Kean.

17. Leonard, Dick (42). A Tahltan Indian who accepted his brothers-in-laws' invitation to trap on the Cross line. Crow.

---

[60] Below, pp. 350–354.
[61] Below, pp. 330–340.

a. ———, Thelma (35). A Nelson Indian.

Ralph (15), who died in 1945; Gerald (14), Joyce (11), Bill (7), Nora (5), Thelma (2)

18. Man, Old (51). An Upper Liard Indian of mixed Indian ancestry who was early orphaned and spent the greater part of his youth in the service of white men. He has been married three times, his first two wives being sisters and half-Cree women from Fort Nelson. His life and personality are presented in Appendix A.[62] Crow.

a. ———, Mrs. (62). A Slave woman from Fort Liard who married her present husband seven years ago. She has no living children. Classified Wolf.

Louisa (15), Old Man's only unmarried daughter; for a brief personality sketch see Appendix A.[63]

19. Maza, Louis (37). Born a Dease River Indian, he joined the Upper Liard tribe following his marriage to his maternal cross-cousin. Old Man is Louis' father's brother. Crow.

a. ———, Allie (26) [8]. A quarter white Upper Liard Indian. Eleanor is her husband's daughter by a previous marriage to her sister and Marie is Allie's child by a white man and therefore three-quarters white. Wolf.

Eleanor (14), Marie (9), Loreen (3), Sonny (0.8)

20. Metša, Old (c. 70). Originally a Nelson Indian, she had passed most of her life at Frances Lake before her death in the Liard River valley during the winter of 1945.

21. Mountain, Dick (c. 32). A Dease River Indian.

a. ———, Annie (c. 25) [2].

Annette (8), Billy (5), Minny (4), Davis (2)

22. Nolan, John (30). A quarter white Indian who was born of a Bear Lake (Sekani) mother and a Kaska father. He now traps along the Muddy River. Wolf.

a. ———, Alice (20). Part Nelson and part Dease River Indian. Crow.

Eric (2), Ernest (0.6)

23. Nolan, Marie (24). A quarter white Indian who is married to a white man whose trap line is along the Muddy River.

24. Plover, Dorothy (22). An illegitimate child, she was raised by her Tahltan stepfather near Dease Lake. She is married to a much older white man. Her two children are illegitimate and half white. Dorothy's life and personality are presented in Appendix A.[64] Crow.

David (3), Conway (0.2)

25. Prince, Edward (27). A Nelson Indian. Wolf.

a. ———, Lois (21). A Nelson Indian who lost one child through miscarriage. Crow.

26. Skipper (72). A Dease River Indian. He now lives with his two young granddaughters. Wolf.

27. Suza, Lady (45) [20]. A widow whose deceased husband's English name was Donnelly. She was born a Nelson Indian but has spent most of her life at Frances Lake. She is a maternal aunt of Nick, Peter, and Xavier Lang. Classified Crow.

Raymond (18), Donald (14)

28. Tom, Peter (20). Early orphaned, he was taken as a partner by Louis Maza. His parents were Slave and Mrs. Man is his paternal grandmother. Classified Crow.

29. Wiley, Irene (17). An Upper Liard Indian who is a quarter Cree. She was deserted by her Frances Lake husband. Most of the year she lives with her stepfather's brother, River Joe.

---

[62] Below, pp. 316–330.
[63] Below, pp. 354–356.
[64] Below, pp. 340–350.

Each of the Wiley girls listed below has had a different father; eventually the half-Cree mother (a sister of Old Man's first two wives) married River Joe's brother, Old Wiley. Irene's baby is illegitimate. Wolf.

Irma (2)

30. Wiley, Mary (20). Originally a quarter Cree Upper Liard Indian, she moved to the Cross trap line with her husband who died in 1945. She now lives with her brothers-in-law and cares for a three year old sister, Charlotte. Wolf.

31. Wiley, Stella (22). She is a quarter white, a quarter Cree, and half Kaska. In 1944 she was widowed and also lost a son. Wolf.

Laura (3); Anne (6), who was adopted by Mildred Lang

SETTING

THE KASKA AREA

THE fifteen thousand square miles constituting the intermontane region occupied by the Kaska Indians west of the Rocky Mountains are divided between uninhabited mountainous terrain visited for hunting and trapping, and wide, rolling river valleys in which a sparsely distributed population carries on the bulk of its activities. Running away from these river valleys the country becomes increasingly hilly as it proceeds toward the eastern Rocky Mountains and the western Cordillera (Fig. 1). North of Frances Lake and south of Dease Lake these mountain systems come close together to provide the natural frontiers of the Kaska area. About halfway up Dease River from Lower Post, an offshoot of the Cordillera—the Cassiar Mountains—transects the country from northwest to south-east. Other minor ranges, including the Simpson Mountains, traverse the region between Frances Lake, on the north, and the Liard River, on the south.

The mountains provide sources for the numerous rivers and creeks that drain the country. All of these waters flow into the Liard River, which empties into the Mackenzie, and, eventually, reach the Arctic Ocean. The rivers are generally fast and shallow and marked by many sloughs. Their crooked courses are interrupted by numerous places where the current is swift and turbulent and by several narrow canyons which are impassable. A number of small lakes are also scattered throughout the area.

The climate of the country alternates between hot summer days with cool evenings, and cold winters in which the temperature hovers around twenty degrees below zero and even reaches sixty or seventy degrees below. Frosts set in around the middle of August and by early September the few deciduous trees have lost their color. Several weeks of intermittent rainfall can be expected after the first of September. When this period ends, the willows and poplars are free of leaves. By late October the rivers run with slush, small lakes and sloughs are frozen, and ice is beginning to form along the shores of the larger streams. Dry snow falls from the middle of October. After the middle of November even the larger rivers are covered with ice except for a few stretches of swift, open water. Winter has set in. In the Upper Liard area snow reaches a depth of fifteen inches by Christmas and three or four feet by the end of January. Around the beginning of March the dry, powdery snow of winter becomes moist under the warmer sun and the prevailing westerly wind (the Chinook), and the surface of the snow begins to form a thick, heavy crust. In April the river ice begins to break and the streams run with ice floes. The northern latitude of the area is associated with long days in summer. In late June and early July the sun rises at about 2:30 A.M. and sets about 10:30 P.M. Complete darkness is absent during this period. In winter long nights are the rule, the sun rising about 9:30 A.M. in December and setting at about 3:00 P.M. Because of its low position on the southern horizon, however, the winter sun is not warming.

The country, part of the circumpolar boreal forest belt, is marked by a predominance of coniferous flora. The principal species include red and black spruce and jack-pine; balsam

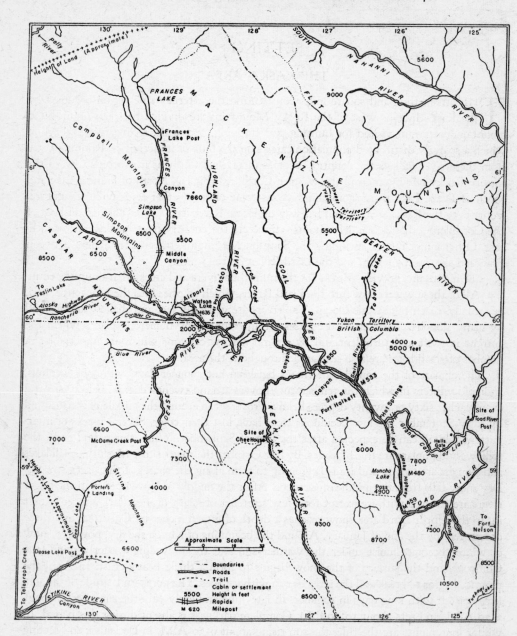

FIG. 1. Map of the Cassiar and Adjacent Area.

occurs at the higher elevations. Along the rivers and creeks, as well as in the forest, there is a profusion of red willow. Also interspersed in the forest are patches of quaking aspen (locally called poplar), birch, and cottonwood. The area contains many edible berries, including the strawberry, soapberry, low and high bush cranberry, raspberry, and blueberry. Along dry sloughs there is often a profusion of coarse grass, while niggerheads are found in an occasional swamp.

Animal life is quite abundant. Represented are large game animals such as the moose, woodland caribou, sheep, and goat and fur-bearing mammals like the lynx, mink, wolverine, otter, fox, coyote, wolf, beaver, and marten. Deer are rare. In the high mountains gopher and groundhog are numerous. The ubiquitous red squirrel is heard chattering everywhere and the spruce forests are overrun with the small trails worn by the feet of the Arctic hare (locally called rabbit). Fish are generally abundant in the lakes, mainly lake trout, whitefish, and jackfish (or pike). In the rivers the principal species are trout, grayling (sometimes called bluefish), and sucker.

The mosquito is a plague until the middle of August; the small "no-see-um" becomes a nuisance at about the time when the mosquito disappears and remains until late October. The gray mouse is a household pest whose numbers foil any attempt at eradication. Birds include the robin, crow, hoot owl, whiskey jack (or Canada jay), and various winter species like the grosbeak. There are also such fowl as the duck, goose, ptarmigan, willow grouse, and spruce hen. The two latter species are sometimes collectively referred to by the Indians as "chicken," although a distinction is recognized between them.

The name "Kaska" is the conventional term adopted by anthropologists to designate a number of linguistically and culturally related Athapaskan Indian bands or tribes living in the area of northern British Columbia, southern Yukon Territory, and Northwest Territories in Canada.[1] The present monograph is the result of work done with four of these tribes, but does not include the Espato·tena, who dwell in the Northwest Territories, east of the Rocky Mountains and are ethnographically unknown. The term Kaska is largely synonymous with the less satisfactory designation, Nahani, which, although formerly used by the Kaska to refer to neighboring Indian groups, is not employed as a term of reference within the society.

The four tribes under discussion are locally identified with particular geographical regions, which are in turn definable by the rivers and lakes constituting their main drainage channels. Except possibly in British Columbia, where trap lines are now formally registered, the boundaries between tribal units are not precisely recognized by the members of any tribe. Figure 2 shows the locations of the four Kaska tribes and their hunting and trapping districts, although only the second two listed below call themselves Kaska.

1. The Frances Lake Indians, the most northern tribe, live around Frances Lake, Simpson Lake, and the upper Frances River.[2] Their country extends from the Pelly River watershed on the northwest to the Mackenzie Mountains in the east.

[1] Osgood, *The Distribution of the Northern Athapaskan Indians* (1936), 13.

[2] The Albees on their walk up the Frances River in 1942 found the first signs of Frances Lake Indian camping grounds above the middle canyon of that stream. Albee and Albee, *Family Afoot in the Yukon Wilds* (1942) 614.

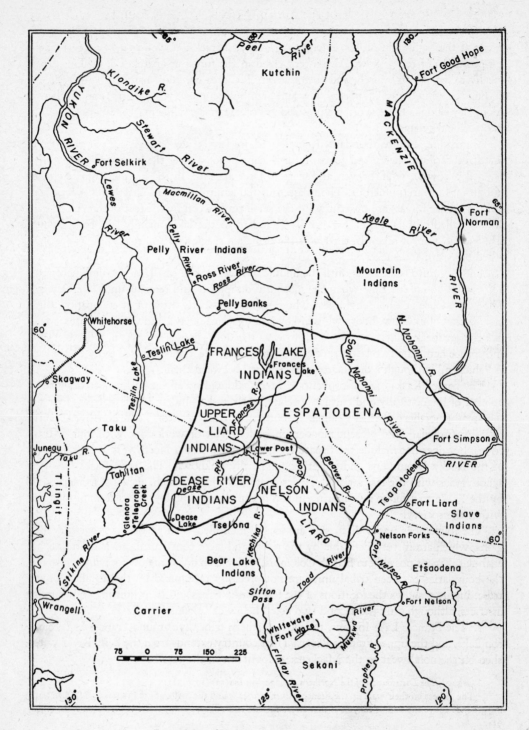

FIG. 2. Map of Kaska and Adjacent Indian Groups.

2. The Upper Liard Indians. This tribe consists of six families living along the Liard River from about eighteen miles north of the Alaska Highway crossing above Lower Post to within a hundred miles of that river's source. Their trapping ranges from the Cassiar Mountains on the west to the Simpson Mountains in the east, where they frequently encounter members of the Frances Lake Tribe.

3. The Dease River Indians are designated in the Indian Affairs Branch census as the Casca Band. They occupy the basin of Dease Lake and Dease River north to Lower Post and also range west along Blue River and McDame Creek to the Height of Land.

4. The Nelson Indians are the most easterly of these four tribes.[3] They live east of Lower Post on both the north and south banks of the Liard River and range up the Hyland, Smith and, for a short distance at least, Muddy (or Kechika) Rivers. Families trapping south along the Muddy River meet the Tselo·na and Bear Lake Indians (both Sekani groups). A number of Nelson Indians trapping south of the Liard and up the Muddy River appear to have identified themselves with the Tselo·na through intermarriage. Eastward, the Nelson people hunt to the Rocky Mountains and in the past crossed these ranges to trade at Fort Nelson, from whence they derive their name.

In 1944–45, Lower Post, located at Milepost 620 on the Alaska Highway (Pl. 1), was the main trading post serving all of these tribes. A smaller outpost, supplied by air freight, served a portion of the Frances Lake Indians. Less than five years before, however, trading posts were in operation at McDame Creek, eighty miles up Dease River from Lower Post, and at the head of Dease Lake.

To the south and southwest the Kaska are adjoined by the Tahltan Indians, trading at Telegraph Creek on the Stikine River. To the west, across the barrier of the Cassiar Mountains, the Dease River and Upper Liard Indians occasionally meet the Taku Indians trading at Teslin Lake Post. Beyond the Taku are the Tlingit Indians, occupying the Alaska panhandle. On the north the Kaska are bounded by the Pelly River Indians (Tutchone nation). To the northeast are the Mackenzie (Mountain) Indians and, east, the Espato·tena and Slave Indians of Fort Nelson, Nelson Forks, and Fort Liard. The Slave refer to the Kaska as "Grand Lakers," which is apparently a translation of tutšo·tena, the present day Kaska term of reference for the Frances Lake people. Occupying the middle and upper Muddy River are the Sekani bands already referred to, who divide their trade between Lower Post and Whitewater (Fort Ware), on the Finlay River.

[3] This statement would not hold if the present monograph included the Goat Indians, or Espato·tena, who trade into Forts Liard and Simpson. In the system of classification adopted for the Northern Athapaskans, these people have commonly been grouped as Kaska (see Osgood, The Distribution of the Northern Athapaskan Indians [1932], 396). Since such classification is primarily on a linguistic basis and because no study of the Espato·tena has yet been reported, the validity of their classification with the Kaska may legitimately be questioned, especially if reason for doubt can be advanced. Contrary evidence comes from Old Man stating, on the basis of brief acquaintance with this tribe, that he could not too well understand their dialect. This suggests that the provisional grouping of the Espato·tena with other Kaska tribes may be incorrect.

A somewhat cursory examination of the dialect of the Tselo·na people tends to warrant their exclusion from the Kaska nation, despite their proximity to the latter. See Jenness, The Sekani Indians of British Columbia (1937), 5, 10; Osgood, The Distribution of the Northern Athapaskan Indians (1932), 17.

THE KASKA PEOPLE

Physically, the Kaska are American Indians with considerable white admixture. In skin color the Kaska range from the light tan of *métis* to medium brown. In spring when the people return to the post their faces often show blanched spots, apparently the marks of severe frostbite. The eyes are characteristically black, although brown and blue eyes occur in children of *métis*, and exhibit the epicanthic fold. Two men were noted who had rims of blue around the dark irises. The hair is generally straight, black, and thick. Old men and women have their hair streaked with gray. Bodily hair is normally light. Stature ranges from medium to small; obesity is infrequent. The faces of most of the people are relaxed and calm but otherwise expressionless, except when they smile or laugh (Pls. 2 and 3). Some individuals have sharp and pinched features, giving the impression of considerable inner tension.

As far as could be observed, the physical development and maturation of the Kaska child parallel that of American children, and are subject to the same vicissitudes when neglect and ill-treatment occur in infancy.[4] For example, at eighteen months Lenny Lang walked, but without perfect coordination, showing a tendency to run. He had four middle incisors, four lateral incisors, and four molars. He did not yet talk. At eleven months Terese Donnelly sat erect, crawled a little when permitted, and had four teeth—the two lower incisors and the two upper canines. She could pull herself into a sitting position by holding onto a support. At four months Sonny Maza smiled, kicked his legs, and showed one tooth just appearing. On the other hand, Irma, the daughter of Irene Wiley, who was starved and neglected during her first six or eight months of life, at twenty-one months pulled herself upright holding on, crawled and smiled but could not stand alone nor talk. Her teeth seemed normal. Old Man reported that little children, from about one to two years of age, are eager to pull off their clothing, a phenomenon also noted in American society.

Menarche occurs between fourteen and fifteen years, several girls having developed pregnancies between fifteen and sixteen years of age. The age of senile impotence could not be established, but may be inferred as occurring relatively late since River Joe, aged about sixty-three, complained of unsatisfied sexual desire following the death of his wife while Old Kean, aged seventy-four, tried to persuade a woman to live with him and actually lived with her for a week or so during the summer. One woman, aged forty-five, several times manifested strong sexual drive during intoxication. In appearance, women age quickly. No signs of senility were manifested by any of the two or three men aged sixty and over. Such signs, however, were observed in one woman, Old Metša, whose age was about seventy.

A tabulation of population figures for the Dease River, Upper Liard, and Nelson River Indians is shown in Table 2. Little reliance can be placed on the accuracy of reports before 1944, since no distinctions were made between tribal groups. All figures are from the Reports of the Department of Indian Affairs,[5] unless otherwise specified.

In 1945, the ethnographer estimated the population of the four Kaska tribes to total

---

[4] See Gessel and Ilg, *Infant and Child in the Culture of Today* (1943).
[5] Canada, *Annual Report of the Department of Indian Affairs* (1914–1934).

TABLE 2. KASKA POPULATION

Tribe	1875	1887	1914	1917	1924	1928[8]	1929	1934	1944[12]
Dease Lake	105[6]	70[7]	70	70	64	150	64	137[10]	74
Upper Liard and Frances Lake			79	84	82	80	80	95	42[13]
Nelson River			89	106	123		141[9]	91[11]	59
Total			238	260	269		285	323	175

about 200.[14] Mooney estimated 500 for the aboriginal population of the total Kaska area.[15] Although it cannot be denied that Kaska population has suffered some decline since 1840, the magnitude of this seems exaggerated. We doubt that the aboriginal population exceeded 300.

About 50 per cent of the Kaska are adults over sixteen years of age (Table 3). Adult males slightly exceed adult females, the ratio being 1:.725. Among children, girls are more numerous than boys by a ratio of 1:1.175. During the period from June 1944 to July 1945 we noted eleven births which suggests a birth rate of at least 55 per 1000 population. Of these births five, or about 45 per cent, occurred in spring. Seven were female and four male. The

TABLE 3. AGE AND SEX DISTRIBUTION OF POPULATION—MARCH 31, 1944

Tribe	Men	Women	Children Under 16		Total
			Boys	Girls	
Dease River	20	14	16	24	74
Upper Liard	14	9	8	11	42
Nelson River	17	14	16	12	59
Total	51	37	40	47	175

[6] French and Ware, British Columbia Posts; No. 7, McDame's Creek Post (1923–24), 395.

[7] Dawson, Report of an Exploration in the Yukon District (1887–1888), 200. This reference, like the preceding, is to Indians trading at McDame Post and no tribal specifications are given.

[8] Allard, Notes on the Kaska and Upper Liard Indians (1928), 24. The author confesses that his estimate of 150 people trading at McDame Creek probably includes Sekani and Nelson Indians.

[9] The constantly rising population of the Nelson Indians seems to point to a confusion of Nelson and adjacent Sekani people like the Tselo·na.

[10] This figure probably includes forty odd Indians classified as "Grahame Nomads" in earlier reports, and this term probably refers to the Tselo·na.

[11] The reference is to "Nomadic McDame and Liard District."

[12] Canada, Stikine Indian Agency Census (1944).

[13] Includes only three Frances Lake Indians.

[14] This figure is based on the 175 people trading into Lower Post and listed in the government's census of 1944 plus an estimated thirty Frances Lake Indians for whom no census data could be obtained. The figure does not include the Espato·tena.

[15] Kroeber, Cultural and Natural Areas of Native North America (1939), 141.

average age of the mother at first conception can be estimated to be about sixteen, the range being reported from thirteen to nineteen. The father is generally about five years older than the mother. Considering the existing families with more than one child, we found that families had from two to six living and one or two deceased children. It must be realized, however, that these are not yet completed families and will produce further children. No difference in fertility could be noticed between women married to white men or Indians.

The Kaska are not a healthy people. The most common illnesses noted during the period of field work were tuberculosis, poor teeth, influenza, dysentery, colds, skin diseases, such as impetigo, and red eyes. A few cases of gonorrhea were treated by the army physicians. No undue frequency of accidents was noted. The only serious one during the fall of 1945 in the Upper Laird tribe was the case of an elderly man who fell while intoxicated and sprained his back.

Children tend to have particularly bad teeth. Two children, aged three, had lost the two upper middle incisors and several children showed extremely bad tooth decay. Influenza epidemics occur occasionally and in the fall of 1944 a dysentery epidemic spread from the town of Lower Post up and down the Liard River. At Smith River five Nelson Indian children were reported to have lost their lives from this disease and an upper Liard Indian woman and child also died. Sporadic outbreaks of dysentery continued during the the summer of 1945. Eleven deaths occurred in the period from September 1944 through August 1945. This indicates a death rate of at least 55 per 1000, equalling the birth rate. Of these deaths seven were of children, one a newborn baby.

HISTORY

According to the Old Man, an Upper Liard informant, the Kaska Indians of that region believe themselves to be descendants from the Tlingit through the Ross River (Pelly) Indians. The progenitors of the present day Liard River Kaska originally moved south to explore the Upper Liard country and remained there. It seems worthwhile to consider this bit of traditional history. Pelly and Ross Rivers mark the headwaters of the great Yukon drainage system and their confluence represents a point which would be relatively easy to reach by moving up the waterways from Bering Sea. From the head of the Pelly River, migrants could continue toward the interior by crossing the Pelly River-Frances Lake divide, thus striking the Liard River drainage system. Once across this barrier the vast stretch of intermontane basin lying between the Rocky Mountains and the Cordillera would lie open. If such a theory of migration into the intermontane basin is to be sustained, the cultures of the tribes extending from the Yukon River would have to show a reasonable degree of similarity. Although evidence is still lacking for the groups north of Frances Lake (for example, the Pelly River Indians), similarity is found between the Kaska (but excluding the Nelson River tribe), Tahltan, and Carrier. Masks, potlatching, line dancing instead of circle dancing, and dual organizations are some of the traits common to Alaskan and the Athapaskan tribes of west-central British Columbia but lacking among the more easterly Slave and Sekani groups.

The above migration theory would deny the derivation of the diagnostic traits from the Northwest Coast, although the subsequent development of such traits may have been effected from that culture area. It seems likely that at least the northern portion of the Northwest Coast area (Tlingit and Haida) and the adjacent interior Athapaskan cultures enjoyed a common origin in Alaska and that at some time a culture prototypical to these moved up the Alaskan river systems. From the headwaters of the Yukon we may then postulate two streams of migration, one down the Chilkat, Taku, and other rivers to the Pacific coast and another into the intermontane basin. A third course of migration probably proceeded eastward from central Alaska and may have been the stream that brought the Kutchin and Mackenzie River peoples to the further inland area.[16] Since this early period there have, of course, been many many other movements into and out of the area. Our informant may be referring to one such known movement of Tlingit to the Pelly River when he traces the descent of his people from such an amalgamation.[17]

Aboriginal culture.[18] Prior to European contact, Kaska society was organized into a number of autonomous, fluid bands consisting essentially of a nuclear family with such additional relatives as sons-in-law, parents' siblings, and aged grandparents. The band lacked formal organization, leadership being exercised by a mature man, who was also a capable hunter. The remaining members were probably held together as much by guarantees of subsistence as by the emotional ties of kinship. Little organization other than some ties of kinship operated between bands. Such kinship ties gained their emotional reinforcement primarily from frequent interpersonal contact, but had no direct function in binding together the various bands constituting a tribe. Tribal identification was relatively weak and depended primarily on close similarity of dialect. A matrilineal, dichotomous social organization prevailed in the western portion of the Kaska area (including the Frances Lake, Dease River, and Upper Liard River tribes) but was of limited social importance.

In summer a number of bands of one or more adjoining tribes assembled around a fish lake that guaranteed a fairly dependable food supply. From this base the men could go out to hunt and the women could set lines of rabbit snares. In the fall these larger units broke up, and small bands or individual families traveled to the surrounding mountains where large numbers of groundhog and gopher were snared, dried, and cached for winter use. Moose were hunted with snares and bows and arrows and the meat preserved for later consumption. With the onset of winter, the families once more congregated at a fish lake and here spent the coldest part of the year. Occasionally young men were sent to the moun-

[16] Such a theory is not incompatible with Sapir's inference from linguistic sources tracing the Tlingit, Haida, and Athapaskan languages to a proto-Na-dene language (Sapir, *The Na-dene Languages, A Preliminary Report* [1915], 557–558). It is interesting to note that Teit's Tahltan informants reported that the Tlingit formerly "occupied from time immemorial a considerable part of the interior north of the Tahltans, including most of the drainage basin of the Taku, and nearly all the northwestern headwaters of the Yukon, north almost to latitude 62 and east to the Pelly Mountains and the height of land dividing Teslin waters from the Upper Liard." Teit, *On Tahltan (Athabaskan) Work*, 1912 (1912), 484. My own theory has been very strongly influenced through discussions with Professor Osgood.

[17] Old Man's paternal grandfather was a Tagish (or interior Tlingit) Indian. Projection of his own ancestry into tribal history may, therefore, have led to confusion regarding traditional history. His maternal grandmother, however, was an Upper Liard woman.

[18] This material represents a very brief abstract of a larger body of data which is now being prepared for publication.

tain caches to bring back a supply of meat. Winter was also a time when caribou were hunted and sometimes men traveled up to the mountains to secure goats and sheep. The food supply, however, was not sufficient to eliminate some periods of starvation. In such emergencies, the people sought for neighboring bands who might still have a supply of meat. When food was really scarce some people even ate human flesh but they were punished if their deed was discovered.

Men set weirs and nets for fish, hunted, and made the necessary implements and weapons to carry out these and other activities, while women collected supplementary tubers and berries, made camp, and helped pack the household equipment or draw the toboggans. Women also prepared the clothing, utilizing the tanned skins of the moose and caribou and furs of the fox, marten, wolverine, lynx, and rabbit. Clothing was tailored and consisted essentially of a long dress with leggins for the woman and a coat and trousers for the man. Both sexes wore parkas, breech cloths, moccasins, and a variety of headgear. Personal appearance was enhanced by tattooing and piercing the nose and ears for bone and wood plugs. Men and women painted their cheeks and wore simple bone and tooth armbands and necklaces. The hair was not cut, but men removed their facial hair.

Aboriginal Kaska society was completely dependent on environmental resources for food, clothing and tools. Each family constituted an independent economic unit, capable of preparing required artifacts and carrying out all the routines necessary for survival. Two related families commonly shared the temporary branch lean-tos which were the standard dwellings. The floors were covered with spruce brush, upon which beaver and other furs were spread for bedding. Fire was made by striking together two pieces of rock and catching the spark in dry tinder; when traveling in cold weather women carried fire on poles. Cooking utensils consisted mainly of spruce bark vessels in which water was heated by means of hot stones or of woven spruce root kettles hung quite high above the fire.

Travel was essential to the economic life. Temporary spruce bark canoes, rafts, dugouts, and boats made of untanned moosehides were used on the water. Rude log bridges were built across the narrow streams. In winter snowshoes were indispensable for the deep powdery snow and wooden and frozen skin toboggans were also used. Small children were carried in moosehide sacks lined with moss.

Although the lack of tribal organization and formal social control made interpersonal quarrels within the society inevitable, overt ingroup hostility was kept to a minimum by the individual's own personal distaste for aggression. Between neighboring Indian groups, like the Tahltan and Pelly River people, mutual fear and suspicion were rife and often flared into sporadic warfare motivated by a need for vengeance or the desire for women. While women were taken captive in war, men and children were usually killed and often callously tortured. Scalping and the degradation of enemy corpses were common features of warfare.

The arts included wood carving, pyrogravure, porcupine quill work, and rock painting. Dancing was a feature of the potlatch, a celebration commemorating a deceased relative and marked by the exchange of food and manufactured objects between moieties. At these festivals, which were observed only by the western Kaska bands, the dancers used wooden masks or skin costumes. The tambourine drum was the only musical instrument. Songs were composed to express love and mourning as well as for amusement. Hide-the-stick gambling games were very popular. Other sports included wrestling, boat racing, tug of war, hide and seek, and skill or strength contests.

Marriages, including those with captive women, were regulated by rules of moiety exogamy and incest avoidance, but unions between certain cross-cousins were favored as were marriages between two sisters and two brothers. Residence in marriage was generally matrilocal and unions were not final until a period of bride service had elapsed. Polygyny was practiced by men whose hunting ability enabled them to secure sufficient food and skins to support two wives and many children. Plural wives were always sisters. Fraternal polyandry was resorted to under such special circumstances as that of an old man who was too weak to supply all the resources required by his family.

The conception of the supernatural revolved around the recognition of a number of beings, some of which were believed hostile while others were regarded as friendly. Special respect was also extended to certain animals, including the otter, mink, and weasel. These animals were never killed. A belief in a supreme deity was loosely developed, but individuals relied primarily on their own supernaturally derived power for security and help. Such power enabled men to hunt successfully and also functioned in curing. A wide variety of ritual observances were associated with hunting activities not the least of which was avoidance of the danger which a woman and her biological functions held for a man's power. Sexual abstinence preceded and followed hunting, while during menstruation and parturition women were isolated. At menarche a girl used a quill tube for drinking water and scratched herself with a stick rather than with her fingers. Every person was a potential shaman who could cure illness through his supernatural power. Certain curers, however, attained greater prestige than others and men of this rank sometimes became rivals who competed in public conjuring. Shamans effected cures by sucking disease from the body, imparting their power to water which the patient drank, singing, and receiving confessions from the sick. Plant medicines were limited and were administered by anyone. Shamans could also sorcerize, but this behavior does not appear to have been widespread.

Death was attributed to both sorcery and natural causes. Old and infirm people might be abandoned and left to die. The corpse was buried in summer but cremated in cold weather. Following a husband's death, his widow underwent a period of restriction in which her activities were controlled by her brother-in-law whom she might later marry. After death the spirit of the deceased was believed to continue its existence in an afterworld.

Historic contacts. Kaska contacts with the Tlingit probably antedate the arrival of the white man in the western part of the area. In the late eighteenth century, after the Europeans had visited the Tlingit villages along the Alaska panhandle, these connections became intensified since the coastal Indians, including both Tlingit and Tahltan, became middlemen in the fur trade between the Europeans and the more interior groups. Two Tlingit tribes, the Taku and Stikine Indians, from their geographical position and reported evidence, may be assumed to have maintained such relations with the Kaska (Fig. 2). Furthest north were the Taku people, occupying the area around Taku Bay and lower Taku River.[19] Krause asserts that they went up the Taku River and across the high passes

[19] There is some question if this refers to a branch of the Tlingit or to a Tahltan tribe which, according to Field and Jenness, later became infiltrated by Tlingit people. Today, in Lower Post, the Teslin Lake Taku are referred to as Tlingit. See Jenness, *The Indians of Canada* (1932), 396; Field, Unpublished Manuscript (1913).

of the Cordillera toward the headwaters of the Yukon River, where they traded with local Indians.[20] The headwaters of the Taku are about thirty miles east of Teslin Lake, at present a Taku Indian village, which adjoins the territory of the Upper Liard Indians. According to Lees numerous trails lead into the Teslin Lake area from the Pacific Coast and a 150 mile trail runs from Teslin Indian village to the Upper Liard area.[21] To the south the Stikine, or Stakhin, people utilized the Stikine River to carry on "a lively trade with the Indians of the interior."[22] The latter designation certainly includes the Tahltan but may also refer to the Kaska. From the upper Stikine River trade goods were further distributed by the Tahltan, who reached the Kaska on Dease Lake and, via overland trails from Telegraph Creek, the Upper Liard Indians at Albert (now Cormier) Creek, twenty-three miles west of Lower Post (Fig. 1). The mouth of Albert Creek is now the site of the bridge by which the Alaska Highway crosses the upper Liard River. According to River Joe, Tahltan traders also reached a point about fifteen miles further up the Liard. Here they established themselves in "tents." The chief's dwelling is said to have flown a flag and to have been surrounded by the tents of the "boys" who accompanied him. From this statement it would appear that Tahltan trade with the western Kaska continued until relatively late in the period of historic contact. The standard of value in this trade may be gauged from the report that an empty lard can sold for one beaver skin.[23] Krause says that some Tlingit Indians traveled as far east as Fort Simpson, which they reached in six days.[24]

. Relations between the Tlingit and the inland tribes, whom the former called Go'nana, were not always cordial. Swanton reports that the Tlingit valued the Athapaskans "for what could be gotten out of them but otherwise looked down upon as a lower race."[25]

The first Europeans. Several dates can be advanced for the first meetings between the Kaska and Europeans. The earliest probably occurred shortly after 1800, following the establishment of Forts Simpson and Liard. Soon after the amalgamation of the Hudson's Bay and the North-West Companies in 1821, a trading settlement was built at the confluences of the Smith and Liard Rivers known as Fort Halkett.[26] In 1834, J. McLeod, a trader of the Hudson's Bay Company, left Fort Simpson "and ascended the Liard to explore its upper waters—hoping, if possible, to cross the watershed and find some stream running to the Pacific." He traveled to where Lower Post is today and then ascended the Dease River, eventually reaching the Stikine after passing through Dease Lake "which he named after the Arctic explorer."[27] Four years later (1838) McLeod established a trading post on Dease Lake.

Billy Barre reported a story which may refer to the post that McLeod established on Dease Lake. The Indians discovered peculiar chips of wood floating down the water, and

[20] Krause, *Die Tlinkit-Indianer* (1885), 103. See also Swanton, *Social Condition, Beliefs and Linguistic Relationships of the Tlingit Indians* (1908), 396, 414; Olson, *Some Trading Customs of the Chilkat Tlingit* (1936).

[21] Lees, *Geology of the Teslin-Quiet Lake Area, Yukon* (1936), 1–2.

[22] Krause, *Die Tlinkit-Indianer* (1885), 111.

[23] Barbeau states that the Tahltan also reached Frances Lake where they traded with the Hudson's Bay Company. Barbeau, *Mountain Cloud* (1944), 15, 28–29.

[24] Krause, *Die Tlinkit-Indianer* (1885), 111.

[25] Swanton, *Social Condition, Beliefs, and Linguistic Relationships of the Tlingit Indians* (1908), 411, 414.

[26] Voorhis, *Historic Forts and Trading Posts* (1930), 79.

[27] Pike, *Through the Subarctic Forest* (1896), 55.

realized that these could not have been made by beaver. To resolve their curiosity, they traveled up the river and found a house. A white man showed them how these chips of wood had been made with an ax but extensive conversation between the two groups was impossible. The following year the trader returned with an interpreter from the east and now people began to bring their furs to the house in exchange for tea, tobacco, and other European goods. According to Old Man, the Tahltan Indian once tried to kill the trader at Dease Lake. A shaman, however, seized the killer's wrist and wrenched away his knife. Although the "doctor" cut his own hand, he saved the storeman's life.

Old Kean reported having heard that the Kaska people first encountered the white man at Dease Lake. The trader subsisted entirely on dry meat which the Indians prepared for him. A white woman is said to have lived with this man. Informants several times mentioned that in those days the traders asked Indians to pile up their pelts alongside a rifle. When the skins reached the top of the gun, the trader accepted the pile in exchange for the weapon. According to Old Man, the Indians were extremely shy of the early white men and talked to them only with their heads down or otherwise averted.

In 1840, two years after the establishment of Dease Lake Post, Robert Campbell, an explorer for the Hudson's Bay Company, started out from Fort Halkett and reached the site of Fort Frances at the foot of Frances Lake. Here he built a dwelling which he called Glenlyon House after his Scotland home. In 1843 he constructed a trading post which was first named Frances Lake House in honor of the explorer's wife. The name was later changed to Fort Frances.[28] The sight of white men with whiskers at Fort Frances is said to have greatly frightened local Indians who thought that the strangers were wild animals. At the sound of a rifle the people fled in terror. Also the Indians would at first not eat bread. The trader, through his interpreter, explained the use of the tobacco pipe to the Indians, stating that smoke was drawn into the mouth the same way as milk from the mother's nipple. Thus the Indians learned to smoke, although at first they were repulsed by the strong smell of tobacco.

There now follows a period when many of these early trading posts were temporarily or permanently abandoned. Dease Lake was deserted in May 1839.[29] It did not resume operation until many years later and was again closed in the summer of 1945. Fort Frances was abandoned in 1851, following the looting of the post by the Chilkat (Tlingit) Indians. It reopened in 1880 but was again abandoned. A new post was finally built at the foot of Frances Lake by Jack Hilditch about 1936. It was soon acquired by the Hudson's Bay Company under whose management it continues. Fort Halkett was closed in 1865.[30] Its timbers and stone fireplace may still be seen a short distance off the Alaska Highway. The trade was absorbed by Forts Nelson, Liard, and Toad River Post near the mouth of Toad River on the north bank of the Liard. This latter post is not mentioned by Grouard,[31] who states that after the closing of Fort Halkett those Indians who had been provisioned there

[28] Campbell, *Discovery and Exploration of the Pelly (Yukon) River* (1883); Voorhis, *Historic Forts and Trading Posts* (1930), 69; Burpee, *Campbell of the Yukon* (1945).

[29] Pike, *Through the Subarctic Forest* (1896), 56.

[30] McConnell, *Report on an Exploration in the Yukon and Mackenzie Basins* (1890), 43D. However, Voorhis gives the year as 1875. Voorhis, *Historic Forts and Trading Posts*, (1930), 79.

[31] Grouard, *Souveniers de mes soixante ans d'apostolat dans l'Athabaska-Mackenzie* (n.d.), 102.

found themselves "thrown into complete poverty" and in the spring of 1867 brought their furs to Fort Liard. Two groups were reported to have come there at the time, Mountain People and Bad People, but neither group brought their families. Toad River post was abandoned about 1890.

Meanwhile, in 1872, Sylvester built a store at the junction of McDame Creek and Dease River. In 1876, after selling this establishment to the Hudson's Bay Company, he contemplated building a "lower post" on the south bank of the Liard near the confluence of the Dease (Pl. 1, D).[32] The Indians living on the north bank, however, complained that when the ice was running they could not cross the river. Since the south bank tribes were already trading at McDame Creek, Sylvester was particularly anxious to reach the more northern bands. Following their suggestion he built on a flat almost a mile below the present site of Lower Post, i.e., below the confluence of the Dease. This is the present site of the abandoned RCMP barracks which were built in 1926. Before 1887 the site had been abandoned for a new store erected where Lower Post stands today. In a short time Sylvester's business was acquired by the Hudson's Bay Company. After 1896 the company built a larger store and warehouse but maintained Sylvester's building as an auxiliary warehouse until 1945, when the structure was demolished.

Important developments took place in the western area between the abandonment of Fort Halkett and the construction of Sylvester's Lower Post. While gold had been found along the Stikine River as early as 1861, it was in 1872 that the bars of the Liard yielded traces of this metal around the ruins of Fort Halkett. In 1873 profitable strikes began to be made at Thibert's Creek at the foot of Dease Lake. Gold hunters in large numbers now began to pour into the country via the Stikine River and in June 1874 the population, exclusive of Indians, was estimated to have reached close to 1500 persons.[33] Many of the miners quit the country with the approach of winter. At this time a Negro, Harry McDame, discovered gold on McDame Creek, where Sylvester operated a trading post. The name of the post was eventually altered from Sylvester's Landing to McDame Creek Post. The news of the gold strikes continued to travel and the influx of miners developed a busy traffic on the Stikine River. In 1874 the Province of British Columbia improved the portage from Telegraph Creek on the Stikine across the Height of Land to the head of Dease Lake, opening a sixty-two mile pack horse trail. By 1876 the population of the Cassiar district reached about 2000 and included a large number of Chinese laborers. The production of the region quickly declined until, in 1887, Dawson found only four or five whites and forty Chinese still at work.[34] In this period three hundred head of cattle were brought overland from the upper Fraser River.

Sometime in the late 80's a Frenchman, Jean La Montagne, opened a trading post at the mouth of the Muddy (Kechika) River. This establishment was soon moved fifty miles up the Muddy River and named Chee House. The post was abandoned early in the twentieth century, when La Montagne, the reputed father of the late Mrs. River Joe, moved to

[32] Voorhis describes Lower Post as being "at the confluence of Dease and Frances Rivers forming the Liard" and describes the post as an outpost of Fort Frances. Voorhis, *Historic Forts and Trading Posts* (1930), 106.

[33] Dawson, *Extracts from the Report on an Exploration made in 1887 in the Yukon District, N. W. T.* (1898), 308–309. See also Pike, *Through the Subarctic Forest* (1896), 56–57.

[34] Dawson, *Report of an Exploration in the Yukon District* (1887–1888), 81.

Nome, Alaska. Goods to these Muddy River posts were first floated down the Liard by scow, a trip entailing passage through Forty-Mile Canyon. Later freight for Chee House was packed cross-country by horse from McDame Creek. A Fraser River Indian, Packer Tom, was in charge of this operation.

In 1887, Dawson visited Lower Post, which he described as "situated at the edge of a terrace forty feet in height on the left bank of the Liard, about half a mile above the mouth of the Dease. It is of a very unpretentious character, consisting of a few log buildings. In the vicinity the woods have been entirely destroyed by fire."[35]

Pike was the second traveler to traverse a large part of the Cassiar and to publish an account of his journey. In 1892, "On 19th August, early in the morning, we reached Sylvester's Landing at the mouth of McDame's Creek, the headquarters of the Hudson's Bay Company's district of Cassiar. A casual glance at once shows the contrast in the appearance of this western trading post as compared with any of the company's establishments in the same latitude on the eastern side of the Rockies. The slovenly log buildings, the row of Indian shanties in close proximity to the master's house, and the absence of any attempt at regularity in the positions of the various storehouses, compare unfavourably with the neatly kept forts on the northern lakes, where the Hudson's Bay Company has held undisputed sway for a century."[36] Lower Post he describes as another "unpretentious establishment" consisting of "A small store, a log hut for the man in charge, and a few rough buildings belonging to the Indians." A man named Smith is reported to have been the manager.[37]

During his visit to Lower Post, Pike heard a rumor that some of the tribes northwest of the divide "intended to bring their canoes across the portage and make a raid on all the whitemen and Indians whom they met on the Liard and Dease, and had even hopes of plundering the Hudson's Bay Post at Sylvester's Landing."[38] Another version of this story was heard in 1944 from Fred Allen, a white trapper, who received it from a Nass River métis, Herbert Hankin. In the 90's an Indian woman informed P. Agnell, the Hudson's Bay representative in Lower Post, and his assistant, Hankin, that Pelly River Indians were coming to attack the settlement. The Indians came but approached the post only to sell some skins. After the exchange had been completed they made their camp a short distance upstream. That night Agnell awoke to hear a dog growl. He looked out and saw Indians crawling toward the store. Seizing his gun the trader flung open the door and shot into the ground. The Indians explained that they had come to sell the Company some additional pelts.

Pike gives an interesting picture of native health in the Cassiar at the time of his visit. "Once we visited a large lake 20 miles to the westward of [Lower] post,[39] and laid in a

[35] This statement seems to indicate that Dawson found Lower Post situated where it is today. In 1944 the burned area to which he refers was covered with second growth poplar and willow. Dawson, *Extracts From the Report of an Exploration made in 1887 in the Yukon District, N. W. T.* (1898), 314.

[36] Pike, *Through the Subarctic Forest* (1896), 60–61.

[37] Pike, *Through the Subarctic Forest* (1896), 68.

[38] Pike, *Through the Subarctic Forest* (1896), 139.

[39] This is clearly a reference to Watson Lake, one of the most important fish lakes in the vicinity and now the site of a modern airport.

supply of whitefish, which we caught in nets under the ice, in great quantities. Here we found a band of Liard Indians hunting and fishing. Sickness was prevalent in the camp—very few of the men were well enough to hunt moose, and they had come to the lake to be sure of making a living. A melancholy spectacle the camp presented; half a dozen pits in the snow lined with pine brush, a little more pine brush stuck up as a wind-break, and no other shelter from the weather. Lying in their blankets were the sick men, some of them evidently never to get up again—dying among the moose hair and fish guts . . . 'Oh! We're always like this,' the chief explained, 'since the white men came to the country. In the old time, my tribe was powerful, but now many of my people die every winter. Some children are born, but they are no good—they die soon.' "[40]

In another place the author comments further on the depopulation of the Kaska area. "The remnants of the once numerous tribe of Casca Indians presents a good example of the rapid deterioration of natives, caused by free intercourse with whites—especially, perhaps, with a class of whites which is always to be found in mining camps . . . . No pious missionary has ever penetrated into Cassiar to point out these matters to the Indians . . . . Perhaps it is too late to begin, as at the present rate of mortality, the Cascas will be extinct in ten years time, and the banks of the Dease and Liard depopulated."[41]

In 1897 and 1898 a second influx of miners entered the area, this time en route to the Klondike gold fields. Two principal routes to the central Yukon passed through the Cassiar region. One involved travel up the Stikine River to Telegraph Creek. From this point the miners could use the Dease, Liard, and Frances Rivers to reach the northern divide across which they would find the headwaters of the Yukon's tributaries. Another route was overland from the Stikine to Teslin Lake and thence by river to Dawson. The overland trail from Glenora and Telegraph Creek to Teslin Lake presumably corresponds to the route followed by the early Tahltan traders visiting the Upper Liard Indians. There was still a third but less used means of access to the Yukon. This was from Edmonton, Alberta, to the Finlay River (via the Peace) and then up Finlay and Fox Rivers to Sifton Pass and down the Muddy to the vicinity of Deadwood Lake. From here the trail leading to Chee House ran to McDame Creek where river travel could be resumed. Johnston reports the latter route to have been traversed in 1898 by Inspector J. D. Moodie of the Northwest Mounted Police.[42] According to Old Man, a pack horse trail was cut at this time stretching from Lower Post to Frances Lake along the banks of the Liard and Frances Rivers. The trail is now said to be largely overgrown but the trees still show where the bark was rubbed by the bulky packs.[43]

The Klondike bound miners passing through the country at this time are still recalled as a group by the local Indians. A number of Upper Liard Indians, some serving as guides to the gold seekers, are reported to have followed the migration to Frances Lake and across

[40] Pike, *Through the Subarctic Forest* (1896), 98–99.
[41] Pike, *Through the Subarctic Forest* (1896), 61–62.
[42] Johnston, *Gold Placers of Dease Lake Area, Cassiar District, B. C.* (1926), 40A.
[43] For some details of the miners' hardships as they pressed through the Cassiar see Tollemache, *Reminiscences of the Yukon* (1912), 23–52. Also, Dennis, *Life on a Yukon Trail* (1899), 377–390, 457–466.

the divide. Some of these Indians settled around Frances Lake and Pelly River and remain there today.

Ideas of Christianity had undoubtedly long percolated through the Kaska area from the eastern peoples who were near the Oblate settlements on the Mackenzie and Fort Nelson Rivers. An Oblate made a brief visit to Fort Halkett in the middle of the nineteenth century, but no direct contact with religious leaders began until relatively late.

Around 1900 a Protestant missionary, Pallgrave, began to visit the Kaska. His preaching, which was conducted out of doors, was strongly directed against witch torture, but he also taught a few men the rudiments of writing. Selecting influential men he encouraged these to exert a moral influence on the other people. After freezing his foot by stepping into an overflow (water seeping through river ice), Pallgrave was replaced by English. The latter minister is reported to have remarked that he found the Kaska "too wild." He was followed by Thorman whose son, Fred, is the current Protestant minister at Telegraph Creek. About 1925 a Catholic church and mission school were established at Telegraph Creek. Sometime toward the close of the nineteenth century the Prophet Cult made its appearance in the Kaska area. The movement appears to have been inspired by Catholic ceremonialism and its weak development in the Cassiar was probably at least in part a result of the limited influence of Catholicism on the Kaska tribes.[44]

Among the Pelly River Indians, where the Upper Liard Indians encountered this movement, the leader of the cult was Gušai·š ("Helps the People"). This man was a Ross River shaman who affected ragged clothes, refused to cut his hair, and carried a drum. He is said to have been provided with a piece of skin on which was drawn a picture of people following in a line to heaven.[45] At assemblages, the prophet talked of God and sometimes threw pieces of meat and fat into the fire, also feeding small pieces to people. He told the people not to eat moose feet or they would be unable to use their own feet.[46] He also stuck a small piece of a feather into the hair of every person present. To some Indians he distributed amulets, consisting of smooth flat stones, the size of a quarter. These, he directed, were to be sewn into a piece of skin and worn next to the heart suspended from around the neck.[47] On other occasions he sang from a skin which was shaped like a book and accompanied himself on a drum. It was said that if blood dropped from the "book" good luck could be expected in hunting. The prophet often demonstrated his power by predicting the arrival of strangers. Gušai·š did not care for the Protestant missionaries, claiming that they did not speak the truth. He was, however, favorably disposed to the Catholic Church.

A Kaska Indian, George Steele, who had spent many years in Fort Nelson before re-

[44] Spier, however, points out that the Prophet Cult of the Northern Athapaskans may have been influenced by the Prophet Dance of the northern plateau. See Spier, *The Prophet Dance of the Northwest and Its Derivatives* (1935).

[45] "Maps" of this kind were a common feature of the Northern Athapaskan Prophet Cult. See Honigmann, *Ethnography and Acculturation of the Fort Nelson Slave* (1946), 132–134.

[46] Both the taboo on moose feet and feeding the fire are aboriginal religious elements which, in some form, still survive among the Kaska today. The feeding of meat and the distribution of feathers mentioned below hearken of communion.

[47] This practice seems to have been influenced by the Catholic scapula.

turning to Lower Post, is said to have had possession of a map showing trails to heaven. The map, Indians reported, found its way into the hands of Catholic missionaries and was blessed by the bishop. In the Dease River area, a ceremony occurred that may have contained overtones of the Prophet Dance as described by Spier. A shaman would play his drum and sing while the people danced. This was referred to as "praying to God." The shaman also dreamed to foretell the future. As a result of participating in the dance, men secured good luck for hunting. The Bear Lake Sekani are also said to have had a prophet who performed a "kind of Mass." Further west the Taku developed a movement along similar lines. The prophet would preach and once, while he was doing so, his wife took a knife out of his pocket, as he was not supposed to carry a knife while performing religious rites.

Recent history. Between 1908 and 1910 the Kaska and Tahltan Indians pooled resources with other British Columbia tribes to fight the Registered Trap Line Act of the Province. According to local informants a Kaska spokesman, Ena?inta ("He Watches the People"), declared that the Indians had existed before the white man and could continue to live without his laws. The Indians demanded the right to trap anywhere without interference, but their case was lost. The anthropologist-folklorist, James (locally, "Jimmy") Teit, aided the Indians in this legal move and was secretary of the intertribal organization.[48]

Around 1904 the Hudson's Bay Company's monopoly of trade in Lower Post was challenged by John Hyland, who built a store in that settlement which, twenty-two years later, was sold to Oscar Anderson. In the late thirties the establishment was acquired by Bill Strong who already owned a trading company in Telegraph Creek and had formerly traded up the Taku River. He named the establishment Taku Trading Company and continues to operate it through an agent (Pl. 1, B).

In 1913, in a report to the National Museum in Ottawa, Poole Field, a local prospector and trapper and formerly a Hudson's Bay trader in Fort Simpson,[49] commented on the prevalence of tuberculosis among the Cassiar tribes. "Tuberculosis seems to be the strongest of all diseases amongst them. A few years ago they were dieing off fast but it seems to have killed all the sickly ones and left the strongest and healthy ones as they are now on the increase and very little sickness amongst them of any kind."[50]

The year 1920 saw a strike of a different character from those made by miners take place in the Dease River basin. The Indians employed to line boats up that river struck for higher wages. The Hudson's Bay Company at McDame Creek had been paying liners $2.50 a day; they now demanded $5.00 daily. The work was hard and required long hours. Lining began at five o'clock in the morning and often continued until eight at night. Six men were required to pull the boat, while in the craft were a captain and tiller man. The leader of the strike was Big Joe, a Pelly River Indian, and under his leadership the strikers won their demands.

For many years reports of witch hunting emanating from the Kaska area had given those tribes an unfavorable reputation. In 1924 this notoriety was intensified when Fred Allen, a

[48] See Boas, *James A Teit* (1922); Boas, *James A. Teit* (1923). The allegation of Indians that Teit absconded to the United States with the funds of this organization (see below, pp. 153) is patently false and deserves serious refutation.

[49] Godsell, *Romance of the Alaska Highway* (1944), 87.

[50] Field, Unpublished Manuscript (1913), 10.

local white trapper, found the body of an Indian, Moccasin, in the Liard River at Little Charlie Slough, thirty miles below Lower Post. The body suggested murder and Allen reported his discovery to the Mounted Police. When they arrived at Lower Post he led them to the scene. The body, however, was missing. Nearby the police found the camp of several siblings of a prominent Nelson River Indian family. The body was finally unearthed and five Indians taken to Prince Rupert, B. C., for trial.[51]

Witch-fear apparently reached the Kaska from the Pacific coast Tlingit via the Tahltan Indians. Informants declared themselves unfamiliar with the techniques of witchcraft and denied that the phenomenon was related to aboriginal sorcery.[52]

In June 1926 a second police patrol was dispatched to Lower Post "to enforce greater respect for the law."[53] This mission was under the command of Inspector T. V. S. Wunsch, assisted by Sergeant J. R. Paton. Accompanying the party was Father E. Allard, O. M. I., en route to take up missionary work with the Kaska Indians. In July of 1926 a mild influenza epidemic attacked the native population at Lower Post as well as the police party. Sergeant Paton reported: "I find that colds and chest trouble are very prevalent in this district, chiefly attributable to their mode of living." Between August 18 and September 1 the police, together with Fred Allen, made a canoe trip to Frances Lake, where, however, they encountered no Indians. The hundred and fifty mile journey upriver took eleven days. The police remained in Lower Post for the winter. In January 1927 Paton got both his hands badly frostbitten while transporting fish from Watson Lake by dog team. One finger had to be amputated at the joint. Later that season, Wunsch suffered an attack of snowblindness.

After his arrival Father Allard opened a church and school at McDame Creek, where he also undertook a brief ethnographic study of the Dease River and Upper Liard Kaska. The priest estimated the total Kaska population to number about 150, including, he thought, "individuals from neighboring nomadic tribes, namely of the Upper Liard, Fort Grahame, Fort Nelson, and also a few from Fort McLeod and Bear Lake, British Columbia."[54] He reported informants to the effect that "the Kaska Indians were very numerous before the coming of the white man which took place about 1878, the time of the first gold rush in the Cassiar." In 1942, while traveling on upper Dease River, Father Allard was drowned near a slough which now bears his name. About that time Father Carpentier, O. M. I., entered the country and built a mission at Dease Lake Post, while the Rev. Pierre A. Poullet, O. M. I., succeeded Father Allard at McDame Creek.

At this time the Cassiar district was opened to ready access by the outside world through the extension of a northern air route from Edmonton. In 1925 occurred the first air flight to Lower Post.[55] It was ten years more, however, before an air route from Edmonton to Whitehorse, via Lower Post, was surveyed, opening the way for the first weekly mail

[51] British Columbia, *Report of the Superintendent of Provincial Police* (1925), X14; also Canada, *Report of the Royal Canadian Mounted Police* (1926), 18-19, 24.

[52] For a historical and psychological study of the dynamics of witchfear among the Kaska see Honigmann, *Witch-Fear in Post-Contact Kaska Society* (1947).

[53] Canada, *Report of the Royal Canadian Mounted Police* (1927), 81-84.

[54] Allard, *Notes on the Kaska and Upper Liard Indians* (1928), 24.

[55] Wilson, *Northwest Passage by Air* (1943), 111-118.

flight between those points in 1937. The route was operated by Yukon Southern Airlines, later absorbed by Canadian Pacific Airlines. In 1939 an airport site was surveyed at Watson Lake, about twenty-five miles from Lower Post, and connected to the town by a well worn Indian trail. Funds for the construction of the airport were released in 1940, the year in which mail service to Lower Post was increased to twice weekly. In 1941, when the construction of the airport was begun, mail service was stepped up to three times a week. In 1941 the partially finished airport was turned over to the joint control of Canadian and United States governments. Watson Lake is named for a Yorkshireman, who came to Lower Post about 1897 en route to the Klondike. He remained in the Cassiar to prospect and trap, marrying a Kaska Indian woman by whom he had several children. He died in 1938.

A new wave of activity struck the Cassiar in 1941 when the two North American governments began to enlarge Watson Lake airport for military occupation in connection with the second World War. Vast quantities of supplies and materials were shipped into the country via the Stikine waterway. The portage road from Telegraph Creek to Dease Lake was graveled and widened and a number of sternwheelers (locally called "tunnel boats") and barges were constructed at Dease Lake Post for service on the lake and river. In July 1941 the first barges reached Lower Post with supplies for the airport. A road was built extending from the settlement to Watson Lake.[56] In 1942 construction activity was stepped up with the undertaking of the Alaska Highway (first called the Alcan Highway). Thousands of civilian and uniformed construction workers began to appear in Lower Post for what slight recreation that isolated settlement afforded. In that same year the Hudson's Bay Company abandoned its McDame Creek post, transferring business to Lower Post where, in 1944, a modern store and warehouse were built fronting the new Highway (Pl. 1, c). The Roman Catholic mission also moved to Lower Post and another church was built at Watson Lake to accommodate the Catholic civilian and military personnel quartered on that huge installation. The B. C. Police constable and game warden were shifted from McDame Creek in 1944, and for a time occupied quarters near the Hyland River, twelve miles east of Lower Post, where a large construction camp was located. In 1945 these government services also located in Lower Post.

Our period of participation and observation of Kaska society covered the period from June 1944 to September 1944, when interaction between the Highway workers and Indians was still fairly high, and from June 1945 to December 1945, when this interaction had all but disappeared. Our work also followed after over a century of contact between native and western culture. The nature of this contact must now be briefly examined, since from it developed a large part of present Kaska culture.

ACCULTURATION

Three main and several less important agents of acculturation may be recognized for their influence on aboriginal Kaska culture. In the main group we can distinguish the traders, missionaries, and police. Of lesser importance in promoting culture change were the miners, trappers, and soldiers who came into contact with the native population.

---

[56] These vessels are now stored on the Indian reserve about a half mile below Lower Post. Their lumber, although available to Indians for boat construction and other purposes, is rarely used.

The most important of all of these agents of culture change were probably the fur traders and missionaries. Although similar agencies had been established in the east for almost one hundred and fifty years, general penetration of the Kaska area was effected only about one hundred years ago. As was pointed out above, resident missionaries have been in the heart of the region only since 1926. In the east, however, missionary influence has been effective far longer and it may be suspected that Catholic teachings permeated the area from eastern centers. Intensive contact with police has also been increasing since about 1926.

All of these agents of acculturation represented a more complex culture, strikingly different from that of the Kaska. In general the influence of these intrusive groups may be divided into changes which they promoted in the technical aspects of Kaska culture and changes promoted in the social aspects of the native way of life. Expressed in other terms, changes were effected in the adaptive aspects of the culture as well as in its adjustive features.[57] The degree of change in the adaptive aspects of the Kaska culture far surpassed that which resulted in the adjustive patterns. The technical changes were better understood and were received far more eagerly than the ideological teachings of the missionaries or the commands of the police. As a result of these readily accepted innovations, most of which greatly facilitated the life of the society, the people, in two or three generations, lost most of their ability to understand how the aboriginal society managed to exist under former conditions. Informants repeatedly referred to the hard life under aboriginal conditions when people lived in the bush "same like game," when there were "no clothes, just skin," and hardly any food but fish and meat. Today there is no tendency for people to idealize the ability of their grandparents to adapt to the environment with the resources of the aboriginal culture. The past is done with and nobody wants to abandon technical improvements for a return to former patterns. The same satisfaction is expressed toward those ideological and emotional features of western culture which have been most firmly accepted by the people, like Christian belief in God, heaven and hell, and the end of intertribal warfare. Nobody hearkens back to aboriginal religious concepts, although some features of this former adjustment continue to survive and have become blended with Christian religious concepts. Retroflective sentiments are, however, directed toward the abundance of moose and caribou in the past.

Looking upon the end result of acculturation more closely, it is apparent that adaptive changes have penetrated almost every aspect of the technical culture. White foods assumed great importance in the native diet, causing important changes in the economic life. Men ceased to concentrate excessive interest and energy in fishing and hunting, and devoted more time to trapping for furs. The flintlock musket and double-barreled percussion cap shot gun replaced the bow and arrow and spear. The crossbow was also introduced, with its stock shaped like a gun stock, and was used until guns came down in price. Canvas tents and log houses replaced the temporary brush shelters, as greater permanency took the

[57] In analyzing Kaska culture we will frequently find it useful to distinguish between its adaptive and adjustive aspects. Adaptation is used with reference to the physical environment, while adjustment is directed to the social, supernatural, and psychological environments. Man thus adapts to the natural environment but adjusts to other individuals, gods, spirits, and to himself. Any behavior may simultaneously serve both adaptive and adjustive functions.

place of frequent mobility. Stoves, blankets, candles, and matches became standard house-hold equipment. New and better tools, including the hammer, saw, steel knife, ax, and nail, permitted the construction of the more permanent dwellings and of tables and raised beds of hewed lumber. These tools, plus the drill, also facilitated the construction of the snowshoe, toboggan, and plank boat. The ax became indispensable for cutting wood to use in stoves. Clothing came to be prepared of wool and cotton cloth, superior to moosehide in warmth, and sewing became less tedious through the use of steel needles, cotton thread, and, finally, sewing machines. River travel and transportation was facilitated by the outboard motor, while the overland transportation grew easier when horses were introduced by the gold seekers. Deadfalls were displaced for trapping fur-bearing mammals by spring traps. Native cordage was abandoned in favor of rope and thread. Tanned skin is used largely for moc-casins and mittens. The bow and arrow, stone knife, stone points, and lance ceased to be manufactured. Bone and tooth ornaments were replaced by glass and metal jewelry; native face paints by cosmetics. Tattooing also disappeared.

Following acceptance of many adaptive techniques and resources from western culture, the Kaska became highly dependent upon these innovations. Today river travel without the convenience of an outboard engine is almost unthinkable; sewing is often postponed until a sewing machine can be obtained; hunting is impossible without a gun. This de-pendence upon recently acquired technical processes complements the previously discussed absence of any idealization of previous patterns of adaptation.

In the adjustive sphere of the culture the important introductions of white men in-cluded a new language—English—with its system of numeration and of ordering time and weights; a new religion, Christianity, and a new system of social control.[58] The Kaska were also faced with the necessity of adjusting to a new ethnic group, the whites. While the native language continued to be spoken within the society, other adjustive patterns dropped out, such as belief in many native supernaturals as well as many avoidances and taboos. Shamans ceased to be the curers of the society. Warfare stopped, and people became subject to the system of institutionalized justice introduced by the government. After the arrival of resident Catholic missionaries nuptials began to be celebrated with religious rites and many marriages acquired a legally binding character. In local summer schools, priests started to give Kaska children elementary training in reading and writing; a few older boys and girls were sent to boarding schools located outside of the Cassiar. New patterns of amusement were introduced, including listening to recorded music, face-to-face ballroom dancing, and poker. More recently the radio has become a popular instrument, while the United States Army permitted a number of young people to see occasional motion pictures.

The early traders tried to institute some degree of government among the Indians in order to improve the collection of fur. They appointed "chiefs," whose main duty was to stimulate energetic trapping. To enhance their status, some chiefs received certain distinc-

[58] The French language never developed in the Cassiar as it did in the Mackenzie Basin. Contact with the French was restricted to the eastern fringes of the Kaska. Once the Cassiar was thoroughly penetrated (about 1870), the day of these traders was over and the Hudson's Bay Company was using English and Scotch represen-tatives. Missionary influence was also late; when the French-Catholic Oblates arrived they readily accepted Eng-lish as the second language of the people.

tive articles of clothing, like colored coats. Men selected for leadership were usually influential "talkers" and were annually provided with food to be distributed at a feast or apportioned to families. This type of government has now been replaced by a still looser form, chiefs being designated by the Indian Agent. Present day Indian leaders have practically no social functions.

From trappers, miners, traders, and other visitors to the region, the Kaska gradually accumulated a knowledge of the "outside"—the cities of the American continent and foreign countries. Illustrated papers and magazines increased the vividness of this knowledge and by their aid some adults laboriously learned to read. Through these agents of culture change, the Indians also acquired an appetite for alcoholic beverages as well as the knowledge for preparing them. In recent years, the presence of United States soldiers in the area greatly influenced the Indians' opinion of "Americans," stereotyped attitudes toward this group being formed which differ sharply from those held about Canadians.

In many respects, however, the ideological and emotional aspects of Kaska culture do not follow the pattern of the white society, and processes of child socialization still adhere to aboriginal lines. Certain traits were only partially accepted or, being adopted, received a different interpretation by the Indians. Many adaptive and adjustive features of the aboriginal culture remain, sometimes slightly modified, alongside the newly acquired patterns. In certain parts of the Kaska area (notably Frances Lake), acculturation has proceeded more slowly than in others. Because some individuals were raised by white fathers or in the service of white men, differences in ideological and emotional acculturation must also be recognized as occurring between individuals and families constituting the society.

The end product of these hundred years of contact between western society and the Kaska Indians is present day Kaska culture.

TECHNICAL CULTURE

LIKE all societies, the Kaska Indians are faced with the problem of surviving in a physical environment. In this division we will discuss Kaska culture as it is directed toward maintaining adaptation to the climate, weather, and natural resources of a specific geographical area, while at the same time it strives to preserve life and comfort by satisfying the physical needs of the human organism.

ANNUAL CYCLE

The economic life of the Kaska tribes is closely bound up with the exploitation of their forest surroundings. During the summer months, the people live leisurely around the trading post, relying upon the traders' stocks for almost all of their requirements. The means to buy these goods, however, is the money received for fur that was trapped during the previous winter and spring.

A good time to begin studying the annual cycle is in August or September, when the people, by quitting Lower Post, put an end to their relatively idle summer. Returning home to the winter settlements and trap lines is always undertaken with great eagerness since, among other rewards, it means relief from the expensive diet of canned meat and other staples and promises a welcome supply of fresh meat and fish. The months until early November are occupied with hunting, drying meat, working hide, building or repairing cabins, and manufacturing equipment like toboggans, sleighs, and snowshoes, which will be necessary for winter trapping. With the first heavy snowfall, hunting becomes of secondary importance and trapping begins for fine fur. This activity is often interrupted around Christmas for a visit to the trading post by men and boys. Here skins are sold and additional food purchased for transportation home. Two or three such trips may be made in the course of a winter. With the arrival of March, beaver and muskrat trapping starts and when this period ends in spring, the people are ready to undertake their summer visit to Lower Post, where they arrive in late May or June.

CAPITAL

Against this bird's eye view of the round of Kaska life, we now take up in detail the economically productive routines of the people. All of the exploitative and technological processes to be described depend on a remarkably small accumulation of capital or producer goods, much of which is of negligible intrinsic value.

A large portion of the capital goods used by the Kaska is not manufactured by the society but is purchased from traders. Such goods include guns, traps, fish nets, sewing machines, snare wire, horses, most tools and implements, matches, vessels, and utensils. Pack dogs are domesticated locally although small hunt dogs are purchased from Tahltan Indians. Other products, equally important in carrying out adaptive routines, are manufactured by the society. Included here are ladders, windlasses, packsacks, dogpacks, lines, wedges, and skin stretchers. The construction of most native manufactures, however, depends upon basic tools and implements, like knives, canvas, thread, pulleys, needles, and drills, which are purchased from traders."

Animal husbandry. The dog and horse are the only domesticated animals. Two types of dogs are utilized, pack dogs and hunting dogs. Pack dogs average about twenty inches from the ground and are of no particular breed (Pl. 7, A and B), while hunting dogs are much smaller. A pack dog becomes useful at about three years and is at his prime in his fourth year. When a dog is six years old signs of weakness begin to appear and his load must be lightened. A family owns from two to five dogs.

Relatively little care is manifested in the breeding, care, and feeding of these animals. An example of poor care was manifested by Nitla who, returning from a hunt early one morning with his dog's nose full of porcupine quills, did not remove these until four o'clock that afternoon. The feeding of dogs is a haphazard procedure, although in general they are more conscientiously fed in winter, when they are required to do more work, than in summer when they are little employed. The animals are also said to eat more in cold weather. Dogs are fed once a day, in the evening. Their food generally consists of purchased dog meal mixed with table scraps and water. Meat and fish are fed to dogs only if these foods are abundant. When traveling in winter, a small piece of lard may be added to the dog meal. If meat is scarce and the supply of meal exhausted, dogs may be fed with a mixture of white or whole wheat flour and water to which a small piece of lard is sometimes added. In winter especially while traveling, food for dogs is served warm. "Just like people like hot tea," Harry Lang explained. In a year, it was estimated, three dogs consume about six hundred pounds of dog meal, although this amount can be reduced if sufficient moose and caribou are killed. Trapped animals, such as marten and lynx, are also boiled and fed to dogs by some people. Louis Maza and River Joe, however, reported that they never fed such meat to dogs. "If you do, never catch anything next time."

No systematic attempt is made to train dogs beyond intimidating the animals from attacking people or from rushing upon slain game. Formal training, by means of consistent reward and punishment, is completely lacking nor was any evidence seen of a personal affectionate relationship between dog and master. Dogs are rarely admired but often verbally pitied. Typically a dog cowers in front of his master. Some animals, however, are designated as being better trained than others and quicker to obey commands. A man used to better trained dogs finds it exasperating to use another person's poorly trained animals. A rather unsuccessful attempt is made to restrain dogs from indiscriminate barking. Such noise interferes with sleep and is also thought to frighten game out of the neighborhood. Barking dogs are therefore quieted by lusty shouting or by picking up a stick and flinging it in their direction.

In early winter, women and girls prepare brush shelters to house these animals during the cold months. In temporary winter camps, brush is placed on the snow for the dogs to sleep on. Dogs are never permitted in the house or camp. Although pups are given considerable freedom around a camp, after six or seven months they, like full grown dogs, are always kept tied a short distance from the residences. An exception to this rule occurs when meat is scarce and dog meal exhausted. In December 1945, when the ethnographer's party arrived at River Joe's place, three of that man's dogs were seen foraging through the settlement while two others had been sent to River Joe's son-in-law, Louis Maza, because of the report that the latter had killed two moose.

Most people call their dogs in English. Some of the names given are: Tobacco, Paper, Yukon, Boiler, One Dollar, Spotty and Wolverine (also called Long Face in the Kaska language). Dogs are generally owned by men, but women and children usually prepare their food and feed them.

Little attention is paid to keeping dogs free from fleas or lice, although wood ashes applied to the animal's hair is regarded as effective in killing these pests. An efficient way of removing porcupine quills from a dog is to empty a porcupine's bladder on the affected parts. The urine stops the quills from penetrating further and the needles can then be painlessly withdrawn.

A few Nelson Indians own horses purchased from points outside of the Kaska area.[1] A family generally owns two or three horses and the winter mortality of the animals is apparently high. Horses are used as riding animals by both sexes. Boys from the age of twelve experience great enjoyment galloping and often ride bareback. Western type saddles are generally employed and preferred for riding. The main function of horses is to pack supplies from the trading post to the winter settlements, but they are also used in summer and fall to pack meat from a moose kill. One or two people in the Upper Liard River district considered purchasing horses with which winter outfits could be transported overland northeastward from the Alaska Highway. Other Indians maintained that horses are suitable east of Lower Post because there the snow is not very deep and horses can winter out. On the Upper Liard, however, the deeper snow would make winter feeding a serious problem. No grain is purchased for the winter feeding of horses. Some men showed considerable affection for these animals and also demonstrated a knowledge of equine qualities.

Weapons. Large and small caliber rifles are used in hunting. The single-shot bolt-action rifle, firing a short or long .22 caliber cartridge, is mainly used for fowl and small game like rabbits. It is also used to kill furbearing animals, such as lynx, wolf and coyote, when these are found alive in traps. The relatively low cost of this gun permits extensive distribution. It is the first weapon which the adolescent boy or girl is able to use and own. The larger rifles of Canadian or American manufacture, firing a .30/30 or /.30/06 caliber shell, are used for killing large game like the moose and caribou. These guns are also regarded as necessary protection against the danger of bears. Their ownership is restricted to men, older boys, and women.

Considerable interest and discussion revolves around the types of shells available for large caliber rifles. Long shells are preferred in the .22 size. Hard point large caliber car-

---

[1] According to one informant the horse was introduced from Fort Nelson, presumably by members of the Nelson Tribe. If true, this would put the date of the introduction of the horse after 1920, or after this animal reached the Fort Nelson Slave (Honigmann, *Ethnography and Acculturation of the Fort Nelson Slave* [1946], 114). According to Old Man, however, the Kaska certainly *saw* their first horse many years earlier, when the Klondike miners passed up the Liard and Frances Rivers' valleys. It is also possible that the horse was originally introduced from the south, via Forts Grahame and Ware, rather than from the east, and it is also well to remember that horse packing for big game hunters has long been an important occupation at Telegraph Creek. In 1944–45 a number of white packers kept horses around Racing River, 150 miles east of Lower Post, and also at Teslin Lake. Indians purchased horses during this period from a trucker, who brought the animals from Dawson Creek.

tridges, bearing what is called a "steel" point, are considered superior to soft point shells. The former are said to kill quicker and this especially recommends them for use against an animal like the grizzly bear. "Go right clean through," Nitla said, explaining the force of the steel tipped cartridge. A soft point shell, on the other hand, may be stopped if it strikes bone. It is understood that the point of the cartridge must be neither too long nor too heavy, else it will lose in distance, dropping low. Beyond this there is no interest in ballistics.

Constant watchfulness is exercised in the handling of guns. A loaded gun will never be used to test ice or as a walking stick nor are .22's kept around camp with a loaded chamber. Fourteen year old Donald Suza expressed disapproval of the ethnographer keeping a loaded .22 in the cabin. "What for you load gun?" he demanded. Asked if this was not good sense, he replied: "Yeah, no good."

Most young men are capable of making repairs on a gun, such as adjusting the sights or sawing down the barrel and constructing new sights. Testing the firing power, range, and trajectory of rifles is one of the reasons for target practice. Much of this firing, however, is not designed to test the weapon but rather the shooter's marksmanship. Target practice is never seriously competitive. Girls were not observed to use guns for this purpose in camp. According to Old Man, however, girls are apt to target shoot when in the bush. Older men tend to condemn this shooting as wasteful. Old Man mildly scolded Donald Suza for target practice. "What you want to shoot water for? You can't eat water." But both Old Man and Old Kean admitted to target shooting in their youth.

Tools. Certain essential tools are found in every household. Women's tools include scissors, needles, thimbles, and steel awls. A married woman generally owns her own ax, butcher knife, file, and tanning tools. The latter include a metal scraper, used to remove hair from moosehide, and a skin softener. Scrapers are manufactured by men from discarded files. The handle of the file is removed and the metal pounded flat on both ends. The flaring ends are then bent in opposite directions and sharpened. The center of the tool is wrapped in cloth or moosehide to provide a grip. The skin softener is prepared from a piece of green wood eighteen inches long and about three inches in diameter. The surface is rounded and smoothed along most of the stick. One end is split and a thin stone, about three inches long and chipped to a thin edge on one side, is inserted. This end is then bound tight with a strip of canvas or moosehide and lashed with cord. Men's tools include the long handled ax, knife, hammer, awl, T-square, drill, plane, and file.

Each sex keeps its own tools in repair and cutting tools like the ax, knife, and scissors are always found well sharpened. Sharpening is done with a six or eight inch file, care being taken to always sharpen blades on axes in such a manner as to avoid a ridge and secure a gently tapering thinness which will assure a deep cut and prevent dangerous glancing. Certain tools are found in almost every winter settlement and may be used by both sexes or by more than one family: the one man crosscut, whip, and Swedish type buck saws, shovel, rake, pick, and mattock. Ownership of a carpenter's rule or measuring tape was not observed. Men sometimes make measuring sticks out of a straight length of willow. This is axed off sharply at one end and laid against the object to be measured, the sharply cut end against one end of the object. At the opposite end of the object the stick is notched and again sharply cut off. The size of the pole now corresponds to the object measured and is light enough to carry wherever an article of corresponding size is to be manufactured. An object to be fabricated in dimensions to match another article may also be compared to the latter by means of a length of string in which a knot is tied at the required length. Thus in the construction of a coffin, the length and width of the deceased were observed to be taken with a piece of string. The height of the reclining body, however, was ignored, hence the coffin was made too low.

Wedges for splitting wood are manufactured as required. They are cut from the lower portion of a black spruce sapling and sharpened with an ax to a long tapering blade. Chips of wood are used as wedges in whip sawing. The back of a long handled ax head is used as a maul.

The implements associated with most cabins are a broom, funnel, and a dustpan cut from a five gallon oil can. One family used an eagle wing as a whisk broom. When cooking is done on open fires, the tea stick is an indispensable piece of household equipment. It consists of a green willow pole, five or six feet long and an inch or more in its greatest diameter. The heavier section of the pole is sharpened and thrust into the ground at a forty-five degree angle to the fire. The upper section of the pole is notched for the handle of the kettle. The pole may be turned aside from the fire in removing the vessel. In a few days, when the ground becomes too soft to support the pole, a rock may be placed on top of the buried portion of the wood and another stone thrust into the apex made by the pole as it leaves the ground. Tea poles are discarded when they become dry or charred. When meat is roasted in front of open fires smaller poles, about three feet high are cut, and thrust into the ground almost vertically, the meat being hung on a sharpened point.

A considerable amount of apparatus is manufactured. In front of each cabin is found a sawhorse for sawing wood. This consists of a bedlog about six inches in diameter and five or six feet long. Close to each end two spruce saplings, about four feet long and an inch and a half in diameter, are driven into the ground so that they cross each other at about a thirty degree angle. The wood to be sawed is placed in these angles. The bedlog is sometimes also used in splitting sawed lengths of wood. In the bush near the settlement are one or more saw pits. Ladders are made to reach caches. The rungs are either set in holes or nailed to side pieces. At either end of the ladder braces are nailed to the side pieces of lumber. For carpentering, a felled tree is levelled with an ax and raised on two stumps to serve as a workbench. Another piece of apparatus is used for bending green lumber in the manufacture of toboggans and sleds (Fig. 3, F, and Pl. 6, A). About six feet long, this consists of the lower trunk and part of the root of a spruce tree. Unnecessary portions of the root and trunk are trimmed away so that the wood exhibits a natural curve which is hewed and planed on its upper surface. Two poles, about two inches in diameter, are nailed to either side of the trunk. Where they project a few inches in front of the root, a crosspiece about eighteen inches long is lashed. The space between the root and crosspiece holds the lumber inserted for bending.

Traps, which are an important category of capital goods, are generally purchased, but a few men still build deadfalls or set two or three snares for wolf and coyote. A trapper generally owns from thirty to fifty steel traps of various sizes some of which are given to wives and children. A limited number of snares constructed of wire cable are also purchased by most families. +

Fur destined for commercial channels is dried on fur stretchers. The several kinds of stretchers may be classified into two types, those used to stretch fine winter fur and those used for beaver skins. Winter fur stretchers are of two sub-types. The first, which may be designated as the keel variety, consists of a flat board known as the stretching board or mould. The dimensions vary according to the pelt for which they are designed. Cut from the wood of a packing case or a piece of hewed poplar or spruce, a keel stretcher for mink is about fifteen inches long, three inches in its greatest width and about a quarter of an inch thick. The edges of the board are crudely bevelled. The foreward portion of the mould tapers sharply for an inch or so to hold the head of the skin being stretched. The keel for a mink stretcher consists of a piece of wood somewhat shorter than the length of the stretching board, half an inch thick, and two inches in its greatest width (Fig. 3, D, a). Along one side of its width the wood is perfectly level. In use this side of the keel is placed on top of the mould. Once inserted in the pelt with the pointed end under the head, the keel is lifted from the stretching board with a wedge consisting of any piece of wood about four inches long, an inch wide, and an inch thick.

The second sub-type of winter fur stretcher may be designated as the keelless variety (Fig. 3, D, b) and consists of two moulds separated by a wedge. These stretchers are used for furs like lynx, fox, coyote, wolverine, and wolf. Two pieces of hewed spruce about one and one quarter inches thick are used in the preparation of the mould. They are finished with an ax and planed smooth. For coyote and lynx skins each board is about six feet long and five to six inches across at the widest portion. The upper portion of each board tapers to a sharp point for about the foreward three inches. The rest of one side is gently rounded. The other side is level for about three quarters of the length. The wood is then sharply rounded to provide a handlelike end about a foot long. These boards are inserted into the skin so that the level sides are together. Between them is inserted a wedge, four feet long and tapering to a sharp point from a width of about four inches. The wedge forces the stretching boards apart thus spanning the skin. Including the time occupied in finding a suitable tree and hewing the lumber, about four hours are required to make a pair of these moulds.

A beaver stretcher is made by bending a green black spruce sapling, about seven feet long and an inch and a half in its widest diameter, into a half oval. A crosspiece, consisting of a spruce pole four feet long is lashed across the open end of the oval. The skin to be stretched is lashed to the stretcher with fine babiche, small holes being cut in the pelt's rim about two inches apart.

The frame used in cleaning moosehide is made by providing a ridge pole about twelve feet long and three or four inches in diameter. One end of this pole is lashed or nailed to a tree at a point about twelve feet from the ground. The other end is generally supported in a forked stick or may also be lashed to a nearby tree. Two poles three inches in diameter and about ten feet long are tied to this ridge pole with their lower end resting on the ground in a forty-five degree angle. The space between these poles is somewhat greater than the

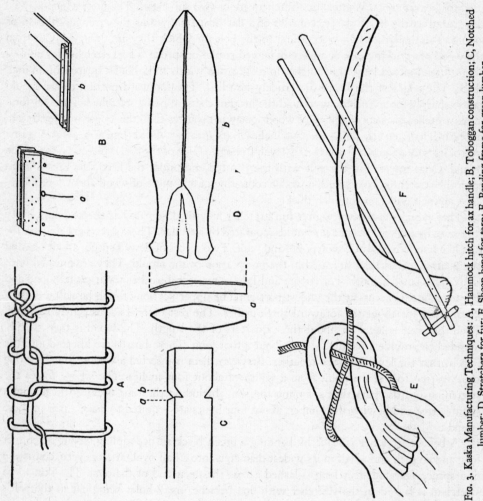

Fig. 3. Kaska Manufacturing Techniques: A, Hammock hitch for ax handle; B, Toboggan construction; C, Notched lumber; D, Stretchers for fur; E, Sheep bend for tarp; F, Bending frame for green lumber.

hide which is to be cleaned. Another pole is placed across the lower portion of the horizontally leaning poles and lashed in position. The skin is then perforated and fastened to the frame. When hides are to be softened, they are fixed on a smaller frame, consisting of four poles, in which the side poles are anchored in the ground perpendicularly (Pl. 8, D).

Construction of most apparatus and all tool making is done by men. Young girls sometimes make stretchers for squirrel skin and women commonly erect the poles for stretching and softening moosehide.

Machines employed by the Kaska have either been purchased from traders or adapted from white sources. Among the machines in the former category are sewing machines, owned by women but purchased by men, and outboard motors, the property of men. A pulley is a common possession and in the fall is used in conjunction with an improvised winch to pull boats out of the water. The winch is made by driving two poles about four inches in diameter and five feet long into the ground about six feet apart. Each pole is grooved on the side which is away from the water and about six inches from the top. A smooth green pole, about four inches in diameter, is fitted into these grooves to serve as a winch. The pull of the boat is sufficient to keep the winch from slipping out of the grooves. A handle is made by lashing a green spruce pole, about two feet long and two inches in diameter, at right angles to the winch.

Every household uses such cooking utensils as frying pans, straight kettles varying in size from one to five quarts, coffee pots, bowls, plates, cups, silver plated spoons and forks, wash basins, and washtubs. A few families have also accumulated china cups and dishes. Bottles and jars are generally saved for storing homebrew and may also function as baby bottles, candlesticks, and sugar bowls. The fifty pound drums in which dehydrated milk is purchased are used to store rice and flour. Empty sugar and flour sacks are widely used to contain tea, rice, meat, and many other commodities. Discarded oil tins are used for storing gasoline and kerosene.

Domestically manufactured utensils include moosehide gun cases, embroidered with silk thread, needle cases, made of scraps of cotton cloth, sewing kits of velvet fitted with pockets and embroidered with silk thread, and envelopes of birch bark containing sinew line or pounded beaver castors.

Productive capital. In general the producer goods needed by an individual or family, both home constructed and purchased, are found in every settlement. Thus each family is in an equal position to secure or create necessary consumer goods. Even if an object is not owned by an individual, it may generally be borrowed from others within the winter settlement or from nearby neighbors. If not immediately required by the owner, such articles are readily loaned, and rent is rarely or never demanded. If an outboard motor is loaned, the borrower is only expected to supply his own gasoline. When dogs are loaned, it is with the sole stipulation that they will be reasonably well fed and otherwise cared for. In short, the necessary productive capital is widely distributed or generally accessible.

EXPLOITATIVE ACTIVITIES

During nine or more months of the year, from the middle of August till late in May, the Kaska Indians are actively occupied in exploiting the resources of their sub-Arctic environment. This section describes the methods of securing the principal raw materials—berries, brush, water, wood, game, fish, fur, and garden produce.

Collecting. Berries, moss, spruce brush, spruce gum, and eggs are collected. In summer the tops of the wild onion plant may be pulled for use in soup, and a parsnip-like tuber is sometimes dug. Most berry picking occurs in late summer, but girls may still pick a few high bush cranberries while visiting the rabbit lines in early winter. When women and girls return to camp with berries, they may offer a share to women who did not participate in the picking. Men will often stop while traveling to pick from an abundant supply of blueberries or low bush cranberries.

Moss is pulled from the ground and piled in a small piece of canvas which is folded together for transportation. In winter the woman scrapes away the snow with her hands or snowshoes and uses an ax to chop out a frozen area of moss. After the moss is dried out it is used to pad children's diaper cloths. When used to chink log cabins, moss is not dried. Spruce brush for use as a camp floor is cut by the women. A number of small trees may be dragged into camp and then trimmed. More rarely, a little brush is obtained by cutting away the lower branches of a standing tree. Spruce gum is peeled off a red spruce tree in the course of traveling and chewed immediately. In June or July a hunter occasionally finds the eggs of spruce hens or willow grouse. The eggs are gently shaken or tapped to ascertain if there is a young bird inside; should this be the case, they are said to be returned to the nest.

Water is obtained from rivers, streams, and lakes in one or two quart covered cooking vessels by the women. In winter the ice of the river is chopped through and this must be done several times a day or else the hole will soon freeze over again. Snow may be melted to secure water. Stagnant marsh water is avoided whenever a better source of running water is not too far distant.

Collecting wood for fuel is time consuming in the winter season. An open camp fire in summer or fall imposes relatively little effort as far as fuel gathering is concerned. Most families wait till twilight to gather a large enough supply of poles to keep the fire going until bedtime. In winter, gathering fuel for an open fire is more laborious, since enough wood has to be collected to provide heat till morning. Except for rotten spruce wood used in smoking hides, it is ideally the man's task to bring wood into camp. In practice, however, women and girls assist. Keeping a stove going in winter requires so much fuel that it is not possible to rely on the supply of dead wood lying around a settlement. Therefore, in order to insure an adequate winter wood supply for a settlement, sufficient trees must be dried two or more years in advance. Two methods are used for drying trees, burning and girdling. In the former procedure, small tracts of timber are fired when the wind is right. The fire kills the trees and in a year or so the wood is dry enough for fuel. More often red spruce trees, from six to twenty inches in diameter, are girdled. This process will dry a tree in about two years. Jackpine is sometimes dried by felling a number of trees, cleaning off the limbs, and then stacking the poles upright against a clump of willows to dry. In about three years this wood will be thoroughly dry, although half-dry jackpine is used in open fires and green jackpine is burned in heaters. A sufficient amount of wood is rarely cut to last more than a short time. Each spring there is usually a severe shortage of wood, and any deadwood lying around the settlement, including discarded artifacts, is utilized for heat.

Green timber is used for lumber. Beyond finding a thick trunk of reasonably straight grain, little selection enters into picking trees to be used for ordinary manufactures. The selection of a birch to be used in constructing a toboggan is more carefully made. A fairly wide diameter is desirable so that three rather than four pieces of lumber will provide sufficient width for the vehicle. Straight grain is also sought. Finally, the tree must be healthy and without any sign of rust on the bark to within two feet from the ground, since it is the lower portion of the wood which is best suited for bending.

Hunting and fishing. The greatest emotional interest is invested in moose hunting, which requires considerable persistence and initiative. Yet in all hunting the person usually sets out with the same self-confidence and expectation of success. This attitude was character-istically expressed by Old Kean who said: "I never hunt yet. Bye and bye hunt all right. I kill him." Louis Maza once said: "We're gonna set fish net. We're gonna catch them." River Joe proclaimed himself to be a good hunter: "See track, follow him anyplace. Get him all right." Several times before setting out on a hunt, individuals mentioned dreams which contained a reference to fish or meat. These were interpreted as favorable omens for the forthcoming venture. Such dreams may be regarded as further aiding the hunter's and fisherman's self-confidence. Another important factor regarding the optimism that charac-terizes hunting is the fact that a person rarely sets out on a major hunting trip out of a sense of duty or urgency. Only chicken and rabbit hunting, in which the hunter knows from experience that he can expect some success, is undertaken as a routine activity out of necessity. The hunting of larger animals, however, always rests on the hunter's enthusiasm and eagerness. Pressure is of little avail if a man does not choose to hunt.

The moose, as mentioned, is the most important game animal hunted by the Kaska, al-though in winter the caribou is equally important for food. Throughout the year adolescent boys and young men hunt rabbits. Porcupine are killed whenever the opportunity presents itself, despite the fact that in British Columbia a law prohibits this. Bears are not sought but are usually shot when encountered. If meat is short, a man may illegally shoot a beaver. In early autumn, men occasionally visit the mountains to hunt and trap groundhog and gopher. Hunting by Indians, except for porcupine and fur bearing animals, is not restricted by game laws.

A man planning to hunt moose generally prepares to be gone several days and expects to travel a radius of fifteen miles or more. Parts of country containing flat marshy stretches with, perhaps, an overlooking ridge are favorite spots for such hunting. Stretches of burnt timber are also visited for moose. A moose hunter's equipment always includes a large caliber rifle, a short handled ax, nails or line (in the event that he wants to return to camp on a raft), a sharp butcher knife wrapped in a rag, and matches. Food is also taken, the amount depending on the time the hunter expects to be gone but always including flour mixed with baking powder and tea mixed with sugar. These supplies partially fit into the hunter's pack. Blankets and ax are packed on a dog. Food is generally prepared for a man by his wife, who asks her husband how long he expects to be gone. If two or three men hunt together each takes his own food.

Moose are hunted individually. The hunter heads for a likely area and searches the ground for signs. When a track has been located, he estimates its freshness from the moisture of the torn soil, from the freshness of excrement, and from willow shoots, torn while the animal was feeding. By the size of the hoof prints, he is able to say if the animal was a bull or a cow. Should the tracks be two days old or more, they are abandoned; otherwise the hunter sets out to follow. Tracking requires careful walking and moccasins are always worn. The tracker avoids stepping on dead wood and is cautious not to break or snap twigs as he passes through brushy places. He watches the wind so as to approach the animal with the current blowing from the latter's direction. When the trail veers from the wind, the hunter abandons the track and, heading with the wind, makes a half circle so as to come on the moose a mile or so further on. Should he come out below the moose, he judges the character of the country before him and the signs of the track. If he knows the area ahead to be thickly covered with willow and other brush, and if the evidence in torn soil, droppings, and bruised twigs is very fresh, the hunter suspects that the animal is only a short distance off, feeding or lying down. Again the hunter makes a half circle calculated to bring him close enough to the unsuspecting animal to venture a shot. Sometimes such a circuit brings the hunter up ahead of the moose. He must then retrace his steps, circling back to where he believes the moose to be. Often deep brush intervenes in the hunter's pursuit, causing him to lose his game either by missing the trail or by frightening the animal with noises. To these difficulties must be added the hazard of coughing. Returning from a moose hunt in the fall of 1945, Old Man said that the hunters coughed so much from colds that they frightened all moose away. When he was out tracking and a paroxysm of coughing threatened, Old Man threw himself flat on the ground to suppress the noise. In the fall, when moose are breeding, the haphazard tracks of the bull are hopeless to follow, and tracking is abandoned, since the bull "never rests." At this time a hunter will try to attract a bull or cow within range of his gun by imitating the bull's call or by rubbing an old moose horn or scapula on a tree.

9:19:45 (Old Man's place). Seven miles northwest of Old Man's Place is a point along a ridge known as Moose Hill. A number of moose have been killed from this elevation, the place overlooking a marshy willow flat where moose are fond of feeding. Harry headed here to call moose. He stopped and called at a point further below on the ridge but nothing responded.[2] At Moose Hill, Harry called again. In about five minutes he saw a cow moose appear on the flat below him. He shot once and missed. Quickly he injected a hard point cartridge into his rifle and, as the running animal appeared in an open space, shot again. The second shot went through the neck killing the moose.

Late winter, when the snow is crusted, is a favored time for hunting moose. Then the animal is said to be easy to kill because, sinking into the snow, he cannot readily escape the hunter who remains on the surface of the crust. Dogs are rarely used in moose hunting.

The moose is butchered immediately after killing, the work being done on a carpet of spruce or willow brush. The general procedure is to remove the head of the animal, skin the carcass, sever the limbs, and then, after gutting, cut the rest of the body into quarters and remove a few ribs and some tenderloin for transportation back to camp. Certain parts of

---

[2] The following morning when the ethnographer and a party passed this place they saw tracks of a bull crossing Harry's trail. The bull had apparently come to the spot after Harry's departure to investigate the latter's call.

the gut, such as the colon fat and kidney fat, as well as the heart, liver, and head are cached with the meat, the cache being protected by covering it with additional green willow or spruce brush. The hunter packs only enough meat for all families in camp to eat. A wife generally distributes this meat after her husband's return. The next morning, each family sends representatives to pack home a share of the kill. Nobody is necessarily invited on such an expedition, but everyone is free to join.[3] Dogs are taken as pack animals or, in winter, are harnessed to a toboggan. The hunter generally accompanies the group, leading the way. When the meat place is reached, tea is started and the viscera of the dead animal thrown to the dogs. Everybody then sets about butchering a quarter of the carcass and appropriating the meat. The whole procedure is fluid and unformalized, resting solely on each individual's initiative. No one exercises leadership or direction. Tea is ready by the time the meat has been divided. A lunch is generally prepared by roasting several ribs or tenderloin steaks in front of the fire. Leg bones are also roasted and then cracked for the marrow. When eating has been completed, the dogs or toboggan are packed and the party returns home.

Moose hunting, as well as big game hunting in general, is undertaken by a man, although there are no restrictions preventing a woman from engaging in the activity if she feels capable of doing so, particularly if she has no one to supply her with meat. In the fall several families will travel fifteen or twenty miles to a good "moose place," where a base camp is established from which individuals go out to hunt.

The amount of time and energy consumed in moose hunting may be judged by an inspection of the data in Table 4. It must be noted that this was the fourth year in which moose were reported to be extremely scarce in the Upper Liard River area, where these incidents were observed.

TABLE 4. AMOUNT OF TIME SPENT IN MOOSE HUNTING—1945

Personnel	Time Spent	Results
Louis Maza and Peter Tom	Seven hours	Three duck
Louis Maza and white man	Five hours	Nothing
Nitla	Three days	One porcupine
Harry Lang	Ten hours	One cow moose
Hans Donnelly and Nitla	Two days	Nothing

The time schedules are difficult to summarize in a table. For example, on October 1 Old Man left for a moose hunting trip. His son-in-law, Hans Donnelly, left to join him on October 3, together with Louis Maza and his family. On October 5 Old Man's remaining son-in-law, Harry Lang, joined the hunters, accompanied by Nitla. Harry and Nitla reached the base camp of the hunters just in time to help eat a bull which Hans had killed on the previous day. During the remaining three weeks that all except one man in this group hunted, not one other moose was killed, although several were missed. Harry and Nitla

[3] Such sharing of meat is strongly expected. Old Man referred to a cousin of River Joe who refused to share meat. If someone approached this man while he was butchering and asked for a share of the kill, the latter would reply: "No, go get meat yourself." Such behavior met with strong disapproval.

stayed out hunting a total of ten unproductive days, Hans sixteen days, and Old Man twenty days—a total of forty-six man days in which only one moose was killed.

Harry Lang's journal for 1940 was analyzed to discover the number of days spent hunting and the amount of game killed. The figures are presented in Table 5.

TABLE 5. AMOUNT OF TIME SPENT IN HUNTING—1940

Date	Number of Persons	Results
April 23		"No luck"
April 24		One caribou
May 1		"4 or 5" caribou
May 5		"No luck"
May 8	2	Four caribou
May 9	2	One caribou
May 10–11	3	One beaver, one moose
May 16–18	1	One beaver, one moose
May 23		No luck
May 24		One caribou
June 3–4		One moose
June 27		No luck
July 2–8		Two moose
July 9		One bull moose
July 11		One bull moose
August 6–24	2–3	Three bull moose; four goats
August 25–31	2–3	Three bull moose

The brief period studied reveals both more time invested in hunting and greater success in this activity than were manifested during the term of field work. An explanation for the intense hunting may lie in the fact that during the winter of 1939–40, Harry's settlement ran short of food.[4] As a result, it seems likely that not enough time could be spent trapping to permit a leisurely summer in Lower Post. Hence the summer was utilized for hunting, the meat being important for seeing the family through till fall.

Caribou are generally sought after the beginning of December, when small flocks begin to descend from the mountains to river valleys. They are far easier to hunt than moose, and it is often possible to shoot several on the frozen river without moving far from the settlement.

A rabbit hunter can operate in a radius of a mile or two from camp and seldom spends more than two or three hours daily at his work. With a .22 caliber rifle and a game bag or packsack, the hunter starts in the late afternoon, seeking a place where black spruce grows thickly. Walking carefully, he peers under the brush and watches spaces between more distant trees. In 1945, a man generally managed to return with one or two of these animals after two hours in the bush. Rabbits are skinned and cleaned by women, to whom the hunter turns over the catch when he returns to camp. Rabbit hunting is usually done by

[4] See below, p. 103.

adolescent boys and men, although it is also attempted by any girl old enough to handle a gun.

Porcupine are either shot or clubbed to death. Lacking a gun, Paulette Donnelly once axed down a jackpine on which she had seen a porcupine sitting. As the tree fell and the animal began to wobble off, Paulette went in pursuit and clubbed it with the back of her ax. After a porcupine is killed the hunter builds a fire and burns off the quills. The animal is then laid on a carpet of brush for butchering. A cut is first made on the ventral surface of the body, extending from the neck to the anus. The stomach and intestines immediately fall from the body cavity. The small intestine is carefully cut free, in order to preserve its blanket of fat. This organ resembles a string of link sausage, and is emptied by being pinched downward from the junction of each link. The heart, liver, and kidneys are left in the carcass, which is packed back to camp with the small gut.

The duck and goose are hunted in spring and fall, and the spruce hen and willow grouse, throughout the year. Chicken hunting, like rabbit hunting, is generally motivated by the need for meat but girls frequently kill these birds while tending to the family's rabbit line. Generally the birds are plucked immediately after being killed, when the feathers are easy to remove. Success in hunting chicken depends largely on encountering a sizeable flock of feeding birds. A man may also return to a spot where he killed several spruce hens to shoot those which escaped but which remained in the neighborhood. With luck favoring him, a hunter will sometimes return from a fowling trip with six to nine birds. When a man's bag is as large as this, he may send some of his catch to other families in camp.

Most fishing is done in lakes and rivers before the formation of ice. The commonest fish caught for food are the grayling, river trout, lake trout, and jackfish. Fishing trips are motivated by a desire for fresh fish as a change from meat, or by the necessity of securing nourishing food for dogs. Fishing is done with a baited or fly hook and with nets. In the fall, when fish travel into a slough to spawn, a net may be strung at the entrance to such a place. Nets are hung with floats about eight inches long and four inches in diameter prepared from spruce wood. Flat stones about two inches wide and three inches long are selected for sinkers. The stones are tied to the lower end of the net at ten inch intervals. Fish line is used for this purpose, the rock being secured in a running noose and the upper end of the line fastened to the net with a double overhand knot. Several feet of manilla rope are added to each end of the net and secured on shore to a piece of drift wood or an overhanging willow. Sometimes fish are driven out of a slough into a net by shooting, the concussion sending several stunned grayling and trout to the surface. When several hours will be required to transport fish to camp, they are often gutted at the fishing site. If fish are to be carried only a short distance, they are strung through the mouth and gills on a thin willow shoot, the ends of which are then twisted together. Near camp a man or boy may fish alone. Generally men only use lines, but either sex may set a fish net. In the fall, a whole family sometimes travels several miles to a likely fishing spot and spends the day there eating fresh roasted fish. Often a family or two men will travel up to ten or fifteen miles to a fish lake, camping there for several days or a week and accumulating a dozen or two large jackfish and lake trout.

Only the rabbit is trapped exclusively for food, setting and visiting rabbit snares being the daily task of women and girls, and is work greatly depended upon to keep a family supplied with meat from day to day. A woman will set from three to six snares at a time. The most common rabbit snare utilizes a trigger stick and spring pole and is constructed with stout cotton line. The spring pole must not be too heavy or the rabbit will be jerked off the ground so abruptly as to break the snare line. Brass wire is also used for snares but without a trigger stick; instead a simple noose is formed on a firmly anchored toggle (for example, a small felled jackpine). Such toggle snares are said to have been introduced into the Upper Liard district by Mrs. Man, a Slave Indian from Fort Liard. Rabbit snares are located above rabbit runs, generally where such paths cross a trail. The noose is placed about three or four inches from the ground. After a heavy snowfall the snares must be raised above the surface of the snow, else they will be passed over by the animals. A tour of the snare line, which is always located close to camp, never takes longer than about an hour. If a snared rabbit is not dead when a snare is visited, the woman will choke the animal by wringing its neck.

Fur trapping. What animals are trapped for fur varies according to the resources of the region. Most areas can be depended on to yield lynx, squirrel, fox, weasel, mink, and wolverine. Marten, an animal whose fur commands the highest prices, is found on high ground, but not all trap lines extend to the mountains. Similarly, not all people are fortunate in having well stocked beaver creeks on their territory. In trapping, the Indian is governed by the game laws of the province or territory in which his line is located. In British Columbia, the season for winter trapping begins on November 15, while in the Yukon it opens November 1. In both places this season ends with February and gives place to the open season for beaver and muskrat. In British Columbia the beaver season extends from March 1 to April 15; in the Yukon it ends on June 15.

Even before the season opens, the trapper should be preparing for his winter work. Some of the duties that must be attended to are packing food to the camps and cabins located along the trap line; building new cabins, caches, or tent frames on the line; cutting new trail over areas of the line hitherto not systematically trapped, and repairing existent tents, cabins, stoves, and caches. White men engage in much more intensive preparation for trapping than the Indians. This is recognized by the latter. As Old Man said early in September, although the trapping season in the Yukon did not begin until November, "some white men start out this time. They pack their grub away. Get everything ready. The boys they wait, then they put their stuff out. I could do it now but I feel bad." Old Man's son-in-law, Harry Lang, moved some food to his base cabin on November 2. For the previous ten days he had been prevented from crossing the river because of running ice and slush. Old Man, who did not have the problem of crossing a river, had his wife move some food to a half-way cache on November 2. Both men started setting traps on November 4. Old Man's other son-in-law, Hans Donnelly, did not start setting traps until November 10, when he also first moved some food to his line camp.

Only unmarried girls and, sometimes, a man's wife confine their trapping to within a day's journey from the winter settlement. Men generally begin trapping from a base camp located from eight to fifteen miles from the home cabin. A man sets up to thirty miles of traps, generally in a circle or semicircle. To cover this circuit may take a week, longer if additional side lines are set radiating from the main trail. Once the traps are placed, they should be visited once every ten days or oftener, in order to remove fur and worthless prey like rabbits and squirrels. Frequent visiting of a trap line is important for several other reasons. In the first place, leaving animals in the traps too long increases the danger of losing them to wolves, wolverines, and coyotes. Also, if a movable toggle is used, the animal before it dies may drag the trap a considerable distance. If not discovered in time, subsequent heavy snowfall will conceal the tracks and carcass of the animal. Finally, the more often a man resets sprung traps, the more fur he can expect to accumulate. In practice, the ideal schedule is rarely followed. A man returning home to visit his family and to obtain additional food often delays returning to his trap line for a week or more. In December his routine is badly broken by a longer absence from the trap line, this time for a visit to Lower Post to obtain new supplies. Illness of the trapper or a member of the family may further delay his return. It can be estimated that trap lines are revisited on the average of about once every two to three weeks.

The pattern of covering trap lines is revealed in the chronological record of events that occurred in Old Man's settlement. These notes are abstracted from the ethnographer's journal.

11:2:45. Harry left this morning to take traps and food to his cabin. Earlier in the morning Mrs. Man and Elsie Lang left to take food to a cache halfway to Old Man's trap line. Mrs. Man returned early, but Harry returned after night fall.

11:4:45. Despite snow, Old Man and his wife left at about ten o'clock to go on their trap line. At about one o'clock Harry Lang and his family left for their base camp. Raymond and Donald Suza returned from Lower Post with additional food and traps for Old Man.

11:5:45. Hans explained that he cannot go to his trap line until he has finished his snowshoes. It snowed most of the day.

11:6:45. Harry returned to fetch his sleigh and snowshoes. He will leave again tomorrow.

11:7:45. Harry left for his line cabin at about two o'clock. He planned to stay until November 20. He will then return for more food or, if he has skins, will go to Lower Post.

11:8:45. Hans said he would start for his trap line tomorrow.

11:9:45. Hans delayed his departure for one more day and spent the afternoon improving several miles of winter trail running to his trap line from the settlement. Old Man and his wife returned in the late afternoon for additional traps.

11:10:45. Hans got off for his trap line today with his brother, Raymond.

11:11:45. Old Lady Metša died.

11:15:45. Hans and Raymond returned to secure dog packs, the former explaining that the snow was not yet deep enough for toboggan travel. Harry and his family also returned, having been summoned to help bury the old lady.

11:16:45. Beer drunk.

11:18:45. Old lady buried.

11:20:45. Old Man set half a dozen traps across the river.

11:21:45 to 11:24:45. The boys hunted, and Hans shot one moose.

11:26:45. Harry and his family returned to their trap line. Old Man explained that his wife's illness is delaying their return. Hans planned to return to his line today, but postponed departure in order to permit Raymond to finish a pair of snowshoes.

11:27:45. Hans and Raymond left for the trap line.

12:1:45. Old Man visited his short line across the river but returned without fur.

12:4:45. Old Man and his wife (who was still feeling ill) left for the trap line. Harry returned with one lynx and two fox.

12:7:45. Hans returned with two lynx and one fox.

12:10:45. Started for Lower Post.

Most trapping is done with the aid of metal traps obtained from local trading stores in various sizes. A well equipped trapper sets fifty or more traps. If he is diligent and well supplied he sets traps at about a quarter mile intervals.

The trap is set in a locale showing animal tracks or at a spot which is reputed to be favorable or lucky for trapping a certain species of fur bearing animal. A fox or lynx trap is generally set with the aid of two trees. One of these, a tree two or three inches in diameter, is lightly grazed with an ax about twelve inches from the ground. About half a teaspoonful of scent or bait is smeared on the exposed wood, and the trap placed at the base. The second tree, a low sapling about an inch thick, is cleaned of branches and used as a fixed toggle— the chain of the trap being slipped over the tree. If two trees are not found in conjunction at a likely place, a free toggle, a pole two or three inches in diameter and six feet long, is used and lodged under a large piece of deadwood. Heavier toggles are employed for animals, like the wolverine, which would chew through a thin sapling. The trap itself is set on a thin layer of brush in order to prevent it from freezing into the snow. Four or five bare twigs, about ten inches high, are set at both sides of the trap as a pen and are designed to force the animal to come straight to the bait and thus step into the open trap. The stick used to smear the scent on the blaze is placed to the rear of the trap as an additional lure. To set a trap in this fashion takes about five minutes. The favorite bait for lynx, fox, mink, and other animals is a mixture of ground beaver castors mixed with lard or butter. A dead squirrel caught in a trap may also be left for bait. Bread or meat is regarded as suitable bait for weasel, while oil of cassia is used for marten, mink, fisher, and coyote. Canned sardines may occasionally be substituted for beaver castors. Sometimes no bait or scent is used and the trap is set blind in the middle of a trail, being covered with a little dry grass. Indians are not generally interested in the experimental approach which white trappers lend to their work, but a number of Nelson Indians reported utilizing bright paper and coffee tins to attract animals' attention. In addition to metal traps, most men also set four or five wire snares for wolf and coyote.

By the time a trapper revisits his trap line, the animals caught have generally frozen to death. If they are still alive they are either shot in the head with a .22 or, if not savage, clubbed to death with a stick.

The general practice is for every adolescent and adult in a family to set traps in the territory agreed upon as his part of the trap line. Sometimes, however, two men, related or unrelated, may set traps together in a single area. Generally one of these "partners" is a youth who is often referred to as assisting his companion. Although the two men operate together, each really traps independently. That is, the fur caught in the traps which he sets (whether these traps are owned by, or loaned to, him) is his own. The same principle obtains if adolescent girls or married women set traps given to them by a husband or father; the fur caught becomes their own.

With the arrival of the beaver season a family may leave the winter settlement and move to an area near a beaver resort. Beaver, being less difficult to obtain than fine fur and earning high prices, is regarded as the most important fur to trap. The beaver season, therefore is eagerly awaited and an individual whose territory contains a well stocked beaver creek is regarded as being a favorable position. Resources in beaver are often referred to as the "Injun bank" and an average trapper can expect to almost double his winter earnings during this season. Beaver trapping differs from winter trapping in that it requires considerable immersion in water, so that it is often accompanied or followed by colds and other illness.

Gardening. In the spring the men in most families plant a small garden in the winter settlement. The standard crops are potatoes, turnips, carrots, and radishes. The gardens remain unweeded while the people spend the summer in Lower Post and usually, being unfenced, are constantly raided by rabbits. Gardens are not of great economic importance. Their yield is generally small and never included when a man estimates the amount of food which his family will require for the winter.

Foresight. There is little manifestation of any realistic attitudes of conservation among the Indians, although the need for such a policy is recognized. To illustrate, Old Man complained that low bush cranberries and raspberries had almost disappeared from the neighborhood of his home. He blamed this on the indiscriminate picking. He also alluded to the large scale moose and caribou hunting that had formerly been possible in the Upper Liard River area. In one year the family's hunters brought down eighty-two caribou and moose. In 1939 Old Man's son-in-law, Harry Lang, told his father-in-law that if they continued to hunt "every day" they would "clean out" all the game. Old Man didn't believe Harry then. "Game come anyway," he told the young man. In 1945, when moose were scarce, he was more inclined to believe the younger man's advice. Old Man also reported a beaver colony near the winter settlement where the beaver "must be old as me." They are never trapped, he reported, being left for "seed." Old Kean, another Upper Liard Indian, was reported to leave marten areas alone for two or three years in order to give the animals a chance to breed.

The Indian's appreciation of the necessity for conservation is well illustrated by his attitudes toward the ruling of the Yukon Government in 1945 declaring beaver trapping to be closed for three years. Hans Donnelly was aware of the fact that the supply of Yukon beaver had become seriously depleted, especially as a result of the indiscriminate killing of these animals prior to 1938, when a law went into effect prohibiting their shooting. Despite his understanding that policy of conservation aimed at rebuilding these depleted resources, he resented the closure and agreed with the point of view expressed by Nitla who said: "Somebody say beaver closed three years . . . what he gonna live on, the people? Better open that beaver. Government look after his boys. . . . Springtime, just sit down one place, out of money, poor luck, too bad. Oh, beaver open, pretty good, best way. Marten closed, pretty good, best way. Government smart, he do it all right. . . . Soon men starving he gonna eat that beaver meat. No smart; that's why he say that closed. Marten, you eat nothing. Just skin. That meat you throw away. Better marten make him closed."

TECHNOLOGY

The principal techniques followed by the Kaska in processing the raw materials obtained from the environment are: woodworking, the making of cordage, skin working, and firemaking.

Woodworking. In recent years, because of the arrival of mill sawed lumber in Lower Post, the necessity of preparing this material by whipsawing and hewing has been reduced. In 1943 lumber began to arrive in the town via the Alaska Highway. When many construction camps along the road were demolished during the summer of 1944, the United States Army permitted the Indians to secure enough lumber gratis (the people paying only for transportation in white men's trucks) to complete cabins in Lower Post. In the fall of 1944 a commercial sawmill began operation near the town, and in the spring of 1945 a number of Upper Liard Indians, seeking to finish log cabins, bought lumber from this source for transportation to winter settlements. Nevertheless, in the bush, Indians are still often forced to depend on whipsawed and hand hewed lumber for necessary construction.

Poplar and red spruce are selected for the manufacture of coffins, beds, tables, and other household objects. Birch is preferred for toboggans and sleighs, while thin black spruce saplings provide snowshoe frames. Dry wood is regarded as easiest to whipsaw or split, but only green trees are used in preparing snowshoes, sleighs, and toboggans.

The first step in woodworking, after the tree has been felled and cleaned of limbs, is to cut the trunk into one or more sections the length of the desired lumber. When lumber is to be prepared by hewing, the trunk is usually split down the center. Several procedures are used in this process. In the case of poplar, the pole is first partly split by axing along a straight line and then completely split with the aid of a wedge. As the halves split apart, the wedge is removed and inserted further along the cut, or a second wedge may be inserted before the first is withdrawn. Small poplar, up to about four inches in diameter, is not split before being hewed. In the case of birch selected for a toboggan, only the lower ten feet of the tree are used, cut close to the ground. Before attempting to split birch, the surface is lightly hewed on two directly opposite faces. In this process the outer and inner bark are axed away together with a thin section of wood. Along each of these levelled surfaces a groove is cut, about one inch deep and three quarters of an inch wide. This work is done with an ax. To split the wood, the log is deeply axed along the length of one of these grooves. When the end is reached, a single strong ax blow usually causes the wood to split in half at this point. A wedge is now driven deeply into the split end. The worker goes beyond the wedge, toward the center of the log, and here again deeply splits the pole with his ax. Removing the wedge from its first lodging place, he drives it into the wood at the point where he has just axed. He continues this process until the log splits in half.

The split log to be hewed is propped against the branches of a spruce tree. Using a sharp ax the worker proceeds to ax away the rounded section of the trunk. Starting in the middle a series of gashes are cut through the bark into the wood until the bottom of the log is reached. Returning to where these gashes began, swift short strokes of the ax remove chips of the bark and wood. This process is repeated on the inner surface of the split log where, however, there is relatively less wood to remove. Hewing continues until the required thickness of lumber is achieved, although a piece of lumber is not hewed thinner than about one inch. Further thinning is obtained by planing. During the course of hewing, the log is reversed and what was the upper section is now hewed down from the middle. The work must always be done carefully in order to avoid a warped or uneven board. The hewing is little more than planing done with an ax. In preparing birch for a toboggan, considerable width is sacrificed in the lumber by the practice of hewing the inner section of the split trunk almost as much as the outer, rounded section. This is done in order to preserve that portion of the wood which bends more readily and which lies toward the outside of the standing tree. It also assures a stronger piece of lumber, since the softest wood is said to be on the interior near the core. Hewing is usually completed at the spot where the wood was obtained. The boards are then carried into camp where they may be further planed or seasoned and bent.

Two men can split a piece of poplar, seven feet long and about seven inches in diameter, and hew two boards, two inches thick, in about twenty-five minutes. Nitla, working more painstakingly, hewed an unsplit piece of poplar, seven feet long and four inches in diameter, in about thirty-five mintues. To split two birch logs, ten feet long and six inches in diameter, and hew three pieces of lumber, each an inch thick, occupied Hans Donnelly for about five hours. He worked patiently and carefully and seemed preoccupied with his task. Actually, however, he often stopped work to communicate some thought that was passing through his mind, generally one unconnected with the task at hand. He also solicited the ethnographer's opinion of what was being accomplished.

Lumber is whipsawed on saw-pits which stand in some nearby part of the forest where large trees are available. If a log cannot be moved to a saw-pit, it may be whipsawed by being felled across a fallen tree, or else it is blocked up with pieces of wood. In such cases whipsawing becomes a laborious operation in which one man must crawl under the log while the other stands at the upper end of the saw. Before whipsawing, the wood is generally cleaned of its bark. Guidelines for sawing are made along the length of the log by means of a string which has been rubbed with a piece of charred wood. Two men hold the string, one at either end of the log. One then picks up the line and allows it to snap against the wood, leaving the imprint of a straight line.

Thin poles, such as are used in making snowshoe frames, are hewed or trimmed with a butcher knife. Straight grained black spruce, about one inch in diameter, is selected for this purpose. Each pole is cut an inch or two longer than the desired length of the lumber and brought into camp. In cold weather the wood is thawed before being worked. With a knife, the pole is now trimmed on two directly opposite sides to a thickness of about five-eighths of an inch in the center but thinner at one end. The width of the original sapling is retained and even the bark is left on the wood at this point. The pole is now ready to be bent in order to serve as half a snowshoe frame.

Lumber is generally planed with a carpenter's plane and sawed with a Swedish buck or carpenter's saw, but in an emergency both these operations may be performed with an ax. To cut lumber with an ax, the ax is first driven straight into the wood at the point where the separation is desired (Fig. 3, c). The wood is then axed from below at a forty-five degree angle to the first cut. Further axing takes place at the apex of each angle, the blade driving straight into the wood until the separation is effected. In cutting with a saw, the T-square is used to mark off a straight edge. If sawing must be done along the length of a board, a charcoal line is used to mark off a level edge.

Wood may be bent on a bending frame or by hand. Toboggan boards are bent and dried on the bending frame described above. That portion of a piece of lumber which was lowest in the standing tree is inserted to a depth of about three inches into a space provided at the lower end of the frame. The upper end of the lumber is then forced back until it approaches the deepest section of the curve of the frame. It is now lashed to the upper end of the apparatus with rope while a second and third piece of lumber are similarly inserted and bent. When all the wood to be bent is in the apparatus, the pieces are simultaneously further bent against the curved surface of the frame, being forced as far back as possible (Pl. 6, в). To prevent the wood from splitting during this process, cleats, a quarter of an inch thick and three inches wide, are nailed across the piece of lumber, the nails extending into the bending apparatus. When the lumber has been forced back as far as possible it is firmly lashed in position and left to dry.

The wood for snowshoe frames is bent by hand. Taking the thinnest portion of the wood, which will be the front of the snowshoe, the worker puts it under his foot and gradually bends the rest of the pole upwards. A notch is cut about half an inch from the front end but no other notches or holes are cut at this time. A rope or piece of babiche is then fastened from the tip to a point further back on the wood and is pulled taut enough to retain the desired bend. When both parts of a rim have been bent they are roughly lashed together in the form of the finished snowshoe. A block of wood takes the place of the struts in keeping the rims a proper distance apart and also helps to bend the rims further. The whole shoe is then spanned with a lever (Pl. 10, D) and dried in the warmth of a cabin.

While trees are sometimes allowed to dry before being worked into lumber, in the construction of toboggans and snowshoes, lumber is dried after it has been worked and bent. Drying is generally done in a house or tent, where there is a stove, and takes from three days to a week. Although it is recognized that long term sun drying is superior to quick indoor drying, no cases were observed in which objects had been made in the spring or summer and allowed to dry outdoors until winter.

Woodcarving with an ordinary butcher or pocket knife is a technique used in making toys, stirring spoons, trigger sticks, and other implements. Wood carving is done by men; the worker drawing the knife toward himself as he works.

Cordage. Although nails are indispensable for joining wood in constructing coffins, houses, and other large objects, line is widely employed in a variety of repairs and manufactures. The principal native lines manufactured by the people are cut from tanned and semi-tanned caribou or moosehide, or stripped from moose and caribou sinew. Line from fully tanned skin is prepared by cutting a piece of soft hide into a continuous strip up to a half-inch in width. Before being used a new piece of tanned skin line is tugged between the hands to stretch it.

Semi-tanned skin line, commonly known as babiche, is cut from caribou or moosehide from which all the hair and flesh has been cleaned and which has been soaked in water to soften. Moosehide babiche is much stronger than that made from caribou skin. The pieces of hide selected generally consist of the four outer edges which, in order that the skin could be lashed on the tanning frame, were perforated during the tanning process. Each strip is about ten inches wide and the length of one of the sides of the stretched moosehide—from five to seven feet long. The strip is cut away from the semi-tanned hide and soaked in a dishpan until it is soft and pliable. To cut the strip into line, two women seat themselves on the ground facing one another, about two feet apart. One woman, holding the hide, inserts the point of a pocketknife to penetrate the material. This hole is made about fifteen inches from one end of the strip of hide (hereafter referred to as the lower end) and one quarter inch from the cut (unperforated) edge of the strip (hereafter referred to as the inner edge). The second woman now picks up the lower end of the strip and holds it taut as the first worker, still holding the hide fifteen inches from the lower end, runs the blade down through the lower end of the material. About eight quarter inch wide strips, fifteen inches long, are successively cut in this fashion. The cutter now takes hold of the strip of hide fifteen inches further up and her assistant likewise moves her grip. The first woman runs the knife from the upper end of each previous cut to the point at which she is now holding the material. The second woman holds the hide taut and separates each strand of babiche as it is cut from the rest of the skin. In this second cutting, each successive strand is cut about one half inch shorter than the previous strand. Again the cutter seizes a new hold on the rectangular strip of hide fifteen inches closer to the upper end. The same process of cutting is repeated until the upper end of the strip has been reached. Before cutting the last fifteen inch length, the cutter slits a hole at the upper end of the hide and in this slit inserts the index finger of her left hand. She holds the strip taut with this finger as she cuts, terminating the first cut about an inch below the hole. Each successive cut, except the last, continues to stop a half inch below the previous termination. The last cut goes through the upper end of the hide. Turning to the remainder of the strip of hide the cutter repeats the same process of cutting which we have just described. As the outer edge of the material with the lashing holes are approached, the cutting is done as carefully as possible. Strands may be cut more narrowly than one quarter of an inch as the cutter skirts the inner edge of one of these holes. These holes are also used as cuts, the knife continuing its operation at the upper end of each. The ragged outer edge of the hide, to which short lengths of cut moosehair still adhere, is discarded and the lengths of babiche are terminated before the upper end of the material is reached. When a rectangle of hide has been cut in this fashion, the worker has a number of bundles of babiche. Each bundle has about eight strips of babiche, a quarter inch wide and about seven feet long, connected at the upper end. These bundles are hung in the open air until dry. As babiche is required, the strands are cut free from the connecting hide. When observed, the cutting of babiche line was done within a tent and without particular emotional expression. Occasional comments were exchanged regarding the progress of the work, or attention was directed toward one of the women's babies.

Before being used, babiche line is moistened. Subsequently, the line dries hard, shrinking somewhat, and thereby providing a secure lashing. Babiche finds wide employment, being used to fill snowshoes, lash handlebars on a sled or toboggan, lash shafts on a sled, and for numerous repairs on axes, toboggans, dog harnesses, and elsewhere when strong line is desired and where the fastening does not have to be frequently undone.

To prepare sinew line, a block of caribou or moose sinew, about one and a half inches wide, fifteen inches long and one sixteenth of an inch thick, is softened by running it through the teeth. Holding the strip in one hand, the worker runs the blunt edge of a knife blade against the surface of the mass. This operation squeezes some of the moisture from the sinew, making it more pliable. Loose strands of sinew are grasped between the index finger and thumb, pulled free, and set aside. When these loose strands have been exhausted, the worker using her fingernails, picks strands away from the block and then strips them free. This continues until the entire block has been separated into individual strands of line. Each of these strands is now placed on the woman's knee and twisted. This is done by moistening the flat of the fingertips with saliva and using them to rub the sinew strand toward the body of the worker. The ends of each strand are then twisted by twirling them between the moistened thumb and index finger. The strands are preserved for sewing moccasins and mittens. All line is manufactured by women. In addition to native cordage, people use ma-nila rope, sewing thread, brass wire, and insulated copper cable for sewing and lashing.

The principal knots used are simple ones and include the single and double overhand, the "choker" or running noose, the slip hitch, and the weaver's knot or sheet bend. The running noose is used to fasten stones, used as sinkers, to a fish net. The slip hitch is widely used when a knot is required which can readily be opened. It is employed, for example, to tie tent ropes to guy posts or to hang up bags of food. The sheet bend is used to secure two ends of line and is also employed to fasten a length of line to the corner of a tarp (Fig. 3, E). The split handle of an ax is sometimes bound together with babiche applied as a marline or hammock hitch (Fig. 3, A). When a moosehide or beaver skin is lashed to a stretcher it often secured at the beginning with a lark's head or cow hitch. This knot is also occasionally used in beginning the filling of the center panel of snowshoes. Women also braid a woolen line from yarn, making a four strand sennit braiding which is used to hold mittens around the neck.[5]

Skinwork. Two types of skinwork may be distinguished: the skinning and stretching of fine furs designed for commerce, and the skinning, stretching, and tanning of moosehide and caribou hide used in domestic manufactures.

Fur bearing animals, which are trapped or shot, are usually brought into camp before being skinned. In skinning a small animal, such as a squirrel, weasel, mink, or muskrat, the animal is placed on its back, the hind legs outstretched. With a sharp pocket knife, a cut is made at the extremity of one of the rear legs extending through the skin to the muscle. The cut is continued up the leg, across the undersurface of the body and to the pads at the lower end of the other leg. In making this incision, care must be taken not to cut through the mus-cle tissue and expose the viscera. The cut passes anteriorly to the anus and male genitals. After the cut is completed the animal is seized by one of its hind legs and the index finger of the other hand inserted between the skin and muscle tissue at approximately the second joint. Using the finger, the skin is loosened all around the leg at this point. When this is done the skin is stripped away from the lower portion of the leg and paw. The same process is repeated on the opposite hind leg. The skin is now pulled away from the upper portion of each leg. Upon reaching the body, the finger is inserted under the skin to loosen it from the lower region of the animal's back. A second cut is then made extending in a semicircle from the first horizontal cut posteriorly around the male genitals and anus. Following this incision, the index finger is again inserted between the skin and the back muscle of the ani-mal and worked toward the tail. Upon reaching the tail, the finger joins the thumb to pull

[5] See Graumont and Hensel, *Encyclopedia of Knots* (1942), 224; pl. 112, Fig. 2.

the cartilage from the tail skin. The animal is then grasped by the hind legs and the skin stripped away from the rest of the body, up to the ears, in a few swift pulls. When the head is reached considerable cutting is necessary before the skin can be successively removed at the ears, eyes, and mouth. The skin is removed with the undersurface of the pelt exposed. In this condition it is now mounted on a stretching board (or mould) and any tears or bullet holes mended with needle and thread. The rear legs are tied to the stretcher with a few turns of babiche or cotton cord; the tail is left free. The keel of the stretcher is inserted below the belly surface of the pelt and supported from the stretching board by a scrap of wood about an inch high. Small skins are left to dry outdoors for about three hours. The pelt is then reversed on the board and left indoors for a day or two of further drying.

Larger fur bearing animals are skinned in the same general way except that severing the pelt from the underlying muscle tissue becomes a much slower task, requiring constant cutting. At almost every half-inch, the skin must be freed from the muscle tissue with the aid of a sharp knife. Large skins are dried on keelless stretchers, short sticks of wood being inserted into the forelegs and supported by wedges to hold the legs extended. The pelts are left to dry for several days.

Beaver skins are stretched and dried by being lashed on a semicircular stretcher through holes cut along the outer edge of the pelt. Babiche is used for this lashing. The skin is dried outdoors for several days. In drying skins outdoors care must be taken lest stray dogs discover the fur and try to eat it. For this reason stretching skins are often kept on a roof.

Skins are stretched as large as possible. Either a man or woman may skin and stretch fur; generally the work is done by the person who trapped or shot the animal, even adolescents skinning and preparing skins which they catch. Dry skins are rolled up but not folded, as this would damage the fur.

Raw fur pelts to be used for trimming personal garments, are usually tanned. The inner surface of a skin is rubbed with bear grease and left to soften. At the end of about a year the pelt is soaked in water and hung out to freeze and slow dry. When half dry, it is brought back into the house to thaw and finish drying. The skin is then softened by scraping the inner surface with a chipped stone softener.

The first step in the preparation of tanned moose or caribou hide is the fleshing of the skin after it is removed from the animal. This process removes any shreds of muscle tissue remaining on the hide. The skin is roughly cleaned of flesh on the woman's knee, the worker using a butcher knife. When this has been done, holes are gashed along the sides of the skin and it is then lashed to a stretching frame. Two women may now cooperate in the fleshing. The workers sit or kneel on the lower end of the hide, partially supporting their weight on the bottom log of the stretching frame. Six inch, keenly sharpened, butcher knives are used. The worker holds a piece of flesh between her thumb and index finger and cuts it loose from the underlying hide. When it is cut free the fingers take another hold. The cuts are carefully made, the woman sometimes pressing down on the back of the knife blade with one hand to guide the instrument's pressure as it slices pieces of muscle free from the hide (Pl. 8, A). The knife is constantly cleaned during this process, by being wiped on a cloth or scraped against the poles of the stretching frame.

After the hide has been fleshed, generally on the following day, it is reversed on the stretcher for the next step, scraping, which removes the hair from the animal's skin. The hairs are cut short by holding them away from the hide with the fingers and then cutting with a sharp butcher knife. This is first done on the lower half of the skin. The upper portion will be cleaned when the lower hide is completely scraped of hair and the skin turned around. Following the preliminary cutting, the short lengths of hair remaining are scraped away from the hide (Pl. 8, B). The scraper is held in both hands, the work being done with powerful downward pulls on the tool.

When the skin has been cleaned, the sides containing the lashing holes are trimmed off and used in the preparation of babiche. The hide is then thrown across poles and allowed to dry for a day or two high above a smudge fire. Now the softening process begins. This consists in soaking the hide in a mixture of moose brains (which have been allowed to decompose for a week or so) and hot water. The mixture is prepared in a dishpan and left to stand for a day or two. Baking soda may be added to soften the water. The hide is soaked in the mixture for two nights. After that time it is removed and the moisture forced out of the material by wringing the skin with the hands. Selecting a spruce stump, about three inches in diameter, the woman trims the uppermost eight inches of the wood leaving a section about one inch in diameter. Holes are cut in one side of the hide and these are fitted over the peg. Holes cut on the opposite side are placed over a pole three feet long and an inch in diameter. Holding this pole the worker twists the damp hide, squeezing it free of moisture. She continues this process for about an hour, the hide then being left overnight with the pole lodged behind the stump. The next day the hide is untwisted and the pole removed. Grasping the hide along the free edge, the woman pulls in order to stretch it as far as possible. The skin is then removed from the stump and spread over a horizontal pole to dry. When dry it is again soaked for two nights in the moose brain mixture and again wrung out, stretched, and dried. A third soaking, wringing, stretching, and drying follows.

The skin is now again lashed to a stretching frame and softened by being scraped with a chipped stone or a dull ax blade set in a wooden handle. This softener is grasped near the stone with one hand, while the other hand holds the opposite end of the stick. The stone end is then rubbed against the hide with as much pressure as possible (Pl. 8, D). A portion of skin is scraped until all trace of the dull yellow color is removed and the hide shows a snowy white. First the upper portion is scraped, the hide then being turned around in order to duplicate this process for the lower portion. Softening a hide may be carried on for two days, the worker, sometimes with the help of her sisters, working about four hours a day. When the skin is as soft and pliable as a blanket it is ready for the final smoking (Pl. 8, C). In preparation for this, the skin is sewn into a tube about two or three feet wide and six or seven feet high. The top is also sewn together. The tube is supported with a tanned skin line from a pole or a group of poles. Underneath it a smudge is created in a shallow hole surrounded by sticks to keep the tube open. The hide is left hanging over this smudge until the interior has acquired a deep yellow-brown color; it is then reversed and the other side smoked. The tanned hide is now opened up and hung over a horizontal pole in the house to dry, after which it is ready for use.

The general process of tanning a hide may run over two or three weeks or even several months. Several days are occupied in simply waiting for the hide to dry following various steps in the process. The most difficult part of the work lies in removing the flesh and hair. Two women can do this in about ten or twelve hours. A family will sometimes purchase a hide which has been fleshed and cleaned and then finish the tanning; such a skin sells for from six to eight dollars. Each softening of the hide takes two people about eight hours. The final smoking must be carefully watched and, depending on the size of the skin, occupies from forty-five minutes to an hour and a half. A fully tanned moosehide represents about fifty work hours; a small caribou skin, somewhat less time.

Fire. Two general types of fire may be distinguished, fires made in stoves and campfires built outdoors. Stove fires are built from small dry kindling split from a section of log and shaved toward one end with a knife. After the kindling has caught, larger sections of cut wood are added. Outdoor fires are generally built with kindling obtained from the dry small limbs found toward the bottom of spruce trees. A large double handful of these twigs is collected and thoroughly broken into small bits. Larger wood is also collected and set to one side. After the kindling has been well broken up, so that it forms a compact mass, it is ignited. When the fire is well caught, the pile of brush may be tipped over from behind and lightly pressed down. Now larger sticks are added. In winter, snow is first cleared from a fireplace before a blaze is set, and a thick layer of brush placed on the ground in front of the fire to prevent moccasins from becoming wet in the melting snow (Pl. 7, D).

People are very much at ease around open fires, readily passing things over the flames and handling hot sticks without any sign of timidity. When working outdoors in fall or winter, men and women generally build fires behind them to keep warm. In standing or sitting around an open fire, people keep their backs to the blaze. If they face the fire, as sometimes becomes necessary, they look over rather than into the flames. This habit avoids the temporary blindness that follows prolonged, nocturnal exposure to bright light. To keep wind from fires, a tarp is sometimes erected on the windward side. In cold weather such protection has the additional function of directing the heat of a fire into the camp. Prevailing attitudes, expressed by men and women, tend to emphasize the smoke, draft, and other inconveniences associated with open fires as compared to stove fires. Smoke is regarded as detrimental to children's health. There is also the fear that children may burn themselves playing around an open fire.

Heavy smoke fires for smoking hides are made from rotten spruce wood which may be mixed with a little green spruce brush. Green spruce brush and green wood are collected for the light smudges used to keep flies off drying meat or for the preliminary smoking of hides.

Care is always taken to prevent campfires from spreading. A shallow trench is dug around the embers with the toes or with a stick, and the loose dirt kicked into the coals. Damage to dwellings from fire is not an unfamiliar experience to the people. Tent fires are especially common; three occurred during the period of field work. Two of these blazes were caused by candles being left too close to the roofs of wall tents while the occupants went to sleep.

Kerosene lamps and candles are in common use and a few families also own Coleman lanterns which are operated with gasoline. People are cautious in their use. Flashlights are owned and used. They are a source of amusement in late summer when two groups of young people, meeting at night, try to blind each other with the beams.

EXCHANGE

A portion of the resources, namely furs, which are derived from the environment, are not directly utilized by the Indian but, after being briefly processed, are converted into consumer and capital goods which have their origin outside the Kaska area. In other words, trapped and stretched pelts are sold or traded. Unlike the white trapper, the Indian confines his interest in fur to the immediate process necessary to convert his fur into cash. Except for rumors of price trends, which he occasionally picks up in Lower Post, he has neither knowledge nor interest in those factors of the world market that ultimately determine the valuation placed on his pelts. Similarly the Indian largely fails to appreciate the economic forces that determine the price of the commodities which he buys. As a result hedging, that is, holding skins from the market in expectation of an increase in value is never practiced.

The value set upon the Indian's fur by the white traders of the North, as well as the prices which the Indian is required to pay for the necessities of living, are both largely controlled by a series of intricate mechanisms involving the economic system of western society, over which the local traders lack control. However, despite the fact that price and value are largely determined by conditions of the world market, differences occur in the amounts paid for fur and prices charged by different traders. The Indian is aware of these local variations. He also knows that competition between local trading companies is apt to benefit him by increasing the amount he receives for fur and by lowering somewhat the prices that he must pay for goods. Table 6 indicates the approximate prices paid for common furs in Lower Post in spring, 1944.

Competitive bidding by traders is common. As the trader inspects the pelts and appraises their value the Indian stands back matter-of-factly without speaking. No emotion, not even interest, is betrayed in his features. When the bid is written out and read, the furs are put back in the sack from which they were taken, still without a word of comment. If later the Indian comes back, dissatisfied with the bid of the trader's competitior, he will signify that he is now ready to sell.

Theoretically the Indian can sell his fur to the highest bidder and with the proceeds buy what equipment and food he needs from the cheapest selling trader. There are several reasons why this procedure is rarely followed. In the first place, a trader short of ready cash frequently offers the seller a good price for fur, provided that the catch is turned over to him in order to settle an outstanding debt or in trade for additional merchandise. Such a transaction is almost pure barter. Another reason for failing to take advantage of the open market is the fact that a trapper may feel obligated to let a particular trader have part of a catch, regardless of the value which this trader sets on the skins, in order to exhibit his ability as a trapper and thus maintain future credit standing with that firm. While such transactions deprive the Indian of some of the value of his fur, they are never resented. Someday, illness or poor luck may make the good opinion of one or both traders important. Individuals recognize strongly the advantages in being friendly with "storemen."

TABLE 6. SOME FUR VALUES—SPRING, 1944

Fur	Value
Beaver	Extra large and blankets, Northern BC's, good colors, $47–$51. Ordinary large, $38–$41. Large medium, $30–$31. Medium $21–$23. Small $16–$17.
Red fox	Yukon's, $13–$15. Ordinary types, $10–$11. Low grades, $1–$2.
Cross fox	Silvery type, $27–$31. Ordinary types $14–$16.
Silver fox	Full silvers, good sizes, $34–$38. Platina types up to $88. Wringnecks and white faces $34–$41. Half and three quarter silvers, $20–$25. Ordinary full, $25–$27. Inferior and off color, $9–$13.
Lynx	Extra large and large, good colors, Yukon's, Northern BC's, $62–$74. Ordinary, $56–$63. Mediums, good colors, $41–$50. Smalls, $25–$30.
Marten	Extra large and large interior BC's and Yukon's, dark and dark browns, $86–$100. Mediums and smalls, $36–$54. Extra large and large Yukon's, light browns and pales, $54–$58. Northern BC's extra large and large light browns and pales $44–$50. Mediums and smalls, light browns and pales $25–$27.
Coyote	Northern BC's, good average sizes, $8–$10.

Most fur is sold by men, a husband or father often selling his wife's or daughter's fur. The proceeds of such sales are reapportioned, each person getting money or credit for the skins which he or she trapped. Since the man spends the greatest time trapping, he naturally also accumulates the largest number of skins. In turn he is responsible for supplying the necessary supplies and food required by the family.

Sometimes a man is reluctant or unable to take his furs to the post and entrusts a friend with the task of selling one or two skins and buying a few necessary goods. The friend may be paid for this service, receiving about five dollars a day for his journey. "Sometime you lose your fur for good," Old Man pointed out dourly. "I did with John Kean. I need cartridge. I let him have one lynx. He got fifty dollars for lynx and buy gun for it. I never got my lynx."

When the furs are sold, the seller is informed of the amount of his credit standing or receives an amount in cash. He is now ready to buy supplies.

Shopping is a leisurely business. Generally a man buys the food and necessary supplies for a family, women confining themselves to the purchase of dresses, yard goods, and occasional necessities. Whenever possible, men and women will select food items or examine clothing which can be reached without going behind the counters. Children go to the stores for candy and fruit. The Indian announces his wants individually, asking for a certain amount's worth of goods without demanding the unit prices of the items. Thus: "Fifty cents soap," or "Dollars worth oranges." Looking around the trader's shelves, he tries to recall what the family lacks. If his wife is there, she may prompt him in her own language.

Often the clerk or storekeeper suggests staples. Many times, after the goods have been packed in a cardboard box and the clerk has turned to wait on a new customer, the purchaser will remember needs originally forgotten. Storemen are used to the idiosyncracies of Indian trading and seldom express any annoyance or impatience. For Indians there is no value in driving a sharp bargain. There is no haggling about price. In part this may be due to the fact that the people still lack a refined sense of the value of money. Furthermore, their reserve and unobtrusiveness are not the personality traits which are customarily associated with shrewd bargaining. Goods purchased are entered on a statement which is marked "Paid," if the buyer pays cash. In either cash or credit transactions, the buyer receives a duplicate of his statement. These are rarely retained and as a result allegations reflecting on a trader's honesty are not infrequent. At times complaints of dishonesty have been turned over to the Indian Agent or policeman, whose duty it then becomes to investigate. Often the individual who feels he has been cheated is content just to voice his complaint to friends. The validity of these complaints is difficult to estimate.

Most of the money received by Indians is spent in Lower Post. Occasionally clothing is ordered from a large mail order house, the independent trader with the poorest stock of goods or the missionary filling in the order blanks. In 1945 Nick Lang and his brother Peter visited Whitehorse where they bought practically all their winter outfit as well as an automobile for cash. Local buying is particularly heavy following the arrival of a new shipment of goods by boat or truck. At such times the stores are always crowded with people curious to see what has been received.

Only one or two individuals have opened savings bank accounts in outside cities. These bank by mail through the traders or missionaries. Their accounts are of not more than three or four years standing and are quite small. More common ways of temporarily saving money are to secret it in a corner of the house or leave it on deposit with the traders in Lower Post, where it does not, however, gather interest. Actually little cash is accumulated. In practice most people behave according to the description Nitla gave of himself: "Cash money nothing for me. I got cash money, spend it like nothing."

HOUSING

Although housing in Kaska society obviously functions to provide protection from the exigencies of climate, additional factors interfere to prevent any perfect correlation between dwelling form and seasonal usage. One such factor is the mobility of the society demanded as a consequence of the exploitative activities on which subsistence depends. Hunting and trapping frequently require temporary camps, the forms of which alter little in summer and winter. Housing is also influenced by the cooperation, time, and effort involved in building a log cabin. The fact that not everyone is ready or able to meet these requirements results in several families living in easily made shelters both summer and winter. Tarps, tents, and houses, therefore, provide shelter in any season of the year, even though the appropriateness of a house for winter comfort is generally recognized.

A gross correlation between dwelling form and status is discernible. From the standpoint of age, for example, a mature man is generally able to meet the costs involved in constructing one or more houses. An unmarried youth, however, never owns a house. Similarly the family of a poor trapper may be unable to afford canvas for a wall tent and so be forced to spend the summer under a tarp. In winter he can secure the materials for a log cabin without monetary cost but, unless assisted by his wife, will often find it difficult to secure free cooperation in assembling the logs. Poor people, therefore, are distinguished by the fact that they own only one house and that of a relatively small size such as could be assembled with a minimum of effort.

Kaska dwelling forms are open camps, tarps (or fly tents), mosquito tents, wall tents, tent frames, and houses. No matter what type of dwelling is used, occupancy is almost always by a single family. In cold weather, during visits, or in the event of death, two families may share one shelter. Such arrangements, however, are always recognized as temporary. Houses and tents occupied for more than one night are always located within easy access to a river or lake. Mildred Lang once expressed surprise at a white man building his home on the Highway, a mile from the river, and said that she preferred to be able to look out on the river from her home.

Camps. Open camps are always temporary and consist of a fire and a pallet of spruce brush for a bed. In cold weather such a camp is surrounded by a wall of brush banked with snow. A fly or tarp is constructed out of eight ounce canvas and is generally about seven feet long and seven feet wide. The fly is erected by supporting the canvas lengthwise on a ridge pole resting in two forked sticks. The ridge pole is two or three feet higher in front than in the rear, and the corners of the tarp are tied to four guy posts, three or four feet high, which are driven into the ground at an angle leaning away from the shelter. The sides of such a camp are usually open but may be piled with poplar or spruce brush for protection against direct sun in summer or wind and cold in fall and winter. Food, clothing, and other goods are stored at the rear or along the sides of the shelter, while a fire is built in front. In winter the fire is backed with brush or a small canvas windbreak. Tarps are used in summer for permanent shelters. In winter men use them as overnight camps while traveling along a trap line.

Single or double size mosquito tents made of muslin are generally purchased ready-made for two or three dollars. They are provided with ties which are attached to front and rear poles about six feet high and to shorter guy posts planted at each corner. No ridge pole is required. Easy to erect, such shelters are used during the summer by adults, adolescent boys and unmarried men. They are primarily sleeping tents designed to provide protection against insects. A tarp is sometimes erected over a mosquito tent to provide additional protection from long rain.

Wall tents are generally made from eight ounce canvas in varying sizes which are referred to as four, five, or more strip tents. A strip of canvas is thirty inches wide; sewing requires about three inches of overlappage, so that a four strip tent is about nine feet long and seven feet wide. The greatest height is about six feet. Wall tents are supported from a ridge pole and are anchored to six guy posts (Pl. 9, D). These shelters are widely used as summer dwellings. In winter, with the walls enclosed by a tent frame, they serve as permanent residences. A man may also erect one or two wall tents on his trap line for temporary winter use. In summer such camps rarely contain heating appliances but in winter a stove is always used. Food, clothing, and bedding are commonly stored at the sides and back of a wall tent.

Since the dwelling forms so far described are often temporary and frequently moved, the Indians have, to a considerable extent, systematized the procedure of making camp. Either a man or woman may set up camp; sometimes both cooperate in the task. The first objective is to find a level piece of ground. Former campsites are generally avoided as is the brush close to such a site, since this area has probably been used for toilet purposes. If the site selected is not already free of underbrush, it is cleared. The branches are cut off close to the ground and the stumps dug out. Next poles must be found. Poplar saplings, which are naturally provided with strong forks at convenient intervals, are preferred as supports for the ridge pole. The ridge pole is generally a slim, straight, red spruce. After these poles have been cleaned of branches, and, in the case of the ridge pole, of rough bark, they are transported to the camp site. The front and rear poles, designed to support the ridge pole, are here sharpened with an ax. In this process the circular trunk is tapered to a point by being axed on four surfaces. The pole is then thrust into the ground until firmly anchored. The tent is slipped over or tied to the ridge pole and the latter fitted into the forked supports.

Camp making presents different problems in a spruce forest lacking poplar. Spruce trees do not have strong forking branches. Hence, instead of being supported in a forked stick, the rear of the ridge pole is sometimes lashed or nailed to a conveniently located spruce tree while in front of the tent two spruce saplings are crossed, thrust into the ground, and lashed. The ridge pole is then placed into the crotch. In winter, when the ground is frozen, a tent is erected with poles which are simply crossed and lashed without being anchored in the ground.

After the tent is erected, the ground inside the dwelling and immediately in front of the entrance is covered with spruce brush. The brush is placed with the thicker end of the branches extending in one direction—either toward the back or side of the tent. Subsequent branches are partially thrust under the brush already laid.

During fair weather, if people stop traveling in the early part of the day, tents are not erected until nearly nightfall. Fire, however, is made immediately and sometimes brush is put down to make sitting on the ground more comfortable.

Tent frames. We come now to relatively more permanent shelters. A tent frame consists essentially of a four or five strip wall tent set inside four walls made of horizontal poles. The walls are a little over two feet high and usually contain a door. In summer, tent frames of lumber are sometimes used in Lower Post but generally tent frames are made of logs and used primarily as winter dwellings by a family which lacks a cabin. They are usually constructed by men; a widow, however, may build her own tent frame. The following observations give the procedure followed in tent frame construction.

9:23:45 (Old Man's Place). Hans Donnelly used green jackpine poles, averaging about four inches in diameter, for his tent frame. He cut the poles about one-eighth of a mile from the campsite and packed them home on his shoulder. His brother Donald (14) fitted the poles and put them in place. The corners were joined in bowl shaped trenches which were chinked with moss before subsequent poles were placed in position. After each pole was placed in position, it was lightly hewed along the upper and inner surfaces (Pl. 6, c). The two brothers worked for about five hours.

9:24:45. Hans worked alone today and finished the walls of the tent frame. He laid the logs to a height of five poles, or about two feet, and explained that chinking would be done after the shelter was completed. When all the poles had been set in place, Hans proceeded to cut a door-way, sawing through the first three logs and about two inches into the next log. On this log the baseboard of the entrance was nailed. The entry was cut about two feet wide.[6] After the logs had been cut through, they were hewed on both sides of the entry. A doorjamb and door were then constructed out of hewed poplar, the door being attached to the inside of the door-jamb with three moosehide hinges, five inches long and two and a half inches wide (Fig. 4, c). A simple bolt was made out of a piece of poplar, four inches long, one and a half inches wide, and one inch thick. A single nail was used to secure the bolt to a base on the doorjamb. The bolt now could be turned to make it fall across the door, thus locking the latter from the inside.

When Hans finished the door he began to level the ground within the tent frame. Using an ax he removed roots and dug out moss. In this process he depressed the floor level of the structure a few inches below the lowest log. After this he went into the bush and secured two forked poplars on which to support the ridge pole. The latter consisted of a straight red spruce, about two inches in diameter. The supporting poles were placed about fifteen inches in front and in back of the tent frame. More care was taken in planting these poles than is usually taken for a wall tent or tarp. The poles were also higher than usual, because of the fact that the tent frame allows the tent to rest a foot or so above the ground. To lift the ridge pole with the tent attached, Hans used a forked stick, two feet long. When the ridge pole was in position Hans discovered it was too high. The supporting poles therefore had to be cut several inches. Guy posts were set outside of the structure to support the walls of the tent. The canvas hung inside of the frame, where it was nailed against the walls with cleats made of hewed spruce saplings. Hans worked about eight hours.

Houses. There are several types of houses. Classified according to materials and construction, there are houses of mill sawed lumber and houses of logs. Considered with regard to function, there are home cabins located in the winter settlements, which are occupied with few interruptions from September to April; line cabins built in the brush, which are temporarily occupied while a man and his family are living on the trap line, and summer houses which some families occupy while living in Lower Post during the summer (Table 7).

TABLE 7. RELATIONSHIP OF HOUSING MATERIALS TO HOUSE FUNCTIONS

House Types	Milled Sawed Lumber	Logs
Home Cabins	Not used; recently floors and roofs of milled sawed lumber have been constructed.	Used almost exclusively with the exceptions noted in adjoining column.
Line Cabins	Not used.	Used exclusively.
Summer Houses	Used almost exclusively.	Formerly used but now abandoned.

[6] When the doorjamb was in place the entry proved to be too narrow, and this provoked considerable amusement.

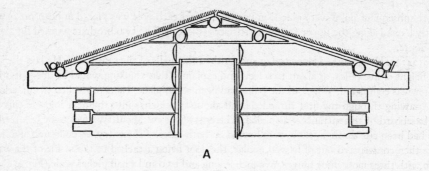

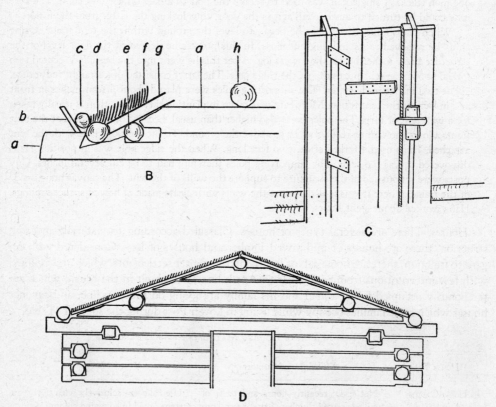

Fig. 4. Kaska Construction: A, Older type log cabin; B, Roof support in older type cabin (a, Width logs; b, Wedge driven into a drilled hole; c, d, e, Supporting logs; f, Dirt; g, Roof pole; h, Auxiliary ridge pole); C, Door for tent frame; D, New type log cabin.

The details of the construction of frame houses will not be presented. Despite their growing importance, they are limited to Lower Post, where lumber is readily available and where summer occupancy does not require the greater warmth of chinked log walls. Such houses are sometimes built with the aid of a skilled white carpenter. If white assistance is used, it is generally for the purpose of sawing and fitting the frame and rafters. Varying in size, the frame house averages about fifteen by seventeen feet and generally contains only one room. The interior of the walls are usually faced with heavy blue paper, sold locally by the roll, while the exterior is covered with black roofing paper. The roof is covered with a double layer of roofing paper but is not shingled. A frame house generally contains two windows and a door, together with such modern hardware as a doorknob and metal hinges.

Log cabins vary in size according to their functions. Home cabins are larger than trap line cabins, averaging about fourteen by seventeen feet as compared to ten by fourteen foot line cabins. As mill sawed lumber has become available for roofing and flooring, the size of home cabins has tended to increase.

A man generally requests his son or son-in-law to help him build a log cabin or else he may hire young men to assist him. Either the width or length of the house may be set parallel to the river. Doors never open away from the river. There are, however, no rules for orienting a house, and an individual will build on any site that suits his fancy, quite without regard to the situation of neighboring structures. Damp or mossy places are avoided for house sites as dampness is known to cause the bottom logs to rot. Low buildings are disliked as they are thought to "carry sickness."

When the builder has decided upon the dimensions of a cabin, he proceeds to cut red spruce logs to fit his undrawn plans. For a durable home cabin, the poles selected are about ten or more inches in diameter; in a line cabin they average about five inches. The bark is removed from the logs, which are then transported to camp and stacked until assistance becomes available to put them in place. Putting up the walls is regarded as the hardest part of constructing a cabin. As each log is set in place, a bowl shaped trench is axed about six inches from the end of each log. The trench is wide enough to support the following log. An older cabin observed lacked these trenched corners. Instead the end of each log was hewed almost square for a distance of about six inches from the end, leaving a rectangular tongue. These tongues were placed upon one another and at right angles, making a tight, close joint. This construction is said to have been introduced in the Upper Liard area by a Tahltan Indian. Both types of corners are shown in Figures 4, A and 4, D (see also Pl. 10, D). Since logs are rarely cut to exact dimensions they may be trimmed after they have been put in place. This is sometimes done in the course of construction and sometimes after the construction is completed (Pl. 6, D). Often it is only partially done. Window frames are cut after the walls have reached the height of the window opening. A home cabin generally contains one or two windows; a line cabin seldom contains more than one window and sometimes has none. The doorway is similarly cut after the required number of logs are in position and the doorjamb added after the rest of the structure is finished.

The construction of the roof is one of the most important tasks in housebuilding. Three ridge poles are generally used in a home cabin; a smaller line cabin, however, may have only one center ridge pole. Very large home cabins sometimes contain five ridge poles to support the heavy roof. The first, or auxiliary, pair of ridge poles is put in position after the last log has been laid along the length of the building and another along the width. This width log, as well as all subsequent ones added above it, is cut more narrowly than the under-lying logs. Two ridge poles, as well as the center ridge log, project about two feet in front of the building and thus provide support for the foreward eaves. The width logs, on which the first pair of ridge poles is laid, project about three or four feet on the outside of the building. On these projections are placed two lengthwise running logs used as braces to support the roof poles and the packed dirt, which is generally used for roofing. In the older type of log cabin this point of construction is somewhat complex and is illustrated in Figure 4, B.

When the central ridge pole is in position, the roofing is begun. Where lumber is not available, poles, five or six inches in diameter, are hewed on what will constitute the interior face and set close together on the ridge poles. The bottom ends of these roof poles rest on the brace logs previously described and illustrated. Sometimes split poles are used in roofing. Harry Lang's cabin contains forty-five logs, or a total of ninety split poles. The old type cabin illustrated, contains sixty-eight spruce poles, 6'5" long, lightly hewed on their inner face. A square hole is left to accommodate the stovepipe, and the roof is then covered with moss. Dirt, to a depth of about six inches, is then piled on the moss and packed firm. Instead of a pole and dirt roof, a piece of eight ounce canvas is sometimes used for roofing. If a mill sawed lumber is used for the roof, it is covered with a double layer of roofing paper. Older cabins may be floored with split and hewed poles. Today floors of mill sawed lumber are the rule. Line cabins are usually floorless, the ground being covered with spruce brush.

Cabins are chinked after construction is completed. Chinking consists of moss or mud applied from the outside of the building while on the interior the spaces between the poles are stuffed with moss, old clothing, or sawdust. On both the interior and exterior walls, wide gaps between the logs are sometimes chinked with thin spruce saplings nailed in place. To add further protection from wind and drafts, wrapping paper and cardboard are nailed against the inside walls. Windows are all purchased readymade in Lower Post and trans-ported to the settlements. A home cabin can be completed in about ten days, if two or three men are available for the work. A smaller line cabin can be built in two or three days by two men. Housebuilding is always done by men.

Sentiment generally favors a house to an open camp. On the other hand, some older people are reluctant to move into a house before the weather turns really cold. Mrs. Man wanted to remain in a tent as long as possible and not hole herself up "like a bear."

Only rarely are cabins dismantled and moved to a new site. Occasionally cabins, which have not been kept in good repair, are wrecked after a new cabin has been constructed.

The completion of a new house is sometimes marked by a drinking party. In Lower Post, River Joe celebrated the completion of his house with a dance. Men who built cabins ex-pressed strong pride in their achievements. Nick Lang, who was building a large house in Lower Post told the writer: "First time pretty hard; next time, by God, easy!"

Furnishings. A limited amount of furniture is found in cabins and houses; less in tent frames. A tent contains no furniture other than a stove in winter.

Home cabins and tent frames may contain a table, simple benches, and sometimes a bunk, besides a cook stove and an airtight heater. In Lower Post, houses often contain single cots acquired from construction camps along the Alaska Highway. At least one family in each settlement usually owns a radio which is not, however, always in working order. Shelves consist of wooden packing boxes nailed with their backs to the log walls. Food, clothing, and other equipment is piled on the floor, stored under bunks, or suspended from poles stretching across the width of a cabin.

Away from Lower Post practically all furniture is locally manufactured out of hand hewed poplar or whipsawed spruce. Besides benches, spruce tree sections, ten or twelve inches in diameter and eighteen inches high, also serve as seats.

A cabin or camp often presents an untidy picture of a great many articles stored in any available space. Old Kean's tent frame presented an extreme picture of disorder. Here the tables were littered with tins of jam, butter, syrup, half used packages of macaroni, and other food left over from several meals. Food was stored under the tables and even in the center of the floor. The bunks were piled with guns, clothing, tarps, and miscellaneous objects.

Griffin has described the interior and furnishings of one of the older cabins in Lower Post (perhaps Mrs. Dickson's house) as he saw it during April 1943. " . . . we go into one of the cabins, stooping to pass the low doorway and straining our eyes in the dim light. Beyond a bed in one corner and a stove in another there is little in the place. The woman sitting on the bed regards us apathetically, but the eyes of the boy beside her are bright and full of curiosity. Two men are bent over some pelts laid out on the floor, marten and lynx. Hudson asks them what the trapping was like this winter and one of them replies laconically, "No good. Too cold.""[7]

In summer, bedding consists of a single sleeping bag or a pair of heavy woolen blankets. In winter a second sleeping bag may be used or additional blankets. Bunks are sometimes covered with dry grass. Some families have acquired single size camp mattresses from construction camps. In daytime, when people sleep on the ground in cabins or tents, the bedding is rolled into a huge roll and stored in the rear of the dwelling where it becomes a backrest for the occupants.

In winter, spruce brush is laid in front of the entrance to a cabin or tent frame, or a burlap bag is thrown immediately inside the door of a house. Here a person scrapes the snow from his moccasins before the warmth of the building causes the melting snow to wet his footwear.

Cabins with floors are swept every day or so with a broom. New brush is laid in tents and floorless cabins about once every two weeks, the old branches being discarded. Every fall cabins are rechinked where necessary and additional sod may be piled on the shallow spots of a dirt roof. Heavy snow is removed from the roof of a sod cabin and from the tops of tents. Cleaning and chinking are done by women, while a man keeps the roof in repair. If tents burn or otherwise become damaged, a woman takes down the shelter and sews a new piece of canvas into the damaged area.

Mice are household pests. Dwellings often contain mousetraps, most of which are of native manufacture. To make a mousetrap, a man takes a piece of wood, fifteen inches long,

[7] Griffin, *Alaska and the Canadian Northwest* (1944), 127.

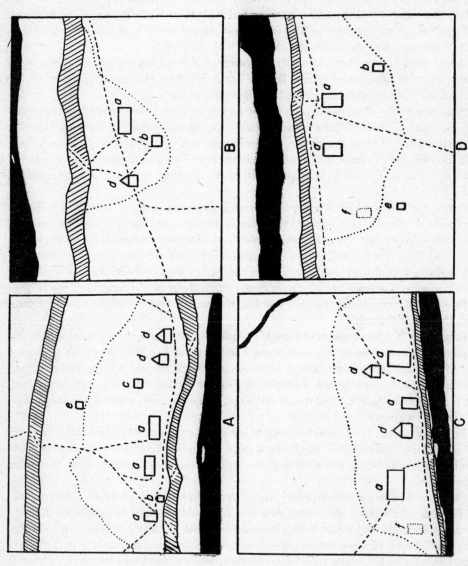

Fig. 5, Four Winter Settlements (Upper Liard River): A, Old Man's place; B, Louis Maza's; C, Old Kean's; D, River Joe's. (a, Cabin; b, Walled cache; c, Open cache; d, Tent frame; e, Latrine; f, Burial place. Broken lines show trails; dotted lines represent the limits of cleared area.)

and carefully whittles it to a smooth round surface. About seven inches from either end he tacks a piece of cardboard or tin, about three inches long and two inches wide. This makes a narrow platform. On one edge of this platform a bit of bait, such as rice or bacon rind, is placed. The stick is then fitted into holes cut in the sides of a four gallon oil can, from which the top has been cut away, and about half filled with water. A mouse running out along the stick to reach the bait must step on the platform. The weight of the animal causes the platform to upset plunging the mouse into the water. When the trap failed to reduce the mice in his house, Old Man one night tried to shoot these pests with a .22 rifle. He placed a little rice for bait on top of a ridge pole. Hearing a mouse approach the food his wife focused a flashlight in the direction of the animal. The mouse froze in the glare of light and old Man tried to shoot the thief. His eyesight was too poor, however, for him to kill any mice in this way.

Nonresidential buildings. A few nonresidential structures are built or used by the Indians. Such buildings include latrines, caches, and bunkhouses.

Latrines are not common. They are not built while the people live in Lower Post but are sometimes found around the home cabins. Little care is taken in their construction. They may be constructed with a piece of canvas over a frame of poles, or they may be built of log walls covered with canvas like a tent frame. Old Man dug a latrine and covered it with an old mosquito tent. He was about the only member of his family to use the structure.

A cache is found near every home cabin and is designed to afford protection to winter food stores from mice and bears. The simplest type is a platform made of two inch wide poles; it is about five feet square and rests on four posts, three or four inches in diameter and eight feet high. The goods to be cached are placed on the platform and covered with a tarp which is then tied down. More substantial caches are rectangular walled structures, about six feet wide, seven feet long, and five feet high, erected on a platform of heavy spruce poles. The platform itself rests on posts raised about ten feet from the ground. The walls of the cache are built of spruce poles, four or five inches in diameter, and fitted with a pole and dirt covered gable roof. A ladder is used to mount to the narrow platform left in front of the cache, while entrance is through a narrow opening about four feet high. The poles supporting a cache have strips of tin, ten or twelve inches wide, obtained from four gallon oil cans, nailed around them about halfway from the ground. The smooth surface of the metal prevents mice from climbing the poles.

Bunkhouses are not specially constructed but consist of cabins or tent frames which were abandoned after a new dwelling was constructed. Such shelters are sometimes used in winter by visitors to a settlement and contain little more than a stove. Guests provide their own bedding and kitchen utensils. Any unoccupied dwelling may also be used as a workshop for winter carpentering and skin work.

When Mrs. Man, a Slave Indian, first came to Old Man's settlement, she built a "tipi," such as she had been familiar with in her own country across the mountains. She utilized this structure as a workhouse and cookhouse, the open fire permitting the broiling of meat. The construction was described as a circle of closely placed poles covered with moss and dirt, and with an opening at the top for a smokehole.

Settlements. The semi-permanent winter settlement consists of a family's caches, home cabin, bunkhouse, and the residences of sons-in-law. From here the people go out to hunt, fish, and trap from early fall to late spring. Such a settlement is generally identified with its oldest resident, who lives here with his family and anyone else who has been invited or accepted to trap on the owner's trap line. Due to the long period in which brush and fire-wood have been gathered around most settlements, the surrounding area is generally well cleared and presents a spacious open appearance in the otherwise forested environment. An attempt is made to keep the immediate environs of a settlement free of willow and other brush (see Fig. 5).

As has already been pointed out, the structures in a settlement are arranged without regard to pattern. Generally they are on one side of a worn and narrow path which skirts the river. From the settlement, trails radiate to other settlements, to Lower Post, and to the trap line. It is not unusual for settlements to be moved a short distance up or downstream and even across the river. Such moving probably occurs when the wood supply in a vicinity becomes exhausted.

Garbage and slop, which is not fed to dogs, is commonly poured over the cutbank. Behind the settlement, in the toilet brush, one encounters piles of moosehair and discarded clothing.

TRAVEL AND TRANSPORTATION

The most important of the exploitative activities discussed—hunting and trapping—can be efficiently carried on only after the people have moved from the relatively populous trading center to the isolated winter settlements. Here it is once more necessary for each family to spread out across the surrounding country to intercept game and fur. Since a considerable portion of the resources derived from the environment are not directly consumed, but are exchanged for traders' food and capital goods, movement back to the trading post is also essential. In brief, Kaska society is, by adaptive necessity, extremely dependent upon mobility.

Two types of travel and transportation may be distinguished for the Indians, long distance and local movement. The first type includes the movement of people with their furs and belongings to Lower Post and their return to the winter homes with food and other supplies. The distance involved in such travel varies, depending on the tribal district and the location of the winter settlement within it. Generally in this form of transportation, goods must be hauled from fifteen to seventy miles. The second type, local movement, designates the mobility of people and goods taking place within the tribal district. Such local travel includes the movement of persons from the settlements to temporary hunting and trap line camps, to fishing sites, and to neighboring winter settlements.

In order to avoid the needless duplication of the words "travel and transportation" it may be pointed out that practically all travel involves the simultaneous transportation of goods. Similarly transportation cannot be accomplished without travel by the owner or his representative. In general a person rarely undertakes more than a day's travel without company.

Summer travel is carried out over trails and rivers. In winter people generally travel over trails, although they also utilize the frozen surfaces of rivers and lakes. Summer trails are generally narrow, cleared only enough to permit the transit of dogs and people traveling in single file. Winter trails are better cleared and cut wider, in order to accommodate loaded toboggans and people on snowshoes. Travelers in summer may follow part of a winter trail, but generally the latter are direct routes while in summer people must bypass lakes, sloughs, and the bends of rivers.

Both summer and winter trails are marked by blazed trees which, in a well wooded area, are spaced about a hundred feet apart. In addition, men who are hunting in an unfamiliar region may make temporary blazes to guide them on their return to camp or on a subsequent visit to a meat cache. Temporary blazing consists of breaking willow branches in the direction taken. Sometimes a forked stick is planted in soft ground and another thin pole laid in the fork to point direction. In early fall, a safe crossing on newly formed ice may be marked by three or four foot long poles stuck in the snow.

Trails usually follow the contour of a country. They never adhere to the meandering courses of rivers but always portage across points of land or, in winter, arms of water, in order to save distance. A trail usually ascends a ridge diagonally rather than proceeding straight up the face. In winter, the open face of such a diagonal ascent may be bulwarked with small black spruce trees laid lengthwise along the trail. Such a bulwark guards a toboggan from sliding down the otherwise open hillside. Spruce poles, roughly trimmed of brush, may also be extended from an ascent into the branches of trees growing below the trail. Such poles are placed about four feet apart and also serve to prevent a vehicle from overturning, should it slip from the ridge. Further protection is achieved by banking ascents with snow which is kicked from the overhanging slope with snowshoes.

Windfalls are removed from winter trails if they are small enough to cut with an ax and light enough to lift aside. Otherwise fallen timber may be axed in half and pushed down into the snow. When a heavy windfall blocks a trail, small sticks and snow are kicked up to make an embankment, on which the toboggan can pass over the osbtacle, or else the vehicle is lifted across the block. Winter trails are maintained by whoever uses them. A man making his first trip to the trap line in autumn will cut whatever overhanging branches and windfalls obstruct his passage. With the first snow he will bulwark ascents to ridges and cut more brush. Anyone else using the trail is free to benefit from these improvements.

In summer, trails cross small creeks by means of bridges constructed by felling from one to three trees, four or five inches in diameter, across the stream. These are trimmed of branches and moved close together. Bridges are also constructed by throwing down four or five saplings, two or three inches in diameter. Large rivers are crossed by rafts.

Many points along trails and rivers are designated by place names. Such identifications are freely coined and usually originate from some outstanding feature of the site or from some memorable event associated with that place. Thus a long ridge overlooking a wide stretch of country is called See the Country. A lake is known as Excited Lake, Old Man explained, because "People come there. They stay one night. They don't know how to go on, go back, or cross the mountain. Talking, talking; finally fighting [arguing] going on. They turn back." River Joe calls a slough below his winter settlement by the name of his daughter, who was born there in a temporary camp. An island in the Liard River is known as Natsitsi ("Long Face") Island. Natsitsi was one of Old Man's dogs. One year, as the family was traveling home on the river, the dog began to bark when the boat approached this land. The vessel was brought close to shore and Natsitsi allowed to jump out. He promptly began to run down a bear which the men, following behind, were able to kill. Since then the island has been called by the dog's name. Many lakes are designated to refer to their stocks of fish; thus Jackfish Lake and the numerous Fish Lakes dotting the area.

Land transportation. Burdens are packed by men and women; animals, the dog and horse, are used to carry goods; and the sleigh and toboggan are employed to move supplies. In recent years people have begun to hire trucks for transportation along the Alaska Highway to a point from which they can reach the winter settlements by foot or boat. One Indian has purchased a used sedan and a number of other men spoke of purchasing half-ton pickups as soon as trucks became available. Pack sacks are manufactured by women from twelve ounce canvas. Each member of a family owns a pack sack, small children using theirs to pack a few pieces of bread and bannock to eat in the course of a journey. Guns are transported in moosehide gun cases provided with a carrying strap, but may also be carried across the shoulder by holding the forward end of the barrel. While hunting a man holds his gun in the crook of his elbow, supporting the trigger guard on his wrist so that the barrel points toward the ground. A sawed section of a tree trunk is sometimes impaled on an ax which is then swung over the shoulder. An additional section may be mounted on another ax and carried in the free hand. In general people do not pack more than thirty or forty pounds; whenever possible human packing is avoided.

Wooden pack saddles of native construction are used for horse transportation. Horses pack up to 250 pounds and with this load can travel up to forty miles a day. To cover this distance, however, requires an early start with camp made around noon. A horse, it was explained, cannot be worked all day without being injured.

Dog packs are canvas sacks, which are slung over the animal's back and secured under the neck and body. The sacks consist of two pockets, about two feet long and fifteen inches deep, sewn to fit on either side of the animal. Each pocket is fitted with three inch wide insets at the ends in order to allow expansion. An area, about seven inches wide, is left between the pockets to fit over the dog's back. Flaps, seven inches wide and fourteen inches long, are sewn at both ends of the center area. These serve to protect such contents as blankets, tarps, and tents which are packed so as to extend from one pocket into the other. An additional protection is provided by sewing a strip of canvas, about twenty-four inches long and twenty inches wide, on the open edge of one pocket. This extends across the top of the pack and is tucked into the other envelope, covering the contents of both. A strip of tanned skin, about two and a half inches wide, is sewn along the outside of each pocket, about two and a half inches from the open edge. These tanned skin strips are sewn only along their bottom length, the upper edge being perforated with six one inch holes spaced equal distances apart. Any piece of cordage is laced through these holes back and forth across the animal's back from one pocket to the other, thus securing the contents of the pack. Halfway down each end, on the outside of each envelope, a tanned skin tab about two inches wide and five inches long is sewn. These four tabs are perforated with one and a half inch holes. About a foot and a half of tanned skin line is tied to one tab at the front end of the pack and a similar length to the tab at the back end. The front line passes under the dog's neck and ties to the corresponding tab on the opposite pocket. The rear line passes under the animal's belly and is secured to the tab on the opposite side. When dog packs are used to transport fresh meat, they may be lined with an additional piece of canvas to absorb some of the blood. The bottoms of packs are patched with canvas or tanned moosehide, when they become worn. Dog packs are manufactured by women. Dogs can pack up to forty or fifty pounds, but loads are generally limited to about thirty-five pounds for a stretch of twenty miles. Among the Upper Liard Indians, women and girls were always seen to pack dogs (Pl. 7, A). A Nelson Indian reported that among his people men pack horses as well as dogs. Men everywhere, of course, pack dogs when traveling without families.

When transporting goods by dogs in summer, one or more persons generally start out ahead of the animals. However, the dogs may be guided by chains until about a quarter of a mile from camp. The chorus of eager barking that arises from a camp, when dogs sense one or more of their companions being packed, is evidence of their eagerness to travel. In winter, dogs follow in the rear of people with snowshoes who break the trail. Traveling in winter, especially over crusted snow, often cuts a dog's foot. When this happens, rest stops are always marked by cutting a little brush which is thrown down for the animal to rest on.

The Kaska use both toboggans and sleighs. The toboggan is regarded as best suited for travel in the soft dry snow of winter. Although a sleigh is sometimes used in midwinter, it is recognized as being particularly adapted for traveling on the top of the crusted snow in late winter and early spring.

Toboggans are either purchased from traders or manufactured locally. The description of hewing and bending wood for toboggans has already been presented. The vehicle is normally constructed with three or four pieces of freshly hewed birch pieces, about twelve feet long, six inches wide, and three sixteenths of an inch thick but the toboggan whose construction was observed and is here reported fell considerably short of these specifications.[8]

After the first two feet of the boards have been bent to produce a curve, they are removed from the bending frame. The cleats, which held the boards together in the bending process, are left in place until all of the crosspieces have been put in position. The exterior sides of the two outside boards of the vehicle are first planed where they have been bent. This planing narrows the front of the vehicle, the reduced nose curtailing the hazard of hitting sticks and stumps along a trail. Such hazards might easily fracture the wood, particularly if the toboggan is traveling rapidly in cold weather. The next step is to substitute crosspieces for the temporary cleats. All of these crosspieces are manufactured of slightly dried birch. On the inner and outer surfaces of the extreme forward portion of the toboggan, two crosspieces are nailed. These are about three inches wide and three quarters of an inch thick (Fig. 3, B). All of the exterior edges of these crosspieces are bevelled with a knife, the bevelled surface being about one eighth of an inch wide. After the pieces have been put in position, the front of the toboggan is trimmed with a saw and planed to insure a smooth and even surface. The second crosspiece is less carefully finished, consisting of a

[8] The toboggan was made by Hans Donnelly whose narrow doorway has already been referred to. Hans is a small man and may unconsciously pattern objects to his own dimensions.

split spruce sapling, about three quarters of an inch in diameter. While the inner surface of the pole is carefully planed, the outer bark is not removed. This crosspiece is nailed about a foot below the first pair and at the lowest point of the rising curve. The worker next cuts four crosspieces two inches wide and a quarter inch thick. These are placed along the body of the vehicle, beginning at the extreme rear and about twenty inches apart. They do not, however, extend the full width of the toboggan but to about three quarters of an inch from each side. On that side of the crosspiece which is to fit against the toboggan boards, the worker cuts two grooves at points about one inch from either end. These grooves are cut about three quarters of an inch wide and half an inch deep. To cut these grooves, they are first outlined with a pencil. The extremes of the groove are then sawed to the proper depth. Using the tip of a butcher knife as a chisel, the worker removes the wood between the cuts of the saw. The blade of the knife is also used to trim away uneven edges of wood. The outer edges and corners of each crosspiece are bevelled. The piece is then nailed to the toboggan, the nails being driven down from the upper surface. The excess length of nail coming through the wood of the running surface is bent back toward the rear of the vehicle.

Old Man pointed out that this was an unsatisfactory way of constructing a toboggan since the bent nails would work away from the boards when the vehicle was in use. Also wear on the boards, such as would be produced by traveling over windfalls, would soon expose too much of the nailed surface. These predictions were fulfilled. After his first trip with the new toboggan Hans removed the nails and drove them into the vehicle from the running surface. Old Man pointed out that many people join the crosspieces to the runners with babiche line. When this is done, the worker first drills a hole through the thickness of the crosspiece and then makes two holes through the runners. The line is countersunk where it passes under the body of the vehicle.

When all of the crosspieces are in place, the running surface of the toboggan is planed smooth, care being taken to avoid the projecting nails. The rear end of the boards are sawed even with the last crosspiece. A three quarter inch hole is drilled in the exact center of the front of the vehicle between the two center boards and directly below the forward pair of crosspieces. Here the guide rope, a piece of manilla line about a half inch in diameter and four yards long, will be tied. Two holes, half an inch in diameter, are then drilled in the front of each of the outside running boards immediately below the forward crosspieces. In line with these holes, grooves are cut in the outer bevelled edges of the forward cross-pieces. From these holes lines, of double twisted babiche or insulated copper cable, bend around the front of the vehicle and are then drawn back to the first grooved crosspiece where they are fastened together. These lines serve to prevent the curve from leaving the toboggan when the wood becomes damp. On each side of the toboggan, between the first and last grooved crosspiece, a tight babiche or insulated wire line is strung. The line passes through the grooves and is fastened to the rear crosspiece. This lashing is used to secure the dog harness, and under it passes the cordage that secures goods on the toboggan.

An attempt was made to note the emotions expressed by Hans during the construction of a toboggan. He was somewhat uncertain if the materials available were adequate for the task. For example, he was dissatisfied with the fact that one of the boards was hewed from black birch instead of white, fearing that the knots would cause it to split. In putting together the vehicle he worked carefully, but inevitable accidents occurred. Several times the partially dried wood used for crosspieces split when nailed in place. Hans did not go out of his way to rectify these damages. In other words, he revealed no evidence of a drive toward perfection. He was always aware of the limits of the material which he was using but was not well satisfied with the finished product. About half-way through the construction process, Hans expressed the desire for sufficient skins with which to buy a commercially manufactured toboggan during his Christmas visit to Lower Post.[9]

Toboggans are built by men. When carrying a passenger, this vehicle is guided by handlebars. The construction of these was not observed. Their principal feature is a pair of curved wooden handles secured together with crosspieces and lashed to the toboggan. The handlebars are placed about ten inches from the rear of the vehicle, leaving a small space on which a man can stand. The partially enclosed cariole was never seen in the Kaska area.

From three to six dogs are used to draw a toboggan. Dogs are hitched one behind the other, one dog being consistently employed as a leader. The fanwise type of harness is not used and, indeed, would not be adapted to the wooded brushy country of the area. Dog harness is made by women from one and a half inch canvas webbing and includes a collar made of tanned moosehide stuffed with moose hairs and sewn with babiche. The traces are secured to the collar, while a cinch strap, containing two or three small sleigh bells, is fitted around the dog's back to keep the harness in place. The harness of each dog behind the leader is fitted with steel rings which are attached to inch long steel snap fasteners at the end of the traces. These fasteners are also used to harness the last dog to the lashing of the toboggan.

A man generally packs the toboggan but may be assisted by his wife. The heaviest load is placed in the rear of the vehicle. The goods are set on the floor boards, cooking pots and frying pans being placed on top of the main load. The outfit is then covered with a large canvas tarp which is tied down to the toboggan's lashing with several pieces of manila rope. The rope is first secured to the lashing with an overhand knot. Passing across the top of the load it bends under the lashing on the opposite side of the vehicle and is pulled tight before being drawn back to the first side. This process continues to the end of the cordage which is then tied to the lashing with a single overhand knot. A new piece of cordage is taken and the tying continued. Cut or uncut wood is also lashed down in this fashion. Lunch for people traveling is placed in a packsack, which is tied between the handlebars when this apparatus is in use. When children or women ride on the toboggan, they are seated so that their backs rest against the handlebar cross pieces. Folded blankets are placed on the floor boards, an eiderdown sleeping robe is spread on top of these and is drawn tightly around the person's body so that it covers the head like a hood. This serves to keep off falling snow. The covering is then lashed to the handlebars and to the side lashing. When the traveler temporarily leaves this shelter, the blankets are immediately closed in order to prevent the heated, damp blankets from freezing. After the toboggan is packed, the man's wife or a younger boy harnesses the dogs to the vehicle.

[9] Although Hans' trapping luck was rather poor, the fact that the ethnographer was willing to buy his toboggan enabled him to satisfy his desire. The toboggan, whose manufacture has just beeen described, is now in the Yale Peabody Museum of Natural History.

In traveling with a toboggan after a snowfall, it is necessary for someone with snow-shoes to precede the dogs and break trail for them as well as to clear windfalls and bulwark the ascents to ridges. Men or women or adolescent children may break trail. If possible, two persons are used to break trail, one following behind the other. The person guiding the toboggan (usually a man) runs behind the vehicle on snowshoes (Pl. 7, B). Such guidance is particularly important when the trail runs downhill, as it is then necessary to restrain the progress of the vehicle. Going uphill assistance must be given to the dogs. This is generally done by the person whose task it is to guide the toboggan running in front with the guide rope and pulling. The rope is not pulled directly in front of the dogs but from a side. On the diagonal ascent of a ridge the guide rope is pulled from the uphill side of the trail in order to prevent the conveyance from slipping. When handlebars are used, dogs are assisted by pushing the toboggan from behind while on a steep hill further help is given by someone else tugging on the dog harness (Pl. 12, A).

A particular danger in traveling across frozen lake and river surfaces is encountered from overflows. These are produced by sinking ice, through which a small amount of water may seep without freezing. Sometimes overflows are impossible to detect in advance, being covered with freshly falling snow. The unfrozen water quickly forms ice on the toboggan boards and, if the unaccustomed friction causes the dogs to halt, may freeze the vehicle to the spot. When a toboggan runs into an overflow and the forming ice begins to hold back the dogs, quick help is given to assist the animals. As soon as the vehicle is on dry snow it is tilted to one side and the ice knocked free with the back of an ax. Remaining ice is scraped free with the ax blade. Sometimes this is not sufficient to remove all the ice. Then the toboggan must be unpacked, a fire made, and the ice melted loose, after which the boards are allowed to dry. Despite the recognized danger of overflows, a suspicious spot of ice is often run over swiftly in order to avoid a lengthy detour. To guard against such danger spots, the person breaking trail often secures a long pole and, well in advance of the vehicle, tests the ice before each step. When not in use the toboggan is turned upside down, on its side, or is leaned against a building with the rear portion resting on the ground. It is rarely placed on a sleigh rack.

The construction of the Yukon sleigh was not observed. Such vehicles, made from birch, are from seven to nine feet long and are far heavier than toboggans. Their construction was probably learned from white men. The basis of the conveyance consists of two runners, which are several inches longer than the floor boards of the body. The runners are three inches wide and one inch thick. After being bent they are fitted with readymade steel runners that are attached with screws. The floor slats of the sleigh are made of birch wood; four pieces of lumber are required, each four inches wide and about a half inch thick. They are held together by crosspieces, five inches wide and half an inch thick. The crosspieces are placed twenty inches apart, their number depending on the length of the vehicle, and are secured to the floor boards by means of carriage bolts. The floor of the sleigh meets the upturned runners in front but along the rest of the vehicle it is supported about four inches above each runner by stanchions, five inches long, four inches wide, and three inches thick. These blocks are spaced about ten inches apart beginning about four inches from the rear of the sleigh. The body and runners are joined to the stanchions by means of screws. Sleighs are usually provided with handlebars, which are about eighteen inches high and much longer than those found on toboggans. Instead of fitting on the rear of the conveyance, the handlebars of a sleigh extend about halfway to the front of the vehicle where they are screwed in place. A lashing of babiche runs along each side of the sleigh body and is used for tying down the load. Shafts are employed with the dog harness. These are cut from green spruce poles, about six feet long and three inches in their greatest diameter. They are attached to the sleigh by means of babiche. The line passes through a pair of holes drilled in the most forward stanchion on each side of the sleigh and through corresponding holes drilled at the lower end of each shaft.

Sleighs are packed the same way as toboggans and their management follows similar principles. When not in use they stand on one side or else are stored on sleigh racks. When left standing with the runners in the snow, ice forms which must be knocked off before the vehicle can be used.

Toy sleds, about three or four feet long, are played with by children around the winter settlements.

Foot travel is the commonest form of overland summer travel, although some Nelson Indian children and women ride horses when long distances must be covered. In winter, children from five or six years of age generally walk, while younger children are packed on the mother's back or else ride in sleighs and toboggans. No particular type of foot-gear is regarded as most suitable for land travel in summer, although moccasins are preferred for hunting. In winter moccasins are always worn and, under these, snowshoes.

Snowshoes have several functions. By relieving the strain of plodding through deep snow and the problem of slipping on an unevenly packed trail, they reduce fatigue in winter travel. They also facilitate travel, since a person can go faster on snowshoes than by plodding through deep snow unaided. Finally these aids are necessary in breaking trail for dogs, and therefore increase the daily distance which these animals can cover.

Snowshoes are of two types. The first, used for hunting and trapping, generally equals the wearer's height in length and is about a foot wide. These are used when a man desires to travel cross country as rapidly as possible, the size of the webbed area preventing him from sinking too deeply into the snow. While such "big snowshoes" are known, their use was not observed among the Upper Liard Indians during the period of field work. The second type is used in breaking trail for dogs and vehicles and for hunting or trapping. Their length is also apportioned to the height of the wearer, a five foot man generally wearing snowshoes about three feet long and ten inches wide. Left and right foot snowshoes are recognized, the greatest curve of the wood being on the outside of the foot. Snowshoe frames are prepared by men and the panels are almost always filled by women. The details of lacing and of the foot lashing follow the style which has been traditional since aboriginal times and will not be described here.

In contrast to what has been said for other areas,[10] the Kaska Indian tends to walk on

---

[10] A detailed description of putting on, walking, and turning with snowshoes will be found in Osgood, *Ingalik Material Culture* (1940), 349–350. The picture he gives there is in complete agreement with what was noted among the Kaska. Personal use of snowshoes revealed that it takes no more than two or three hours to become used to them in walking. Learning to turn takes longer time, and a number of days are required before their presence on the feet ceases to be consciously noted. So far as their indispensability is concerned, there can be no question.

snowshoes much as he does without them, the feet being lifted sufficiently for each shoe to clear the frame of the other. In climbing a hill, the toes are bent sharply so that they will extend down through an unfilled space at the front of the center panel. In this way the toes secure an anchorage in the packed snow. In breaking trail, the hardest kind of winter travel, a person can generally cover about fifteen miles a day with such footgear. This distance can be doubled if trail is already broken.

Following use, snowshoes are usually brought into the house and carefully dried, after which they may be stored outdoors. Repairs on snowshoes are frequently necessary. A split frame is secured by willow splints, which are cut in a few minutes and lashed to the fractured wood with babiche.

Water transportation. In summer the Kaska use rafts and plank boats. Only Old Kean owns a plywood canoe of commercial origin, which he sometimes uses for fishing. Rafts are built by men where trails cross wide rivers and are also used by hunters who wish to float downstream to camp. They are about seven feet long and from three to five feet wide, being constructed from red spruce poles some four or five inches in diameter. Two crosspieces, consisting of spruce saplings about two inches in diameter, are used to hold the logs together. The poles are generally aligned in water and the crosspieces attached with nails. In the fall, when rivers run cold, rafts are built on skids near the shore and pushed into the water when completed. When the vessel has reached its destination, it may be left on the shore for use by other travelers or it may be taken apart and the poles allowed to dry for fuel. In spring, larger rafts are sometimes built in order to float a family downriver to the trading post with dogs, fur, and household equipment.

Rafts are managed with the aid of poles, which serve as sweeps and also function when the craft must be pushed away from drift piles. Accidents with rafts are not infrequent, the use of these vessels being regarded as particularly dangerous in spring and fall, when rivers run with ice. In the spring of 1944, Stella Wiley lost her seven year old son when a raft on which two adults and three children were traveling hit a drift pile and capsized. Her winter's catch of fur was also destroyed.

Plank boats are owned by many families and are either built by Indians from mill sawed lumber or are purchased from white men. They average about eighteen feet in length and are about three feet wide. For long distances, propulsion is always by means of a gasoline driven outboard motor. To cross a river, however, boats are poled or rowed. Oars are of native manufacture, being large and crudely cut from a piece of hewed lumber, and characterized by a narrow blade, which is roughly ridged, and a thick shaft about five feet long. Oars are used with steel oarlocks.

To cross a river with a strong current, the boat is dragged as far upstream as possible and is then pointed upstream from the shore. As the boat moves toward the center of the river and the current is felt to swing the prow around, the rower on the lower end rows hard while the person on the upper end pulls more easily. To curtail further the force of the current, weight is generally placed in the back of the craft. Men and women as well as adolescent children row and pole boats.

A boat lacking motor power may be pushed by another vessel which is equipped with an engine. Pushing is regarded as more efficient than lashing one boat alongside another, although this is also done. When a boat is to be pushed, manilla line or a pair of spruce saplings are used to fasten the vessels together. If poles are used, one end of each pole is bent to fit into the gunwales of each boat where the ends are lashed. This device is said to prevent the boats from breaking if they drop down a shelf of swift water. If two boats are used in conjunction, dogs generally ride in the forward craft and passengers with goods behind.

Once, in rainy weather, Louis Maza erected a mosquito tent in his boat. The tent was placed over a pair of bent spruce saplings anchored in the gunwales and forming an arc. The front and rear ties of the shelter were attached to the gunwales. Under this shelter rode Louis' wife, infant son, and Irene Wiley with her baby. Louis and his fourteen year old daughter, Eleanor, alternated running the outboard. The ethnographer met the party as he and Nitla were fishing downriver in a plywood canoe. Louis signalled to Nitla and the two vessels were lashed together side by side with only a slight reduction of speed on Louis' part. The journey was then resumed with all the passengers in the larger vessel.

In fall, boats are removed from water and stored high on the shore in order to prevent the spring break-up from smashing them.

Routine of travel. In contrast to the leisurely life of the Indians in camp, considerably more determination marks travel behavior once a journey has been undertaken. An effort is made to begin long journeys by getting a start early in the day, in winter sometimes an hour or two before sunrise. The demolition of the camp and the packing of the household equipment is undertaken by women while men transport the goods to boat or toboggan. When the tent has been taken down, the poles which supported the structure are left standing. This, however, is scarcely for the convenience of the next comer as only rarely will one family camp in another's campsite. Farewells, beyond a casual good-bye, are rarely taken, even when a family expects to be gone for a long period.

On walking trips, rest stops are frequently initiated by the leader of the party, but these stops are of only brief duration, particularly in winter. Smoking is a common feature of such rests. People try to cover at least half the distance of a day's journey before pausing for lunch. Lunch stops are marked by a fire and the preparation of tea; they seldom last more than forty-five minutes.

In the course of winter travel, fire is always made as soon as any member of a party complains of serious chilling. If gloved hands perspire in the course of a journey, they are exposed to the cold until chilled and then regloved; this prevents the mittens from becoming damp with perspiration and freezing. Should the fingers become cold in walking they are held lightly clenched within the mittens and the arms swung. Against the dampness absorbed from falling snow, there is no protection while traveling. When camp is reached, however, clothes are thoroughly dried or changed for fresh garments. The blanched faces of some people returning to the trading post in spring indicate that individuals are often careless or unaware of the danger of frostbite. No chances are taken with wet moccasins, however, and footwear is promptly dried or changed should it become wet.

Camp is generally made shortly before dark. If women accompany the party, they now take over the task of cutting poles and laying brush while men transport the necessary things from the craft or vehicle and perhaps start a fire. Unneeded supplies are left in the vessel covered with a tarp. If goods must be unloaded from a boat before reaching the final destination of a journey, they are stored on the shore and, if rain is expected, placed on poles and covered with a tarp. In contrast to the absence of farewells, greetings are warm. People meeting in Lower Post after a winter's absence in the bush always shake hands with expressions of pleasure.

Indians are usually enthusiastic about travel. The same anticipation and pleasure marks a family's return to Lower Post in the spring which characterizes their start home in the fall. Hunting trips, when the decision has been made to start, are always undertaken with exuberant optimism and enjoyment. Less eagerness marks the start of a trap line tour. There is a commonly expressed attitude of disdain for "sitting one place all the time like white man." Any prolonged camping in one spot quickly becomes tiresome and dull. This ennui is manifested in several ways. People complain of how much it is costing them to live in town; a man remembers that soon the bull moose will begin to run and lose his fat, hence the time to get meat is running short; somebody else expresses pity for the "starving" dogs who need fish and meat. Often the decision to move is made with little warning. One day may be spent finishing new dog packs or belatedly buying supplies, and the next morning the eager barking of the dogs gives notice that the family is off.

Despite the frequency of travel, families seldom move solely for pleasure and rarely go beyond the limits of the tribal district except to visit the trading post. A man's youth is ideally a time for wider travel but such longer journeys never succeed in permanently luring a man from the Kaska area. As Nitla explained it, people in a strange place are apt to become lonesome for their country and this homesickness takes considerable time to wear off. Before it has had a chance to disappear, the youth has started back to his people.

FOOD, DRINK, AND INDULGENCE

Few Indians, except possibly some members of the Frances Lake tribe, any longer strive to maintain themselves primarily on game and fish. Although meat and fish are of both gustatory and economic importance, they are not in themselves depended on for subsistence, survival being closely bound up with the foodstuffs supplied by white traders. In winter when the Indians are far from the trading post and heavily dependent on the goods which were transported in the fall, an adequate supply of food is an indispensable guarantee against hunger anxiety. Food also has capital value. A sufficient stock of accumulated food-stuffs means that, once the trapping season opens, time and effort can be concentrated in the business of getting skins rather than diffused between hunting and trapping. Hunting is ideally to be pursued in autumn, not only because at that time game is fat from rich summer living, but because then time is available for this activity and the meat obtained will allow purchased provisions to stretch through the winter. Fishing in late summer and fall is of similar economic importance. These reasons explain in part the strong emotion which Indians invest in a supply of things to eat. They also help to demonstrate why the value of food in Kaska society is comparable to that of money in our own.

The Kaska refer to two kinds of food, meat and "grub." Meat categorically includes fish and any game animals or fowl killed for eating. Grub designates any food purchased from the traders, including flour, rice, canned meat, and fruit. Each family is expected to supply its own grub and this principle is rigidly adhered to in summer, when the people live in Lower Post within easy contact of the stores. In winter, however, shortages of grub frequently arise and a family often has to be assisted until it has accumulated sufficient fur to undertake a journey to the trading post to restock depleted supplies.)

Periods of hunger often occur among the Kaska. There are several reasons why this happens. A man sometimes errs in estimating his winter outfit. Often a minimal supply of grub must be shared with more unfortunate relatives. A man may also lack the money or credit to buy sufficient food. When any one or a combination of these conditions occur, and the family cannot kill sufficient meat to take the place of grub, acute and serious food shortage results. Hunger is never pleasant to the Indian, yet the average man and women is able to accept temporary periods of food shortage without manifest alarm and overtly tends to minimize such experiences. Despite the anxiety concerning food, most people do not carefully ration their winter outfits. As a result, shortages are discovered only when the supply of a particular commodity is already almost exhausted.

A period of hunger was reported to have occurred in Old Man's settlement during the winter of 1939–40. All the grub had been eaten and there was no meat. Included in the several families living in this settlement at the time were Old Wiley, his wife, and children; they had not purchased a winter outfit. "They always had no grub. Old Wiley never trap," Old Man explained. "Girls, gee they tough; they strong. They didn't feel no hungry. They sing around, cut wood." After four days with scarcely any food, Old Man's son-in-law, Harry Lang, killed a dozen chickens, and then Old Man brought down nine more fowl. Everybody ate chicken. The following day Harry left again to hunt moose. He killed one moose but lost another. "I got one marten," Old Man related. "I got seven skin that time." He took the marten and traveled to a white man's home twenty miles upriver. This white trapper gave Old Man "nearly two hundred pound grub for one marten. Here it is, we come back with load of grub. Here it is, they all left. They went to Excited Lake. We got to Excited Lake. Everybody hungry." The people had already consumed the whole of Harry's moose. "We come in with grub. I think it last about three days." In March, Harry took Old Man's skins to Lower Post from where he returned with a sledful of grub.

Associated with the familiarity of hunger is the fact that people are always ready to accept food. A gift of food is recognized as one of the most important presents. In children the desire for food shows itself starkly, being as yet unmodified by socially patterned inhibitions on emotional expression. Young boys entering the ethnographer's home and seeing his children eating stared avidly and sometimes snatched at leftovers which were abandoned on the plates.

For most of the Indians the ideal diet consists of a balance between meat and grub. These need not necessarily appear together at every meal but some meat in the course of a day is regarded as indispensable. Either a diet of straight meat without grub or straight grub without meat is regarded as unfortunate. Not only is a straight grub diet less appetizing, but people are aware that reliance on such food causes staples to diminish rapidly and therefore increases the danger of running short. Living on straight grub also involves a greater expense; meat is free, but grub must be purchased at relatively high prices. Only one or two old women, like Mrs. Man, are content with a straight meat diet accompanied by little more than tea and sugar. The strength of this woman's emotional dependence on meat is indicated by the fact that, in September 1945, she expressed the conviction that she would die if meat did not soon arrive in camp. She refused to eat bannock, beans, or potatoes. "What you're gonna live on?" Old Man asked. "I drink tea," she replied stolidly. Old Man and his sons-in-law, however, all complained that they felt poorly when forced to eat straight meat.[11]

Meat itself is ranked in order of preference. Highly preferred is moose, caribou, sheep, and porcupine meat. Fat is greatly relished and all meat is improved if it contains fat. From October, when the moose begins to run, and throughout the winter, bulls are tough and their meat contains little fat. They then are regarded as "no good eating," in comparison to the cow, which is rich and succulent with fat. During most of the fall and winter, rabbits are staple food, occasionally supplanted by chicken. Too long a diet of any meat becomes displeasing and creates a desire for fish. Little or no fishing, however, is done in winter.

Certain meats are not eaten, including squirrel, wolverine, fisher, fox, weasel, and wolf. Some people also avoid eating marten and lynx. Rabbits are rejected if they are unusually thin, or if a "white stuff" is found in the lungs. Many people refuse beaver fat, claiming it is too strong and "works on the stomach like epsom salts." A moose killed by wolves is likewise not eaten.

In winter, staples, apart from meat, include beans, macaroni, white flour, sugar, dry whole milk, tea, coffee, rice, oatmeal, lard, baking powder, yeast, and dry fruit (mainly apples and raisins). Soon exhausted are such luxury items in the winter outfit as cocoa, bacon, butter, potatoes, cheese, canned sardines, dry salmon, cornflakes, sweet crackers, jam, dry eggs, onions, and sugar syrup or honey. Meat is generally eaten with rice, macaroni, beans, or, when available, potatoes. Bannock generally follows the main course. When possible this bread is spread with butter, jam, or cold bacon grease. Cooked dry fruit is also frequently eaten for desert, but most of this product is reserved for making wine. Oatmeal is prepared for breakfast, as are cornflakes, and hot cakes.

In summer fresh meat occupies a more limited place in the diet, being replaced by canned meat, bacon, dried salmon, and salmon bellies. The latter two fish foods are imported from Telegraph Creek, where they are said to be put up by Chinese merchants. In this season, fresh eggs are commonly eaten, canned milk supplants powdered milk, and canned fruit takes the place of dry fruit. A very few fresh vegetables are received from white gardeners in the fall or may be harvested from native gardens. Berries, oranges, apples, tomato juice, canned vegetables, and cheese have important places in the summer diet. Bannock continues to be made but the people also purchase pies, doughnuts, sweet and soda crackers, and pilot bread biscuits.

In general, particularly when meat is short, the winter diet is poor and nutritionally

[11] There is evidence for believing that if the organism is used to a mixed diet of proteins and carbohydrates and is then subjected to a straight meat or protein diet, a painful readjustment is required. Similarly a readjustment from a protein to a mixed diet also takes time and too sudden a switch is said to produce cramps and illness. White bushmen in the North have developed a system for making the transition from a straight meat to a mixed diet. Phillips, Unpublished Manuscript (1944).

inadequate. A generously estimated intake of 1850 calories a day is insufficient for work which requires from 2500 to 3000 calories for both sexes. Vitamin C is almost completely lacking; the amount of vitamin D received in the diet is low and can hardly be supplemented by the weak winter sunlight. Such minerals as calcium, iron, and copper are also poorly represented. So long as a mixed diet can be maintained, a proper balance of carbohydrates and proteins is assured, but in winter, personal experience revealed the intake of fats to be too low. As a result, considerable sugar is craved and eaten. In summer the diet is more nutritional and the only deficiency seems to be in vitamin D, but this can then be supplemented by sunlight. It may also be pointed out that the early months of living in the bush are associated with a somewhat better balanced diet than the later months, when most of the luxury items have been exhausted.

Moose and caribou meat are the principal preserved foods. A few fish are sometimes dried in the fall but seldom last more than a few weeks. Berries may be preserved by boiling and storing in unsealed glass jars, but they do not last until winter. A few families were reported to mash up dried low bush cranberries with bear grease in the fall for winter consumption.

In summer and early fall, when fresh meat is in danger of rapid spoilage, it is preserved by drying. The meat is boned and cut into a single slice, about a half-inch thick and from eighteen to thirty inches long. These slices are hung over a pole, which is supported between two forked sticks, and exposed to the sun. Underneath the meat a small smudge fire is built to keep away the flies. The meat dries in a day or two and is then removed to the house or cache, where it may be hung or stored in empty flour sacks until eaten. A few rabbits are sometimes also dried in this way, the skin and viscera being removed and the animal hung up by the hind legs until dry. In later fall, when flies have disappeared, larger pieces of meat are hung outside the cabin without a fire and left to dry or freeze. If game is killed in winter, only sufficient meat for a few days is brought into camp, the rest of the animal being left in the bush on a platform cache. People return to such a "meat place" when more meat is needed. Food preservation is the work of women.

In order of frequency, meat is prepared by boiling, frying, and broiling. Staples, such as dry fruit, potatoes, rice, and oatmeal, as well as the fins and heads of trout, are always boiled. The water is not poured off these foods but eaten. In camps as well as in the winter settlements where there are stoves, meat and fish are both fried or boiled. Porcupine is generally roasted but is also boiled. When porcupine has been cleaned of hair and gutted, with the kidneys left in place, it is split lengthwise on either side of the backbone. The quarters are axed off and the backbone is cut into three sections. The meat is skinned after it has cooked or roasted. Moose tongue, rabbit and beaver meat are also usually boiled.[12] The heads of the moose, caribou, and porcupine are always roasted before an open fire and are regarded as delicacies. Moose bones are split and the marrow used in the preparation of soup. At a moose kill young people often throw the lower leg bones into a fire to cook the marrow, which is then scraped out of the split bone and eaten. When broiling meat, a portion of the kidney or colon fat is often simultaneously roasted and portions of meat and

[12] The same information has been reported for the Mackenzie River Indians. Phillips, Unpublished Manuscript (1944).

fat eaten successively. Some people smear cold lard on lean fried meat in order to improve the flavor. The large colon of the moose is cut open, scraped, washed, and then fried in lard. If lynx is eaten, it is generally boiled with a change of water. Berries are eaten raw and also cooked with sugar. Eggs are both fried and boiled.

Flour is generally prepared in the form of bannock, which is also known as baking powder bread, less often as yeast bread. In making bannock two tablespoonfuls of baking powder are added to two cups of flour with a half teaspoonful of salt (hunters usually carry flour already mixed with these ingredients for making bannock). Two tablespoonfuls of sugar are optional for the dough, as is a teaspoonful of cinnamon. One cup of water is added to the dry ingredients, and the mixture stirred with a spoon. The dough is then formed into a single round loaf, which is usually scored, or into individual round rolls, about two inches in diameter, and placed in a frying pan to fry in deep fat until brown on both sides. After both sides have browned, the bread is revolved on the edges until these are brown. Some-times bannock is baked in a moderate amount of fat in a moderately hot oven, the loaf being basted with melted shortening before closing the oven. At an open fire bannock may be either fried or baked. In baking, the frying pan is set at an angle in front of a hot fire so that the heat is reflected on the dough, which has been spread with melted shortening. An even browning is assured by revolving the loaf as one part browns. Not until baking powder has been exhausted do people trouble to make yeast bread. The bread is baked in an oven or, if a stove lacks a baking compartment, in a straight kettle set on top of the stove and surrounded with hot rocks.

Special foods are not prepared for children. During the day they may ask for bannock and spread it with sugar, cooked berries or, when available, jam or butter. In summer a favorite with children is "ice cream," which they prepare from soap berries placed in a bowl and mashed with a wet spoon. Three parts of sugar are added to one part of berries and the mixture beaten until a thick froth appears. Children up to adolescence are also fond of fixing a mixture of dry milk and sugar added to a little water; the thick cream that results is eaten with a spoon. In winter "ice cream" is sometimes said to be made of powdered milk mixed with snow and sugar.

Throughout the year people eat three main meals a day, one upon arising, another toward the middle of the day, and one in the evening. If the family expects the return of one of its members late at night, tea and other food is often kept warm awaiting the person. In a cabin, meals are eaten from a table; in tents, food is eaten on the ground. Old Man reported that his present wife had to learn to eat from a table. For a long time she refused to do this but ate alone on the floor of the cabin while her husband and his children ate from the table. She still does all her sewing and other work on the floor, setting her sewing machine on an overturned box. A family always eats as a unit. Only on meat packing expeditions was sexual division of eating observed, the men and boys cooking their own food at their own fire, and women at another. Unless they are ill, people eat heartily rather than sparingly but without hurry or noise. The upper part of the body may be slightly bent toward the plate, but a person does not eat hunched over his food. Meals are accompanied by conversation and care is always taken not to waste food. Only inedible scraps are fed to dogs.

Dishes are generally washed as soon as a meal is completed. Hot or boiling water, with or without soap, is used for dishwashing and a wet cloth used to remove grease and food particles. In traveling, dishes are washed less carefully, often being merely rinsed with hot water and allowed to dry. Washing dishes is women's work unless men are eating alone.

Beverages.[13] In the last twenty or twenty-five years the Kaska have learned the process of fermentation from white men and today frequently prepare their own wine and beer. The principal alcoholic beverages consumed by the people are malt beer, fruit wines (both of which are domestically manufactured), whiskey, and rum. The two latter beverages are surreptitiously obtained from white men. Also consumed are such alcoholic products as lemon extract, hair tonic, after shave lotion, and stomach tonic.)

Malt beer is the beverage most commonly manufactured by the Indians. One can of malt, which is obtainable from local traders, with five pounds of sugar and one or two yeast cakes added to warm water produce about five gallons of beer. Sometimes a handful or two of fruit, such as raisins, oranges, or berries, is added at the time of setting the malt beer in the hope that fermentation of these will increase the alcoholic content. Fruit wines are made from raisins, prunes, dried peaches, or dried apples; rice may be added. To make five gallons of wine requires a total of ten pounds of fruit or grain, five pounds of sugar, and one or two yeast cakes. A five gallon barrel is filled close to the top with water and the mixture allowed to ferment. In summer, wines are prepared from soap berries. Any brew containing these berries, may be referred to as "bear drink" or "bear medicine."

Beer or wine is set in either a wooden barrel or in large aluminum and enamelware cooking pots. In Lower Post, brews are almost always set in the bush, away from the camp or house, in order to prevent detection by police and missionaries. When this is done, there is danger that the cold nights of autumn may interfere with the fermentation process. To prevent this, hot rocks are sometimes placed alongside the barrel, or the vessel is covered with a tarp and partially buried in the ground surrounded by hot rocks and ashes. Indians estimated that a malt beer is completely fermented in three days, while a fruit wine requires about five days to reach full alcoholic potency. Nevertheless native wines are rarely allowed to set longer than three days and beer is sometimes consumed after it has been working only twenty-four hours. The alcohol in malt beer, when given a chance to approach complete fermentation, rarely exceeds five per cent. Wines may contain up to about ten per cent of alcohol. No rigid division of labor is apparent in setting brews, women and men both preparing the beverages. In Lower Post, people rarely make more than five gallons of beer or wine at a time. At home, if visitors are present to participate in the drinking, ten or more gallons may be prepared.

The principal nonalcoholic beverages consumed are tea, coffee, and milk. Tea with sugar but without milk is the favorite daily drink of most people, strong tea being said to make a man feel strong. The beverage is brewed until quite dark and is then heavily sweetened. A house or camp generally has a ready pot of tea standing near the fire, and people drink some several times a day. Tea made with water obtained from snow is praised for its finer taste. Most families drink coffee at least once a day, generally for breakfast. It is made weak and is always taken with milk and sugar. Children alone drink milk. Evaporated milk diluted

---

[13] See also, Honigmann and Honigmann, *Drinking in an Indian-White Community* (1945).

with water is used in summer. In winter, powdered whole milk, which is easier to transport and which cannot become damaged by freezing, is generally prepared.

Stimulants and condiments. Tobacco has attained wide popularity in the Kaska area and is smoked, chewed, and, in the form of snuff, held in the mouth without chewing. While a few older men smoke pipes, the majority of men and women prefer cigarettes, particularly the American brands to which they have been introduced by soldiers and civilians engaged on work along the Highway. Boys begin to smoke at about the age of nine and girls at about fourteen. In Lower Post, people commonly buy readymade cigarettes (at thirty-five cents a package). Including the many cigarettes that must be given to friends who temporarily lack "smokes," a person consumes a pack of cigarettes a day. In the bush, nearly all smokers roll their own smokes, an exception being Old Kean who supplies himself with a winter's supply of "tailor mades." For rolling, the stronger tasting rice paper (Chanteclair brand) is generally preferred. Donald Suza was the only person observed to moisten dry cigarette tobacco by first rolling it in his hand and then breathing into his clenched fist. Only rarely is a supply of smokes rolled in advance of a journey. Young girls, however, sometimes preserve partly smoked stubs in empty match boxes and use these while traveling in cold weather, when rolling cigarettes is difficult. Men who are playing cards, gambling, or drinking may request an unoccupied youth or wife to roll smokes for them. In smoking cigarettes are generally held between the thumb and index finger, the hand being cupped around the glowing tip (Pl. 5, c). They are smoked until quite small and are then usually thrown into the fire or, in summer and fall, stamped out with the foot.

Both men and women take snuff orally. When the supply of prepared snuff is exhausted, a person may prepare his own by mixing cigarette tobacco with white wood ashes on a piece of cardboard. The mixture is spread thin and heated in front of a fire. While snuff takers as well as tobacco chewers also smoke cigarettes, for most people smoking is not a satisfactory substitute for the other forms of tobacco. The chewing of plug tobacco is almost entirely restricted to men.

The principal condiments used by the Kaska are salt, pepper, cinnamon, ketchup, pickles (in summer), Worcestershire sauce, and prepared mustard. Older folks, not having been brought up to use salt often use it sparingly, but for most people it is an indispensable feature of the diet.

Standard of living. Unlike the situation prevailing with respect to capital goods, which are easily constructed, readily available, or freely loaned, the distribution of consumer goods varies more sharply among different families. The principal factors making for an unequal standard of living are: differences in hunting ability, luck in hunting, health, the degree of incentive invested in trapping, the character of a trap line, and the willingness of a man to work for wages during the summer. Families in which there are several able hunters and persistent trappers are better provided with consumer goods than families consisting of old or infirm people or those whose productive members are reluctant to exert themselves.

The average combined winter and spring earnings of a Kaska family are about $2000. A very few men earn as high as $5000 a year; others earn only from $700 to $1000. In appraising these figures it must be remembered that families often have several children and unproductive old people who must be fed, and that prices for food and most supplies are very high in the North.

A large portion of these earnings goes to pay back the credit extended by traders the previous fall. The balance is used by the family to live in Lower Post during the summer at which time cash is paid for everything purchased. The record established by a man in trapping in turn determines the amount of credit which will be extended to his family the following fall to be used in purchasing food and supplies for winter consumption. Credit, however, is not the only factor determining the distribution of consumer goods in winter, since there is a limit to the amount and quality of food that can be transported to the settlement. The number of moose and other game animals which can be killed in the fall and winter also has an important bearing on the family's standard of living.

TABLE 8. MINIMAL BUSH STANDÁRD OF LIVING

Item	Price	Item	Price
50 lbs. flour	$ 6.00	5 lbs. oatmeal	$1.00
4 lbs. lard	1.00	¾ lb. butter	.65
¾ lb. tea	.75	1 lb. jam	.25
4 lbs. baking powder	1.00	1 lb. bacon	.60
12 lbs. sugar	2.10	2 cakes face soap	.25
12 lbs. beans	2.00	2 cakes laundry soap	.25
25 lbs. rice	4.50	1 lb. chewing tobacco	1.00
1 lb. cheese	.70	1 lb. cigarette tobacco	1.00
3 lbs. dried milk	2.00	2 pkgs. cigarette papers	.30
1 lb. salt	.50	10 pkgs. matches	.35
5 lbs. barley	1.00	12 candles	.50
100 lbs. dog feed	17.50	50 large cartridges	2.50
8 lbs. dried apples	2.50	50 .22 cartridges	.90
5 lbs. raisins	2.00	Needles, thread, etc.	1.00
3 lbs. macaroni	$ .50		
			44.60

Because money is generally plentiful in the spring after a family returns from trapping, the unequal standard of living is not generally apparent in Lower Post. Almost everyone has money to spend for new clothes, canned meat, fresh fruit, pies, doughnuts, cigarettes, candy, and whiskey or rum. An average family's expenses for these months in Lower Post amounts to about $700. Women, and particularly adolescent girls, spend a large part of their winter earnings for clothes; buying many blouses, slacks and jackets when they arrive in the post in the spring, or ordering these garments from mail order houses. Men and boys tend to confine clothes purchases to necessary items and generally secure these on credit in the fall. Their surplus money goes largely for alcoholic liquors.

In winter, the inequality shows up more sharply. A minimal standard of bush living is shown in Table 8. This indicates the amount of food and necessary supplies which a family consisting of two adults and one child, and owning four dogs, requires in one month. The prices are for Lower Post and must be almost doubled for gauging living standards at a remote outpost like Frances Lake.

If the monthly rate is multiplied by the nine months that the average family spends in the bush, it will be seen that a *minimal* standard of living away from the post for a family of this size requires the expenditure of about four hundred dollars. Most families, of course, spend more than this.

It is interesting to compare the minimal requirements shown in Table 8, which were obtained from Indians, to the monthly ration alloted to an indigent adult (or child over twelve) by the Indian Affairs Branch (Table 10).

From bills, which he had preserved, it was possible to reconstruct at least part of Old Man's winter outfit for 1942. His purchases, made for a family of four at one store, are listed in Table 9 and may be regarded as quite average. Many of the items were probably dupli-

TABLE 9. PART OF OLD MAN'S WINTER OUTFIT—1942

Item	Price	Item	Price
224 lbs. white flour	$27.00	10 lbs. lard	$ 3.35
50 lbs. wheat flour	6.00	5 boxes corn flakes	1.75
25 lbs. rice	5.00	16 lbs. jam	6.75
150 lbs. sugar	26.60	4 lbs. salt	1.00
16 lbs. brown beans	3.20	1 slab bacon	4.90
14 lbs. navy beans	3.50	10 lbs. lentils	2.50
17 lbs. white beans	3.40	1 carton candles	8.50
10 lbs. corn meal	1.90	1 suit	30.00
5 lbs. macaroni	1.10	10 No. 3 traps	25.00
50 lbs. dry milk	32.00	1 doz. No. 0 traps	5.75
25 lbs. raisins	10.00	1 doz. No. 1 traps	6.00
25 lbs. prunes	8.50	1 pr. pants	7.50
8 boxes .30/30	17.00	1 mackinaw	12.00
1 carton .22 long	5.00	½ case eggs	10.50
10 lbs. tea	12.00	1 ax	2.50
11 lbs. coffee	13.75	snare wire	8.25
5 lbs. soup mix	1.25	1 dunnage bag	4.00
2 cans egg powder	2.50		
7 lbs. syrup	2.50	Total	$329.95
10 lbs. butter	7.50		

cated in his purchases at the other trading company, with other items, like dog feed and matches, added.

A complete winter outfit, including replacement of capital goods, totaling in all about $500, would last Old Man, his wife, daughter, and his wife's granddaughter until Christmas, when most of these purchases (excluding capital goods) would again be duplicated. From these data it may be estimated that a family of two adults and two children with several dogs requires an outfit costing about $1000 for the winter stay in the bush.

Data have been presented showing first, the Indian's own estimate of a family's minimal monthly food requirements, and, second, some of the food which an average family takes into the bush for winter living. Table 10 represents the monthly rations allotted to Indians

TABLE 10. SCALE OF MONTHLY RATIONS FOR INDIANS ON RELIEF[14]

Item	One Adult	Two Adults
Flour (Canada approved)	24 lbs.	36 lbs.
Rolled oats	6 lbs.	9 lbs.
Baking powder	1 lb.	1¾ lbs.
Tea	1 lb.	1½ lbs.
Sugar	2 lbs.	4 lbs.
Lard	3 lbs.	5 lbs.
Beans	5 lbs.	5 lbs.
Rice	2 lbs.	3 lbs.
Cheese	1 lb.	1½ lbs.
Dried milk	2 lbs.	3 lbs.
Salt	15¢ to 20¢ per month	
Matches	15¢ to 20¢ per month	

who, because of age or widowhood, are presumed to be unable to trap sufficient furs to maintain themselves. Lacking even such essentials as soap and dried fruit, these rations are evidently expected to be supplemented by meat and fish supplied by relatives or friends or caught in rabbit snares. The allotment is bitterly criticized by most Indians.

DRESS AND ADORNMENT

Clothing is used for protection and modesty but relatively little attention is paid to dress as a channel for expressing vanity. Although new and attractive clothes are greatly valued by girls, only one or two young women are characterized by any demonstrable narcissism in this respect. Most women are not careful in the way they dress, change clothes relatively infrequently (although more often than men), and wear garments that are stained, worn, and ill fitting.

In summer men wear two piece suits of knitted cotton underwear with long sleeves and drawers. Over this are trousers of cotton duck or worsted, and a flannel shirt with long sleeves. The trousers are often khaki colored, the shirt blue or gray. The collar is left open and in very warm weather several additional buttons of the shirt and undershirt are undone. Trousers are supported by a leather novelty belt which is often quite wide and gaudily studded. Heavy woolen socks are worn over ankle high leather boots which are usually laced from the outside in, instead of from inside out. A few of the older men wear slipper moccasins.

A wide variety of headgear is fancied.[15] Young men are attracted to "cowboy" hats or wide brimmed Stetsons. Older men usually wear disfigured snap brim felt hats. Other types of headgear appear and disappear as fads take hold. In 1944, Tahltan Indian youths from

[14] The list is dated January 3, 1944. Children under twelve years receive half this ration. "This ration," the list reads, "is set by the Indian Affairs Branch at Ottawa and merchants must not change either the quantities or commodities without written permission from the local Indian Agent."

[15] In conversation, Dr. Cornelius Osgood has pointed out that a taste for novelty in headgear seems to be characteristic of aboriginal and contemporary Northern Athapaskans and is also found in the Northwest Coast. For some types of headgear see Plate 2.

Telegraph Creek were distinguished by their homemade white canvas sailor caps. In the early summer of 1945, most Kaska youths were wearing these caps, a number being sold by local Tahltan families at two dollars apiece. In August of that year, a new fad appeared when Kaska girls began to make caps of blue cotton cloth shaped like the overseas caps worn by the American Army and the Royal Canadian Air Force. During the warmest part of the day men and boys may go hatless.

In winter men don heavier woolen underwear and woolen trousers. Leather shoes are now abandoned in favor of large moccasins supplied with an ankle wrap of canvas. These are worn with one or two pairs of woolen socks and blanket duffel. A heavy woolen shirt, with a sweater or purchased parka, are also worn. The most common winter hat is made by covering heavy broadcloth with beaver skin, and is provided with large flaps which, when let down, protect the ears and face (Pl. 5, A). Large mittens, with a wide cuff covering the lower end of the sleeves, are always worn when traveling. In spring, when the ground is wet, ankle high rubber shoes are common.

Summer garb for women includes flannel bloomers and either a flannel undershirt, rayon slip, or blouse. Corsets and girdles are not used, although Mrs. Maza was attracted by these garments in the illustrated mail order catalog and expressed the desire to buy a girdle. She thought it would help her to feel better. On top of these undergarments is worn a cotton dress, which in younger girls is tucked into cotton or worsted slacks. During a period when women's slacks were difficult to purchase, several girls wore men's black trousers. A bright colored blouse is generally added over these garments and sometimes also tucked into the slacks. Older women, however, may wear two long dresses, or an extra skirt and blouse. Old Lady Metša always wore a pair of men's trousers under her skirt and petticoat.[16] While some younger girls go without stockings, the majority wear mercerized flesh colored hose or black ribbed cotton stockings. Low or medium heel oxfords are the most common type of footwear, except among older women who wear moccasins with canvas ankle wraps. Girls often go hatless; older women cover the head with a rayon scarf. In winter these basic garments, except for the shoes, remain the same, although for traveling heavier slacks may be put on. Black ribbed stockings, sometimes worn double, are common in cold weather and there is added a woolen or poplin windbreaker or heavy woolen sweater. Wide duffel moccasins and duffel mitts, both worn with blanket duffel, are standard winter garb. Head-gear consists of a woolen scarf which may also be wrapped around the neck.

Young boys wear knitted wool-cotton undergarments plus overalls or long trousers and a flannel or cotton shirt. In summer, moccasins and oxfords are seen less often than rubber overshoes. Young girls wear flannel bloomers and a shirt covered with a cotton dress. Cotton stockings and oxfords or moccasins complete their ensemble. In cold weather, children of both sexes don woolen overalls, black ribbed cotton stockings, a sweater or doeskin cloth windbreaker, wool toque, commodious moccasins, and mittens lined with duffel.

Little variation in dress is observed corresponding to moderate changes in temperature. Summer garments are worn till quite late in the fall, eventually with the addition of a jacket or windbreaker. In summer, a jacket or sweater is sometimes added toward evening. When

---

[16] According to Nitla, Pelly River Indian women wear "breeches" instead of bloomers under their skirts.

it rains, rubbers may be put over moccasins but little hesitancy is shown by adults or children in allowing the feet to become wet.

Most clothing is purchased from local traders; a little from a Canadian mail order house. Some items are domestically manufactured by women, including girls' and women's dresses, children's underwear and overalls, moccasins, mittens, duffel, and caribou skin shirts for men's hunting wear. The material for dresses is obtained locally and the patterns of the finished article always follow those of commercially finished garments. Sewing machines are widely used in dressmaking. The pattern for children's one piece long winter underwear is shown in Fig. 6, c. Two of these pieces are cut. In sewing it becomes necessary to cut away the upper from the lower portion at the waist and sew them together again in proper alignment. An opening is cut in the front, from neck to waist, and fitted with buttons and button holes.

Moccasins and mittens are cut from tanned moosehide, only babies' moccasins being prepared from the softer caribou hide. During the period of field work most families were short of hide, although partially tanned skin was available for further processing. It was only in late October that two such skins were finally smoked; they were immediately sewn into garments. The foot portion of the moccasin is cut by folding a piece of moosehide, of the required length and width, once along the length (Fig. 6 E, I, a–b) and then cutting out the curved forward portion indicated by the broken line in the figure. The worker often goes over her cut to assure a smoothly flowing line. The heel (x–y) is cut after the tongue has been sewn to the foot part, and after the heel has been partially sewn from the top (c–c) for about one inch (II). The tongue (III) is cut by folding a rectangle of moosehide or caribou hide, about one half the size of the footpiece, on the diagonal (d–e). The cut is then made as indicated by the broken line. In an adult's moccasin, the tongue is placed about one inch from the forward edge of the footpiece and the sides of the skin are then gathered up and sewn to the edges of the tongue giving the blunt toe (IV). Sometimes the tongue is covered with a piece of black velvet or otherwise decorated before being sewn to the footpiece. If the moccasins are to be of the slipper type, a cuff about an inch wide is sewn from the upper edge of the tongue all around the open portion of the footpiece. In winter, ankle wraps of eighteen ounce canvas are sewn around this part, and tanned moosehide laces are affixed. Laces may be attached in two ways. Either a single piece of line is threaded in and out around the heel and side of the moccasin and then two equal lengths left free to tie around the ankle wrap or two equal pieces of line may be passed through narrow slits cut on either side of the front opening and held firm with a single overhand knot.

The pattern for a child's mitten is illustrated in Fig. 6, B. Four pieces of material are cut to pattern (I). In two of these, thumb openings are made. Two thumb pieces (II) are cut, and folded, (a to c), and sewn (ac to b). The thumb is attached to the body of the mitten with point (ac) matching (a'c') and (f) matching (f'). The back and front of the glove are then sewn together. For an adult, the cuff portion is cut a great deal wider, so that the upper width of the cuff exceeds the widest part of the hand section by about three inches. Mitten duffel are cut in the same general style but are, of course, smaller than the gloves which cover them. Sinew line is generally used to sew mittens and footwear. When moccasins become worn they are frequently patched, the patch being sewn on the inside of the

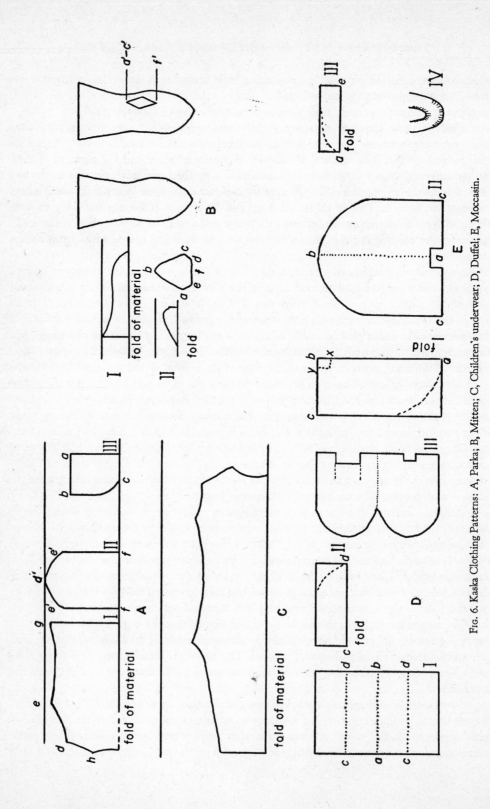

Fig. 6. Kaska Clothing Patterns: A, Parka; B, Mitten; C, Children's underwear; D, Duffel; E, Moccasin.

shoe, so that the sinew will not be subjected to too much wear. Mukluks are rarely seen but may be purchased locally from traders.[17] Piping is inserted in the seams of moccasins and mittens, serving less as decoration than to prevent the penetration of cold.

Children's foot duffel often consists of a woolen or flannel rag simply wrapped around the foot; sometimes rabbit skin, which has been dried outdoors in cold weather, is used for this purpose. Adult duffel is cut from old woolen blankets, the pattern being said to follow an old moccasin pattern which was abandoned a long time ago. Material of the required size is first folded along the diagonal (a–b) as shown in Fig. 6, D, and is then again folded along (c–d). The rectangle of folded material thus obtained is now cut along a curved line. What will be the upper layer is now cut as illustrated by the broken line and the garment sewn around the toe and side thus making a loose slipper. The heel is sewn to within an inch of the bottom of the lower layer, which is then cut to square off the heel and sewn. An ankle wrap of the same material is added, but no lacing is used to keep this part in place since the outer moccasin lacing will do so. Felt insoles are sometimes worn as additional duffel.

Although aboriginally the Upper Liard Indians made the parka, today there are only a few women who know how to cut this garment, which is usually purchased. Native parkas are manufactured from doeskin cloth or canvas. Mrs. Man made a parka during the period of field work (Fig. 6, A) and explained that in her country, around Fort Liard, the garment continued to be manufactured. Two pieces are cut of the parka body (I) and sewn together back to front (h–d) and (e–g). The front of the parka is cut down from the neck as indicated by the broken line. The sleeve (II) is sewn from (e') to (ff) and then attached to the body (e') matching (e), and (d'), (d). The hood (III) is sewn from (b) to (c) and then attached with opening (a–b) being sewn to the neck. In the sewing, point (b) matches the back center of the neck, and points (a) the front center of the neck on either side of the cut. When the hood is open it will be seen that there are two points (a). This pattern undoubtedly reflects the influence of commercially manufactured garments.

Women's dresses, underwear and stockings are worn for about a week before being laundered. Men may wear their clothes for two weeks or longer before washing. Girls or women wash clothes in galvanized iron tubs which are set on the ground or floor (Pl. 10, A) Water is heated on an open fire and poured into the tub, soap powder also being added. The laundress sits on a low box or fallen tree, or squats on the ground over the vessel. Washboards are not employed, although these are available at the stores. Squeezing the soapy water out of the garment with the right hand, the woman at the same time twists it between her two fists in a circular movement. The entire garment is gone over several times in this way. Clothes are not rinsed. When clean, the article is stretched to shape and thrown over a line strung near the camp. In traveling, garments, especially diaper cloths, are often spread on willows to dry. There is no common washday, a wife or daughter doing this task as the need arises.

Adornment. The principal ornaments worn by women are a rosary and a variety of hair ornaments, including combs with artificial flowers, clips, ribbons, and barrettes. Sometimes girls appear at dances with curlers in their hair. Men wear rings and arm garters. Both sexes frequently have wristwatches.

[17] On Christmas morning (1945) Harvey Cross, a Nelson Indian, wore a very decorative pair of mukluks.

Moccasins and mittens are usually decorated by being trimmed with strips of raw or tanned fur (rabbit, fox, or beaver) or by the addition of an embroidered floral design. Slipper moccasins may be decorated with a second tongue of white caribou hide or a piece of colored velvet sewn to an underlying moosehide or canvas tongue. The cuffs are sometimes bordered with embroidered pinked black velvet or dark blue doeskin cloth about an inch wide. The principal embroidery stitches are the outline, cross, and chain stitch. The first two are used for floral designs, while the latter is employed to embroider borders along the upper and lower edges of the cuff trimming on slipper moccasins. Since the war it has been difficult to obtain glass beads, so that beadwork designs on moccasins have been largely replaced by silk embroidery. Native and even purchased parkas are trimmed around the hood and cuffs with fox or wolverine fur, the latter being preferred for this purpose because it does not frost. In general, clothing decoration is limited.

Men shave once or twice a week. Some of the younger men several times sought to encourage mustaches during the period of field work, but only two older men permanently displayed this feature. Men's hair is cut by anyone who owns shears and clippers. In winter the hair is allowed to grow long and thick, and the only attention it receives is a casual morning combing.

Women do not comb their hair while traveling, but in camp and at the trading post the younger women exhibit considerable consciousness of their coiffures. A favorite headdress is to wear the hair rolled over the forehead and sometimes all around the head (Pl. 5, B and D). The rolls, however, are uneven and wisps of hair are always falling loose, even the ribbon or rag used to keep the roll in place being exposed at many places. Many young girls comb the hair straight to the sides and allow it to fall over the neck (Pl. 3). Older women dress the hair by braiding it and putting it up at the back of the head, or by parting it on one side and pinning it at the sides with bobby pins and barrettes.

Cosmetics gaining favor include lipstick, powder, nail polish, and perfume. Since the local selection of lipstick shades is limited, no effort can be made to match it to the shade of complexion. The same lack of matching enters into the use of nail polish, which is often crudely applied and not given sufficient chance to dry. A popular amusement of girls is to paint the fingernails of men, boys, and very young children. Perfumes are in great demand among girls and women. Cosmetics begin to be used at about the age of thirteen or fourteen; older women, beyond the age of thirty, are little interested or experienced in this behavior.

ROUTINE OF LIVING

Discussion has ranged through the principal economic techniques by which individuals adapt to the environment to secure the satisfaction of their needs. Certain residual needs, rest, cleanliness, and elimination now remain to be considered. Following this material we will examine the effort and motives which underlie the technical activities that have been described.

In summer young people tend to rise late, after ten or eleven o'clock, and seldom go to sleep before midnight. Unmarried boys keep even later hours, with darkness assembling in some camp to play cards, strum guitars, and wait until the older people have gone to sleep; then they begin to tease the unmarried girls. On a night when there is a dance, young married couples, often with children, seldom go home until well after midnight, while un-married people remain abroad until three or four o'clock in the morning. Older people as well as very young children retire and rise early.

In winter everyone tends to retire early in the long northern night, and people seldom arise before the sun—about nine o'clock in the morning. On the trap line or while traveling earlier rising obtains.

Indians retire fully clothed, except in summer, when moccasins and outer clothes are sometimes removed by the younger people. In winter, an extra sweater and dry moccasins may be donned before going to sleep as additional protection against cold. Following a day of winter travel, people are always careful to hang moccasins, socks and duffel in a warm dry place where these garments will have a chance to dry thoroughly. Despite full aware-ness of danger from burning, people frequently place damp moccasins too close to a fire causing them to scorch.

People sleep on the back or side and always cover their heads with blankets or eider-downs. In summer this habit serves as a protection against mosquitoes, while in winter it is imperative for warmth. According to many people's admission, the Indian tends to be a light sleeper. In summer one hears frequent complaints of having been unable to sleep due to the sounds of trucks, crying dogs, or young people "running around."

A person seldom washes more than once a day and then it is upon arising. The hands, arms, face, and neck are generously lathered with soap and rinsed in a washbasin. Bathing is rare, except in summer when boys and girls may go swimming. Nevertheless the people appear clean and emit no offensive body odor. Their clothes and hair, however, smell of wood smoke. Little attention is paid to head lice and nits, most children being afflicted by these pests. Sometimes washing with gasoline is used to get rid of body lice. One very old woman was observed to search her clothes for lice which she would crack with her teeth and eat. A few young people were seen to clean their teeth upon arising, but the extent of this practice seems limited.

Extreme reticence marks the function of elimination. When in a group, a person will never announce that he is going to the toilet but says "I go out," or else simply slips away unobtrusively. Such a departure never meets with comment. People also avoid looking when they see a man or woman going off into the brush alone, and the uncleared toilet area near a camp is generally avoided except for its purpose. Although young men will urinate and defecate in the presence of one or more friends of their own age and sex, urinating is always accomplished by facing away from another person, thereby concealing the genitals. Men urinate in a standing position. Women are much shyer than men and always go a con-siderable distance into the brush to perform these bodily functions. While adults will never urinate or defecate in the house, an exception is sometimes made for very young children who, in cold weather, are permitted to urinate in a tin can. Children are also not obliged to move as far into the brush to eliminate as adults, and when very young often do so only a few steps from a camp or cabin. People always avoid urinating on a trail; instead they turn to one side, even when wearing snowshoes. Adults were reported to defecate two or three times a day. Twigs or moss are used to clean the anus.

No shame is attached to spitting or clearing the nose. Many men spit constantly and do so anywhere except in a house containing a lumber floor. In their homes, people who chew tobacco or take snuff generally expectorate into a small tin can containing an inch of water which is kept standing under the bed. Members of either sex are often seen bending from the waist and studying a stream of mucuous for signs of blood. Both sexes generally clean the nose by blowing it between the thumb and index finger, then wiping the hand on the side of the trousers or dress. Nose picking is frequent.

The English word "work" has restricted significance among the Kaska, since it is almost exclusively applied to hiring out to white men for wages. Hiring out for woodcutting, lumbering, freight handling, and working for government survey parties, is seldom under-taken except in case of necessity. Duties outside the society which require special abilities, such as piloting river boats, are far more satisfactorily regarded by the Indians. Since the completion of the Highway, opportunities for such work are no longer available. During the building of the airport, a number of men hired out to contractors and this period is looked back on with considerable pleasure, chiefly because of the excellent remuneration and the gifts (food, cigarettes, and liquor) that were received. Women do not hire out for wages, although some women earn a little money making dog packs and moccasins to order for white trappers.

In general Indian men find it far more pleasant to be their own supervisors in the per-formance of their own socially patterned tasks than to hire out and work for either white men or other Indians. While certain of these necessary duties are more or less congenial to specific individuals, no evidence could be obtained of tasks which were generally regarded as onerous or unpleasant. In several interviews Nitla saw the Indian man's typical round of activities as a somewhat futile and painful way of existence. He tended to pity himself and compared the Indian's life to that of the white man who "just sit down one place." On one occasion he said: "By goodness, man hard time. Move the camp around . . . go after camp. I go hunt around that way. Make fire, hunt. Sometime get no moose. Second time hunt moose again. No moose. Woman set snare, bring rabbits, meat. Sometime pack berries home. Cook, mix, eat. Another man hunt moose. Who lucky for game, get moose. Pack home. Give that man a piece of meat. After, people move camp. Make the dried meat. Sit down. Soon finish game. Hunt the moose again . . . woman find porcupine sometime. Find two. Clean 'em. That man want porcupine. Kids he send them. Give half sometime . . . Hunt moose, two men apiece each. Woman stay, just watch the camp. Have to go a long way to shoot the moose. Sometime lost moose . . . Oh, hard luck! He's stuck. He keep one dog, hunt porcupine. Dog he find porcupine. He not find porcupine, nothing to eat one day. Sleep. Kids he soon crying . . . Mother mean. Hell! My goodness!"[18]

The principal incentive for accepting work with white men or other Indians (as in housebuilding) is the need to earn money for summer living following a poor trapping season. Men who have had a successful trapping period are, of course, completely uninterested in hiring out. Nick Lang said frankly that he disliked working for wages because such work

[18] It must be noted that Nitla is referring to the way of life of the Frances Lake Indians who, in an area of high prices, cannot get sufficient fur to buy a winter's supply of food and so are highly dependent on game for subsistence. This in turn curtails their opportunities to trap. Thus they are inextricably caught in a vicious circle.

did not permit him to earn enough money. During the building of the Watson Lake airport he did river transportation using his own boat and earned eighteen dollars a day. He quit because meals were inadequate and the contractors wouldn't increase his wages to twenty-five dollars a day. Even when there is a direct necessity to earn additional money during the summer, work habits are apt to be sporadic. White men, who have had experience with Indian labor, try whenever possible to arrange payment on a piecework basis. Even this fails to spur production. Although work is often accepted enthusiastically, with optimistic visions of the rich rewards to follow, enthusiasm seldom endures and jobs are readily abandoned for various reasons. Often the opportunity to join a drinking party results in the interruption of production. In summer, the heat is given as an excuse for knocking off. Dances, with resultant late sleeping, also cut the number of hours that can be put into such work. One youth quit a job with a survey party because too much tax was deducted from his earnings. Finally the potential productive capacity of the Indian is restricted by the leisurely pace at which he is accustomed to working.

The Indian's motivation in connection with work for white men was very well demonstrated when, in early autumn, the Upper Liard Indians decided to spend a couple of weeks at the Highway Crossing before going upriver. They planned to earn money cutting timber for a white man's sawmill. The men set out from Lower Post full of enthusiasm. They calculated the number of trees that could be cut in an hour and estimated their daily earnings hopefully. For two days most of the men worked about four hours a day. On the third day, a brew became ready and no one worked, while on the following day hangovers made everyone reluctant to exert himself. On that day Richard Day and Edward Prince decided to return to Lower Post. They had become involved in a brawl with Upper Liard Indians and felt themselves unwanted in the community. Four days later Louis Maza and River Joe cut some more logs, for which they were promised free lumber to use for construction in their winter settlements. This finished the woodcutting and now everyone began to talk of getting home to hunt before the moose started to run.

When people work for themselves, the chief incentives may be classified as securing food to eat, securing fur which can be traded for food, maintaining cultural expectations of comfort and cleanliness, and, finally, providing necessary equipment, such as snowshoes or toboggans. Another motivation arises from the pride which most people experience in their achievements. Despite these motivations, only slightly more effort is invested in socially patterned tasks than in activities undertaken for whites. Although it is recognized that certain tasks can be completed within a specific period of time (a hide can be cleaned in two days, a toboggan can be finished in three days, twenty trees can be cut in one day), meeting a time limit is not a strong incentive and rarely are such standards met in practice. Few men trap as much of an area as they are capable of covering. Success in hunting and trapping, although requiring some knowledge of animal habits and considerable skill in tracking, is primarily founded on perseverance. This fact is appreciated by the Indians, but success is also ascribed to luck. Some men are very "lucky for skins" or game, others are not. Persistence and determination are also undermined by the attitude that one should not be too anxious for fur. "If you wish something too much, that game don't want to get into your trap." Procrastination is habitual. Despite the insistence of Louis Maza and others that they had to leave the bridge to start moose hunting before the bulls began to run, no serious hunting was done before the bulling season was well advanced. The advisability and need of setting a fish net was once discussed for several days, but the net never got set and dogs continued to be fed on fast disappearing dog feed.

Ideally hard work persistence, and "rustling" are highly evaluated. Advice to a young man stresses the importance of early rising and of always doing something. One morning Old Man remarked: "Nitla sleeping yet. Maybe that's the reason he's got nothing . . . used to be Harry [Old Man's son-in-law] like that. Used to talk about his kid hungry. He tell me this time: 'You're right. What I'm gonna do? My kid hungry. How I'm gonna feed?' I tell him: 'You gotta rustle for yourself'." Yet neither Old Man nor Harry Lang gave any evidence of "rustling" during the period that observation was possible. The period of hard work and great drive was always being planned and was constantly imminent but never materialized.

Except when traveling, there is little tendency to begin necessary duties early in the day. Women generally get up before men and start the fire, although ideally a man should do this in very cold weather. If men get up first, they may start a fire and then hang around doing nothing until a woman wakes up and prepares breakfast. Women, usually having assistance from daughters, seldom spend more than a few hours a day doing housework. In Lower Post, where duties are even fewer, much time is spent by the family visiting or sitting around the various trading stores, meeting friends, and engaging in desultory conversation. Periods of strenuous work by men—housebuilding, hunting, and trapping—are always succeeded by several days devoted to relaxation. On the whole, the tenor of life appears unhurried, relaxed, and even-flowing.

CONCLUSION

The technical culture just described presents a picture of Kaska Indians' adaptation to the demands of their inner and outer environments. The exploitation of the game and fur resources of the Cassiar region may be regarded as the hub of this adaptive process. Game is directly consumed and so forms an important item in the native economy. Fur is briefly processed and exchanged for capital and consumer goods which the society requires to supplement environmental resources and domestic technology. This is a bald summary of the essential sequences constituting the adaptive routines. We now propose to evaluate the data presented in the preceding sections. The question we want to answer is: how successfully do the Kaska solve their adaptive problems?

The evidence leaves no doubt of the genius which Kaska society possesses for adapting to the exigencies of its northern environment. One of the most serious problems, securing protection against cold, has been so well beaten that almost never do we hear of serious frostbite. With the aid of proven devices, like the snowshoe and toboggan, travel remains unimpaired by the loose powdery snow. Winter travel and the efficient transportation of grub to the trap line are, of course, indispensable to the modern trapping economy. Obvious conveniences like the gun, steel traps, outboard motor, stove, and sleeping bag scarcely need having their adaptive utility stressed. In short, the Kaska are apparently well equipped technically and materially for carrying out behaviors that insure life and comfort. Yet when we examine the demographic data and view the amount of illness in the society we encounter situations in which adaptation is unsuccessful.

An inescapable conclusion is that Kaska society stands in a precariously balanced condition so far as its comfort and survival are concerned. The population was reduced by at least one-third within the last hundred years. During the period of study, the death rate probably equalled the birth rate, although effective means of birth control are not employed. The Kaska are not a healthy people. All of these facts are indicative of the threat faced by the society in solving the problems of survival. The society itself, however, cannot be held entirely accountable for failure to meet this threat. In the last hundred years the people have encountered many novel problems for which they were not prepared with traditional solutions. Illness, for example, probably increased after the Dease River and Klondike gold rushes. In confronting illness at the close of the nineteenth century, the people lacked even shamanism with which to fortify themselves psychologically against the menace of disease.[19] It would seem that as far as the high death rate and extensive morbidity are concerned, Kaska society is suffering the effects of culture contact. White diseases have taken their toll of the native population not only because the people were less resistant to disease (although their resistance leaves something to be desired), but also because once these illnesses were introduced, the Indians did not receive the same medical protection which reduces mortality in the white society.[20]

So far we have exonerated the society from failing to preserve the health and life of its members by pointing out that the strain of adaptation became considerably itensified following white contact. We will now consider some aspects of Indian motivation and behavior which, although ostensibly oriented toward survival, are actually contributing to discomfort and illness. The first of these is nutrition. At least during the winter, a majority of the society appears to suffer from inadequate caloric intake plus vitamin and mineral deficiencies. The consequences are seen in reduced energy and heightened susceptibility in disease. Malnutrition extends to children, in whom it may be seriously impairing physical and psychological development. The responsibility for undernourishment cannot be blamed upon a lack of education, since professional advice in food consumption, valuable as it may be, is after all limited to only a fraction of the world; nor can it be ascribed solely to acculturation. The causes for malnutrition appear to lie in the attitudes of the Kaska themselves as well as in conditions of acculturation. To dispose of the second point first, it seems likely that foreign penetration of the area within the last ten years (including the building of the Highway, airports, and the noise of aircraft) have resulted in a severe dislocation of game.[21] Such disturbances probably also followed influxes of gold seekers into the country and must be regarded as temporary. Currently, however, they appear responsible for the dearth of meat

[19] Honigmann, *Witch Fear in Post-Contact Kaska Society* (1947), 236.

[20] Marchand, *Tribal Epidemics in the Yukon* (1943), 1020. Honigmann, *Ethnography and Acculturation of the Fort Nelson Slave* (1946), 28.

[21] Williams points out that "the noise of road building, including roar of machinery and blasting, has obviously driven wild life back from the Highway. With the quieter conditions of post-construction days, wild animals will doubtless return. . . ." Williams, *Geological Investigations Along the Alaska Highway from Fort Nelson, British Columbia, to Watson Lake, Yukon* (1944), 3.

(which appears to be particularly severe in the Upper Liard region, which lies east of the Highway and along the air route), and for the consequent reduction of proteins and fat in the native diet.

Malnutrition, however, is also a consequence of the fact that people going into the bush in the fall are not in possession of sufficient purchased food for winter consumption. Grub often becomes exhausted before it can be replenished and for weeks adults and children are then forced to live on a diet of bannock or fatless bread, beans, fatless rabbits, and a little fruit. To understand the reason for such shortages requires an examination of the attitudes and behaviors with which the Kaska Indians approach the business of living. The gist of these factors reveals that the people are not able to insure the realization of their own ideal of an adequate standard of living. Little effort is made, for example, to secure more meat in the fall than is immediately consumed; hence there is no surplus which can be preserved for winter consumption. Such preservation would make grub stretch further and is, in fact, an ideal of the people. This observation is not made without being aware that resources of game have been disturbed by technological developments in the Cassiar. Admittedly that disturbance makes hunting more difficult and less rewarding. The fact is, however, that men tend not to hunt until a supply of meat is exhausted. Ideas of futurity, therefore, have little influence in determining hunting behavior. Trapping is similarly relatively little motivated by ideas of futurity. The long delays likely to ensue between visits to the trap line (delays which are ideally condemned by the people themselves), and the haphazard methods of trapping all result in an accumulation of fur too small to permit the supply of an adequate winter diet the following year. Furthermore, there is no realistic evaluation of the amount of food that will be required for winter consumption. Partly because of straitened circumstances and also for psychological reasons, which will be discussed in connection with the ethos of the society, people underestimate their needs and commonly forget important items of grub. Such neglect may lead to borrowing in the same or neighboring settlement, with the result that other families are quickly reduced to shortage.

As we have pointed out, few men buy their winter outfits for cash. The proceeds of the winter and spring fur sales quickly disappear to make up deficiencies occurring in the course of the winter bush life, to pay debts contracted the previous fall, and to live during the summer in Lower Post. People, therefore, live from hand-to-mouth, and if sickness enters the circle and disrupts winter trapping, severe disorganization must follow. Winter illness means the debt remains unpaid, additional credit is withheld or drastically reduced, and malnutrition with its evil consequences becomes intensified. A potential means of supplementing the winter's work by contracting labor to white men is neglected even by those men who do poorly in trapping and have most need for additional sources of income. The reasons for this reluctance to engage in wage work may be defined structurally (i.e., with reference to alternative or conflicting economic patterns) and psychologically. A structural explanation for the lack of interest in working for white men is to be found in the fact that another way of making a living, trapping, is readily available to the Indian. He can usually obtain a nominal amount of credit or otherwise secure (as, for example, by becoming an older man's helper) the minimal capital goods necessary for such independent production. Psychologically, as will be demonstrated in connection with Kaska ethos, the Indian prefers to be his own boss and for this reason trapping is more congenial to him than wage work. Furthermore the greater returns from trapping overshadow returns from contract labor.[22]

In large part, as we have indicated, the Indians have failed to solve novel or intensified problems which are concommitants of the penetration of the Kaska area by foreign agents. Partially, however, the failure to secure efficient adaptation is also an inevitable product of the Indian's system of motivation. No attempt can be made to assign any guilt for the conditions we have just described. The Kaska are no more to blame for their failure to provide themselves with adequate nutrition than the Canadian and American governments can be held responsible for disturbing the balance of game in the area. We have simply tried to define the efficiency of the Indian's system of maintaining health, life, and physical comfort in relation first, to the demands of the human organism and, second, to the resources of the external environment. We have done this with the assurance that the basic values of survival and comfort were shared by the Kaska themselves. Certain other implicit judg-ments, such as the need of self-exertion and planning in the pursuit of getting a living, are more immediately derived from the anthropologist's own society but are also ideally ac-cepted by the Indians.

To sum up the conclusions drawn from the technical culture, we can say first, that the resources of the society—specifically, technological knowledge—are adequate for the task of adaptation to the traditional problems presented by the environment. Second, where problems have been introduced by culture contact, like the displacement of game and ill-ness, the Indian possesses few aids for meeting their threats. Finally, the Indian has not learned to fit himself into the modern trapping economy and as a result suffers from malnu-trition, which increases his susceptibility to disease.

[22] If we contrast Kaska society with our own, we find in the latter certain conditions supporting the system of wage labor which are completely unknown to the Indians. American society, for example, has made contract labor well nigh indispensable to survival. Without wages few people in our society possess the skills required to make a living. The loss of status resulting from joblessness is another factor maintaining the wage system in America. Unemployment, no matter how unavoidable it may be, results in placing the worker in an inferior social role with consequent loss of prestige. Finally, our society does not freely or easily provide opportunities for set-ting up independent production.

SOCIAL CULTURE

THE second major division of Kaska culture to be described, is derived from those ideas and activities which reflect the individual's adjustment to other individuals. In many situations such adjustment is essential for the execution of adaptive behaviors but it also represents the solution of additional problems arising out of interpersonal relations. Social culture has been divided into three subdivisions: interpersonal organization, ranging from the family to local groups; interpersonal relations in the larger society, including property, governmental, legal, sexual, and other relations between individuals; and those interpersonal relations entering into the lifecycle.

ORGANIZATION

FAMILY

The nuclear family in Kaska society consists of a married couple and their true or adopted children. Such a group is sometimes augmented by the presence of additional relatives, as for example, an aged or widowed grandparent, an orphaned grandchild, or the orphaned children of a mother's sister or father's brother. A family may also contain temporarily the unmarried siblings of either spouse. The Kaska family corresponds closely to the settlement described above in which the group occupies a single residence. If more than one family live in a settlement, they usually occupy separate dwellings.

Authority in the family is ideally invested in the husband, although actually the wife is consulted in all important considerations and may also originate action by influencing her husband's decisions. The authority of the husband is maintained even if the family happens to contain a grandparent. Although under conditions of matrilocal residence, a father may offer advice to his son-in-law, such advice is not given in an authoritative fashion and, once the marriage is established, does not dispute the authority of the husband. The importance of the father is also reflected in the fact that, despite the system of matrilineal moieties, family names follow the patrilineal line.

Functionally the family is of great importance, constituting the primary economic unit of the society. It is able to provide its own capital goods and to exploit the environment in order to secure necessary consumer goods. Cooperation tends to be restricted to the family, but even here it cannot be demanded except from a young, unmarried son or daughter. A young married couple will generally trap together, but once children are born, the man will look to others for trapline companionship and assistance. Helpers secured in this way enter what may be described as a *protégé* relationship. That is, the partner is often a related or unrelated youth who is taught the art of trapping, freely loaned traps, and extended the privilege of using the trapping territory. Such a partnership is founded primarily on congeniality and is readily dissolved. Sometimes a family takes along a mature girl or young widow. The girl helps the wife in household duties, but may also trap, using resources which are loaned her by the family with whom she resides. "They live on you. They get no money and live on you, helping till they get husband."

124

Although the number of exceptions seems to be increasing, the recognized form of residence in all but secondary marriages is matrilocal.[1] Secondary marriages, where the man is already established on his own trap line, follow independent or patrilocal residence. One of the primary factors that seems to be undermining the custom of matrilocal residence is the inheritance of trap lines. In one instance this economic factor led a man to insist on both matrilocal residence for his daughter and patrilocal residence for his son. River Joe first expressed resentment when his daughter married outside of the Kaska area and took up residence in her husband's community several hundred miles away. "Where he get girl, stay there," Joe stated and pointed out that his daughter had access to a good trap line which could adequately support the couple. A few months later his son, Ted, became interested in a part Tahltan girl from the upper Dease River. Now the father affirmed that when his son married, he should remain on the family trap line. Where a young unmarried man holds ownership in a productive family trap line, or where he is anxious to acquire his own (as was Louis Maza), matrilocal residence is temporary, merely fulfilling the conditions of bride service and lasting only a year or two. When an Indian girl marries a white man independent residence is always followed.

Interesting information was obtained regarding a man's adjustment to the country in which he must operate after marriage. "First time pretty hard for me," Hans Donnelly reported. "I don't want to hunt nothing. I don't want to get lost. Now all right." From this instance it would appear that a man can learn the terrain and routes of a new area in about two years. There is no evidence that matrilocal residence poses any difficult problems of social adjustment for the man. He assumes the authority in his own family, lives in his own dwelling and, except for offering meat and other assistance to his father-in-law, pursues his own economic interests.

Adoption of young children is often practiced to increase the size of the nuclear family. The principal motives are the desire to insure future economic assistance and to provide care and subsistence for an orphan or half orphan whose surviving parent cannot effectively do so. While there are no fixed rules defining adoption, in general the relationship is assumed to be permanent and any measures taken by a surviving parent to abrogate it are regarded with resentment. Nevertheless adoption is often temporary and children often reclaimed by parents or by parents' siblings. Adopted children ideally achieve the status of true children. Manifestly, however, they may be overworked and sometimes are even more deprived of emotional satisfaction than true children. There is reluctance to adopt children who, it is feared, are not normal or healthy.

The private life of the Kaska family is not easy to observe. This is due to the social isolation maintained by the family, as well as to the slight interaction that is manifested publicly between spouses. While several newly married couples revealed signs of close emotional attachment, it is not usual for older ones to demonstrate any considerable amount of affection except possibly when intoxicated. Terms of endearment also seem to be lacking in the conversation of husband and wife, although a number of men (especially when drunk) were observed to address their wives as "mama." The general pattern of relations between marriage

[1] Generalization based primarily on Upper Liard River data.

partners may be summarily described as one in which the husband is rather consistently dominant or assertive and the wife relatively passive.

The principal material substantiating this pattern comes in the expectations of one spouse from the other and their fulfillment. Ideally the husband expects from his wife not only the obvious conveniences of living, such as a well kept house, prepared meals, clean clothes, and thrift, but usually also economic assistance, sexual faithfulness, loyalty, and personal comforts. These demands are all provided by most women. Thus a wife provides economic assistance through rabbit trapping, fur trapping, and even hunting. She supplies the raw materials for making moccasins and mittens, snowshoes, and line. While adultery occurs, it is not common and never flagrant. A wife is also careful not to gossip about her husband, nor does she criticize him before strangers. She offers him many small physical comforts, bringing tobacco, rolling cigarettes, putting on the husband's shoes, fetching his tools, and caring for him in illness. In addition a woman is more careful of her personal appearance when she expects her husband to return from a trip. A wife will also not absent herself from camp for long periods while the man is at home.

A woman, on the other hand, expects her husband to provide the principal food supply for herself and children; she demands sexual faithfulness and loyalty, but she is not so ready to demand smaller emotional comforts comparable to those which she herself is called upon to make in the marital relationship. She does, however, like her man to remain with her in camp when he is not otherwise occupied. Men are conscious of their economic obligations but are somewhat less reliable in fulfilling the other expectations. They certainly do not fulfill these to the extent that they are met by women. In the event of a wife's illness, however, most men demonstrate concern and solicitation.

Between spouses who have been living together for a long time, there is evidence of considerable and deep emotional attachment. Old man confessed that when his second wife died he became extremely depressed, took to drinking heavily, and even attempted suicide. River Joe, a very recent widower, likewise spoke of his depression and worry. In a man or woman such emotional dependence is often rationalized as economic dependence, this motive being given as one of the main reasons for a widower to seek remarriage. On the other hand a number of widows were known during the period of field work who showed no desire to remarry. This indicates that, despite his greater assertiveness, the man is, in many respects, emotionally more dependent on his wife than she is on him.[2]

One of the warmest, if not the warmest, interpersonal relationship in Kaska society is that existing between siblings, particularly between sisters and between siblings of opposite sex. It is significant that this quality of sibling relations, as expressed by the use of kinship terms, tends to be projected into other social relationships characterized by strong affection and friendship. Thus lovers sometimes exchange brother and sister terms of address, while two men, whose friendship is particularly warm, may call each other "brother."

Four terms are used to distinguish between siblings and are extended to parallel cousins. While the pattern of warm sibling relations is also commonly extended to such cousins, especially where maternal cousins are thrown into association under conditions of matrilocal residence, it is in the nuclear family that age is most important in determining sibling

[2] See the discussion relating to the status of adult women below pp. 197–198; 291.

behavior. Sometimes age status is counteracted by the dominance of a younger sibling, but in general the older boy or girl is from childhood permitted a measure of authority and responsibility over younger siblings. Early in life children are made aware that they must protect and care for younger or weaker siblings, and these attitudes also tend to persist through life. Thus a widow, who has lost her parents, is assured of care by married brothers or sisters. Siblings are taught not to fight or tease each other, and boys are warned not to ridicule their sisters for fear that their mouths may become twisted. The ties between siblings do not relax with marriage and the custom of matrilocal residence often serves to keep sisters together. The most demonstrative greetings are exhibited between sisters who have been separated, while within a matrilocal settlement, sisters exhibit the most gracious and spontaneous cooperation. Among men the sibling relationship is less demonstrative and more apt to be marked by friction. Between like sexed siblings there are no taboos on sexual conversation. Brothers and sisters will shy away from this subject and may also embarrassedly avoid any situation in which a sibling of opposite sex is in sexual interaction.

KINSHIP

Individuals related by blood or affinal ties are designated by terms of kinship. While kinship organization defines certain permitted and restricted forms of behavior (including marriage) between relatives in general, as elsewhere in the Northern Athapaskan area it is not important for regulating interpersonal relations far beyond the nuclear family. The emotional ties of kinship depend primarily upon frequency of interaction for their reinforcement. Nevertheless, through marriage the kinship system does relate families within the society and to some extent the frequency and intensity of social interaction tends to be partially determined by such relationships.

The elementary kinship system of the Kaska is relatively simple and, with minor variations of dialect, applies to all the tribes in the area. Some terms are rapidly falling into disuse. Thus frequently the grandchild term is unknown, the native mother and father terms are ignored in favor of "papa" and "mama," and cross-cousin terminology is confused.

A list of the kinship terms, ignoring tonal modalities, is presented below. The parentheses indicate that the enclosed sound is subject to elision. The term "my" is to be read before each English equivalent.

(e)stsi·'e	MF, FF, FSisS (m.s.), WF (m.s.), HF (w.s.)
(e)stsu'	MM, FM, FSis, FSisD (m.s.), WM (m.s.), HM (w.s.)
eta'	F
ena'	M, MSis[3]
(e)stšu'e	S, BS[4]
(e)stu'e	D, BD, SisD
(gu)ti·'e	eB, elder male parallel cousin, WSisH (older than ego)
(e)tšit'le	yB, younger male parallel cousin, WSisH (younger than ego)
(e)ta'te	eSis, elder female parallel cousin, HBW (older than ego)

[3] so'a is an alternative term for MSis

[4] esi'ye is sometimes used for parallel cousin's son, the term signifying "stepson."

(e)ta'tze	ySis, younger female parallel cousin, HBW (younger than ego)
(a)sla'	MBS, FSisS (w.s.), HB (w.s.), WB (m.s.), SisH (m.s.), WSis (m.s.)
ekle'	MBD,[5] FSisD (w.s.), HSis (w.s.), SisH (w.s.), BW (w.s.)
(e)sta'	FB
seze'	MB,[6] SisS
(e)stša'	SS, DS, SD, DD, SW
se'lige	H
(e)si·'on	W
(e)spa'	WSis (m.s.), BW (m.s.)
senaze'	DH

It will be noted that the system makes no provision for the great grandparent genera-tion. Individuals do not know their genealogies beyond two generations, and when nec-essary, more distant relatives are referred to by the grandparent terms.

The kinship system of the Kaska corresponds to the Crow type. There are four sibling terms which are extended to parallel cousins. Father, mother, son, and daughter are char-acterized by separate terms. Only two terms are in general use for the parents' siblings; these distinguish the father's brother and the mother's brother. The father's sister is called "grandmother" and the mother's sister is generally referred to as "mother." All siblings' children, except the sister's son, are called "children." The sister's son, however, is called reciprocally by the maternal uncle term. Provision is made for two grandparent terms and one grandchild term. Overriding of generations within blood relatives occurs only when a man is referring to his father's sister's son, father's sister's daughter, or when either sex is referring to the father's sister; all these relatives, as well as parents-in-law, are classified as grandparents.

The relationships between individuals constituting the nuclear family have already been discussed. Here behavior between the most important residual relatives remains to be examined. A grandparent's attitude toward the young grandchild is generally indulgent and lenient. If the individuals involved in this relationship are in frequent contact, a warm bond may develop between them. A grandfather may tease his grandchildren, but neither he nor the grandmother exercises discipline unless they are acting as foster parents to the child. A grandfather's advice to his grandchild is not always heeded and, while a grandparent is entitled to respect, he cannot expect his word to be accepted as inspired wisdom or law.

The relationship of parent's sibling to sibling's child varies according to the parent's sibling involved. The strongest ties are between the mother's sisters and their children. Because of the custom of matrilocal residence, these relatives are usually in frequent inter-action. In the presence of her own or her sister's children, a woman generally refers to her married sister as "mother," rather than by the Christian name or sibling term. This prob-ably helps to condition the warm relationship of the mother's sisters and sister's children. Children may also call their maternal aunt by the mother term, but an aunt who is too

---

[5] A man may also call his MBD (e)spa'. The ekle' and (e)spa' terms are frequently used interchangeably, especially for siblings' spouses.

[6] ete'za is an alternative term for MB.

young to be married is addressed with her given name. Sisters share in the care of one another's young children for short periods. Following a woman's death, the surviving children are often brought up by a surviving sister, the rationalization being that the aunt is
"the same like mother." A mother's sister will rarely exercise discipline to a particularly
annoying sibling's child, and then only if the mother is not present. On the other hand, if
the aunt is young, she is often unmercifully teased by a five or six year old youngster.

The relationship of the father's brothers to children is ideally close, the children being
referred to as equivalent to true children and the paternal uncle the "same like father,"
although he is not called father. A man's brother is sometimes given the care of his children,
following the death of the true parents. The relationship warrants respect on the younger
person's part and sexual matters are never brought up in the presence of the paternal uncle.

A woman's brother refers to his sister's daughter as his own child, but the relationship
between these relatives weakens when the man leaves the parents' camp following marriage. A reciprocal term is employed between a boy and his mother's brother. It was said
to be all right to "talk fun," i.e., refer to salacious matters, with the mother's brother. The
relationship of a child to its father's sister could not be observed.

The pattern of cross-cousin terminology may be summarized as follows:

	(m.s.)	(w.s.)
FSisS	(e)stsi'e	(a)sla'
FSisD	(e)stsu'	ekle'
MBS	(a)sla'	(a)sla'
MBD	ekle' or (e)spa'	ekle'

Marriage between father's sister's daughter and mother's brother's son is prohibited.
On the other hand, father's sister's son and mother's brother's daughter "can talk to each
other" (i.e., they are permitted sexual teasing) and are preferential marriage mates.

One of the most important social relationships obtains between father-in-law and son-in-
law. With an industrious son-in-law, a man can retire from active hunting and restrict himself to trapping some nearby stretch of line, while the younger man goes to a more remote
part of the trap line and keeps the family supplied with meat. The son-in-law is also expected to offer his cooperation for housebuilding and other tasks in which the older man
may require assistance. The ideal expectations patterning a son-in-law's behavior are often
not fulfilled. Old Man had two sons-in-law living in his settlement and complained that
both did not hunt often nor far enough and that they were not industrious trappers. In
most observed cases, relations of the son-in-law to his father-in-law were characterized by
respect and reserve coupled with a little good-natured kidding. There was no evidence of
submission on the part of the younger man. Frances Lake men tend to show extreme shyness
of the father-in-law. "They keep it like a hundred years ago," Old Man observed. Referring
to his own youth, he illustrated the changing norms that are slowly crystallizing in this
relationship when he said: "I used to talk fun with father-in-law. He shy but I laugh."

Extreme reserve tends to characterize the relationship between a man and his mother-in-
law, but there is no restriction on these relatives remaining in one another's presence or on
their eating and drinking together. When observed between Harry Lang and Mrs. Man,
the mother-in-law avoidance seemed sustained more by the old woman's shyness and em-

barrassment than by the son-in-law's avoidance behavior. Even when intoxicated, Mrs. Man never relaxed in her reserve.

Between sisters' husbands, who call each other "brother," there is evidence of good friendship and some cooperation. Such brothers-in-law often hunt together and frequently visit each others camps. They also constitute trapping partnerships. Talk of a sexual nature is not supposed to occur in the brother-in-law's presence, because "he's married to my sister." Between a man and his wife's sister there is generally good natured interaction; a man may tease this woman, and she may offer to help him in some task requiring assistance, particularly when his wife is absent. Women avoid unnecessary intimacy with this relative. Thus Louisa Man returned a gun while only the ethnographer (classificatorially her sister's husband) and her brother-in-law, Hans Donnelly, were in the cabin. She would not enter but handed in the gun through the open door. During intoxication direct sexual approaches were several times attempted by Old Man's sons-in-law toward their unmarried sister-in-law, Louisa. The latter firmly resisted their attention.

In general, the Kaska feel little need to phrase interpersonal relationships with non-relatives in kinship terms. The reasons are apparent. Kinship in itself is of slight importance in defining relations beyond the nuclear family, and the intensity of wider social relations is governed by frequency of interaction. It is consistent, therefore, that only the most intense and persistent relations with nonrelatives are marked by use of kinship terms. Non-relatives are most frequently identified as grandfather, brother, sister, and by the sibling-in-law terms; the son, daughter, and parent terms are avoided in such situations.

Several instances of artificial kin relationships were observed. If two persons of considerable age difference are thrown into association, the younger person may refer to the older by the grandfather term. The behavior toward this conventional grandparent may vary from respect to teasing. The older person himself is generally familiar and indulgent toward the artificial grandchild, whom he addresses by the given name.

In 1945 Old Man was host to his daughter's husband's mother, Lady Suza, who was also his current wife's father's sister's son's wife. Old Man took to calling her "sister." All his daughters called her "grandmother."

When the ethnographer and his family became guests of Old Man they were also vocatively classified within the kinship system. The ethnographer's wife was called "older sister" by Old Man's daughters. This correlated with the expectation of matrilocal residence, in which a daughter brings her husband to her parents' settlement to live. The ethnographer logically became a son-in-law. The ethnographer's children were not called by kinship terms except once when Louisa Man addressed David (4) as "younger brother." The expected term here would have been seze' ("my sister's son").

Young men who are not related but are interacting in a drinking party often address one another as "brother-in-law." As pointed out above, sibling terms may be used between sweethearts. When kinship terms are extended to non-relatives, they are almost always employed vocatively rather than referentially. A stepmother is referred to and addressed as "mother" and "mama."

Among men, between whom there is no relationship, the given name is generally used as a term of address and either the given name or the full name as a term of reference. A man refers to an unrelated married woman by the first name of the husband with the prefix "missus." Between two women, the given name is generally employed.

LARGER SOCIAL GROUPS

Social organization beyond kinship is of slight functional significance in Kaska society and, even more than the kinship system, is largely of categorical importance. The organization of the Kaska nation into tribes occupying loosely defined geographical districts has already been discussed.[7] There are four tribes known as the Frances Lake, Upper Liard River, Dease River, and Nelson Indians. The degree of emotional identification is relatively slight and would seem to be highest among the Upper Liard Indians. Here, however, relations between intertribal neighbors are, as we shall see, riddled by considerable suppressed antagonism. Although there is a tendency to restrict marriage within tribal units, many marriages have taken place between these units with a consequent diffusion of tribal membership and identification.

No single pattern for determining membership in a specific district or tribe seems to obtain. Old Man reported that a man belongs to the country of his father. He called himself a Liard River Indian, although his father was a Pelly Indian and his mother belonged to the Liard River tribe. In general a person seems to belong to the tribal district or tribe in which he was born and raised, regardless of the tribe from which his parents originally came. This is not final, however. A man who changes his residence with marriage, generally becomes identified with the country in which he takes up residence and begins to trap. For a time, he continues to be referred to as belonging to the district from which he originally came. As his roots grow deeper in the adopted district, he begins to be identified with that tribe. Because of the frequent shifting of residence that occurred up to about thirty years ago, and the frequency of tribal intermarriage which still continues, the districts present a far from perfect correlation with tribal designation. For example, the bulk of families in the Frances Lake district are reported to have originally lived in the Upper Liard River region. Of the four family heads known as Upper Liard River Indians, only one was born in that region and his youth was spent in many parts of the total Kaska area.

Most of the Kaska Indians are divided into two nonlocalized, matrilineal "sides" or moieties, the members of each of which feel vaguely related.[8] Although these sides are identified by the names of two animals, the Crow and Wolf respectively, there is little thought that a person has actually descended from a wolf or crow. Since neither of these two animals is customarily eaten, it is meaningless to talk of totemic food taboos. Both animals are readily killed, however, and the wolf is trapped for its fur as well as for the bounty paid on the pelt. The importance of the moiety is slight. Formal organization is lacking, there being no executives and no mechanisms to bring about the unified functioning of the group as a whole. The principal functions of the moiety lie in the regulation of marri-

---

[7] See above, pp. 32–35.

[8] Writing in 1928, Allard gives the impression of a number of unilateral kin groups. "The tribe," he says, referring to the Kaska," is divided into sibs, such as Wolf (tsi yo nih), Crow (niska), Bear (sis), etc." No evidence of more than two exogamous groups could be adduced. By the Bear "sib," Allard is probably referring to the Bear Lake Indians, who trapped up along the Muddy River and traded into McDame Creek and Lower Post. Allard, *Notes on the Kaska and Upper Liard Indians* (1928), 25.

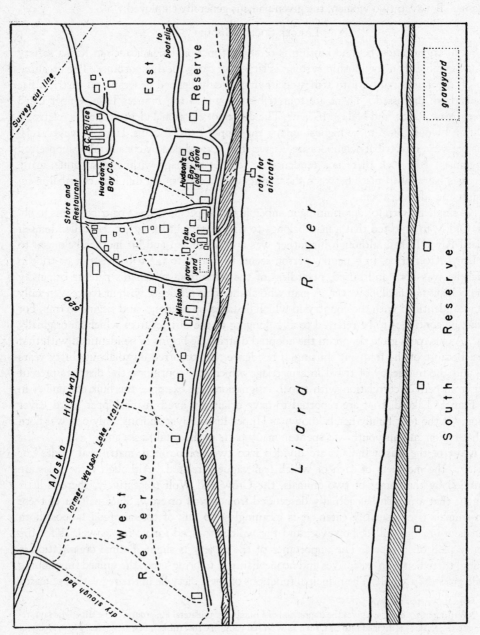

FIG. 7. Plan of Lower Post, showing Indian Reserves.

age through the rule of exogamy and the organization of potlatches. The former function constitutes the manifest explanation for adhering to these divisions. Thus River Joe explained that the moieties, going far back in time, serve to prevent anyone from getting "mixed up" and marrying a too closely related person. Any ideas of the superiority of one side over the other could not be adduced.

Certain individuals identified with the Kaska Indians lack affiliation with any side. These are either Slave Indians, who have married into the Kaska nation, or else members of the Nelson tribe. The latter people never followed the moiety pattern of their neighbors. Such individuals generally receive a conventional moiety identification when they marry a member of either exogamous group. No gesture is made toward formalizing such allegiance, the person being verbally identified with the appropriate side or being told to eat with that side at a potlatch. A woman whose moiety membership has been determined by convention transmits this affiliation to her children. There is no question, however, but that such conventional affiliations are less binding than more clearly established moiety membership. Children of a woman whose affiliation was established by convention are often permitted to marry endogamously and even the grandchildren of such a woman are recognized as having extremely weak ties with other members of their side. Sometimes an effort is made to regularize the apparent endogamy of such marriages by having one of the spouses alter her moiety membership. Thus Old Man married the Cree-Kaska daughter of a Cree woman from Fort Nelson. The first Mrs. Man was commonly regarded as a Crow. After she married Old Man, a Crow, however, she was designated as a Wolf. Some people were encountered who had "forgotten" their side and thereafter married girls whom, they later discovered, belonged to their moiety. Louis Maza married a Wolf woman although he himself had been born of a Wolf mother. He later changed his membership to the Crow side. It must not be supposed that such forgetting is common. Louis blamed the priests for having "mixed up" the people regarding their moiety affiliations.

All of the Kaska Indians and Sekani who trade into Lower Post (but excluding the Frances Lake people who generally frequent their own trading post), local white traders, the missionaries, white trappers, and government functionaries may be recognized as members of the community—a "maximal group of persons who normally reside together in face-to-face association."[9] A number of Tahltan Indians from the area southeast and south of Lower Post also frequently visit the settlement and these may be recognized as temporary members of the community. The one or two Tahltan families who maintain permanent residences in Lower Post are, of course, full fledged members. Social interaction between these people is largely restricted to summer and is maintained through visiting; attendance at dances, church, and school; friendship; marriage; gambling and loitering. The total community, as has already been described, gathers in the spring and is dissolved in late summer, when most of its members disperse to their trapping districts and winter settlements. Community interaction during the Christmas and other winter visits to the post is primarily supported through visiting and encounters in the restaurant and bunkhouses.

The Indian section of the community (hereafter referred to as the Indian community) tends to divide itself into three sections, roughly corresponding to the tribal groups trading

[9] Murdock, et al., Outline of Cultural Materials (1945), 29.

in to Lower Post. Each of these groups maintains its residence on one of the three Indian reserves adjoining Lower Post (Fig. 7). On the south bank of the Liard River are the camps of most of the Dease River, Nelson River, and Sekani people; on the north bank, east of the trading stores are other Nelson Indians and two Tahltan families, while west of the trading center and church, the land is reserved for Liard Indians. Such local divisions is traditional but not compulsory. Members of all these tribes occasionally shift their camps to reserves predominantly occupied by tribal neighbors. The growing custom of erecting permanent summer houses, however, will curtail this practice. Although discouraged from doing so by the policeman and Indian Agent, Indians occasionally camp off the reserves in proximity to the camps or houses of white trappers.

The community as a whole is split into two ethnic divisions, Indian and white. Visiting, intermarriage, and social functions tend to be somewhat restricted between these subdivisions but there are many exceptions to this statement. Dances and gambling games organized by Indians are often participated in by white trappers. Where marriage between an Indian woman and a white man occurs, each normally maintains most intensive social interaction with his own ethnic group. Separate winter accommodations, or bunkhouses, for Indians and whites are maintained by the two largest trading companies; one independent trader, however, does not at all attempt such segregation.

The Indians do not take an interest in improving conditions in the community or on their reserves. Such improvement was once observed in 1944 when a government bulldozer was employed by some white men to level off their properties in Lower Post. Inspired by this scene, River Joe engaged the operator for the task of constructing an automobile road to the end of the Upper Liard River Indian reserve. He proposed to pay for the work out of contributions secured from other Indians but ended by paying the major share of the costs himself. Since the road now opened the reserve to visits by the policeman's car, he and other Indians soon regretted his enthusiasm.

SOCIAL STRATIFICATION

Kaska society is both casteless and classless. While superficial differences of social behavior obtain between families—for example, in the type of houses built, the number of dwellings owned, or the annual income received—any operational significance of such differences is completely absent. If we regard classes as abstractions based on habits of groups in a society,[10] or if we regard class differences as based on associated interest differences,[11] we must conclude that the Kaska cannot be divided along class lines.

The members of the community emphasize few status differences apart from those associated with age and sex. Political status is ascribed from outside the Indian society and will be discussed below. Ethnic stratification is unemphasized. Younger *métis* are sometimes referred to for a few idiosyncratic traits of behavior, but are not distinguished from the rest of the society in terms of life goals or interests and are not subjected to any differential forms of behavior originating from other members of the society.

[10] Dollard, John, Seminar on Social Structure and Individual Orientation. Yale University, 1943.
[11] Kardiner, *The Psychological Frontiers of Society* (1945), 341-342.

SPECIALIZATION

The unimportance of formal social organization in Kaska society is correlated with a limited development of occupational specialization. Thus specialists are of little importance, many men's and women's tasks are freely interchangeable, while age governs occupation

TABLE 11. SEXUAL DIVISION OF LABOR IN REPRESENTATIVE OCCUPATIONS

Occupation	Normally Done By Men	Normally Done by Women	Frequently Done by Opposite Sex	Normally Done by Either Sex
Collecting	O	X	O	O
Getting water	O	X	X	O
Cutting trees	X	O	O	O
Hauling uncut wood	X	O	X	O
Hewing	X	O	O	O
Trapping				X
Hunting Large Game	X	O	O	O
Hunting Small Game	X	O	X	O
Fowling	X	O	X	O
Fishing	X	O	X	O
Care of dogs	O	X	X	O
Gardening	X	O	X?	O
Woodworking	X	O	O	O
Cordage making	O	X	O	O
Skin tanning	O	X	O	O
Commercial skin stretching				X
Cutting firewood				X
Making fire				X
Tool making	X	O	O	O
House building	X	O	O	O
House cleaning	O	X	O	O
Erecting tent	O	X	X	O
Cooking	O	X	X	O
Making brew	X	O	X	O
Making clothes	O	X	O	O
Washing clothes	O	X	O	O
Marketing furs	X	O	X	O
Buying food	X	O	X	O
Human packing				X
Packing dogs	O	X	X	O
Making snowshoes	X	O	O	O
Filling snowshoes	O	X	O	O
Managing toboggan or sled				X
Managing boat	X	O	X	O
Medical care				X
Care of children	O	X	O	O
Preparation of corpse				X
Gravedigging	X	O	O	O

only insofar as it affects strength or capacity. Regional specialization is completely lacking.

In the absence of any professional occupations—there being no people who wholly devote themselves to such activities as carpentering, tanning, or hunting—only a limited amount of individual specialization may be noted. Some men are regarded as excelling in the manufacture of boats, snowshoes, or in carpentering while certain women are well known for their skill in sewing and cooking. Such professionals are occasionally approached for assistance in carrying out a task like boat building and are paid for their work. In general, however, such services are rarely requested.

A summary of the division of labor is presented in Table 11. It must be pointed out that this tabulation is based on manifest behavior which, in some cases, differs from the ideals of the society. For example, Louis Maza reported that a man's job is to get wood, brush, and water for the camp while the woman lays the brush and does the cooking. Actually few if any men haul water, none gets brush, but some do haul heavy wood.

Table 11 shows that out of thirty-eight representative occupations, eight are normally performed by either sex and at least thirteen additional ones are frequently done by both sexes. Few tasks can be rigidly allocated to either men or women. Although certain occupations ascribed to men are not normally done by women, women can in an emergency fulfill these tasks. Such work includes big game hunting, cutting trees, and even building tent frames. Men too, in an emergency, can tan skin, make babiche, wash or repair clothes, sew moccasins, and fill snowshoes. In general, however, men do not like to perform women's duties.

No occupations are clearly demarcated by age categories, ability rather than age determining when tasks may be performed. Children, particularly girls above the age of six or seven, perform such household duties as getting wood and water, making fire, tending rabbit snares, sewing, and washing clothes. Girls from about eleven years of age assist in such heavier or more complex female activities as tanning skin, making camp, lacing snowshoes, or preparing cordage. Mature girls and women, however, take the executive role in carrying out these activities. Boys from fifteen years commonly engage in male allocated tasks like cutting trees, hewing, woodworking, trapping, and hunting, but if they are below that age little more than occasional assistance in these tasks is expected of them. No activities are taboo to old age. An old person keeps performing his customary duties until the nature of the work exceeds his physical powers. As a matter of fact it is this dwindling ability, rather than accumulated years, which defines old age.[12]

INTERPERSONAL RELATIONS

Related to what has already been said of the relatively slight importance of social organization in Kaska society is the fact that interpersonal relations are primarily restricted within the family during six or seven months of the year. Visits between winter settlements relieve this pattern somewhat, but it is mainly during trading visits to Lower Post that such interpersonal relations involve larger segments of the society. The highest degree of social interaction occurs during the summer, when members of the several tribes make their residence in that town.

[12] See below pp. 198–200.

LANGUAGE AND COMMUNICATION

The division of Kaska speech into four mutually intelligible dialects has already been discussed in connection with the tribal differentiation of the Kaska nation. These languages belong to the Athapaskan stock and, like most of the divisions of that group, are tone languages.

In addition to understanding the speech of the members of other Kaska tribes, most people can also manage to understand non-Kaska speakers from surrounding areas who use more distinctive Athapaskan dialects. The mutual intelligibility of the dialects has probably contributed to reducing the need for any marginal language. Some men understand and can speak a little Chinook, but this jargon is never used within the community.

To whites and, to a lesser degree, among themselves, the Kaska speak a variety of English which follows some of the rules of that language but possesses distinctive features of its own. Thus, for example, the feminine gender is usually ignored and the pronouns "he" or "him" are sometimes applied to both sexes and neuter objects. In replying to a question employing the negative, "Yes" is largely used instead of "No." Thus, "You don't know that story?" is answered, "Yes," if the speaker wishes to indicate a lack of knowledge. In speaking English, the sound l is substituted for r by most adults. A few French words have entered the language; *merci* is sometimes used for "thanks" and the adjective *li* is occasionally employed for "the." Several Tlingit words (like *gultšis* for "thank you") are also employed.

While orthography is of minor importance in this monograph, a brief statement of the signs used to represent some sounds occurring in the kinship terminology and elsewhere should be given. The vowels are:

i·as in English *eat*
i as in English *it*
e front unrounded, somewhat like English *let*
æ as in English *hat*

Final vowels usually receive the weak stress found in the last sound of English *sofa*. A dot following other vowels than i indicates lengthening; in the case of i the dot signifies a high front unrounded vowel. The diphthong aj is pronounced as in English *my*.

Consonants are as in English, with some exceptions. The t is formed with the tongue against the lower teeth and is slightly voiced before most vowels. The dorsal lateral spirant ł is pronounced as in the Welsh. Other consonants include the voiced and voiceless dorsal spirants, γ and x; the glottal stop, ʔ; the voiceless apical slit spirant θ, and the frontal spirants š and ž.

All of the data for the present study were collected in English, and, since some of this data has been published verbatim, some attention may be paid to the English vocabulary of the Kaska. The following list of words and phrases indicate the principal local usages developed for English words.

ANYBODY, *pron.* Everybody, as "anybody eat."
BOSS, *n.* A person who has the right to act upon, order, and care for an object, animal, place, or person, thus, "I'm boss for that woman."

BOTHER, *v.t.* To annoy; to approach sexually with or without the object's willingness; to meddle with something; to disturb; to coerce.

BULLSHIT, *n.* Nonsense; a lie.

CAN'T, *id.* Will not; won't; may not; don't want to, as, "I can't do that."

GRUB, *n.* Any food received from white source other than meat.

HE, *pron.* He; she; it.

HIM, *pron.* Him; her; it.

LOTS, *adj.* Many. As, "Lots of people."

MUST BE, *id.* Probably.

NEVER, *adv.* Not for some time, as, "I never hunt"; not ever.

NEWS, *n.* Unfavorable report, as, "to hear his news"; gossip; information.

NOTHING, *n.* Anything; as, "I never see nothing"; no.

PACK, *v.t.* To carry; to load, as, "to pack dogs"; to steal; to carry off.

Obviously all of these as well as all other words carry specific connotations for the Kaska which are sometimes different from their meanings in American speech. Thus a word like "lots," denoting "many," may be used to refer to a group of ten persons with the emotional expression that we would reserve for a mob of hundreds.

Several cases of speech defect were noted. One girl, eight years old, stuttered slightly. A young man was pointed out as speaking little and as being unable to command the communication of sentences of any length. The defect was regarded with amusement and was even joked about in the young man's presence. Cases of deafness and mutism were also reported.[13]

For insults and vituperation, recourse is generally had to English. The use of such terms is stilted, as though there were no clear realization of their meaning. In situations of emotional stress, delivery is more rapid and under such conditions speakers also manifest a tenseness of the body, including the face, which affects the vocal cords.

The Kaska Indians are not a gesticulating people, and the number of socially patterned gestures are relatively limited. Anger is expressed by frowning and by a narrowing of the eyes; shame and embarrassment, by covering the face with the hands and turning away the head. The latter gesture is most common among girls, being rarely used by boys and men. The explanation offered for the gesture was that the feeling of self-consciousness and shame is so intense that the individual does not want others to see her face. Affection, particularly between young people, either of the same or opposite sex, is generally expressed tactually but not by kissing. When the ethnographer's two year old daughter sought to kiss Ann Wiley (6), the latter demurred and cried, "Shame!" When the attempt was repeated, Ann sought to distract the younger girl by calling her attention to something else. Mirth and exuberance (the latter rarely) are released in infectious laughter. Acute hostility may be expressed in refusing to talk to, or look upon, a person, as well as by a sullen, dark facial expression. These are the most common signs used to communicate emotional states, although there are other socially patterned means for the individual to express more personal emotional states. Further discussion of emotional expression is reserved for a later section.

In narration, the hands and arms are sometimes used to aid communication. Thus to de-

---

[13] See also the discussion of linguistic theory; below, p. 230.

scribe the progress of a boat in rough water, the hand dips up and down as the arm is slowly moved from one side of the speaker's body to the other. Shooting of a gun is illustrated by holding the left hand close to the speaker's face, the fingers close together touching the thumb. The other arm is outstretched, the fingers held in the same position and directly in line with the left hand. When the speaker mentions the gun being fired, he spreads out the fingers of both hands in a quick, flaring, movement.

An obscene sign frequently demonstrated by boys and sometimes by girls is made by clenching the first with the thumb inserted under the index finger. This signifies coitus. In dancing hand pressing is often used as an erotic overture. A number of conventionalized gestures are used in the gambling game, including the indication of number by raising the corresponding number of fingers. Other signs include shaking the head up or down in affirmation or from side to side to express negation. The arms are used to express size. The left arm is stretched out, palm sideways, and size indicated with the right hand being placed at a right angle to the appropriate point. The point where the index finger joins the palm is marked off to indicate small size; the inside of the elbow or close to the shoulder are points marked off to show larger dimensions. To indicate height, the arm is outstretched palm sideways, the thumb slightly raised and the fingers close together. Height is indicated by the lowest portion of the hand. Nudging may sometimes be used for communication as, for example, to demand silence.

Aboriginally the Kaska possessed no writing. The syllabaries introduced somewhere in the Athapaskan area by Catholic and Protestant missionaries were not developed in the Cassiar. Traders took the pains to teach a few individuals to read and write simple words, but only a score or so Indian men are literate and less than half a dozen women. Today most children of from seven to fifteen receive a few weeks of instruction in writing and reading each summer in the Catholic mission school. Adults set a high value on literacy and many parents express the desire that their children master these abilities so that they will be able to write simple messages to the traders, read bills, and otherwise help the older generation adjust to modern conditions. Young children do not often share these attitudes, but some young men, like Nitla, spend several hours a week laboriously trying to learn to write words and coherent sentences. Several times Nitla asked the ethnographer for lists of familiar words such as the terms for commodities, local place names, and stock phrases ("I am going hunting,") which he could copy when the need arose.

Simple journals, often little more than calendars marking off the passage of the days and months, are kept by several young men. They contain brief notations of outstanding events (arrival of visitors, hunting data, departure from the trading post, etc.). Sometimes the writer forgets to enter a day in his journal and then his calendar is awry. Excerpts from the journal kept by Harry Lang in 1940 are given below; the original spelling and punctuation are preserved. Bracketed words are the ethnographer's.

Aug. 1.th 1940 Stay at Lower Post, yet.
Aug. 2.th 1940 Start from Lower Post
Aug. 3.th 1940 At [Joe] place. We camp.
Aug. 4.th 1940 Start camp at Frances River.
Aug. 5.th 1940 We get Home upper [Old Man] Creek.

Aug. 6.th 1940 We start for Lakes.
Aug. 7.th 1940 [John Keats] meet as on trail.

. . . .

Aug. 25.th 1940 We go to mountain for shap [sheep].
Aug. 26.th 1940 We stay at the mountain yet.
Aug. 27.th 1940 We go down to Lake.
Aug. 28.th 1940 Old Man [Wiley] and me and [Billy Barre] hunt moose Kill one moose.
Aug. 29.th 1940 I kill two Bull moose. and We goe home, for the camp.

Young people occasionally make photographic records with simple folding or box cameras; these are generally pictures of friends and relatives. The films are mailed to large cities for developing and printing. Great pleasure is found in looking at photographs, even after they have been seen many times before. Informants were also pleased to show a copy of the *National Geographic Magazine*, for May 1942, containing the record of the Albees' trip through the Upper Liard River valley and showing pictures of both deceased and living people.[14]

People communicate from one bank of a river to another by shouting; young men may also whistle. In the bush two smoke fires are said to be the signal for distress. Generally, if a person becomes lost in the bush, he fires a large caliber rifle and then waits for an answer. If he is injured, he may fire a number of shots in quick succession. Between winter settlements located as many as eight miles apart, gun fire is sometimes used for signaling.

In winter, if anyone leaves a settlement for a visit to the trading post, he is sure to be given messages to the storemen requesting additional supplies and a small increase in credit. These messages are usually laboriously pencilled by someone who can write, verbal messages being ignored by traders unless accompanied by cash. Notes are sometimes left at cabins when the occupants go away. Such notes commonly explain the reason for leaving and give the destination of the occupants.[15] Ordinarily Indians have little occasion to write letters. When they wish to do so, help is usually solicited from the independent trader in Lower Post.

Visitors between winter settlements, or in summer, from other parts of the area, disseminate news. Such transmission generally occurs at informal gatherings, perhaps while the visitor is refreshing himself with a cup of tea. News circulated in this way includes accounts of illness, death, luck in hunting, and the progress of house construction, as well as the activities of traders and other white people. Such accounts very rarely contain personal items unfavorable to a subject, gossip of this kind being either suppressed or withheld for more intimate occasions.

PROPERTY

Among the Kaska Indians, property—that is, those social relationships controlling the use and alienation of some subject matter[16]—tends to be of relatively little importance.

[14] Albee and Albee, *Family Afoot in the Yukon Wilds* (1942).

[15] Albee and Albee, *Family Afoot in the Yukon Wilds* (1942), 690. The specimen note given by the authors is very similar to ones which we encountered three years later.

[16] Murdock, *et. al., Outline of Cultural Materials* (1945), 24.

The things, around which property relations revolve, are quantitatively slight and qualitatively of little intrinsic value. Associated with these conditions, is the fact that interpersonal adjustments with reference to the subject matter of property have not been rigorously formalized. In recent years, however, the accumulation of stores of purchased winter food and capital goods has increased. One result of this accumulation may be seen in the conflict between such divergent property conceptions as loose personal control and strict private ownership. It is apparent that the growing amount of material goods is making the absence of concepts of strict personal control disturbing. We are therefore probably dealing with a transition period, in which property conceptions are becoming more rigorously formulated and ideas of strict personal ownership gaining in importance. These points should be borne in mind in reading the following material.

As near as could be learned, the subject matter of property includes the land but stops short of the fauna that pass over the land. The control of land, however, gives the owner the exclusive right to kill fur bearing animals on his territory but is less explicit about conferring exclusive privileges of killing game animals and birds. In one case, Old Kean protested when a white man announced his intention of hunting moose on the former's trap line, but generally little attention is paid to where a man hunts or fishes so long as he restricts trapping to his own territory. Ownership does not usually include the flora unless it has been affected by the owner's labor. Thus dried trees are ideally recognized as belonging to the person who killed them, although others do use such wood for fuel. Property is not extended to include spouses or children; a person may express authority over children but he would not claim to owning them.

All property is conceived of as privately owned. Ownership confers certain powers over the subject matter of property, including ideal control over permanent alienation and use. This ideal control indicates that the owner has the right to refuse the loan or transfer of his property in case of another's need. Manifestly, however, this right is restricted. The closer property relations involve the members of a settlement, the more limited is a man's control over the use of his property. Different categories of property are variously correlated with the right of use or access by others. Capital goods are probably most highly correlated in this respect; personal objects, like clothes, least; and grub, intermediately. Implicitly, the owner recognizes that his ownership fails to give him full power of control, so long as others lack and need his possessions. Often refusal to transfer needed objects is indirect; the owner may beg that he does not have what is needed. Such indirect refusal to lend further points to recognition of the limited control which is actually exercised over many possessions. There are, however, thick-skinned individuals who refuse to acknowledge the unformalized right of others to use their property and who, directly, strive to maintain full control. Such people are disliked and are branded as stingy or cranky. It is interesting that such people often try to defend their action, as though recognizing the lack of social support for their behavior. It must be pointed out that few people acknowledge their limited control willingly or generously. Conversely, most people never strongly express their right to use another's property.

A few examples of property relations may clarify these principles. Old Kean said one day that he had almost three year's supply of food at his place. He added with unconcealed annoyance: "All winter people I feed." Chronically this man complained of his sons' thefts. He was widely regarded as cranky and ungenerous. Similarly Old Man told the ethnographer that he didn't want to buy too large a supply of dog feed. If he did, he said, his sons-in-law would feel too free to use it. Light was thrown on attitudes toward too exclusive control of property when Leonard Dick stayed a night in Mrs. Dickson's unoccupied cabin in Lower Post. The next day he moved out and into a tent, despite the fact that his son was ill. We asked Old Man why Leonard did this. Old Man replied: "Maybe he hear kick coming. That's why he move out. Hard to get around that woman. She's mean . . . Anybody come around his place, she grab ax." The following day Old Man commented: "Some people pretty bad. Kick about it if you use their cabin or stuff winter time in bush. We do it just the same."

The principal forms of real property are land, houses, and caches. Each family head may be regarded as owning his trap line, a piece of territory varying in size from about two hundred to five hundred square miles. In British Columbia these trapping areas have been clearly mapped for each individual and the ownership is registered. Here trap lines are relatively small. In the Yukon, however, registered trap lines have not yet been introduced and considerably more confusion pertains to the boundaries of such a territory. Disputes over limits are not infrequent in the Yukon and, when these are called to the attention of the Royal Canadian Mounted Police, they are generally adjudicated by fixing some waterway as the boundary. It is rare for such questions to be referred to the police. Generally a man who feels that his trapping privileges are being infringed upon remains content to complain to his friends and to gossip unfavorably about the infringer. There is apparently no severe shortage of trapping ground and most trap lines are far from completely exploited. Trap lines are owned by men with only two exceptions noted. In these two cases women received their lines from husbands.

Use of a trap line is freely granted to all the members of the owner's primary family and may also be apportioned among a man's younger brothers and, temporarily, to a partner. Following marriage of a daughter and matrilocal residence by a son-in-law, the head of the household assigns an area of the trapping territory for the use of the young man. A son-in-law refers to this area as "mine," and only when pressed will he recognize the fact that final ownership is still invested in his father-in-law.

Houses are built by men, but their ownership is theoretically vested in woman. Tents also belong to women; they are sometimes manufactured by women but may also be purchased by men. River Joe, who is part Taku Indian (a tribe which has probably been more strongly influenced by coastal Indian attitudes than the Kaska), expressed an atypical conception of house ownership when he indicated that houses may be linked through female relatives. Thus his house, which was owned by his deceased wife (a member of the Wolf moiety) was said to be linked to the house which his son-in-law, Louis Maza, had built and transferred to his wife (also a Wolf). Both houses were "just the same," River Joe affirmed.

Movable property includes all items of capital goods, meat, grub, skins, vehicles, clothes, and other personal belongings. Children are not regarded as owning property until they approach maturity. "Children got nothing," Old Man said. "Just they eat. When full grown, they have their own stuff. They get money from daddy or sometimes they good trappers and pick up their own stuff." A child's money is its own, even when held by parents, and should not be spent without the owner's consent. The traps used by a wife or child belong to the man, but, as already pointed out, any fur which is caught in them belongs to the individual trapper. The man hunts and buys food, but once food is in camp it is controlled by the woman. A woman will seldom alienate any grub without first consulting her husband.

Property transactions. Three main forms of property transactions can be distinguished: appropriation, alienation by gift, and alienation by lending. Other forms of alienation, such as destruction, renting, and selling either occur rarely or not at all.

Appropriation often takes place when a son or son-in-law helps himself to his father's or father-in-law's goods without having any formal right of access to such property. Harry Lang appropriated a number of his father-in-law's tools, which he subsequently loaned to the ethnographer, designating them as his own. When Old Man saw these tools he pointed out his claim of ownership but beyond this made no effort to resume control. Old Kean's adult sons several times appropriated their father's cigarettes and food. This made the old man angry but, beyond buying new locks for those that had been broken, he was unable to enforce his control. In early summer, Old Man had cached a large portion of the subsequent winter's outfit at Louis Maza's place. In the fall Old Man expressed the fear that Louis Maza was using his dog meal and other goods. Asked if this was "all right," Old Man resignedly replied: "That's all right. Maybe he figger that's because I use his boat." On another occasion, as he was packing for a journey, Louis Maza's partner, Peter Tom, produced a flashlight. Louis picked up the light and said he would "hold" it until Peter came back, adding that he could use a flash if he had to look for something at night. Peter responded without a word to the appropriation. When people are drunk, they often quite uninhibitedly appropriate food. One night Old Man was sleeping off a drunk in Lower Post. When he awoke he discovered that his friends had helped themselves to a carton full of canned meat and fruit, leaving only the empty box. "Not stealing," Old Man said in response to the ethnographer's question. "Just they hungry and thirsty and eat." He was, however, far from pleased. In the Yukon, where trap lines are not registered, even trap lines may be appropriated. When Old Wiley died, leaving several daughters, the Wiley line was appropriated by his adjoining neighbors, Louis Maza and Old Wiley's brother-in-law, Old Man. Old Man, however, explained that he had originally given the ground to Old Wiley after the latter had followed him in settling on the Upper Liard. The appropriation of the Wiley line was resented by at least one of the Wiley daughters who, after the ethnographer returned to Lower Post from Old Man's place, interrogated him as to where the old man was trapping.

In gift giving, there is a wide gap between theory and practice. Ideally: "Who's poor luck, help him out little bit," said John Kean. "Help one another. Lazy man never think what he's going to live on . . . I help him out. I think . . . might he be better next winter. Might he help me sometime." He explained that a stranger in camp is always asked if he wants to eat. A friend, however, is told to help himself to food. "We don't worry about it. Glad to do it." Only when a man persists too long in living on another person's generosity would he be told to go into the bush and trap for himself. Even then a generous man will ideally stake a friend to a hundred dollars or so for capital goods and food.

Manifestly we can classify gifts into two kinds, those made spontaneously and those which follow a request for assistance. The meat of large game animals is always readily distributed, even when a family is living with unrelated people. Other spontaneous gifts are made relatively rarely and then only in well defined cultural contexts. The most common of these presents include purchased trade goods; manufactures, such as moccasins; meat, berries, and brew. A few people exchange purchased trade goods at Christmas. Native manufactures may be given by a woman to her husband or brother. Spontaneous gifts, excepting meat, are frequently reciprocated within a few days or weeks and such reciprocity is usually expected, although not clearly formalized. Hospitality may be recognized as a special form of free gift giving, but is not carried to extremes and few people visit for any length of time without supplying their own grub. Persistent demands for hospitality are, first covertly and then soon overtly, resented, since, particularly in the winter settlement, the supply of grub is limited and often barely enough to see a family through to spring.

Most gifts follow a call for assistance. Such requests may be outright, but are more generally advanced by implication. It is far more satisfactory if a person has his offhand statement of being low on raisins or moosehide fulfilled by a gift of such goods than if he has to request the objects directly. Although requests are commonly fulfilled, this is not necessarily done in a spirit of generosity and the realization of covert resentment operates to reduce calls for help. In return for his response, however, the donor enhances his reputation for generosity. Nevertheless this reputation dare not be too widely advertised, for fear that it will boomerang in the form of additional requests. Actually more people were described to the ethnographer as being stingy than were praised for their generosity. The reluctance of most people to make demands for goods or grub, particularly to non-relatives, also prevents a person's generosity from being abused. It is more or less understood that following assistance, the recipient will reciprocate the favor when he is called upon to do so. Actually many people chronically seek help without being able to contribute anything but cooperation in return, and this they are usually very unwilling to offer. The result is that the onus of giving rests upon a few older men who have been able to accumulate food and goods and who are generally extremely resentful of the role in which they are placed. Their antagonism reveals itself in ungenerous giving which in turn does not pass unnoticed and stimulates resentment in neighbors.

Loans differ from gifts in that they are made with the stronger expectation of the return of the object or its equivalent. Capital goods, as we have shown, are readily loaned. Grub, on the other hand, being more valuable, is more reluctantly shared in this fashion. Loans of money are occasionally made in summer with no interest being charged. It is not infrequent that loans fail to be repaid. Old Man reported lending skins to his son-in-law, Hans, who needed supplies but had no money. "I did it," Old Man said, "but he never let me have it [back]. If he stranger man, I bother him, but no use—he marry my daughter."

A final word may be added concerning the relatively rare incidence of the destruction of goods. This is limited to the worn clothes of the deceased, which are burned or abandoned after death, the rationalization being that they may carry disease and in this way threaten the surviving members of a family. A tent in which death has occurred is also sometimes abandoned for the same reason. Food of any kind is never destroyed.

Inheritance. Like most of the property transactions already referred to, the processes of inheritance are poorly formalized. The amount of inheritable goods is small, the most valuable being the trap line, but no cases of real property inheritance were recorded. Indians spoke of their children or their sons-in-law receiving a trap line but in no case had anyone attempted to make provisions for such inheritance. Since men usually take up residence in the wife's country, it is reasonably likely that inheritance would fall to either a man's daughters or to his sons-in-law. Hans, Old Man's son-in-law, opined that if his father-in-law died, he would obtain ownership of the trap line which he was now using; after him the line would go to his brother-in-law, or preferably, to his brothers, who would then continue to support his wife. This, however, was largely wishful thinking. Old Man himself felt that his trap line should go to both his sons-in-law. His statement, however, was not intended as a testamentary disposition, and there is no evidence for believing he was much concerned with the matter. River Joe's attitudes regarding the marital residence of his children may be recalled as pointing to one individual's desire to insure the inheritance of his trap line by his children. Such an expectation contrasts with Old Man's readiness to have his property pass to sons-in-law and emphasizes the unformalized patterns of inheritance. It must be remembered, however, that Old Man has no sons and only a fifteen year old unmarried daughter. He also has two sons-in-law already trapping on his line, whereas three of River Joe's sons-in-law have set themselves up independently.[17]

Other goods left by a deceased are generally kept by the surviving spouse who may sell them or apportion them among her children according to sex, a woman's objects going to girls, and a man's to boys. Inherited property so disposed of includes mainly dogs, guns, traps, snowshoes, tools, jewelry, and clothing. A deceased child's possessions, including clothes, are divided among the siblings. No report was heard of disputes about inheritance.

GOVERNMENT

Lacking governmental institutions of their own, the Kaska Indians are subject to the Dominion Government and, depending on their location, to the local government of Yukon Territory or the Province of British Columbia. In the present section we are chiefly interested in the Indian's relationship to these governments. We will emphasize the individual's attitudes toward federal and local authority rather than discuss the functions of these authorities in any detail.

The Kaska Indians are, with a few exceptions, wards of the Dominion of Canada. The exceptions are the relatively few women who, having legally married white men, were enfranchised as citizens and the one or two young men who have had their names removed from the "Indian list," i.e., successfully petitioned for the status of citizenship. Such individuals often deny that they are Indians and emphasize their equal-to-white status.

In general, the people regard the abstraction, government, as a "boss" whose functions

[17] In a letter dated January 5, 1944, F. R. Butler, Game Commissioner of British Columbia states: "Should the holder of a trap-line die without making any provision with regard to the transfer of his line, then the line and his estate automatically come under the control of the Official Administrator for the district, and generally such official contacts this office and has the trapline transferred to a relative of the deceased holder, or he asks for permission to sell the trap-line and equipment thereon so that any money derived therefrom may be turned into the Estate." In Yukon Territory, where trap lines are not registered, transmission following death is probably handled by the Royal Canadian Mounted Police, when called to their attention.

are manifold. Thus, referring to the impending visit of the forestry inspector from White-horse, Edward Prince once remarked that everything has a boss: "People have boss, game have boss, even stick [that is, timber] have boss!" To understand the attitudes of the Indian toward governmental authority, the significance of that word, "boss," must be thoroughly understood.

Within the native community, no man can exercise absolute power over any other adult. Parents are "boss their children," and it is even said that a man is "boss his wife," but the authority of these roles is not arbitrary and rarely abused. Furthermore, between adults authority has no meaning. An individual responds to the originations of another indi-vidual only when he stands to gain by such submission or when he cannot tactfully refuse agreement without endangering the harmony of his relationship to the other person. Obedience of an adult to the originations of another member of the Indian community never occurs because the originator possesses a status which of itself requires submission. Between Indians of equal status, that is, of relatively the same degree of maturity and of the same sex, a thorough-going laissez faire prevails. Considered by itself, the Indian community is an atomistic society in which every adult claims autonomy and independence. For example, Old Man once sent a message to his neighbor, Louis Maza, asking the latter to join him in a moose hunt. Louis went on the hunt but almost immediately decided to turn back, be-cause he was worried about his infant son's health. When appraised of this decision, Old Man said in effect: "It's up to you. I'm an old man and I can't see to shoot moose. I hoped we would hunt together but you do what's right. It's up to you." Those last words, "Up to you," are frequently heard when adults discuss plans and come to a disagreement. A person with richer experience may state his reasons for disapproving of a projected course of action, but if a younger man does not choose to heed the advice, the matter will usually be dropped. Obviously there are men who try to make their will prevail, who are dominant and assertive. Such men may hold authority within a group of brothers and their wives, but throughout the rest of the community they are generally disliked.

The English verb, "to boss," is used by the Kaska with two different connotations. When used in the sense of exerting authority it often connotes criticism or disapproval. In its wider meaning, however, the term denotes the right and ability to order and care for an object, animal, place, or person. Usually, as we have indicated, government is conceived of as a boss in the first sense, as a meddling and bothersome authority whose sovereignty is sometimes even branded as illegitimate. Thus Old Kean complained vigorously that the governments did not help the Indians. He denied governmental sovereignty over the area, and referred to the legitimate authority of a Ground Boss who would someday soon come to regain his dominion. No Indian admits or accepts the authority of a government to censor his drinking. Such authority is perceived as presumptuous and autocratic. In terms of the prevailing atomism of Kaska social life, it is almost inevitable that any activities of the Dominion and local governments in pursuit of their regulative functions should be resented and productive of anxiety. This situation was especially aggravated during the summer of 1945, when reports reached Lower Post that a wire fence had been erected around the Tahltan Indian Reserve at Telegraph Creek, 250 miles south of Lower Post. Although the ostensible reason for the fence was to demarcate Indian lands and protect children from the portage road's truck traffic, the Kaska Indians reacted to the fencing by construing it as a move to keep the Tahltan imprisoned on the reserve.

Only as far as such governmental services as aid to indigent Indians, free hospitalization, medical care, and gifts are concerned, do the Kaska accept the political authority of the whites. When these services are found inadequate or are, for any reason, interrupted, resentment is quickly expressed. Old Man reported that a former Indian Agent had given people fish line, nets, and cartridges. Under this agent's administration indigent Indians had also received not only rations, but a sizable winter outfit. Since then two new agents have served the community without giving gifts to the population. Many people therefore feel that the current Indian Agent is misdirecting government money which should go toward the Indians' general welfare. As a result of this chain of circumstances, the current agent is disliked and the governments are in little favor.[18] Louis Maza compared the position of the Kaska to the Indians of the United States. He had heard that in the latter country, the Indian is well treated, receiving adequate medical care as well as treaty money, while in Canada the natives are ignored.[19]

As far as the individual can be said to conceive of his political status, he is mainly concerned with his rights and privileges as an Indian and inclined to overlook any duties or liabilities to which he may be politically subject. He comprehends government as an agency which is supposed to take care of all the Indians—not only of indigent people—to the extent of protecting their trap lines from encroachment, supplying them with food when game is scarce, and providing medical care and hospital facilities. Education is not as strongly endorsed as these other rights. Furthermore he demands that on the Indian reserves, the people should be immune from government interference. Only in case of misbehavior on the "white reserve" is governmental authority recognized.

The Indian resents the duty of bearing arms. No Indians were drafted from the Kaska tribes in the course of the second World War, but several threats of conscription were rumored, all meeting with decidedly negative reactions from young men. According to Nitla, the government did not treat the people well. Consequently the Indians have a hard life and therefore can have no business to fight in the "government's war." Conscription, he opined, should be reserved for people who enjoy nice homes and comfortable living. Little resentment is expressed toward paying taxes on trapped furs. The sums paid, however, are quite insignificant when compared to the total value of a catch. Old Man and others pointed out that the Indians were getting no return for these revenues, and again alluded to the former Indian Agent who had made a return to the people in the form of gifts.

Political authority in the Kaska area is represented by the Royal Canadian Mounted Police, the Provincial Police in British Columbia, and the Indian Agent. This authority is most immediate during the summer, when the community is grouped in Lower Post within

---

[18] Superficially the lesson for applied anthropology seems plain: let the governments assume the roles of a protecting and providing boss and their legitimacy will be strengthened in native eyes. Actually such a role would be difficult to fulfill, although progress could certainly be made, first, by extending more abundant rations and medical care, and, second, by reducing, through tact, the severity of regulation.

[19] In northern British Columbia, west of Fort Nelson, Indians do not receive treaty payments as they have never concluded treaties with the Canadian government.

easy range of supervision. During the rest of the year, after the people have dispersed to their trapping districts, the authority becomes greatly relaxed. Only rarely do police operate far afield from the trading post.

Apart from the representatives of the provincial and Dominion law enforcement agencies, and the Indian Affairs Branch, political authority is nominally invested in native chiefs. Theoretically, each tribe or district is supposed to have a chief. Actually, only the Nelson people have such an executive and he is apparently expected to represent the whole Kaska nation. The chief is appointed by the Indian Agent for an indefinite period without remuneration. The duties of the chief are poorly defined, but he may be regarded as a *liaison* officer between the government officials and the people.

The current chief is personally a rather ineffectual person whose nominal authority in no way increases his prestige among the Indians. Since no prerogatives are attached to the office, it is not surprising that his status is not different from that of any other mature adult. The general attitude toward the chief is one of criticism for his failure to be more assertive in the service of his people. Old Kean expressed his opinion of the current chief in the following words: "Just like kid. Never talk nothing. Just sit down one place. That's why nobody go down there [i.e., to the east reserve]. Just stop alone." The fact that the chief does not belong to Old Kean's tribe is undoubtedly a factor influencing the latter's attitude. Observation failed to support the old man's statement that the east reserve was deliberately avoided by the bulk of the society.

When the chieftainship was vacant several years ago two Upper Liard men, Old Kean and Old Man, rejected offers of appointment to the position, the former because he felt himself to be too old and the latter because, not receiving payment for his service, he thought people would not listen to him. River Joe is reported to have sought the office unsuccessfully.

It has already been pointed out that the principal governmental activity, with which the Kaska have experience, is regulation. The most common subjects of such regulation are trapping and drinking. In the exercise of their regulatory functions the governments, through their agents, do not act in a manner calculated to allay the Indian's antipathy to authority. In the past there are said to have been police officers willing to overlook many minor infractions of laws applying to Indians, particularly those applying to drinking. Currently policemen, whose problems have greatly increased as a result of the opening of the area by the Alaska Highway and the subsequent influx of strangers, are much more rigorous. During the period of field work they frequently acted as detectives, patrolling Lower Post late at night and visiting camps in order to apprehend misdemeanors.[20] As a result most of the people have learned to be constantly wary of the police. Young men, even if innocent of any offense, often flee and hide when an officer is reported to be approaching. In short,

---

[20] It is not uncommon for provincial and Dominion police to enter a tent or cabin without a warrant if they have reason to suspect drinking. While Indians are unaware of the powers of a warrant, they resent the invasion of their privacy. From white men Indians have learned to question the right of the Mounted Police to operate in British Columbia, where a local police organization is maintained. The Mounties explain that they are free to operate anywhere in the Dominion of Canada when engaged in the enforcement of national revenue (liquor) and Indian regulations.

the police are disliked and this attitude is readily transferred to the governmental stereotype constructed out of the individual's experience with law enforcement.

LAW AND SOCIAL CONTROL

The atomistic structure of Kaska society is associated with a complete lack of formal social control beyond that which has been introduced following the absorption of the group into the larger white society. There is a tendency for the people to remain as much as possible aloof from the white man's law or system of justice, interpersonal grievances within the Indian community rarely being brought to the adjudication of white courts. As a result, all cases heard have as their complainants the police, Indian Agent or white men.

The principal individual incentives compelling adult conformity to the Indian and white expectations of behavior are guilt, shame, warnings, precepts, and fear of sanctions. Guilt and shame are inextricably related in patterning conformity to the Indian standard of values, although they are notably weak in making behavior conform to those expectations of the white society that apply to drinking, brewing, trapping, and hunting. Guilt and shame may be identified as conscience or superego pressure. Nitla defined this mechanism well when he said that an individual knows if he does evil. "He know it in his brain. Everything bum. You better stay alone." Conscience may often drive a person to make amends with the individual whom he has offended or it may prompt him to excuse his behavior, blaming it on somebody else. In the case of John Kean, who began living with his brother's wife, strong antipathy and aggression appeared to those people who, he thought with some reason, were criticizing his conduct. On one occasion he tried to slough off responsibility for his actions by laying the blame on Adele, the woman with whom he was living, and even on his brother. Forgiveness does not always erase the pang of conscience, as witness River Joe and Louis Maza the morning after a drinking party that had been accompanied by considerable violence and disorder. Although Mrs. Maza forgave her husband for having hurt her and River Joe was assured that his aggressive behavior had not seriously harmed anyone, both men appeared extremely shy and discomfited. They protested to the ethnographer how "sorry" they felt about the fracas which they had begun. In general, however, the Kaska superego does not seem harsh. Once the situation of default is past, the offense tends to be quickly forgotten. No evidence was adduced of a lingering sense of guilt (although it was looked for) nor of the long persistence of any need for atonement or expiation.

Rather slight effort is made within the native community to induce adult social conformity by means of warnings and precepts, although the missionaries and police make stronger use of this technique. The priest frequently warns Indians of imminent police and supernatural sanctions, while the police threaten suspected wrongdoers with fine and arrest. Because of the reluctance of an Indian to interfere in another person's business, warnings and advice are entirely limited to relatives and close friends. River Joe was afraid to exert himself in the relationship of John Kean and Nitla's wife, for fear that word of his interference would reach the Lower Pelly River tribe to which Adele belonged and whose members would then be "down" on him. Louis Maza also emphasized his powerlessness in this direction. "I can't say nothing. That not my business. I never tell nobody what to do." One of the main reasons for such lack of interference is the fear of arousing resentment and hostility, but it also seems to spring from the individual's personal desire to be left alone; hence he respects another's privacy. Such attitudes, however, do not always inhibit gossip, which is derived from latent antagonism or which sometimes functions as a vehicle of social control.

The chief sanctions imposed by the Indian community include gossip, ostracism, and supernaturally derived insanity. Fine and arrest are the formal sanctions imposed by the white society. Gossip is the common result of failure to share grub and capital goods or control aggression, and also follows adultery. Since gossip is also an expression of inter-personal hostility, its functions are wider than social control. As might be expected, the dual uses of gossip succeed in complicating its utility as a means of social control. That is to say, people often use gossip more as a retaliatory device than as a sanction, and this in turn arouses antagonism in the wrongdoer even when it leads to a modification of behavior.

Ostracism is an ideal sanction which in practice tends to be avoided for fear of giving too direct offense to a defaulter. Nitla vouched for this ideal pattern when he said that an aggressive person, one who is "too much mean, swear, cranky," will be avoided by the people. "Nobody look after that kind of man. Everybody he don't want him." A man who becomes aggressive under alcohol may be quietly left out of a drinking party, although nobody would refuse an invitation to share *his* brew. On the other hand, if the offensive person appears on the scene of a beer drink, there is no way to prevent him from joining the group.

Insanity and deformity are supernaturally derived sanctions which are popularly feared to follow infractions of moiety exogamy and other forms of incest. Insanity is also believed to occur: "If you think about girl too much . . . If you want to play with girl too much."

Fines are feared not so much because they deprive one of wealth than because they involve appearance in court and expose the individual to questioning and public censure. Arrest is the most dreaded sanction, and this fear is reinforced by the frequently repeated story of one of River Joe's sons. Several years ago the youth was arrested on the complaint of a white man for a marital offense. Found guilty, he was sent to prison for one year. The incarceration is widely supposed to have affected him mentally, although other reports blame his subsequent break-down on a too intense interest in girls. At any rate, upon his release from prison, the young man showed psychotic reactions and once more had to be removed from the area for confinement. He is still a patient in a mental hospital near Van-couver. This incident is very much in the memory of the people and helps to confirm the strong fear of arrest. Nobody was jailed during the period of field work, one reason for this being the lack of jail facilities in Lower Post. In 1945, however, a jail was built in the town and the constable is reported to have promised that it would be readily used if necessity demanded. Imprisonment outside of the area is reserved for serious crimes involving sen-tences of a year or more.

Offenses against life and the person are rare. Premarital sexuality, especially when it occurs among sixteen and seventeen year olds, could be construed as a crime according to national law but tends to be ignored by the police (who would have difficulty securing evidence), and is not regarded as a serious offense by Indians. In the past, one or two girls at McDame Creek have been sent to reform school for pronounced sexual delinquency.

Adultery probably occurs more frequently than is known, but the offense is generally kept within the family and from police knowledge. Incest may also occur more commonly than is suspected. This is implied in the statement of Old Kean, blaming several cases of physical deformity on the fact that people are too "mixed up." Within the Indian community, drunkenness is scarcely considered as criminal and is regarded as good "fun" so long as it does not lead to violence. Lying is disliked but is not strongly resented. Braggarts, who overindulge in "bullshit," are secretly criticized and ridiculed.

Many property offenses are condoned with the realization that the owner must be careful not to give the impression of selfishness. A few individuals are widely known for their tendency to steal and such people receive careful watching. Indian caches and those of white trappers remain free from violation except in case of hunger, and even then will only be approached by the rare person with a pronounced predilection for stealing. Government supplies along the Alaska Highway were rarely disturbed by Indians, who had abundant opportunity to observe instances of disrespect for such property by their white neighbors. The accusation of trap line infringement is sometimes voiced, especially with regard to beaver trapping. Some white men are almost paranoiac in their suspicion that Indians are poaching on their lines, but most white trappers regard such intense insecurity as an unwarranted quirk of thinking. Several years ago Edward Prince was arrested and fined for hunting beaver on a white man's territory. It is not unusual for a number of youths to plan the stealing of a brew that is ready for drinking. No moral hesitation and little secrecy is apparent in such behavior, as anyone would agree who has seen a tract of bush alive with people hunting for a reported beer keg. The finders try to finish as much of the beverage as possible before they in turn are discovered. Young children often show a predilection for stealing small gaudy trifles, like toys, but are severely punished if discovered by parents. In the case of property offenses by adults, discovery generally leads to recrimination, a demand for the return of the stolen goods, or suppressed hostility. Offenses connected with the nonfulfillment of credit obligations to traders are rare. Such defaults would quickly result in the blocking of further credit and few persons could sustain this penalty. Between individuals, failure to repay loans may lead to recrimination and hostility.

Since most crimes and misdemeanors are discovered in Lower Post, which is in British Columbia, justice is largely administered by provincial officials. Punishable offenses discovered by the police do not generally lead to an open statement of arrest nor is the individual given his liberty under bail, since to announce arrest leads to the danger that the offender will remove himself from the community. Within three or four days following the offense, word circulates through the town that the magistrate will hold court in the afternoon. The policeman then informs those Indians, who have been "under arrest," that their trial is due that day.

According to provincial law all offenses, other than major crimes, regardless of the plea of the defendant, may be tried by a civil magistrate without a jury. For some years cases have been tried by elderly white prospectors, but in 1945 the police constable from Fort Nelson several times flew to Lower Post to act as magistrate. All hearings are conducted in English. Court is held in the Hudson's Bay Company's bunkhouse which is normally reserved for white trappers. A few boxes serve as seats for visitors, while the arresting provincial or Mounted Policeman acts as prosecutor and witness. In no case observed was an accused Indian put under oath when he appeared before the court. The following examples of trials, abstracted from field notes, illustrate judicial process in Lower Post.

7:11:45. When Louis was called before the bar, he leaned forward comfortably on the table behind which the magistrate was seated. The latter told the accused to stand up. Louis obeyed but in a moment again leaned forward listening to the charge being read. Again the magistrate had to command the accused to stand erectly. Louis pleaded guilty to having been intoxicated and was fined fifteen dollars and costs. The arresting constable then reminded the magistrate of an additional penalty obtaining if the accused, an Indian, refused to divulge the source of the liquor. This section of the statutes was read to Louis, who was then asked where he had obtained the beverage. Louis affirmed that he had found it in the bush. Sarcastic questions expressing the magistrate's disbelief of this reply could not shake Louis from his story. The constable then spoke up, saying that the accused was probably telling the truth and that there was no reason to doubt his word. Further sentence was thereupon suspended.

8:7:45. Three Indians and one white man were arraigned on charges of intoxication. Peter Lang was called first. This was his second offense under the liquor statutes. After the charge had been read he was asked how he pleaded. When Peter failed to understand the question, he was asked directly whether or not he had been drinking liquor on the night in question. Peter denied drinking liquor, adding that he had drunk only a bottle of beer. Manifestly annoyed, the magistrate tried to explain that beer and liquor were both alcoholic beverages and therefore denied to Indians. "You evidently think you're allowed to drink beer but not whiskey." Peter again denied drinking whiskey. The magistrate insisted that if Peter admitted drinking beer he had also been drinking liquor. Misunderstanding, Peter tried to maintain his innocence from the charge by interjecting the common term for an untruth—"bulfshit." The magistrate at once sharply reprimanded the Indian, saying: "Don't you dare use language like that in court." Peter did not grasp the rebuke and answered: "That's what I say, that bullshit." The magistrate looked hopeless but let the word pass. He did, however, appeal for an interpreter who could speak the language of the accused. None was forthcoming. It was finally established that Peter Lang realized his offense. His plea was recorded and he was fined sixty dollars and costs, with the alternative of two months in jail. He accepted the fine and was then asked where he had secured the beer. Refusal to answer, he was warned, could lead to an additional fine. Peter said he had found the beverage in the bush. This irritated the magistrate, who was apparently inclined not to believe the answer, although he finally accepted it. Peter was warned that a third offense would certainly earn him imprisonment with hard labor.

The second defendant was Nick Lang who pleaded not guilty to the charge of intoxication. Two witnesses testified under oath to having seen Nick manifest signs of intoxication. The first witness was the Mounted Policeman, who had accompanied the provincial official on the night of the arrest, while the second was the local constable himself. Both affirmed having seen the defendant walking "unsteadily" and "staggering." Nick declined the opportunity to question the witnesses, but said he had been getting water with a lame foot when he had encountered the police. The magistrate found him guilty and imposed fine of fifteen dollars and costs, with the alternative of spending a month in jail. Nick chose the fine. Under further questioning he too insisted that he had found the liquor in the bush. This explanation angered the magistrate, who warned that he would be very severe if he ever returned to Lower Post and again heard that story.

The third defendant was a young Bear Lake (Sekani) Indian man, who was temporarily stopping in Lower Post following employment with a government survey party. While the legally worded charge was being read the accused unthinkingly turned his back on the magistrate. For this he was sharply rebuked. Pleading guilty, the youth was questioned concerning the source of the liquor. He affirmed that soldiers had given him a bottle of rum. The magistrate sarcastically remarked that such generosity to Indians was difficult to understand, since most soldiers were themselves short of liquor. He then imposed a fine of fifteen dollars and costs, and adjourned court while the defendant, in company with the provincial policeman, went to friends trying to borrow the money. The boy came to the ethnographer's cabin and there found Daisy Joe, an Indian woman, whose common law husband was a white man. The policeman had recently caught this woman in the company of her husband carrying a gunny sack of beer. Now, suffering from severe toothache, she was uneasily waiting to see if her offense would also come to trial. When the boy asked Daisy (a nonrelative) for money, the policeman became suspicious and remarked: "Maybe that's where you bought the liquor!" This accusation was firmly denied by both parties as well as by Daisy's white husband.

Trials are conducted so as to be punitive as well as judicial. Several times we heard the magistrate making an attempt to frighten the Indians from drinking. There is no question but that the people are afraid of court proceedings, although they are never sufficiently intimidated to reveal the true sources from which liquor is secured. Thereby they protect their access to those sources. Most of the time court proceedings are conducted on a level of formality and a plain of experience quite foreign to the Indians. The efforts of the magistrate to command respect and proper courtroom demeanor are both pitiful and amusing.

Ingroup Relations

In this section, cooperative action and conflict within the Kaska nation as a whole is considered. In the section immediately following discussion will take up relations between Kaska and non-Kaska individuals.

It is in keeping with the atomistic character of Kaska society that cooperation within a tribe or within the nation as a whole should be unknown. No mechanisms for bringing about the unified functioning of these groups are available and group sentiment is transient and ephemeral. Under such conditions it is not surprising that the development of social policies has scarcely gained even a foothold in the group. About thirty-five years ago, under the direction of a white man, James Teit, the Kaska were involved in an attempt to further group interests by supporting a social ideology.[21] The movement was directed toward the preservation of the Indians' right to trap anywhere in the country without being confined to registered trap lines, which were at that time being introduced in British Columbia. As the first task of implementing this social policy, the Indians contributed money which was to be used to institute legal proceedings. Teit, however, is alleged to have absconded with the funds collected. At any rate, the policy met with no success. Even in this group movement, as reported by Old Man, we can detect the spirit of individualistic opportunism at work. "We're trapping Yukon side. White man tell us, 'Yukon trappers put up five dollars. B. C. trappers put up one hundred dollars.' They do that. Old Chief put up five hundred

---

[21] We have adopted this term from Kardiner who uses it to refer to "a system of ideas which seeks implementation by action to gain or preserve certain interests," Kardiner, The Psychological Frontiers of Society (1945), 371.

dollars. That's his kids. He's got maybe five kid. Each put up one hundred dollars. *He figger he gonna take whole Hyland River*. Old Kean put up one hundred fifty dollars. My brother put up ten dollars. They say from Lower Post three thousand dollars going." The imputed motive of Old Chief (which we have italicized) is significant, since it points out the lack of ingroup solidarity and the self-centeredness of the individual. Old Chief received his designation from white men and should not be regarded as an executive whose legitimacy was derived from the native society.

Today only unorganized and diffused traces of social ideologies are encountered. All of these emphasize better governmental care of the Indian and consist mainly of pleas and complaints which never achieve a stage where they are implemented by action. Interest was shown toward a Canadian Commonwealth Federation (C. C. F.) organizer who came to Lower Post in 1945. Old Man, who heard of the man indirectly from John Kean, spoke approvingly of the "new government" and thought it would "do something" for the Indian.

Interpersonal antagonism characterizes most of the relations of men in the area and is even the most prominent feature of interpersonal relations within a tribal district. Despite the ideal attitude commanding a person to mind his own business, the common expression of this latent hostility is through malicious gossip and backbiting. Such expression, however, is confined to good friends and older men who are not apt to carry the calumnies back to the subjects. Young men and most women show a strong and consistent reluctance to gossip or criticize, and it is only in an unguarded moment or during intoxication that their feelings are permitted escape. The careful control on the expression of hostility is related to the Kaska Indian's great fear of giving offense to people and thereby damaging his own reputation. Old Man illustrated this tactfulness abundantly. He felt that Old Lady Metša had to be given a good funeral for fear of otherwise offending her daughter, Lady Suza. Following the death of her mother the latter was received in Old Man's house as a temporary accommodation, but the old man soon regretted his action as he began to perceive that Lady Suza and her youngest son, Donald, were depleting his stock of grub. He was extremely reluctant however, to take any action that would give offense. Instead he complained to the ethnographer of his guests' eating habits and criticized young Donald's laziness. A large part of his resentment was expressed in the socially permitted form of tormenting the latter youth for his indifferent work habits.

The hypocrisy between even good friends is striking. Old Kean and Old Man had spent a sociable evening drinking brew together and complimenting each other. Two days later Old Kean criticized Old Man bitterly. He accused the latter of illegally trapping on both sides of the Liard River, affirming that the other man had no right to cross the stream. Then he alluded to Old Man's long association with white men and implied that Old Man was beginning to think of himself as a white man. He ended up by branding his friend as "full of bullshit," that is, a liar. A few days later Old Kean aired his resentment of River Joe, whom he accused of trying to be the boss of the whole country. He fancifully threatened to put River Joe in jail.

Similar attitudes prevailed in the relationship of Old Man and River Joe. Together the two always appeared to be good friends, but behind the other's back Old Man was tirelessly critical. He indirectly warned the ethnographer not to be taken in by River Joe's friendship, stating that River Joe quickly tired of people and then discarded them. Old Man periodically resented Joe's past criticism of the present Mrs. Man. According to Old Man, River Joe had sneered at this marriage to an old woman and urged his former brother-in-law (Old Man had married sisters of River Joe's brother's wife) to find a young girl. Old Man expressed little sympathy with River Joe's widowhood, claiming that the latter had once called himself a Taku Indian, and why didn't he go to those people now in order to find a new woman. In his turn River Joe warned the ethnographer not to live with Old Man and compared his own settlement, with its clean, well floored houses, to Old Man's floorless buildings.

The same note was struck by Louis Maza, who jeered at the poor accommodations which Old Man could offer the ethnographer and pointed pridefully to his better quarters. Louis' attitudes were echoed by his partner, Peter Tom. Derogatory attitudes were expressed by Old Man regarding Louis Maza. He said that out of meanness Louis was not allowing his partner, Peter, to live in the former's new home but was forcing the youth to sleep in an old tent frame. This appears to have been a total misconstruction of facts, since Peter had previously boasted that the tent frame would become his own when Louis moved into his new house.

We also heard Peter Tom criticize River Joe for turning against people who ate his grub. This antagonism may be explained by the fact that after having lived with one of Joe's daughters for a year, Peter found his plans to wed the girl legally frustrated by the older man's sudden change of mind. Peter also asserted that Hans Donnelly did not treat his wife well, forcing her to haul and cut wood. There is reason to believe that even a neighbor's economic hardship is often experienced as gratifying. An indication of this comes from the amusement with which travelers' news of poor luck in hunting and trapping is received in the winter settlements.

All of these illustrations come from one tribal district and show the character of the attitudes existing between close neighbors. Even within a single settlement there may be antagonism, especially if members of two unrelated or affinally related families live in proximity. Thus Harry Lang accused his brother-in-law's, Hans, mother of having "talked" about him and thereby influenced Hans to build his own tent frame and cease sharing Harry's house.

One function of interpersonal hostility is to reduce any feeling of ingroup solidarity and thus to reaffirm the atomistic social structure. Between people of different tribal districts even stronger antagonisms prevail. Such people are often referred to as strangers or as "different people." Thus one afternoon Louis Maza expressed his suspicion that the people across the river were drinking a brew. He added, "No use we go over there. Those different people. They never treat." Asked for his opinion about the Cross brothers, who were Nelson Indians, Old Man replied that he didn't know the Cross "bunch" but said that, according to Mary Wiley, who had lived with them as an affinal relative, they were "pretty hard to get along with and always talk about other people." He also reported River Joe's decision that the Nelson people were "no good." When Richard Day was asked his opinion of Edward Cross, he stated that the latter is disliked by many people. All he would add by way of explanation was: "He lies." Later Richard added that he would not associate with Edward for fear of imperiling his friendship with age mates. Even older children show characteristic behavior toward companions from other districts. When Donald Suza first appeared in Lower Post, after fourteen years spent at Frances Lake, a number of youths approached and inspected him, calling him: "Stranger." They then threatened to hurt him. Donald remained submissive. An hour or two later the same boys had fully accepted the visitor. In these attitudes and behaviors toward members of contiguous and mutually intelligible Kaska tribes we see the beginnings of the ethnocentrism which will be discussed in connection with intergroup relations. In a last analysis the true ingroup among the Kaska is probably the nuclear family.

Any overt expression of hostility in quarrels and ingroup violence is rare. When people are sober there is consistency between ideals and behavior so far as the control of aggression is concerned. Even the possibility of inviting quarreling is forestalled by the fact that many people are quick to flee from any such threatening situation. Although one or two dominant and assertive men appear more ready to face disharmony, in general the pattern for both sexes is rigorously to suppress and ignore all open expression of hostility.

Intoxication sometimes alters this picture. In this condition, a number of men show readiness to revive old grudges and air antagonisms without fear of provoking violence. In English, the drunken quarrelers hurl insults replete with obscenity at one another in an attempt to provoke an initial act of violence. Before the mounting hostility can reach this level, women with their young children have generally retreated to a safe distance. Often the provocations to violence remain unaccepted by either party, and the quarrel peters out in a last disgusted exchange of insults. Sometimes, however, the challenge is taken up and blows begin to be exchanged. While fists are used at first, this form of fighting soon yields to wrestling, the aim being to throw the opponent and then choke him into surrender. Weapons of any kind were never observed to be employed in quarrels. Sometimes a woman will try to separate two men who are fighting, but generally women are too timid to venture close. Old Man was rather outstanding among men for his consistent tendency to forestall aggression at beer drinks; he also broke up many fights. Antagonism following such quarrels is rarely prolonged, although the resentment may continue covertly and motivate additional aggression during a subsequent drinking party. Sometimes in intoxication a bullying type of behavior appears. Louis Maza once manifested such behavior when he asked Nitla, a very pacifistic youth, to wrestle him. Nitla immediately declined. Louis then rudely took away a dipper of coffee which Nitla was drinking, but again the latter displayed no emotion. Turning his attention elsewhere, Louis picked up a nearly empty tea pot and emptied the grinds on Edward Prince, at the same time winking to the ethnographer. Edward ignored the slight and remarked: "Must be raining." Only an hour or so previously, when both had been much drunker, Edward and Louis had quarreled bitterly, but now Edward was sobering up and refused the implicit challenge evident in Louis' behavior.

Family life is not characterized by quarreling. Ideally a man feels entitled to beat his wife if he suspects that she has been untrue to him, but not all men avail themselves of this permitted behavior. Several husbands (including Hans Donnelly, Edward Prince, and Louis Maza) are noted for aggression toward wives when intoxicated. One such quarrel was ob-

served between Louis and his wife, Allie. Perhaps because she was herself partially intoxicated, Allie showed no fear when her drunken husband began to beat her. Several times she
half-heartedly ran away. Once Louis caught her by the hair, knocked her to the ground, and
began to punch her with his fists. With some effort the ethnographer and Old Man succeeded in separating the couple. Allie still stood her ground, and only with difficulty could
she be urged to run away.

All open expression of hostility is socially condemned. Since alcohol is understood as
causing most aggressive behavior, there is a feeling that individuals prone to violence are
not good drinkers. As we have shown, this idea does not lead to the realistic exclusion of
such men from drinking situations. Once the aggressive person returns to sobriety, he
strongly regrets his behavior.

INTERGROUP RELATIONS

Relations between Kaska speaking Indians and non-Kaska people are generally restricted.
The greatest amount of such interaction is carried on with Tahltan, Bear Lake, and Tselo·na
neighbors; also with the whites. Most of the Kaska have heard of the Pelly River Indians
to the north, but interaction between these two groups is rare.

Socially patterned attitudes toward Indian groups who reside outside of the Kaska area
are characterized by an ethnocentrism which is expressed mainly in unfavorable opinions
and is most strongly directed against the Tahltan. Least does it influence relations with the
nearby Sekani tribes, into which considerable marriage has occurred. While Kaska judgements of their neighbors tend to extol the ingroup, any direct expression of ingroup exalta-
tion is rarely heard.

It is commonly felt that the Tahltan Indians are too aggressive, while the latter people
in turn look down on the Kaska as uncouth "bush Indians." The Tahltan, as Old Man
pointed out, in their attitude toward the Kaska are influenced by the memory of their
ancestors fighting these more northern Indians. Mildred Lang expressed a typical attitude
toward the Telegraph Creek people when she said: "Too many Tahltans here. They're too
tough. Fight too much." She also resented two local dwelling Tahltan families as being too
"high toned," i.e., they tried to maintain a social exclusiveness which sometimes led to
directly snubbing certain Kaska Indians, including herself. River Joe indicated that marriage
between Tahltan and Kaska people is to be discouraged. The few marriages of this type,
however, seem to be well established. On another occasion, when River Joe was intoxicated,
he is reported to have become openly abusive of the Tahltan, claiming that they had no
right to live in Kaska country. To the ethnographer he said that the Telegraph Creek
Indians always get into fights when they have been drinking. The tenacity of Kaska attitudes toward these neighbors may be gauged from the fact that in 1945 a local restaurant
lost considerable trade when the management was given to a Tahltan family. Although no
organized boycott occurred, many Kaska kept their promise not to spend money in that
place. Our evidence thus corroborates what Morice saw around 1900, when he wrote:
"Even to this day the Kaska resent the Tahltan's assumed or real superiority, and will not
be confounded with them as co-members of the same tribe."[22]

[22] Morice, The Nah·ane and their Language (1900–03), 520.

In contrast to the Tahltan, the Bear Lake people, with whom considerable marriage has taken place, are accepted with little discrimination. Attitudes toward the Pelly Indians are also less hostile. The feeling of the Kaska is that the latter people are far less acculturated, that they still rely primarily on meat for food, and that they are therefore more hardy. There is a half-laughing tendency to admire this hardiness, which suggests some ambivalence of feeling. Old Man opined that the women of one lower Pelly River tribe, the Selkirk, were all unfaithful. "You sit in camp, if you're married to Selkirk woman, and your wife sees another man. When you go out and you come back you find your wife gone with kids. Selkirk Injuns always like that."

Not much is known of the Slave Indians who dwell to the east beyond the Rocky Mountains. When Louis Maza heard that these people lacked the potlatch, his immediate judgement was: "Just like dog." Then he wanted to know if they didn't abandon the bodies of their dead anyplace, without troubling to inter the corpses. When this was denied, he nevertheless praised the care with which the Upper Liard people treated their dead.

Contradictory attitudes are often manifested by the Indians toward the whites. White people who are not "high toned," associate with Indians, and participate in the latter's activities are treated with a great show of enthusiasm and friendship. These attitudes were markedly expressed toward the American soldiers and construction workers who, in visiting the area, were not only cordial to the natives but also generous, giving the latter gifts of food, liquor, and other objects. Occasionally less favorable sentiments toward whites betray themselves, as when Old Man requested an Indian youth to help him run a white man's boat, saying that he didn't want to rely wholly on "stupid" whites. Resentment toward American troops was also aroused in Indian youths when these soldiers monopolized native girls. River Joe once sent a complaint to the commanding officer of the RCAF, claiming that Canadian Air Force men had disturbed his camp in the middle of the night while looking for girls. Joe was, however, proud of his friendship with American soldiers and civilians, although fully aware that his unmarried daughter and niece were the chief reasons for his popularity. The Kaska are cognizant of the fact that many white men regard them as inferior and often spread distorted reports of Indian customs. Such attitudes, although covertly resented, do not lead to quarrels unless Indians have been drinking. Occasionally white men also take it upon themselves to criticize an Indian girl's promiscuous behavior. The girl usually reacts by denying the allegations and indignantly branding her accuser a "liar."

White men who demonstrate hardihood in their adaptation to the environment and who are good hunters, quickly meet the Indians' approval. Whites who fail to develop such abilities are pitied rather than condemned. A number of Kaska men (including Richard Day and Old Man) are characterized by strong ingratiatory behavior toward whites. Old Man frankly emphasized such demeanor as a valuable technique for getting along with white men, by which he meant receiving gifts and favors—especially liquor—from them.

SEXUAL RELATIONS

In this section the interpersonal relations arising out of the socially patterned sexual impulse are discussed. Recent studies have shown that societies differ in the values and attitudes which they place on sex, and we shall accordingly pay close regard to these covert aspects of sexual interaction.[23]

The Kaska tend to avoid idealizing the sexual relationship. For the most part there is little demonstration of affection in public.[24] Although young married couples show considerable devotion to one another, the closest bonds between sexual partners appear only after marriages have endured for some time. There is evidence for assuming that tender feelings are inhibited, and that romantic affection is most readily expressed by simply maintaining proximity to the loved object. Little evidence of romantic passion was adduced. Commenting on the blind devotion which a white man was showing Dorothy Plover, Mildred Bates said: "White man more crazy than Indian about girl. Don't think Indian man do that." Richard Day, a métis who had been educated at a Pacific Coast boarding school, admitted having been in love, but described the effect as so unpleasant—he could neither eat nor sleep—that he did not want to risk the experience again. Love, he explained, appears after a man has had sexual intercourse with the same girl several times.

Only the man's ideals of female erotic beauty were secured. Such ideals emphasize even, white teeth; coordinated eyes; a well shaped nose; and long, well combed hair. One informant, adding the qualities of tallness and plumpness, said that he did not fancy too prominent breasts. Breasts, with the exception to be noted below, have little erotic significance. Attractive clothes appear to enhance a girl's desirability, but informants denied any erotic significance for perfume or cosmetics.

The attitudes guarding against exposure of the genitals have already been indicated in connection with the discussion of defecation and urination. It may be added, that strong shame is not attached to the exposure of the breasts. A nursing woman will freely uncover the upper part of her body in public, and Irene Wiley once went swimming in mixed company wearing only a pair of bloomers.

Shyness in the presence of the opposite sex is more strongly developed in girls than in boys, although it is by no means lacking in the latter. It is hard to gauge how much of a girl's coyness and reticence represents expected social behavior and what part is a sincere expression of confusion, fear, and embarrassment. The proportion of these motivations undoubtedly varies among different girls. There are several girls, like Irene Wiley and Flower Joe, who can never be upset by sexual attention. Younger and less promiscuous girls, however, are quick to become conflicted and alarmed by too direct a sexual approach, and even young married women will often reflect genuine disturbance when they encounter sexual attention from strange men. In the man, intense shyness soon becomes inhibited in accordance with the social expectations.

Among themselves, young men often discuss sexual topics and would readily do so upon the invitation of the ethnographer, once his company became familiar. Always, how-

[23] For recent studies stressing the social determinants of sex see Ayau, *The Social Psychology of Hunger and Sex* (1939); Seward, *Sex and the Social Order* (1946), and Honigmann, *A Cultural Theory of Obscenity* (1944). The insight that sex is multiply determined, rather than constituting a primary determinant (as Freud postulated), stems largely from Adler. See Wexberg, *The Psychology of Sex* (1931), and Maslow, *Self-Esteem (Dominance-Feeling) and Sexuality in Women* (1942).

[24] The display of affection in public is increasing among youths who have been outside to attend boarding school and is also evidenced by Tahltan young men and women.

ever, they kept their voices low and maintained a cautious watch to prevent interruption. While alcohol still further reduces a man's sexual inhibitions, there is evidence to believe that this process takes much longer in the girl. The belief that girls will readily succumb to sexual advances when intoxicated could not be verified. Unless people are intoxicated, little direct attention is paid to sex. Obscenity is limited, and mainly expressed in gestures. Discussion of sexual processes tends to be avoided.

Three types of sexual stimulation may be noted and usually follow in sequence. These are communication by means of conventional signs, teasing and rough-housing, and, finally, a direct sexual approach involving the genitals. All of these types of approach are distinguished by the fact that they do not rely on words; as we shall show, the whole sexual episode can easily be executed without speech.

The principal conventional signs serving to manifest sexual interest are winking and hand pressing. The latter is a common means for boys (and sometimes girls) to express sexual attention toward a dancing partner. Agreement to the invitation implied in the gesture is indicated if the partner returns the pressure. In many women the sign (although it may be returned) provokes a storm of real or affected embarrassment. Pinching the face and thighs are other gestures used to manifest sexual interest.

Among young unmarried people, teasing and rough-housing are the commonest ways of sexual stimulation, serving as a means of overcoming the difficulties related to a verbal sexual approach. Obviously a direct solicitation to coitus would not succeed in the society since, under such circumstances, most unmarried girls would immediately run away in embarrassment or fail to respond. Furthermore direct sexual solicitation would be embarrassing to the boy. Teasing and rough-housing are usually limited to nighttime, when boys encounter girls in Lower Post or around a house where a dance is in progress. Often girls initiate these actions. It is interesting to note the inception of the behavior in fourteen or fifteen year old girls, who throw bits of orange peel at young men in the safety of daylight and run off laughing as the boys threaten to catch them. Such provocation is, of course, not yet clearly sexual. At night couples often slap at each other with willow branches, push one another, or girls try to snatch boys' hats. All such actions soon lead to the girl's running off with the boy in pursuit. When the boy has caught her, usually with the girl's consent, the couple will wrestle until one or the other is thrown down. In this wrestling the boy manifests the first direct sexual approach to the girl.

As we have indicated, the third form of sexual stimulation, a direct sexual approach involving the genitals, follows a period of teasing and rough-housing and comes when the young people have moved far enough away from other people to be safe from observation. It is usually reserved until the boy has caught his partner in a dark, secluded place, preferably in thick bush. Sometimes it occurs in any social situation when intoxicated boys (more rarely a bold, intoxicated girl) initiate such behavior regardless of observers. Boys normally experience some hesitation in advancing to this form of stimulation, unless they feel sure that the girl will not resist too strongly. Should several boys operate in a group much less consideration of the girl's possible resistance obtains. Generally, some indication of the girl's willingness has already appeared in her teasing or, more importantly, is indicated when she allows herself to be caught. Direct stimulation usually involves a boy touching a girl's genitals through her clothes or pressing the front of his body against hers, forcing her to remain against him. Sometimes a bold, intoxicated girl will cling against a boy's body, without, however, touching his penis. If sexual intercourse does not immediately follow, the boy may subsequently find many opportunities to caress the girl's body. For the most part such caresses are directed toward the hips and genitals. An interesting exception to the rule that breasts are not used as sexual zones comes from two young men, who had been outside to school, and in sexual situations grasped girls' breasts.

Intercourse is always carried out in privacy, usually at night, and is accompanied with little or no verbalization. A period of foreplay, in which the young man handles the girl's vulva and clitoris and presses his body and face close to the partner's, proceeds the act of coitus. During the foreplay the boy helps the girl remove her slacks and bloomers, but usually these garments are not entirely removed, the girl simply withdrawing one leg. The girl avoids the sight of her partner's nudity and carefully conceals her own sexual parts with her slip, dress, or blanket. Rarely will a girl assist in intromission. During coitus, in which the common ventroventral position is occupied, there may be some kissing. The coital rhythm of the male is described as slow and oscillating or wavelike, rather than sharp or jerky, with just a bare increase of tempo as ejaculation approaches. It would appear that not all girls attain the orgasm. The man's orgasm is relatively quickly attained and there is evidence that he is not concerned with waiting for his partner's climax. Following the orgasm there may be a brief period of relaxation in which additional kissing and close embracing occurs. In this post-coital relationship the girl is described as soothing and comforting.

Sexual intercourse is behavior which requires considerable patience and time. Both partners, after having signified their interest in the act, must wait until all strangers have retired or until older people are asleep. A boy's patience is also tested when there are rivals for a girl's favor at hand. Premarital sexual relationships do not ordinarily include an unmarried girl spending the night with her lover. While there is no evidence for assuming any shame or sadness immediately following coitus, the following day sees an embarrassed avoidance of unmarried sexual partners.

Up to this point we have described the pattern of sexual stimulation and intercourse for unmarried couples in summer. Variations occur in winter when the group is smaller and outdoor interaction difficult. In that season, sexual relations between unmarried people are often limited to occasions of visits. Then a boy will come to a girl's bed in the cabin after her parents are asleep. The older folks, if awakened, are said not to notice such behavior. Between husband and wife, as between an unmarried couple who have had sufficient opportunity to become sexually familiar, the period of sexual stimulation is limited to a more direct sexual approach which does not, however, always ignore foreplay, some wives being reported to arouse their husbands manually. Boys in general appear to be eager to secure new sexual partners and only as a last resort accept a willing partner who is apt to be one of the community's more promiscuous girls.

Attitudes toward sexual intercourse describe the situation as "dandy." Nevertheless there is some ideal uneasiness regarding too excessive indulgence as well as premature indulgence. Eighteen is commonly given as the age when sexual relations can safely be begun. Most girls begin when they are fifteen or younger, and boys when they approach seventeen. Situations prohibiting intercourse are not consistently recognized. A number of youths say that they would not have intercourse with a girl who is menstruating; they will, however, permit a girl in this condition to masturbate them. Other boys deny such inhibitions or else utilize a condom with a menstruant. Men are generally reluctant to have intercourse with a girl who is feared to be venereally diseased, but will do so if condoms are available. "French safes," as condoms are locally designated, were largely secured from soldiers and construction workers during Highway construction but are now sold by one of the independent traders who secures them through truck drivers hauling from Dawson Creek. Coitus is not avoided before a hunting trip; in fact a man who expects to be away hunting for some time may make a point of securing intercourse before leaving.

When intoxicated, most of the younger men are keenly interested in describing their sexual prowess. They recount such feats as attaining several orgasms or copulating with three and four different girls in a single night. Sexual capacity is also spoken of as the ability to "wear out" a girl. One story is told of three boys who exhausted a girl by having intercourse with her twice each. Boys will reveal the names of their sexual partners only to close friends, and even this is rare unless a youth is intoxicated. From observation it is apparent that much of this conversation tends to exaggerate the frequency of coitus. It is probable that in summer an unmarried man has intercourse about once in seven or ten days. Since there are fewer unmarried girls available for this purpose, the frequency of coitus is considerably greater for this sex, averaging perhaps three or four times a week in summer for promiscuous young women. Along with the high value invested in sexual capacity, goes a concern for the size of the penis, a large organ being regarded as desirable and commendable.

That the male's interest in sexual capacity and genital size may point to a fear of impotence is indicated by material collected from and about one thirty-two year old man. He was reported to suffer from acute impotence on two occasions. In an interview with the ethnographer, he once denied that virility declines with age, affirming that some old men are "stronger for girls" than young men. In a dream reported before specific reports of his incapacity had been obtained, he told of being in the company of his brother when he was attacked by a grizzly bear. "My gun stick. I get nervous. I try to take shot at him, My gun got no power. Goes ʃʃʃʃʃ—goes out quick . . . I take all shells and put new shells in. He run around. He don't bite me. I get mad at grizzly bear. I holler at him: 'You better get away or I hit you with that gun.' " The informant tended to deny the interpretation equating the gun with the penis and the dream's situation with sexual incapacity. The rejection was inconclusive, however, the man saying that to kill a dangerous animal in a dream was a promise of effectively combating illness. "You kill him, that's lucky. You're safe . . . you're not going to die. Gun is great thing when you're dreaming."

Acute impotence under the influence of alcohol was denied by several informants, who reported an aphrodisiacal effect from liquor and brew.

Ideally, premarital sexual intercourse is disapproved of, particularly for girls. Parents, when they venture to speak of the matter, warn girls to avoid sexual relations before marriage, citing the dangers of illegitimacy and venereal infection. Such behavior may also be criticized, scolded, or otherwise punished. One girl, thirteen, who was showing a tendency toward promiscuity, was reported to have been beaten "just like dog" by her mother, who herself has a widespread reputation for past promiscuity. Parents, however, are often willing to condone some premarital sexual experience in older daughters if it avoids promiscuity and leads to marriage. There are few if any unmarried girls above seventeen who can be regarded as virgins or who conduct themselves in such a way as to discourage sexual advances.

Several factors are responsible for this hiatus between ideal and manifest. The first is the delayed age of marriage in the contemporary society. In the past, when the ideals of premarital morality were originally formulated, marriage for girls occurred within a year or two after menarche; now it is often postponed until eighteen or nineteen years of age. Secondly, the post-pubescent girl is often given considerable autonomy and independence, parents relaxing supervision in the face of the girl's demand for such freedom. In the past this relaxation of control would have been correlated with the young woman's adult status and channelized in marriage. If supervision is maintained into late adolescence it is resented by the girl; sexual promiscuity may then be a means of expressing revolt and independence. Finally, most of the parents of adolescents were themselves raised under social conditions similar to those obtaining today, and a great number have borne children out of wedlock. These facts are known to girls, and probably help to undermine parental sanctions.

Despite the fact that premarital promiscuity is disapproved of, girls who manifest such behavior are not ostracized or avoided by other members of the society. In 1944, when a number of girls were almost nightly accepting truck rides with soldiers, one or two older men sought to remonstrate with some of these young women. The girls resented this interference, one telling Old Man that her activities were none of his business. Another girl, June Barre, accused him of having done the same things in his youth. River Joe often criticized his brother's daughter, Irene Wiley, for her promiscuity, and unsuccessfully advised her to marry. To the ethnographer Joe complained of this girl who, refusing marriage, nevertheless would not live alone. "Maybe she look for husband, but don't think so," he said. "Anyway, none of my business." Despite his criticism of Irene's behavior, River Joe never refused to feed or shelter the girl and often expressed concern about her poor appetite.

Two types of extramarital sexual relations may be distinguished in Kaska society, adultery and permissive sexual relations. Unfaithfulness in marriage is probably more common among men than women, since married women only rarely have an opportunity of meeting lovers under suitable conditions of privacy. Adultery is condemned when it occurs in either spouse and frequently leads to quarrels. It is also reported to be not uncommon for a man to beat an adulterous wife, although aggression between a husband and wife's lover is rare and apparently avoided. A woman who sleeps with a married man fears the jealousy and hate of the wife and dreads provoking the latter to physical violence. In general unmarried girls tend to avoid the sexual overtures of married men. Children born from a wife's adulterous relationship are frequently rejected by the husband.[25]

Permissive extramarital sexual relations are unformalized and any evidence of such behavior is carefully guarded, particularly from white people. Wife exchange is sometimes reciprocally arranged between two married men who are good friends or partners. In such

[25] See below, p. 177.

cases the wife is informed of the husband's decision. According to Nitla: "She can't say no. I'm her boss." He added: "No matter if friends, and you give her kids. So long you not sick." However questionable such ideal control of the husband may be, the fact is that a wife will often be fully willing to act as a partner in such an arrangement, because she herself desires the husband's friend and finds any other means of gratifying her desire difficult. She may even add her insistence for such an exchange to her husband's, in the event that the other partner remains aloof from the proposal. A rare variant of this pattern is for an unmarried man to supply his married friend with an unmarried girl in exchange for sexual access to the latter's wife. Frequently extramarital sexual exchanges are arranged under condition of intoxication. Wife lending also occurs to oblige a man who is away from his wife.

Evidence of the direct sale of sexual favors was noted in only one young woman during the period when American troops and construction workers were crowding Lower Post. Although other promiscuous girls undoubtedly received money and gifts of cigarettes, candy, and lighters from soldiers, the motive behind their behavior does not appear to have been primarily pecuniary. Most girls were willing to exchange sexual access for truck rides and the stimulation of erotic situations. Local white trappers also make efforts to secure Indian girls as temporary sexual partners and in return generally give them money. Since no girl relies to any extent on such financial remuneration, a pattern of prostitution may be questioned and other motives inferred. Such motives include a desire for sexual interaction and a reluctance to offend persistent white men.

Incest is regarded with abhorrence and there is a tendency to classify as incestuous any sexual relationship between relatives (other than the paternal male and maternal female cross-cousins) closer than third cousins and between members of the same moiety. Not only would discovery of an incestuous relationship arouse strong public opinion, but such behavior is thought to lead to insanity in the guilty couple and deformity in the offspring.

The only forms of atypical sexual relations known to occur in Kaska society are rape and manifest homosexuality. Since premarital sexual intercourse is often carried out in a manner suggesting rape, particular attention was paid to the definition of this form of behavior. Informants agreed that pursuing a girl in order to win sexual access to her is not necessarily rape. They pointed out that rape can occur only when a girl unmistakably resents a man's attention and fights him for her freedom. One is still left unclear as to how much struggle is required to demarcate the typical from the atypical. Field notes contain several incidents in which from two to six youths were observed dragging girls into bushes or vacant houses. On one occasion June Barre, the youngest promiscuous girl in the community, requested the company of the ethnographer's wife en route to a dance. She was asked if she ran from boys in order to tease them or because she was afraid, and replied that she ran because she was frightened. Yet the ethnographer's wife once interrupted a situation in which three older youths were struggling with June. The boys ran off but the girl, instead of retaining her safety, quickly went into the night alone. Obviously the ambivalence which girls seem to manifest in sexual situations makes it difficult to recognize rape. The fact that girls traveling at night are often accompanied by partners helps somewhat in making a distinction. When such girls accede to sexual demands expressed through teasing and pursuit, they separate willingly. Any reluctance to separate or any assistance furnished by a girl's partner indicate unwillingness or at least unreadiness for intercourse.

Homosexuality can be divided into two types, overt homosexuality and behavior which seems indicative of repressed or inhibited homosexual tendencies. The former behavior, although socially condemned, nevertheless occurs secretly, generally in the form of mutual masturbation. Informants reported overt homosexuality to occur in both sexes following puberty and to be largely a consequence of sexual frustration. "No girl, can't catch," Nitla explained, "he stuck for girl, some man do that. Girl, can't catch a man, do that, bother girl." Apart from social disapproval if discovered, the behavior is not associated with any specific sanctions.

Overt homosexual tendencies are often publicly demonstrated between intoxicated men. Several such instances were observed. When Richard Day, Edward Prince, and the latter's wife were drinking in the ethnographer's tent, Richard, after gesturing toward Edward's penis, began to simulate masturbation of the latter. This was really frottage, as Edward was fully clothed and the hand did not rest directly on the genitals but in their vicinity. On another occasion Old Man was drinking and, turning to Richard Day, spoke of how he had teased and wrestled with the latter when Richard was a small boy. He began to speak of men "fooling" with boys the way they "fool" with women. He gestured playfully toward Richard's genitals and referred to the youth's "little worm." At a later party Old Man told his son-in-law, Harry Lang, to give Donald Suza a cup of brew. Harry put his arms around the boy and drew the latter to his knee. He called Donald, "My little sweetheart." Donald bore this patiently but Old Man cried: "Shame, mustn't do that."

Behavior suggesting hidden homosexual impulses is revealed by unmarried adolescents of both sexes. It is chiefly manifested in embracing, wrestling, and by a youth playfully coming up behind another young man and pressing his body close to the latter. Sometimes a swift coital-like rhythm is manifested in these embraces. On one occasion Flower Joe was observed playfully simulating the strumming of a guitar on her cousin's, Irene Wiley's, breast. Irene showed no reaction.

No particular value is associated with male continence. Carefully regulated sexual be-havior (that is, the avoidance of excess) may aid a man to live long and bring "good luck," but some sexual experience is nevertheless regarded as desirable. Continence may actually be as dangerous as excessive sexuality if it leads to "worry about girl." In such cases a man may "Lose his brains, go crazy." Therefore the advice is: "Better get married."

The idea of a woman remaining a lifelong virgin was regarded as amusing. The informant rejected this notion as an impossibility and stated that if a woman of thirty, who had never been sexually initiated, were to see a man, "She grab him. She sleep right there. More worse than dog." However the informant thought it very unlikely that young men would ever permit a woman to get that far into life without some sexual experience.

RECREATION

No one who has learned to know the Kaska people can doubt their great love for recrea-tion or "fun." Necessarily reduced to a minimum during the family's isolation in winter, recreational patterns flourish during the summer in Lower Post. The formal amusements are: drinking parties; participation in festivals, particularly the potlatch; music; dancing, and gambling. The less important informal recreational patterns, which we will discuss first, include: idling, conversation, humor, and visiting.)

Informal. Idling is a feature not only of the summer period in Lower Post, when families may be seen gathered in the shade of the mission buildings or the traders' stores, but is also the pattern of the long winter evenings after the family has finished supper. Rarely are individuals seen loafing alone, the tendency always being for a man to seek company when he has free time available. People from more than a single family, when loafing in a group, tend to separate according to age and sex; the women and children gathering by themselves, the men lolling a short distance away. In such groups people often sit with their backs to each other with no thought of discourtesy. Generally the space separating individuals is not great; children cluster near the mother and the women, as well as men, sit in close proximity. In the evening idling in the center of town is often enlivened by the rough-housing and wrestling of boys and unmarried young men and girls. In winter it is sometimes accompanied by making figures out of a folded handkerchief or pulling string figures.

A special form of idling occurs when the community gathers on the river bank in Lower Post to watch the arrival of the boat from Dease Lake with freight and passengers from Telegraph Creek and Wrangell, Alaska. The boat is often heard when it is still out of sight, around the tongue of land dividing the Liard and Dease Rivers. News of its approach circulates quickly and soon the bank is lined with people watching the slow approach of the vessel as it ascends the river (Plate 11, c). The crowd is quiet but eager, these occasions marking one of the high spots of the summer stay in the post. However, the introduction of the Alaska Highway has probably deprived the event of much of its old time emotional appeal. Now families often idle in front of the restaurant facing the Highway, where the arrival and departure of trucks may be silently studied. It was in this setting that the ethnographer was reintroduced to his Indian friends upon his return to Lower Post in June 1945.

In the family as well as in other groups there is a relatively low value on conversation. While in American society interpersonal situations are mainly sustained by conversation, and any sign of its lagging is often a signal for the group to disperse, in the Indian community verbalized social interaction is of only incidental significance. A group is organized on the basis of the presence of its members. Thus Kaska social life is not characterized by loquacity. Even during visiting, conversation is intermittent, commonplace, and slight. Gossip, as already pointed out, is never expressed in large groups but is confined to conversations that include no more than two or three well acquainted individuals.

Kaska humor is neither richly developed nor subtle in its construction. The society boasts no *raconteurs* noted for their ability to tell a series of funny stories nor is there a large stock of jokes. Nevertheless, the people are always ready to laugh and a person like Old Man, who does not confine "talking fun" to drinking situations, enjoys considerable popularity.

Several functions of humor may be noted. A joke is often used to make light of a difficult situation, either one facing the humorist or a person present in his audience. Several examples may be given. When Nitla's wife sought to leave her husband in preference for the latter's brother, Nitla continued to live with the couple. The situation provoked Old Man to tease the boy saying that the latter was "keeping it like old times" by sharing his wife with a brother. This brought out laughter. Another example was manifested when Peter Tom and Richard Day returned from several hours of fishing with only a two inch sucker. Richard said: "We caught a whale," and held up the insignificant prize. One evening Taku Indian visitors from Teslin Lake arrived in the post. Old Man promoted laughter when he said: "You come a long way. When you're up to fifty you won't do that." The reference was to himself and his own weakening capacities.

Humor may also function as a social sanction or as a means of expressing displeasure. For this purpose a joke is sometimes employed by an old man desiring to censure youth. Old Kean one day exclaimed: "In old days used to be sing. Young boys sing—like bull moose. This time young boys just run around like hell; run around all night!" The same sanctioning quality in humor may be noted in the designation of the pilfering whiskey-jack (or Canada jay) as "Hudson Bay bird." On another occasion the provincial policeman had come upon a number of intoxicated men. After the official had retired Old Man promised that soon he would prepare a big brew. Before people drank it, however, he would post a big sign at the entrance to the western Indian Reserve warning the police to keep out under penalty of provoking trouble.

A final function of humor is its use to blunt the sting of an emotional situation in which the individual feels discomfited or embarrassed. In such situations the discomfort may be so great as to interfere with the quick juxtaposition of two incompatible ideas—the principle on which Kaska jokes rest. The missionary one day asked Old Man why he didn't go to church. Old Man replied: "If I go to church I don't get any younger!"

It will be noted that all of these functional types of humor contain what may be called an element of incongruity, only the content of the joke being selected for the function. The juxtaposition of two incongruous ideas, or the appreciation of an incongrous situation, are the sources of most Kaska humor. Incongruity provokes laughter in the appearance of a boy with close cropped hair, and in the designation of a small child as "grandmother." Incongruity is the spring for the age jokes which are so easy and popular. An example of the latter comes from Nick Lang talking to an elderly man. Nick pointed to himself as an old man while his companion was described as a youth. Incongruity determined Old Kean's laughter, when the ethnographer read him the low prices for staples advertised in an Edmonton newspaper. It is also the root of the popular Athapaskan joke in which a man teases a boastful hunter saying that the latter could only kill a porcupine, one of the easiest animals to capture. One day Eva Ardo told Old Man that he spoke too slowly. The latter promptly replied: "I'm no machine!" and aroused a storm of laughter. Seeing a young man carrying a newly purchased packboard Old Man stopped and said: "What you packing? You're not a horse. What for you got saddle?" This was regarded as quite funny. Another incongruous picture is presented by adolescent girls parading with young men's broad brimmed Stetsons. The mechanism also determines the laughter which Indians are quick to direct against the mispronounciation of their language by a white man. Non-sexual exhibitionism, which provokes laughter, may also be interpreted in the light of incongruity. Old men are fond of approaching a group and shouting convenient nonsense in a loud voice. This always provokes a laugh. Similar behavior appears in the incident of Nitla picking up a slim volume containing a gospel. He solemnly crossed himself and spoke the Sign of the Cross in Kaska. His friends laughed riotously.

Customarily visits are never exchanged across sexual lines, but rather between members of the same sex. The only exception to this rule is the fact that an elderly man will sometimes visit a camp in which a mature woman lives alone. Men and women exchange visits through-out the day, but in Lower Post there was noted a tendency for a few women (including Mildred Lang and Marie Nolan) to limit their visits to after supper.

Like most sociability, pleasure in visiting comes from social proximity rather than from conversation. Although individual loquacity varies, in general people tend to say little during a visit (to the discomfort of white hosts!), the situation often resembling a roomful of disparate individuals. This constraint is lacking when members of a family visit together but grows more pronounced when comparative strangers from outside the tribal district pay a call.

Hospitality is not expected as the necessary response of a host toward a visitor. In fall or winter, when visitors have come to the winter settlement from a long distance, tea is generally asked for or poured by the guest from the host's everready supply. If a traveler has brought no grub, he may be invited to eat (he is always free to help himself should there be meat in the host's camp), or he may, without shame, ask for food. A family coming to visit for sometime does not depend on such hospitality but brings its own grub, meat, and blankets. Before this food supply has been exhausted the guests will probably be gone.

Visitors enter a house or tent without signaling although Indians usually rap before entering a white man's cabin or speak upon approaching his tent. Formalities do not always mark the end of a visit. While some men have adopted the white pattern of calling a farewell, most people ignore this nicety and silently take their departure. A certain etiquette marks a visit which is directed toward making a request or borrowing something. Upon entering the house, the visitor stands quietly for a few minutes, perhaps paying attention to the host's children. Then the business matter of the visit is stated and when it is settled, de-parture is in order. If the call is made in order to return a borrowed object, like a plate, the guest always remains for several minutes after the transaction has been completed.

Formal. Beer or wine is generally made, or liquor purchased, with the intention of shar-ing it with close friends at a drinking party. A man is always host at such parties, which may be held in a tent or cabin or, for safety from the police, in the brush a short distance away from Lower Post. Guests are usually limited to members of the host's tribe, who have been selected by factors of reciprocity and congeniality. Occasionally a white man joins an Indian beer drink. Solitary drinking is unknown, if beer, wine, or liquor is available in quantities of a quart or more.

Everyone drinks from the same cup. The host dips the cup into the liquid (which is never strained) and hands a helping to each guest. In the case of bottled liquor, the bottle is passed around the company starting with the host. Sometimes an after-shave preparation or hair tonic is mixed with beef-iron stomach tonic and a few ounces served to each visitor in a cup. With few exceptions an Indian drinker, man or woman, drains his cup without once removing it from his mouth. The style of slow drinking (that is, sipping interspersed with conversation) is referred to as "white man's drinking" and, although encouraged by a few older men, meets with little response. After everybody has had a helping there may be a brief pause before the next round is begun. Servings increase in frequency and the pauses shorten as the degree of intoxication progresses. In the space between rounds, both sexes smoke many cigarettes and indulge in conversation, the nature of which quickly becomes unrestrained. Men generally outnumber women at drinking parties, although in the winter settlement the whole family drinks, even five year old children being permitted beer and wine. In general the Indian quickly shows the effects of alcohol.

Nobody is ever severely criticized for being drunk nor are there severe guilt feelings on the following day, unless under intoxication behavior occurred which the individual has cause to regret. Drunken behavior includes recklessness, quarreling, physical aggression, singing, joking, depression, and expressions of heightened sexuality. Sometimes a form of behavior occurs in which violent aggression is coupled with complete breakdown of cerebral control. We will return to this behavior later, and here discuss the more common manifestations of intoxication.

Recklessness during intoxication is illustrated by the incident of a number of boys, ranging from seventeen to twenty-one, stealing a white man's car. They blew a tire, burnt out the battery, and finally ran the vehicle into a ditch where it was abandoned. People recognize that in the extreme cold of winter, recklessness may be fatal to an intoxicated person. An older man, however, generally remains aware of this danger. Thus one Christmas Old Man saw the necessity for keeping sober while everybody was drinking. It was very cold and he feared that if everyone became intoxicated the fire would go out and the people, particularly the children, freeze while they slept without blankets. He also warned Louis Maza, upon the latter's arrival, not to get drunk before tying the dogs and putting down brush for the animals' comfort.

Quarreling frequently occurs in the course of drinking parties but only one instance of murder under such conditions could be recalled for a period of about fifty years. Hostility rising to the surface during intoxication is quickly forgotten once the individual recovers. Sometimes there is a tendency to play down and forget all the unpleasant elements that occurred in the course of drinking and refer solely to the "fun" that was had.

While the Kaska tend to avoid sexual allusions in conversation when sober, especially in the presence of women, in drunkenness such references are readily forthcoming and the strongest obscenities or the most suggestive jokes freely uttered. Drinking is also accompanied by weakening control of direct sexual behavior and young men are often eager in soliciting coitus verbally. The sexually stimulating effect of alcohol is recognized by the Indians; although men condone this effect in themselves, they believe it wrong for girls and women to drink. Intoxicated women get "too crazy," they say.

Drinkers are reluctant to end their intoxication and when one batch of beer or wine has been exhausted eagerly inquire into the whereabouts of another. Usually this search fails and men end up producing money for bootleg whiskey or extracts and hair tonics. Only rarely does a woman like Mrs. Man put aside a few bottles of the beverage for use in recuperating from the effects of hangover. Mrs. Man's tendency is known, however, and men, after finishing a batch of brew quickly beg her permission to tap the hidden cache.

Potlatch. Apart from Christmas parties tendered to children by the missionaries, the most important festival is the potlatch. This occasion is ideally a presentation of food by the members of one matrilineal moiety to those of the other and is designed to honor the memory of one or more deceased members of the hosts' side. The "Wolf party" observed in 1945, however, included guests belonging to both moieties and was organized and financed by a Crow man and his Wolf daughters. A few days after the Wolf party, Louis Maza apologized, explaining that he was "a little crazy" the day of the potlatch when he had let both moieties eat. He blamed his confusion on having been intoxicated the morning of the festival. His apology indicated that people had commented on the mixing, regarding it as incorrect. Louis stated that the subsequent Crow party would not be mixed. His promise was partly fulfilled, in that eating was limited to adult guests of the Wolf side, but children belonging to both moieties were served. Prior to 1945, the last potlatch in the Kaska area is reported to have taken place at McDame Creek around 1930.

Ideally a potlatch is organized by a deceased person's brothers or maternal uncles. Manifestly, however, fathers, daughters, and husbands were observed to organize these parties. The male organizers undertake the task of securing the food to be eaten, while sisters and female parallel cousins cooperate in the cooking and serving. The Wolf party, which was designed to honor the memory of Mrs. River Joe who had died nine months previously, was directed by River Joe and his son-in-law, Louis Maza (both Crow), while the food preparation was under the control of Joe's several Wolf daughters and their parallel cousins. This potlatch, like the following Crow party, was celebrated in Louis Maza's large home. Financial support was contributed by a majority of the members of the Wolf side, about $120 being collected. The functions of the party, as stated by River Joe, were to "help" the deceased, to have "fun," and to "Make good time for [in memory of] my missus." A chronological record of events marking the first potlatch of 1945 is given below.

6:11:45. In the presence of River Joe, Old Man explained that there might be a potlatch in memory of River Joe's wife who died last October. He explained that Skipper or the latter's brother could "make" such a potlatch, because they belonged to the dead woman's side.

7:1:45. River Joe went to Teslin Lake in order to fetch his daughter and the latter's Taku Indian husband.

7:5:45. River Joe returned from Teslin Lake in his son-in-law's truck. He was fired with the idea of giving a "potlatch party" for his wife but quite resented the notion that this would be an old fashioned procedure, pointing out that at Teslin village the Indians all observed this custom.

7:6:45. River Joe and his sons-in-law, Louis Maza and the Taku youth, went to the Hudson's Bay Company with the latter's truck. Here they bought a large quantity of food and piled it in the back of the vehicle which then proceeded to Louis' home where the cooking would be done. River Joe announced he would collect money from the members of his wife's side who were camping across the river.

7:7:45. Today River Joe's daughters cooked and baked for the Wolf party tomorrow. River Joe said that his daughters were giving the potlatch for their mother, but that he had also contributed fifteen dollars to the expenses. "Me boss that party. Bye and bye somebody lose his missus. He boss for him." He agreed that the decision for a potlatch was (could be?) in the hands of the widower. Louis Maza indicated that the potlatch might last for six days and refused to consider the possibility of the police blocking it as a result of the meningites quarantine attached to the reserve where his house is located.

7:8:45. The final preparations for the potlatch were delayed five or six hours, because Louis Maza had been extremely drunk last night and was still sleeping early in the afternoon.

6:00 P.M. River Joe's daughters set the potlatch tables on the floor of Louis' cabin.

6:30 P.M. River Joe went to the missionary to borrow a large pot for brewing coffee.

6:45 P.M. Louis Maza took his boat across the river to bring back potlatch guests. People started to walk up the river road from town to Louis' house.

7:00 P.M. Louis and Joe held a conférence at which Louis suggested that both Crow and Wolf people eat. River Joe said: "All right, I guess."

7:30 P.M. River Joe suggested (for the ethnographer's benefit?) that somebody pay Dorothy Plover's grandmother to start the potlatch dance and teach it to others. The woman apologized and said that she did not know the dance too well.

7:40 P.M. Louis explained that the potlatch could not start until those people who had gone to church for the evening service were dismissed by the missionary.

8:00 P.M. Louis went to the guests who had come for the party and requested their dishes and eating utensils. He took these into the house and helped his sisters-in-law to arrange them around the tables. When the dishes were in place Louis began to point to people, telling them "Go in, eat." Men began to file in. The old men without wives sat themselves against the west wall of the room. The soup was brought to them, but they waited before eating until all others who were to eat at the first sitting were in their places. After the soup, the dishes were rinsed and filled with two varieties of canned meat and fish (sausages, a slice of bacon, and salmon), mashed potatoes, and peas. Tea was also served. All the food was put on the plates by River Joe's Taku son-in-law and brought to the guests by Joe's daughters and paternal niece.

8:10 P.M. The cassocked priest drove his truck up to the door of the potlatch house and called in to ask if Richard Day and Peter Tom wanted to ride to Watson Lake with him (the two youths were employed there to cut wood). The boys did not reply and avoided meeting the gaze of the priest. When the missionary left with his exhaust exploding loudly, Louis Maza said: "That's not the only job in the world." "To hell with him," River Joe added. Although the two hosts did not mention it, they seemed annoyed with the priest's unceremonious behavior.

About twenty-two adults and children ate at the first sitting. After finishing the meal the guests helped themselves to the cakes, cookies, jam, pies, and doughnuts which were set in the middle of each table. Sugar, butter, and canned milk were also provided. During the eating, Louis Maza sat on the bed with his wife, who was recovering from a complicated parturition. Children entered and left at will, coming to parents when they wanted some delicacy and then running out again. A number of children hung around the door looking. Most people, when they had finished eating, turned their cups down on the plates and filed out of the building without a word. A few men patted their stomachs and remarked what a good meal they had eaten. As one man left the house he shook hands with River Joe whereupon the latter said: "Tomorrow come again." While people were leaving, River Joe repeated the announcement that fruit was available in boxes piled along one wall; nobody heeded his suggestion. The dirty dishes were removed and rinsed by the servers, assisted by Joe's Taku son-in-law.

9:00 P.M. The second sitting began to enter the potlatch house. As Dorothy Plover's grandmother entered she did a little dance, shifting from one foot to the other, one hand with the index finger erect raised from the elbow. This provoked a ripple of amusement.

9:30 P.M. A few people entered the building for the final serving. Wolf women from the Dease River tribe took over the task of serving and dishwashing, giving River Joe's daughters and niece a chance to leave the house.

In contrast to the enthusiasm invested in the preparations for the party, there was very little emotional display at the meal itself, and several signs were observed of people being ill at ease. Thus it was necessary for Louis Maza repeatedly to urge people to go into the house and eat. Except among some old men, there was little sign of gaiety or festivity. As each man filed into the building he removed his hat and silently took his place. Conversation during the meal was slight.

Plans to revive the old fashioned potlatch dance were not fulfilled. A number of older people were finally persuaded to line up and execute a few movements, but this behavior was not spontaneous and the embarrassed laughter of the younger folks apparently disconcerted the dancers.

After having eaten, the guests gathered outside the house where two fires were built against the chill of the evening. Five gallons of coffee were heating alongside one fire. Louis Maza several times distributed cigars and cigarettes around the two circles of guests as well as oranges to the children, who were enjoying a riotous time. After the dishes had been washed by the women of the Wolf sib, the guests reentered the house to retrieve their cups, plates, and tableware. Considerable confusion resulted in this distribution and many people were unable to find their own objects. Even Louis Maza lost several of his own utensils, all of which suggests that some people, who had not come with tableware, went home with utensils not belonging to them.

On the day following the potlatch meal, a number of Crow people returned to Louis' house where his wife and her sisters distributed packages of food, tins of jam that had never been touched, fruit, and cake left over from the party.

The second potlatch on July 13 was designed as a return party by the Crow moiety. Louis placed himself in charge of the preparations and was assisted by his father-in-law. The cooking and serving were undertaken by Dorothy Plover, her cousin, and the ethnographer, who was conventionally designated as a Crow. The food was cooked in the residence of a white trader and transported to the potlatch in Louis Maza's boat. In Louis' house it was kept warm on the stove. The potlatch this time began at one o'clock in the afternoon and was completed by six o'clock. Behavior held to the same emotional tenor that was described for the first party except that considerable amusement was furnished by the several white trappers who attended while intoxicated but who caused no trouble. No attempt was made to introduce dancing, although a social dance in Liard Tom's house was announced as a part of the festival and took place later in the evening.

Music. The only musical instruments played by the Kaska are the violin and guitar. Many men are accomplished "fiddlers," while most boys and girls can play accompaniments on the guitar. All musical ability is patiently self-taught and is motivated by the individual's personal desire to learn. A new tune is generally picked up by listening to a Tahltan Indian visitor play it. The Tahltan, in turn, learn new melodies by listening to the recorded words and music. Such double, and sometimes triple, transmission by ear results in a melody often being considerably altered from its original form. The most popular tunes include: "I Know What It Means to be Lonely," "Take Me Back to Tulsa," "My Dixie Darling," "Wabash Cannonball," "Red River Valley," and "You Are My Sunshine." These are not only played at dances but are often sung or whistled around town and camp. Local Tahltan youths have improvised words to "Wabash Cannonball" which contain the refrain "Yukon cannonball." The prevailing theme of most of these songs is nostalgia, expressed as a longing for a loved and remembered place or an idealized woman. When played by the Indians, all of these melodies are transposed to a minor key, which further accentuates the nostalgic quality of the words and music. An undercurrent of gaiety and vivaciousness is introduced by the four-fourths time in which the tune is rendered. A number of people also own portable phonographs (locally called "gramophones") on which a variety of music, ranging from reels to ballet, is played.

Young men sometimes improvise short songs around commonplace activities. These are also sung in a minor key. Thus Nitla, while preparing to go hunting, sang of how he was going to get a moose. Song composition becomes freer when young men are intoxicated. Drunk in Old Man's camp one night, Peter Tom strummed his guitar and improvised a song around an incident that had occurred earlier that day. The words went:

> I spit blood this morning
> I don't want to die.
> Ole-o-lady o . . . [yodling].

Dancing. One of the most popular recreational features are the dances marking summer evenings in Lower Post. Early in the summer, with many young people in town, such dances are held almost nightly. They are attended principally by young people, married or single, and by one or two white men. When the American soldiers were in the Kaska area a number showed up at these dances until the Army declared Lower Post out of bounds. The music is furnished by a violinist and one or two guitarists. Dances begin around midnight, when it is starting to get dark, and may continue to three or four o'clock in the morning. Later in the summer, as the nights get longer, dances start earlier. When a group of people want to dance they first ask the recognized musicians to play. The players receive no remuneration for their entertainment, although soldiers and white men sometimes collect a purse for them. The next task is to find a place to dance. River Joe's home, an unfinished trading store, and a deserted bunkhouse belonging to one of the trading companies were all well regarded as dance houses in 1944–45. Most of the time such accommodations are made available without charge; several times, however, River Joe sought to collect money from visitors attending dances in his house. He defended his behavior by speaking of the public dance hall at Teslin Lake to which admission is charged. Few people paid the requested fifty cents.

After a dance has been announced people congregate outside the building, while the players take their places at the back of the house near a lamp or candle. Several tunes go undanced before sufficient dancers venture inside the house or before people feel relaxed enough to go on the floor. Boys who have been drinking get the dancing underway more quickly, the availability of liquor, beer, or wine always making a more spontaneous and lively party. Within the dance house, the sexes line up along opposite walls of the building. When a man wishes to select a partner, he crosses the room and stops before the girl of his choice. She rises and, looking away from her partner, begins to dance with him. A girl continues to avert her face throughout the dance. The man holds his partner lightly and rarely is there any conversation between the couple. When the music has stopped, the girl turns swiftly and returns to her place while the man joins his friends across the room or else stands outside the building until the next number is begun. Sometimes women too go outside. Men frequently dance while wearing their hats and, unless it is very warm, girls continue to wear their coats. Both sexes often dance holding an unfinished cigarette in their hands. In form, Kaska dancing may be described as a one-step, but some men in leading proceed in a monotonous walk-like step that has earned the soldiers' approbation, "Lower Post shuffle." The Tahltan do a square dance, but few Kaska Indians know this form. Waltzes are rarely played and are not well danced. White trappers when intoxicated are fond of introducing a variant of the one step. Calling, "woodpecker!" they execute the step by banging the heels forcefully on the floor instead of shuffling. Intoxicated young Indian men sometimes dance in this manner, and drunken musicians create considerable amusement by speeding up the tempo of playing, forcing everyone to dance rapidly. Occasionally a white man will fiddle for a dance. His playing is slower than the Indians' and he frequently interchanges the one step with waltzes, schottisches, and polkas to which the natives do not dance confidently.

One of the primary sources of enjoyment in dancing comes from the movement and rhythm. There are, however, other functions of a dance which contribute to its popularity. The first of these is the excitement which, even without the aid of alcohol, serves to break down the emotional remoteness of the people and, like the gambling games, leads to some of the most intensive social interaction in the society. Dances are also popular because they are among the few situations facilitating sexual interaction. Soldiers and civilian construction workers employed on the Alaska Highway recognized this function and often utilized dances to recruit Indian girls for sexual purposes. Complaints by traders and missionaries led the provincial and Mounted Police to pay surprise visits to dances and order out of town all strangers found there. Indian dances are also visited by the police to detect evidence of drinking. Dances found in progress after midnight, Saturday, are ordered closed under the terms of a provincial law forbidding Sunday dancing.

Gambling. In contrast to dancing, not much time is spent in gambling. Card games, such as poker and blackjack, are played during the summer and winter but are emotionally less intense than the stick games, which take place for a few consecutive nights each summer. When interest has been aroused in such a game, someone proposes that it be played and word travels through the community. Gradually people make their way to the designated spot. Gambling generally takes place some distance from town, since experience has taught the Indians that the resident missionary and traders are likely to be displeased if kept awake by the sound of the drumming.

In preparation for gambling someone first cuts eleven tally sticks from green willow branches. These sticks, each about a foot long, are peeled and one end sharpened so that they can be thrust into the ground. The next task is to choose two sides. This is done informally, but the man who is most prominent in the choosing becomes the captain of his team. Each team usually contains an even number of men—from four to six. A youth is then designated to manage the "drum," which may consist of a frying pan, a four gallon oil tin, or a tambourine drum specially prepared for gambling. The drum stick is a plain piece of thick willow.

A fire is made and a large amount of dry wood collected. Facing each other, each team kneels on a blanket at opposite sides of the fire. The drummer places himself to one side of the blaze while the spectators crowd opposite him or stand behind the players. Before the game begins each player selects, or is suggested, an opponent from the opposite team with whom he bets. All players generally bet the same sum—generally twenty-five cents a game. It is then decided which side shall open the playing, and all of the tally sticks are thrown across the fire to this team, which we will designate as the guessing team. The opposing side will be referred to as the playing team.

When the guessing team is ready, the drummer moves behind the line of playing men and begins the gambling rhythm, a staccato six-eight beat. Each man on the playing team holds a coin in his hand. Drawing the blanket over the knees, the men on this side bend low, hands under the blanket and, bobbing their bodies up and down to the beat of the drum, individually decide in which hand to secret the coin. When all are ready they straighten up, kneeling and holding up clenched fists. Their bodies and arms continue to bob to the drummer's rhythm. Most of the players also accompany the drum by chanting "tš-tš, tš-tš, tš-tš" in the same time. The captain on the guessing team is now required to guess in what hand his opponents carry the token. This is done in certain conventionalized gestures and without words. Once the captain has pointed out his decision, the players must reveal their hands. This is done swiftly, without the swaying bodies once losing the rhythm of the drum. The open hand is exultantly flung out with obvious glee to show that the guesser has missed, and the coin is then quickly slapped into the open palm of the exposed hand as the lucky player gets ready to play again. Everything counts on swiftness, and the captain must be quick to note how many men he has "killed"—that is, how many he has guessed correctly—and to remember how the others played so as to anticipate their next move. Then for each person left in the game, the captain (or his neighbor) throws a tally stick across the fire. The playing team does not wait for this signal, but is already busy continuing the round. Again the hands come up and the captain, trying to estimate what his opponents will have done this time, claps his hands and points. Swiftly he is shown his failure. More of the tally sticks go across the fire. The longer a side can outwit the guesser, the greater the excitement and the more exultant the triumph of the winners. Those who have been defeated, however, kneel quietly next to their playing team mates. Eventually the guesser will have succeeded in eliminating all of the opponents and the first round of the game is over. In the second round the original guessing side hides the coins; the drummer now stands behind these men and the captain on the other team acts as the guesser. The success of a man as a guesser can be estimated by the number of tally sticks which his side is able to retain in the course of eliminating the playing side. If the process takes eight or nine sticks, the original guessing side is manifestly at a disadvantage when it is their turn to play. A game is won by the side which first secures all the tally sticks. With no sticks to play, the losers now pay the forfeit previously agreed on and a new game is begun.

Often the game is immediately continued after a side has won all the tally sticks. When this is to be done the captain of the winning side calls "Twenty-one!" One round only is played in twenty-one. The number of sticks won in this round is subtracted from the total number of sticks and the remainder thrown across to the losing side. The sticks won in twenty-one are the handicap against which the losing side starts guessing in the next game.

The outstanding features of gambling games are swiftness, excitement, and movement. The aim is to confuse the guesser by as much distraction as possible. Intense emotion is concentrated in the playing and the rests between games, when losers throw over their forfeits, are very welcome. These rests are often prolonged when a winner fails to catch his forfeit and must hunt for it in the grass, or when a winner has to give his opponent change for a bill. If a man loses and has no money to pay his bet, he may continue playing and owe his opponent the losses. White men who gamble are often confused by the custom of a man temporarily leaving the game to rest, eat, or urinate. Nobody represents him on his team but, unless he clearly indicates that he is "through," the absentee player continues to participate in the winnings or losses of his side and is obliged to pay his forfeits or entitled to collect his winnings.

Confident players can afford to burlesque while they are hiding, particularly if they are playing against a naive captain. Louis Maza, for example, after withdrawing his hands from below the blanket, provocatively stretched one fist toward the fire, placing the other behind his back. As was obviously expected, the captain indicated the hidden hand. Triumphantly Louis displayed the token in the outstretched hand. Sometimes games become contests between two dominant personalities who enjoy reputations as capable players, as when Louis Maza played against Nick Lang, each being captain of one team. Repeatedly both of these men would kill everyone on the other side but the opposing captain, and the game would continue with one captain matching his wits against the other. The swiftness of the game facilitates cheating, and sometimes games break up with considerable hard feeling as one side accuses the other of unfair playing. In general, the Indians are not good losers and resentment often makes its appearance in the form of nagging and muffled derogatory remarks concerning the opponents. It is obvious that the game is not played for the financial stakes but rather for the excitement and pleasure which the gambling promotes.

LIFE CYCLE

Birth and Infancy

Although in 1945 one woman, Dorothy Plover, gave birth to a son in the hospital at Whitehorse, most women continue to bear children without white medical assistance. Whenever possible an attempt is made to keep the expectant mother in a winter settlement where experienced female help will be available to assist in delivery and postnatal care. This assistance is not always possible, however, and sometimes (especially if birth is premature) an older woman is forced to deliver her own child or is assisted by her white husband. No case was heard of an Indian man aiding parturition. During the summer at Lower Post, a mature woman is generally called upon when labor becomes severe. The duration of labor noted was from three to nine hours, the latter for a fourth pregnancy.

Delivery is with the parturient in a sitting position. The cord is cut with scissors, and mother and child are then washed with warm water. The baby, its legs laid straight, is wrapped in blankets with the hands bound to its sides and placed in bed next to the mother. The afterbirth is thrown far away in the bush or may be hung in a tree. No special precautions are taken with premature babies.

Following birth the baby is not fed for one day and is then put to the mother's breast. The parturient usually remains in bed for four days to a week, and during this period her husband or grown daughters take over the household duties. In summer a mother may be seen carrying her infant through town within two weeks after delivery and by this time she has also resumed most of her customary duties (Plate 4, c).

Children born out of wedlock or conceived in adulterous sexual relations are regarded as illegitimate. All illegitimacy is deplored, but the incidence of premarital motherhood appears to be quite low. The child of an unmarried mother may be cared for by the girl herself or entrusted to the care of grandparents. Once illegitimate children are grown, their status is not different from that of other persons and no evidence of discrimination against them could be observed.

The only two cases observed of extreme rejection of infants involved illegitimate children. Irene Wiley gave birth to Irma a short time after she had been deserted by her husband, who disapproved of her promiscuity. She did not want the infant, neglected its feeding and care, and often abandoned it in her mosquito tent for long periods while she went riding with soldiers. One cold night in August, 1944, Irene's father's brother's wife found the eight months old baby uncovered and so cold that it had to be washed with warm water. Although news of this incident reached the police, who publicly reprimanded the mother at a dance, Irene did not improve her care of the infant. Commenting on the child Louis Maza once observed: "That baby raise himself. Nobody take care of him. Mother don't care. Never change him . . . Some people tough. Me, I can't do that." River Joe, Irene's paternal uncle, said: "My heart sick I hear that baby cry. Sometime I take care of him." The extent of his care, so far as could be observed, consisted of occasionally feeding Irma sugar cookies. In 1945, when Irma was about two years old and retarded in her development, Irene began to manifest somewhat more attention toward the child.

A second instance of a young mother neglecting her newborn illegitimate infant occurred after the *métise* woman's husband had refused to permit her to keep the child. Although the putative father, a married man, was easily identifiable, no effort was made to induce this man to accept responsibility. Instead both parents left the baby in a tent at Lower Post while they went to visit friends two hundred miles up Dease River. The child was subsequently cared for by the mother's sister and later somewhat reluctantly adopted by its maternal grandmother. For her behavior the mother is reported to have been censured by the Indian Agent during his visit to Lower Post.

Children are usually named soon after birth, a Christian saint's name being decided upon by the parents or suggested by the missionary if the baby is brought for baptism. Sometimes naming is neglected for several months after birth. If, during this time, a friend suggests an appropriate name it will be adopted by one or the other parent. Thus the ethnographer named Nitla's baby during the summer of 1945. In addition to a formal personal name, a family occasionally coins a nick-name for a child, but the range of such names is limited. Two common English nicknames are Boss and Piggy.

Children born in Lower Post are usually brought to the mission a few weeks after birth for baptism. The ceremony is little emphasized by the parents and is often delayed until the matter is pressed upon their attention by the priest.

Infants are breast fed, occasionally receiving supplementary bottles. No rationalization for the extra feeding could be obtained. A large variety of bottles are used for this purpose including, besides the regular nursing variety, beer bottles and even small perfume bottles with a mouth wide enough to fit the rubber nipples locally purchased.

Suckling is a casual process of which the woman exhibits little concern. A young infant is nursed outdoors, in traders' stores, and in church whenever it frets or cries. Whereas a baby nurses as it reclines in the mother's lap, an older child, who can hold itself erect, often suckles as it perches on the mother's knee while the latter is eating, idling, or even carrying out such tasks as scraping moosehide (Plate 8, A). No fondling of babies was observed during the nursing situation. An older child may signal its desire to nurse by touching the mother's breast or, if it can crawl or toddle, pull aside the nursing mother's loosely fastened dress. It is recognized that a mother's milk is affected by her diet. Most often, particularly for a small infant, the supplementary bottle is held by the mother, but sometimes it is tilted on the baby's body supported by a light pillow or folded blanket. The contents of a bottle are warmed for a young baby.

Weaning from the breast generally occurs before two years, but some children nurse until they are three years old. Earlier weaning occurs when a baby is displaced by the birth of a sibling. However even young babies are given a solid piece of meat or fat to suck, and the amount of solid food gradually assumes a larger place in the baby's diet as weaning approaches. During weaning, milk continues to be served in both the bottle and cup. Crying for the breast leads the mother to pick up the baby and carry it, but if this does not lead to soothing, nursing is permitted. An older child who remains persistent in his attempts to nurse may be mildly criticized and teased about his infantile habits. Pacifiers are also used in weaning. Weaning is not abrupt and most children appear satisfied to accept the bottle as a substitute for the breast.

Kaska society is infant centered. This is brought out in the ready affection and attention devoted to babies. It is also illustrated by the fact that in this society it is not an older sibling who cares for the infant while the mother does the housework. Rather the reverse holds true; a woman with a nearly adolescent daughter has little to do but take care of a young baby. Often even the lap baby is left to the care of the older sibling, while the mother devotes all her time to the infant. Ideally children are desired and, unless there are too many of the same sex, there is no preference for either boys or girls.

Bodily care of the infant is manifested in diapering, washing, clothing, and packing. Diaper cloths are pieces of flannel of various sizes. About seven or ten layers of such material are laid out and the child placed in the center. These cloths are then passed between the baby's legs and pinned at the sides. Sometimes a layer of dry moss is placed in the center of a single piece of material to aid in absorbing the infant's excreta. Diaper cloths are changed when the outermost layer becomes damp. In addition to these cloths, the neonate wears an undershirt and dress, blouse, or rompers. He is generally closely bundled in a clean blanket which is snugly pinned around the body so that the legs lie straight together. In warm weather the hands are exposed (Plate 4, C). While the infant sleeps, the blanket is loosely thrown over his face. With this binding the child is placed in the baby pack and carried on the mother's back. After a few months, blanketing is replaced by rompers, overalls or a long dress, and a sweater. Long cotton ribbed stockings (essential for summer protection against flies, mosquitoes, and other insects) and diminutive moccasins complete the costume. The head is covered with an embroidered cap. Diaper cloths continue to be used until the child is about a year old. In the morning and at night the baby is washed with warm water.

A fancy baby pack is sometimes made of velvet and wrapped around the baby in a manner similar to the blankets. Along one side and at the bottom the bag is fitted with lacing. The material of the pouch is bound tightly around the infant whose head is kept covered with a cap or with an inner blanket. The sack is supported on the woman's back in a wide shawl, but not by shoulder straps. When packed in this way, the baby faces the mother and often leans forward on the mother's back or shoulder while sleeping.

Baby packs are used only a relatively short time. By the time the baby is about six months old, the velvet bag has been discontinued in favor of a shawl or blanket in which the infant is bound as it sits astride the mother's back (Plate 4, B). This packing is used when the mother is traveling and also when she is working around camp. Older siblings or young aunts may also pack small children in this fashion. Older children are sometimes carried facing the mother in packsacks such as are used to carry meat and other supplies. These containers are fitted with holes through which the feet can extend. Sometimes an ingenious pack is made of canvas or ticking cut like coveralls with long trousers but lacking sleeves. This pack, used for children from two to four years old, is supplied with carrying straps that pass over the mother's shoulder. In such a container the child also faces the mother. Beyond the age of six months the mother begins to carry the baby in her arm or on her hip as she moves around camp. Sometimes a shawl extending around the mother's shoulder is used to support a baby astride the hip, but usually the only support is the mother's arm.

Children are always content on the mother's back, never kicking or squirming. Much of the day the year old baby is left free to crawl around the camp or cabin but always under the watchful eye of the mother. At night it generally sleeps with the mother; sometimes, however, a small child is placed in a hammock of blankets which is suspended over the parents' bedding. A baby is always laid on its back, never on the stomach.

Another aspect of infant care, protection, is illustrated by the mother's reluctance to leave a small baby alone. Small babies are rarely left in another person's care for more than a few hours. Even though the child could be cared for by an aunt or grandmother, most mothers will not leave camp to travel any distance and allow an infant to remain behind.

Up to about two years of age the baby is rarely or never punished and is the recipient of considerable attention, not only from the mother but also from its father, siblings, grand-parents, and aunts. Although, as we have pointed out, the Kaska are an emotionally unex-pressive people, they do demonstrate considerable affection toward the neonate and infant. A number of terms are employed to express devotion toward young children. Two of these are, tena zonzæ ("little man") and mamazæ ("little mother"). Babies are rarely permitted to cry without some relative making an attempt to comfort or distract them. Emotionally expressive behavior toward babies includes bouncing the infant in the arms or on the back, mouthing its fingers, cuddling, holding its face close to the adult's, kissing the cheeks, uttering nonsense syllables, and praising it with kinship terms, like "my younger brother."

Fathers are also seen handling and playing with babies, and often refer to their young off-spring with pride. Despite these patterns of good infant care and unstinted attention to the baby, occasional instances were observed where mothers slapped or roughly shook restless and fretful year old babies.

Unless the expected course of maturation fails to appear, parents manifest only casual interest in promoting an infant's development. Occasionally a mother will seek to support a young baby in an upright position. Only once were parents seen walking while supporting a fifteen month old between them. The removal of the half-year old child from the baby pack or from tightly bound blankets also affords the child an opportunity to develop through exercise. While the appearance of the first teeth is noted by parents, little attention is focussed on this phase of development. No attempt is made to discourage finger sucking nor is this behavior much manifested by babies. Attitudes toward infantile sexuality were not observed or reported. In its early years, of course, a baby, being closely bound and heavily diapered, has little opportunity to explore its genitals.

CHILDHOOD

The transition from infancy to childhood among the Kaska is informally recognized as occurring at between three and four years of age, when the child becomes "half smart." As is customary in child study, we shall anticipate this transition somewhat and refer to childhood as that period of life which follows shortly after the infant has taken its first steps and which terminates with the onset of puberty.

Although the first attention to sphincter control comes between one and two years of age, it is never harshly introduced at this time nor is it seriously expected to take hold so early. At that time, especially if it is summer, diaper cloths are abandoned and the mother begins to take the child with her when she goes into the bush for her own needs. Verbal explanation and encouragement are little used while the child is so young. As explained by one mother of six children, the toddler is expected to wet himself. "That time he wet his pants. Pretty soon I take him to toilet. Pretty soon he tell me." Scolding was denied. "I never say nothing. He learn himself." In summer the eighteen month to two year old child is allowed to play without pants or with pants (or bloomers) in which a long slit has been cut in the crotch. This device permits him to eliminate without soiling his clothes. Another practice is to don the child's moccasins as soon as he wakes in the morning and send him outside the house to urinate. Ideally parents also recognize the advantage of preventing the youngster from drinking any liquids during the hours immediately preceding bedtime.

No serious notice is taken of wetting or soiling before two and a half or three years of age. Even four years is sometimes tolerantly regarded as too early an age at which to demand complete cleanliness training, and often children continue to wet at night until this age. Generally, however, the child is expected to be trained at three and from then on begins to be scolded for daytime failures. "Look you dirty boy," Dorothy Plover said to three year old David before she changed him, "You dirty your pants." Some parents also introduce spanking at this time to enforce sphincter control. When enuresis occurs in older children, the sleeping place of the child may be padded with moss which is discarded every morning. Together with learning habits of sphincter control, the child also acquires certain attitudes toward the excreta. The strongest attitudes of disgust are directed toward the feces, which are regarded as "dirty" and repulsive.

The development of childhood is accompanied by a definite change in the care which the infant has been accustomed to receive from its mother. This aspect of the parent-child relationship, whose characteristics will now be described, may be defined as withdrawing from the child his principal source of affective gratification. The pattern is not to be confused with direct rejection; the child continues to be loved passively and cared for in the family. What occurs is an emotional withdrawal of the mother, who in infancy was the chief source of affective stimulation. The mother becomes less responsive to the child's demands, less eager in her attention, more remote and disinterested in her appreciation. Stated positively, the mother becomes more concerned with herself than with the child, or, if there is now a younger sibling, more preoccupied with the infant than with the lap baby.

If the emotional rejection is correlated with the birth of a sibling it often has its initiation at about eighteen months, when the child is beginning to toddle. However, children often nurse until they are two years old, so that generally the mother does not begin to withdraw in her affective relationship until the youngster is between two and three. The process is both a gradual and an unconsciously motivated one. Its behavioral manifestations are many. For example, the child's crying is no longer responded to with the spontaneous attention that this behavior earned in infancy. "Don't cry for nothing!" the mother sharply scolds, as she continues with her work. Fretting for attention, which begins to appear in the two year old, is less tolerated, and the mother reprimands the child for clinging to her garments or body. For long journeys, children continue to be packed up to four or five years of age but around camp fretful demands to be carried and cuddled go ignored. Stella Wiley was exceedingly passive with two year old Laura. One time Laura was observed to crawl into her mother's lap. Stella accepted the child without any demonstration of interest. On another occasion Laura was clinging to her mother's skirts, whining and crying "mama." Stella continued placidly smoking and talking to her sisters, as though unaware of any distraction. Comfort is often withheld even if the child is hurt or frightened. Four year old Marie Lang had been vaccinated and came out of the mission crying. She ran to her grandmother, Mrs. Man. The latter made no direct effort to comfort her. For a few moments the girl sat quietly alongside the woman. Then she began to cry anew and threw her head into Mrs. Man's lap. Fleetingly the latter put her hand close to the child's head. Then she was distracted and turned to scold a noisy boy who was playing too close. Marie continued to sob loudly but Mrs. Man remained passive and unattentive.

Mildred Lang is in many respects one of the warmest women in the community.[26] Waiting for a ride at the Highway crossing her adopted daughter, Ann Wiley, started to fall asleep. She leaned her head on Mildred's arm. The latter shoved the child's head away saying: "Oh, go away you." Ann then leaned her head on a bridge girder and dozed. By the time a child is five or six years old, a clearly defined pattern may be observed in which comfort is no longer sought from the mother. The child has learned to endure pain by itself. Now children are sometimes seen weeping in solitude and sucking the first two or three

---

[26] She was warmly regarded by her nephew, Harry Lang, whose care she undertook for many years. See Harry Lang's autobiographical sketch below, pp. 332–333.

fingers when unhappy. Withheld emotionality is displayed when an injured child runs to a nearby parent. The usual response of the latter is to scold the youngster for his wild behavior and then to briskly dust his clothes. Any overtures of kindness and affection are readily responded to, however, and girls in particular never lose a responsiveness to caresses and bodily contacts by older siblings and other women.

The father, who has never been as demonstrative as the mother in his affectional handling of the infant, retains some of his more moderate warmth, and we have even observed instances of a father picking up a lap baby whose fretfulness went unnoticed by the mother. Thus when Richard Cross, five, hurt himself while playing he ran to his father, who lifted him and tried to distract him from crying by pointing out a horse across the river, murmuring: "Crying bad animal." Although the man's attention to young children is limited by his economic activities, several instances were noted of children, ranging from four to six, developing close attachments to their fathers, while the mothers were occupied with the care of younger siblings. Under such circumstances fathers often pack youngsters while traveling. Louis Maza once spoke of how, when Eleanor was four years old, he packed her on his back while climbing to the timberline to trap marten. In 1945 Loreen was his constant companion, trailing him all over Lower Post. Generally, however, such close attachment between father and child affords little satisfaction to the boy or girl other than the opportunity to remain in the parent's company. Physical contact between the two is always brief. In some cases dependence of the child on the father is continued into later childhood. While generally it is the boy who, beginning at about seven or eight, occasionally accompanies his father trapping and hunting, often daughters enter this relationship and, in thus carrying on their early emotional attachment to the father, learn skills which are usually expected to be transmitted to sons.

When, as frequently happens, the family through death is deprived of the presence of one or both parents, the process of emotional rejection becomes more severe. Over ten per cent of the children in Kaska society at the time of field work had lost either one or both parents. Emotional withdrawal is particularly strong in the case of adopted children and orphans who, although they may receive physical care from foster parents or grandparents, receive little emotional gratification. One exception to this statement was observed in the behavior of the Cross brothers' mother, who was raising the four year old son of her late daughter. The child was never seen separated from this very old lady who would sit with his head in her lap, murmer to him constantly, and devotedly keep flies and mosquitoes away from his face. This is extremely atypical behavior toward a child of that age.

Obviously the pattern of family relationships which has been described offers a child little opportunity for exhibitionism. However, sometimes the visits of relatives and friends temporarily transform the family into an audience ready to laugh and applaud the child's behavior. It is interesting to observe the eagerness with which young children from four to six respond to such stimulation. Beyond that age, however, adult interest in children is slight and, as we shall see, when it appears is most often practical and educative.

If the child continues to live with both parents, the father is ideally regarded as the most important disciplinarian. Usually, however, it is the mother who actually punishes. The ideal aim of punishment is to make the child submissive to, or "scared" of, the parents. Such

submission is theoretically valued, because it is felt to create an atmosphere in which parents can most effectively direct the development of socially expected behavior. To "please"
a child too much is to spoil him and make him "wild like squirrel." Manifestly, few demands
are made on the child for the first six or seven years. During this period obligations of obedience are slight. Following these years, the economic role of the girl begins and may be
accompanied by somewhat greater regulation of her activities, but for the greater part of
the time children of both sexes are left to their own devices.

The Kaska family does not reveal a picture of authoritarianism run riot. There is no
tendency to deprecate the child and force his humility in relation to parents. While one or
two fathers are tyrannical, the father's role is reduced in importance by the fact that he is
often absent from the family hunting and trapping. During such periods the mother assumes
control of the household and operates independently—that is, without referring authority
back to her husband. There is no evidence that punishment is ever delayed until a father's
return to camp. There is also no reason to believe that the mother is laxer than the father
in dispensing punishment or that children more readily obey the latter parent.

Scolding, corporal punishment, and threats are the principal techniques employed by
parents to maintain discipline. We will consider these forms in sequence. Scolding is employed for minor failures to behave according to parental wishes. Children who play near
the river or climb down the cutbank are scolded. Playing in mud and dirt, fighting, nagging,
and masturbation are also reprimanded. Any wild or unruly behavior, such as shouting or
horsing around, may bring rebukes, especially if the child is a girl. Sharp reprimands to prevent very young children from touching objects like violins or candles also fall in this category of discipline. Watchfulness and scolding are often abandoned if the parent becomes
distracted, but sometimes scolding is reinforced by threats of corporal punishment, a
mother breaking off a twig or picking up a stick to emphasize her warning. Scolding is
closely related to that form of discipline known as "talking to" a child, that is, advising the
youngster of socially approved standards of behavior, and, in the case of a girl, may persist
until marriage.

Corporal punishment is utilized for more serious offenses or persistent disregard of
parental advice. Stealing, childhood sexuality, uncontrollable play, and deliberate disobe-
dience are punished by beating. Corporal punishment is ideally disapproved of for children;
"good people," it is said, "don't lick their kids." Manifestly there are indeed a number of
people who apparently refrain from using force upon children. On the other hand there are
a few men who are widely known for their authoritarianism and for the vehemence with
which they inflict corporal punishment. This extreme of behavior is generally disapproved.
Most parents go no further than shaking a child or pummeling it with the clenched fist.
Generally the upper part of the child's body is beaten. Spanking the buttocks was never observed. Corporal punishment for boys is generally discarded long before puberty. A girl,
however, may be beaten by her mother as long as she lives in the family.

A number of threats are used to instill fear in children, with the object of making the
latter's behavior conform to the parents' wishes. Children are kept from leaving camp in
Lower Post by being warned of the dangers of trucks and horses and, in the winter settlements, are made afraid of vague dangers of the bush, wolves, and the menace of night.

Children who want to play outdoors at night are warned that an owl or other animal will come around and get them. To keep children from wandering off in the bush, threats of the danger of getting lost are frequently employed. Old Man several times warned the ethnographer's son of the danger of wolves. At the same time he deplored his fourteen year old daughter's manifest fear of these animals. To control masturbation and premarital sexuality, children are warned of insanity. Control through threats, except with regard to sexual behavior, is rarely continued beyond childhood. Certain types of discipline are apparently absent. Shame, humiliation, and ridicule are not employed against children. Punishment in public is rare and when it occurs is never done with the aim of public humiliation.

Discipline is restricted to the family and is rarely shared by other adults. A man even refrains from disciplining his wife's child by a former husband and a woman maintains a similar reserve toward her husband's previous children. Beyond infancy, a mother often entrusts her children to the care of grandparents and other relatives. Thus when Peter Lang went to Whitehorse, he brought four year old Marie to Mildred Lang's home with the girl's blankets and went off. Mildred was not too pleased with her brother's act, and said that Peter's brother's wife could very well have taken care of the child. The amount of care received in such circumstances is often negligent and little supervision is exercised. More authority is exercised when care is delegated to siblings, older siblings often being firm disciplinarians who do not hesitate to follow scolding with corporal punishment. In general, however, relations between young siblings are close and warm and rarely marked by aggression or hostility.

Unrelated or related adolescents are an important source of attention to young children. Boys from twelve to eighteen often demonstrate a genuine affectionate interest in younger boys and girls, with whom they arrange games and provoke chasing. Lying in a camp, an adolescent boy becomes fair game for youngsters who climb on him and generally exploit his tolerance. Adolescent girls are also affectionate toward younger siblings as well as to unrelated children. Largely, however, this attention depends on the adolescent's momentary disposition and is extremely transitory, the older boy or girl soon tiring of the play or else becoming distracted by other interests. Nevertheless a lifelong warm relationship is developed with these older playmates, especially when they are maternal aunts or uncles who live in close proximity to the growing child.

Two aspects of childhood remaining to be considered are routine bodily care and protection from danger. Beyond infancy, the child receives less systematic bodily care. Washing and clean clothes are often neglected and mealtimes are erratic, particularly when older children in Lower Post venture away from home and play in neighboring camps. An effort is sometimes made to have children of up to nine or ten years of age in bed by ten o'clock, but usually they are allowed to remain up until the parents themselves are ready to retire. Except in the extremely low temperatures of winter, parents show little concern for the child's physical comfort; around camp children are rarely asked if they are hungry or cold, nor is notice taken of wet clothes or moccasins. However, in traveling with a boat or toboggan, bread is kept available for a young child. In winter great caution is exercised to assure the child's adequate protection from the environment.

Protection from danger includes keeping very young children from playing with sharp implements, going into the forest alone, leaving the house in cold temperatures, approaching the gunwales of boats, and venturing near river banks or too near a fire. Failure to heed such advice is punished by scolding or with threats tended to inspire fear. As children pass the age of five the river is no longer forbidden as a place to play nor are children prevented from handling scissors, knives, or axes (Plate 10, B). By that age they have learned to be careful of open fires and stoves and limit their activities to the main part of the community or winter settlement, never venturing into the bush alone.

Education. Most education for living is received by the child in the course of performing routine activities. Such education is unformalized and undirected. Our characterization above of the training of dogs reflects some of the features of the child's education. Instruction and direction are rarely explicit. "Do this," is the formula, and the child is left with the task of working out the details of an activity for himself. If the young girl is asked to make a fire and tries to light large pieces of wood without first splitting kindling, the task will be taken over by an adult. The child may then observe the correct sequences for the completion of the activity, but few people trouble to drill these into the learner. Sometimes generalized instructions are furnished to children who, in carrying these out, often become confused. Thus we observed one fourteen year old girl make tea by putting the leaves into cold water. Nobody referred to the muddy quality of the beverage. The same kind of teaching was used with the ethnographer. Activities were illustrated but never explained in detail, the exposition of principles being ignored. On the second day of a journey with dog team and toboggan, the handling of the vehicle was entrusted to the ethnographer without a word of instruction regarding the technique of managing the dogs. Meanwhile the guide walked on ahead, rapidly breaking trail, so that when the traces fouled and the dogs rebelled, he had to retrace almost an eighth of a mile. Another observation that is worthwhile making so far as education is concerned, deals with the relatively narrow range of stimulation available to children, particularly in winter, when youngsters lacking toys are confined to small cabins and rarely interact with parents.

The girl's education is derived from her household duties and begins quite early. From the age of six or seven, she hauls water and packs wood. A few years later she learns to cut and sew moccasins, often practicing with scraps of moosehide; tends the rabbit snares; cuts wood; washes clothes, and helps with simple cooking—all by following the examples of her mother or older sisters and with a minimum of verbal instruction. A young girl may at first rebel at economic chores and seek to shirk them, but by the time she is nine or ten years old the rebellion has almost totally disappeared and she is only anxious to complete her duties quickly so as to have free time available. Boys' education begins somewhat later, at the age of eight. Now they begin to accompany fathers or older brothers on short fishing, hunting, and trapping trips. The boy learns masculine skills by observing older men prepare snowshoe frames, hew lumber, or manufacture implements, vehicles, buildings, and tools. While the boy assists older men in these activities, by collecting firewood and handling tools, his real economic contribution begins much later than the girl's. Not until he is near puberty, does the boy begin to manufacture apparatus on his own or go out to hunt large game with an agemate.

As early as the age of three, a child begins to try using snowshoes. Such learning is gradual, but by six the child is already able to cover ten or more miles with these travel aids. Children begin to feed themselves at about three years of age.

No effort is made to give a child sex instruction, and since people rarely discuss sexual topics, children are limited in the information which they may acquire about this subject. Sexual prohibitions are explained obliquely and with many euphemisms, so that the prevailing attitude toward sex as something highly personal and restricted cannot fail to be transmitted. On the other hand, some awareness of sexuality may be gained when a child loiters in the mixed company of adolescents and unmarried young people, who engage in sexual teasing and sometimes make threats or references without regard for the presence of youngsters. Since parents and children sleep in the same dwelling room, it is likely that children are early exposed to sexual activities, the meaning of which is not explained. When adults are intoxicated there is also a relaxation of sexual taboos from which youngsters are not protected. A sense of modesty begins to be inculcated in the child when he is three or four years old, and children of that age will not urinate or defecate in the presence of other people. Now the mother also warns a child of any indecent exposure in a public place.

Some effort is indirectly or directly made to inculcate induration to pain, fatigue, and cold. Young children of five and six are often required to walk up to fifteen miles with parents who are bound for a trap line or hunting place. Minor ailments are seldom regarded as an excuse for delaying such journeys. In winter some parents directly advise an older child not to try to keep his hands warm all the time but to get used to having the fingers "half frozen." In that way, it is explained, they will become better able to withstand cold. Children are also warned of the dangers present in the environment when the temperature is very low; for example they are taught that in such temperatures the bare fingers or mouth must never touch metal.

With regard to formal education, most of the parents are ready to send their children to summer mission school and, at least in early years, try to insist on such attendance. Schooling is not valued for opportunities which it opens for the child, but rather for the advantages it offers parents. Commenting on his grandson's education, River Joe expressed this attitude when he said: "Me boss that kid . . . I raise him. Learn something, he good for me that way." The school in Lower Post follows a leisurely program of instruction. Counting and reading occupy a fractional place in the curriculum, which also attempts to teach religion, values of cleanliness and hard work, and even includes the teaching of French and English folksongs.

In 1945 the mission, in conjunction with the Indian Affairs Branch, sent eight children ranging from five to twelve years old to a Catholic boarding school at Grouard, Alberta, 700 miles south of Lower Post. Here they will receive two years of education. Heretofore such outside education has been limited to one or two youths going to the mission boarding school at Lejac, on the Pacific Coast.[27] The value of such short term education is, of course, limited. Richard Day and Harry Lang, who were both educated in boarding schools, are capable of simple writing with poor spelling. In Harry, education also contributed to some dissatisfaction with the limited stimulation of Lower Post.

Many young children, from four to eight, express relatively little animation or spon-

[27] The school was built with Government funds and is taught by nuns. See Carroll, *The Vicariate of Prince Rupert* (1945), 14-15.

taneity in play. Most of their time is still spent close to the parents, sitting quietly or amusing themselves with desultory activities. This pattern conforms to the ideal for children's
behavior. Parents try to restrain the exuberance of children. "Quit raising hell!" Mildred
Lang called to Ann Wiley, six, who was dashing to and fro excitedly.[28] Nitla once remarked
on this ideal when he compared Indian to white children. Indian children, he said, were
"quiet all the time" while white children never sat still but ran around constantly and nois-
ily. He confirmed the ethnographer's objection that not all Kaska children could be characterized as quiet. Some Indian children, he admitted, were "wild" in their play.

One of the outstanding features in the play of native boys and girls is the absence of
cooperative activities, that is, enterprises that could not continue or would be disturbed
if one of the participants withdrew. Most play may be characterized as parallel activity in
which two or three children do the same thing although each remains primarily engrossed
in his own routine. Thus children fish with bent pins, drag boats in the river, or run with
home made wheel toys, each playing independently but gaining pleasure and stimulation
from the presence of companions. The height of cooperative play is attained in later childhood, when an older boy wheels youngsters in a trader's wheelbarrow or in games of throwing balls. Girls begin camp play at about five or six and the game continues to adolescence
but is little cooperative. "I lay down," a young child exclaims, whereupon the others follow
suit. Older children may set up more elaborate "camps" in which broken stoves are used to
heat tea or even to cook rabbit, but such make believe play as acting out the roles of husband
and wife does not appear, each child remaining his own personality. Older children, including boys, sometimes join youngsters in building small camp fires on which water is boiled
in vacuum tins and tea leaves with sugar added. The beverage is then shared by the group.
Parents were not observed to participate in children's games.

Imaginative play is also limited in young children. Small cut out animals are prepared
from cardboard by older children and used to act out sequences of moose hunting. Paper air-
planes, made by folding and trimming a piece of heavy paper and then adding cut out wings
and propellers by means of slits, zoom through the air and are identified as Japanese or
American. Wooden guns, cut by fathers, are used by boys to shoot imaginary moose and
enemies. The older folks also cut wooden boats out of poplar and cottonwood for a young
child. A piece of tin may be cut in the shape of an outboard motor and fitted with a propeller
that revolves when the boat is dragged in the river. Such craft are tied to a sticks that enable
their owners to sail them several feet from shore. For girls there are dolls purchased at the
traders'. Such babies are put to sleep in a wooden box, which we once saw a young girl
dragging behind her. Generally, the number of toys into which a child can project fantasies
is limited. Children show little inclination to share toys, and the attempts of other youngsters to appropriate objects may provoke aggression or flight. Generally there is little overt
hostility in children's interpersonal relations and all manifestations of such behavior are
promptly discouraged by parents.

Young dogs and puppies provide young boys in Lower Post with a popular source of
amusement. Youths ride these animals like horses, tie objects to their tails, roll around with

---

[28] It is interesting to note that during school recess, the missionary urges the children to run and jump
around rather than idle in quiet groups.

them, and sometimes inflict blows without cause. Horses are also plagued and teased by boys whenever the opportunity presents itself. This sport leads to punishment when it results in complaints to parents from the animals' owners, who fear that the teasing is making the horses too shy. Older boys, from ten into adolescence, take keen delight in riding bareback along the river road and directing their mounts into a cluster of girls.

From five to six boys often make crude rolling toys out of the cover of a vacuum tin. The disc is nailed to a willow or poplar stick and the nail bent where it emerges from the other side (Plate 10, B). The child runs pushing the wheel before him. Youngsters try to cut thin brush with axes, explaining that they are cutting trail. In winter children, ranging in age from five to late adolescence, enjoy sliding down cutbanks to the frozen river on tobog-gans or small sleighs made by older uncles or parents. Only the bitterest cold interrupts this sport. By seven or eight, boys make their own slingshots, to use in shooting at trees and birds. Boys of twelve are sometimes seen testing their strength picking up heavy weights and trying to lift the nailed boards of a table top. This is also the age for target practicing with .22 caliber rifles, although hunting for small game has already begun.

In contrast to boys, girls generally play less impetuously and more quietly. Some exam-ples of girls' activities have already been given. In addition the girl's fondness for represent-ative and decorative art must be mentioned. Most girls have copybooks of crayon colored drawings, many of them conventional floral patterns such as are embroidered on moccasins. Sometimes street scenes from illustrated magazines are copied. With a stick, a girl draws extensive curvilinear designs on the level snow of a frozen lake. Another popular activity of older girls is to cut masks out of paper bags. These are bizarrely outlined and colored with lipstick and charcoal, and worn to visit neighboring camps or cabins, whose occupants the children try to frighten.

Boys of five and six often make themselves nuisances by teasing older girls. Such teasing leads to pushing and wrestling in which the older girl's strength often succeeds in defeating her tormentor. Teasing between the sexes continues to puberty (when it gives place to sex-ual provocation), and is usually conducted in a spirit of fun rather than with any intent of serious aggression.

Following the period of infancy and, as we will see, arising partly out of the emotional rejection to which the young child is subjected, there develops in children a sense of youth-ful responsibility, independence, and self-reliance such as is noticeably lacking among chil-dren in western society. Many attitudes of parents go to sustain these character traits. People rarely condescend to children. There is little encouragement of make believe play; even a youngster of four or five may be told that he will never catch anything by fishing with an unbaited safety pin. Parental attitudes are also not designed to encourage depend-ency trends. Although the child is dependent on the parents for all the necessities of life, it is rare for the latter to stress this dependence except in order to reaffirm their dominance in the socialization process. Often parents stress *their* dependence on the child, the need for his help in the present and the importance of his economic role in the future. In carrying out parents' wishes, children are not exposed to suffering loss of dignity or self-respect, such as might arise were ridicule and humiliation features of the socialization process. The independ-ence of the young child is not frustrated by confronting him with autocratic demands to do things according to the detailed specifications of adults; rather the child is given an opportunity to work out for himself the details of many cultural tasks. The responsibility accorded to a twelve year old was vividly demonstrated in Lower Post when five children, ranging from seven to twelve, climbed into a boat to cross the Liard River. The oldest boy could not start the outboard motor and the vessel began to drift down the swift current. He gave orders to his compaions, and four children seized the oars, two on each side, and in that way they crossed.

Correlated with the child's early development of independence and a sense of personal responsibility is the fact that children, especially girls, are not long exempt from making economic contributions to the family. It must be realized, however, that in a society where only relatively brief periods of intense labor are regarded as necessary and in which duties are undertaken leisurely, without compulsion, there remains abundant free time which children may claim for themselves. The Kaska girl, like her mother, is not a household drudge and the economic obligations of children do not restrain either sex from play or from social interaction with agemates.

ADOLESCENCE

The period from puberty to marriage is a relatively short one for the Kaska girl and only slightly longer for the boy. It is a time which marks the full growth of the independence for which young people have been prepared since early childhood. No social recognition marks the transition to puberty in the boy or girl.

Menarche is handled so privately by a girl's mother that sometimes not even the father is aware that his daughter has reached physical maturity. Sequestration of menstruants has only recently disappeared.[29] Apart from the fact that some men refrain from sexual intercourse during catamenia, there are paractically no disabilities restricting girls' behavior at this time. Since women are reluctant to speak of menstruation, even to other women, the subject was not a suitable one for obtaining detailed information. According to Paulette Donnelly, no absorbent is worn to catch the menstrual flow. Observation suggests that younger women often change from slacks to dresses when the flow is in progress.

For the girl puberty is accompanied by few major changes in her economic role. She has been using a small rifle for a year or two and has already been given the task of running her mother's rabbit lines. With her mother or sister she has started trapping and earning money from fur that came into her traps. The pubescent girl is generally an accomplished sewer, able to make dresses or moccasins, and has sufficiently observed the processing of moosehide to be able to carry out the task herself. In a word, she is as adult in her experience as her physiological capacities permit. Beginning with puberty a mild avoidance relationship, phrased as shyness, begins to develop between many girls and their fathers. This persists even after the girl is married. "Used to be Anna like my heart," Old Man said. "Now she grow up I wouldn't talk to her. Injun like that."

The economic role of the boy has not been as fully developed as the girl's; that is, unlike his sister, he has not been given as many opportunities to learn his socially expected roles

[29] For information regarding what must have been one of the last case of puberty sequestration see Dorothy Plover's autobiographical sketch below, pp. 342–343.

by performing them. Around puberty the boy's education begins as an independent trapper and hunter. Unlike the earlier trips with his father, this is more serious work. If he is acting as the *protégé* of an older man, his winters are occupied in hauling and cutting large supplies of winter wood, hunting rabbits and chicken for daily food, and guiding the toboggan. If the youngster shows himself willing and eager to do and learn, the relationship between the partners is warm and comfortable. If, however, the youth shows a tendency to lie in bed on cold mornings and is slow in executing his expected tasks, his life is plagued and made miserable. Father, uncle, and brothers lecture to him about his laziness and may even plant practical jokes on him. Thus late one morning, while Donald Suza was sitting up in his sleeping place sipping coffee and eating a late breakfast, Old Man planted a thin stick behind the youth's back. When Donald lay down again after his repast the stick snapped, but not before it had sharply jabbed into his back. If the boy is afraid of the bush (in other words, if he has not unlearned the socially patterned attitudes of childhood), he is "talked to" and cajoled. From the life history material collected, it is apparent that adolescents often have to "unlearn" fear of the forest when they begin to travel alone, but this seems to have been successfully accomplished in most men and even in many women.

For their activities adolescents receive more praise than they have hitherto been accustomed to. A girl's sewing is pointed to with pride by a mother or father. A girl who can shoot rabbits, chicken, and porcupine is flattered and may be called "my little boy." A boy who begins to hunt is praised less lavishly for small game (although his bag is always welcome), but his first moose or caribou marks an occasion of considerable excitement. By his ability, diligence, and persistence as a hunter and trapper a youth creates his reputation in the community just as a girl develops her prestige through domestic skills. These attributes prepare the adolescent's way to marriage.

Considered from an overall point of view, adolescent activities range from work to play. They include hunting and fishing trips, bicycle riding, dressmaking, swimming, and horsebacking riding. At this age the boy's teasing of girls assumes a sexual quality. The adolescents, as has already been described, often show a considerable fondness for younger children but also spend long periods in association with adults. Musical instruments have been toyed with since a child was nine or ten; adolescence, however, is the time when serious efforts are made to master the violin and guitar. Now, too, boys and girls make their first shy appearances on the dance floor. They also begin to drink. At first this drinking is casual, representing the acceptance of adults' hospitality, but by sixteen or seventeen, most boys demonstrate a keen appreciation of alcoholic release. Masturbation, although regarded as highly shameful, is reported to be quite common for both sexes between thirteen and sixteen years of age but disappears once sexual intercourse is initiated. In summer, with the season's opportunities for social interaction, adolescence becomes a time of carefree holidaying. Responsibilities and duties are largely forgotten as the bush is forsaken; life revolves around dancing, music, gambling, drinking, and sexual relations.

An important behavior which makes its appearance in the later years of childhood and continues through adolescence to marriage is the formation of intrasexual friendships. Just as one seldom sees an unmarried boy and girl walking or talking together, so rarely is an adolescent seen abroad without a friend or companion of the same sex. Boys, having greater freedom of movement than girls, have a wider range of friendships. Girls, particularly around the time of puberty, have their friendships restricted to female siblings and girls living in an immediately adjacent camp.

Fluidity tends to be a feature of such friendships, but during the period when a particular relationship exists it is often marked by close affection and exchange of confidence. The emotions of friendship are rarely expressed verbally, but are abundantly demonstrated tactually. Such expression is most strongly developed in girls, who are often seen holding hands, sitting close together, hugging, and wrestling. Boys, too, often sit resting against each others' bodies. Sometimes a boy creeps up behind a friend and embraces him tightly from behind, whereupon the other tries to lift him up or shake him loose. Such horsing around often leads to wrestling for sport.

Although adolescence may be thought to offer advantages in the way of less direct supervision, greater independence, and more opportunities for achieving prestige, there seems to be no haste in either boys or girls to grow up. Although two sisters may be only two years apart, and one may use lipstick or begin to tease and be teased by boys, the other does not presume above her age, and shows no haste to emulate her sister. She seems content to wait for the physiological signal that will denote her maturity. Meanwhile boys do not bother her. Such younger girls often act as companions to older friends, when the latter attend dances or walk around in the summer night. In this role they are often able to increase their sexual knowledge.

The boy's freedom during adolescence is greater than the girl's, just as his whole childhood has been marked by fewer obligations and duties. Girls of fourteen and fifteen continue to be scolded and forced to assist in household tasks, but there is evidence for believing that now this direction begins to be resented, leading to negativistic behavior. At this age girls, following a family quarrel, often leave their families to live with married sisters or maternal aunts. In late adolescence boys may also leave home and live in another settlement, but this step is generally a preparation for marriage.

What is the adolescent's orientation in life? What are his ambitions and aspirations? We sought to ask such questions but rarely received clear or decisive answers. Irene Wiley refused to try to think of her future and shook off all such inquiries. A typical expression of personal orientation comes from Carl Leonard, a literate fourteen year old boy of mixed Tahltan and Kaska parentage. Asked what he wanted to do when he grew up, Carl replied: "Work at something; little work. Build house. I want to trap most." Did he want to go outside of the Kaska area?"Sometimes I go out, just for trip." Why did he want to build a house? "Live inside." What was the goal in trapping? "Catch something on trap." What about money? "Yeah, make a little money." What is money good for? "Buy some things." If he had a great deal of money what would he buy? "Buy some grub, clothes for myself, buy good blankets. That's all."

From this not unrepresentative instance we may conclude that the Kaska adolescent's aspirations do not significantly outrank the generally low level of aspiration patterned by the society. The adolescent's goals are formulated within the conventional realm of experience; his personal ambition is limited. In later life the adult will retain these qualities as distinctive features of his personality.

Marriage and Adulthood

Marriage in Kaska society is essentially an unformalized contract between two individuals, the husband and wife. Only secondarily is it also a relationship between the man and his wife's father, to whom he becomes indebted for a certain period of cooperation or bride service. The latter element in the marital relationship appears to be gradually weakening in importance, with marriage becoming solely an interpersonal relationship between two people. Kaska marriage does not build up a set of important reciprocal relations between affinal relatives.

Marriage may be regarded as marking the transition from physiological maturity to social adulthood. Although adult economic roles and some measure of adult responsibility have been fostered on the boy and girl by adolescence, it is with marriage that the full burden of economic responsibility descends on the man and woman. Now the curtain is rung down on the carefree pursuit of fun by adolescents. This consideration is important in understanding the conscious motives to delay marriage.[30] Richard Day explained his reluctance by pointing out his current sexual freedom, which would be hampered by a wife's interference. Eva Ardo said: "I don't want to get married. Too hard time. That man lazy, what I gonna do?" Other informants were content to claim that they were too young to marry.

On the other hand marriage is recognized as the proper way of life. People cannot live comfortably alone. Children are desired but cannot be well brought up without a father. It is also ideally believed that once marriage is entered, it should become a permanent union of one man and one woman. The primary qualities desired of a husband are persistence and ability in hunting and trapping as well as a congenial temperament. A wife is desired who combines skill with attractiveness and modesty. While a man might prefer to marry a virgin, there is little manifest reluctance to marry a girl with sexual experience who has the desirable qualities expected of a wife. A woman who has acquired a reputation for adolescent promiscuity is not regarded as an ideal wife.

Police and missionary advice is cited by the Indians to back up the opinion that marriage at too early an age is undesirable. Although a number of marriages have recently been contracted between fifteen or sixteen year old girls and nineteen year old men, opinion holds that neither spouse should be below nineteen or twenty. Another argument maintains that premature marriage (presumably because it would be accompanied by premature sexual intercourse) results in a loss of blood and early aging. It is apparent that governmental and religious agents are attempting to discourage early marriage with the cooperation of Indians. Nevertheless, native attitudes disapproving of early unions are often ignored in practice.

Besides being governed by the principle of moiety exogamy, marriage is forbidden between any relatives closer than cousins and any cousins other than a girl's paternal cross-cousin and, complementarily, a boy's maternal cross-cousin. The marriage of such cross-cousins is regarded as preferable. Several existing marriages also reveal an approved pattern in which two sisters marry two brothers. Marriage with a white man is permitted and sometimes encouraged. Hesitation is sometimes expressed toward marriage outside of the part-

[30] Compare Parsons, *Holding Back in Crisis Ceremonialism* (1916).

ner's tribe or with Indians outside of the Kaska nation, but plans for such unions are not seriously blocked if previous marriages have helped cement relations between such groups, and if the match itself is regarded as a good one. It may also be noted that a desirable marriage between members of the same moiety is readily condoned if one of the partners, or a partner's mother (sometimes even a maternal grandmother), has been only conventionally classified with the side and originally came from a tribal district lacking dichotomous organization.[31]

Marriage may, as usually happens, be directly negotiated between the boy and girl or it may be originated by the father of a marriageable daughter. Generally a boy proposes to a girl, who either indicates her acceptance or rejection or else refers him to her father. Consultation between the boy and his sweetheart's father is regarded as the desirable and correct way of negotiating marriage. Old Kean complained that nowadays many couples agree to live together without consulting the girl's parents and, as a result, worthless men often succeed in marrying good girls. The pattern of consulting the girl's father may be only indirectly accomplished, as when a shy youth requests permission to trap with a man, leaving the more fundamental motive of his petition to be inferred. The prospective father-in-law is ideally regarded as an arbiter qualified to pass upon a youth's suitability as a husband. During the period of field work one instance was noted of a confident and headstrong part-Tahltan girl asking a boy's father for permission to marry the latter's son. This behavior was recognized as atypical and was pointed to as an unfavorable sign. "That means they're not gonna stay together long," Old Man opined. "Better if boy run after the girl." River Joe, whose son was being sued, appeared less concerned with this aspect than with the fact that there was distant kinship between his and the girl's family. He invited the ethnographer to trace this relationship and was pleased to learn that the children were distant cross-cousins.

The second pattern of marriage is illustrated when, as sometimes happens, a man with a marriageable daughter keeps watch for a likely son-in-law. If among the unmarried young men (or white men) he notes one who is unrelated and who is not by birth a member of his daughter's moiety, he may invite the prospective son-in-law to trap with him for a winter. This situation, once the boy accepts the invitation, is calculated to bring the young people into intimate association. If the couple decide to stay together, the man's visit assumes the character of bride service and a marriage is recognized.

In cases where marriage has been initiated by a young couple and approval has been received from a girl's father, the son-in-law changes his residence to the winter settlement of his fiancée and begins an indefinite period of bride service, which is ideally stated to last about a winter but which really has no formal termination in cases where matrilocal residence continues permanently. The boy hunts for his father-in-law's family and traps on the latter's trap line. Fur that the youth accumulates becomes his own, the family looking to the young man mainly for additional meat and necessary assistance. Sexual relations are implicitly permitted during the period of bride service, so that this relationship is often tantamount to marriage. In at least one instance, however, the expectations of a young man

[31] See above, p. 133.

(Peter Tom) were dashed when, after a period of living with his sweetheart, the girl's father (River Joe) forbade the legalization of the union by the missionary.

The English word "married" is generally reserved by Kaska speakers to designate unions which have been sanctioned by the Roman Catholic missionary. Approximately four out of five families with children have been instituted with religious sanction and the ideal attitudes of the people are strongly in favor of such "church marriages." "Married more better," River Joe explained. "No married, people split all the time that way." Generally by the time religious recognition of a marriage is sought, the couple have already "stayed together" in the girl's family for a year or more. Such staying together, once it has continued for a time, can be said to constitute "Injun married" or "blanket marriage."

From the foregoing it will be clear that no hard and fast line can be drawn between the period of bride service and the inception of a marriage relationship. Often the two gradually merge one into the other and it is mainly by the boy's behavior toward the girl that a state of marriage can be diagnosed. If the boy appears in public with his finacée, buys grub for her, and if they share their own dwelling, then marriage has occurred. Even these diagnostics may lack clear significance, however, in the case of an unattached older adolescent girl who seeks support for the winter by living with a youth (who purchases a joint winter outfit) but in the summer returns to independent living.

Following marriage, the woman gradually becomes known by the man's surname. The husband builds a cabin or tent frame near his wife's parents' dwelling. The form of marriage is always monogamous and has been so during the past forty years.

One rather exceptional instance of what might be considered as true polyandry was noted. For five years Dorothy Plover had been married to a white man who acknowledged some slight degree of Cree ancestry. He was much older than Dorothy and by him she had borne one child. In Lower Post, while continuing to live with this husband, Dorothy simultaneously began to live with another and also much older white man (her first husband's employer), who allegedly fathered her second child. After some months, Dorothy's first husband, although he continued to refer to the woman as his wife, moved a short distance from the town and Dorothy began openly to live with the putative father of her second baby. This behavior was commented upon rather unfavorably by several Indians, who referred to Dorothy's revival of an "old fashioned way." Dorothy's father, a Tahltan Indian, raised no serious objection to the second union when he visited Lower Post.

Non-support, cruelty, and infidelity are the reasons commonly given for divorce in Kaska society. Divorce is simply accomplished by separation, although when a church wedding has occurred this form of divorce is of course not sufficient to bring about legal dissolution of a marriage. Several years ago the remarriage of an improperly divorced man led to his arrest and imprisonment and the incident is still recalled as an illustration of the binding nature of church marriage.[32] Within the society little notice is taken of separation unless it occurs between a couple who have been married for some time and have children. In divorce, children remain with the mother unless they are old enough to prefer the father and able to care for themselves. Statistics on divorce were difficult to obtain. The incidence is undoubtedly high in marriages which do not have a legally binding character but here,

[32] See Old Man's autobiographical sketch below, p. 323.

as we have mentioned above, unions of older girls (like Irene Wiley) with unattached men are sometimes so transitory as to warrant doubt of their classification as marriages.

Community reactions to divorce may perhaps be best illustrated by giving in some detail an incident occurring during the period of field work. In the spring of 1945 Nitla brought his wife, Adele, and two year old daughter from Simpson Lake to his father's home on the Upper Liard River. Here the couple put up in a cabin belonging to Nitla's brother, John Kean. John had been married twice previously. His first wife died in childbirth while the second woman, Anna Man, left him. Following Nitla's arrival at Old Kean's place, John became interested in Adele and she reciprocated his attention. When the Upper Liard Indians moved downriver, where some of them spent the summer camping at the Highway crossing, Adele and her baby joined them and lived with John while Nitla went on to Lower Post. Here Nitla complained to friends about his brother's behavior. Community sentiment was with Nitla and against John, who was spoken of as having "stolen" his brother's wife.

Although the marriage of Nitla and Adele had never been religiously solemnized, the missionary, hearing of the separation, decided to try both to effect a reconciliation and at the same time give the marriage a binding character. With the diocesan bishop (who was visiting in Lower Post) the priest went to the Bridge. However his attempt to talk with Adele was unsuccessful, as the girl refused to leave her tent and the clerics were forced to abandon their efforts. Since by this time the affair had become common knowledge, rationalizations seemed called for. To friends Adele explained that she had left her husband because the latter did not treat her well. She alleged that Nitla did not leave her with enough wood, and that he often left her without food for several days. She pointed out that Nitla did not even have a tent to house his family. These conditions, she maintained, forced her to live in John's accommodations and to share the latter's food.

Most of these charges were denied by Nitla, who at once began efforts to secure some food and a mosquito tent. He accused his brother of having fought him and asserted that he did not want to lose his wife and particularly not his daughter.

Meanwhile John Kean was also on the defensive. Twice he threatened Old Man with physical violence for interfering in the affair. Steadfastly he denied that he wanted to keep Adele, explaining that he was merely looking after the girl in his brother's absence at Lower Post. To Nitla, however, John was reported to have explained that Adele preferred him and what could he do if she refused to leave him alone?

The summer drew to a close without the matter being settled. John and Adele returned upriver first and again began living together in John's cabin. When Nitla arrived he was given sleeping space in the house but relations with his wife were strained and the couple did not have sexual relations. Now for the first time Old Man began to refer to Adele as John's "missus." In other words, public opinion began to recognize that a divorce and remarriage had occurred. Nitla, bowing to the inevitable, took his property from John's cabin and, in the face of his brother's angry protestations, went to live at Old Man's place. Here Nitla dictated a letter to his father-in-law at Simpson Lake affirming that he had always treated his wife and child well and that he had not abandoned them. The purposes of the letter, he indicated, were to counteract any malicious rumors which John might circulate and to keep himself in his father-in-law's good graces. He suspected that John would take

Adele to Simpson Lake and would probably try to persuade the girl's father to recognize Adele's new relationship. Shortly after this Nitla left Old Man's place to go to Lower Post.

From this point on it was no longer possible to remain clearly in touch with events as they transpired. Apparently Nitla returned to his father's place and found that, as a result of a series of bitter quarrels, Adele and John had become estranged. In mid-December John reported to the ethnographer that Nitla and Adele were living together on Nitla's father's trap line.

The case is admittedly open to several interpretations but it may serve as an illustration of the interrelated attitudes underlying divorce and of the rationalizations adopted by each member of a triangle to defend himself in the face of public opinion. It is interesting that, despite adverse sentiment, Adele and John were not avoided by other young couples (including John's former wife), but that John and Adele were often reluctant to show themselves in public. Nitla, who felt he had right on his side, found no social pressures he could employ to reestablish his control over either his wife or child. Eventually he was forced to withdraw. In one of his last interviews at Old Man's place he gave some indication of the strength of his emotional reactions. "Can't sit down one place," he said. "Too much worry. Can't stay here. Good-bye—sometime get meat." Asked what he worried about, Nitla replied: "I worry. Your missus stay alone for other man, you can't feel good. I go down Lower Post. He keep my girl too. He say he never keep your girl. He just fool for me . . . Crazy man! No good for woman. That first girl he can't keep it. He get it again. He lick him too. . . . Sometime too much think about it. I don't want to stay here. Too much think about it. . . . Well, he hurting my heart now. I can't let him go my kids. No matter how many mile I go, I can't forget my kids. My kids he hold your mother for me now."

While widows are noticeably slow in seeking a new spouse, both divorced and widowed men are quick to seek remarriage. Generally such secondary marriages are more easily accomplished by widowers than by divorcees, since the reputation of the latter is seldom calculated to inspire a woman's confidence. Often a young man who has lost his wife through death will ask her parents for one of her sisters; such a request is readily granted and this may be regarded as a preferred form of secondary marriage. Older men who have been widowed tend to marry widows. Bride service does not occur with a remarriage if the husband already possesses his own trap line and independent residence. Such a man will, however, generally stand ready to assist his father-in-law in any major piece of construction.

Pregnancy. Like childbirth, pregnancy is not marked by excessive concern or anxiety either in the case of the mother or other people immediately concerned with the process. In the early period of pregnancy the woman exhibits little concern with her own health or with the safety of the fetus. Pregnant girls were observed bicycling and wrestling into the fifth and sixth months. Housework duties and even traveling are continued until the time of parturition. Sometimes this lack of concern results in accidents. Thus John Keans' first wife, who was almost ready to deliver, died in a sleigh upset that promoted miscarriage. Commenting on this lack of precaution, Old Man said: "They're not smart. She don't know what's wrong. . . . That's why she die." In the later period of pregnancy a woman is sometimes shy and retires from public appearances. At no time is a woman's pregnancy discussed or commented upon, the process being politely ignored.

Status of women. An adequate picture of the status of women in Kaska society must include consideration of several interdependent factors. These include the ideal attitudes of men regarding women, manifest behaviors of men toward women, and women's attitudes and behaviors toward men.

Ideally men recognize no intrinsic difference in intelligence between the sexes. On the other hand, by virtue of his activities, a man regards himself as superior to a woman. Because he traps and hunts, and through these activities supports a woman, he is "better" than she is. Old Man, who refused a direct answer to the question of which sex was superior, somewhat obliquely pointed out that a man who has lost his wife can be independent of a woman, making his own snowshoes, moccasins, and so on. Sexual antagonism of men is sometimes betrayed in derogatory remarks about women. Such remarks are: "He's just like woman," or "He's worse than woman."

Manifestly we find a woman to be economically dependent on a man although not necessarily on her husband. In marriage men perform the principal economic routines, supplying the household with most consumer and capital goods. It is interesting to note, however, that many men are reluctant to hunt or trap for long periods without the company of their wives. Old Man's statement that a widower can get along without a wife is belied by the events in his own life; he became emotionally upset, suicidal, and alcoholic following the death of his second wife and has been married three times. Such observations offer convincing proof of the fact that men are not content to live alone. Rather, a mature man's existence without a wife is sometimes characterized as "being hard time." Women, on the other hand, show a greater readiness to live independently and, as widows, do not show the eagerness to remarry which is revealed by men. A widow, perhaps with the aid of a daughter or sister, often becomes economically self-supporting, hunting moose and trapping as well as tending to female allocated duties. The woman's greater capacity for independence is probably related to the fact that men rarely do women's work, while as children women are in a position to learn many of the duties of the opposite sex and are better prepared to be self-sufficient. Matrilocal residence in marriage also operates to reduce both a woman's emotional and economic dependence on her husband. Finally, the status of women is further benefited by the fact that the society does not restrict a woman's activities by limiting them. Despite the fact that she may have several children, a woman will often move camp several times a year, accompany her husband traveling, and generally show no sign of being tied down or frustrated in a wide range of behavior. This freedom gives her opportunities to gain further knowledge of male allocated techniques and routines which may someday be useful and thereby lowers her degree of dependence.

We do not, however, find any pronounced reflection of a woman's potential independence and self-sufficiency in her marital relationship. Although in most families a wife is consulted before her husband makes any major decisions, there are few women who display dominant or matriarchal characteristics although sometimes a man's ineffectualness leads his wife to assume a firm command over family matters. Women generally reveal passive and compliant personalities and are willing to follow the lead of their husbands.

The expression of masculine striving in some girls seems to reflect a discontent with the less prestiged, more unexciting activities of women. Several such expressions were collected. Before her marriage, Paulette Donnelly is reported to have told her father: "I want to be like boy. I want to rustle, make little money." She didn't want children, feeling they were too much trouble, and inquired for contraceptive information. The spontaneous exclamation of Paulette, "I'm just as good as man!" when she one day killed a porcupine with an ax, is further evidence of the same trend. Another of Old Man's daughters was on her deathbed when she said to her father: "Don't try to save me. I'm no good to you. I can't break trail, I can't hunt, I'm only a girl."[33] In conversation women often speak rather boastfully of their exploits when hunting big game. Several women were reported to have attempted to induce sterility by magical means.[34]

To sum up the pertinent data reflecting the status of women, it can be said that the society enables the feminine sex to develop a considerable degree of independence and that such freedom is welcomed. The behavior of masculine striving is additional evidence of the woman's search for sexual equality. On the other hand, men's attitudes toward women and the marital relationship give women little opportunity to express independence, and force them to take a subsidiary role which is somewhat inferior to that patterned for men.

OLD AGE[35]

The Kaska define old age primarily by its biological correlates. Physically, as Old Man pointed out, "When people get old they get stiff and cramp everywhere. When they turn around, everything sore." General weakness and debility affect the body. Eyesight and hearing become impaired. As a man ages his hunting ability is one of the first things to decline. Stamina is drained off, "just like electricity." Louis Maza observed that when he was young he would go anywhere for moose. He kept on the move all the time, traveling all hours of the night. But now, at the age of thirty-seven, he is beginning to feel incapable of such exertion. The day after having indulged in too strenuous activity he wakes feeling unrefreshed and unrested. "You open your eye, feel you get up. No. Go back to sleep again. Old do that." Old age is also stated to be a time when very early experiences of an individual often vividly return to memory—"just like reading book."

Ideally old age is regarded as a period of wisdom derived from abundant experience. Old people are sometimes thought to possess strong supernatural power which has enabled them to hold on to life. Such idealization of age, however, is no obstacle to characterizing a clumsy or inept performance by assessing the actor as "like old man." In carrying old clothes, blankets, and other objects from the cabin which was to be occupied by the ethnographer, several girls began to chant: "Metša blanket," "Metša coat," and so on, for each hoary article which they brought out. The reference was to a partially senile old woman of

[33] Masculine striving was rewarded in aboriginal Kaska society at the expense of a woman's sexual satisfaction. A young girl, protected against conception by magical means, was brought up in the clothing and role of a boy, being trained to do a man's work. Her hunting ability was regarded as tied up with virginity, and she was expected to defend herself strongly against seduction. Slightly different patterns for assertive women to adopt men's roles (without, however, denying themselves sexual satisfaction) have been reported from Plains and other American Indian tribes. For a review of the literature see Seward, *Sex and the Social Order* (1946), 119-121.

[34] For details of such techniques see below, pp. 231-232.

[35] The collection of data for this section was considerably influenced by reference in the field to Simmons' *A Prospectus for Field-Research in the Position and Treatment of the Aged in Primitive and Other Societies* (1945).

that name who lay ill in the settlement and to whom they were humorously comparing the discarded belongings. The myths and folktales show no evidence that the aged were ever glorified. On the contrary, they idealized the stamina and ingenuity of youth while reflecting pity and sympathy for the old and helpless.[36] Sixteen year old Carl Leonard said: "I don't want to be old man. I want to be young man as long as I live. Old man, they say, hard time. Nobody carry around your things. That's why old no good. Young man always do something. I don't mind to be old, but not too old. Too old no good. Someplace you want to go, you can't go."

Anxiety is the principal emotional component with which the individual adjusts to growing old. While the aging person is resigned to the inevitability of his increasing debility, he nevertheless reacts to it as a threat for which he realizes there are no social bulwarks. There is no compensation for old age in Kaska society which takes the place of initiative in hunting and trapping. When the individual feels his capacity to endure the effort of these activities being reduced, he realizes, especially if he is a man, that from now on his self-sufficiency and independence will be seriously limited. Since the man is the principal economic provider of the Kaska family, old age is far more anxiety provoking to the male than to the female. The solidarity of women, their warmer interpersonal ties, and a woman's training for a relatively dependent status all assist in providing her with greater emotional security in age than is afforded the man. The latter, trained for the role of independent provider and taught to rely on his powers of endurance, finds it difficult to relax. His insecurity is starker and less relieved.

The manifest adjustments to old age are found first in the reduction of a person's activities. A man will curtail his trapping activities, giving the more remote portions of his territory to sons-in-law or younger brothers. He may continue to hunt with a group or go out alone for a day, but extended hunting trips are abandoned and more of the old man's time comes to be spent idling around the camp or house. Increasing criticism of youth also appears to mark the male's transition to a new segment of the life cycle. A woman too restricts her activities with age, although she has long been used to receiving assistance in household activities from daughters. For a long time she may continue to sew, apportion food, and maintain a firm control of household activities, Between husband and wife signs appear of emotional ties becoming more tightly knit. Each spouse expresses concern with the other's health. The woman worries if her husband leaves the camp and remains away too long. In both sexes there is more illness. Older men indulge in reiterated descriptions of physical symptoms. Such illness further interferes with the performance of customary duties, while the symptoms are sometimes used as rationalizations for curtailed activity. With the onset of menopause, some women also complain of headache, abdominal pains, and general despondency.

As long as an old person avoids senility and retains an interest in his household, family, and friends, he is not treated differently from other adults. With senility, however, helplessness and dependence become more extreme; the individual is left more alone, is not consulted regarding decisions, and may even be neglected.

In Old Man's camp lived a partly senile old woman. Old Metša, who was being cared for

[36] See Teit, Kaska Tales (1917).

by her daughter, Lady Suẓa, and a foster son, Nitla. With Lady Suẓa most of the time was her youngest son, Donald. From these relatives Metša received a minimum of care and little compassion. Frequently her fire was permitted to go out and rekindled only after her pro-longed moaning and shrieking brought attention. Nitla complained several times of being unable to sleep at night or of being awakened by Old Metša's demands for fire. Old Man too complained of being kept awake by the sick woman's moaning. Because of her lice and uncleanliness, all except Metša's daughter were reluctant to come into contact with the old woman, although on the boat journey to Old Man's place illness and debility made it prac-tically impossible for her to climb into the vessel unassisted. On the boat she sat isolated from the other travelers and most of the time crouched in the prow near the dogs. Early in October everyone in camp left on a hunting trip and abandoned the old woman in camp with only the ethnographer's family. According to Nitla, they went on the hunt only after feeling sure that Old Metša's health was improved, and that she was able to do small things for herself. Four or five days' supply of wood was left, but little food other than sugar, oat-meal, and flour. During this period the old woman once more relapsed into serious illness (perhaps because of too liberally helping herself to sugar, for which she had an inordinate fondness) and was unable to keep her fire going. The wood also became exhausted. Among the last people to return from the hunt was Metša's daughter.

Youth shows little sympathy with the debilities and weaknesses of old age. No courtesies are developed toward the old. So long as a camp contains food, however, a helpless old per-son will not be allowed to starve. The aged are also entitled to rations provided by the Indian Affairs Branch. Unless there are particularly devoted children, however, it is likely that the standard of living of the very old must go below that of the average member of the society.

SICKNESS[37]

Sickness is apt to strike at any point along the life cycle and its classification following old age is solely a matter of convention. Here we will deal with those aspects of illness which affect the person's interpersonal relations. The Kaska Indian, with rare reprieves, is forced to live in close association with illness, either his own or that of some member of his family. While all illness is not necessarily serious, concern with symptoms occupies a large portion of the adult's attention. Young people, in contrast, often underestimate the seriousness of sickness.

Little concern with the implications of sickness for the future is manifested, even by those men who are most concerned with their symptoms. Yet incapacitation through illness may have serious economic consequence. Illness in the fall, for example, can prevent hunting and frustrate the accumulation of meat for the winter. If serious ill health occurs in the winter it hinders trapping. The following spring, with insufficient fur, a man can do little more than pay off the credit extended to him the previous year before beginning to run up a new and higher debt. Several men were caught in this vicious circle.

The economic burden resulting from a man's sickness must, in greatest part, be borne

[37] Field work in connection with sickness was greatly aided by the use of Ackerknecht's *On the Collecting of Data Concerning Primitive Medicine* (1945). For other information concerning ideas of sickness and medicine in Kaska society see below pp. 245–246.

by the individual and his immediate family. A father-in-law and son-in-law may assist each other if poor health strikes, but such assistance is limited to gifts of food or casual labor (cutting a little wood, making an occasional trip to the trap line) and never extends to gifts of money. Problems arising from sickness are shouldered as inevitable, but promote considerable self-pity and despair. A sick person is neither neglected by his spouse or parents nor exceptionally well treated. Illness is generally not catered to, and a sick adult or older child, unless he actively resists, is rarely excused from work. There are, therefore, few satisfactions to be derived from illness, although men often use their symptoms as justifications for inactivity or procrastination. In general people do not remain in bed until they are seriously sick. A patient may sit a great deal or, if an old woman, crouch on the ground, but is slow to lie down.

As far as treatment is concerned, any man or woman may assume the role of therapist, a role conferring little status or prestige. Generally a parent ministers to a child, a husband and wife to each other. There is still a residual belief that certain individuals, particularly older men like River Joe, possess supernaturally derived curative power. This belief, however, serves no important function and such reputed shamans are no longer requested to practice. An incident reported by Old Man illustrates contemporary attitudes. Five or six years ago Willy Wiley accidentally shot himself through the hand. The boy's father, Old Wiley, refused to consider Old Man's resolution to send the boy outside for medical treatment. "Fortune gonna heal it," Old Wiley said, refering to the concept of supernarural power. Old Man replied: "Fortune not gonna help." The latter's opinion prevailed, and Willy was flown to Fort St. John, where the injury was successfully treated. In native therapy, medicine is rarely forced upon an unwilling patient and even adolescents are usually permitted to control their own treatment. Thus Old Man reported that his daughter, Louisa, had been prescribed "T. B. medicine" by the Canadian Air Force physician at Watson Lake Airport. The medicine was given to Old Man with instructions that the girl take it daily. "Doctor tell me, 'Make her take it'." Nevertheless Old Man left it up to Louisa to treat herself. "I don't think she take it yet," he remarked several months later.[37a]

The most important therapy comes from outside the Indian community. Since their stay in the area, the Roman Catholic missionaries have dispensed a limited amount of simple medication, and white trappers also from time to time provide first aid and simple remedies for Indians encountered in the bush. During 1944 and the greater part of 1945, highly qualified medical therapy together with limited hospital facilities were available from Canadian and United States Army physicians, dentists, and nurses who were stationed at Watson Lake Airport to serve the air forces. The facilities for such care were readily used by the Indians until they were withdrawn in the fall of 1945. Several times Canadian and United States doctors made unofficial visits to Lower Post, where they advised patients who sought them out. In January 1945, an United States Army physician parachuted from a plane near Smith River, to help curb a dysentery outbreak that has already claimed the lives of several children. When his work was done, Indians guided him out of the bush to the Alaska Highway.

[37a] Information received during the winter of 1948–49 revealed Louisa to be a patient in a hospital far south of the Kaska area.

Currently the Canadian government provides qualified medical attention for Indians at two hospitals, one for Yukon Indians in Whitehorse and another for Indians of British Columbia at Fort St. John. The former hospital is about three hundred miles from Lower Post, while the latter is about six hundred. To secure admission and permission for air travel to either hospital, the missionary or police must radio the Indian Agent at Telegraph Creek. Should the agent be away from his office, traveling in the performance of his duties, a reply to the wire giving authorization for transportation and hospitalization may be delayed for several days. Such delay occurred during the summer of 1945 in the case of a young victim of spinal meningitis. The boy was in delirium for three days before authorization was received to fly him to Whitehorse, where he died and was buried.

A nurse and physician employed by the Indian Affairs Branch visit the Indian community at Lower Post each summer and suggest medical or hospital treatment as required. The Mounted Police remain vigilant for evidence of venereal infection, and when a source of such disease is reported insist on the patient receiving prompt treatment. These precautionary attitudes contribute to the fact that the degree of venereal infection, despite the recent large influx of strangers, is relatively slight.

Native attitudes toward hospitalization vary. A number of men expressed admiration for the air forces' hospital at Watson Lake and also spoke well of the care they had received in the government hospital at Whitehorse. Other people severely criticized the regimen of public hospitals, some without themselves having been patients. Speaking of the Whitehorse institution, where he had gone to have a dislocated hip bone reset, Old Man claimed that the wards for white patients are superior to those reserved for Indians. Asked how he liked the hospital, he answered: "I didn't like it. You smell something." The odor, he said, reminded him of death and was absent in the white wards which he had casually visited. He admitted that the staff of the institution had "treated me fine." Another informant complained that the same hospital had starved his young daughter, feeding her only bread and water twice a day. He asserted that the hospital employs doctors at government expense who try to starve Indians to death.

DEATH

Death, the separation of body and soul, is a condition that usually results from old age and from serious illness or accident. In holding these notions of death, the Kaska are not stoic fatalists resigned to dying. For the individual, his family, and friends the final moment is to be avoided and delayed as long as possible. Death, a bad thing in the contemplation of which the Indian is never at ease, not only represents a tragedy for the deceased, but also introduces danger for the surviving members of the latter's family as well as other members of the community who may come into the orbit of the event.

The living organism represents a union of body and soul or, as the latter is referred to by the Kaska, wind.[38] Some people also reported the spiritual existence of the shadow, but did not clearly differentiate this concept from wind. Although death represents a final dissolution of the body-soul relationship, certain temporary alienations may occur without neces-

[38] Throughout this section the words "soul" (wind) and "spirit" will be used with certain definite meanings. The term soul refers to the spiritual attribute of the body. Upon death it becomes a spirit. The visible manifestation of a spirit is referred to as a "ghost."

sarily bringing about the end of life. Thus dreaming represents a condition in which the soul temporarily leaves the body and "walks around." At this time it may "find out something—what you're gonna do." Should the soul travel too far from its proper locus, the life of the sleeping person may be endangered. Old Man reported that he awoke one night to find his second wife hardly breathing. He chafed her wrists and rolled her body. "Finally wind come out." He asserted that her soul had traveled too far from the body which, as a result, was close to lifelessness. Old Kean referred to the mobility of the soul when he declared: "My tajuš know lots of things. Just like man it go anyplace."

Following the final and permanent alienation of the body and wind, the spirit is believed to linger around the place of death for an indefinite period of time, generally from three days to a week. During this interim period the spirit is regarded as malevolent, being particularly dangerous for children below the age of puberty and to those relatives who have offended the deceased in life.[39] Even a child's spirit presents such danger to living children and especially to surviving siblings. The intent of the spirit is to secure a child to accompany it in the afterworld, while toward relatives who have injured it, the spirit seeks vengeance. Four days following Old Metša's death, Old Man commented on the two fires that had recently broken out, one in Hans Donnelly's line camp and the other in Hans' wife's tent. Although empirical explanations for both accidents were readily advanced and discussed, Old Man thought that Old Metša's spirit was also at work. "This old woman suffer. Nobody cut wood for her. Hans never cut wood for her; nobody come around. . . . Used to be old people believed it." It was pointed out that Hans' tent had burned eleven hours before death occurred. Old Man agreed but added: "Old woman just about all in that morning."

During the period shortly after death, a spirit may also communicate to people through the crackling of burning wood. When this phenomenon is heard, a small piece of bacon or other food is thrown into the stove as an offering to the spirit. Old Man revealed that Lady Suza had been seen to respond to such a signal, while her mother's unburied body remained in camp, by throwing a bit of food into the stove. Following the period of sojourn (or, according to one informant, immediately after death) the spirit travels to the afterworld.

Occasionally spirits return from the afterlife and manifest themselves in human sounds and activities. Sometimes they are also seen in human guise although, lacking tangible existence, they cannot be felt. Fear of ghosts is not an intense or prevalent characteristic of the Kaska. One experience of this kind was noted. Ten days after Old Metša's death, Old Man reported that he, his wife, Lady Suza, and Paulette Connelly were awakened by the sound of footsteps in the snow outside the cabin. A moment later they heard the sound of ripping canvas. Old Man expressed fear that one of the dogs had gotten loose and was breaking into the adjoining tent, where the old woman had died. Paulette arose and lit a candle. As soon as the light appeared, all sounds ceased. Paulette left the house but could find no tracks in the snow. Upon checking the dog shelters, she found all the animals in place. The next morning Old Man looked around, but also failed to locate any tracks. We asked Old Man his opinion of the phenomenon. "I figger maybe ghost come back," he said. "That woman suffer too much."

[39] Compare Opler, An Interpretation of Ambivalence of Two American Indian Tribes (1936); Opler, Further Comparative Anthropological Data Bearing on the Solution of a Pyschological Problem (1938); also Honigmann, Northern and Southern Athapaskan Eschatology (1945), 469.

Suicide. All evidence agrees that completed suicide is very rare in Kaska society. On the other hand, observation and communications agree that attempted suicide by men is of frequent occurrence and very likely to appear during intoxication. There is a general pattern for such attempted self-destruction. In the two cases of the sort observed during field work, the weapon selected was a rifle. As he brandishes the weapon the would be suicide announces his intention in an emotional outburst. This becomes the signal for interference to block the deed. One or more men leap forward to wrest the gun from the intended suicide's possession and toss it out of sight. The would be victim is now usually emotionally overwhelmed by his behavior. This pattern is illustrated by Louis Maza's behavior during intoxication.[40] Several times during the afternoon Louis had manifested aggression toward himself, crying: "I don't care if I'm killed. I don't care my life." After several hours of such emotional outbursts interspersed with quarreling and aggression toward his companions, he seized his large caliber rifle and threatened to kill himself. Old Man threw himself on the gun and as the two men grappled for the weapon, Louis succeeded in firing one wild shot. John Kean and the ethnographer ran to the camp and together wrenched the gun from the drunken man. John fired the shells in the chamber and Old Man tossed the gun half-way down the cutbank. No punishment or other discrimination is reserved for attempted suicides. The individual is comforted and in the future, while intoxicated, he is watched lest he repeat the attempt.

Dying. The recognized signs of death are scarcely noticeable breathing, a grasping for breath, and a faltering weak pulse rate. When these actions cease completely and the movement of the heart can no longer be felt, the individual is considered dead. As soon as signs of impending death are noticed, it is customary to summon relatives and friends, who may attempt any medication or treatment which suggests itself to retain life. Attention is also focussed on the expiring person's last words, which are apt to be remembered for some time. When death is believed to have taken place, one of the relatives feels the person's pulse or heart. If these are silent, the news is circulated to other members of the settlement or community. The nearest kin of the deceased retire from any but the most essential activities and begin to weep. Friends of the mourners will try to comfort them and bring them out of the depression. "When people feel bad," Old Man said, "we try to make heart strong." Mourning for death always appears genuine and painful, but when observed did not manifest itself in uncontrollable emotional outbursts.

Immediately after the fact of death has been established, two friends or distant relatives, who are of the same sex as the deceased (and who may belong to the same moiety), wash the corpse with warm water from head to foot. The body is invested in clothing as new and as attractive as possible and is finally wrapped in a length of cotton cloth or other material four or five yards long. Away from Lower Post this is apt to be a cotton print material originally purchased for making dresses. The cloth is laid out on the ground and the body placed lengthwise upon it, face up, the legs stretched absolutely straight, the arms folded across the abdomen. Excess yardage is allowed to extend beyond the head. The edges of the material are brought over the body, pulled tight and pinned with safety pins. The excess

[40] For a description and analysis of Edward Prince's suicide attempt see Honigmann and Honigmann, *Drinking in an Indian-White Community* (1945), 594–595.

yardage at the head is then folded across the face. The shrouded body is laid on a blanket, a towel sometimes being used as a head rest. All the belongings of the deceased are removed from the death house to await distribution or destruction. When Old Lady Metša died at Old Man's place, her knees were found to be almost irremedably flexed from the fact that she had spent so many years kneeling and sitting on the ground at her work. After the body was shrouded, a packsack filled with clothing was placed across her knees in order to level them. When questioned as to why flexed knees were undesirable, Old Man explained they would require the construction of a larger coffin.

After the body has been washed and dressed it is left in the house or tent where death took place until the completion of the coffin. Some people may, in winter, keep a small fire burning near the body and also maintain a vigil candle. In general, however, the death place is avoided as much as possible and children are not permitted to play nearby.

Burial as soon after death as possible is the ideal and construction of a coffin is begun almost immediately. Several reasons are given for the desire to inter the deceased so quickly. In the first place, the removal of the spectacle of death relieves the bereavement of close kin. The evidence of death is also a reminder to others of their past losses and hence is depressing. Finally, the intense mourning of close kin, which is apt to be relieved by the final disposition of the corpse, is also depressing to neighbors. During the period that the deceased remains in the tent or cabin, the other occupants of the dwelling live with friends or erect a new residence.

Any other disposition of the corpse than burial in the ground is distasteful. A body should also be intered in a "nice place." "If they throw in the water," Edward Cross said, "No good. People can't go see graveyard."

The construction of the coffin is generally undertaken by a man who is recognized as being skilled in the task. He is assisted in the whipsawing and planing of the lumber, although in Lower Post readymade lumber is purchased. Before whipsawing begins, the measurement of the corpse is taken with a piece of string and considerable care is taken not to cut more boards than are required. If extra lumber remains after the completion of the coffin, somebody else in camp will die. The lumber is trimmed to make the foot portion of the coffin several inches narrower than the head (Plate 12, c). The scene of the construction of the "box," as the coffin is referred to, is not avoided. When the coffin and its cover are completed, their exterior surfaces are covered with a layer of any available material. This is tacked on the four exterior sides of the box, overlapping into the interior and along the bottom; it is also used to cover the exterior of the cover. When the draping of the coffin was observed in connection with Metša's burial, Paulette Donnelly helped her husband cut the material for his grandmother's coffin while that man and his brother-in-law tacked the goods in place (Plate 12, b). The finished coffin is transported to the place where the body is waiting. After the body has been placed in the box and the lid hammered into place, the coffin is transported to the burial ground. A small burial area is generally located close to each winter settlement, the few graves being marked by simple crosses on which individuals' names are sometimes crudely pencilled. Sometimes a fence is constructed around the graves, "So dogs don't come around" (Plate 12, d). Two large graveyards are located in Lower Post. These are maintained in an extremely poor condition, being thickly overgrown with aspen, willow, and weeds. Crosses mark most of these graves and there are also a few wire fences. One grave house may also be seen; apparently it covers a Tahltan burial.

The following record of Lady Metša's funeral was made at Old Man's place, November 18, 1945.

A sleigh was used to transport the completed coffin to the death camp, Raymond Donnelly setting himself between the shaft bars to pull the vehicle. When he arrived at the tent frame where the body was waiting, Harry Lang assisted the youth in carrying the box through the narrow entrance, which Mrs. Man later axed away in order to facilitate the coffin's removal. Harry and Raymond placed the body in the box as Mrs. Man, Lady Suza, and Paulette Donnelly watched from the entrance. At this point it was discovered that the sides of the coffin were too low, so that the head of the deceased protruded. Hans was called and dispatched to the carpentering place for additional short pieces of lumber, which could be inserted as wedges to support the lid above the projecting head. Hans found some lumber which Old Man had hewed for skin stretchers and these were axed to fit the width of the coffin and increase the height of the back end of the box. The sides thus left open were covered with the draping that had previously been allowed to overlap the undersurface of the cover.

The coffin was carried out of the tent by Harry and Raymond and placed on a sleigh. Paulette lashed the box to the vehicle, while Raymond began to hitch up five dogs. The men and boys retained the usual emotional imperturbability during this work, but Paulette and her sisters, Anna and Louise, chatted unconcernedly and even laughed at the ethnographer's photographic activities. Meanwhile Harry and Hans had gone into the latter's tent to drink tea and warm up (the temperature was more than twenty degrees below zero, Fahrenheit). When they were through they secured a pick, mattock, and shovel and returned to the carpentering place to prepare a cross out of a red spruce sapling about two inches in diameter. Raymond meanwhile started the sleigh toward the graveyard, riding on the back part of the way. Behind followed a straggling procession including Old Man, his wife, Lady Suza accompanied by Louisa Man, and the ethnographer. When the going became steep and the weight too heavy for the dogs, Raymond suggested that the mourners proceed. He and Louisa, with the ethnographer's assistance, then aided the animals up the steep incline to the burial hill (Plate 12, A). Meanwhile Harry and Hans caught up with the funeral procession and quickly went ahead to prepare the grave.

Early in the morning a large fire had been built on the gravesite in order to thaw the ground for digging. The burned wood was now raked away and the men took turns digging through the still frozen earth with pick and mattock. Raymond, Old Man, and the ethnographer assisted in shoveling the dirt out of the hole. A stick was used to obtain the dimensions of the coffin and to guide the progress of the gravedigging. The work went slowly. In the lower portion of the ground the soil was not yet frozen, and here somewhat faster digging was possible. Nevertheless, darkness overtook the workers before the hole could be excavated to a depth of between four and five feet. Meanwhile the women stood on green brush around a fire which Louisa had kindled thirty feet behind the grave. The evening was intensely cold and overcast, the gathering darkness rapidly obscuring the attractive view which the ridge afforded of the snowcovered Simpson Mountains to the northeast and the Cassiar range to the west.

Two poles, about two inches in diameter, were laid at the upper and lower ends of the burial pit and two similarly placed poles spanned the top of the shaft. The coffin was carried to the grave and rested on the latter poles. The women now moved close to the grave. A quarter inch rope was twice passed under the coffin. With this rope one man lifted the upper end of the box, while two men supported the lower portion. The top poles were pulled free. The man at the upper end of the pit ordered the lower end to be lowered as far as possible whereupon he let his own end drop into the grave, the length and width of which barely accommodated the coffin. The rope was then pulled up. Old Man, removing one mitten, bent down and tossed a handful of earth on top of the coffin. Mrs. Man and Lady Suza followed suit, but without removing their mittens. Harry and Hans then began to shovel dirt into the grave and the other people started returning to the settlement. During the digging of the grave only Lady Suza was tense and mute. The other people, including the working men, chatted of many things without any show of constraint.

Mourning by closely related kin may continue for several months, morning being a time when a woman will feel particularly sad and apt to cry. In time the intensity of mourning wears off. It is, however, often promoted when women are intoxicated, weeping or even sobbing for long deceased children being a characteristic feature of women's drinking.

Sometime after the interment of the deceased, the clothing worn by the individual at the time of death is burned. Any other possessions, such as packsacks and blankets, which are worn out or old and not desired by relatives as mementos, are also destroyed. Other possessions, like guns, files, axes, and snowshoes are distributed to relatives and friends. Good quality blankets and eiderdowns, after being kept out of use for a time, are thoroughly washed with soap and water and rinsed for future use by members of the deceased person's family. Certain decorative possessions, such as fancy moccasins or an ornamented dog harness, are kept as mementos by a surviving parent, a spouse, or child. A woman may also keep her dead mother's tanning tools. Old Man reported that he could never leave his present home for if he started to "move around" he would lose clothing and other objects that had been associated with his dead son and to which he wanted to hold on. He still used his deceased daughter's silver plated cup, referring to it as "the ghost cup." The dwelling in which the person died remains uninhabited for a week or two and is then reoccupied. Sometimes a tent frame or tent is permanently abandoned following death.

Following the death of a husband or wife, young children may be raised by the surviving spouse or given in adoption. A man will generally entrust the care of his children to his mother-in-law. When Mary Wiley's husband died in the spring of 1945, the latter's brother, Edward Cross, took the widow to his trap line. Old Man explained that Edward did not want his sister-in-law to "run around" too soon after her husband's death. It is felt that a widow should wait at least a year before seeking new attachments. Following the death of her husband, a woman retains his name until she remarries.

As participants of the Roman Catholic Church, most of the Kaska have been taught to pray for the dead. Such prayers, however, are rarely said outside of church services. Following the burial of the body, there is little tendency to revisit the graveyard. In the fall of 1945, River Joe asked his son-in-law, Louis Maza, to construct a fence around the plot where Joe's wife and Louis' baby were buried. Following the completion of the fence, he placed a purchased gravestone over his wife's grave. A few days before this occasion Joe accompanied his son-in-law to Old Kean's place, where the rest of the Upper Liard Indians were temporarily staying, and invited them to share a brew. There would be a "little party," he explained, to celebrate the erection of the stone and the completion of the graveyard fence. A few people braved the autumn rains to go the ten miles. Ideally, about one year after a person's death, a memorial potlatch should be celebrated by the members of the moiety to which the deceased belonged. The deceased is remembered for about two generations.

CONCLUSIONS

In this section we propose to evaluate the manner in which the Kaska secure their goal of interpersonal adjustment. In contrast to the technical culture, where the effectiveness of behavior was judged by the maintenance of life and human efficiency in the physical environment, a sharply defined comparable statement for the social culture is not easy to formulate. Tentatively it may be suggested that the adjustive behaviors of any society can be evaluated from their operation in imposing adequate control on the expression of interpersonal hostility (deference), keeping at a minimum seriously conflicting attitudes and behaviors (consistency),[41] and insuring sufficient morale to keep the members of the group together and satisfied (stability). It also seems impossible to consider adjustment without some reference to the goals of adaptation, whose achievement is influenced by various aspects of the social culture.

Before going on to examine how well the Kaska manage to meet these minimum standards of adjustment, we will briefly review the over-all quality of Kaska social structure and interpersonal relationships. Kaska social culture may be understood once it is realized that the Indians conceive of interpersonal adjustment atomistically, that is, as lying in the avoidance of as many intense and close human relationships as possible. Somewhat paradoxically (at least from a western point of view), it may be said that the Kaska pattern interpersonal adjustment in terms of interpersonal avoidance or, at least, restraint. In social life this note is correlated with an absence of rigid social organization and of devices for securing wide group identification, cooperation, and unity. The pattern is reflected in the kinship system which, as was pointed out, is not important in regulating interpersonal behavior far beyond the nuclear family. Beyond the household, interpersonal relations tend to occur between individuals rather than between relatives whose statuses and roles are symbolically, sharply defined. Such a kinship structure is consistent with a society in which the frequency of social interaction is low for the greater part of the year. If, however, unrelated persons do enter close association with ego, kinship terms are usually quickly applied in order that, one infers, ego may more assuredly anticipate the results of his behavior on another as well as the nature of the behavior to which he will in turn be subject. The social atomism of Kaska life is further revealed in the relative unimportance of the moiety and is also connoted by the nature of the marriage contract, which primarily involves only two, or at the most three, people. Since marriage is not important for joining family groups, we find no tendency to elaborate the event; in fact, no crises points in the life cycle are ceremonially elaborated. One of the functions of ceremonial elaboration would seem to be the subordination of the individual's role in an event to the social group whose symbolically expressed recognition is regarded as essential. In Kaska society little note is taken of transitions made along the life gradient. Finally we may consider the demonstration of atomism by the absence of

---

[41] Benedict has stressed continuity between points of the life cycle but we are now extending such consistency to other aspects of social life. See Benedict, *Continuities and Discontinuities in Cultural Conditioning* (1938).

strongly patterned forms of interpersonal cooperation, which are, however, also not demanded by the nature of most of the adaptive behaviors. The family is the primary economic unit in Kaska society and receives little assistance from beyond its circle. Even within the family, cooperative undertakings often rest on a voluntary basis. The *protégé* relationship is an unformalized cooperative unit which depends on the implicit assumption that it must be immediately (not eventually) profitable to both parties. At any time a partner may withdraw from such a unit and there is no sanction that can effectively force his subjugation. A similar note occurs in the father-in-law relationship. When a youth feels he can make his living independently, he may discontinue matrilocal residence as readily as he abrogated his *protégé* status. Economic sanctions cannot effectively be employed to control behavior at any of these points. For one thing, the execution of ego's adaptive activities does not require him to be submissive in order to secure economic cooperation. Furthermore, the moderately ambitious youth always has the possibility of securing economic aid through credit extended by white traders. Although this assistance may at first be small, it is usually sufficient to assist in setting up an independent producer.[42]

In a wide range of interpersonal behaviors, including sexual relations, visiting, and the relations of parents and children, we see the operation of isolating patterns which, by failing to bring individuals into close and intense interaction, give Kaska social culture its atomistic quality. Only in the excitement of drinking parties, gambling, and, to a lesser extent, in sexual relations and dancing, are these attitudinal screens relaxed in order to permit relatively intense, uninhibited interaction.

So far we have discussed the atomistic basis of Kaska social culture, mentioning in passing the integration of this style of living with the adaptive routines which do not require extensive cooperation. We turn now to an examination of the stress points in the social culture and the manner in which the conflicts arising around these points are solved. It is here that we shall apply the criteria of deference and consistency.

Most of the stress in Kaska interpersonal relations arises in the sphere of property and generates latent antagonisms that become expressed in drunken aggression and gossip. We have pointed out that although a person is not able to manifest complete control over the use and alienation of goods, ideally such exclusive ownership seems desirable. These data must now be considered in the broader orbit of social structure, in which the individual is defined as owing few obligations outside of the nuclear family, and which provides few sanctions compelling people to share grub, trap lines, and tools. Apart from the father-in-law relationship such sharing is not, for example, included in the ideas of kinship behavior extending to relatives beyond the nuclear family. However, and perhaps partly as a result of the perilous balance between life and death in the Kaska winter environment, people expect help in emergencies without, however, being able to demand it by reference to explicit standards. As a result of the interplay of these conditions, the demands for sharing are not *consistent* with the ideal notions of complete control.

How are the conflicts arising from such divergent values solved? In the first place, the

[42] Social atomism need not always be associated with equality of opportunity. Among the individualistic Chuckchee, for example, the young man's independent start in life is hampered by the selfishness of adults who withhold from him necessary means of production.

conflict rarely becomes overtly expressed. As indicated, most people share food with only covert resentment, which, however, is not successfully hidden in interpersonal relations (perhaps because such resentment is expected). People are also reluctant to make excessive demands for assistance, and this serves to reduce the situation's inherent disharmony. When the conflict occurs, the expression of resentment is further suppressed in accordance with the strong attitudes directed against quarreling and other forms of aggression. Antagonisms growing out of property conflicts do lead to gossiping, the results of which soon become known to the subjects. One consequence of calumny is to contribute to the reinforcement of the primary individualistic quality of social relations and the weak development of in-group feeling. This consequence, however, is again congruent with the expected character of social life.[43] Another consequence of calumny is the building up of latent hostility which, while avoiding interpersonal violence, leads to feelings of insecurity and being disliked. In the discussion of Kaska ethos we will examine these feelings at greater length and point out their significance for *personal* adjustment.[44] Here we may conclude that property introduces conflicts in interpersonal relations which are handled in so restrained a manner that they do not violently disrupt social life. In other words, inconsistency in the sphere of property relations does not necessarily imperil deference except during intoxication when, as among the Navaho, aggression is readily forgiven.[45]

To a lesser extent occasional failure to furnish cooperation is another conflict point in Kaska society and one which, when it occurs is susceptible to an analysis closely similar to that offered for property. In fact if we were to substitute the cumbersome term "social sharing of goods and services" in the discussion of property, and make a few other revisions in what has been said, we would be able to cover both property and cooperation in the same discussion.

To digress for a moment, the persistence of the potlatch seems significant in this setting of conflicting property values and minimal cooperation. In that festival, money is often contributed by a group of moiety members who extend beyond kinship ties and the tribal group. Apparently the occasion offers satisfaction in overcoming the reluctance to share, and provides a formal means of demonstrating a degree of generosity which, because it takes place in summer—a time of plenty—is not economically threatening. The pleasure in potlatching is reciprocal; the hosts' moiety derives satisfaction in preparing and serving a relatively lavish meal, while the guests enjoy the bountiful food and gifts which are so unequivocally offered. Since not all contributors can serve in the distribution (the organizer's family seems to derive the greatest prestige), we can understand the desire at the first potlatch in 1945 to let both sides eat, that is, to participate directly in the more intense emotional aspects of the feast. Unfortunately this aroused criticism, exactly why or in what quarters (whether in the hosts' or guests' moiety) we are not certain.

[43] But may not be congruent to the personal needs of the Kaska as human beings.

[44] Obviously adaptive and adjustive conflicts may also affect personal adjustment. At this point, however, we are trying to focus mainly on the structural aspects of adjustment *between* people and omit all extended consideration of psychological adjustment which we will have abundant opportunity to study in connection with the dominant motivations that underlie the structural picture here being delineated.

[45] Kluckhohn, *Navaho Witchcraft* (1944), 54.

Old age and illness may be regarded as stress points in interpersonal relations, although the conflict is primarily a personal one, the individual experiencing his declining or debilitated capacities as heralding loss of prestige. It is consistent with atomistic living that the old should receive no preferential treatment or compensations in the way of being looked to as social or spiritual leaders. Temporary illness often promotes a degree of intrafamily cooperation but the amount is not sufficient to offset the loss of the patient's productive efforts and the same conclusion may be drawn with regard to old age. From this we can see how essential are the energies of each member of the group for survival and how limited any possibilities for cooperation. The burden of personal responsibility is tremendous in Kaska society and accidents interfering with its fulfillment costly in terms of comfortable living.

This responsibility is related to one of the most important inconsistencies in Kaska life. As already pointed out in the conclusions to the technical culture, individuals, particularly men, are unable to fulfill adequately the requirements of their economic roles. The Indian is not able to direct his energies in hunting and trapping toward his own ideals of what constitutes an adequate standard of living. In the description of Kaska ethos and its development we will discuss the personal maladjustment resulting from those aspects of the boy's socialization which fail to prepare him to maintain economic initiative. Here it may be said that certain personality trends associated with the effects of emotional rejection interfere with the mustering of more than minimal effort. Such extra striving is required by contemporary conditions of life, particularly so when an individual, due to some emergency, must provide for others beside himself. Failure to be endowed with the necessary initiative to overcome such crises interferes not only with the solution of adaptive problems but also complicates interpersonal relations between a father-in-law and son-in-law and intensifies the social conflicts of old age and illness. A father-in-law becomes dissatisfied with a youth who does not meet the *ideal* standards of initiative (for which the boy was not prepared) while the aged and ill must face the prospects of debt and poorer living because they cannot unload their responsibilities on a young man. Apart from the failure to inculcate the ability to carry through economic responsibility, parent-child relations further complicate a youth's eventual social role by forcing him to acquire a fear of the bush which must later be unlearned.

Relatively minor inconsistencies appear between the postponement of the age of marriage and resultant parent-child conflicts promoted by girls' excessive premarital sexuality. Little social conflict appears in the sphere of sexual relations. There is, for example, no hiatus between marriage and "normal" premarital sexual experience. Men are not reluctant to marry nonvirgins, although they may balk at marrying girls who have a reputation for promiscuity. In marital sexuality, the forms of permissive extramarital sex relations (which seem likely to make their manifestation where individuals are in close interaction) probably contribute to the reduction of socially disruptive adultery. In Lower Post, however, the size of the community and the presence of strangers does not always make it possible for a husband to anticipate when a relationship may lead to adultery, or else he finds it difficult to act unembarrassedly on such an anticipation. The result is that he sometimes fails to counteract effectively the threat of adultery with wife lending or wive exchange. In the smaller settlements such a safeguard is probably often effective in reducing marital conflict. Although adultery may imperil deference in the family, it does not lead to an expression of hostility against the wife's lover and there is no evidence of a woman actually fighting her husband's mistress, even though this threat is feared.

As far as the stability of the society is concerned, the atomism characterizing social relations is related to the fact that there is little discrimination directed toward groups like *métis* or bastards. Foreigners, particularly the Tahltan, are warmly disliked and differentially treated but are, of course, by definition not members of the in group. This raises the significant point that the stability of Kaska society cannot be accredited to the mutual identification of the group's members, since even within a tribe the degree of such identification is slight. Rather we must explain Kaska morale atomistically as resting on the feeling that life in the group is congenial for the individual because it offers him an adequate opportunity to carry on interpersonal relations in the manner for which his personality has been conditioned. The satisfactions afforded by the technical culture, despite the fact that they have been importantly modified by acculturation, are still congruent with the patterns of interpersonal adjustment demanded as a consequence of the socialization process. Such satisfactions, therefore, are subjectively greater than any that would be afforded by life outside the society. Boys who have spent a brief term in boarding school may enjoy the stimulation of outside places, but apparently they are not attracted to the forms of interpersonal organization present in the white society. Thus they are not attracted to the employer-employee relationship even as this occurs in Lower Post. Nevertheless, it may be suggested that the hiatus between the increased responsibilities introduced with contemporary economic life, the increased effort that must be invested in trapping, and the ideas of futurity which are demanded as part of the trapping economy all contrive to undermine some portion of the Indians' morale. This is especially true because of the fact that socialization procedures have not become modified to fit the individual for participation in the new technical culture that is evolving. How effectively this discontinuity will be solved is a question for future research.

Another important threat to morale comes from the activities of the government agents whose behavior is totally at variance with the key forces of the social structure. Authority, direction, and supervision are producing considerable uneasiness in the Indians since effective flight is difficult. Significantly, in 1945, a number of men promised that the following year they would not spend the summer in Lower Post but would camp near the Highway crossing or on the east bank of the Dease River out of reach of the police.

Summing up, Kaska social behavior and attitudes may be described as adequately providing for the maintenance of deferent human relationships within the group, although certain inconsistent points, particularly in the spheres of property and personality development, introduce stresses in interpersonal relations. Despite these stresses and, in some cases, because of their deferent handling, conflicts within the group are not so severe as to promote instability, although the pressure of an organized authoritarian white society is considerably lowering morale by undermining the satisfactions which the Kaska have been accustomed to find in their atomistic social setting.

IDEATIONAL CULTURE

THE third major division of Kaska culture is built principally around the ideas and attitudes which the Indians direct toward the supernatural, natural, and social environments. These ideas, in many cases underlying behaviors described in the technical and social cultures, serve both adaptive and adjustive functions but in addition fulfill the important need of securing the individual's personal adjustment toward his known universe. Through these thought patterns the Indian strives to understand his experience.

In this division we will describe beliefs ranging from the fields of religion to natural history and human biology. We will discuss behaviors toward the supernatural environment and present activities illustrating the motivating role of other ideas. An attempt will also be made to understand the patterned, conscious and unconscious, thought and emotional processes of the people, and to outline the breakdown of rational control which occurs in some Indians when under the influence of alcohol or in mental disease.

NUMBERS AND MEASURES

Although the western system of numeration has been universally adopted in the Kaska area, few individuals are capable of extending such reckoning beyond one hundred. Arithmetical calculations are limited to simple mental addition and subtraction. No ritual or symbolic significance of numbers could be obtained.

The standard English system of weights and measures is in use, but the ability to understand these is not evenly developed. Most men have a fairly clear conception of mass measures, such as pounds, but a much more limited comprehension of length. When traveling along the crooked courses of rivers, Indians often refer to distance in terms of the number of points of land that must be rounded rather than the mileage that remains to be covered. There is keen interest in translating the distance between two known locales into miles but individual estimates are often widely at variance. White men are regarded as authoritative sources of such information, the ethnographer's maps being several times utilized in order to measure the distance from Lower Post to individuals' trap lines. Volume measures are also difficult for people to estimate, especially if a container is larger than five gallons.

In sewing the method of measurement is to compare the material to the span of the hand or the length of the arm. Rules, measuring rods, and squares are not used in carpentry or sewing.

Most Indians own clocks and pocket or wrist watches. These, however, are not primarily used to order time since most people are unable to read the dials and the measurement of time, like other measures, is only gradually being learned. Disagreement between time pieces is often considerable, especially in winter when, if a clock stops and there is no radio, the owner is only poorly able to guess at what hour to reset the instrument. The confusion resulting from Lower Post being on the boundary of two time zones is also partly responsible for the discrepancy between time pieces in summer. Individuals are not governed by time in the performance of customary activities.

By means of journals or by marking off the passage of days on a small calendar, an effort is made to keep track of the date. Alongside the use of this calendrical system, attention is still paid to dividing the year by moons. Instead of following the aboriginal system of referring to each new moon by a descriptive word or phrase (as, for example, "Moose moon" to designate the month when moose are fat), an effort is now made to correlate the moon with the western calendar system. This leads to some confusion. Thus the new moon around August 12, 1945 was referred to as "August moon" by one man but as "September moon" by another. However, opinion generally identifies the moon with the name of the following month. The Indians have kept track of the years only since about 1914. "Before we don't know years," Old Man explained. It may be added that since then, the Indian's memory for years is also not too reliable. As a result of the earlier ignorance of years, few older informants are certain of their ages. Some attempt has been made by the Indian Agents to determine ages by reference to the person's development at the time of the Klondike gold rush in 1898 or the outbreak of the European war in 1914.

The seasons are not precisely correlated with the calendar months in the thinking of the people and such "natural" divisions of the year hold considerable popular interest. The first dry snow, occurring in late October, is the beginning of winter. Spring comes when the crust of the snow begins to melt and the ice goes out in the rivers. Summer is the subsequent, relatively brief period of hot days, while fall follows when the deciduous trees begin to lose their color. Fall is also the time when game is fat and the bull moose begins, or is expected to begin, to run. All these phenomena are looked for and their appearance is associated with important changes in cultural activities.

LORE AND LEARNING

Kaska culture is characterized by little speculative or abstract thought. Aboriginal myths represent the limit of cosmological speculation and, in some cases, have become fused with western religious ideas. This may be illustrated by the creation myth obtained from Nitla.

The world was made by Jesus. At first there was a flood of salt water and only the sky was above the deep. Jesus then told the rat to plunge into the water and bring up some ground. The rat tried but "couldn't make it." The water was too deep and he died. Then Jesus sent a small duck (a species with a distinctive head and a cry like "rrrrr")[1] down under the water to get ground. "He catch the ground. He come up, let him go. Ground soon grow and make big and bigger." The earth grew from the size of a little island. Jesus then sent a wolf down to see how big the ground was getting. The wolf began to run around the island but never came back. "Too big that ground. The wolf become game." Everything in the world originated from Jesus.

"Jesus, he make Injun. No Injun first time. Jesus think about it. Make ground, willows, anything grow. No hill, nothing. Just like dirt the ground. He make lots of birds; leave 'em anyplace. Birds sit down and sing. This ground alive. Birds live and grow." Then Jesus made the whitefish, trout, grayling, and other fish. They were intended as food on which the Indian could maintain himself. Jesus also created the moose and caribou. "These Injun grub. If man lucky he get this grub; if hard luck maybe he lost his game."

Then Jesus created the Indian. The first man was made out of mud and ashes, Jesus tracing the human figure in the soil—"head, legs, arm, hair, eye, anything." Jesus left the image and it was like a man asleep. When Jesus spoke to the figure, however, it couldn't answer. It couldn't

[1] This would seem to be one of the crested species of duck.

breathe. "He think about it." Then Jesus brought a small bird and threw it into the clay mouth of the image. Again Jesus spoke to the man and this time the figure replied with speech. "He talk damn good."

Jesus thought about what He had done. He decided that He ought to make a girl for this man. Giving the man some "lunch," Jesus told him to go to sleep. Then cutting into the man Jesus removed a left rib—the last rib. He put this under the blanket next to the man. When the man awoke a woman was sleeping alongside of him. Jesus told the man to "keep" the girl. He told the couple to raise children. When the man and woman died, Jesus said, the children would marry and they would have children and so there would always be people in the world.

Aboriginal elements are more sharply delineated in the myth of the origin of the sun and moon,[2] which was obtained from the same informant.

At first there was no light, just perpetual darkness. The sun and moon had a boss and were kept in a cabin where they furnished never failing light. The keeper of these bodies had a wife, who had a daughter. This girl drank water in which there was some dirt. She was unsuccessful in purifying the water and as a result of swallowing the dirt conceived and gave birth to a boy. The boy "grow smart quick." When he was able to walk around he began to cry and demanded the moon to play with. His grandfather assented and gave the moon to the child. The boy rolled the moon back and forth in the cabin until it accidentally rolled out the door and away. From then on moonlight appeared.

The next day the little boy began to cry for the sun. The grandfather heard him and exclaimed: "I'm tired of hearing that crying. Give it to him." So the mother gave the child the sun as a plaything. The boy rolled the sun back and forth until it too rolled away. Now the family found itself in darkness. They went to sleep. In the morning upon awakening they found daylight everywhere. "Good now. No more hard time."

Although lacking a comprehensive sample of Kaska speculation, we may nevertheless provisionally seek to classify their reflective thought. Ontologically the people are, of course, supernaturalistic in their conceptual perspective. That is, they tend to refer ultimate explanations of being to a principle which is beyond nature. Today this being is generally identified as an anthropomorphic God. It is not surprising to find this ontological theory associated with the metaphysical duality of mind and matter. Such dualism is evident in the notion that a person's thoughts can influence the capture of game and fur because of a power which is continuous with man's mind and also controls the animal world. Dualism also manifests itself in the idea of divination, in the ethical conceptions of free will and predestination, and in the belief that human life depends on the correlated functioning of body and soul. Explicitly, of course, the notion of metaphysical duality has never been formalized in Kaska philosophy.

One characteristic of epistemological thinking stands out clearly, the relative nature of truth. The Indian does not regard his thinking in absolutist, or universal, terms of validity. "That's what Injun believe," Old Man would say, implying the realization that white and other people have conceptual systems which differ from that held by the Kaska. Knowledge to the Indian is derived from experience and tradition. Since not all peoples have the

[2] The same tale occurs among the Kutchin and also the Tlingit. See Chapman, *Notes on the Tinneh Tribe of Anvik, Alaska* (1907), 8–10; Pinart, *Notes sur les Koloches* (1872), 797–798.

same experience nor identical traditions, there follows the readily accepted assumption that the world contains different kinds of knowledge and different truths.

Despite the fact that the Indian lacks the ability to formulate ideas in strict chronological sequence (we have already referred to the difficulties experienced in securing chronological life histories), he may be credited with a historical sense. Examples of native history have been presented in reporting the traditional ideas of Kaska origins and the memories of life in the aboriginal society. This material is distinguished by its static, rather than dialectic quality, no attempt being made to relate the events which are described. As pointed out in connection with acculturation, the Kaska are not attracted to the past. There is relatively little interest in hearkening back to aboriginal times, certainly no sentimentalism. Only occasionally will a contemporary incident move some man to describe the event as similar to behavior which was commonplace in former days. Such historical attitudes promise that in one or two more generations the ability to report "old fashioned" life will have entirely disappeared.

ETHICS

Ethically and morally, as well as philosophically, the Kaska are inclined to be relativists, particularly when non-Indian behavioral norms are discussed. Thus people asked the ethnographer if it was true that white people sometimes married their parallel cousins, whom the Kaska classify as siblings. An affirmative answer met with no criticism or repugnance. Moral relativism is noted chiefly in connection with marital and sexual behavior; aggression and lack of generosity are not so tolerantly regarded. In the latter fields, the Indians tend to recognize more absolute values. Thus the second World War appeared to confuse many informants, and local traders are often criticized for neglecting to meet the Indians' standard of generosity.

The Kaska express the same theoretical conflict between free will and determinism that is familiar to students of western society. As evidence of determinism we may cite the fact that a person is thought to be bad because he has "bad blood." This evil disposition is inherited, so that an evil man produces evil children. Opposing these ideas is the belief that an evil person can be taught to control his behavior. It is possible too for a good man to produce bad children, since it is often through error that good people commit evil—they "make mistake." Although this conflict between free will and determinism comes out in interviews, in everyday life there is little question of the moral accountability of the individual.

Abstract ethical ideals, like righteousness and justice, have little meaning for the Indian. When forced to concern himself with formulating ideal conceptions of human nature, he is primarily concerned with such concrete individual and social virtues as generosity, industriousness, pacificity, courage, skill, and (in women) marital chastity.

The ideal man is first of all generous. He gives good gifts and helps out a friend who is in need of food or of some capital goods like traps or cartridges. A good man is not pugnacious or "mean"; he is disinclined to unfriendly gossip and hypocrisy, nor does he seek to exert authority. He avoids talking unfavorably about his friends, is not cranky, and will not fight unless unduly provoked. Putting these traits more positively, virtue may be recognized in a pleasant disposition. A good man is ready to laugh and eager for fun. When he drinks he enjoys himself, but "he don't fight nothing." Finally, the ideal male reflects industry. He is, as Nitla explained, a "good trapper. He watch his trap line. Every two days he look his traps, fix his traps. He hunt too." He keeps his house well supplied with meat, wood, and grub. The ideal man shows courage without being foolhardy. "Somebody fight him, he tell him: 'Don't fight.' He save his life that way." Associated with the idea of courage is the ability to withstand discomfort. A good man must be "tough," able to travel long distances on foot, while bearing up under cold and hunger. In his ideal proportions a man shows skilfulness; he traps well; can make necessary tools, apparatus, and vehicles, and undertake a variety of repairs. Male informants did not report marital faithfulness as an ideal masculine virtue.

The primary qualifications for the ideal woman are faithfulness, thrift, industry, and skill. "You got a good woman," Nitla explained, "He can't leave you. Me, I want him. [If] I teach that girl: 'You leave him, that fellow'—that kind of woman no good. Good woman—try, try I get him—he don't want me. That number one woman. Smart woman." Not only does the concept of marital faithfulness include an absence of extramarital promiscuity, but it also denotes a wife's devotion to her husband, her care for his welfare and comfort. A woman's thrift also reflects her virtue. Thus Old Man often praised his wife for the manner in which she earned money by trapping and selling her own fur, saving the proceeds. So far as a woman's industriousness is concerned: "Good woman wash clothes, do something, cook anything. Fix the plates. Damn number one woman. That woman just the same queen. She catch fur too. She help her man. Best one." Feminine virtue includes skill. A good woman can cook well, trap effectively, lace good snowshoes, and make outstanding moccasins and clothes. A skilful industrious woman will not visit around too often but spends most of her time keeping her camp in order. Courage is not valued in a woman. Generosity, with those objects which a woman controls, and absence of aggression are further female virtues. An ideal woman may drink, but in doing so she "look after her man; wouldn't bother another man. Just talk fun."

RELIGION

Religious beliefs are of minor importance in Kaska life and the culture includes no religious ceremonials beyond the Mass and other introduced Catholic devotions. The general conception of the supernatural consists of an imposition of Christian (Catholic) attitudes on vague and disappearing elements of native belief. Both the Christian and the aboriginal elements are loosely comprehended, although an attempt has begun in the mission schools to formalize Christian beliefs in children. The general orientation of the religion tends to place all natural phenomena, including human life, in a universe controlled by supernatural agencies or "bosses." Since the techniques for soliciting this supernatural power are little stressed the individual—as well as all of nature of which he is part—would seem to enjoy a kind of fatalistic existence. This deduction is partly belied by the fact that the relative absence of supernatural supplication does not stem from attitudes of fatalism, but rather from an empirically grounded idea that in everyday things the individual's persistence and activity must also be counted on to solve problems of living.

Three main orders of the supernatural environment are distinguished by the Kaska. The first of these contains the executive agencies of natural phenomena—the "bosses" of the

clouds, water, earth, and animals. Although these bosses are often referred to in anthropomorphic terms, there is evidence that the executory forces behind the natural phenomena
are not always so understood. The second supernatural order is reserved for an anthropo-
morphically conceived Supreme Being, an aspect of religious thinking that was probably
strengthened following white contact. The final order of the supernatural includes the devil.

Of the nature bosses, our data permit discussion only of the executive agency operating
behind the animal world. Although there seems to be no clear idea as to whether the real
animals encountered in the forest are individually capable of knowing the intentions of men,
or whether it is a superior intelligence behind the fauna which has this ability and operates
through the creatures, the latter reading seems best to fit the facts. This, however, is only
one of several possible interpretations. A better deduction (for which there is no clear
evidence) might be to regard the spiritual components of the real animals as mystically
identical with the total supernatural realm in whose intelligence man and the various
species participate. We will assume that it is the supernatural animal realm which possesses
final intelligence and power and which, somehow manifesting itself through the forms of
real animals, bestows supernatural power on men. This intelligence is also capable of
frustrating the efforts of a trapper, who desires fur "too much," by keeping the animals
away from that person's traps.

The relationship of the Supreme Being to the nature bosses was never expressed and
probably has never been speculated upon. From statements of informants it is possible to
see this Being as superior to the lesser supernatural agencies and as a kind of final and
creative authority. The Supreme Being is identified as God or Jesus. As is indicated in Nitla's statement that Jesus is "head man" and "boss of this ground," Jesus and God are sometimes thought of as one; at other times, however, Jesus is referred to as the son of God.
Nitla spoke of Jesus having been killed by hostile soldiers who were instigated to their
deed by a wealthy but evil king. By His death Jesus made a trail upon which the people
could reach heaven. Prior to His killing, people could not achieve heaven but had to "stop
this side." The Supreme Being resides in heaven and is the final judge of the actions of men.

The conception of the devil was not much better elaborated. In general he seems to
be the boss of evil, operating through people who are hereditarily or wilfully disposed to
follow his influence. The devil is also capable of controlling the actions of certain animals
which he apparently created, such as the grizzly bear. By instigating the grizzly to kill men,
the devil can claim the spirits of the animal's victims.

Mythologically there is a fourth realm of supernaturals, mainly cannibalistic monsters,
like the giant frog, jackfish, and elephant, which formerly menaced people and are still
occasionally feared, perhaps because of their association with the devil. A few people spoke
of these creatures with manifest emotion and sincerity. Two persons, Old Kean and his
grandson, twelve year old Jack, identified a number of the Rorschach inkblots as such
mythological monsters.

Both people and animals (who, a long time ago, were also people) may sometimes
possess supernaturally derived power. The acquisition of such power by individuals is
no longer of great social importance, but few individuals were willing to discuss the concept
frankly. When intoxicated, however, several young men were reported to have announced

their possession of power, tracing it to the agency of animals. As near as could be learned, power (which is sometimes called "medicine") denotes that the person is under the protection of an animal supernatural on whose assistance he can rely. Any animal or game bird can bestow such benefits on an individual, who may solicit their interest by isolating himself in the bush. Apparently, however, purposeful isolation is not essential in order to obtain supernatural help, a person sometimes receiving an indication of such attention without any effort on his part. The acquisition of power is signalled by a vision or, perhaps, a dream in which an animal manifesting human attributes speaks to the individual. Sometimes a vision is not readily forthcoming even when solicited and was in fact denied to Nitla who said: "Some people go stay in brush alone. Got medicine. I can't make it, me. I'm too young. I'm just try first time. Nothing see me . . . Something don't want me." He was not disturbed on account of this lack of success.

A different type of supernatural power, one that is more readily talked about, promotes aid and protection. This may be acquired through possession of religious symbols like crucifixes, prayer books, and rosaries. Many people carry such objects on their persons whenever they leave camp. Once Nitla said that he would request the "mission man to give cross for me and wife. Grizzly bear can't bother that one. Somebody say that way. I believe him." Lowering his voice the informant added that a crucifix would also keep a seducer away from a man's wife. It would protect both the husband and woman from sexual aggression. A few weeks later Nitla was seen wearing a rosary around his neck. Small gospels distributed by the priest are also carefully kept. Paulette Donnelly embroidered a moosehide "Bible case" to contain one of these slim volumes.

Occasionally occurrences are interpreted as resulting from a favorable disposition on the part of the supernatural environment. Thus a man may ascribe his luck in killing a moose to the fact that he has had the cooperation of the animal realm. Many more times, however, references to luck are simply offhand mentions of a fate whose character the individual is not troubled to analyze.

Two states of existence are possible for the spirit in the afterlife. For those whose lives were free from evil there is heaven and everlasting happiness; for the evil there is hell. Just as heaven is identified with God, hell is associated with the devil. This correlation of an afterlife with the morality of the spirit's earthly career is not perfect, however, since, regardless of his conduct, any person killed by a grizzly bear must go to the bear's "daddy" —the devil. Although hell is recognized as an unpleasant place, few people admitted any realistic fear of it.

The idea of praying for the welfare of the dead is known to some informants as a result of church attendance. This suggests the beginnings of belief in a third, temporary state of spiritual existence—purgatory.

Alongside the idea of spiritual immortality remains a belief in reincarnation, the rebirth of the spirit in a child who, as he grows older, recognizes the world as a place where he has already been. One or two children were mentioned who had revealed this déja vue experience.

Several forms of divination are practiced more or less seriously by a few Indians. Sometimes the leaves in a tea cup are inspected in order to foretell the results of a prospective hunt. Seeing the outline of a game animal, like the moose, in the cup promises successful hunting. Another oracle is used to determine how many lynx (or any other specified fur animal) will be found in a person's traps.[3] The oracle is executed by winding a string around a smooth round stick according to prescribed directions and then placing the apparatus under one's pillow for several hours, after which the string is unwound. If, instead of falling free, the string is found looped around the stick one or more times, the practitioner is promised that number of pelts.

Omens of luck are more numerous than signs of misfortune. Hiccoughs promise good fortune, sneezing the receipt of good news. Burning wood also provides an omen. "When you think of something and fire crack," Old Man said, "That's ghost telling you 'yes' or 'no.' He knows your mind." In other words, the sound of the fire clears a doubt or confirms a decision in the listener's mind. Another omen is the tingling of a woman's breasts. This sensation often predicts the quick return of a woman's long absent son or of some other relative.[4] Many dreams are portents of good and bad luck. The revelatory functions of dreaming will be more fully discussed below. Sometimes dreams of hunting include a familiar bit of country; the dreamer then knows that he has received a communication from the animal realm and that if he hunts in the locale shown in the dream he will certainly meet success.

Almost every person has one or more older relatives whose dreams and powers of intuitive prophecy he respects. In the community as a whole these people enjoy no standing as prophets, but their own family and immediate relatives listen to the revelations with great seriousness and frequently recall instances in which predictions were validated. Fortune telling mainly pertains to events like the arrival of visitors, the conception of a child, or the return of friends. Old Kean was exceptional in expressing a predilection for more ambitious prophecy, a tendency which was largely ignored by everyone except his grandson. Thus he stated that "bye and bye" the world would again disappear, as it once did, in a flood. All the Indians would be wiped out in that disaster and white men would take over the country. Asked if the Indians deserved such punishment, Old Kean affirmed they did and alluded to the fact that incestuous relations had made the people "all mixed up." A year previously he had opinioned that the then current war would "clean out" the white man. "Something boss that make water, big rain, and ground," he pointed out. This force was going to rectify evil in the world, particularly the evil of wholesale killing.

Many supernatural sanctions underlying and explaining avoidances still observed in Kaska society have been lost, and it is quite likely that soon all of these unrationalized observances will be discontinued. Still held by some people is the belief that to make snowshoes in summer, or before there is snow on the ground, invites the danger of death. Another taboo forbids a woman to drink any liquid for twelve hours before smoking a moosehide, else a wet hide will emerge from the process. The care exercised not to cut extra coffin lumber lest another person die has already been mentioned. Those men who have acquired supernatural power from animals observe a taboo on eating all or some part of the benefi-

[3] See Honigmann and Honigmann, A Kaska Indian String Oracle (1947).

[4] Among the Hottentot, "If a woman's or young girl's breasts itch, they say: 'My son, my cousin, or some near relation will soon arrive' ". Hahn, Tsuni ||Goam, the Supreme Being of the Khoi-Khoi (1881), 87.

cent animals' flesh. Some fathers warn their sons not to eat moose marrow, the explanation being that marrow will destroy the boy's endurance and thus limit his moose hunting ability. A number of families avoid feeding their dogs the meat of trapped animals explaining: "If you do, never catch anything next time." Considerable respect is shown to the bear. Coming across a bear, River Joe once refused to kill the animal, vaguely explaining his behavior by saying that the meat was not good to eat. On another occasion the ethnographer's four year old son several times threw a bear paw into a brush fire. Each time Donald Suza pulled it out and finally threw the part into the river. He would not reveal his objection to burning the paw. In discussing the incident Old Man explained that the Frances Lake Indians continue to regard "many things" as "bad business" and added that Lady Suza will not eat bear meat.

The only religious rites and ceremonies in which the Kaska participate are those officiated by Catholic missionaries. Such ceremonies include baptism, prayer, Mass, confession, and communion. During the summer, nightly devotions in Lower Post bring many people together to recite one or two decades of the rosary. The prayers are said in English, although a few people also know them in Kaska. Apart from such occasions, prayer is limited. River Joe said that during his wife's illness he had prayed for her improvement. The woman died and Joe is reported to have expressed resentment that his prayers were not answered. During the summer, Mass is celebrated every morning but in winter it is limited to Sundays. How well the symbolism and liturgy of the rite are understood could not be learned. When attending church services the sexes generally separate, men sitting on the left side of the building and women on the right.

Many people go to confession about once a year to confess such sins as drinking, swearing, and sexual offenses. The confession, according to Old Man, is prompted by the priest asking questions like: "Did you swear?" and then requesting the number of times that the offense was committed. Following confession the people may receive communion.

Christmas is the most important ceremonial holiday. In the winter settlements its celebration is sometimes begun on Christmas eve, when a brew is drunk; drinking may continue for several days. If the people are in the trading post, Mass is attended Christmas morning and, sometimes, an afternoon church party is given for children. In the summer of 1945, a religious ceremony occurred in connection with the consecration of the new church in Lower Post. The rite was performed by the bishop of the diocese and was witnessed by all the Indians then in the community. On the following morning a solemn high Mass was celebrated by the bishop assisted by two missionaries. Both ceremonies were marked by considerable glamor and quite appreciated by the Indians.

Attitudes of the people toward the priests vary, but in general are marked by respect and some tendency to ingratiation. In the case of many people one of the reasons for attending religious rites is a desire not to expose themselves to the direct attention of the missionaries. The priests, who are young men, try to be friendly and democratic and appear to be sincerely interested in the Indians' temporal and spiritual welfare. Any direct interference of the missionaries in the life of the people is resented and may lead to an informal boycott of the church and school. Old Man stated that once when a missionary reported him to the police for drunkenness, he remained away from church until the priest suitably apologized. In 1944, when the priest, annoyed by the sound of the gambling drum, angrily shouted across the river, a number of people kept their children home from school for a few days.

A Protestant missionary formerly visited this area annually, so that many Kaska have at some time attended Church of England rites. Some Indians were first baptized by Protestants and later by Catholics. The attitude of Dorothy Plover indicates what would probably happen if rivalry between the Protestant and Catholic churches ever developed in the Kaska area. She said: "I go to any church, English or Catholic. I go to make the priest feel happy."

As a liaison between the mission and the people, there is a church chief, an office originally set up by Father Allard, the first missionary in the Kaska area. The functions of this official consist principally of informing the people of rites and devotions. "He call us to go to church. He just stand up outside. Let anybody go in. Then he come behind." The position is at present held by an extremely shy and retiring widower, who many years ago was elected by a show of hands. Only one youth, Richard Day, regularly assists the priests in celebrating Mass. He seldom alludes to this role and receives no social prestige from his status.

REACTION TO NATURE

During the many years that the Kaska have occupied their subarctic forest environment, observation and speculation have enabled them to accumulate a considerable body of knowledge concerning natural phenomena. Many of their beliefs, being used to guide hunting and trapping, have been thoroughly verified by pragmatic testing. By permitting individuals to make an efficient adaptation in the climatic, floral, and faunal environments, such empirical knowledge can be considered as having offered the society a measure of control over nature. Other ideas about the environment are primarily descriptive; for example, relating types of weather with certain winds, recognizing varieties of snow, identifying trees with types of soil, and classifying the temperatures of riparian waters with their sources.

Meteorological beliefs. Generally the Indian is less concerned with predicting weather from day to day than he is in long range forecasting based on experience. Thus it is pointed out that September always brings a long rainy period, snow will fall heavily around the middle of October, the end of November is often marked by a spell of mild weather, and intense cold can be expected shortly before Christmas. These predictions are often fulfilled within reasonable margins of error. In short range prediction of weather, the condition of the sky at sunset and sunrise is the principal indication of trends. Thus black clouds in the north at sunset promise warmer weather; as Old Man expressed it: "Warm weather, that's his pillow. He lay down there." A red northern evening sky also signifies a warm day. A crimson eastern horizon in the evening indicates a cold night, while a similar sky at dawn points to warmer weather. In winter, when open stretches of rapid water are clearly heard toward evening, cold weather may be expected.

Certain winds are recognized as accompanying types of weather. These winds are not identified with the cardinal points, although observation has fixed the quarter from which they blow. Upper Liard Indians speak of a cold wind coming from the east or southeast;

a bitter cold wind, termed "ptarmigan excrement," blowing from the north-northeast, and the warm Chinook originating in the west.

A number of predictive beliefs are associated with snow. On the Upper Liard, when snow comes from downriver (south-southeast) it will generally continue for several days; coming from upriver (north-northwest), a snow flurry will soon stop. Commenting on the intermittent flurries of snow in late October, Old Man described snow as "just the same like army. Bunch go for a while; then nobody." In winter such intermittent snowing indicates heavier snow to follow. "Injun say it listens for next heavy one coming." Several varieties of snow are recognized, including the wet snow associated with the beginning or end of winter, the dry powdery snow of midwinter, and the crusted snow of early spring. To protect cut boards from freezing into moist snow when stored on the ground, they are always laid across poles or on a thin layer of spruce brush. Other adaptations to climate have been discussed in connection with clothing, shelter, and travel.

No particular beliefs about the rainbow or aurora borealis were adduced. Equinoxes are apparently not recognized, although the longest and shortest days of the year are pointed out. In March, when the weather turns warmer, small children are often frightened by the heat waves that radiate from river ice and then get reflected back on the frozen surface as shadows. No unusual significance is attached to this phenomena, which receives an empirical explanation. Fog in winter is sometimes interpreted as an indication that a black bear has cubbed.

Attitudes toward types of weather are consistent among the Kaska population. People do not like hot weather or persistent rain. On the contrary, winter, with its crisp cold, is looked forward to, but it is thought that cold weather requires a period of adjustment. People explained that they often felt the cold intensely in October, although by November and December they no longer minded it. Rain or snow are regarded as unsuitable conditions for traveling and, unless the matter is urgent or the journey already underway, people will rest until the weather has cleared. In summer after a rain there is a tendency to wait before starting a trip until the brush has dried. Changing weather, alternating between warm and cold, is thought to make a person weak. "November cold," Old Man said, "then you feel strong."

Ethnozoology. A sample of animal knowledge was obtained principally from one informant, Nitla, who tended to divide the species according to whether they had been created by God or the devil. Most animals are good, that is, they were created by God. The devil, however, made the frog, mink, otter, wolverine, coyote, and grizzly bear. These animals are generally regarded as hostile or dangerous to man. According to Old Man: "All kinds of game smart." It will be seen, however, that although intelligence is an attribute of all animals, the distribution of this trait is differently apportioned among the various creatures.

The rabbit and beaver are two examples of "smart" animals. The rabbit (Arctic hare) is intelligent because he is hard to capture, running even from the faint sound of snowshoes. Nitla thought that rabbits became somewhat less canny in hot weather, when they are easy to snare; Peter Tom said that very cold weather and snow made these animals less intelligent and easier to trap. Throughout the year rabbits inhabit brushy places, sleeping on top of the ground or snow. From the deep thicket where he secures himself against dan-ger, the hare runs trails to feeding areas. Rabbit snares are always set across such trails. The animal eats willow, spruce, and jackpine foliage as well as a variety of bark—in fact, "he eat anything," even human and dog urine. The female breeds about four times during the summer, the period of gestation lasting about one month. The litter generally gets dropped in the shelter of a large windfall and may contain up to eight young. During some years rabbits are known to fall off rapidly, dying by themselves. This is thought to be due to their eating harmful food. The intelligence of the hare is demonstrated by the fact that the animal is believed to avoid a snare which smells of tobacco (apparently because this smell, foreign to the environment, signifies a human enemy). Before visiting the rabbit lines, women and girls are careful to wash their hands. Like the fox, the rabbit is also quick to learn. If he has once or twice narrowly escaped from a snare, he will afterwards recognize traps and give them a wide detour.

Beaver are found in lakes, rivers, and creeks. During the summer this animal moves around freely, leaving his winter dwelling in June not to return during the period from July to September. Upon his recursion, he builds a house or repairs a previously occupied dwelling by adding poles and additional mud. In fall the beaver industriously accumulates a cache of willow branches for his winter food. These he stores outside his house by thrust-ing them into the bed of the lake or stream. "Just the same Injun they live," Nitla pointed out. "Injun got no grub, he can't live. He got to bring grub here [to the settlement]. That way he live. Beaver just the same. You fix your camp good, no air, no cold got through. Beaver can't live outside. Inside hot, more better." A beaver house may contain four or five adults. The inhabitants of such a dwelling are known to fight amongst themselves, skins often showing the tears received in battle. Mostly such aggression is directed toward a strange beaver, who tries to join a colony in which he does not belong. This provokes resentment and attack on the part of the permanent members. The animal breeds during the winter, with the young being born in June. A litter may contain from four to six young. Low water in winter is often fatal for a colony of beaver, who starve to death when the ice freezes so thick that the animals lack sufficient room to move in obtaining food from the caches. When beaver exhaust their cached food, they may break through the ice in search for additional edible material. Again thick ice can be fatal if it frustrates this effort. Generally a cache lasts until April, at which time the ice is already going. Feeling his house disturbed, a beaver usually leaves the dwelling and enters the water. If the animal smells a campfire, he will not leave the water. The beaver's tail helps him to "steer" while swimming.

Less intelligent animals include the black bear, grizzly bear, and mink. The black bear is regarded as intelligent when he is fat in fall time. Then he is quick to flee from danger. In spring, however, when the animal is "poor" and the female has cubs to protect, the bear will readily attack other animals and even men. In summer, bears eat berries and grass, oc-casionally fish, beaver, and other animals. In October the bear dens up in a hole which has been tunnelled into the ground or the side of a small hill. The den is piled with dry grass for warmth. Before entering this dwelling, he scratches up the trees in the vicinity; "like he write his name," Old Man commented. In winter a hunter seeing fresh bruises on trees knows that he is in the vicinity of an occupied bear den. The black bear breeds in June, the young being born toward the end of the following March. A litter of a young bear contains about five cubs; an old bear may have only three young. One Indian, Peter Lang, spoke admiringly of a white man stationed at one of the U. S. Army kitchens near the Hyland River who had trained a young bear to come to him for meat. This man once told Peter to try to lure the animal with such a prize. The bear was wary, but the white man spoke to it, telling it not to be afraid of Indians. Peter tried again and the young bear put his paws on Peter's shoulders and ate the meat that the Indian held out. Peter was much impressed with this experience.

The habits of the grizzly bear do not differ radically from those of the black bear. In summer he travels around eating berries, grass, moose, beaver, and fish. Should he kill a large animal like a moose, he covers the uneaten portion of the carcass with leaves and dirt. When he is hungry, he returns to this cache to feed further. In November or early December (depending on when he begins to lose his fat, generally later than the black bear), the grizzly returns to a former den or tunnels into the side of a steep hill. Here he holes up against the cold, sustained only by his fat. The grizzly breeds in June (according to Louis Maza the grizzly runs in October), and the young are born in the den around the following March.[5] A litter contains four or five cubs, depending on the age of the parent. People have great fear of provoking or even encountering a grizzly, although when met every effort is made to kill the animal. The meat is eaten by some people, the grease being described as excellent for bread, and is also fed to dogs. The grizzly is described as "not smart." As Nitla put it: "He see you, he fight you." If the enemy is stronger than the grizzly, the latter will suffer for his foolhardiness. "Just the same German, tough heart. He catch man. One time he slap you, your neck off just like nothing. You tough, he start to fight you, you shoot him just like nothing." Informants agreed that the grizzly was not particularly dangerous in late fall. According to Old Man, in the fall, if a person turns aside from a grizzly's charge, the animal will keep running in a straight line without following his intended victim. In spring, however, a grizzly, especially one with cubs, will follow an enemy everywhere.

Mink live chiefly on rabbits, muskrats, and fish. For fish the animal plunges into a river or lake, the hind legs, with their scissorlike action, propelling him at a good speed. The tail of the mink is said to "steer" him and facilitate a quick turn. The animal inhabits the neighborhoods of rivers, creeks, and lakes and can be caught by setting traps along such bodies of water. The mink breeds in March, the young being born in June. Nitla did not know the size of the litter: "I never see inside his guts." A litter is generally dropped inside of an abandoned beaver house. "Mink can't make house nothing. He got too small hand." The meat is never eaten and is not used for dog feed as it is said to induce vomiting and to be exceptionally strong. The mink is not regarded as an intelligent animal. "Just like pup. You put bait on tree, you put trap here, he smell fish, he come right over. No smart."

Some other animals, like the lynx, are known to be constantly on the move, roaming over wide stretches of country in search for food. Other species, like the marten, restrict

[5] According to Seton, the grizzly mates in June and bears its young about six months later (Seton, *Lives of Game Animals* [1929], II, 32–35). The idea, reported by a Nelson Indian, that midwinter fog is a sign of a black bear cubbing, indicates that some people know bears to drop their young around December and January. Nitla was apparently not aware of this fact.

themselves to a particular area. Throughout the year the lynx moves "anywhere" in search of rabbits. "He can't stay one place nothing." In cold weather the animal takes refuge in deep brush, that is also a good place for finding rabbits. The lynx breeds in March and drops its litter of up to six young in June. Marten winter in dens. In February, when this animal begins to breed, he travels a short distance. A marten's litter generally consists of six young.

A considerable body of knowledge is available concerning the moose and caribou. Both species are known to visit good mountain feeding grounds in spring. In early fall the moose returns from the high land in search of country where there is as yet no snow. The caribou comes down in early winter, driven to lower ground when the deep snow makes food hard to find. Considerable interest is manifested by men in when the bull moose begins to run, for then the animal becomes hard to kill and travels extensively. In summer, however, "just right. Stay one place. Easy get them." In addition, as already stated, both the cow and bull are fat in summer, and therefore delicious eating, while in winter only a cow has fat, the bull being lean and tough. To be edible a moose must be quickly killed. For this reason the meat of an animal killed by wolves is not eaten. Then "the moose die slow," Old Man explained, and the meat is filled with "foams." A popular belief, not much honored, regards moonlight as a good time to hunt moose. "Moose not smart that time," some people believe. Caribou are not expected in the river valleys until late December or early January. In the mountain rimmed country of the Upper Liard River their arrival is eagerly expected, for they promise abundant and easily obtained meat.

Any youth who has spent some time in the bush accompanied by an older man is in possession of many hints for hunters. Thus he knows that the best time to hunt squirrel is in the morning, when the animal feeds. In the latter part of the day "they lay down someplace." Spruce hens are easy to kill, since, when they are frightened, they fly only a short way. Willow grouse, on the other hand, fly a long distance if startled and are then difficult to locate. A man is warned that he must be cautious in hunting the wild goat. When this animal encounters danger, he sometimes lies down and pretends to be asleep but attacks as soon as the hunter comes close. Old Man recounted one such experience. "Pretty near I grab it with my knife. I mistake. Lucky I shoot. When you come close just throw themselves down like dead. When you come close they kill you."

Ethnobotany. The use of plants for medicine will be reported in connection with ideas about medicine. Knowledge of trees is relatively limited and connected with the practical utilization of forest products. Two kinds of spruce trees are distinguished, the red and black varieties. Both grow in soft ground, where there is plenty of deep soil, the wood being soft and easy to chop when dry. Dry red spruce makes a hot fire. Spruce is used for snowshoes because of its lightness, birch being regarded as too heavy for this purpose. Poplar grows on hard ground. "Damn good wood," said Nitla. "Damn best wood." The wood burns well when dry and easily worked when green. Like spruce, birch trees also grow in soft ground. When dry the wood is too heavy for a good fire, but its strength makes it particularly suitable for toboggans and sleighs. Hans Donnelly thought black birch to be inferior to the white variety for this purpose, because the former contains too many knots. Because of its susceptibility to rot, birch cannot be used for cabins. Jackpine grows on hard ground where ashes and rocks occur. Like cottonwood, it is valued as a hot, slow-burning fuel and is burned in heaters even when green. Balsam is found in high mountains on rocky soil. The wood is good for fuel when dry and is easy to chop. The brush is particularly comfortable, its soft-ness being compared to silk. People also regard the odor of balsam brush as highly pleasant.

Miscellaneous. Cosmic phenomena have stimulated relatively little speculative thinking among the Kaska. There is, for example, no clear idea if the moon and sun are male or female. Nitla had once vaguely heard that in May the moon is a woman. This may be a reflection of the Catholic belief regarding May as the month dedicated the Virgin Mary. There are no ideas of the moon affecting human behavior. The big August moon is a sign that game is fat but the planet itself does not influence the growth of game. Eclipses are noted with wonder but no interpretation of their cause or function could be obtained.[6]

Some men, notably Old Man and River Joe, possess a good knowledge of hydrographic phenomena, like the ability to "read water," which has been derived from long experience working on traders' river boats. It is widely recognized that rivers like the Liard, which rise in mountains, freeze quickly. On the other hand, rivers like the Frances and Dease, which have their sources in large lakes, take longer to ice over. People desire river ice to form quickly, as this assures a smooth surface that is ideal for toboggan travel. In hauling wood on sleighs and toboggans, the vehicles are often run on the smooth shore ice of rivers.

Directions are not related to the cardinal points and few Indians could indicate north or south. References to direction are generally by the courses of rivers or by known land-marks identified with place names.

HUMAN ORGANISM

In this section are reported knowledge and attitudes concerning the structure and functioning of the human body as well as information, based on reports, observation, and clinical testing, regarding socially patterned psychological processes. It is obvious that some of the data consists of popular, scarcely formalized beliefs, which may vary considerably between different individuals, especially between members of different tribal districts. Some of the ideas may be survivals of aboriginal conceptions. These, however, in contemporary Kaska thought are associated with attitudes which have undoubtedly been acquired from missionaries and other white men. As in the case of religion, no attempt has been made to classify aboriginal retentions apart from introduced ideas, our purpose being to describe the content of knowledge regardless of its sources.

Bodily Structure and Function

The pattern of human growth is compared to the development of other aspects of na-ture. "Anything in the ground he grow. Soon big grow; no more he grow. Injun just the same." Growth of the body is a function of bone development. Girls mature more rapidly than boys.

Weather, food, and heredity are the principal factors determining the growth process. Summer is a more favorable period for human development than winter, so again it would seem as though the organism is viewed as developing in harmony with the rest of the

---

[6] Nitla remembered an eclipse of the moon which he had witnessed two years previously. He still recalls the phenomena with wonder. See his autobiographical sketch below, p. 352.

natural environment. Food is a stimulus to growth, and grub a better aid to development than straight meat. Because of the role of hereditary factors, children come to resemble their parents in height as well as appearance. The cycle of bodily growth is thought to be most intense before the age of fifteen, when it may be hindered by sexual activity. In maturity, sexual intercourse promotes the rapid growth of a girl's breasts. During early childhood, frozen elbows or knees may also retard a child's development, while accidents to the head are feared because they lead to an arrest of growth. Following physiological maturity, excessive sexual indulgence is thought to lead to rapid and early aging. In old age the growth process in both sexes partially reverses itself. Speaking of an aged person Nitla said: "He grow back again pretty soon." Seven stages of growth are popularly recognized. These are:

Baby (or not smart)	Up to about the age of three
Half smart	From about three to seven
Enough smart	From about seven to twelve
Half big	From about twelve to seventeen
Enough big	Adult
Half old	An adult with grown children
Old	Over fifty but depending on the individual's abilities

The ideal proportions for the human body were defined by Nitla as moderate: "Half pretty big, pretty good." There is some evidence that small men are sometimes sensitive about their stature. For example, it was reported that while drunk Skipper once offered to fight when another man referred to him as a "little man."

Human blood may be strong or weak, the quality, as well as the initial blood itself, being derived from the parents. Weak blood leads to illness and debility but may to some extent be strengthened by a diet containing sufficient meat. Food in general renews the blood. Exercise has a tonic effect on the blood, making it "work." The circulatory system is visualized as continuous throughout the body, the blood even passing through such extremities as the little finger. By tying a line tightly around the tip of this finger, the circulation of the blood may be arrested.

The body hair serves in securing warmth. The eyelashes are an aid to induce sleep; their removal may also lead to frequent tears. One informant had heard of a man who had lost his eyelashes and began to shed copious tears, without, however, suffering from insomnia. The absence of the eyebrows is regarded as extremely grotesque.

Concerning the head and features, children, as already mentioned, are believed to inherit the facial characteristics of the like sexed parent; a boy comes to resemble his father, a girl her mother. The most important parts of the head are the ear, nose, mouth, and brain. Within the ear is a tube connecting the outer to the inner portion of that organ and between these two divisions is a thin diaphragm which registers sound. The nose is both an organ of smell and an adjunct of breathing, serving as a channel for the expulsion of the air taken into the lungs through the mouth. The mouth functions in taste, breathing, and the ingestion of food. The teeth are necessary to chew food preparatory to swallowing. Their principal constituent is bone, and the exposed portion is believed to be softer than the part which is contained within the gums. The loss of the milk teeth occurs in childhood after they have been "worn out." In the adult, however, wear results merely in shortening the exposed portion. Meat is particularly wearing on teeth, grub tending to sharpen them. "Sweet stuff" may induce tooth decay, which is also influenced by the inheritance of poor dental equipment. The brain is the seat of intelligence, thought, and reason. Mental capacity is primarily derived from parents as a product of heredity.

The most important of the internal organs are the liver, stomach, heart, and lungs. Injury to the liver may produce death. The liver also functions in coitus, the sexual act fortifying that organ and keeping it "black." Prolonged sexual abstinence may cause the liver to become white and sick. If the stomach swells, injury to the liver is often suspected, while injury to the former organ is greatly feared lest its occurrence be followed by fatal damage to the liver. The heart is compared to a watch or clock; besides being the seat of emotion, it is a regulator of life and once it stops beating death is inevitable. A damaged heart can never be completely restored to normal functioning. The lungs are organs of breathing, and in this task are closely related to the activity of the heart, permitting the latter organ to perform its regulatory activity.

With regard to the surface of the body, a thick skin is beneficial because it is less easily broken than a thin surface. Skin color is both inherited and environmentally conditioned, the dark skin of the Indians being regarded as produced by a combination of such factors as heredity, an excessive amount of meat in the diet, and persistent exposure to sunlight.

Reactions to bodily processes. Urination as well as defecation are, as has already been indicated, activities to which people usually attend in privacy. Urine is regarded as the product of ingested liquids, which pass through the stomach and thence out through the genito-urinary system. The yellow color of human urine is the result of drinking tea; water is said to produce a colorless flow. Feces are the final product of ingested and digested food. The odor of the feces is brought about by their stay and decay in the body's hot interior. Constipation is caused by poor digestion, the stomach and intestines not "grinding up" food quickly enough. The feces may be hard when a man has eaten tough meat, and in that condition their passage may cause bleeding. Loose stools are the result of eating soft foods. Gas accumulated in the stomach and intestines is released through farting. Persistent farting follows overeating. Most people are careful not to fart in company and teach children to control this reaction.

Dermal reactions, such as itching, are produced by skin irritations or lice. In the case of irritations, scratching should be avoided in order to prevent the infection from spreading. No shame is attached to scratching. Blushing occurs when the blood rushes to the face. It may occur in both sexes as the result of shame or anger but is most common in girls and women. Fever is believed to come from white men but is also regarded as a condition arising from "too strong" blood. When perspiration results from strenuous activity, it constitutes a loss of the water contained in the blood. Too great perspiration makes a man weak. In illness, sweating represents an attempt of the body to rid itself of disease.

Facial reactions reveal the individual's predominant disposition and transitory moods. Smiling occurs when a person "feels good"—"he think about skin." Laughter is thought to be most common in young people, who are quick to respond to a joke. A man who is half old, however, is no longer so ready to laugh. Laughter is also related to idleness and good health, so that when a man is working or ill, he has little inclination to exercise this faculty.

Frowning is a sign of anger or disapproval. Sneering could not be explained to the informant and, in fact, was not observed among the Kaska.

Sneezing and a running nose are generally symptomatic of a cold, although sneezing sometimes indicates that a person will receive good news. The nasal discharge originates between the eyes at the head of the nose. A running nose is preferred to nasal congestion and consequent shortness of breath, which may, it is thought, lead to death.

Among ocular and auricular reactions, weeping is regarded as caused by sadness and depression. Winking is a voluntary response with humorous and sexual overtones. Ringing in the ears constitutes a phenomenon likely to occur when a man is too much alone, but may also be produced by accumulated ear wax. "Seeing stars" may be brought about by excessive heat or a disordered stomach as, for example, a stomach poisoned from bad water.

No ideas of shame or embarrassment are attached to most oral reactions, a person feeling free anywhere to hiccough, yawn, or eat, although most people refrain from spitting on a lumber floor. There is some self-consciousness about coughing in a strange camp, for fear that the owner will consider the response "dirty" or unhygienic. Hiccoughing is the result of an overstuffed stomach, which causes some food to lodge in the esophagus, blocking the passage of wind and causing air to be taken in huge sudden gulps. Hiccoughing is sometimes regarded as an omen of good luck, promising meat or fur. No means is known for relieving this condition. Yawning is a sign of fatigue, but may also be a product of hunger and consequent weakness. It is relieved by a cup of tea. Spitting is regarded as ridding a person of excess mucus secreted by the nose and mouth. Its prevalence has already been discussed. Constriction or irritation of the throat, such as may come from smoking, leads to coughing, although sometimes this reaction originates from a disturbed stomach. Swallowing the "wrong way" is dangerous, because it may result in food being carried into the lungs where it may decay; "pretty soon man die."

Vocalization, or speech ability, appears when a child becomes half smart. Shortly after birth, however, a mother may wipe her index finger around the baby's mouth to insure that the child will not be mute. As the child grows, he begins to make meaningful sounds and finally, informants said, begins to imitate words uttered by the parents. In this way language is acquired by each successive generation. The people believe their own language easier to learn than English.[7]

Digestion is primarily promoted by the stomach grinding up food. The intestines continue the digestive process by further grinding. Illness results if, for any reason, the digestive ability of the stomach become impaired. Digestion renews the blood—"cleans" it. If this

---

[7] A mythological account of the origin of linguistic diversity offered by Nitla is interesting because of the fact that it is almost an exact transcription of the Eleventh Chapter of Genesis. The myth follows: Originally all the people spoke only one language and there were only white people. They piled a great structure up in the air trying to reach the sky. Then the white people went to sleep, planning to finish the tower on the following day and cut through the sky. During the night the poles they had erected collapsed. "They can't make it up there. They make trouble. The pile slide down everything. Tomorrow try we talk this fellow; he can't make understand nothing what you say. Another fellow try. Can't hear nothing. All men different talk." Gradually groups of people withdrew and taught one another the language of one of their members. These groups now began to disperse to different countries and there further developed their languages. At this time too the Crow and Wolf moieties developed and the Indians became distinguished from white people.

cleansing did not take place, a person would soon die from the effects of bad blood coursing through his body. The manner in which the blood and stomach interact with each other was not clear to the informant, who emphasized that blood could not enter the stomach or intestines without endangering life.

The sexual impulse in the male is believed to originate in the genitals, whose excretory and sexual functions are closely under the influence of the kidneys. The kidneys stimulate sexual desire when they become "too rich." The testicles are responsible for erection, and their excision also causes sexual desire to diminish or disappear. In a woman the uterus arouses desire, while a stimulation of the clitoris increases the tension and, in copulation, leads to orgasm. In coitus each partner produces equivalent secretions. In the male the semen originates in the kidneys; the origin of the vaginal secretion is not known. These secretions are regarded as akin to blood, intercourse therefore resulting in a mixture of bloods.

The Kaska have no theory to explain menstruation, Nitla dismissing the question by referring to the process as "God business." He added his own version of a common attitude toward the menstruant: "No good for man . . . keep away from it that kind" and expressed the belief that intercourse with a menstruating woman tended to promote quick conception. No evidence of menstrual pain or discomfort could be obtained. As we have evidence of girls being periodically indisposed, it might seem that dysmenorrhea is not common. Amenorrhea is reported to have followed miscarriage in Lois Prince. In some women menopause is associated with headaches, abdominal and back pains, and general despondency.

Coitus, as was pointed out, leads to an interchange of the blood of the sexual partners; the man receives some of the woman's blood and the woman some of the man's. Conception, apart from spiritual reincarnation, is a result of the amalgamation of the bloods in the uterus, while in pregnancy the uterus, which has "caught" the male semen, begins to grow, surrounding the embryo with water. Apparently subsequent coitus of the woman may influence the embryo's development. This is suggested by the statement that if a woman, who has conceived, is unfaithful to her husband, the resulting mixture of two men's blood may result in damage to the forming organism. A child thus influenced in its embryonic development will be born "mean," that is, with an aggressive disposition.

Despite the ideal desirability of children, formulae for limiting as well as promoting conception are known. Only one formula for helping a woman to conceive was obtained. This prescribes that eating fetal rabbits will promote quick conception. While coitus during menstruation is said to facilitate conception, the practice is not specifically recommended for barrenness. The primary motives for having children include a desire "for company," but are chiefly economic. It is expected that when children grow old enough to hunt and assist in housework they will become economic assets making it possible for parents to retire from many routine tasks.

Mary Wiley and Paulette Donnelly stated that they did not want children. Another girl, Lois Prince, following a miscarriage decided that she did not again want to conceive and sought to induce sterility by piercing the afterbirth of the stillborn fetus with porcupine quills. This method of sterilization is said to be restricted to the Nelson Indians. When Mary Wiley sought to prevent conception, she followed an Upper Liard Indian custom.

Taking a three foot long piece of a bear's small intestine, she tied it around her abdomen next to the skin. This belt was worn for ten days. Although married for three years, Old Man reported, Mary has not yet produced a child. More direct methods of contraception are limited. The condom (locally called "French safe" or "safe") is not used as a contraceptive, its employment being mainly confined to protecting boys against venereal disease. One woman, who is married to a white trapper and has six children, reported having unsuccessfully used chemical suppositories purchased by mail in order to avoid pregnancy. Another childless woman, who has been married to a white trapper for six years, was reported to have advised washing vulvae and vagina with hot water following intercourse in order to control conception. The number of children a woman brings into the world is not a prestige point in Kaska society nor is barrenness a disgrace. These attitudes may therefore be regarded as supporting the desire of some women to avoid pregnancy. A family with many children is sometimes referred to as "tell ducks," because this species reproduces prolifically. There is also a belief that if a family has no more than seven children, then all will live. To have more, however, increases the danger that many will die. "Maybe true," Old Man remarked. "Look at River Joe. I had nine; pretty near all I lose." Too many pregnancies are also regarded as quickly aging women.

Old Man reported that among the Upper Liard Indians, children are always spaced two years apart, leaving a year between pregnancies. No evidence could be obtained that such spacing is deliberate. Systematic contraception and prolonged sexual avoidance of a woman following childbirth were both explicitly denied. "I know myself," Old Man insisted. "My wife like that. I never sleep alone. Every other summer baby start." The significantly high rate of summer conception, already pointed out,[8] was further corroborated by Old Man. Out of six children born to him, four were probably conceived in the period of June and early July. An explanation for the phenomenon may lie in the fact that the generally increased social stimulation of summertime in Lower Post, together with the greater privacy of tent living, and the opportunities for couples to retire to the privacy of the bush in this season, may provide greater opportunity for coitus and increase sexual stimulation more than life in the crowded winter cabins. In other words, the relatively greater frequency of summer conception is to be explained by the interaction of climatic and social factors.[9]

Motor habits. In general the Indians are relaxed in everything they do, never awkward, and exhibit few postural signs of tension. Many motor habits in connection with the performance of cultural activities have been described in other portions of this report and only certain general motor patterns, such as sitting, walking, hand preference, and hand-shaking remain to be discussed at this point.

In sitting on the ground, a man rests on his heels with his legs drawn under the buttocks, his knees apart. Often, especially outdoors in warm weather, men squat on the flat of their feet, the knees drawn up below the chin close to the body. In front of a campfire or stove and in a tent men generally recline, resting on one elbow, the legs outstretched. All three of these postures are avoided by women. A woman typically sits on her heels with her legs

[8] See above, p. 37.
[9] Compare Montagu, *Climate and Reproduction* (1939).

drawn straight under her, the buttocks resting on her ankles and calves, her knees close together. In other words, she sits while kneeling. Often a woman kneels as she works, her buttocks only slightly resting on the calves of her legs, the knees close together. Young girls, especially if they wear slacks, often assume less conventional positions. In walking, both sexes maintain a relaxed, erect posture and do not slouch. They retain this erectness into old age, three men from fifty to seventy being observed who showed no slouch. People are predominantly right-handed and regard left-handedness as amusing. The common hand-shake lacks vigor, consisting of a limp clasping of hands.

PSYCHOLOGICAL PROCESSES

Important organs for sensory perception include the nose, tongue, eyes, and ears. The length of the nose is believed to be correlated with an individual's olfactory acuity—the longer the organ, the more far-reaching the sense of smell. A fantastically long nose, the informant said laughingly, would enable a man to smell a moose while with only a short nasal passage a person is able to detect odors only a brief distance away. Taste is an ability of the tongue, related to the fact that this organ is covered by an extremely thin membrane. Taste is regarded as a guide to the edibility of food. Since the function of sight is transmitted by heredity, having many offspring will result in the diminution of this power in children, while the parents will also develop weak eyes. Such diminution of sensory power through reproduction is not a feature of other perceptual processes. Blindness may also appear as the result of an exclusive meat diet.

Emotions. The heart, operating in conjunction with the blood, is the center of emotion, particularly of such feelings as love and hate. The expression of these emotions, however, is mediated by the brain or thought—a noteworthy instance of Kaska thinking being quite in agreement with the latest psychological theories of emotion as a function of the viscera and the cerebral cortex. If a person's heart is "good," hate and violence are impossible for him, even in the face of malice or aggression. Apart from violent emotions like rage, fear, and, for women, pain and excitement, language is rarely used as an adjunct of affective expression.

Curiosity is strongly developed toward unusual features in the immediate environment. The people are intensely interested in any novelty introduced into the community; the ethnographer's glasses, pens, the army trucks, the flush toilet at the Watson Lake mission, purchases of neighbors—all were handled or examined with unrestrained curiosity. Sometimes curiosity prompts even nasal and oral reactions. One day Irene Wiley picked up a handful of fresh sawdust and smelled it. Following her, Anna Lang picked up a pinch and tasted it with the tip of her tongue. At Irene's suggestion, Anna also smelled it.

Fear in the face of a recognized danger is readily expressed by adults and children. Women are particularly prone to show fear, shying from strange dogs, horses, and automobiles and also expressing great dread of wolves. Men are not immune to this emotion. While Nitla and his brother, John, were helping the ethnographer erect a tent, they encountered some hornets from which they fled to a safe distance, at the same time showing manifest fear. In men excessive fear of wolves or fear of the bush is reluctantly expressed and when shown is combatted with ridicule. It is believed that intense chronic fear, or anxiety, may result in death. Old Man told a story of a white man who was very frightened of a dead body. "Maybe because he scared he gonna die." It so happened that this man did die within a short time. "He so scared, I think, that's why. Any you think about something danger when it's time to go to bed, you dream about it. Maybe that's why fellow scared he die."

Men do not generally cry out in pain; women, however, quickly exclaim, crying "Ajya!" until the stimulus is removed or reduced. Men commonly try to suppress any too demonstrable manifestation of excitement. A fresh moose track may produce a tensening of the hunter's body and a whispered remark, but little more. The sight of game promotes a swift, calculated move to a man's gun. In speaking about a hunt or kill, a male narrator's voice reveals little intense emotion but is quite level and matter-of-fact, only a young man smiling as he tells about his success. Women, however, never attempt to inhibit signs of excitement or elation stimulated by game or successful hunting. Any sign of animal life near camp is for them a signal for turbulent running and shouting which, as Old Man ruefully pointed out, quickly drives the game away. At Old Man's settlement, Anna Lang one day dropped a bundle of fresh brush which she was carrying and ran to the river bank. She called something to her sister, Louisa, who was alone in the house. Louisa dashed out of the cabin and called to the ethnographer's wife: "tate, Anna sees fox other side!" Anna ran into the ethnographer's dwelling urging the latter to hurry out with his rifle. Under Anna's urging, the ethnographer shot and missed the fox. Louisa excitedly repeated: "Shoot it, shoot it!" Running, Anna called Lady Suza who, coming with her rifle, also shot and missed. The fox finally ran into the brush. As Anna turned away she chanted: "I saw fox today!" Later, Lady Suza visited Anna and the two women, after discussing the event, began to exchange stories of animals that they had previously encountered and shot.

A frequent pattern of reacting to an embarrassing or otherwise presssing interpersonal situation is by flight from the scene, women in particular being quick to flee when they feel discomfort in social relationships. In both sexes, embarrassment or heightened self-consciousness often finds expression in coughing. Two women returning to a dance from the toilet brush were observed to cough as they entered the house and took their places. When such a reaction occurs in an interpersonal situation involving two people, it seems to serve as an excuse for hesitating or not answering some embarrassing or inconvenient question. For example, our informant, Nitla, denied that people ever coughed when embarrassed or ashamed. We pointed out that he had coughed just previously, when the subject of anal reactions had been introduced. The informant explained that a throat tickle must have occurred simultaneously with the question and had promoted his coughing. He added that smoking (he had been smoking) also stimulates coughing. It would seem that such emotionally motivated coughing is an unconscious phenomenon.

Conscious mentation. Thinking is ascribed to the brain. Several reasoning processes are demonstrated by the Kaska, including analogy, empirical induction, and deduction. Analogy is used frequently in explaining animal behavior on the basis of human behavior, while examples from other aspects of nature are sometimes also used to illustrate or explain human processes.

Induction is here defined as mentation leading to empirical knowledge or belief which, being derived primarily from perception, is alterable as perception reveals new data.[10] Perceptual knowledge, if true, leads to prediction and control. The success of these processes furnishes pragmatic proof of the validity of empirical beliefs. Deduction, of which mysticism is an example, is knowledge derived primarily by conception. Since purely deductive knowledge involves premises not derived from perceptual experience, such beliefs are not readily altered.

Inductive reasoning underlies many of the Kaska Indians' beliefs that guide behavior in the exploitative and technical aspects of the culture. The people have observed, for example, that marten remain in one region and do not travel indiscriminately like the fox or lynx. This empirical datum opens the possibility of control of the animal; marten may be most efficiently trapped by trapping them in the same area annually or they may be conserved by protecting them from trapping for several years. Other examples of empirical thought in Kaska society, some of them absurdly simple, are listed:

> A fire will thaw frozen ground.
> Wet garments on body parts are fatal in very cold weather.
> Scratching an infected skin spreads the area of infection.
> Blood endangers life if it enters the stomach.
> Death follows the stoppage of the heart and pulse beats.
> Old age reduces a person's stamina.
> Birch wood is hard and therefore suitable for a toboggan.
> Babiche is strong and useful for furnishing a firm lashing.
> Dogs need more food when they work hard.

Reasoning which is primarily deductive is the basis of ideas concerning taboos and dreams. In these cases a traditional belief is accepted as an unalterable premise from which certain events are assumed to follow. Many examples may be given. To drink water before smoking a moosehide results in a wet hide; to dream of a sexual situation promises female game to a male hunter; blood circulates through the entire body and, since the little finger is one extreme of the body, all blood must pass through this point. Any isolated failure of the expected behavior to follow in these sequences is usually not sufficient to influence the suspension of belief in the premises. Failures in the occurrence of expected sequences are also readily overlooked. On the other hand, when the expected sequence does occur, this concurrence may be emphasized as evidence of the validity of the premise.[11]

[10] Scientific method, then, is merely a special form of empiricism in which perceptually derived knowledge is formally tested. As Kardiner has pointed out, scientific method is a peculiar achievement of western society. Empiricism, however, the basis of scientific method, is worldwide in its distribution, although particular societies probably differ in the degree to which they rely on either deduction or induction. See Kardiner, The Psychological Frontiers of Society (1945), 406; Wilson, The Analysis of Social Change (1945), 70–71; Hallowell, Some Empirical Aspects of Northern Saulteaux Religion (1934).

[11] Krige distinguishes three rational processes in Lobvedu society—mystical (or non-natural), magical, and empirical (which he calls scientific). The Lobvedu, he points out, do not discriminate between a magical and empirical apprehension of the universe. but they do distinguish between supernatural and natural. We feel it worth reemphasizing that all of these forms of thinking proceed logically or rationally. It is likely that such distinctions

Unconscious mentation. Dreams for the Kaska are not consciously motivated at the will of the subject and are, therefore, to be classified as unconscious behavior. The native interpretation of dreams is primarily mystical. Much dreaming is regarded as offering a glimpse into the immediate future, and is thought to be produced by the spirit of the dreamer traveling abroad from the body thereby encountering destiny. Sometimes a full stomach promotes dreaming. According to Old Man, a dream is easy to remember, "If you lie in one position; if you turn around you forget."

Two categories of dreams are distinguished by the Kaska, good and bad. The former promise something desirable that will soon occur to the dreamer, and there are certain patterned dream situations and symbols which are always interpreted as indicating that a person will soon secure meat, fish or fur. Thus Hans Donnelly once said: "I dream for fish . . . I set fish net, that's the way I dream." Asked the meaning of the dream, he replied: "I think lucky for skin this winter." Louisa Man reported: "I dream I eat meat; a cow moose. Fat meat." She paused and added: "Soon you eat fat meat."[12] Bad dreams represent situations and symbols which frighten the subject or indicate impending misfortune. Thus to dream of water portends danger of a person drowning; anyone dreaming in this way is well advised to stay away from a river or lake for some time. To dream about gopher or groundhog indicates that the dreamer will soon go hungry. Bad dreams are often anxiety dreams and may be motivated by current fears and illness. Mrs. Man woke up gasping after dreaming that she had fallen in the water. She had been ill with a severe cold for some time and both she and her husband had been worried. Dreaming of a grizzly bear is a frequently encountered, socially patterned anxiety dream which is sometimes interpreted as indicating the approach of cold weather. To dream of an airplane also promises "bad day coming." Young girls are particularly likely to have anxiety dreams featuring attacks by grizzly bears or by strange men. The significance of this experience will be explored in connection with Kaska ethos.

The manifest content of Kaska dreams is often easy to discover, as the following example indicates. Early in October Nitla returned from Louis Maza's settlement to Old Man's place in order to follow Old Man and the latter's sons-in-law to a stretch of burnt hilly country, where the people planned to hunt moose. Upon arrival Nitla told the ethnographer "I dream for meat, burnt hill. They go this way. Me, I go behind. Ahead people go. They kill meat. Last night I dream that." The manifest content here reflects the purpose for which Nitla was to set out on the following day. A wish-fulfillment element is sometimes also quite clear in some dreams. Most dreams of meat and fish are probably expressions of a desire for these foods or for good fortune in general. The degree to which Kaska dreams are amenable to analysis by other psychoanalytic concepts of dream dynamics will be apparent when a number of dreams have been studied in connection with other expressions of the dominant motivations of Kaska personality. In general, it may be pointed out, Kaska dreams

---

of thought can be validly applied in other societies. The whole field of comparative thinking (or, more broadly, comparative philosophy) merits more attention. Krige, *The Magical Thought-Pattern of the Bantu in Relation to Health Services* (1944).

[12] It is interesting that Japanese dream interpretation also regards dreams of fish and fishing as signs of general future success. Ten Kate, *Beitraege zur Kenntnis des japanischen Volksglauben* (1912), 401; Miura, *Ueber japanische Traumdeuterei* (1905), 294.

present no unusual problems so far as the application of European and American derived explanatory concepts is concerned.[13]

Abnormal states. In this section attention will be directed to reactions arising as a result, of the disorganization of the processes by which individuals normally adjust to reality. We will consider some processes of disorganization produced by alcohol and mental illness. A characteristic form of manic-like behavior occurs under conditions of alcoholic intoxication and may be superficially compared to running amok. The following examples are from field notes.

7:22:45 (Lower Post). An Indian woman had been drinking most of the night with white men. Early in the morning she rushed into the ethnographer's cabin, waking his family. Her hair was disheveled and emotionally she appeared to be in a state of intense agitation. She half fell, half threw herself on the floor alongside our bedding and began sobbing and moaning incoherently. Following attempts to comfort her, she finally quieted down and permitted herself to be led home. No sooner had a few clothes been taken off than she rushed out of the house in her petticoat and stockinged feet. Sobbing anew she rushed into the home of a nearby white man and, climbing into his bed, began to kiss and lie on top of him. The man tried to urge her out of the building but she would not be persuaded. Instead she began to plead, saying: "You want full blooded Injun? You like a full blood Injun? I like you." This began to annoy the white man who swore in anger and ordered her out of his home. At this point the woman reacted with even greater rage and began a stream of obscenity which provoked the man to try to push her out the open door. Once more the ethnographer and his wife sought to calm the woman and finally succeeded in bringing her home. All attempts to get her to bed were resisted. She was too agitated and disorganized to relax. Another white man came into the house and she began to demonstrate affection toward him, calling him "brother-in-law." With great tact this man escaped the situation and the woman was finally persuaded to go to bed. She now sought to send a message to a white trapper who could supply her with liquor. At the same time remorse and shame appeared in her behavior. She began to cry and told the ethnographer's wife not to bother with her, that she wasn't worth any attention. She also revealed how a white man had forced his way into her home the previous evening and insisted she take a few drinks. It was not long before her resistance to drinking had broken down. After this period of self-recrimination she fell asleep.

As the day progressed the distracted woman secured more liquor until she finally wound up in the restaurant where, becoming abusive, she had to be told to leave. For a long time she could not be found but in the evening a boy informed the ethnographer that she was sleeping under some willows in a downpour of rain. When discovered she was suffering from severe chills and complained of a painful headache. Otherwise she was quite subdued except for occasional moaning. After taking hot tea, soup, and aspirin she went to sleep.

8:14:45 (Lower Post). During playful sexual advances made by Edward Prince toward Peter Tom, the latter suddenly became angry, seized Edward, and in a few minutes was choking him in the crook of his arm. Peter called on Edward to surrender, while the latter sought to dig his fingers into his opponent's back. When Old Man and Mrs. Man pulled Peter off, the youth

---

[13] The conclusions Seligman draws from Ashanti dreams and dream interpretation also largely apply to the Kaska data. Like Ashanti dreams, Kaska dreaming shows wish-fulfillment as well as conflict elements. In interpreting dreams, the Kaska (like the Ashanti and western psychoanalysis) often reject the manifest content, but do not generally attribute meanings that are opposite from the dream's manifest content. Rattray, *Religion and Art in Ashanti* (1927), 204.

was trembling violently and sobbing. Mrs. Man finally succeeded in leading him a short distance away. Here the old lady (who was herself intoxicated) tried to comfort Peter, her grandson, and drew his head down on her lap. After a few minutes he calmed down somewhat and moved to rejoin the men. Edward began anew to make obscene and derogatory references about Peter. For a while the latter was content to reply in kind. Suddenly he sprang to his feet again, as did Edward. Each was ready to fight. Taunting one another they moved to level ground above the riverbank where Peter swung in rage but missed his opponent. Old Man and his wife pulled the two apart but Peter tore himself free from his grandmother and went off by himself sobbing and otherwise revealing intense agitation. His unsuppressed rage and hostility expressed themselves when he viciously struck at some willows with his clenched fist. In a little while he was again calm.

8:22:45 (Bridge). Drinking had been going on for about six hours. River Joe began to abuse Richard Day for sleeping with Irene Wiley (his brother's daughter) and for never giving her food or money. Richard did not reply, but River Joe called on his son-in-law, Louis Maza, telling the latter what was angering him. In an immediate outburst of rage Louis turned on Richard, but the latter quickly fled to Edward Prince's camp, Louis following. Meanwhile, expressing his anger to himself, River Joe began tearing down his niece's mosquito tent, carrying some of her blankets to his own camp. Irene stood off abusing her uncle, calling him "crazy old man" and "crazy dog." At the same time Louis was systematically demolishing Edward Prince's tent, from which all occupants had fled. Louis' rage was not yet abated and he once more set out to look for Richard, rushing into the ethnographer's camp and accusing the latter of harboring the youth Frustrated in his search, Louis now began to direct aggression toward his wife. When Mrs. Maza finally ran off with her classificatory sister, Irene, Louis began a frenzied search for her, lurching through the camp area in a drunken stupor. After he was unable to find her, he announced that he was going to shoot himself and fetched a rifle from his tent. The gun was torn from his grasp and emptied whereupon the wrought up man finally began to calm down.

9:13:45 (Old Kean's Place). Adele Kean had been drinking fruit wine for several hours. During this time she had manifested direct affection toward her husband's brother, John Kean, with whom she had been living for several months. After their guests had gone, she began to demonstrate violent behavior, smashing furniture and other objects in the cabin. In an effort to quiet her, John locked the girl in the building. This still more infuriated her. She removed her brother-in-law's high power rifle from its place on the wall and threatened to shot through the door and kill John. The latter rushed into the cabin and secured the gun. The couple now began to quarrel bitterly, Adele promising John that she would surely kill him on the following day. At this point Irene Wiley returned to the house and tried to quiet the distracted girl. Adele inexplicably directed her aggression toward Irene, and began to tear the latter's hair. In return Irene struck Adele in the face, causing the latter's nose to bleed. John had meanwhile awakened the ethnographer, asking him to stop the girls' fighting. When the ethnographer entered the room Adele lay on the bloody floor sobbing violently and complaining that Irene and John had hit her. With intense anguish she wailed over and over: "Ajya mama! Ajya mama!" In the bunk her child began to cry, but Adele paid no attention. Finally Paulette Donnelly came around and staunched the flow of blood. She then led Adele to the latter's bed where Adele continued to moan and call for her mother.

While all drinkers do not break down into such catastrophic emotional behavior, alcoholic intoxication has a noticeable effect in releasing emotionality—excitement, aggression,

and grief. A number of older women are well known for the ease with which alcohol in-
duces melancholy in them; they signify intoxication by beginning to sob for a deceased
daughter or son and refuse to be comforted.

Inquiries regarding mental disease in the Kaska area brought reports of several cases in
which individuals of both sexes were described as "going crazy." All of these cases follow
a pattern of manic-like behavior involving indiscriminate aggression and violence. Mental
disorder is ascribed to several causes, including moiety endogamy, family incest, excessive
sexuality, and worry.

Mrs. May Wiley was described by Old Man as "a little crazy." "She always making
trouble. She always trying to be better than anybody. Mean. She chop the house, she want
to fight us. She talk outside. Harry Lang told me: 'Don't go out. Let her come in. We'll fix
her.' She chopping outside [at this point Old Man showed the ethnographer a single ax slash
on the doorframe of the house in which the latter was living]. She wouldn't go in. When she
feel like to fight she always like that. She treat his own kid good but sometimes when she
lick her kid. I don't know how many times she pound Irene." Mrs. Wiley died about two
years after the incident of the chopping. At the time of her death "they say just kind of
quiet; she never speak a word."

Another woman was described who had developed mental illness and killed her grandson. A week after the homicide she died. Her husband, Old Ajen (from whom Iron Creek
on the Alaska Highway just below Lower Post is named), had also become "like John Kean;
hollered, sang 'doctor,' and he try to kill his wife." He was finally hospitalized in Vancouver
where he died. It was said that both husband and wife were Crow and had married despite
the rule of exogamy. Mental disorder was ascribed to this offense. It is interesting to note
that John Kean was also deemed "crazy" by both his father and his brother, Nitla. Both
said that John's aggressive behavior should be reported to the police. Old Kean told the
ethnographer that John had several times threatened to kill him.

Old Man identified the late Mrs. River Joe as "not all there," and referred to some of
her questions as evidence in point. For example, she couldn't understand why the ethnographer was writing about Indians. On the occasion of a dance in a trader's store, she wanted
to know why flour and sugar had to be stored in a dance place. Old Man said she had been
"like that" for six years. About 1912, River Joe is reported to have exhibited manic behavior. He sang and cried wildly, went into other people's camps and tried to kill his wife,
who had to hide in the bush for a week. He did not try to harm others. In a month he was
improved. About two years ago, following his arrest, one of River Joe's sons was taken out
of the Kaska area because of manifest mental disorder.

Without attempting to classify these symptoms, it may be pointed out that all but one
of these cases of mental breakdown involve mature men and women and otherwise also
conform to the manic-depressive syndrome.[14] About twenty years ago, according to Harry
Lang, the Nelson Indians were visited by what appears to have been some kind of group

[14] Czaplika has distinguished two forms of Arctic hysteria among the Siberian aborigines. The classical,
compulsively initiative form of the disease, she points out, is common in young people, but the violent form occurs between thirty-five and fifty years of age. Czaplika, *Aboriginal Siberia, A Study in Social Anthropology*
(1914), 315–319.

hysteria in which people for no known reason fled from their camps and sat in the snow. This may represent an outbreak of true Arctic hysteria with compulsive suggestibility.

PERSONALITY

Rorschach's Test was given to twenty-eight Kaska Indians. Although at first instructions were closely followed and each card was shown a second time, in order to perform the inquiry and to invoke further responses, it was soon discovered that two showings made the test too long and irksome for these people. Particularly children grew restless when required to sit through a detailed inquiry, while most adults showed little sign of becoming more at ease as time over the cards increased. The situation often grew so painful that it was necessary to beg the subjects to remain for a few more minutes. To overcome this difficulty, it was determined to conduct the inquiry simultaneously with the initial presentation of the cards. While this procedure in part upset the standardization under which the test was constructed and is commonly administered, it may be expected that the results obtained have not been seriously impaired. Of the twenty-eight protocols collected, thirteen are based on two showings of the cards, the inquiry here being conducted in accordance with standard procedure. In the case of girls and women, most of the tests were administered by the ethnographer's wife.

Rorschach records were obtained from fourteen adult males and five adult females. Nine children under sixteen years of age were tested, five boys and four girls. Although the number of cases is limited, in general the psychological homogeneity of the population is demonstrated.

The mean number of responses for the adult group is 22.16, the range being from three to ninety although only two individuals gave more than thirty-six responses. An important qualification to be added is the fact that slightly over fifty per cent of the subjects produced fewer than eighteen answers. The mean number of responses for the children's group is 15.5, the range being from six to twenty-nine.

The tabulation of responses according to location is shown in Table 12.

TABLE 12. TABULATION OF RORSCHACH RESPONSES ACCORDING TO LOCATION

	Adult Mean (N=19)	Per Cent	Child Mean (N=9)	Per Cent
W	3.53	14	4	25
D	11.47	54	10	64
Dd	6.63	30	1.55	10
S	.53	2	.11	.7

An inspection of these figures reveals the adult manner of approach to be (W), D, Dd S!!!! while the child approach is W, D!, Dd S! In other words, among the adults as a whole we find a very high overemphasis of small detail responses with an underemphasis of whole answers, whereas in children a somewhat better balanced picture obtains.

In Table 13 is presented a tabulation of the responses according to determinants. The distribution of these responses reveals significant differences from the distribution of determinants in American society, the most important being the very low number of color determined responses and the high number of form percepts which even characterizes the child group. In both groups we find a M: sum C relationship in which M exceeds the sum of the color scores; in adults the mean ratio is 1.16:.97, while in children it reads 1:.56. A similar tendency is found in the ratio designated $(FM+m):(Fc+c+C')$. For adults this relationship reads 3.32:.9 while in children it is 2.78:.44. About thirty-seven per cent of the adults and thirty-two per cent of the children's responses were produced on the last three cards. The $W:M$ ratio in adults is 3.53:1.16 while in children it reads 4:1.

TABLE 13. TABULATION OF RORSCHACH RESPONSES ACCORDING TO DETERMINANTS

	Adult Mean (N=19)	Per Cent	Child Mean (N=9)	Per Cent
M	1.16	5	1	6
FM	3.32	15	2.67	17
m	0	0	.11	.7
k	0	0	.11	.7
K	.37	2	.11	.7
FK	.32	1	.11	.7
F	15	67	10.22	66
Fc	.63	3	.33	2
c	.16	1	.11	.7
C'	.11	.7	0	0
FC	.47	2	.56	4
CF	.26	1	.11	.7
C	.32	1	.11	.7

The responses presented according to content are shown in Table 14. This tabulation is noteworthy for the high number of animal responses found in both the adult and child categories. In adults the ratio $(H+A):(Hd+Ad)$ in 11.52:5.79 while in children it is 9.1: 1.67.

Responses distributed according to their popularity or originality are shown in Table 15.[15]

In Table 16 is tabulated the number of failures to attend to any of the cards. This is expressed as a percentage of the number of people potentially able to respond to this blot.

It is significant that five per cent of the adult group failures (or about forty per cent of the total number of adult rejections) occurred on the last three cards. This would indicate color shock, an interpretation confirmed by an inspection of many records. One third of the failures in children occurred on these all color cards. Cards V, VI, and VII also show a significantly large number of rejections and inspection of the protocols confirms the interpretation of shading shock, which may also partially explain the rejections of the first card.

[15] In scoring an answer popular we were guided by Beck (Beck, *Rorschach's Test: I Basic Processes* [1944], 191–195). Any response occurring more than once in the group as a whole was also scored popular.

TABLE 14. TABULATION OF RORSCHACH RESPONSES ACCORDING TO CONTENT

	Adult Mean (N=19)	Per Cent	Child Mean (N=9)	Per Cent
H	1.68	8	2.22	14
Hd	1.74	8	.67	4
A	9.84	44	6.88	44
Ad	4.05	18	1	6
Aobj	1.26	6	.22	1
At	.47	2	0	0
Sex	.05	.2	0	0
Obj	.63	3	2	13
N	.74	3	.68	4
Pl	.42	2	.89	6
Geo	.05	.2	0	0
Fire	.05	.2	.11	.7
Clouds	.16	.7	.11	.7
Blood	.11	.5	0	0
Abstract	.32	1	0	0
Stone	.37	2	0	0
(A)	.11	.5	.78	5
(H)	.11	.5	0	0

TABLE 15. TABULATION OF RORSCHACH RESPONSES ACCORDING TO POPULARITY

	Adult Mean (N=19)	Per Cent	Child Mean (N=9)	Per Cent
P	12.05	54	10.3	66
O	10.11	46	5.2	33

An application of the Rorschach data to the problem of ethos will be presented later. At this point we propose to describe briefly the personality structure of the Kaska Indians as revealed by the sample tested. As judged from Rorschach records, the average Kaska adult reveals himself intellectually as a concrete and practical thinker who avoids levels of abstract or generalized speculation. He is shown to be uncritically preoccupied with discrete and relatively minute facets of existence. When this excessive interest in petty details is considered alongside the low production of human movement responses, the Kaska adult is demonstrated as unable to release his imaginative processes in creative thinking. Although the ability for such thought is present, its expression is inhibited by other personality factors. Children are less concerned with minutiae. They seem to be freer to grasp relationships within broader frameworks without, however, being more able to utilize imagination in this process.

Emotionally the average Kaska is disclosed as tense, inhibited, or constricted. The ability

TABLE 16. TABULATION OF THE NUMBER OF REJECTIONS TO EACH RORSCHACH CARD

	Adult Mean (N=19)	Per Cent	Child Mean (N=9)	Per Cent
I	4	2	2	2
II	1	.5	0	0
III	2	1	1	1
IV	0	0	0	0
V	2	1	1	1
VI	4	2	1	1
VII	2	1	1	1
VIII	2	1	0	0
IX	4	2	1	1
X	4	2	2	2
Total	25	12.5	9	9

to be emotionally stimulated by inner experience (fantasy and imagination) or by external situations are both lacking. Socially detached, affectively cold and undemonstrative, the Indian personality can be characterized as emotionally immobile and blocked. This constriction prevents the individual from freely grasping or understanding all aspects of his world and undoubtedly is related to his indefinite, hesitant, and limited intellectual approach. Correlated with constriction is a circumscribed range of interest. The Kaska Indian is an introvert who, having removed himself from the stimulation of his environment, confines himself to a subdued and suppressed individualistic career in which even internal stimulation is not permitted to develop.

That this emotional aloofness is psychologically defensive is suggested by the evidence of a severe anxiety, whose origins go back to very early experiences of the individual. Paralyzed by this basic tension, the personality seeks a narrow course of safety between inner apprehension and external fear. As a result people in interpersonal relations tend to be indirect, suspicious, reserved, and uneasy. There is constant fear of being overwhelmed, dominated, or exploited. The awareness of this danger results in a self-centered existence in which emotional spontaneity is reduced to a minimum.

MEDICINE

The Kaska Indians understand the principle of contagious disease and ideally recognize more hygienic techniques for preventing illness than they display in behavior. For example, although it is believed that such diseases as colds and tuberculosis are transmitted through contact with a person who has these illnesses, little care is taken to forestall physical interaction with reputed carriers. Again, while in principle the danger of using another's cup or table utensils is understood, tableware, especially at drinking parties, is often interchanged without rinsing. At the two potlatches given in 1945, each guest was told to provide his own cup, plate, knife, fork, and spoon. The plan miscarried, however, as many people neglected instructions. While dishes were washed between servings, the water was not boiling nor was it changed.

Nevertheless some instances of preventative medicine can be given. Most men are cautious in having sexual intercourse with suspected carriers of venereal disease; the condom as well as urination following coitus are recognized as safeguards against acquiring genital infections. Parents were several times observed to call their youngsters away from one or two children who carried impetigo scars, in one case a seven year old victim of this disease being told: "Go away, you're diseased." In the spring of 1945, following the dysentery outbreak of the previous fall and winter, Old Man burnt the toilet brush near his settlement. He explained that the area had been used by people suffering from the illness. Old Man also dug a new latrine. Following death, old clothes, particularly those which were in contact with a sick person, are abandoned in the brush or burnt. A number of years ago, during a serious flu epidemic in Lower Post, a group of Espato·tena is said to have fled from the town in order to avoid the sickness.

Quarantine control of contagious disease was introduced to the community at Lower Post on July 28, 1945, when the death of a boy from spinal meningitis led the Mounted Police and the provincial policeman to post the western reserve. The quarantine was far from complete, however, consisting of little more than a prominently lettered sign being placed at each of the two main entrances to the area. In addition the missionary sought to segregate the school children from this reserve, while adults were advised to limit their shopping trips into town to once a day. The lax enforcement of the quarantine resulted in its consistent violation by everyone except the parents of the boy who had died (not, however, by his next younger brother). People continued to leave the area frequently, ate in the restaurant and at the lunch counter, and attended church. Few people from other quarters of the community avoided visiting friends or dances in the restricted reserve and two potlatches were even celebrated there during the term of the quarantine. Only the white residents of Lower Post were explicitly warned to observe the posting on the occasion of the first potlatch. Several Indians, including the family of the deceased, expressed annoyance at the theoretical infringement of their freedom introduced by the quarantine, and several times adolescent boys tore up the signs and tossed them into brush where they were retrieved by the provincial policeman and remounted. The quarantine was officially in effect for over a month.

It has already been stated that the Kaska are not an accident prone people. Nevertheless accidents do occur and are generally attributed to carelessness, drunkenness, or "bad luck." Associated with the relative infrequency of accidents is the fact that most people manifest a realistic, though not exaggerated, concern with safety. In case of necessity, however, considerations of safety are readily sacrificed to expediency combined with caution. A person will travel during a snowstorm or in very low temperatures if the journey is important or has once begun. Parents do not worry unduly about household dangers. Sharp tools, scissors, axes, and knives are often left lying around the camp where children are free to handle them. Nobody was observed to take foolhardy chances, however, and when any real threats of danger are pointed out, the advice given is generally heeded.

The treatment of accidents is not developed beyond a simple, practical level. Small cuts and bruises are not treated. More serious cuts are bandaged. It is felt that serious wounds should be kept warm in order to promote rapid healing; this care is especially important in winter. Nosebleed is often permitted to continue without interference, the victim leaning forward to allow the blood to drop on the ground. Excessive bleeding of this kind may lead to attempts to staunch the flow of blood with a cloth and sometimes the little finger is tied with a string to stop the circulation before it reaches the nose. Balsam pitch, when available, is applied to burns. The treatment of snowblindness consists primarily in avoiding exposure to strong light. In an emergency, broken bones are set by anyone who feels capable of the operation and mobility is later aided with a crutch made of a single pole, shoulder height, on which is nailed a semicircular wooden support for the armpit. One report was obtained about an old man who, paralyzed on one side, was provided with a small "sleigh" with wooden wheels. To this a dog was harnessed and thus the man could move around camp.[16] Frances Lake Indians sometimes treat swellings and pains in the joints with a charcoal cross drawn over the affected spot. Patent medicine linaments are used for muscle aches and their application may be accompanied by some massage of the painful area. Frozen members of the body are thawed with snow, which is gently applied but not rubbed in place. Corns, regarded as the pecular affliction of men, are cut out at the root with a pocket knife, "Women can't get it," Old man said, referring to corns. "Maybe because they stay in camp, warm place." In recent years any serious bodily injury, including toothache, has been referred to white medical attention when possible.

Kaska society has formulated no clear and explicit theory of disease. As a result several vague but not necessarily conflicting notions of the origin and cause of illness obtain among different individuals. Thus commenting on his cold, Hans suggested that "wind" must have brought the "cold sick" from "down there," gesturing down the Liard River. The notion of communicable diseases being borne in the air or wind is closely allied to the notion of disease transmitted in interpersonal association to which we have already alluded. In referring to the fact that he and his wife had suffered from dysentery during the winter, Billy Barre said that people were "packing" the disease around with them "just like wind."

Some illnesses, especially cold, are believed to result from exposure to wet and cold. Thus Old Man felt he had caught a bad cold during his walk home from Old Kean's place in the autumn rains. Summer days of strong wind and flying dust usually provoke people to comment on the dust as being injurious to health. The dust raised by dancing on a wooden floor also stimulates complaints from people who ascribe sore throats to this irritant. Another point of view ascribes illness to internal disorders, particularly disorders of the stomach and liver. Louis Maza, in relating the story of his first son's death, said the child had been carried on the back of one of the older girls. He suspected that in the packing one of the baby's ribs had somehow been struck with the result that the liver had become damaged. Death followed in a few days.

Less frequently is the origin of a specific disease ascribed to the spirit of a dead person and rarely to sorcery. Informants were consistent in denying belief in "bad medicine."[17] While recognizing that such attitudes had formerly occurred in the society, today, ac-

[16] The wheel is not aboriginal in Kaska culture.

[17] Kaska ideas about sorcery may be divided into two types, first, those surviving from aboriginal times and, second, "witch-fear," which appeared in the post contact society and lasted until about 1925. See Honigmann, Witch-Fear in Post-Contact Kaska Society (1947).

cording to Nitla: "New people like white man; he don't know." A residual faith in witch-craft may persist among the Nelson Indians. As Old Man somewhat unwillingly stated: "Looks like some people still believe it. I know Nick Lang still believe it." Following the dysentery epidemic of 1944 in the Nelson Indian district, Old Man heard Mary Wiley report: "The people pretty bad yet. They talk about witch." During a discussion of the sporadic cases of dysentery occurring in the summer of 1945 one young man spoke up and said: "Too much war; too much blood. That brings out sickness. Too much people killed."

Some of these theories of disease are at least partially empirically demonstrable. How-ever, even where empirical beliefs apply, as for instance in connection with cold and tuber-culosis, they do not necessarily influence therapeutic or hygienic measures. Isolation of the patient is not practiced in conjunction with these illnesses. Little attempt is made to pre-vent wetting or chilling, except in very cold weather, and in fall children often spend entire days in wet mocassins. Walking long distances in wet brush is avoided whenever possible, but this precaution is generally more a matter of comfort than of preventative medicine.

It is worth pointing out that there is a greater tendency to explain illness in empirical terms than to attribute it to supernatural causation. The typical methods of reacting to sickness, however, are to do nothing, use what patent medicines are available, or refer the patient to white medical attention. Although there is a tendency to defend against anxiety and fear by making light of sickness, there can be little question but that it is usually intensely anxiety provoking to the patient. Undoubtedly this fear of illness is related to the inadequate control which the society experiences over disease. It may also be related to the fear of in-capacitation, which can be expected to assume serious proportions when an adult is ex-tremely dependent on his own resources to make a living and where mobility is of para-mount economic importance.

Most of the medical therapy performed by the Indians is with the aid of patent medi-cines obtained from stores. A high degree of faith is invested in such preparations and sev-eral assorted bottles are often purchased in the fall to be used for what illnesses appear dur-ing the winter. The most commonly used patent medicines include cough remedies, lina-ment, dysentery remedies, castor oil, stomach tonic, liver pills, fruit salts, and Listerine; the latter, however, is largely consumed in lieu of other alcoholic portables. Lozenges for coughs are often purchased and Vicks Vaporub is popular for colds and chest coughs. As-pirin is not commonly bought. Epsom salts are used to "clean the blood" by removing "bad water" from the intestines. River Joe drank a compound of fruit salts daily for this purpose.

Indigenous medication is limited to the use of a few plants products, like balsam pitch, balsam bark, soapberry bush, and willow buds, as well as inhalation, exercise, and the ap-plication of heat.

Balsam pitch is firmly believed in for its medicinal properties, but is not readily acces-sible in the river valleys where most of the people's time is spent. In the fall of 1945, while hunting in the Simpson Mountains, Old Man secured some balsam pitch and put a little in his weak eyes. The pain was intense at first but in the morning he found his sight greatly im-proved. He did not repeat the treatment, as no more balsam was immediately available. Application of balsam pitch is also recommended for impetigo and other skin diseases. The bark of the balsam tree boiled in water and drunk is said to be an effective cure for coughs and for pain near the heart. A cup or two of the stems of the soapberry plant boiled in water provides a cathartic. For a skin irritation on the back of her knees, Elsie Lang was advised by her grandmother, Mrs. Man, to apply a poultice made of fresh or dried boiled fireweed. Two handfuls of willow buds boiled with a pint of water for about twenty min-utes in a discarded food tin (the buds discolor metal when boiled) make a medicine that will cure cold. Doses should be taken at regular intervals. A willow-like plant, known as "moose brush" and growing along the upper reaches of Dease River, is highly regarded for its medicinal efficacy. The stems of the plant are boiled for several hours and the effusion drunk for chest pain and cough. The solution may also be used for washing sore eyes. Stems are kept for reuse, but are discarded after several boilings.

The inhalation of the fumes of dog urine is a popular remedy for cold. A person watches for a place where dogs urinate and collects the soaked wood or brush to use in creating a smudge. People walk back and forth through the fumes, breathing them. This treatment is also thought to be effective in preventing cold. When Louis Maza's baby showed a swollen neck, the father suggested an "old fashioned" remedy. A hot rock, heated in the oven and wrapped in a towel, was applied to the sore area. Exercise is sometimes recommended for therapy. Following a long period of illness from cough and cold, Old Man set out on a five mile walk, planning to fish upon arrival at his destination. "I figger if my blood work, I'm all right."

CONCLUSIONS

It is not likely that any analysis of Kaska ideational culture made with reference to the criteria of adaptive and adjustive efficiency will reward us with greater insight than we have already derived. As a matter of fact, although many of the ideas which we have just discussed may potentially be of great utility in making a living, their value depends upon their behavioral application; to discuss the manner in which the Kaska apply their empirical knowledge, for example, would require repetition of much that we have already said con-cerning the Indians' style of life.

Therefore, in concluding the description of Kaska culture, we shall be content with briefly sketching the structural relationship of a few aspects of ideational to technical and social behaviors. The ideal virtues of men and women, for example, are clarified when the industriousness and skill ideally expected of the man are considered alongside the nature of the male's economic routines and their significance for survival. The Indians are aware of the necessity for hard work in the business of getting a living but do not practice as much as they believe. The economic importance of a woman's industriousness is also revealed in the ethical standards, indicating how important feminine labor is seen to be in conjunction with the man's economic role. Despite men's statements that they can live independently, both sexes are clearly expected to supplement one another, as they actually do. From another point of view, the relative simplicity and unelaboration of ideational material may itself be regarded as functionally related to the primacy of the food quest in the life of the society. Intensive speculation, whether religious or empirical, requires sufficient leisure for at least part of a society plus an intellectual tradition on which to build. Both these conditions are lacking for the people of the Cassiar. Even the sexual life is influenced by the economic pattern requiring long isolation in the bush under crowded states, which because of the private phrasing of sexual matters, are relatively unsuitable for the union of men and women. Therefore we see a higher rate of conception occurring in summer, after the total community has assembled and when climate facilitates finding privacy.[18]

Kaska parents rationalize their desire for children principally in terms of the child's potential economic contribution to family cooperation. Children are wanted because it is expected that they will grow up as staffs upon which parents will find support. This ideal expectation of a child's eventual role is, as we have already indicated, generally doomed to disappointment. Although adolescents make important contributions to family economy, they do not, as adults, provide sources of gratification on which the tired, old, or sick parents may rely with any assurance. The rationalized desire for children, therefore, turns out to be a weak one and it is to be expected that people with the empirical ability of the Kaska should have learned how little they can depend on grown offspring. Assuming that social awareness of the child's increasing disregard of parental wellbeing exists, we find, as a result, an absence of any extraordinarily compelling economic or social motives for reproduction, which in turn is compatible with the desire of some young women to limit their fertility. Contraception, in other words, denies the adult society of no important potential rewards or obligations and hence meets with no disapproval. Other unconscious attitudes associated with the desire to avoid progeny, related to the female pattern of masculine striving outlined in connection with the status of women, will be further explored in the following division of this report. It may also be noted that the native theory of procreation, which derives the offspring from a double mixture of blood, the father's and mother's, and thus implicitly notices the male's role in forming the embryo and fetus, is compatible with the manifest bilateral emphasis of family life in which neither parent is singled out as most important. Such bilaterality is more manifested in Kaska society than the fiction of matrilineal descent.[19]

Finally, attention may be directed to the relationship of the Kaska's blocked emotionality, as revealed in behavior in the Rorschach situation, and the atomistic social structure of the society in which interpersonal adjustment is typically sought by what has been described as an avoidance of social interaction. Significant in this regard is the contrast between the normally unexpressive life of the Indian and the explosive outbursts that sometimes occur with intoxication and in mental disease. It seems likely that the latter phenomena follow an involuntary release of strong inhibitory mechanisms. In this discussion of emotion we are already approaching the sphere of Kaska ethos, to which we will now give extended attention.

[18] We are reminded of Mumford's picture of medieval Europe with the awakening of sex coming in spring. "... the late medieval astrological calendars, which depict this awakening, show the lovers having intercourse in the open with their clothes on. ... For lovers in the medieval house the winter months must have been a large wet blanket." Mumford, *The Culture of Cities* (1938), 41.

[19] According to Richards: "By dogma of descent I mean ... those theories of procreation which express a people's beliefs as to the physical contribution of the father and mother to the formation of the child." Citing the attention which Malinowski and Rattray in their field work had previously paid to this theory, she points out that a society's dogma of descent often correlates with social structure. Richards, *The Political System of the Bemba Tribe—North-Eastern Rhodesia* (1940), 96; see also Evans-Pritchard, *Heredity and Gestation, as the Azande See Them* (1932), 405; Ford, *A Comparative Study of Human Reproduction* (1945), 44.

ETHOS

IN this division we propose to describe Kaska ethos, for illustrations drawing upon the cultural data already presented and upon such additional personality data as may be required. Each of the dominant motivations first will be defined briefly and then described as it expresses itself in behavior. A synthetic interpretation of the Kaska world and self-views follows this portion of the work and finally a theory is offered to explain the patterning of the dominant motivations in the socialization process.

DOMINANT MOTIVATIONS

We have defined the socially patterned dominant motivations as constituting a world of meanings, which influences the emotional significance of internal or external situations and becomes expressed in a human being's motivated response to such a situation. Obviously basic motives do not operate in isolation from the rest of the organism and its environment, but rather interact with nutritional, glandular, climatic, social, and geographic determinants.[1]

Kaska ethos comprises the operation of six basic motivations. Reserving their definition for the present, these are: egocentricity, utilitarianism, deference, flexibility, dependence, and emotional isolation. From the subsequent description of the expression of these motives, it will be apparent that some of these headings could be subsumed under others. Such overlap is to be expected, however, since most behavior is expressive of more than one motive and because we have made no effort to characterize the society by the method of listing independent traits. Furthermore, the dominant motivations must be thought of as interrelated aspects of a single configuration. Their isolation for separate consideration only serves the purpose of convenient analysis.

Little importance should be attached to the words that have been chosen to designate these motivations without referring to their explicit definitions. Words utilized for the characterization of personality in western society often have a loose connotation. When, added to this loose usage, it is remembered that such words also have a significance derived from experience in one cultural context, the danger will be realized of making these symbols do duty for the description of superficially similar phenomena in another cultural context.[2]

---

[1] It is necessary to remember that although all behavior is determined, not all activity is motivated. Decrying the obfuscating, synonymous usage of "motivated" and "determined" Maslow writes: "There are many determinants of behavior other than motives. For instance, one other important class of determinants is the so-called 'field' determinants, Theoretically, at least, behavior may be determined completely by the field, or even by specific external stimuli, as in association of ideas, or certain conditioned reflexes. If in response to the stimulus word 'table,' I immediately perceive a memory image of a table, this response certainly has nothing to do with my basic needs." (Maslow, A Theory of Human Motivation [1946], 42–43.) As is apparent from the example given, Maslow here is not referring to the free association relied upon by psychoanalysis. In discussing Kaska ethos we limit our subject matter to behavior that is motivated by dominant motivations.

[2] A loose cross cultural use of psychiatric concepts may be noted in many studies of national character appering shortly before and during the second World War. See Klineberg. A Science of National Character (1944), 155–156.

A related difficulty arises with respect to the valuational connotation associated with some of the words used to describe Kaska dominant motivations. It is inevitable that the characterization of personality by the use of words which have obtained currency in European and American psychiatry and clinical psychology should be loaded with implicit value. Overtones of value emerge from terms like passivity, dependence, mastery, and ego strength. Kardiner has defended the necessary use of similar terms because of their utility, but has rejected characterizations like "normal" and "abnormal" as pure value or moral judgements.[3] Three cautions may guide us through this predicament. In the first place, psychiatric descriptions borrowed from one cultural context and applied to behavior of non-western societies do not necessarily have the same significance which they enjoy in the psychiatrist's own social group. Isolation, dependence, constriction, and moderate ego tonicity, when applied to the Kaska, *by themselves* never denote positive or negative values; intrinsically they are neither good nor bad. In the second place, terms like anxiety, frustration, fear, and others always denote unpleasant psychological states. Finally, defenses (like passivity) developed against unpleasant states (like anxiety) are to be regarded as either able to resolve, or incapable of resolving, those conditions. Any final appraisal of such defenses, however, involves a psychiatric rather than a moral judgement which, if made, must always take due cognizance of all the relevant facts within a specific cultural context. In other words, the anthropologist choosing to make such an appraisal must prepare himself to estimate objectively the efficiency of a socially patterned defense system in terms of its social consequences.

In discussing each motivation our procedure will be to first give a definition. This will generally be followed by a description of the motive's expression in observed behavior, verbal communication, and inferred unconscious attitudes. Wherever possible the expression of the motive in the Rorschach test situation will also be considered.

With regard to the definition of the dominant motivations, it is our experience that membership in a society which fails to understand an attitude, for example flexibility, makes it extremely difficult to define such a construct in positive terms. We can much more readily say what flexibility is not; for in a society like ours, which stresses order and routine, any absence of these attributes is quickly noted. An attempt is nevertheless made to present, in some degree, an objective and positive definition of all dominant motivations. In discussing the expression of the motivations, attention is centered on the manner in which they enter into many cultural situations; in other words, emphasis is directed as much as possible on the influence exerted by these aspects of personality on the adaptive and adjustive features of Kaska culture.

A word may be added concerning the procedure followed in describing the expression of the dominant motivations in the Rorschach test. The meaning of the response category in every case is clearly given and either generally follows the standard interpretation of that category as formulated by Rorschach experts or else involves an explicitly stated assumption making the interpretation more applicable to the Kaska.

EGOCENTRICITY

Egocentricity refers to a dominant motivation charged with a high evaluation of individualism and personal independence. Interests are self-centered rather than group cen-

---

[3] Kardiner, *The Psychological Frontiers of Society* (1945), 219, 234–237, 252–258.

tered in such a point of view, and tendencies toward altruism and social identification have either a limited development or are absent. The initiation of activity tends to come from within the egocentric individual rather than from others and is correlated with a strong sense of personal responsibility for success or failure.

A striking correspondence is apparent between the egocentric aspect of Kaska perso-ality and Horney's "detached" personality type.[4] The outstanding characteristic of this type, Horney finds, "is a need for *self-sufficiency*. Its most positive expression is resourceful-ness . . . In the detached type the spirit is like Robinson Crusoe's: he has to be resourceful to live. It is the only way he can compensate for his isolation." She goes on to show that "Self-sufficiency and privacy both serve his most outstanding end, the need for utter inde-pendence. He himself considers his independence a thing of personal value . . . It manifests itself in hypersensitivity to everything in any way resembling coercion, influence, obligation and so on." Continuing, she says: "When the detached person's feeling of superiority is temporarily shattered, whether by concrete failure or by an increase of inner conflicts . . . he may reach out frantically for affection and protection." As a psychiatrist working in a par-ticular cultural milieu, Horney sees the goals of the detached personality as "negative: he wants *not* to be involved, *not* to need anybody, *not* to allow others to intrude on or influence him." She stresses the fundamental inutility of such trends in western society. In contrast, however, the similar trend here labelled egocentricity is far more realistic in an atomistic society like that of the Kaska, where everyone is equally detached and relative self-sufficiency is economically possible.

Egocentricity and the tonicity of the ego. Eogcentricity will first be discussed in connection with ego tonicity, variously expressed as ego strength, ego feeling, or self-esteem. Perhaps the simplest definition for the common referent of these concepts is: "The individual's image and evaluation of himself."[5] Here we will include with that definition the psychoanalytic notion of the ego as the partially conscious, executive mechanism of the personality through which, we may assume, the goals of the dominant motivations become realized or meet frustration.

Without at this time anticipating in detail data to be presented in connection with the other dominant motives, we may say that the facts point to the presence of moderately de-veloped ego strength in the average Kaska Indian. Although, as will become clear, many problems are defined by the individual's doubt of his capacity for mastery, there is, on the other hand, evidence for inferring the ability of the ego to master many situations of poten-tial danger. The people survive in an uncongenial environment and are generally optimistc of their capacity to adapt. There is no exclusive readiness to rely on traditional solutions of adaptive problems but a certain ability to experiment. Thus Hans Donnelly reported trying various woods for toboggan manufacture, despite the fact that traditionally the use of birch is specified for this purpose. People are rarely "stuck" in adaptive problems but show a con-siderable amount of resourcefulness and ingenuity for pulling themselves out of danger. Without the ability to make too fine discriminations, we must be content to postulate mod-

[4] Horney, *Our Inner Conflicts* (1945), 75–81.
[5] Maslow and Mittelmann, *Principles of Abnormal Psychology* (1941), 131. Compare Beck's definition of the ego: "a consciousness of values to which the individual clings and which he wants the world to respect." Beck, *Rorschach's Test. II. A Variety of Personality Pictures* (1945), 21.

erate ego feeling, or neither excessively high nor low self-esteem. Such a conclusion seems warranted by the facts considered above as well as by the absence of directly expressed self-pity, the manifest pride in achievement, and, on the negative side, by the tendency to bolster self-esteem, placing the blame for misfortune on others, and showing up the inferiority of others. The readiness to apply empirical thinking also demonstrates a certain degree of positive ego development; on the other hand, we find this type of thought paralleled by mysticism, in which ego control surrenders to unconscious wishes and anxieties.

Beck has postulated that the stronger the ego, the more good form responses will appear in the Rorschach record while poor form answers often indicate personal needs distorting perception.[6] The mean Kaska adult $F+$ and $F-$ scores show a balance in favor of good form responses.

	Mean (R = 22.16)
$F+$	9.21
$F-$	5.84

Despite inability to correlate quantitatively form perception with ego tonicity, these figures confirm the interpretation that the Kaska level of self-esteem is not excessively low and that its strength is probably undermined by the intrusion of passive longings.

Expression of egocentricity. All positive expression of egocentricity in Kaska behavior may be understood as a statement by the individual affirming his ability to accomplish a task upon his own initiative, or declaring his independence from other people. Some situations, however, may overwhelm the person with their complexity or else be beyond his capacities. In such cases a threat to egocentricity, arising in part from the operation of contradictory motives, promotes reactions of guilt and anxiety. By discussing egocentricity as the first of the dominant motivations, we hope to show its important and consciously accepted position in Kaska personality. It is unfortunate that in this advance position we cannot too clearly relate the motive to the other dominant motivations still awaiting discussion. We may, however, refer to egocentricity and utilitarianism as representing the self-asserting and self-sufficient trends of Kaska personality. The expression of egocentric attitudes will first be discussed in connection with technical, social, and religious situations. We will then take up the question of differences in egocentricity between men and women, the general reactions produced by threats to the egocentric goal and, finally the expression of egocentricity in the Rorschach test situation.

Together with utilitarianism, egocentricity dominates most of the technical routines of Kaska culture, investing those activities with conscious meaning. Work becomes significant because it guarantees the person's independence and self-sufficiency or, if adaptive difficulties arise, threaten those aims with failure—that is, imperil the maintenance of egocentricity. Successful hunting, construction, and traveling represent self-assertion.

Independence is assured in Kaska economic life by the fact that most technological activities do not require people to work together for common ends, nor need many persons

---

[6] Beck, *Rorschach's Test. II. A Variety of Personality Pictures* (1945), 20, 21. Poor form answers may also be caused by erroneous perception due to intoxication or excitement.

participate in an activity for its completion. Individualism contrasts Kaska society to a co-operative social group, in which a number of people work *with* one another for the common good (the usual voluntaristic definition of cooperation), and also to a competitive society, whose members tacitly agree to participate in an activity but work *against* one another. Among the Kaska both forms of cooperation are largely lacking and the consequent indi-vidualistic emphasis may be partly understood as a result of egocentric striving. Specific expressions of egocentrism in economic life are abundant. The motive is demonstrated in the personal initiative which governs economic relationships and allows an economic partner to withdraw from such a relationship when it no longer proves congenial. What cooperation exists in the technical culture is primarily on a voluntaristic basis. The economic independ-ence of a family unit rests on foundations of personal independence and responsibility. Psychologically, the family can survive alone because its adult members place a high value on being able to live independently and resourcefully without major external assistance. Egocentric trends are also manifested in the reluctance of people to undertake wage work for other Indians or white men. An individual's values are such that only personal goals are invested with emotional appeal; and the more remote a task from one's immediate interests, the less attractive its valence.

The sense of personal responsibility for success and failure is revealed in the fact that a hunter experiences disappointment when he fails to secure meat and, in spite of the fact that he suppresses manifest emotionality, appears intensely satisfied when he has done well in hunting. This observation is corroborated by the observation that in no case is a successful hunt seriously ascribed to "luck"—personal satisfaction from the exercise of egocentric striving rarely permitting any diffusion of affect away from the ego. Lack of success, however, in order to relieve the sense of failure, shows a tendency to be allocated to supernatural cau-sation. It is in motivating hunting behavior that egocentricity reveals itself most strongly as the positive driving force of Kaska personality. Overemphasis would be difficult in describ-ing the optimism with which the Indian approaches hunting. Self-assured, confident of suc-cess, conscious of a subjective command over the venture, the hunter sees his task as the acme of personal achievement. That successful young women hunters overtly display such emotional reactions (which men inhibit) points up both their eagerness to identify with this male vocation as well as the role's importance for personal self-esteem and satisfaction. Ego-centricity must also be credited as motivating the conquest of early patterned fear of the bush, a victory for all boys and some girls, which permits the egocentric gratifications af-forded by successful hunting and trapping.

Turning now to the social expression of egocentricity, we find independence assured by the atomism of social life—the consequence of a low degree of social identification. The egocentric sense of personal responsibility is related to the fact that a person rarely feels accountable beyond his family, and is apt even to resent criticism from that source. In other words, an egocentrically motivated attempt is made to insulate against awareness of social expectations. It is not surprising, therefore, to find that a sense of guilt is more important for insuring conformity than a feeling of shame. Any attempt to induce shame probably only succeeds to the degree that it generates guilt. External sanctions are also resented be-cause they imperil independence. Here is the root of the Indian's negativistic attitudes to the white man's law and the regulative functions of government. Nitla's words demonstrate the connection between a desire for inviolable independence and the denial of external authority: "Injun nothing boss. He feed himself. He live on the meat. Nothing boss the Injun." Going on, he sought to point out the meaninglessness of authority which is not legitimized by a validated protective role. Game, Nitla said, is fed by Jesus, not by the government. Jesus "make this ground . . . He the boss for it. Well, He make white people, He make game, anything. Well, He boss to anything." The white man made nothing in the native's environment, hence he cannot properly assume authority.

In his ingroup relationships the Indian is also self-centered and nonauthoritarian. He does not seek authority in interpersonal relations, and others can scarcely tell him what to do—initiation of activity must come from within. Egocentricity thus leaves little room for patterns of leadership. Few people know how to direct others effectively and white men who try to originate action in social affairs, like dances or trading, meet with apathy and usually fail to realize their suggestions. In most cooperative enterprises, like berry picking or poling a boat, each participant selects his role with a minimum of direction. Within the Indian community, there is a consistent reluctance to give direction or, except in cases of manifest danger, as in adapting to the winter environment, even venture direct suggestion. "We do it this way," the Indian says when approached for help or advice, the implication being that the pupil may or may not follow the traditional pattern. There is little attempt to force adherence to habitual modes of procedure. Personal standards govern the manufacture of cultural products. For example, Hans Donnelly provoked considerable amusement when he constructed a doorway to his tent frame which only suited his own small dimensions, and built a toboggan that was also smaller than most of these vehicles. Although they may be extreme, these examples are not exceptional. Instead of cultural objects being manufactured in close accordance with traditional forms, we find toboggans lashed with insulated wire cable, and other cultural products utilizing scraps of material salvaged from the refuse dumps behind Watson Lake Airport. Any analysis of material products of behavior confirms the absence of formal patterns and indicates the readiness with which variations are developed.

Self-interest sometimes leads to selfishness, people generally showing little appreciation of values like self-sacrifice. When in danger a man tends to look out for himself or his immediate family. Old Man, going home from a dance at which there had been drinking, saw a car in town belonging to the Mounted Police but warned nobody of what was certainly a threatening state of affairs. On another occasion Dorothy Plover's sister warned her brother, who was intoxicated at a dance, that the provincial policeman was walking through Lower Post. The two young people fled without warning anyone else. Self-interest is revealed historically in the fact that once when a social ideology was adopted (under the leadership of a white man), one Indian at least clearly manifested a primary concern with personal gain. The Kaska Indian's preoccupation with his own welfare is even expressed in his complaint that the government does not help the Indians; in reality the center of reference is the speaker, who sees himself standing to benefit from any generous Indian policy.

In some cases egocentricity is overdeveloped to a point where it motivates deviant behavior. Such an individual neglects to project his desire for independence and personal freedom and tries to dominate others by authoritarian direction. This behavior imperils the individual's value of deference by earning him considerable disapproval and dislike. Authoritarianism, in the few Kaska individuals where it occurs, is too complex for analysis simply as a device for reinforcing selfinterest and independence by controlling other people in much the same way as the normal personality seeks to control the natural environment. In addition, the dominant man in the society may be a particularly aggressive person who, contrary to social expectations, too freely releases hostility. Nevertheless, despite these ramifications men like John Kean, Peter Lang, and Harry Lang may have their deviance partly understood as following from a failure to project the desire for personal inviolability. Instead they attempt to carry over into social relationships egocentrically motivated demands for personal control.

From what has been said, it is apparent that egocentricity motivates the characteristic, individualism of the Kaska Indians. Besides being expressed in the atomistic social structure, we find this note extended into the games which people play. Team organization is rudimentary in the popular stick game, teams being little more than a series of individuals playing together. Members bet against single persons on the opposite side and otherwise manifest little tendency to cohere as a group. It remains to be seen how competitive sports may someday become integrated into such a personality setting.

Egocentricity also finds expression in sex, sexual relations being unconsciously identified with successful hunting and sexual potency with feelings of general capacity and mastery. The evidence for the relationship of selfassertion to sex is indicated in the socially patterned interpretation of sexual dreams. Referring to a dream characterized by his soninlaw's sexual sadism toward a widow, Stella Wiley, Old Man said: "I look for Stella on ice all day—I mean animal." He explained, saying: "If you dream you play with girl and then hunt, you kill a [female] animal." In other words, on the day following the dream Old Man looked for game on the frozen river. The relationship of sex to selfassertion will be more extensively discussed below.[7]

Egocentricity in men and women. We have described the operation of egocentricity in behavior which seeks to maintain independence, selfinterest, and responsibility. Attention will now be directed to the relative development of egocentricity in the sexes.

The ethnographic data have already revealed that some women show a tendency to emulate the roles of men and to anticipate unfavorably the state of motherhood; their behavior is expressive of masculine striving and suggests considerable selfassertion. Although in marriage women are generally content to permit husbands to originate important action and are prepared to offer a number of personal comforts which men do not reciprocate, married women still continue to seek opportunity for realizing their capacities through hunting and trapping. Widows show little immediate inclination to remarry but are often possessed of sufficient initiative and resourcefulness to support themselves independently. All these data express a considerable degree of feminine individualism and independence. They are evidence that, like men, women are also motivated by egocentric striving. A few feminine behaviors suggest less egocentricity for that sex. Women, in contrast to men, have

---

[7] See below, pp. 294–298. For the relationship of Old Man's failing capacities to dreams of sexual potency see the analysis of his personality below, p. 330.

from childhood been trained for a serving role, and this renders them more passive. Within the family, women cooperate more freely. In these situations, therefore, they show a weaker motive of self-assertion and somewhat less self-interest. On the whole, we may conclude that egocentricity seems to be quite firmly patterned in the feminine personality but is sometimes modified by the demands of the woman's marital role.

Threat to egocentric goals. For the present we will limit discussion to threats occurring in the man's personality as a result of failure to realize his egocentric values. Threats to feminine egocentricity can be better understood when considered in relation to other motives. As long as the ego is able to withstand the stresses of living and unable to perceive any conscious conflict of egocentricity and incompatible motives, the Kaska Indian approaches life with confidence. Any interference with the maintenance of egocentric trends, through failure of the executive functions of the ego, is inevitably accompanied by threat and anxiety. In critical situations, when expression of the egocentric motivation is blocked, when independence or self-reliance have been overwhelmed or expect to meet defeat, we find a mustering of passive forms of mastery, such as reliance on luck, withdrawal from the field, procrastination, and hypochondriasis—defenses all, designed for the ego's protection against mounting anxiety, In a society which demands considerable personal exertion in the process of getting a living, in which there are few alternative economic roles to choose from, and in which dependency and passivity are anxiety provoking, we may expect old age and illness to be traumatic phenomena, particularly in men.[8] Hypochondriasis is a common feature of the adult male personality and represents a common type of defense against situations in which the ego feels unable to achieve goals of independence and responsibility. Preoccupation with symptoms as an excuse for achievement, therefore, in part represents a passive withdrawal from the field of struggle. Its appearance occurs mainly in mature men, like Louis Maza and Old Man, but is already begun to be shown by a young married man like Hans Donnelly. Such men are expected to bear the brunt of economic responsibility but exhibit ego tonicity insufficient to support their socially patterned role.

Expression in the Rorschach test situation. We have already alluded to the form answers as related to one aspect of this motivation—self-esteem. Other criteria, applying partially to egocentricity are, those measuring the introversive trends of the personality. Klopfer and Kelley have defined the introvert as "predominantly motivated from within."[9] and this is the general significance of the term as employed by Rorschach workers. If we limit introversion, as measured by the Rorschach technique, to denote the responsiveness of the individual to his own values and ideals (in contrast to extraversion, in which the values are in the environment) we may assume that introversion expresses one important aspect of egocentricity.

Klopfer and Kelley have listed three criteria for determining the relative degrees of introversion and extraversion of Rorschach subjects. These are, the ratio of the number of human responses to the sum of all color answers (M: sum C); the ratio of animal plus inanimate movement to shading, texture, and achromatic color responses ($(FM+m):(Fc+c+C')$ and,

---

[8] This generalization is well illustrated in the case of Old Man, who, during the past few years, has been coming to feel the limitations imposed on his physical powers by advancing years and failing eyesight. See the analysis of his personality below.

[9] Klopfer and Kelley, *The Rorschach Technique* (1942), 221.

finally the percentage of responses given to the last three cards.[10] The significance of these three criteria may be briefly summarized according to their definition by Klopfer and Kelley.

M:sum C   Indicates the balance between promptings from within and stimuli from without as far "as the subject can utilize these motivating forces."

(FM +m):(Fc +c +C') Represents the introversial and extraversial tendencies not fully accepted or utilized.

Cards VIII, IX, X/R Indicates the degree of "responsiveness to stimuli from without which is even less under the conscious control of the subject than the use of action and color elements."

The relevant figures for Kaska adults are given below:

	Mean (R = 22.16)
M:sum C	1.16:.97
(FM+m):(Fc+c+C')	3.32:.90
VIII, IX, X/R	34 Per Cent

In the two ratios, the left hand terms indicate introversive tendencies. The ratio of movement to the sum of the color responses lies in the direction of introversion, although not significantly so. In the second ratio, similar but stronger introversion is indicated. The conclusion follows that, although the Kaska do not seem to be able to draw upon a rich source of inner motivation, their tendency nevertheless is to rely upon themselves rather than to be responsive to pressure from the external environment. In the percentage of responses to the last three cards, the figure of thirty-four per cent is less than the forty per cent automatically expected, any excess of which is significant of external stimulation. The mean percentage given by the Kaska is also not below the thirty per cent level at which underproduction is stated to occur. Inspection of the records, however, reveals that many responses to the last three cards make little use of the color for concept formation. Here too, then, we can speak of a tendency to introversion manifested in the fact that outside stimulation has relatively little effect on the motivational life of the subject. We may conclude that Rorschach analysis tends to confirm the picture of egocentricity as denoting a personality organization in which there is strong interest in retaining independence from outside pressures with primary reliance on personal initiative.

Reference has been made to the expression of independence and individualism in the lack of interest which the individual shows in working for others. Such lack of motivation is reflected in the resistance to the Rorschach test situation, particularly in the high number of rejections.[11]

Résumé. A description of the operation of egocentricity has been offered in which the goals of this dominant motivation were identified as including personal independence, self-centeredness of values, and a sense of individualistic responsibility. Egocentricity constitutes one of the relatively self-assertive motives of the Kaska personality and is associated with a

---

[10] Klopfer and Kelley. *The Rorschach Technique* (1942), 253–254.

[11] For a tabulation of rejections see above, p. 243.

moderate development of the ego. No profound difference in the egocentric direction of the masculine or feminine personality seems to obtain. Under situations of stress, illness, and old age, because of the failure of the physical capacities of the individual, the ego becomes unable to execute the egocentric demands of the personality. This leads the individual to resort to passive forms of mastery which conflict with the egocentric goal, thereby arousing anxiety.

UTILITARIANISM

In referring to an aspect of Kaska motivation, utilitarianism denotes a practical, functional, ingenious approach to the problems of living, and the ability to grapple with the problems resourcefully. The motivation aims toward mastery of experience via concrete, immediate thinking, sparing a minimum of attention for abstract speculation or non-functional elements of craftmanship like beauty, decoration, and perfectionism.

This section will consider the expression of utilitarianism in adaptive situations, personally adjustive behavior, the Rorschach test situation, and, finally, with reference to the Kaska Indian's reality system.

Adaptive expression. Utilitarianism, in motivating practical and ingenious behavior, bears a close relationship to the dominant motivation of egocentricity. As already pointed out, together the two dominant motivations may be described as headed for a goal of self-sufficiency, utilitarianism aiding the achievement of independence by providing practical resourcefulness. Whereas egocentricity sponsors the attitude: "I *must* do this by myself," utilitarianism reinforces individualism with the statement: "I *can* do this alone." Faced with a rigorous and often dangerous environment, the Indian must be resourceful and competent in meeting the problems which he encounters in the atomistic social setting of his making, where cooperation is limited and professional assistance unobtainable.[12]

The role of utilitarianism in motivating adaptive problem solution is well illustrated by the characteristic resourcefulness and ingenuity displayed by Kaska Indians. Consider, for example, the cleverness with which men use common tools as substitutes for more refined implements—the ax as a saw or plane, the knife as a chisel and plane. Despite the Indian's preference for modern tools, he is never hampered when confronted with a necessary task whose postponement is impossible but for which suitable appliances are not available. Ingenuity leads a man to manufacture usable substitute equipment. While making snowshoes, preparatory to visiting the trap line, Hans Donnelly discovered that the settlement lacked small sized bits for drilling holes in the wooden frames. Spending eight to nine hours in heating and beating down the point of a file, Hans succeeded in manufacturing a suitable drill point which he then mounted in a wooden handle. When tools break in the winter trapping districts, where replacements are difficult to obtain, they are often soundly repaired with few other aids than a file, wire, and babiche. We have seen lost firing pins for .22 caliber rifles replaced with filed down nails, and split ax handles serviceably lashed with babiche. No commercial machine or apparatus, other than perhaps the radio (and here curiosity is begin-

---

[12] This statement may be modified if we consider that Indians sometimes secure a little expert mechanical assistance from white trappers in Lower Post. During much of the year, however, such specialized advice is not obtainable.

ning to lead to tentative experimentation), is too complex for tinkering and repairing. Long hours are spent overhauling outboard motors and only as a last resort, when some precisely fitting piece is damaged beyond repair, will the task be abandoned and a new part purchased. A broken ax handle or a shattered snowshoe never suggest the abandonment of a journey, for such accidents can always be repaired with commonplace tools, a splint of willow, and a few feet of babiche. Several men reported encountering moose and caribou while traveling without a knife and butchering the animals with an ax. On one ocacsion Old Man retrieved the shell of the cartridge that had brought down the animal; then, using an ax, he beat the brass into a crude blade, fabricating an instrument with which to finish the butchering.

Utilitarianism is the personality factor on which the society relies for maintaining the mobility which is of paramount importance for economic survival. Considerable practical and ingenious thinking is displayed toward this end. For example, to lighten the weight of guns, men often saw down a rifle barrel, afterwards fitting the weapon with new sights which are then carefully tested in target shooting. A shortened barrel reduces the firing power of a weapon (it is not known if the Indians are aware of this limitation), but also makes the gun more comfortable for long marches in brushy country. Spruce wood, selected in preference to harder birch, for snowshoes represents a similar empirical and utilitarian approach to convenient travel. The prevalent use of bags and similar lightweight containers for food and clothing is another practical adaptation to the economic necessity of free mobility. One autumn, the failure of an outboard motor caused self-sufficiency to be strikingly applied to securing movement when, after a protracted period of delay, Harry Lang and his brother-in-law finally tracked and poled their boat more than fifty miles upriver from the Highway Crossing to Old Man's settlement. Their solution was the only one that could get them home while the bull moose still retained his fat and before the enforced delay, in an area where there was little game, consumed too much winter grub.

Utilitarianism, defined as a practical, functional approach to living, also shapes the attitudes towards acculturation in technical culture. We have already pointed out that the Kaska have been far more ready to borrow technological improvements than they have been to modify adjustive patterns of behavior. This acculturative set is associated with an utilitarian motivated absence of sentimentality for the aboriginal style of adaptation. This may explain the receptiveness which Morice has regarded as a characteristic trait of Athapaskan society.[13] To the utilitarian personality, the past represents a hard way of life, while newer ways of working, traveling, and general living quickly suggest their advantages.

Empirical attention to the zoological, botanical, and bodily environments too stems from utilitarian considerations, giving the practically important habits of animals far greater significance than other aspects of behavior. Kaska ethnobotany is a system of knowledge almost exclusively concerned with the economic values of woods coupled with more obvious observations of habitat. Beyond this, interest is limited. For example, Nitla could give no explanation of how trees maintained themselves or the manner in which they reproduced. Esoteric speculation and mysticism with regard to weather and in connection with sickness and death receive little elaborate development. Interest in such phenomena

[13] Morice, *The Fur Trader in Anthropology; and a Few Related Questions* (1928), 77.

is primarily determined by practical and immediate considerations—their value to ego's self-sufficiency or their threat to his efficient functioning.

The strongly developed practical interest in adaptation leads the Indian to neglect beauty and to be unresponsive to perfectionism as an end in itself—that is, above and beyond the degree required for utility. Embroidery on moccasins, mittens, and gloves is reduced to a minimum or often lacking. Only one or two women enjoy a reputation for fancy sewing, although many more are acknowledged as skillful, practical dressmakers. Oars are particularly crude and unfinished. Experiments made to deduce the emotional aspects of cultural products in connection with clothing and housing consistently revealed qualities of simplicity and nonperfection. Mittens, moccasins, and children's underwear, without being fitted to the wearer's dimensions, are cut with a general impression of size, allowing a little extra so that the final product is always somewhat larger than necessary. The style is baggy, the garment only crudely shaped to the body. Analysis of several log cabins reveals a striking lack of perfectionism. In one cabin some roof poles are partly hewed while many are not hewed at all. Where the logs join at the corners they are often not all sawed off to equal length. Another cabin is only half floored. The interiors of most houses are not painted or otherwise finished. Such housing style permits the inference that the people's primary concern is with utility, adequacy of a structure being defined primarily in terms of the building's use for the obvious function of weather protection. Thus we find walls lined with cardboard to keep out drafts, and moss chinking far more prevalent than the more finished-looking chinking with pole cleats which many white men use. It may be pointed out, however, that the increasing use of mill sawed lumber, which is easier to manipulate than logs, is resulting in larger and, in some cases, more finished looking cabins. While the neglect of nonfunctional artistic production may be partly determined by the fact that Kaska society has not been able to develop leisure time patterns of self-expression, any total picture of this neglect must also take into consideration the dominant motivation toward utility. It is consistent with configurational thinking that such personality values should be developed in members of a society forced to live under rigorous environmental conditions, where energy has to be largely confined to adaptation.

Attitudes condemning waste may be partly ascribed to utilitarian considerations. Food leftovers, instead of being discarded or fed to dogs, are preserved for future meals. At the first potlatch, food remains returned by the servers were scraped from dishes and, after being mixed with the contents of the cooking pots, were served again. Similar economy is revealed toward the possessions of the dead. Destruction of death goods is minimal; only worn or soiled clothes are burned. Valuable goods (like a sleeping robe) are freed from contagion by washing or by allowing a period of time to dissolve the association between object and deceased owner.

Social sanctions supporting utilitarian resourcefulness are not lacking. Both the ideal man and woman are skillful. Young men are quietly proud of their technological achievements and older men of their special technical abilities. A skillful individual is selected for favorable comment and is also favored by a prospective parent-in-law, while an unskillful youth has his behavior deplored. More important than the social recognition of these attributes is the fact that practical skills and ingenuity greatly lighten the individual's adaptive problems, guarantee him comfort, and contribute to survival.

Adjustive expression. Up to this point discussion has been limited to aspects of utilitarianism revealed in adaptive resourcefulness. We now propose to examine the expression of this dominant motivation in the individual's psychological adjustment to phenomena like time, direction, and concept formation.

The Indian's slight concern with abstract systems of generalization is reflected first in the relative timelessness of the people. The best apprehended divisions of time are either based on the alternation between night and day, the passage of seasons, or else derived from the duration of cultural tasks (such as the period of time required to build a toboggan, make snowshoes, or clean a hide). Superimposed upon these relatively concrete divisions of time are the introduced patterns of a more abstract apportioning of the day, month, and year. Why have the Indians been slow in orienting themselves to the latter temporal divisions? Any explanation for this lag must take into account the dominant motivation which is threatened by these more abstract systems. Utilitarianism includes the need to be concrete. The abstract conception of time is meaningless, since it divorces the individual from realistically perceived units which he feels best suited to control.

This point of view may perhaps be better illustrated by abstract spatial orientation. The points of the compass mean little to the Kaska Indian. Instead, he equates himself to things of immediate personal significance, like the camp, a ridge, a range of hills, a river, or the direction of the current. The native patterns of temporal and spatial orientation may also be interpreted by saying that the concrete gives the Indian a sense of mastery, while the abstract means losing control. Mastery, therefore, is an aim of utilitarianism just as it is also related to egocentricity. In his orientation to time and space, the Kaska Indian is expressing both these dominant motivations in an attempt to preserve his self-sufficiency. It follows that any increasing readiness and ability to accept abstract temporal and spatial ideas would have to develop in terms of the native's world and self-views, or would follow from important basic personality changes.

Educational methods displayed in relation to children, with their neglect of principles and stress on learning by doing, also reflect the lack of motive to conceptualize, as well as the lack of interest in planning to which we will now turn attention.

Utilitarianism motivates the person's concrete attention to the present, whose significance is more readily perceived by the personality than past or future. The absence of idealizing or sentimental attitudes toward the past is related to both a focus on practical contemporary problems and an absence of intense interest in the future. As a result of an inability to cathect the past, the individual is unable to systematize his own life history beyond a series of sequential events, and often uninterested in even doing that within an orderly time frame. Examples of the inability to anticipate the future emotionally are provided from the ethnographer's discussion of the possibility that the Cassiar might become more familiar to white people, with a consequent influx of visitors. What would this mean to the Indian? Few men, with whom this potential problem was discussed, reacted to it with more than polite attention. The picture became even more extreme when individuals were hypothetically confronted with their own future. We have seen Gerald Leonard's reaction to this subject marked by a lack of personal ambition or aspiration and little evidence of genuine emotional interest.[14] Gerald is an adolescent. In Nitla, a young adult, we find even less in-

[14] See above, p. 191.

terest in the future. Asked what he would do in, say, five years, Nitla replied in a manner suggesting that the whole notion of projecting himself that far ahead was incomprehensible. "I don't know," he said. "Sometime I want something. Five years more I want something. Sometimes a year I want something. Sometimes nothing. I wouldn't think about it. I don't figure up anything." The question was repeated and the subject echoed it, speaking half to himself. Then: "Don't know. I never think about it. I just look to eat . . . five years more I'm never think. I'm hungry . . . " In other words, Nitla is emotionally bound to the tangible reality of the present. Whereas the future is remote, its consideration inviting a wasteful disbursal of unproductive effort. Here, *now*, are the problems which he is best equipped to solve and that are most important.

The weak emotional valence exerted upon the utilitarian personality by the future is related to the scope of native divination and revelation. In these situations, expecially with regard to intuition and dreaming, we find an expression of concrete immediate wishes. For example, the camp may be expecting the return of a youth, the people waiting for news or supplies which he will bring from the trading post. It is at such a time that a person may experience a dream or omen pointing to the youth's return. Similarly a person who has planned to hunt the following day is encouraged by relatives with optimistic predictions of success. The only example of large scale prophecy came from Old Kean, and his statements, as already pointed out, met with little popular emotional interest.[15]

Expression in the Rorschach test situation. Our discussion has identified utilitarianism in practical and concrete thinking. Several Rorschach criteria may be regarded as indicators of such a style of mentation. Pointing to the percentage of animal associations as one index of "adaptive thinking at a peripheral level," Beck goes on to say: "The percentage of animal associations is the measure of the ability (a) to see what's there, and also (b) to free the perceptual activity from this easiest kind of reaction."[16] Animal responses thus reveal attention to the mundane and not only to specifically practical aspects of living. Klopfer and Kelley concur with this when they relate a high percentage of animal responses to a narrow range of interests.[17] The use of animal responses as an index to a motivation directing attention to practicality and the concrete poses another question. Would not a people closely familiar with an animal environment tend to give more animal responses than a people in an urban area, whose principal experience is with people? Hallowell did not find this to occur among the Saulteaux, where the mean animal per cent obtained by him (47.8) compares closely to that which has been found in western society, namely, 46.87 per cent (S.D., 17.58).[18] The figure for Kaska adults, on the other hand, is significantly in excess of these figures, being 62 per cent. Homogeneity is indicated for the Kaska, since only five of the nineteen adult subjects produced fewer than fifty per cent animal associations. The interpretation

[15] This example gives us another interesting opportunity to test the theory of the deviant as partly socially patterned. In Old Kean we find socially patterned behavior (prophecy) carried to an extreme point of idiosyncratic development, probably in order to express personal insecurity and hostility. See above, p. 14.

[16] Beck, Rorschach's Test. II. A Variety of Personality Pictures (1945), 15.

[17] Klopfer and Kelley, The Rorschach Technique (1942), 214–216.

[18] Hallowell, The Rorschach Technique in the Study of Personality and Culture (1945), 203. Beck, Rorschach's Test. II. A Variety of Personality Pictures (1945), 15.

follows that Kaska adult subjects, when compared to groups of western subjects or Saulteaux Indians, show a greater tendency for mundane and intellectually undifferentiated thinking. We conclude that excessive interest in practical and concrete thinking is revealed in the Rorschach test by a high percentage of animal responses.

Adequate attention to the routine problems of living is further indicated by the position of usual detail responses in the test. The mean adult figure of fifty-two per cent usual detail responses indicates neither exaggerated nor underdeveloped attention to such obvious stimuli but assumes greater significance in view of the fact that whole answers are significantly below the norms determined for western test subjects. This indicates relatively little ability for the Kaska to generalize and conceptualize. These findings are compatible with the percentage of animal responses, and together the three criteria identify the Kaska personality as narrowly concerned with the concrete and obvious features of the environment.

There is also evidence that human movement responses are an index of interest in comprehending the world beyond practical and mundane levels. Beck relates human movement to creativity.[19] Klopfer and Kelley associate human movement with imagination and power of productive thinking.[20] Several human movement responses (M) are generally expected in each record of a "normal" adult in western society and ideally human movement should exceed animal movement associations (FM). Furthermore, if the sum of animal and inanimate movement $(FM+m)$ is more than one and a half times the number of human movement associations, "inhibiting forces" are seen at work, leading to the expression of an "infantile domination of instinctual drives."[21] The pertinent data for Kaska adults follow.

	Mean (R = 22.16)	Per Cent
M	1.16	5
FM	3.32	15
m	—	—

Interpreted by means of the criteria given above, the low mean of human movement responses indicates a limited capacity for imaginative thinking, such as would indicate departure from preoccupation with concrete and obvious problems of daily life. Animal movement is seen about two and a half times more often than human movement, indicating "that a subject is emotionally infantile living on a level of instinctive prompting below his chronological or mental age."[22] To conclude, the avoidance of abstract thinking in the Kaska adult is at least partly related to the basic utilitarian motivation, which focusses attention on practical situations of daily life, whose mastery rewards the individual with feelings of self-sufficiency. Below it will become apparent that adaptation on this level further stems from emotional inhibitions, placed on intellectual creativity, by unconscious needs for safety and protection.[23]

[19] Beck, Rorschach's Test. II. A Variety of Personality Pictures (1945), 24–25.
[20] Klopfer and Kelley, The Rorschach Technique (1942), 276–278.
[21] Klopfer and Kelley, The Rorschach Technique (1942), 280.
[22] Klopfer and Kelley, The Rorschach Technique (1942), 279.
[23] See below, p. 300.

Reality systems. Kardiner has found it useful to distinguish between two types of reality systems.[24] Both have emotional components, but the first is derived from empirical sources while the second is of projective origin, being related to early experiences of the individual. A less developed projective system, Kardiner says, may be correlated with a greater degree of adaptability.[25] It goes without saying that an empirical reality system is also influenced by the individual's early life. For our present purpose we may distinguish between these two reality systems on the basis of whether they rely on empirical or mystical explanations for phenomena.

Utilitarianism among the Kaska is associated with a moderately developed empirical and a more restricted projective reality system. Illness, death, and a host of other experiences tend to be explained in empirical terms, or with reliance on deductive reasoning and analogy rather than on mystical apprehensions. We are thus returned to the earlier formulation of moderate ego strength as a characteristic of Kaska personality. Just as the empirical reality system tends to affirm ego strength, the ethological significance of the projective reality system is to deny the fortitude of the ego. Projective thought comes into operation as a result of the passivity which chronically underlies the person's self-sufficiency. Projective thinking among the Kaska is distinguished by a desire to avoid offense to the supernatural lest trouble befall the individual. Some loose integration of Christian attitudes toward the supernatural has also occurred, the emphasis in these being to solicit help from the super-natural in order to avoid trouble. Many of the dominant motivations, whose operations will now be described, have as their goal a passive adjustment to reality. Among other things we will note their relation to the projective reality system.

Résumé. Utilitarianism has been described to show its functions in assuring the adapta-tion and psychological adjustment of the individual. Characterized by resourcefulness, in-genuity, and concrete thinking along practical lines, this dominant motivation organizes experience in a manner designed to guard against the need for passive adjustments. In as-sociation with a lack of concern for perfectionism, art, and beauty, utilitarianism serves to concentrate energy on elemental survival needs. It is related to a moderately developed empirical reality system, an underemphasis of abstract, speculative systematization, and lack of serious or careful planning toward the future.

DEFERENCE

Deference denotes a dominant motivation directed to maintaining warm human relations, that provide assurance of the individual being liked and respected. The expression of defer-ence is marked by care to avoid arousing anger or hostility and by conscious antipathy to aggression.

First we shall consider the expression of deference in behavior and ideas, followed by consideration of the hostility component in Kaska personality, and opportunities taken for the discharge of aggression.

Expression of deference. The importance of deference in an atomistic social structure need

[24] Kardiner, *The Psychological Frontiers of Society* (1945), 38–46.

[25] "... a society which is dominated by projective techniques lacks adaptability. . . ." Kardiner, *The Psy-chological Frontiers of Society* (1945), 44.

scarcely be stressed and has, in fact, already been pointed out in the evaluation of the social culture. In a society without effective group controls, the unharnessed expression of hostility could rapidly assume suicidal proportions with retaliatory counter aggression permitting little personal safety. Such a society would have difficulty in maintaining itself, the degree of deference (in association with strong instigation to frustration) being inversely correlated with the imminence of social self-destruction.[26] Although cultural instigations to frustration do not appear excessive in Kaska society, the people avoid even approximating a reign of terror in interpersonal relations by encouraging strong and consistent attitudes against hostility. A wide variety of situations may be cited to show how behavior has been organized to avoid the threat of hostile interpersonal relations.

One is immediately struck by the pattern of avoiding refusals when requests are nevertheless not well received. Thus a solicitation for assistance may be met with silence or a cryptic "must be," although the individual has no intention of complying. Often the answer is, "yes," whereupon the commitment is forgotten. Many people made such equivocal promises to the ethnographer during the course of field work, their aim being to avoid offending the ethnographer by direct refusal and thereby, as the Indians thought, arousing resentment. Sometimes a request for assistance will be referred to a supposedly more capable person. The ethnographer sought to persuade several women (who were recommended for their special abilities) to manufacture a parka and a packsack. Direct refusal was never given. Twice the women nominated some more capable worker; once a promise of assistance was given and not fulfilled. From the standpoint of deference such lies, founded on the implicit premise: "Avoid offense in order to avoid trouble," must be regarded as expressions of tact. While a mockery of promises is often disconcerting to white people, it is more than likely that broken commitments do not rankle within the Indian community. Furthermore, in a setting where self-sufficiency is a primary value, requests for assistance are kept at a minimum. Necessary requests are usually carefully and obliquely made. Thus a man going hunting will announce his intention to a friend. Should the latter want to join, he says so. If he fails to answer, the hunter (depending on how strongly he wants game) either postpones the trip or goes alone. When Old Metša died, Old Man, in the presence of the ethnographer, asked rhetorically how assistance for building the coffin could be secured since both his sons-in-law were on their trap lines. Although demurring when the ethnographer offered to carry a message by following Harry Lang's trail, Old Man was obviously relieved to secure an answer to the problem.

Deference is similarly revealed in the avoidance of direct suggestions which might offend an individual. To the ethnographer Old Man sometimes expressed his belief that grouse might be found at certain points near the settlement. After several such remarks, it was perceived that he was obliquely suggesting our hunting these birds. In the same way hints of dwindling meat and grub constitute tactful suggestions that sons-in-law hunt or visit the trading post. Indirect requests avoiding explicit direction illustrate the need to forestall arousing resentment in the interests of deference and the egocentrically motivated desire to avoid dominance in interpersonal relations. From both standpoints, such behavior demon-

[26] For a study of a society without social control and giving minimal attention to patterning deferent personality goals see, Henry, *Jungle People* (1941).

strates tact. An individual realizes his own resistance to authoritarianism and projects a similar feeling into others. He knows that domination must be avoided, because it is likely to produce rebellion or hostility.

The most direct expression of deference is found in the exclusion of face to face quarrels. When a situation becomes too intense and anger has been provoked, women, particularly, often escape the consequences of such provocation by running away. Sometimes, as further illustrated in connection with humor, a joke is conceived in order to relieve a situation of emotional stress. All escape from potential hostility is regarded as intelligent behavior. Actually, remarkably little quarreling or violence characterizes Kaska interpersonal relations. The avoidance of violence is well illustrated in the case of Nitla, Adele, and John Kean, to which several references have already been made. In this marital triangle, Nitla felt considerable hostility toward his brother, but took no direct action against him. Many societies are known in which a husband's violence could safely be predicted for an affair of this kind.[27]

To avoid aggression, people also avoid any direct criticism outside of the immediate family, instead expressing disapproval in gossip. Obviously the need of controlling direct criticism and the substitution of malicious gossip makes for hypocrisy, which is potentially dangerous, since it may also lead to ill feeling and recriminations. For this reason gossip is carefully controlled. Most people when sober are extremely reluctant to gossip, the most consistent manifestation of such behavior coming from older men. Fear of creating offense and trouble is one reason why Indians will rarely report community delicts to the police. Old Kean said that even if he found a dead body in the bush, he would never report it to law enforcement authorities. The absence of sadistic and malicious humor is a further instance of cultural organization toward the goal of deference. Only rarely does humor function toward social control, and then not with the aim of singling out an individual for criticism but rather a group—such as youth. Here, apparently, safety is perceived in number and generality.

The unformalized patterns which we have just described are all directed toward the end of forestalling overt hostility and violence. In addition, we have attitudes decrying aggression. For example, there is no admiration for might and power. The grizzly bear is clearly powerful, but he is the most feared animal in the Cassiar and a common feature of socially patterned anxiety dreams. Because of his very strength, which leads him to court danger by attacking people, the grizzly bear lacks intelligence. Indians fear him exactly as they fear any hostile person who can cause trouble and injury. Aggressive people are regarded as somewhat "crazy" and there is ideally a strong belief that such troublemakers are better locked up or removed from the society. Above all, hostilely disposed people must not be offended; still they are admired by no one.

Opinions about the second World War, which terminated during the period of field work, offer another insight into the expression of deference in ideas. Nitla resented any ex-

---

[27] See, for comparison, Elwin, *Maria Murder and Suicide* (1943), particularly pp. 116–117. The entire book presents descriptions of behavior in striking contrast to that which we are here describing for the Kaska. Obviously, it would be extremely valuable to know something about the basic motivations to which the Bison Horn Maria's violence is related.

pectation that Indian youths should be conscripted to fight and wondered how the government could utilize men to kill, at the same time evading the responsibilities which the white society demands for murder. The government, he opined, was "not smart. He send his boy to the war. . . . You smart, you gotta hold his boy. Then damn good, number one government. He want to make try lots of fun . . . the Jesus, He can't send to war his boy. . . . " Another youth ascribed the cause of the dysentery outbreak to the bloodshed that the war was fostering.

The hostility component. It is well recognized that a certain component of hostility is an inevitable concomitant of the socialization process, and that throughout the subsequent life of an individual additional frustrating or anxiety provoking conditions may strengthen this component. It is also necessary to recognize that a motive like deference may further reinforce the hostility component when it does not permit aggressiveness sufficient opportunity for discharge. Accumulated aggressiveness comes into conflict with deference and is repressed. The repressed hostility provides an area for fecundating anxiety which, in turn, creates fresh hostile impulses—and so on, in a vicious circle.[28] We will now investigate the manner in which this largely unconscious hostility component is kept in check and the conditions under which control is abrogated.

The very fact of repression indicates that aggressive impulses are intolerable to the ego and therefore denied. That individuals deny their hostility is evident from the conscious attitudes strongly stressing the ideal of warm human relations and condemning violence. Dreams often reveal quite a different tenor of thinking. In a person like Old Man, who is frequently occupied in forestalling drunken aggression and who enjoys a reputation for pacificity, there are many examples of dreams expressing unconsciously motivated hostility. One example may be given here.

12:2:45 (Old Man's Place). "I dream that Mrs. Louis Maza couldn't talk no more. They figger her tongue was tied up. And River Joe said: 'John [the ethnographer] getting poor and kids getting poor. He never eat?' he told me. 'They eat.' 'I hear they're starving.' 'No. they got grub yet.' He start to tell me about that woman, Mrs. Suza. 'No!' I told him. 'Because his mother died that's why old woman look after him. I'm not that much crazy!' Funniest dream I ever had."

Old Man was asked if he had dreamed of the current Mrs. Maza.

"No. Louis Maza first wife. She talk, she talk, Finally his mouth quit. Just fall down. I told Mrs. Suza—she want to help—I say: 'Don't help. Maybe she got some kind of fortune.' You know, some people otter doctor. They just drop. . . . After I set my net. Short net, just as long as boat. I just got one whitefish." [What kind of woman was the first Mrs. Maza?] "Mean woman." Old Man denied that she had ever been mean to him. "Just mean to his husband."

This dream occurred on a night when, in order to arrange transportation to Lower Post and to pick up seriously needed additional food, the ethnographer's wife with Old Man's daughter, Louisa, and Elsie Lang were absent from the settlement to visit Louis Maza. The ethnographer's food supply was low and for several days loans had been solicited from Old Man, who was also feeding his son-in-law's mother, Lady Suza, whose own mother had died a month previously. In the dream Louis Maza's first wife loses her voice while her

[28] A more extensive theoretical formulation of these principles will be found in Horney, *New Ways in Psychoanalysis* (1939), 199-204.

father, River Joe, suggests that the ethnographer's family looks ill fed. Here we see Old Man's anxious anticipation of the gossip which will be set in operation when the women reach Louis's place and ask for food. River Joe will surely seize upon this lack of food as a sign that Old Man did not take proper care of his white visitors. Old Man knew that Louis and River Joe both had warned the ethnographer about the "poor place" Old Man had to offer. The dream therefore expresses an aggressive wish that his enemies' tongues should become unable to gossip. By reference to the principle of condensation, we understand the first Mrs. Maza to stand for her father, River Joe; for her husband, and for her sister, the present Mrs. Maza. The first Mrs. Maza was "mean"; this fact helps to explain her selection by the dream work in an attempt to characterize all of her referents as unpleasant people. The evil nature of gossip is revealed in the association to the dreaded otter. Up to this point the dream strives to express Old Man's fear of hostility as well as the accompanying aggression against his enemies.

But the dream also refers to Lady Suza. Apparently (in the dream) River Joe had insinuated that Old Man was cohabiting with this woman. During the previous summer, River Joe had unsuccessfully attempted to secure Lady Suza as his wife. Now Old Man "has" her, at least in the sense that she is sharing his house. Old Man, however, often complained about this woman eating his grub. Is this dream then also an expression of guilt because of his lack of generosity? That suggestion gains support when the conjunction of Lady Suza and the ethnographer is considered. Old Man its chafing under this woman's stay in his home but the ethnographer is also borrowing food which Old Man cannot refuse to lend. In the dream he resents both the woman's and the ethnographer's drain on his limited resources, but feels guilty about his resentment and also dreads being gossiped about as a stingy host. The denial of sexual interest stands for a denial of general, emotional interest in Lady Suza's well being, an interest that Old Man cannot afford to develop. The episode of the short net, which is a reference to Old Man's reduced powers as a food getter, adds more to the interpretation. He secures only one whitefish. That being the case, how can he be expected to provide for so many people? The last note in the dream, therefore, recognizes the essential and unavoidable truth in the gossip (Old Man's settlement *was* short of grub), which Old Man would like to stop, figuratively by tying up his enemies' mouths.

In Kaska society intoxication often results in the release of a portion of the hostility component, and for a number of men such behavior can usually be accurately predicted. Under alcohol rational controls largely disappear, so that an individual is sometimes overwhelmed by the excitement of his unharnessed impulses. This theory explains the outbursts of rage, hostility, and catastrophic reactions that sometimes appear with drinking and of which many people in the community are afraid. Generally, however, drunkenly expressed hostility is not completely undirected. A subliminal measure of control over the labile excitement is maintained, and for this reason drunken aggression is usually focussed upon the continuation of past quarrels, traditional enemies, fancied aggressors, or (as sometimes happens) strangers within the tribal district. It is also noticeable that, following a prolonged series of hostile attacks, swearing, and violence, aggression is finally directed toward the self. A number of men and women were observed who, at the height of intoxication, began to moan, sob, cry for their mothers, or wildly condemned themselves for being "no good."

Sometimes men turned from such a mixture of self-pity and self-recrimination to outright attempts at suicide.

The dynamics of attempted suicide in Kaska society are extremely interesting, their interpretation contributing much to our understanding of deference. The goal of deference has been defined as warm human relations; from the psychiatric standpoint this is equivalent to saying that the goal of deference is love. Consciously, it must be made clear, the Kaska does not so much want to be liked as not to be disliked. The significance of this statement will be further clarified in connection with emotional isolation. Kaska individuals are afraid of giving offense and arousing hostility in a wide circle of human relationships, because they are anxious lest they be disliked. Evidence comes from the fact that people are readily hurt or offended. Thus, Nitla's fear that his father-in-law would hear a false story about how he had neglected Adele led to his desire to tell his wife's father his side of the story so that the latter would not dislike him. Old Man once expressed a complaint that Louis Maza was receiving visitors from downriver, but that nobody was continuing upriver to his place. Visitors are an assurance of popularity, so that a lack of them suggests being disliked. Unquestionably an attitude which fears dislike equals an unconscious fear of the loss of love plus the desire for love. It is against this theoretical backdrop that we may understand the significance of attempted suicide following a sequence of hostile and uncontrolled behavior. By his aggressive behavior the intoxicated individual violates personal standards of deference, betrays hostility, and earns the loss of love. Guilt follows and, while intoxication continues to reduce the efficiency of the egocentric defenses, he reacts to this guilt by a sudden reversal of activity. Aggression and hostility are deflected toward the self and this reversal leads to such behavior as Edward Prince manifested just before he attempted suicide, complaining that he was all alone in the world without relatives; or else the individual announces his intention of self-destruction. The function of this anouncement is clear. It is a plea for help and a defense guaranteeing that the attempt will be unsuccessful. People immediately rush to stop the suicide. This is the would-be victim's pay-off. In the attention he receives, he is assured of the affectionate regard which a moment ago he so strongly doubted. By this time the attempt is a thing of the past. The gun has been safely thrown away, the anxiety of loss of love and assurances of love pile up in the catharsis of emotion that typically terminates a sequence of hostility. From now on defenses can once more restore the emotional isolation of the personality which alcohol tore down. While all self-pity in intoxication is expressive of an unconscious demand for love, not all such emotional expression is immediately determined by aggression released during intoxication. It may also be a result of the affect hunger which the individual feels more keenly while his defenses have been reduced by alcohol.[29] Some reported episodes of psychotic behavior may also be regarded as representing a disintegration of deference and the exposure of the individual to the excitement of hostile impulses which he can no longer control.

Not the whole of the hostility component is reserved for spectacular explosions under intoxication. We have already dealt sufficiently with gossip to make clear the fact that this form of aggression draws upon a chronic store of hostility. Many people are neither gossips nor do they manifest rage and aggression under intoxication. The majority of people are

[29] Affect hunger will be discussed more fully in connection with emotional isolation (see below, p. 287).

"good" drinkers, in whom the relaxation of conscious control is not followed by abnormal behavior.

A few socially permitted forms of releasing hostility are available. The wrestling of young men appears to serve this function. Such behavior (as, for example, when it was observed between John Kean and his brother, Nitla) often becomes grim and serious, only the laughter of the onlookers preventing it from taking the form of a serious expression of hostility. Another potential channel for releasing hostility is gambling. The high appeal of gambling, the intense preoccupation in the stick game, the use of the word "kill" to denote the elimination of an opponent, the joy displayed when the guesser has been outwitted, and the disappointment in defeat, all point to this situation as of great emotional significance. These facts make it likely that gambling is unconsciously conceived as a channel for expressing aggression. The dancelike body rhythm accompanied by the drumming offers an opportunity for a somatic discharge of repressed emotion. When one refers to the intensity with which two dominant men like Nick Lang and Louis Maza played against one another, the scornful clowning of Louis on another occasion, and the fact that gambling games are sometimes broken up through quarreling, the interpretation of gambling as a socially permitted form of releasing aggressive impulses is strengthened.

It is of course obvious that such permitted forms of release, provided they do not culminate in open hostility, are not in conflict with the dominant motivation of deference. Rather an adequate number of such situations might insure the better preservation of the value, by preventing a dangerous accumulation of repressed hostility.

Expression in the Rorschach test situation. There are no satisfactory criteria for judging aggressiveness or its absence in the Rorschach situation. Responses involving scenes of aggression or hostile animals have sometimes been interpreted to indicate aggressive impulses. Both types of answers are inconspicuous in Kaska records. On the other hand, a number of responses to be discussed in connection with subsequent motivations offer insight into how the Kaska behave in social relations in order to reduce the danger of open conflict. The significance of these responses for the question of deference will be pointed out.

Résumé. Data have been presented and analyzed to show the operation of deference as a dominant motivation which defines potentially hostile situations as threatening and patterns their avoidance. The motivation aims at maintaining warm human relations and guarding against threats of the loss of love. Safety lies in tact or (to use a word familiar to the Kaska) in refusing to "bother" others and in evading all situations of being bothered. Under alcohol, inhibitions of hostility sometimes become reduced. Such instances, as well as dreams, reveal a considerable component of repressed hostility.

The efficiency of deference lies chiefly in the fact that it succeeds in curbing open interpersonal aggression in an atomistic society by confining it to relatively harmless forms. As deference results in the accumulation of hostility, from which unconscious anxiety may be generated, its efficacy becomes reduced. Under conditions of a surfeit of hostility and derived anxiety, it is not likely that the goal of deference—warm human relations—will be subjectively realized. Rather, under such conditions, the individual will feel uncertain of how closely he is living up to his demand for deference and also insecure regarding how well he is liked by his society.

FLEXIBILITY

The term flexibility denotes a complex of motivation in which concepts like necessity, hurry, and duty are subordinated to circumstance and personal inclination. The expression of the motivation is marked by relaxed modes of procedure and tolerant, even indecisive, attitudes toward the demands of living. Negatively, flexibility may be described as lacking compulsive trends like rigidity and perfectionism, nor does it stress conscientious attention to routine or careful planning.

Before proceeding to illustrate the general expression of this dominant motivation, an attempt will be made to explain how flexibility is related to the low development of a capacity for realistic planning. Following consideration of miscellaneous forms of expression, closer attention will be paid to procrastination as a feature of Kaska behavior, and, finally, flexibility will be studied from its manifestations in the Rorschach situation.

Planning. Planning is related to the organizing and systematizing capacities of the personality. In connection with utilitarianism, we have already shown how the emotional need for concreteness limits the ability for abstract organization (what might be called the "creative act"). As far as ideas of futurity are concerned, immediate problems and situations are of far greater significance to the utilitarian motivation than prospects which are remote in time. As a result, planning for future goals receives little attention. In the study of the relationship of planning to flexibility, two types of planning are seen. The first organizes behavior in which the end lies in the relative present (building a house or setting a brew) while the second directs behavior in which the goal is in the future (trapping in order to insure a good standard of living the following winter). We will discuss each of these types.

Unless behaving in an habitual manner, the Kaska Indian appears unable to adhere to a sequence of causally related activities whose end lies in the relative present. This was demonstrated when Richard Day and a Tahltan youth announced the intention of setting a brew in the bush. Richard first forgot to buy the ingredients, making it necessary to use the other boy's supplies. It was then discovered that the brew barrel was in Richard's house, where Edward Prince was also living. Because of his tendency to drink unready liquor, Edward could not safely be told of the brew before its completion. The barrel, therefore, had to be secured without Edward's knowledge. A good way of doing this, Richard decided, was to have a dance and, while Edward was fiddling, Richard would slip away and cache the barrel. The dance was held as planned but Richard became interested in "bothering" June Barre, and as a result never left the dancehouse. The brew was postponed until the following day. Often people do not even try to plan their behavior systematically. Rarely do people come to a store knowing in detail what must be purchased. As a result, shopping is a slow process in which the buyer often uses the mercantile display to remind him of his needs. Actually few activities are undertaken with a plan. Either the individual operates through a series of automatic habits or muddles through by making adjustments as required. Watching Richard and his Tahltan companion finally set brew, one got the impression that they had no clearly conceptualized notion of the total process of which the separate acts were parts. After each step they stopped to discuss what was next in order. Such lack of planning often results in being unprepared to complete an activity. A house begun in the fall is often left unfinished for a year, until the builder can, for example, secure additional materials to complete the roof whose requirements were underestimated. Lack of preparedness was evidenced when Irene Wiley, after heating water to wash clothes, discovered that she lacked soap powder.

All of these behaviors, involving planning for relatively immediate goals, reveal not only utilitarian antipathy to conceptualization and systematization, but are also relaxed, indecisive modes of attending to problems of living. They reveal the operation of a flexible motivation that is not bound by rigorous rules. In packing and storage we find a similar lack of compulsive order, no indication of a notion like: "A place for everything and everything in its place." Consequently, houses and camps furnish a picture of considerable confusion, despite which, given time (and time is not a Kaska value), a required object can usually be found. Lack of physical ordering is carried over into the lack of any purposeful ground plan where people camp or in the placing of buildings within a winter settlement. In these situations Kaska behavior is also motivated by personal inclination.

In company with poor systematization, we find grandiose planning. A social event, like a potlatch, gambling game, or dance, for which there is strong anticipation, often results in exaggerated ideas of its scope. An example of this tendency occurred in connection with the first potlatch, when Louis Maza enthusiastically declared: "That potlatch keep a-going." River Joe agreed equally heartily, saying: "Have fun! Six days! Nobody stop that potlatch. Police can't stop him. Injun law!" Obviously the hosts were not buying enough food for six days of feasting but, we thought, perhaps they would initiate various entertainments during the week. Nobody, however, mentioned entertainment. Originally a midday and an evening dinner were planned for the first day of the potlatch. When the shortage of vegetables was noted, the plans were altered, it being decided to eat once, at midday, and then serve tea and refreshments in the late afternoon. The festival actually began at seven o'clock in the evening, with none of the other plans materializing. Such exaggeration was possible, and wishes were free to be expressed, because of the absence of any realistic conceptualization of the total situation.

Unrealistic planning was also illustrated when River Joe engaged a bulldozer to build a a road on an Indian reserve without first ascertaining the cooperativeness of the other members of the community, or whether they would, as he expected, contribute to the expense of the project. As a result of his enthusiasm, Joe paid the major share of the cost himself and subsequently had further cause to regret his zeal, when the road opened the reserve to police cars.

In discussing planning toward future ends, we find ourselves confronted by an apparent contradiction. We have characterized Kaska personality by a tendency to ignore future responsibilities, but we must now account for future ideals like saving, being prepared with grub for trapping, and trapping toward an adequate standard of living during the following year. Partial explanation lies in the relative emotional strength of these conflicting attitudes. One set is more congruent to the basic motivations than the other. This is demonstrated by the fact that, although voiced, future ideals are not easily implemented by action. We may adopt Horney's distinction between beliefs and values to conceptualize the difference more sharply.[30] Beliefs are relatively superficial attitudes, which are not deeply

---

[30] Horney, *Our Inner Conflicts* (1945), 25–26.

rooted in the dominant motivations and produce a weak emotional response. Values, on the other hand, are more congruent with the dominant motivations, emotionally more important to the personality, and become expressed in behavior. Ideas of saving and preparedness also represent beliefs rather recently acquired from white trappers, traders, and missionaries. Their integration with basic motives is still to take place.

Obviously future ideals, when they become conditioned to important values like comfort and survival, are proven desirable from experience. Energetic trapping, for example, is generally recognized as a means of getting a larger amount and richer variety of food. As acquired beliefs assume increasing importance, they promise satisfactions like greater self-sufficiency and resourcefulness, but also become threatening to a personality which dislikes the effort and duty that they entail. In other words, a conflict between goals ensues, flexibility on the one hand, egocentricity and utilitarianism on the other. As a result of this conflict, anxiety is aroused and promotes various defense reactions. The individual talks of working hard, "rustling," and makes other grandiose plans, but shows little effort to carry these projects into practice.

Flexibility, therefore, is revealed in the lack of realistic long range planning, and this gives Kaska culture its superficial flavor of spontaneity and informality. Dances and gambling games may be anticipated for a day or more, but, because nobody feels inclined or (as a result of the underdevelopment of leadership patterns) able to assume the function of rigid organization, seldom get started until quite late some evening. Lumber is hewed and whipsawed when needed and in the quantity required. A supply of cut firewood in the bush is seldom sufficient to last beyond about two months, and more than one or two days' supply is never found in camp. When tracts of land are fired to dry wood for fuel, too little may be dried with the result that by spring people are reported to burn large amounts of green wood. Lack of foresight occurs in connection with buying winter supplies, some things invariably being forgotten. The disturbance occasioned by shortages is usually slight, never leading to recriminations within a family or producing masochistic self-devaluation, such as might be expected from a perfectionistic personality in western society. There are even avoidances supporting flexibility as, for example, attitudes associating danger with the manufacture of snowshoes before there is snow on the ground, or with striving too intensely for success in trapping.

A striking expression of lax planning is encountered in the training of dogs. The Indians attempt to teach dogs to obey a few simple commands, but confess their lack of success in this effort. Old Man admitted that white men trained dogs far more successfully. Much of the poor care and irregular feeding that dogs receive can be traced to the absence of rigidly planned routines in which regular feeding is perceived as duty; thus people often "forget" to feed their dogs.

By way of partial summary, it may be said that relaxed attitudes toward future goals are motivated by flexibility and represent an attempt to preserve egocentric mastery in a setting of moderate ego development. An effort is made to circumscribe the field of participation in order to avoid any too great testing of the limits of personal responsibility for success and failure. We see now why utilitarian preoccupation with concreteness, or intellectual circumscription, is not only self-assertive but also influenced by needs of ego safety. Speculation and planning beyond immediate necessity are anxiety provoking to an ego that does not feel itself capable of coping with the additional problems introduced by too broad a world view.

There are some men, like Nick Lang, who are capable of greater far sightedness and more compulsive work habits than most individuals in the society. In Kaska culture such deviant behavior may be partly understood as the result of a person having learned new defenses against inadequacy, new ways of directing egocentric expression. What personal factors are further involved in acquiring these new habits depends on the individual's life history. To the majority of Indians, flexibility in the setting of moderate ego development make impossible any intensely striving behavior.

Other forms of expression. Many other expressions of flexibility occurring in daily life may be briefly described. Most routine situations, for example, are never marked by hurry or regarded as duty. There are no rigid programs for getting through the day's work; there is scarcely even a conception of what a normal day's work entails. People cook when hungry and wash dishes when the opportunity suits; clothing is laundered when a suitable amount of dirty garments have accumulated; water is fetched when the supply in the house is exhausted; wood is cut or hauled in the evening after depleting the household pile. By comparing the attitudes governing these simple behaviors to the emotional significance which such commonplace routines hold in other groups (the local white trappers, for example), one can understand how little compulsion the Kaska have to work against time or out of a sense of duty and preparedness.

The same quality of being unburdened by duty or obligation also characterizes the socially patterned guilt system of the society. While the operation of a superego pressure toward conformity can scarcely be questioned, there is no doubt but that the Kaska conscience accords with the general loose comprehension of necessity. The Indian reveals no need for expiation, no strong drives for atonement. People are not weighted down with an overwhelming sense of guilt; on the contrary, pangs of conscience are transitory and soon worn off or forgotten. Because the superego does not lead to self-abnegation or self-debasement, it is also congruent with the vital interests of egocentricity. Only during the temporary loss of rational control, as we have described, do suicidal attempts reveal the abrogation of mastery and betray intense pressure of guilt.

The overall expression of flexibility is found in the low development of formalized ways of behaving and the lack of any formal social control. Despite somewhat fanciful references to "Injun law," the society is not interested in codifying activity. There is no authority to define the limits or patterns of adult behavior once these have received their initial direction in childhood. Certain acts are, of course, traditionally expected from everyone, or are required for survival and adjustment, but there are few explicit rules to which the individual's performance must conform. Behavior primarily originates with ego and is often as unplanned by himself as by his group.

Before approaching the operation of flexibility in crises, let us review the functions of flexible modes of procedure so far described. Primarily they represent techniques of maintaining egocentric independence and self-sufficiency by ruling out definitions of urgency in everyday routines. Flexibility offers a means of getting through life with greatest psychic economy. Duty, planning, necessity, and hurry represent patterns of striving which are incommensurate with the potentialities of the Kaska ego.

Procrastination. It is in approaching the expression of flexibility in procrastinating behavior that the functions of defense associated with this dominant motivation become clearest. In subjectively defined crises, the dynamics of flexibility may be understood as an attempt to protect the individual from the anxiety concomitant to any activity which threatens the egocentric, utilitarian, and other motivations with failure to maintain the integrity of the individual. A crisis to the Indian is not only a threat imperiling life (here, however, procrastination would scarcely be attempted), but is any situation in which he is confronted by a need for action, the rewards of which are highly uncertain or that compel more effort or cooperation than is congenial to his egocentric disposition. Procrastination, therefore, is to be regarded as an unconscious maneuver for escaping unmanageable stimuli crowding upon a personality directed toward individualistic self-sufficiency or emotional isolation. Such crises occur in both the adaptive and adjustive spheres of the culture.

Examples of procrastination are numerous. When the Upper Liard Indians were camping at the Highway crossing. Louis Maza and River Joe talked for several days of setting a fish net in order to suupplement their dog food. Finally, one evening, they actually got together and began to disentangle the net, only to be distracted by the arrival of some white people. The work was dropped and the net never set. In the technical culture we fully documented the procedure followed in getting started to trap and the delay in trapping that is likely to ensue once a man returns to the winter settlement. When the ethnographer was ready to return to Lower Post from Old Man's place, the tendency to procrastinate assumed vexing proportions. Our own food supply was low. Harry Lang and others were borrowing staples from Old Man, who himself lacked lard and butter and was down to his last two tins of baking powder. A trip to the trading post was urgent and the weather, having turned somewhat milder, made travel conditions excellent. On November 24, Harry complained of his shortages and promised to run his line in three days in order to rush to the post with his brother-in-law, Hans Donnelly. This was either an example of grandiose planning or tactful lying. He left for the line two days later, while Hans, telling the ethnographer he would be back in four days, did not leave till the following day. Harry returned on December 4 (a total absence of eight days) and began stretching his skins. Hans returned on December 7 (ten days after his departure) and brought back part of a cow moose. Meanwhile Old Man left for his line and the sons-in-law talked of waiting for his return, although Old Man did not expect us to delay for this purpose. The meat, of course, reduced the immediate pressure of food shortage, but the small amount of baking powder remaining necessitated the laborious task of making yeast bread. Nevertheless, the trip to Lower Post did not get under way until December 10, and then only after insistent urging and bribing on the part of the ethnographer. Undoubtedly if it were not for this pressure the trip would have been delayed until the return of Old Man, a matter of at least another week.

Most people act quickly in adapting to dangers, like cold weather, and sometimes in emergencies, like illness. More often the typical reaction to sickness is compounded of helplessness, fear, and delay. Such attitudes are both expressive of a lack of techniques for meeting the threat of illness and an attempt to shut out the emotionally upsetting affects of the situation. Thus, we observed Harry Lang refuse to do anything about his wife's badly infected ear and, despite the fact that she was in severe pain, reject the idea that she needed medical attention. Old Man himself was much surprised when Louis Maza made a hurried trip to the airport with his ailing infant son (Louis' only living boy). "What he rush for?" Old Man asked. "There's nothing the matter with that baby."

In adjustive situations, procrastination manifests itself in easy promises which are not regarded as binding. Such promises, as already mentioned, are a way of warding off insistence without hostility and, since they are not made seriously, protect the individual's initiative and independence from tasks requiring unnecessary and troublesome effort. Sometimes promises have the character of grandiose planning, and in that way serve to give a false sense of personal capacity. Thus Peter Tom gained pleasure in assuring the ethnographer that he would guide him downriver to Lower Post and even would lend him his dogs. When this spontaneous promise was subsequently recalled to Peter, the latter again affirmed what he had said. A date was specified for the trip and a reminder sent to Peter, but the youth never showed up to keep the appointment. Later it was also found out that "his" dogs in reality belonged to Louis Maza.

The essentially passive nature of procrastination is revealed following a failure to solve compelling interpersonal problems. Under such circumstances, the individual is sharply confronted with his own helplessness; this leads to consciously expressed worry, signs of unconscious anxiety, and attempts to withdraw from the overwhelming situation.

In Nitla we can see the inability to cope with inevitable interpersonal problems of emotional intensity, for which no society can provide wholly satisfactory solutions. Nitla's interviews, following his wife's desertion, provide a record of chronic worry following from his inability to handle his current problems. The situation confused the husband excessively. He sought help from older men as well as from the priest, but there was little these people could do to solve Nitla's predicament. In early August the young man came to Lower Post to buy a tent in order to remove one excuse which Adele gave for living with her brother-in-law. Having no money and being a comparative stranger in this part of the Kaska area (most of his life was spent at Frances Lake), he could not obtain goods on credit. He was also reluctant to remain in the town to work, giving the excuse that his wife was at the Bridge twenty-three miles away. Despite this excuse, a good part of July and August were spent in Lower Post. His worry and confusion are revealed in the following: "I like to go today. Can't make it. No tent. I hope the Father come down. I hope he do it today. My goodness. I want to get my money [the missionary owed him a few dollars for a day's work at the Bridge] . . . I'm looking for my money. I want to get tent. I get tent, get little eat something, I come back. I get little job. I want some money all right."

When society is unable to provide formal solutions for intense personal problems, their successful solution depends on the relative strength of the ego. For the Kaska, complex problems quickly overwhelm the potentialities of the ego, giving rise to the characteristic response of withdrawal from the disruptive stimulus. Behavior like procrastination, indecisiveness, and vacillation are signs of threat to the ego and also results of the absence of more assertive coping techniques. Obviously procrastination cannot solve vital conflicts in interpersonal relations; we therefore always find in the wake of a passive solution some residual component of conscious worry or unconscious anxiety and repressed hostility. This may be further illustrated with reference to Old Man, who volunteered to help Nitla by speaking to John Kean. As a result of his interference, Old Man earned his former son-in-law's enmity and was even physically threatened by John. Any further attempt to assert himself was now blocked, as much by Old Man's high regard for deference as by his passivity. In the following dream Old Man reveals his anxiety; he expresses his hostility to John by transferring its functions to a stronger and more capable person.

9:5:45 (Old Kean's Place). "I dream a plane land here. Police come out from plane. They tried to slap Nitla's little girl. They figured they'd start John fighting. 'If he look for fight we're gonna take him,' they said. 'Go ahead,' 'I said. They went down. I heard little girl cry. John put his sleeves back and police got him. I woke up. My old lady sit on my feet." The subject denied any conception of the dream's meaning [unconscious resistance]. "Two Mounted Police come off," he repeated. "We'd like to know John,' they say. 'We just find out what he's gonna do.' They took a long time afterwards. . . . They grab him, two of them." Old Man then went on to talk of the lack of any medicines to use for his wife's present illness. He said that the ethnographer's bullion cubes had saved Mrs. Man's life the previous year. "When she start feel bad she like I sit 'long side her all the time. She wouldn't let me go."

The dream portrays Old Man permitting the police (symbol of authority and strength) to avenge him with his passive approval. In the associations he denies his hostility and anxiety, appeals to the ethnographer for the latter's sympathy, and tries to solace his help-lessness by the security of his wife's presence.

Sometimes dreams fail to provide any solution for the latent anxiety and feeling of ego inadequacy which they reveal. John Kean's dream mentioned in connection with sexual impotence, provides such an instance. Another anxiety dream, marked by a lack of any as-sertive solution, is taken from the record of Gerald Leonard (14).

7:6:45 (Lower Post). Sometimes I dream something bad come to you, some bad animal. I jump up in bed. No good. Sometimes you dream you got no gun. Bad animal come at you. No good. Jump up in tree.

A denial of anxiety by the conscious repudiation of worry is a familiar pattern among these people and one that prompts white men to affirm that Indians never worry. Old Man, early in the second season of field work, denied that he worried, but projected such emotions into other men. "I never worry about money," he said. "Some people worry, worry. Like to make lots of money, good time in summer. But I never think about anything. Lots of people worry. Louis Maza, he's the one worries about money. Old Kean, he worries . . . worry about his country, trap line . . . Dick Mountain, he's worry man. . . ." Subsequent data indicate quite clearly that Old Man is not blessed with freedom from anxiety although he quite characteristically seeks to minimize the emotion. In Peter Tom's case worry over having spat blood was revealed only during intoxication and strongly denied when sober.

The essentially passive nature of flexible responses to crises may be regarded as an an-swer to threat experienced by the moderately developed Kaska ego. Crisis situations, whether internal (like anxiety) or external to the individual, are themselves largely the products of unassertive ego functions. Their significance as threatening leads to a renewed attempt by the individual to remove himself from the scene of disturbance without radically coming to grips with the problem.

Expression in the Rorschach test situation. In studying expressions of flexibility in the

Rorschach situation, attention may first be called to the manner in which the test was apprehended by the Indians. Schachtel has pointed out that "unobliging" persons are among those who give few responses to the test "because of their resistance to the test situation as they define it."[31] Evidence of resistance among Kaska adults comes from the fact that, although the mean number of responses (22.16) is normal when judged by western standards, a high degree of deviation (20.9) reveals a significant skewing of scores. Inspection of the adult records indicates the main reason for skewing lies in the fact that ten out of nineteen adult subjects each produced fewer than fifteen responses, while two others produced seventeen and twenty responses respectively.

A clue to the nature of the resistance comes from an examination of the method of approach. For the Kaska adults, approach may be shown as (W), D, Dd S!!!!, indicating significantly greater attention to small unusual than to whole and usual details. A record of this type may reveal an appreciation for unusual aspects of life, but, as Schachtel has pointed out, unusual detail responses "are very often the expression of a definition of the Rorschach situation—and of the subject's life situation in any other interpersonal relationship—in ambivalent terms. On the one hand he 'submits' to the situation defined in authoritarian terms; on the other he evades or rebels against the 'authority' and tries to *assert* himself by clinging to minor details instead of dealing frontally with essentials."[32] Reference back to the resistance inferred from the relatively few associations given by the majority of adults makes it likely that the excessive concentration on petty details among the Kaska can be explained in Schachtel's terms. The Kaska, unable to refuse the test assertively (lest they imperil the value of deference and arouse hostility), vaccillate just as they do in their promises and in instances of procrastination. Petty detail responses "have the function of asserting oneself in a negative or petty way where insecurity and fear block an open and direct self-assertion."[33]

This interpretation now permits us to assess the constraint which adults and children exhibited in taking the test and the discomfort which made it necessary to abandon that portion of the test situation in which the spontaneous responses are redirected to the subject's attention, with the request that he indicate the manner in which he formed his perceptions. The restlessness during the first showing of the cards signalized a threat to the ego from which complete withdrawal was impossible and to which a passive adjustment was offered. In the inquiry, the pressure of the situation grew so severe, the threat so intense (often people refused to answer, looking around as though for escape, and seizing on distractions), that, charitably, the effort had to be abandoned.

We conclude that adult subjects' responses to the Rorschach situation reveal many of the qualities already cited as flexible expressions toward subjectively defined crisis situations. The goal of the average subject was withdrawal from the intensity of the situation but, under pressure of deferent motives, this could not be done self-assertively. Independence was also threatened, and the conflict between motivations produced further unconscious anxiety.

[31] Schachtel, *Subjective Definition of the Rorschach Test Situation* (1945), 433.
[32] Schachtel, *Subjective Definition of the Rorschach Test Situation* (1945), 441.
[33] Schachtel, *Subjective Definition of the Rorschach Test Situation* (1945), 442.

Other criteria of the Rorschach test suggest themselves for verifying flexibility. Rorschach writers have pointed to succession (or the sequential use of wholes and details within the responses to each card) as a measure of intellectual efficiency. Beck points out that succession "demonstrates habits of controlled method," ranging from rigid procedure to the unpredictable procedures of the confused schizophrenics."[34] Succession may also be regarded as revealing effort at mastery of upsetting problems and affects. Due to the small number of responses, succession could not be judged from over fifty per cent of the adult records. We assume that this is in itself of a certain significance as far as the coping techniques of the subjects is concerned. Not only is failure to produce the expected number of responses related to resistance, but it reflects the process of psychic economics referred to above. By refusing to become too concerned with the stimuli, the subjects spared themselves the effort of controlling their procedure. In cases where judgements of sequence were possible, the range of succession types is between orderly and loose. "An orderly succession," write Klopfer and Kelley, "represents in most cases the optimum for intellectual efficiency," while "Loose succession is to be found where mental capacity is not high enough to grasp a logical order fully or where the mental control for maintaining such an order is weakened," as, for example, through emotional interferences.[35]

The conclusion can be drawn that in type of succession Kaska adult subjects exhibit a flexible mode of response. They avoid rigid procedure and reveal a tendency to resist the compulsion of order and planning, due to the fear of straining ego potentialities.

Another feature of the Rorschach test with significance to the present discussion is the ratio of whole to movement responses. Klopfer and Kelley point out that "the quotient W:M can be used as an indicator for what may be described as the relationship between drive for intellectual conquest and personal productive capacity to make these conquests substantial. People with a great predominance of W, say with at least three or four times as many W's as M's, seem always to be lacking in the best use of their creative or productive powers."[36] The mean ratio for nineteen adult Kaska subjects is 3.53 W to 1.16 M; that is, there are about three times as many whole as movement responses. Interpreted according to the former authors, we may conclude that Kaska adults do not express a drive for the intellectual organization or planning of their lives and activities. The question of what constitutes "the best use of creative or productive powers" must vary with the group involved and its cultural standards. By avoiding a high degree of organization the Kaska are living up to the capacities of their ego development and preserving maximum psychic economy. Furthermore, planning is relatively unimportant in many (but not all) aspects of the culture. It is interesting to note, in view of the small number of M answers, Israeli's statement, that the organization of planning "requires daring and bold imagination."[37]

Finally we may note the assumption that movement responses are representative of the activities of the superego.[38] If there is any validity to this observation, the low mean number

[34] Beck, Rorschach's Test. II. A Variety of Personality Pictures (1945), 17–18.
[35] Klopfer and Kelley, The Rorschach Technique (1942), 273.
[36] Klopfer and Kelley, The Rorschach Technique (1942), 277–278.
[37] Israeli, Originality in Planning (1945), 139.
[38] Apfeldorf, Rorschach Theory and Psychoanalytic Theory (1944), 190.

of movement responses (for adults, 1.6) may further corroborate our description of the relatively mild Kaska guilt system.

Résumé. Data have been presented and analyzed to demonstrate flexibility as a basic motivation functioning in many cultural situations to maintain maximum psychic economy by protecting the ego from undue stress and from excessive burdens incompatible with other dominant motivations. In crises flexibility represents a passive defense against stimuli, whose emotional intensity is perceived as disproportionate to the tonicity of the ego and therefore threatening to the self-assertive motivations. Flexibility determines behavior whose predominant aim is to maintain invulnerability by defending the individual from situations with which he cannot cope self-assertively or which seem beyond his capacity to master.

The efficiency of such a form of defense must be judged within a specific cultural context. By protecting the Kaska individual from undue anxiety and excessive stress, flexible modes of procedure are compatible manifestations of a personality whose ego is moderately developed and whose dominant motivations stress independence, deference, and emotional isolation. When forms of defense lead to the accumulation of unsolved problems, worry, and anxiety, or when they interfere with the achievement of other values (like sufficient and varied food and comfort for survival), their efficiency becomes questionable, since they fail both to achieve their own, and block the realization of other, vital goals. While such results sometimes occur with serious anxiety provoking effect, among the Kaska, additional personality features, for example, a noncompulsive superego and a low aspiration level, serve to minimize the affects produced. So long as a reasonable long term balance is maintained between defense systems and anxiety, personality adjustment may be considered relatively adequate, although in any specific situation the upsetting effects of flexible defenses may be readily demonstrated.

DEPENDENCE

In its present usage the term dependence refers to a passive receptive longing for care and affection. The motivation, however, does not lead to submissive behavior but rather causes people to invest with value those persons, goods, and behaviors that represent unconscious equivalents of love and protection. The distinctive note in dependency manifestations is the desire to receive gains without active self-assertion. Grouping dependence with flexibility, we may speak of these as the relatively passive motivations of Kaska personality.

We will first discuss the potential conflict between dependence and the self-assertive motives, then the expression of dependence in social life, and, finally, the patterning of the motivation in men and women.

Conflicts with dependence. Obviously, as a basic orientation of Kaska personality, dependence is at variance with several other basic motivations, particularly egocentricity and utilitarianism, whose joint goal of self-sufficiency it threatens. In its tendency to break through affective barriers, dependence is also in conflict with emotional isolation, but discussion of this point must be postponed until the following section. The Kaska Indian, when he abandons active forms of mastery for passive receptive demands, comes perilously close to subordinating his life to others. For the readily accepted egocentric attitude: "I must live by myself," dependence substitutes an unconscious plea for help in living. It is interesting to note, however, that the potential and seemingly inevitable subordination never fully occurs; egocentricity is never wholly abandoned. The divergent goals exist side by side in fundamental incompatibility but with no evidence of incapacitating disharmony. The reason for this apparent un-neurotic adjustment of the individual lies in several distinguishing features of Kaska dependence. In the first place, the motivation does not involve the surrender of personal initiative to others, except perhaps in old age and illness, when the physical incapacity of the organism necessarily dooms the ego's assertive coping techniques. Parents sometimes express ideal dependence on children, but here a speaker is looking to protection in old age and realistically is not surrendering his autonomy. A second reason why the conflict between dependence and egocentricity is not more severe lies in the fact that under the motivating influence of emotional isolation, the unconsciously directed search for care and protection cannot assume an unequivocal form but must take symbolic guise. Finally, expressions of dependence are not of a kind to humiliate or abase the individual. One can, for example, in Kaska society symbolically demand love and protection in a relatively self-assertive fashion and without betraying too far the behavior's fundamental passivity.

As in the case of flexibility, dependence does not function solely when the person is faced with adaptive and adjustive crises, but rather represents a seeking for safety whose press is experienced throughout life. That is to say, unconsciously, passive receptive attitudes are constantly alert in Kaska personality but are repressed under the influence of self-assertive tendencies. It is this readiness for dependence, in association with moderate ego tonicity, which quickly sets off reactions of acute passivity when strivings toward self-sufficiency become blocked.

Expression. One of the outstanding forms of dependency motivated behavior may be identified as "demandingness," which sometimes takes the form of the individual leeching himself onto people in a position to give. The most direct manifestation of demands is directed toward the government whose regulative functions, it will be recalled, are strongly repudiated. In the cultural background, we have already given a number of examples to illustrate this point. Perhaps the strongest examples of demandingness come from Nitla who, having been raised in the relative isolation of Frances Lake, has had less opportunity to come into contact with regulative governmental functions and so can freely express his conception of authority as a provider. In him the typical expression of dependence stresses the "hard time" of the Indians and the consequent responsibility of governments to take care of these subjects. The associations to one dream reveal an interesting interweaving of conflicting egocentric and dependency motives.

8:1:45 (Lower Post). "I dream that it's winter time; fall time. That much snow [indicates], I dream . . Must be I work in winter time. A lucky dream. I got fly tent, trap." When asked if he wished it were fall time, Nitla agreed and explained: "Man trapping, sometimes lucky dream that way. Man dream that way, he can't die. . . . He feel good. . . . Never know feel bum; feel good." Spontaneously he went on to complain about the noise in Lower Post and how it made a man feel "bum." In Frances Lake Post, on the other hand, things are much quieter; Indians stay in their camps at night and don't constantly walk around. This led to complaints about being "stuck" in Lower Post. The only way for him to rejoin his wife was to get a ride on a truck going straight through to the Bridge, but he was afraid of taking the wrong truck and so being carried to Watson Lake. "Storeman too, he never give anything. No sugar, nothing. No beans, no raisins, matches, .22 shells . . . anything. Man he need it. Can't make it. By goodness . . . Taku [Trading Co.] no good. No give people. . . . Man he got money, he can't get stuck. Man he got the kids, no good. . . . What he gonna eat, my kids? Storeman gotta treat every-thing, all right. Just the same your daddy. Got to give something to eat. . . . Man he kill enough skin, he got a good friend. Man no skin, he got no friend."

Asked for associations to "fly tent" the subject said: "You don't want the snow. You dream about fly tent. . . . You don't want hard time. I got a fly tent up there . . . close to Simpson Lake." Spontaneously Nitla went on to talk about food again. "Just straight flour no good. . . . Make a man feel bum." He emphasized the importance of butter and began to praise a series of white foods, including potatoes, beans, and cheese. Then he appraised chewing tobacco as good. "No tobacco, by goodness, I feel bum."

When his interest began to decline, Nitla was aroused from silence by being asked to talk about his childhood. Following a series of remarks pertaining to food eaten as a child, he went on to describe in detail three accidents he had met with in his youth. When this topic was ex-hausted, Nitla paused. "What else gonna show you?" No suggestions were offered. He went on to describe the hard life of most Frances Lake Indians. Only a few men are lucky in trapping. He discussed the importance of beaver fur in the Indian economy and then finished the hour by roundly criticizing the government for closing the trapping of beaver. Beaver, he explained, was valuable both for its skin as well as meat; why not close marten, the meat of which nobody eats?

Previous to the interview, Nitla had eaten supper with the ethnographer's family. The chain of thinking oscillates between defining the ability of a man to be self-sufficient and the urge to be taken care of. From the associations, it is apparent that these two elements also exist in the dream. The first part of the dream, trapping in fall time, represents the assertive aspect of the personality individualistically striving for survival and comfort. The task, however, is too difficult for the ego, leading to expressions of dependence, like wishing that white men were more generous. Unfortunately, the traders who should be parental protectors, give only after a man has produced fur with which to pay for what he wants. The second element of the dream, the fly tent, introduces the motion of being cared for an protected. "You don't want snow. You dream about fly tent. . . . You don't want hard time." Parenthetically we may note the inadequacy of the symbol chosen to represent pro-tection; a fly tent is a summer dwelling, and only the poorest trapper would use it in cold weather. Associations lead from the tent to the whiteman's food; if this food were abun-dant, the subject seems to say, the Indian would not have to work so hard for a living. Prod-ded to speak of childhood, Nitla perseverates on the theme of food (dependence) and switches to accidents, again pointing out his helplessness. Once more he leads himself out of this dependency stratum and speaks of the exigencies of trapping, but his egocentric motivation hesitates and again passive receptive attitudes appear, leading to criticism of the frustrating government.

It is significant that the Kaska Indian's dependence is largely expressed in terms of re-ceiving food from white men or being well supplied with grub. One explanation for the emotional value of food may be found in the light of dependence. Food represents the protected state of childhood, that existed before parents instituted emotional rejection and is symbolic of the love and care which were lavished on the helpless baby in the early satis-faction of his alimentary needs.[39] We have stated love to be the ultimate goal of dependence. In Nitla we see this expectation directed toward white men—the government, traders, and, indirectly, the ethnographer who had just fed him. Of Nitla's leeching tendency there can be no question. Like several other youths, he always showed up at our house around meal time and never refused to eat. We may conclude that receiving food from white people, or receiving food in general, is unconsciously equivalent to receiving love and security. Psy-choanalysts have long maintained that passivity and orality are related; this relationship is well demonstrated in Kaska personality, where passive receptive attitudes represent a means to acquire security and protection without exercise of self-assertion. A similar note is struck in Louis Maza's dream, related when the ethnographer visited his home in September. He dreamed that a white man told him of a creek where gold could be found. The stranger reminded Louis that the latter had often crossed this creek. "There's gold there," the white man said. "You have a pan, use it. Go there." In associating, Louis tried to figure out to which creek the reference applied. Again in this product of unconscious thinking, a white man is pictured as a benefactor. Louis is a relatively insecure person preoccupied with the idea of getting out of debt. In the dream his goals are passively solved, although there is the realistic note that Louis must still find the gold. Indians are not concerned with pros-pecting for precious metal, so that the occurrence of gold in Louis' dream may have a special but unknown significance for his personality.

During the construction of the Alaska Highway, dependence was inadvertently satisfied by the generosity of American soldiers and civilians who gave the people gifts of cigarettes, food (especially meat), and liquor.[40] The favorable stereotype constructed of Americans may therefore be explained in terms of the significance of their generosity to the Indians. Unfortunately the Canadian soldiers, who subsequently appeared in the area and served for lower pay, have not met the expectations of generosity to which the Kaska had become accustomed. The Indians were already familiar with the traders' lack of generosity, which is founded on a sense of good business. The unfavorable stereotype developed of Canadian soldiers, therefore, represents partly a generalization of experience from Canadian traders to Canadians and is also the product of frustrated expectations.

Closely related to food as a symbol of love is the high value placed on generosity. The language of generosity may be interpreted as: "You are a good person because you give," A demand to receive, founded on passive receptive aims, is implicit in this unconscious defi-nition. It might appear that the demanding dependence of the Kaska, especially as it is ex-pressed toward food, should make a stingy people. Actually we find the Kaska no more stingy than they are spontaneously generous.[41] However, the sharing of grub (not meat)

[39] See Fenichel, The Psychoanalytic Theory of Neuroses (1945), 63.

[40] During the Second World War, peoples in many parts of the globe had occasion to benefit from the well paid American soldier's generosity and probably often responded to it with much the same manifest pleasure as the Kaska. It remains to be learned if the unconscious significance of gifts was the same in all of these cases.

[41] For examples of compulsive generosity see the discussion of Harry's personality below, pp. 336–337.

We may point out here that while Kaska society lacks any ritualistic forms of bestowing authority, aborigi-nally the leaders of a band held people together by their roles as food providers. The early traders recognized some-

is done with extreme reluctance and then usually with the interests of deference closely in view. The criticism of any lack of generosity, however, is a dependency motivated behavior, based on the frustration of this dominant motivation. Excessive generosity, when it ap-pears in a very few Kaska, is probably a reaction formation based on demanding. Just as reception equals the incorporation of love, so giving represents a means of earning love. In psychoanalytical parlance, the desire to incorporate is replaced by the desire to be pas-sively incorporated. The emotion invested in the potlatch is also partly derived from the fact that the central feature of this festival is the giving away of symbolically precious food. Potlatching for the hosts is a public demonstration of the cultural ideal of generosity and in turn gratifies the guests' unconscious passive receptive needs.

Emotional dependence is one of the outstanding features of the marriage relationship. This is revealed in the fact that many men are reluctant to separate themselves from their wives, in the poignancy of a widower's loneliness, and in the jealousy manifested by both spouses. Our evidence suggests this dependence to intensify with time. Among old people, where we find the closest bonds between spouses, strong dependence is expressed in atti-tudes of mutual care, protection, and worry. Mrs. Man was reluctant to allow her husband to leave camp alone for any length of time. Old Man showed himself as much preoccupied with his wife's health and symptoms as with his own. Marriage, therefore, represents a pattern of indulging passivity and must also be estimated for its role in undermining goals of individualism and self-sufficiency.

Another instance of intrafamilial dependence is found in the attitudes of parents stress-ing their future economic dependence on children, and only secondarily admitting the latter's reliance on parents. Such unconsciously motivated attitudes not only do a great deal to sustain the emotionally isolating tendencies of the society, but in turn set up dependency motivated behavior in childhood, like food leeching and the theft of small objects—"sym-bolic thefts of love."[42] We will return to these aspects of children's behavior in describing the development of Kaska ethos.

A study of the cultural background will reveal other situations whose emotional quali-ties suggest the operation of dependence. Several of these may be briefly pointed out, al-though the most we can do is to point to future problems for research. Thus one is tempted to raise the question of a relationship between drinking and passive receptive oral trends. The fact that alcohol promotes passive reactions in these people cannot be doubted. Old Man often related how drinking quickly helped him forget his illness and debility. Alcohol, furnishing a relaxation of overtaxing self-assertion represents a means of withdrawing from the press of life. In his discussion of basic personality in western society, Kardiner pointed out that the nostalgic themes of contemporary music represents the idealization of the pro-tective mother.[43] A similar function may be suggested for the music which is most popular

---

thing of the dynamics of this role and in appointing "chiefs" to direct fur production provided the nominees with flour and tobacco for free distribution. At present the government neglects such traditional and psychologically grounded means of defining the chief's status.

[42] Levy, *Psychopathic Personality and Crime* (1942), 100.

[43] Kardiner, *The Psychological Frontiers of Society* (1945), 369.

among the Kaska and which expresses yearning for a loved and familiar place. The characteristic minor key of Kaska playing may also be pertinent in this connection. We are on more certain ground in once more estimating the roles of charms, magic, and luck in relation to dependence. Harry Lang's journal is liberally spotted with phrases like "lucky today," "poor luck today," and "no luck today." Conversation often tends to account for failure in terms of luck. Although predictive beliefs promising success (few are used to forecast failure) reveal a certain degree of ego tonicity, both as expressions of optimism and pessimism, reliance on charms and divination or ascription to luck denote an individual's relatively passive adjustment to forces on which he feels himself contingent.

While religious attitudes do not sharply stress a person's subordination, in a general way they encourage the feeling of being cared for in a system that pictures human life as primarily passive. Man, like the animal and plant environment, is a part of nature, the operation of whose laws make it possible for him to hunt and trap successfully. Jesus is a protector who takes care of his "boys." The animal realm has a similar role. Heaven is a state of future good to which the individual automatically feels destined. Such optimism, or faith, is both related to egocentric and dependency motivations.

Expressions in the Rorschach test situation. Criteria for interpreting dependence in the Rorschach situation have not been well worked out in the literature. Bochner and Halpern,[44] like Maslow,[45] suggest that responses involving the mouth, food, eating, and drinking may be regarded as signs of orality and therefore potential expressions of dependence. Such responses are not conspicuous in Kaska protocols.

Dependence in men and women. Although there is no evidence for doubting that primary dependence (that is, dependence inculcated in the early years of life) is characteristic of both men and women, characterological differences between the sexes are nevertheless shown in the expression of this motivation. These may be summarized as follows:

Men   Dependency goals are socially discouraged in favor of egocentric and utilitarian considerations. The ego, however, lacks the required tonicity for consistent assertive behavior, thus facilitating dependency reactions.

Women   Dependency goals are socially permitted and even encouraged, but the absence of sufficiently low ego development does not always leave women content with a passive role. Hence they often express socially patterned egocentric and utilitarian motivations which overshadow dependency trends.

Expressed in other terms, women, because of their social roles, and especially after marriage, are permitted to rest back more and expected to manifest more passivity. Men, conversely, are expected to display initiative. In men ego strength is not high enough to support the socially patterned male role; in women, despite early training for a serving role it is too high to make them content with their status and so we sometimes find them heading families, trapping, hunting big game, and otherwise fulfilling roles allocated to men.

Actually this works out to provide a rather neat balance in intersexual relations, but also produces many conflicts which we shall take up in the following section. In marriage

[44] Bochner and Halpern, *The Clinical Application of the Rorschach Test* (1945), 63.
[45] Maslow, *Rorschach Theory* (1944), 52–54.

men are more in need of a women's emotional support than vice versa and women are socially encouraged to fulfill these expectations. Evidence also suggests that men seek what few secondary advantages accrue from illness, but that women are less required to resort to such techniques since their responsibilities are fewer.[46] Widowers, for the same reasons, are also far more emotionally upset upon the death of a spouse than widows, who often delay remarriage. In general, women's socially patterned roles permit them the satisfaction of dependency aims without strong conflict and partly for this reason they are less required to utilize passive receptive techniques like demanding, leeching, and hypochondriasis. They are also spared from the full burden of responsibilities which, in conjunction with a moderate ego development, often moves men to relax into passive forms of adaptation and adjustment.

It has been pointed out that in a social setting enforcing unmitigated feminine dependence, passivity, and submission, we would find evidence of feminine masochism. Following this suggestion of Horney,[47] we watched for such expressions in Kaska women's behavior. We could collect no evidence of dysmenorrhea (here, however, observation was limited and not subject to careful checking), excessive concern with pregnancy and childbirth, or fears of exploitation determining women's fear of sexual relations. All these points listed by Horney are criteria of feminine masochism. While social expectations demand that to some degree Kaska women inhibit their interaction with men, women are not led to look for advantages as a result of regarding themselves as weak or helpless, nor are they predominantly self-sacrificing. Although the woman is economically dependent on the man, her husband is not the sole source of such satisfaction and economic dependence is not serviceable as a channel for woman's emotional dependence on the opposite sex. The absence of feminine masochism is further corroborated by the absence of other social conditions which Horney regards as predisposing to such attitudes. For example, manifestly, women are not discriminately blocked in finding outlets for sexuality before marriage; no cultural value is based on fertility, nor are limits placed on the number of children she can bear. The woman is not restricted to spheres of life built on an emotional basis, rather her ability determines the extent of her cultural participation. There is no surplus of marriageable women to favor their emotional dependence on men (if anything, the reverse is true). However, the male attitude regarding women as an inferior sex represents one condition listed as compatible with female masochistic feelings. Women's unconscious fear of aggression in coitus (to be discussed in the next section), may represent another such condition. On the whole the evidence does not suggest feminine masochism and supports our conclusion that Kaska women are not content to be swallowed in their socially patterned, passive role.

Résumé. The passive receptive goals of dependence have been outlined, together with an account of the conflict between this motivation and the motivations of egocentricity and

---

[46] Kluckhohn has essayed to collect evidence pointing out that in many parts of the world either men or women "are somewhat neglected or occupy low status" and seek means of securing attention through bewitchment, trance states, and neurotic seizures (Kluckhohn, *Navaho Witchcraft* [1944], 49). In Kaska society men, while not most neglected, feel their greater social burdens severely and this is one reason why they often seek attention through hypochondriasis.

[47] Horney, *The Problem of Feminine Masochism* (1935).

utilitarianism. Despite the self-assertive aims of these latter motives, ego tonicity in the Kaska male is not sufficient to permit his personality to resist dependency strivings. Because of the lighter responsibilities of her socially patterned role and the fact that feminine dependence is encouraged, the woman faces less conflict in following her dependency trends. Actually, however, the woman's ego is high enough to make uncongenial a solely passive role.

EMOTIONAL ISOLATION

Preservation of emotional aloofness and social detachment represent the outstanding features of emotional isolation. The motive is founded upon low development of an ability to tolerate affection or to express any considerable warmth in interpersonal relations. The emotionally isolated individual seeks to stay impervious to intense affective stimuli, whether originating within or outside of the organism; emotional ties are underemphasized, strong feelings repressed, and spontaneous affective expression constricted. Emotional isolation, as used here, includes Levy's concept of "affect hunger."[48]

In describing the emotionally isolating motivation of Kaska personality, attention will be directed to its interrelationship with other motives previously described, expression in general behavior, role in determining intersexual relations and sexual constriction, and manifestation in the Rorschach situation. Finally, the occasional relaxation of emotional aloofness will be discussed.

Interrelations of emotional isolation. If the goal of emotional isolation is succinctly phrased as withdrawal from all emotional stimuli, it becomes clear that this dominant motivation is closely related to other basic trends of Kaska personality. This relationship is most obvious with respect to the goal of egocentricity, whose aims have been defined as individualism, independence, and personal responsibility. The Kaska Indian seeks to stand alone, for the most part rejecting cooperative relationships and avoiding intense identifications with any social group beyond the family. Approached from the standpoint of emotional isolation, the atomistic quality of Kaska social structure may now be related to blocked affectivity. The egocentric individual is not only intent upon preserving his independence but also avoids the formation of strong affective ties with neighbors. In the language of psychoanalysis, there is a low development of aim-inhibited libido, or love, which may be directed toward a leader or other members of a group to form a cohesive society.[49] The society consists of a group of people who seek to stand alone and experience the extension of affective ties as anxiety provoking. In contrast, a corporate society is structured where affectional bonds are diffuse and abundant, so that people trust others and are mutually concerned with each other's welfare. Among the Kaska, strong interpersonal ties are little extended beyond the nuclear family, and even the members of this group are characterized by strong emphasis on self-sufficiency and little expression of emotionality. It does not follow that Kaska atomism is founded upon antagonism, since this affect is not only also too intense but also threatens the basic value of deference; the Kaska individual,

[48] Levy, *Primary Affect Hunger* (1937).

[49] Freud, *Group Psychology and the Analysis of the Ego* (1922). Kardiner suggests that in Alor blocked affectivity is also related to the atomization of Alorese social structure. Kardiner, *The Psychological Frontiers of Society* (1945), 170. See also Bateson and Mead, *Balinese Character* (1942), 4, 33, 47, 68.

as we have mentioned, cannot tolerate hostility without experiencing threat of the loss of love. The relationship of emotional isolation to deference in Kaska life is well expressed by Horney's statement that the detached personality is interested in excluding all feeling, "both love and hate. It is the logical consequence of the need to keep at an emotional distance from others, in that strong love or hate, consciously expressed, would bring one either close to others or into conflict with them."[50] It would not be correct to assume that deference in Kaska personality is no more than an attempt to exclude hostile emotions from consciousness. While these two, like all the dominant motivations, are intimately related, many conscious attitudes and behaviors, consistently and strongly expressing antipathy to aggression, warrant consideration of deference as a relative independent motivation.

Expression of emotional isolation. Like Horney's detached personality type, the Kaska Indian is governed by "a general tendency to suppress all feeling."[51] Emotional reactions to crises are the first manifestation of emotional detachment which will be discussed. Typically we find such reactions minimizing and underestimating the significance of critical experiences. Sometimes unconscious defense formations, like denial, are instituted to further ameliorate threats to emotional isolation. As we have seen in connection with humor, a number of older men are particularly prone to use a feeble wisecrack in an effort to evade a strong emotional impact and so restore a sense of mastery in the face of upsetting stimuli. Old Man's joking about Nitla's marital predicament reveals an attempt to alleviate the latter's unpleasant involvement in a tense emotional situation. Similar expressions of emotional minimization occur in the case of death. Weeping and mourning are inevitable when death occurs, but a determined effort is made by the bereaved's more distant relatives and friends to reduce the emotional impact of the situation through comforting words or even humor, and to remove as quickly as possible all evidence of the event which would tend to keep mourning alive and remind others of their losses. Severe hunger crises are also denied by having their emotional significance underplayed, joked about, or replaced by an uncertain optimism expressed as: "We won't starve yet."

Further manifestation of emotional isolation is found in the minimization of affective bonds by stressing economic utility or material comfort. A widower expresses his loneliness and desire for remarriage in terms of requiring someone to cook for him, make moccasins, and satisfy his sexual needs. Adele Kean's preference for her husband's brother was not defended as love but in terms of utility; John, she said, took better care of her than Nitla and was a better provider. Similarly, John never conceded that he was romantically attached to Adele. A man's prolonged absence from camp is not directly discussed with worry or fear for his safety; rather, when Peter Tom remained downriver for several weeks, Old Man expressed the desire to have back the gun which Peter had borrowed and Louis Maza fretted about the dog that Peter was using. The ability of individuals to withdraw from excessive concern and pity for illness and old age is another consequence of emotional isolation operating in an egocentric personality, while the burlesqued and exaggerated farewells of sisters probably also express a tendency to minimize the affect of parting experienced between these close relatives. These are instances in which emotional concern for individuals

---

[50] Horney, *Our Inner Conflicts* (1945), 82–83.
[51] Horney, *Our Inner Conflicts* (1945), 82.

is suppressed. Emotional minimization is designed to preserve maximum psychic economy by warding off exciting stimuli with which the personality is afraid to deal.

As may be expected, inhibition of affectional expression also influences the marital relationship. Despite the tenderness shown between some newly married couples, the evidence of divorce, quarrels, and other interpersonal behavior between spouses strongly suggests that it takes considerable time for affect barriers to break down in marriage, thereby permitting partners to grow close. Horney's observations are applicable here. "In view of all we have said about the detached persons's human relationships," Horney writes, "it will be clear that any close and lasting relation would be bound to jeopardize his detachment and hence would be likely to be disastrous—unless the partner should be equally detached and so of his own accord respect the need for distance. . . . Provided emotional distance is sufficiently guaranteed he may be able to preserve a considerable measure of enduring loyalty."[52] Preservation of emotional distance, however, would appear to be quite difficult where dependency trends are also operative.

We may cite other expressions of emotional detachment in social situations. The disparate individuals constituting a visiting or idling group are constructed by proximity of members but not by intense social interaction through conversation. In this same connection it is appropriate to discuss the patterning of physical contact in the culture. Despite the high development of tactual interpersonal relations, in contrast to verbal relationships, considerable ambivalence seems to attach to such contacts. Intrinsically they are pleasant, supplying a channel through which warm human relations are possible without too great danger. When strong attention is focused on tactual relations, however, embarrassment and confusion are provoked. This is illustrated by young people's reluctance to dance before self-consciousness can be obliterated in a group, in the avoidance of an unmarried boy and girl appearing together in public, and in the tendency for the sexes to initiate sexual teasing by slapping at one another from a distance with willow branches. It is also demonstrated by the segregation of men and women in idling groups or at opposite walls of a dance house. At a dance it is only after some time has passed before inhibitions are sufficiently reduced to permit the sexes to mingle freely outside of a dance place.

It is characteristic of the Kaska Indian to restrain as much as possible his participation in the social and physical environments; he is afraid of revealing himself emotionally, of dropping defenses which guarantee egocentric independence and aloneness. The avoidance of conversational self-expression is one example of restricted participation in the social environment. Folktales are narrated with little emotional expression other than quiet relish or enjoyment. Certainly we noted none of the gusto ascribed to Menomini story tellers, or the "richness of gesture and vocal inflection" with which they identify with folktale characters.[53] In physical movement the same constrictive withholding is practiced. Although physical activity is not marked by tension, but rather is relaxed and free-flowing, people display few gestures and no "grand" expressive movements. Social dancing is done mincingly, or at least in a circumscribed spatial context. In the brief example of an aboriginal dance witnessed at a potlatch, the participants moved only the upper portion of the body,

[52] Horney, *Our Inner Conflicts* (1945), 85.
[53] Skinner and Satterlee. *Folklore of the Menomini Indians* (1915), 235.

raised and lowered the feet, while keeping the bent arms close to the torso. Such constriction of movement seems partly motivated by the need to preserve emotional isolation.[54]

Coughing may also be understood as a means of withdrawing from a social situation whose pressure is found discomfitingly intense or embarrassing. As a reaction to this pressure a person becomes more concerned with himself and perceives, as Fenichel points out, a functional dryness of the throat.[55] Coughing serves to release the tension induced by the social situation and may afford an opportunity for the inhibition of speech—for example, a person need not answer an embarrassing question.

Together with the tendency to remain aloof from disturbing situations which threaten the resources of the personality, a related objective of the detached person is to bridge the gap separating him from others. We have already discussed attitudes toward warm human relations in connection with deference and dependence. For the former motive it was pointed out that by avoiding hostility the Kaska do not so much seek love as they avoid the loss of love, while dependency produces ambivalent feelings in a person who fears that the care and protection he desires undermine his self-sufficiency. To these difficulties, that stand in the way of the egocentric personality's search for love, we must now add the anxiety which warm human relations invite because of their conflict with emotional isolation. Withdrawal of love in childhood not only sets up a barrier against any close interpersonal relationships but also instigates unconscious "affect hunger," or a search for the unacceptable satiation of affection.[56] Passive receptive (oral) trends, expectation of secondary gains from illness, and a reputation for generosity are some previously mentioned means by which the Kaska seek to satisfy affectional insatiety. One oral trend of pronounced emotional significance, alcoholic drinking, deserves further consideration. If the Kaska child's emotional rejection sets up affect hunger, we can understand the role ascribed to alcoholic intoxication as dulling "the pain of loneliness and [putting] the alcoholic in a state where he can fantasy love, at least."[57] The idea of reincarnation may also serve to fulfill unconsciously the unstilled longing to overcome personal isolation. Such a belief, it has been pointed out, may be a symbolic means of fulfilling persistent longings to bridge the gap between mother and child and to deny the even more final interpersonal isolation that follows death.[58] Ambivalent attempts to assuage affect hunger through sexual relations will be discussed below in connection with sexual constriction. Before we can adequately comprehend the phenomena of sexual constriction in the light of emotional detachment, we must review what has already been said about the relations of men and women, adding emotional isolation to the other motives entering into these relationships.

Relations between men and women. We have pointed out that Kaska men are expected to be self-assertive to a degree where they will be able self-confidently and resourcefully to provide food and fur and perform other services required by the family. The society, how-

---

[54] Bateson has pointed out that physical processes of artistic creation are ethologically related to the broader cultural context. His remarks stress an aspect of culture that has hitherto been largely neglected. Bateson, G., Oceanic and Balinese Art. Lecture delivered at the Yale Art Gallery, Spring, 1946.

[55] Fenichel, *The Psychopathology of Coughing* (1943).

[56] Levy, *Primary Affect Hunger* (1937). See also Fromm, *Escape From Freedom* (1941), 19-20.

[57] English and Pearson, *Emotional Problems of Living* (1945), 25.

[58] Deutsch, *Psychology of Women. II. Motherhood* (1945), 175. See also Ford, *A Comparative Study of Human Reproduction* (1945), 35.

ever, also patterns a degree of ego tonicity and conflicting passive motivations in men that make their roles difficult to fulfill. As a result, men often relapse into passivity and dependence which introduces them to increased anxiety. Kaska women, on the other hand, although endowed with self-assertion and independence, are nevertheless expected to serve men and to rely on the male for the principal economic necessities. Inasmuch as their development does not entirely prepare women for an exclusively passive role, their ego tonicity is greater than their status demands. It is strong enough, for example, to permit some women to execute the responsibilities normally expected from men. Ideas of the woman's social role restrict men from comfortably performing many female allocated functions but, as might be expected, women exhibit no difficulties in performing male allocated tasks; in fact they may derive satisfaction from the opportunity to thus identify with men.

If we now approach male and female social roles from the standpoint of emotional isolation we find that in men considerable ambivalence is attached to the emotional comforts derived from association with women. As marriage endures, there is increasing dependence of a man on his wife. These passive trends are productive of male anxiety, first, because they are contrary to the self-assertive motives and, second, because of their conflict with emotional isolation. Turning now to women, we can expect that since women are also trained for assertive forms of mastery, passive mechanisms of adjustment may also be productive of anxiety; this is borne out in the fact that some women seek to avoid this socially expected pattern of adjustment by manifesting masculine striving. On the other hand, the fact that there are social expectations of feminine passivity, and that from the age of six or seven girls are trained for a serving role, make it easier for a woman to relax; her conflict here is exclusively "personal" whereas in the man it is both a personal conflict between motives and a struggle between individual and social demands. However, the Kaska woman to some extent shares with her husband the predisposition to anxiety once emotional isolation is exposed to the threatening emotional intensities of marriage.

The following summary may help to clarify the essence of the foregoing discussion.

Sex	Training	Conflicts
Man	Emphasizes unmitigated self-assertion.	Between socially expected self-assertion and passivity.
		Between self-assertion and dependence on the wife.
		Between emotional isolation and dependence on the wife.
Woman	Self-assertion relieved by some preparation for a serving (passive) role.	Between socially expected passivitiy and self-assertion.
		Between self-assertion and dependence on the husband.
		Between emotional isolation and dependence on the husband.

All of these conflicts lead to anxiety and derived hostility, which further threaten the self-assertive as well as deferent motivations. These conflicts find expression in the ambivalence characterizing the emotional relations of men and women in Kaska society. Illustrations of this ambivalence will now be studied as it manifests itself in male feelings of superiority, men's and women's attitudes toward marriage, in folklore, and in men's unconscious use of sex for aggression. Because of closer work with men, it is inevitable that the illustrations should primarily reflect male ambivalence to women; on the other hand, it is also possible that a woman's frustrations, because of her greater opportunity to relax from self-assertion, her early training in passivity, and her cross-sexed identification with her father in childhood, are less strong than a man's.

Male feelings of superiority to women are expressed when men generalize from their important economic roles on the one hand to a notion of generally superior status. They are also revealed in Old Man's defensive claim that men can, if necessary, do many feminine tasks, like caring for children, making babiche, lacing snowshoes, and cutting moccasins. On another occasion, however, Old Man reported that such tasks were only regretfully performed by men and their necessity considered a hardship. River Joe, too, often complained about a man's difficulties when he lacked a woman to cook and care for the camp. We therefore conclude that Old Man's statement of male self-sufficiency has little basis in manifest behavior and is an expression of male superiority. It represents an attempt to deny the anxiety provoked by dependence on his wife.

Both sexes reveal conscious reluctance to marriage. In men, holding back is defended on grounds of sexual freedom, while in women it is rationalized as a fear of being economically frustrated or physically overworked. Avoidance of marriage may be interpreted both as a fear of the strong emotions that the bond develops and of the dependency which it invites. The period of premarital promiscuity, as we shall see, affords abundant opportunity to satisfy sexuality without too seriously threatening emotional isolation. Furthermore, sex in this period offers full opportunity to express self-assertion, while marriage, with its burdens of economic responsibilities and child care, threatens to tax that motivation in both sexes.

The expression of sexual ambivalence in folklore is illustrated in the story of "The Blind Old Man," selected by Old Man to unburden the anxiety and hostility engendered by his growing dependency.[59] The theme of the tale, an old man deceived by his wife who withholds food, strongly suggests the husband-wife relationship to be marked by distrust and ambivalence. That the woman is able to deceive her husband, shows her to be perceived in a position of superiority and power, which throws light on the man's intense and conflictful emotional dependence. A second tale reveals a similar theme.

THE GIRL WHO TURNED INTO AN OWL

Two brothers shared a wife and lived with their mother-in-law. One day the girl climbed a tree to reach an owl's nest and was turned into an owl. Her clothes drifted down to her mother, who donned them and returned to camp pretending to be the young wife. She placed a roll of blankets in her camp to simulate an old woman asleep. When the boys came home the woman fed them, but as she had no teeth she could only eat tripe. To give the sound of chewing, she put a

[59] See the discussion of Old Man's personality below, pp. 327–328.

piece of charcoal into her mouth. Occasionally the mother-in-law threw a piece of meat to the "old woman." The brothers became suspicious of the old woman's actions and made her tell what had happened. Then they went to the owl's nest and pleaded for their wife to return. But the owl swooped down at them saying: "I'm going to eat you." The brothers became angry and one of them shot the owl with a bow and arrow. The owl failed to die and, referring to the point in its leg, said: "That's going to be my sinew."

This story was told by Old Man after he had been talking to Nitla about the latter's loss of Adele to John. He teased Nitla with living as people did in "old fashioned" days and was reminded of this story. The tale again stresses the deceitfulness of women. Although men are dependent on women, they always suffer a residual fear lest they be deceived or overwhelmed (eaten). In a burst of hostility, men fantasy using their strength to kill the ambivalent object. But male self-assertion, symbolized by the arrow, simply strengthens the woman. The closing incident of the tale might also be interpreted with reference to the self-assertion which men unconsciously invest in coitus. The penis, instead of conquering the female has its strength incorporated by the unassailable sexual object. In other words, men fear failure in their sexual relationships.

Female homosexuality and masculine striving are two elements in another folktale.

A TRIBE OF WOMEN

Two brothers, caught on an ice floe, drifted downriver until they reached Fort Liard. One of the boys was young and not smart; the other was already a little smart. They reached land and found a camp in which there were only women. The women fed the brothers. As the youths ate they saw another group of women return to camp with caribou meat. The leading woman in the camp explained that in this country all male children were killed at birth because they didn't want men. Men, they said, hurt women. Here women "bothered" each other and in that way conceived children who were painfully born through Caesarian section. The older boy told the women how children were born in the country upriver. Then the younger brother saw the "stick gun," which the women used in hunting. To fire the weapon, the hunter hit the back of an arrow with a stick. The younger brother did not believe that such a weapon was practical, and invited the women to shoot him. The women refused but the boy walked off a distance and insisted that they try. So the women killed the younger brother with the stick gun. The older boy then showed the tribe how to bury the dead in a grave instead of under a pile of brush. Later the older brother returned to his own people.[60]

[60] In Arapesh a similar myth occurs "in which a wandering male finds a group of independent women who have flying foxes (flying foxes are the symbol of aggressive, actively sexed, non-material women) as lovers to scratch their vulvas and who bear them only female children. The man marries them. They are pictured as ignorant of the proper order of childbirth (for a male child) so that the first pregnant woman is cut open and dies; after which the man teaches them how to bear children properly. He then grabs all the flying foxes in their tamberan house and burns them up; only one small flying fox escapes and enlists all the birds to avenge the death of the flying foxes. The birds attack the man, cut off his penis and drop it among the women, who bury it sorrowfully. Meanwhile, he has begotten enough sons to continue the race normally." (Mead, The Mountain Arapesh II Supernaturalism [1941], 345–346; see also 378–380.) Not only is the remarkable similarity of these tales, originating in two distant societies noteworthy, but more striking is the fact that both Arapesh and Kaska society pattern ambivalent attitudes to sex which this tale serves to express. In Arapesh the story "expresses the men's fear of the woman's independent sexuality which threatens death." In Kaska the tale, among other things, reveals the danger which emotionally isolated men perceive in too intense sexual interaction.

This tale (told by Old Man) expresses the mystery which women present to men, the masculine striving of women, and man's fear of women's sexual functions. The man's unconscious sexual passivity, suggested by the homosexual element, is indicated in the women's weapon which kills the younger brother.[61] In the younger brother we see passivity so strong that it leads to a masochistic sequence in which the man allows himself to be killed and, through interment, becomes incorporated by women. Thus the theme of the myth is once more expressive of male-female ambivalence.

Other unconscious ideas inferred from behavior and verbalization further expresses the pattern of intersexual hostility. The society, as already pointed out, recognizes the relationship between sexuality and hunting. Coitus and the self-assertive motives are unconsciously related, sexual intercourse being equivalent to the successful killing of game. Such an idea also carries the expression of ambivalent attitudes between men and women. Unconsciously sexual relations are interpreted as conflicts in which men are superior, but folktales reveal that men are as uncertain of their sexual powers as they often are about their economic capacities.

From these data we infer that the man's egocentric and utilitarian motivations strive for unconscious gratification through ideas of masculine superiority over women. The failure of these motives is unconsciously interpreted as making a man like a woman. That this idea should be further expressed in symbols equating the gun and penis is not surprising. The male sex organ and potency in general are perceived as weapons of mastery; this is indicated by the boasts of boys claiming to have "worn out" girls, and is also reflected in the young man's concern with his potency and the size of the penis. Schilder has pointed out that "the male sex organ is a protrusion and can therefore be symbolized by protrusions of another type. Every protrusion may then become a symbol or a sign for activity as well as for masculinity."[62] Any appearance of the gun, arrow, or stick gun in products of unconscious mentation therefore becomes significant. The importance of target practice with rifles is also partly determined from these ideas, and arises from the fact that it ensures self-assertive mastery not only actually (by improving skill) but unconsciously by relieving genital anxieties. Not only are weapons objects of protrusion, but by the Indian's own admission they are also symbols of male superiority and self-assertion, and equivalent to the penis as a weapon of conquest. These symbols emphasize the hostility which men unconsciously experience toward women and also illuminate what the woman hopes to achieve by masculine striving. By denying her capacity to have children and follow masculine allocated tasks, she is embracing assertion through male identification and denying the passivity associated with her body openings.[63] Note that women are not less eager to target practice than boys, only doing so in greater secrecy.

[61] Harry Lang, while intoxicated, once revealed his passivity by fantasying a woman with a revolver. Other examples of Harry Lang's behavior demonstrate his latent homosexuality, suggesting that unconsciously some men identify strongly with the passive female role and invest women with masculine self-assertion, a penis. The illogic of unconscious mentation of course permits such divergent ideas as sexual self-assertion and sexual passivity to exist side by side. See the discussion of Harry Lang's personality below, p. 337.

[62] Schilder, *Goals and Desires of Men* (1942), 153; also Fromm, *Sex and Character* (1943), 24.

[63] Schilder, *Goals and Desires of Men* (1942), 153.

Having established male-female ambivalence, we can now use the data as background for studying the expression of emotional isolation in sexual constriction.

Sexual constriction. Sexual constriction refers to an ambivalent response to sexual situations whose emotional intensity threatens to break down the imperviousness of the aloof personality, and which are further perceived as providing a channel for assertive self-expression and a bridge to warm interpersonal relations. From what has been said concerning the relations of men and women, it is obvious that sexual constriction is also influenced by the unconscious hostility and fear responsible for other manifestations of ambivalence in male-female relations. If we focus on sexual interaction as introducing two people to potentially warm and close association, which threatens the characterological armor against intense emotional impingements, we can understand the function of sexual constriction as a defense system designed to deal safely with dangerous but nevertheless pleasurable sexual phenomena. Sexual constriction is directed not so much against the pleasure aspects of sex as against its affectional aspects.

Manifestations of sexual constriction appear in premarital sexual stimulation, the unconscious definition of the sex act, the development of sexual incapacity, premarital and extramarital promiscuity, and in homosexuality. Our analysis will take up these points in order.

We have fully described the outstanding features of premarital sexual stimulation—preliminary teasing, chasing, capture, struggle, and coitus. In discussing rape we pointed out that it was often difficult to distinguish true rape from typical premarital sexuality; both occur in Kaska society.[64] The pattern of premarital sexual stimulation reflects the ambivalent significance of sexuality to the adolescent personality, and may be compared to a ritual dramatizing an internal struggle in the form of mock rape. Let us review the program of this ritual. Elements of sexual provocation and willingness, often initiated by girls, are followed by expressions of fear and hostility in which boys pursue girls. Finally the girl allows herself to be captured and, apparently only with reluctance, submits to coitus. All of these behavioral sequences are of considerable importance to the actors. Teasing, pursuit, and capture reflect the provocative pleasurable aspects of sexuality on the one hand and the fear of the emotional intensity of the situation on the other. Nobody in the ritual makes any direct gesture of surrender, but each sex makes concessions—the girl by teasing and allowing herself to be caught, the boy by chasing and then taking the initiative in coitus. The behavior in both sexes also affords opportunities for symbolically denying passivity and emotional dependence and for expressing self-assertion.

That girls should sometimes take the initiative in sexual situations is an adjustment to the unconscious coupling of self-assertion and copulation in the male personality and the attendant fear of potency failure. While men everywhere probably experience some fear

---

[64] Brown's observations regarding sex crimes in western culture are applicable to the Kaska data. Such crimes, he says, when committed by men (as most are) cannot be explained by sex alone but also embody "a definition of womanhood . . . not as something to protect but as something to violate." (Brown, *Social Pathology*, [1942], 152.) Neurotic women, in turn, often develop masochistic attitudes welcoming such attack. See Plaut, *Zur Psychologie der Notzucht und ihre forensische Begutachtung* (1930).

of potency failure which conditions their attitudes toward sex,[65] among the Kaska this danger is made particularly severe, first, by the threat of intercourse to a personality directed toward emotional aloofness and, second, by the chronic readiness to expect failure in any emotional crisis. Men, therefore, are ambivalent about taking the lead in sex or else do so, as in rape and mock rape, with real or symbolic aggression, which is supposed to reaffirm their sense of mastery.

The unconscious definition of the sexual act, derived from dreams and associations, confirms the impression of the sexual situation as a kind of mock rape. A typical dream of being pursued, similar to others several times reported by girls, comes from Marie Nolan.

6:30:45 (Lower Post). "Night before I went to sleep. Tom [her white husband] came home twelve o'clock. I said: 'I dream that somebody come to my camp. Who are you?' He said: 'Me.' I get scared and I start to get up. He grabbed me. He said: 'What are you trying to do?' Then I woke up. He said I start to fight him."

Asked whom she thought came into the camp, Marie said she suspected it was a soldier. She was invited to talk about soldiers and revealed that on the evening preceding the dream she had been at the restaurant when one of a group of American soldiers encountered her and tried to lure her into a truck with the promise of a drink. Marie, however, ran away. She was asked to say something more about soldiers. "These soldiers American, but I don't know who they are. I like American people. They're always fine people. I like white people. I always liked them. It must be because there's half-white blood in mine." She admitted that she had always wanted to be like white people and pointed out, with some pride, that her name did not appear on the Indian census rolls.

Marie's dream expresses an ambivalent fear of sexual attack. The fact that the dream occurs simultaneously with her husband's entrance into the camp is significant, since the dream thereby juxtaposes the white soldier and Marie's white husband. Further evidence of ambivalence toward the central idea of the dream, coitus, is revealed in her association to American people, whom she likes, and white people, with whom she identifies.

A somewhat similar dream was reported by eleven year old Elsie Lang.

11:30:45 (Old Man's place). "I dream soldier—they drunk." The scene of the dream was Lower Post, where the soldiers pursued Elsie who sought to escape by fleeing down the cutbank.

Elsie is too young ever to have had sexual intercourse, but the dream may be interpreted as indicating her awareness of this behavior and expresses her dread of, and probably her wish for, the experience. The same girl reported recurrent dreams of running away from attacking dogs.

Eva Ardo admitted a series of dreams reflecting fear of attacks by animals and indicating the unconscious sexual significance of animal dreams.

6:15:45 (Lower Post). "I scared when I dream beaver. If somebody kill him, I never scared beaver. . . . Everytime, that's my dream—otter, mink, beaver. That's all. Is some boy, that otter. Then he come with me and catch me pretty near. I scared. I get away. That mink just the same boy too. Same way I see grizzly bear too. Just the same like a man. Is white man. I scared that grizzly bear. I scared black bear too."

---

[65] Fromm, *Sex and Character* (1942), 24.

6:16:45. "I sleep, I dream grizzly bear . . . I scared. He go up on a tree. Just I see him. He run me that grizzly bear. I run after a little way. I see him a little way behind." The dream was interpreted as a fear of being pursued by somebody. From whom is she running away? "Nobody," Eva replied. "That man he wants me but I lick him . . . I don't want him. Is good worker. . . ."

These animal dreams manifest the girl's fear of sexual aggression. Eva's second dream was reported following a discussion of the men who wanted to marry her and of one, particularly, with whom she was reported to be already living. In both dreams the sexual situation is conceived as attack and reacted to with dread. The intense fear of the grizzly bear, recounted by many male and female subjects, and the preoccupation with the grizzly in thinking suggest that unconsciously the grizzly bear symbolizes the emotional intensity of the sexual situation or any other intense emotional experience. In girls the grizzly bear fantasy takes the form of running away from the animal, just as in life the girl runs from the boys who want to possess her. Although boys admit conscious fear of the grizzly and also dream of this animal, they often dream or talk of overcoming the menace with a gun. In other words, the sexual situation is to be mastered with self-assertive tendencies. Failure to achieve such mastery, as in the dream of John Kean, whose gun failed when he was confronted by a grizzly, is the equivalent of sexual impotence.[66] In view of the male's unconscious definition of the sex act in terms of aggression, it is interesting to note Nitla's communication of the emotions he experienced when, as a ten year old, he saw a couple engaging in coitus. "I say: 'What the hell!' I'm scared. I think I kill woman sometime. I never think. Too young. I'm scared."[67]

Coming now to the manifestation of sexual constriction in sexual incapacity, we find the man's fear of impotence expressed in exaggerated ideas of potency. There is also evidence that girls and women are often frigid in coitus, partly, perhaps, because of the man's selfish sexual technique. Such interferences with the feminine orgastic functions may, however, be expected when the sex act is unconsciously conceived in terms of attack, and where there is strong ambivalence regarding the intensities of sexual interaction. In the man similar ambivalence, plus the fear of being inadequate to master what is defined as a self-assertive situation, may similarly result in orgastic disturbances.

Sexual sanctions further reveal the conflicting appeal of sex. All sexual activity is first of all regarded as indelicate and to be concealed. Children and youths are warned that premature sexuality arrests growth and that excessive copulation causes early aging or leads to insanity. There is probably a connection between the insanity invoked as a sexual sanction and the offense. Mental illness in Kaska society is usually described as running amok and manifesting general lack of conscious control. The intensity of the orgasm may resemble a similar dangerous disruption of control to the emotionally constricted Kaska, the sanction of insanity being projected from the fear of excessive orgastic stimulation. On the other hand, the Kaska regard some sexual indulgence as necessary for health.

If sexual constriction serves to block sexual expression, how can we account for the

[66] See above, p. 162.
[67] See his autobiographical sketch below, pp. 351-352. Also note his reference to the vagina dentata theme in the same place—the fear of death in intercourse.

prevalence of premarital sexual promiscuity as well as the high incidence of extramarital adultery?

Sexual promiscuity in adolescence represents a complexly determined phenomenon, all of whose keys we cannot pretend to locate. Focussing on the motivational aspects of this behavior, with only a passing nod to the awakening glandular processes and the lack of manifest controls imposed on the behavior of adolescents, we can point to this period (when drinking also begins) as providing youth with one of the first opportunities since early childhood to experience release of emotional isolation. Promiscuity is more specifically explicable as affording the egocentric component of the girl's personality an opportunity to express itself in a revolt against her parentally enforced, passive, serving role. At this age too the boy's general self-assertion begins to be important in hunting and trapping, also embracing his awakening genitality; promiscuity means for him chances to prove himself and acquire further prestige. The biologically derived anxieties of sexual failing probably reinforce his drive to succeed in non-sexual fields, while failure in those spheres in turn intensifies potency anxiety. Finally, promiscuity offers a chance to satisfy affect hunger without involving either sex in too close or inextricable emotional bonds—safety lying in the number and variety of partners. Richard Day indicates this in his complaint of having found the effects of being in love so unpleasant that he would not want to risk the state again. He explained that love arises after copulating with the same girl several times and admitted that he avoids persistent intercourse with the same partner.[68]

In marriage, promiscuity is probably often a flight from the anxiety aroused by too intense interpersonal relations between two people. The ambivalence with which the spouses enter marriage foreshadows the insecurity which develops when infatuation wears off and emotional isolation begins to be threatened by the dependence promoted through living together. In view of the Indians' moderate ego tonicity, it may be expected that marriage will also cause a man to feel the pressure of economic responsibilities. A husband who tries to allay this anxiety by too great reliance on his wife invites fresh anxiety from the ensuing conflict between egocentric and dependency motives. Extramarital promiscuity and divorce are attempts to substitute transitory and unthreatening sexual experiences for oppressive marriage relations.

We now come to the expression of sexual constriction in homosexuality. Again it must be emphasized that it is not our intention to explain this tendency fully but only to throw light on some of its motivational foundations. Furthermore, we do not intend to discuss overt homosexual behaviors. Mutual masturbation probably grows out of close interpersonal association but we had no opportunity to study its psychological results. We can

---

[68] There is little doubt that sexual promiscuity is conditioned by the social climate in which it occurs, i.e., that it is structurally related to other aspects of culture. Recent papers have begun to study this problem, from the standpoint of personality in western culture but the results must be interpreted cautiously in view of the fact that the subjects of investigation comprise a selected sample of promiscuous men, namely those who contracted venereal disease. See Wittkower and Cowan, *Some Psychological Aspects of Sexual Promiscuity* (1944), and Watts and Wilson, *A Study of Personality Factors among Venereal Disease Patients* (1945). It has also been pointed out that female promiscuity may be a product of poor emotional adjustment and latent homosexuality. See Dupouy and Picard, *Une érotomanie médicale* (1928).

discuss only the significance of homosexual tendencies like intrasexual friendships and tactual (non-genital) contacts. Bisexual tendencies are most pronounced at early adolescence when the fear of sexuality is apt to be greatest. Homosexual impulses at this time represent an alternative for intense intersexual relations, substituting attachments that do not pose an immediate threat to emotional isolation. Intrasexual friendships further offer an opportunity to satiate affect hunger, particularly through kinaesthetic satisfactions which omit any need of verbal self-revelation. One reason why such associations are continued beyond early adolescence lies in the fact that sexual constriction, founded on a base of sexual hostility, prohibits these satisfactions to accrue from oppositely sexed partners. Homosexual attachments, however, are not completely unthreatening to emotional isolation. This is indicated by the fact that intrasexual friendships are not invested with intense emotion (except, perhaps, between sisters) but are highly transitory and easily abandoned; the partners are readily substituted. In other words, Kaska homosexuality is promiscuous. As in premarital sexuality, when a homosexual association begins to grow too intense, it breaks down and partners are replaced.

As an aspect of emotional isolation, sexual constriction has been described as a conflict between the acceptable pleasure functions and the threatening affectional functions of sex. We have also tried to unravel the complexity with which the Kaska world and self-views condition the significance of sexual situations.

Expression in the Rorschach test situation. Three aspects of Kaska Rorschach performance reveal emotional isolation; first, insensitivity to emotionally exciting stimuli; second, repressed spontaneity, and, finally, indications of emotional anergy.

Rorschach literature recognizes three types of responses as revealing sensitivity to emotionally exciting stimuli. These types are, first, responses making use only of color; second, color responses which are secondarily determined by form, and, finally, form answers which make additional use of color. Before considering their expression in the Rorschach protocols of Kaska adults, let us define each of these groups.

Pure color responses (C) denote an instantaneously evoked, uninhibited, and relatively infantile expression of emotion "without regard to time and place."[69] According to Klopfer and Kelley, they reveal the extinction of all "rational permeation."[70] Color determined form answers (CF) indicate a heightened consciousness of the world to which an individual is aware of being required to adjust his emotional expressions in the interests of affection and social acceptance. "But the center of reference is still himself. He is still gratifying himself."[69] According to Klopfer and Kelley, in the CF response "the consideration of rational elements is not altogether abandoned but the emotional stimulation" predominates.[71] Finally, the form determined color responses (FC) indicate a full acceptance of "the outside world" by an adult who "knows its feelings and feels with it. He reacts with emotions but these are tempered by his regard for how the other fellow feels."[69] Such answers indicate "that the subject is open to the emotional stimulus implied in the coloring but is not willing to

[69] Beck, Rorschach's Test. II. A Variety of Personality Pictures (1945), 30.

[70] Klopfer and Kelley, The Rorschach Technique (1942), 286.

[71] Klopfer and Kelley, The Rorschach Technique (1942), 283.

react to it unless it can be done within the limits of rational considerations."[72]

Any attention to the color cards is, of course, limited by the number of pure form determined responses. This factor will be more fully discussed immediately following the analysis of color reactions.

The relevant scores for adult Kaska subjects follow:

	Mean (R = 22.16)	Per Cent
C	.32	1.4
CF	.26	1.1
FC	.47	2.1
F	15.0 (−5.8)	67.0 (−26.1)

The evidence indicates that Kaska adults make relatively little use of the all-color cards. When color is reacted to, it most often indicates emotional responsiveness determined by social considerations. Nevertheless, the scores show a residuum of self-gratificatory and labile emotionality which is kept under rigid control. The figures may, therefore, be interpreted as indicating a rigid rationing and control of affectivity from within the individual.

Color responses can be summed. When this is done for Kaska adults they yield a mean color score of .97. Compared to western color sums, this is very low and quantifies the disinterest in color stimuli and the inability of strong emotional reactions to be evoked by external situations.

Another quantitative technique for studying emotional reactivity in the Rorschach situation requires measuring the percentage of responses to the all-color cards. In Kaska adults, thirty-four per cent of all responses are made to the all-color cards. For western society the mean is 62.45 per cent (S.D. 25.6).[73] The low mean for the Indian subjects would indicate, according to Beck, that "something inhibitory is happening to the affects." If this inhibition is related to a rejection of the all-color cards, we have "color shock," which in western clinical practice is interpreted to be symptomatic of "neurosis and is therefore in reality neurotic shock. What happens is that . . . the individual becomes more constricted, inefficient, inaccurate, impoverished."[74] Apart from the rejection of the all-color cards, other criteria of color shock include an increase in poor form responses, absent or delayed popular responses, delayed responses, decreased productivity, an ignoring of color as a determinant, and expressions of inability to see meaning. Usually two or more signs of shock appear in a record and are sufficient for diagnosis. Sometimes only one sign may be manifested. The evidence of color shock in adult records is summarized in Table 17.

Four individuals responded with only one sign, nine with at least two signs, and five with three or more signs. Only one subject lacked any of the signs. Color shock is therefore clearly indicated in a majority of those adults who took the test and who reacted with two or more signs. Schachtel warns that "emotional suppressors" are not necessarily clinically

[72] Klopfer and Kelley, The Rorschach Technique (1942), 282.
[73] Beck, Rorschach's Test. II. A Variety of Personality Pictures (1945), 32.
[74] Beck, Rorschach's Test. II. A Variety of Personality Pictures (1945), 37.

TABLE 17. SIGNS OF COLOR SHOCK IN ADULT KASKA RORSCHACH RECORDS

Signs	Number of Subjects Responding (N=19)	Number of Subjects Responding to One Other Sign	Three or More Signs
At least fifty per cent of popular responses to last three cards	4	4	2
No use of color on any all-color card	5	5	3
One all-color card rejected	2	2	2
Two all-color cards rejected	1	1	1
All all-color cards rejected	2	2[75]	
Significant delay on one or more all-color cards	4	4	3
Inability to give meaning reasonably fluently on one or more all-color cards	8	7	3
At least fifty per cent of total F- on the all-color cards	5	3	2
Thirty per cent or fewer responses on the all-color cards	7	6	2

neurotic; before such a diagnosis is valid, the solution adopted to color shock must be studied.[76] Kaska adults, we find, do not respond to color disturbance with an increased number of poor form responses, indicating little relaxation of customary controls in the face of disturbing experience. Rather, shock leads to an avoidance of the whole disturbing situation (no use of color in forming the response, rejection of the all-color cards, momentary disturbance that is overcome). This bears out what has already been said of the Indian's striving to shut such situations out of awareness. Beck also emphasizes that the degree to which color shock occurs is important and warns that "the shock reaction is found throughout all groups of normals. . . . thus it demonstrates the old cliché that we are all, in this high-pressure age, neurotic."[77]

From their performance on the all-color cards, we may conclude that the Kaska Indians are upset by exciting stimuli but are inclined to control affective reactions to such disturbances. Drawing from this interpretation, we may say that the Rorschach situation tends to confirm not only the emotional isolation of the Kaska but also the Indian's deferent manner of escaping emotional provocations to hostility and mastering internal aggression.

Repressed spontaneity is the second expression of emotional isolation revealed by the Rorschach technique. According to Klopfer and Kelley: "Where a human being is afraid that he may not be able to control his emotional impulses, he resorts to an attempt to repress the spontaneity of his reactions and to put in its place an impersonal, matter-of-fact, cold way of dealing with situations. When this form of control plays a dominant role in the personality, we describe the behavior of such a person as *constricted*."[78] The authors define

[75] Both subjects were also marked for presenting fewer than thirty per cent of responses on the all-color cards.

[76] Schachtel, *On Color and Affect* (1943), 405.

[77] Beck, *Rorschach's Test. II. A Variety of Personality Pictures* (1945), 39.

[78] Klopfer and Kelley, *The Rorschach Technique* (1942), 227.

constriction quantitatively; subjects with adequate intelligence whose record contains between fifty and eighty per cent *F* can be called constrictive.[79]

For the Kaska we find the mean *F* per cent to be sixty-seven for adults and sixty-five for children. Furthermore we find this picture of constriction to be unalleviated by any significant use of vista and texture responses, indicating "very rigid constriction."[80]

Bochner and Halpern point out that: "People who repress their emotions, those whose entire life is constricted . . . will show a stereotyped outlook, since inhibition in one sphere necessarily causes related narrowness in other spheres."[81] Lack of intellectual differentiation (stereotypy) is revealed in the high percentage of animal content. Since the mean animal per cent for western control groups is 46.87 (S.D. 17.58),[82] Kaska adults, with an animal percentage of 63 (S.D. 26) are, as already stated, placed sufficiently high in animal content responses to demonstrate such stereotypy and to warrant the conclusion that it is partly a consequence of emotional aloofness. In connection with utilitarianism, animal responses were considered to exemplify the tendency toward practical and concrete rather than specu-lative thinking. We are now in a position to understand further these utilitarian behaviors as in part motivated by emotional isolation. Below we will see from Rorschach evidence that the root of the individual's circumscribed approach to life, his procrastination in the face of danger, and general constriction—emotional as well as intellectual—follow from a deep seated basic anxiety derived in an early stage of development. Rooted in this trauma are utilitarian manifestations like the caution which prohibits the Indian from releasing his imagination and productive powers. Primary anxiety also reduces ego tonicity, from which in turn originates the flexible behaviors designed to protect psychic economy. The basic anxiety to which we refer is derived from the early affectional rejection of the child and continues to be borne by the adult individual. One of its expressions is emotional anergy which, in the Rorschach situation, is revealed by shading shock.

Klopfer and Kelley have associated shading shock "with individuals who have feelings of inadequacy and are afraid of external contact. It seems to indicate . . . that the individual is aware of his personality instability and that the disturbance is deeply rooted."[83] Speaking of "gray-black shock," Beck says: "It signalizes that anxiety which, because its roots lie deep in the very early experiences of the individual, has become a central character force, diffusing his energies and paralyzing him in almost all of life's crises, even the minor ones."[84]

A number of diagnostics are available for judging shading shock. From those suggested by leading Rorschach workers, we have selected six to verify in Kaska records. These are briefly summarized below.

1. Productivity is reduced when shading cards are shown.
2. Form quality declines on the shading cards.
3. Outright rejection of the shading cards occurs.

---

[79] Klopfer and Kelley, *The Rorschach Technique* (1942), 234.
[80] Klopfer and Kelley, *The Rorschach Technique* (1942), 234; also see p. 239.
[81] Bochner and Halpern, *The Clinical Application of the Rorschach Test* (1945), 60.
[82] Beck, *Rorschach's Test. II. A Variety of Personality Pictures* (1945), 15.
[83] Klopfer and Kelley, *The Rorschach Technique* (1942), 388.
[84] Beck, *Rorschach's Test. II. A Variety of Personality Pictures* (1945), 39.

4. Expressions of shock and other manifestations of discomfort and indirect rejection appear when the shading cards are presented.
5. A decline in the number of popular responses appears with the shading cards
6. Texture is avoided as a determinant with the shading cards.

The shading cards are Cards I, IV, V, VI, and VII. Although Card I is not as significant as the others for determining shading shock, since the novelty of the inkblots may influence the subject's reaction to this initial stimulus, it may be included in order to balance the number of shading and other cards. A comparison of the two sets of cards for adults in terms of the criteria of shading shock is given in Table 18.

TABLE 18. EVIDENCE OF SHADING SHOCK IN ADULT KASKA RORSCHACH RECORDS

Sign	Per Cent of Responses	
	Shading Cards	Other Cards
Proportion of total responses	43	56
Proportion of poor form responses	51	49
Proportion of outright rejections	43	57
Proportion of popular answers	40	60
Proportion of texture responses	47	53

Except in the case of outright rejections, the evidence indicates that Kaska adults as a whole did more poorly in the case of the shading cards than with the rest of the blots. That we do not find expected differences in the percentage of outright rejections is probably due to the fact that the non-shading cards contain the color blots, whose heavy rejection has already been discussed in connection with color shock. A summary of the performances of seven adults, prepared with special reference to the shading cards, reveals the uneasiness occasioned by these stimuli and also gives evidence of indirect rejection manifested in expressions of shock and discomfort.

PAULETTE DONNELLY

Card IV. "I don't know this one." Then a pause and finally a response.
Card VI. "I don't know this one." The card was rejected. The record contains no other initial or total rejection.

HANS DONNELLY

Cards I and VI. Rejected without comment. There were no other rejections.

DICK MOUNTAIN

Card I. Rejected.
Card IV. "My gee, what's this now? I never see like this in this country. I don't know. Don't know." The card was rejected.
Card V. Rejected.
Card VI. "Gee whiz! Don't get nothing out of this." Rejected.
Card VII. Immediately the subject exclaimed: "Oh, nothing." He refused the card vigorously.

OLD KEAN

Card IV. "Funny thing. Something like lake. Just like sometimes a man coming up that lake. Injun scared like hell." The subject digressed to speak of a mythological cannibalistic frog.

Card V. "I never see this country like this. Someplace something different too. Just like man. He do something in lake. . . ."

Card VII. "I guess devil like that. Old Devil, he make everything. God make good thing . . . this country I never see that one."

RIVER JOE

Cards V and VII. Rejected. One other rejection occurred in the record (Card X).

EDWARD PRINCE

Rejected all the cards till Card V, gave a response to that and rejected VI and the three all-color cards.

JOHN KEAN

Card IV. The first of two rejections occurred on this card; the second occurred on the second all-color card.

Card VI. "I never see that too . . . looks like bug, two teeth up here [D 7]. . . ."

The evidence of shading shock discovered in Kaska adults' records may be interpreted as revealing a deep feeling of inadequacy or basic anxiety derived from the early experiences of the individual. We conclude that this crippling anxiety follows from the child's emotional rejection. The anxiety may also be regarded as the inhibitory fear which makes the individual recoil from any intense emotional stimuli and motivates him to erect rigid barriers, like those revealed in the high F per cent, and defenses such as we have discussed in connection with the other dominant motivations. It is from this point of view that all of the dominant motivations may be perceived as defenses adopted against threats to still more basic needs, like security and self-esteem.

Release of emotional isolation. Several opportunities occur in Kaska life for the relaxation of defenses against emotional stimulation and the expression of relatively strong emotion in interpersonal relations. Gambling, with its opportunities for releasing aggression, is a situation in which the stimulation of company is greatly relished. Intoxication, as already indicated, reduces the conscious threshold of a number of inhibitions and is a condition in which emotional reactions are readily released. Dancing, with its opportunities for sexual and physical contacts, probably owes a large share of its popularity to the fact that it permits the release of isolating defenses, breaks down detachment, and facilitates bodily contact between young people of opposite sex. Visiting, idling, and potlatch groups have similar functions in partially breaking down social detachment. The whole summer period, in fact, holds opportunities and promises for closer personal relations.

Why should the breakdown of emotionally isolating defenses be enjoyed? The very fact that situations affording release are so popular suggests that the Kaska Indian is not completely satisfied in his way of life, that the guarantees afforded by social detachment also impose a frustration on "natural" tendencies. Whether such tendencies are innate or not, we cannot say. It can be said, however, that the trauma of emotional rejection leaves the person with a sense of impaired capacity, affect hunger, and desire for warm interpersonal relationships. The popularity of dancing, visiting, drinking, and gambling arises in part from the fact that these situations offer opportunities for breaking down attitudinal screens that normally inhibit interpersonal relations. The ambivalence manifested in many of these situations (e.g., the blocked conversation of visiting, the initial reluctance to dance) indicates the primacy of the emotionally isolating motivation to which so many aspects of the culture are geared. The motive can most safely be released in a crowd. When intense release occurs otherwise, the effect is to activate the basic trauma, promoting intense guilt and a feeling of catastrophic breakdown—"absolute worthlessness, absolute rejection."[85] This is the effect of mental breakdown.

Résumé. Emotional isolation has been discussed in relation to the other dominant motivations of Kaska personality. With its roots in the affectional rejection of the Kaska child, emotional isolation strives to maintain the individual's safety from all emotionally intense situations, which are identified as threatening. Emotional isolation inhibits both responses of love and hate and also cooperates with other motivations to pattern intersexual hostility and ambivalent attitudes toward sexual situations.

The accumulated evidence tends to show that out of the trauma of maternal emotional rejection, the Kaska Indian is led to erect an intricate system of defenses designed to maintain safety via the route of social detachment and personal inviolability. In an atomistic society composed of other individuals similarly motivated, this system is often successful. On the other hand, the initial trauma, on which the motivation is founded and against whose reactivation the defenses are maintained, burdens the individual with a constant source of threat and anxiety which must be regarded as intrinsically unpleasant. Furthermore, the craving for love without the means of accepting this gratification impose another almost insoluble frustration on Kaska personality which must also be taken into account in evaluating the efficiency of the defense system.

WORLD VIEW AND SELF-VIEW

We have presented a descriptive picture of Kaska ethos, building an interpretation around six partially conflicting dominant motivations. Our purpose now is to synthesize this description. The Kaska view of the world wavers between an idea that experience is manageable and an awareness that life is threatening and difficult. These opposite attitudes lead to two principal means of responding to adaptive and adjustive problems. For many of the hazards of existence, there are tested problem solutions with the aid of which one can efficiently overcome a harsh and rigorous environment. In these situations it is possible to be resourceful, capable, and masterful. Unfortunately, the context of life offering security is extremely limited. To stay within the area of safety requires constant watchfulness and caution. As soon as experiential boundaries widen, catastrophy may be expected. The uncertainties of life must be avoided lest by testing resourcefulness too sharply they promote failure. Society, like the physical environment, also holds dangers. Here safety lies in avoid-

[85] Maslow and Mittelmann, *Principles of Abnormal Psychology* (1941), 59.

ing interpersonal relations which promise to stir up intense emotions or invite excessive effort against which there are no effective safeguards and which tax the resources of the ego.

Two divergent attitudes toward the self, self-reliance and helplessness, complement the double view of the world in Kaska personality. The most acceptable is the notion of self-confidence that seems to say: "I can do this, but I must do it alone." The independence and self-containment involved in this formula partly rest on feelings of being socially detached, lonely, and afraid. To deny these anxious notes, a person must prove his effectiveness lest by failure he admit his need for social support.

Completely inacceptable is the idea of personal helplessness, the doubt that promises failure and which urges the person to relax from striving. In life's critical situations—and these are frequent and inevitable for an uncertain personality—the responsible feelings of the individual, to his great dismay, quickly give ground. There ensues a blind reaching out for all the things that are equivalent to failure—relaxation from striving, affection, and protection. The person is touched with guilt for his helplessness and threatened by anxiety which he dares not release for fear of further imperiling his safety. So long as the Kaska can contain their physical and social environmental participation within narrow limits, they feel resourceful, capable, and safe; trouble is avoided; life is simple, and the individual is supreme. As soon as the protective boundaries are upset, however, there follows a wave of worry and anxiety that signifies the penalty of failure.

DEVELOPMENT OF THE ETHOS

Our study of Kaska ethos now concerns itself with the development of the dominant motivations in which this system has its roots. In pursuing this aim we find it more significant to concentrate on how learning takes place than on the cultural content which is transmitted by direct learning, although explicit instruction which reinforces dominant motivations will not be neglected. In the words of Bateson and Mead, our assumption is that, "An individual's character structure, his attitudes toward himself and his interpretation of experience are conditioned not only by what he learns, but also by the method of learning."[86] For this analysis, the most significant aspects of socialization may be grouped under five headings: infant care, emotional rejection, parental attitudes and authority, identifications, and activities of later childhood.

Infant care. A newborn infant occupies an extremely favorable position in Kaska society. The baby is carefully kept warm and comfortable and fed whenever it cries. Crying also brings a quick response in the way of other comforts and attention. The early relationship between mother and child is a warm one and during the first two years of life the child is usually in close proximity to its mother, although the manner of blanketing the infant permits little direct contact between the mother's arms and the baby's naked body. Weaning is gradual and tolerant, the satisfactions of suckling being prolonged by continuing to allow nursing from a bottle once weaning is terminated. Punishment is as rare in the baby's life as attention is plentiful.

What are the effects of these patterns of infant care in the personality of the developing

---

[86] Bateson and Mead, *Balinese Character* (1942), 84. Also see above, p. 15.

child and adult? Good maternal care in infancy, by gratifying the child's craving for physical comfort and alimentary needs, may be considered the initial stimulus for the development of feelings of mastery and control and to instill confidence for later investigating and dealing with the external world. It is therefore the basis for the development of egocentricity and self-sufficiency, the self-assertive motives of Kaska personality, which determine the emotional significance of many adaptive situations. The prompt satisfactions produced by crying also condition the child to expectations of being able to control his environment resourcefully, capably, and empirically. In other words, good care in childhood is a strong stimulus for developing the executive functions of the ego. The cherished position of the Kaska baby is responsible for creating active coping techniques in the personality, which later become expressed in attitudes toward the world and self characterized by self-confidence, independence, and ego strength.

On the other hand, as Kardiner has pointed out, a readiness for passive forms of adaptation and adjustment is one of the "bad effects" of good maternal care.[87] Such passivity results primarily from the infant's unconscious idealization of the mother as a powerful and resourceful figure. The satisfactions of Kaska infancy, kinaesthetic and oral, are well nigh complete and extremely gratifying. Their very fullness sets the stage for an unconscious attraction to this period of easy gratification. In later life passive reactions occur when, under situations of stress and crisis, the person unconsciously attempts to restore the omnipotence which maternal gratification encouraged in the very early years of life. The appearance of passive adaptive and passive receptive techniques, in which the person surrenders active striving, are therefore indices of an unconscious process called regression.

Thus we see that in the state of infancy Kaska society begins to shape both the relatively assertive and the passive coping techniques of the personality. It endows the personality with a capacity for mastery and accomplishment by inducing confidence in the self to command the resources of the environment. On the other hand, indulgent care creates a readiness to relinquish such techniques when, under conditions of stress, the ego no longer feels capable of achieving its goals. At what level of aspiration that stress will induce passivity seems to depend largely upon the development of personality beyond infancy.

Emotional rejection. Although the Kaska child receives a good start in life, this favorable situation is soon interrupted when the emotionally isolating tendencies of early childhood are instituted by the hitherto indulgent mother. At about two or three years of age the child begins to be denied the emotional warmth and generous attention to which he has been accustomed. He still receives sufficient nourishment, so long as good food is available in camp, but affectionally he is rejected; attention is withdrawn, fondling and playing with the child discontinued, the mother withdraws into impersonal aloofness. Following upon the initial period of extreme gratification these new attitudes are exceedingly traumatic for development. The self-confident expectations which the child was encouraged to experience toward the world are suddenly disappointed; his capacities for securing comfort and attention fail. There follow feelings of abandonment, of being, reduced to struggling for satisfactions and creating comforts. The consequences of emotional isolation include the blocked

[87] Kardiner, *The Psychological Frontiers of Society* (1945), 345; 347-348.

development of active forms of mastery, affect hunger, institution of the first regressive trends, development of emotional aloofness, and the creation of various projective systems organized to deal with the persistent traumatic effects of this situation. We will now discuss these effects in greater detail.

We have emphasized the importance of good infant care in Kaska society for developing security and encouraging capacities for self-assertion and mastery. Such results are not only derived from social responsiveness to the child's bodily needs but are also built up in the process of inducing affection. The combined effect of these gratifications is to stimulate a congenial view of the world and faith in the self. When affectional stimulation is interrupted by the mother's emotional rejection, the development of the self-assertive aims receives a setback. Although the initial impetus to activity permits a conscious compensatory develop-ment of ego striving to continue (this will be discussed below), the removal of the heartening stimuli to such growth leaves ego strength in a precarious position, which in later life leads to narrowing the field of effective participation and strong readiness to succumb to crises with passivity and regression.

Emotional rejection institutes the first regressive trends because it intensifies the memory of infantile omnipotence. The highlighting of a past and more favorable period of adjustment, together with a simultaneous blow to ego development, help institute a chronic dependence that continues to underlie all forms of active mastery. Affect hunger is one feature of this phenomenon. Emotional rejection leaves the Kaska individual unable to form close emotional attachments for two main reasons. In the first place it must be remembered that the expression of love requires inducement; that is, it must be stimulated by the ex-perience of being loved. When such indirect learning is early discontinued, as it is when the three year old is emotionally rejected, the individual is left without sufficient capacity to cathect love objects. He has not been sufficiently prepared for love. Second, emotional re-sponsiveness may be inhibited by serious affectional disappointments encountered in the course of development. The Kaska child meets such disappointment when expected affec-tional gratification is abruptly withdrawn by the primary source of this reward—the mother. The seriousness of this withdrawal is reflected in the prolonged trauma that characterizes Kaska personality. As a result of that shock, the child becomes afraid ever again to lose his identity in strong love relationships which might once more be destroyed at the individual's expense. Both these factors help to institute emotional aloofness, leading the person to regard with fear all strong love relationships while at the same time he longs for a return to the period when affectional gratification was abundantly available. Realistically, regres-sion is impossible; so the person comes to perceive one avenue of safety in the maintenance of personal inviolability and self-sufficiency. What happens is that emotional rejection secon-darily reinforces the earlier patterned egocentric aim of mastery—independence comes to be valued as an active defense. The fact that such an assertive defense system can be pat-terned testifies to the importance of good infantile care for developing sufficient ego strength to institute such defenses. But emotional rejection also sets the stage for passive receptive techniques, which represent attempted or symbolic regression to the gratifications that were effortlessly available in infancy. Stealing and food leeching in childhood, the earliest ethological expression of this regressive process, originate from the child's awareness that his demands will not be adequately fulfilled. Stealing is largely confined to trinkets and food, objects symbolic of love. Food leeching is a means of securing oral indulgence, the mouth having been the organ most intensely associated with infantile gratification and unconsciously remaining a channel for trying to approximate those early rewards. Since children are punished for stealing, the behavior does not often continue into adulthood but its underlying aims continue to operate in the demandingness of the adult and in the high evaluation of generosity. The fact that demandingness is most directly expressed toward the government and whites, suggests that these sources are unconsciously regarded as parental substitutes who have in abundance what the individual needs and so suggest themselves as suitable sources for restoring the balance of frustrated parent-child relations. The statement of Nitla referring to the traders as "Just the same your daddy" is significant in this respect. The conception of authority, or bosses, as sources of protection also equates these concepts with the early parental ideal.

These facts show how closely emotional isolation is related to dependence. In dependence, the search for love is partially affirmed but in emotional aloofness (which, in turn, is related to the motives of egocentricity and utilitarianism) the need for love is denied. "I don't need anybody," the individual seems to say. While intrinsically this is not true, the expression of aloofness is important because of its effects in keeping down passivity and in encouraging the self-assertive motives. The extremes to which emotional aloofenss is carried in Kaska society are striking. It leads to the isolation of the individual from all intense social contacts and constantly seeks to guard him against internal and external exciting stimuli which might activate the trauma of emotional rejection. The personality characterized by these trends bears many resemblances to Balinese character structure and certain etiological factors in the two situations are also broadly similar.[88]

The development of a psychoanalytic approach to culture and personality by workers like Roheim, Mead, and Kardiner has stimulated interest in the elucidation of projective systems. Such systems are "the records of traumatic experiences . . . excrescences developed from nuclear traumatic experiences within the growth pattern of the individual."[89] Following such a definition we would expect to find the emotional rejection of the Kaska child reflected in projective systems and this is indeed the case. In order to distinguish between "records of traumatic experiences" and the ethological expressions of all early experiences in the ethos, we are using the term projective systems for the symbolic representation of a patterned traumatic experience (or persons related to such an experience) in the socially patterned behavior and ideas of a society.[90] Such representations may be regarded as the symbolic reenactment of the individual's roles in an early traumatic experience and involves the assumptions that the trauma still persists vividly in the individual's unconscious memory and that he is anxious to assume control over it.[91]

The principal projections of emotional isolation are found in the representations of women in Kaska folktales. We have already alluded to the story, "The Girl Who Turned

[88] See Bateson and Mead, *Balinese Character* (1942); Mead, *Researches in Bali* (1939).
[89] Kardiner, *The Psychological Frontiers of Society* (1945), 39.
[90] This definition seems implicit in the work of Mead. See Mead, *Researches in Bali* (1939), 24.
[91] See Fenichel. *The Psychoanalytic Theory of Neuroses* (1945), 120.

Into An Owl," to point out the manner in which this tale served to express Old Man's personality conflicts. Now we turn to another function of this tale, seeing it as the projection of emotional rejection and a representation of the mother pictured as a deceiver. The story also indicates a certain equivalence between the husband-wife and parent-child relationships. The girl's mother, taking the wife's place, symbolizes the equivalence of the maternal and wifely roles. Unconsciously, husbands are children fed by their mothers. They are dependent on wives as they were dependent on the maternal care in infancy, but in the tale the mother reveals her deceitfulness and must be punished. Similar unconscious ideas may also be at the root of the aggression which men direct against women during intoxication, and also in the rejection of the breasts as erotic stimuli in sexual situations. A similar story of a deceitful wife is found in "The Blind Old Man," in which the man again kills the mother equivalent. In "A Tribe of Women" we see represented a flight from parents and the discovery of new mothers. When the younger brother allows himself to be killed by these women he gives into a regressive wish to be incorporated by the mother and attains his passive goal by being buried in the women's camp. That men should be indicated in these tales as experiencing somewhat greater frustration from emotional rejection than women can perhaps be partly explained in terms of the girl's greater opportunities to repair the wound of rejection. This will be discussed below in connection with identifications and childhood activities.

The grizzly bear fantasy may be regarded as another example of a projective system repeating the child's terror upon encountering emotional rejection. The mother is here represented (familiarly, as far as western clinical practice is concerned) in a large and dangerous animal against which the person feels powerless. It is not coincidental that another function of this fantasy is to express the anxiety which girls feel in the face of sexual situations, whose intensity threatens to break down the emotional isolation adopted as a defense against rejection.

Parental attitudes and authority. Parental authority plays a relatively slight and nontraumatic role in the Kaska child's life. Attitudes toward toilet training are not severe and sphincter regulation is not seriously expected before the child possesses the capacities for voluntary control. Punishment is rare and generally limited to situations of defaulting while overprotection has no soil in which to grow. There is an absence of authoritarian supervision such as would emphasize the child's humiliation and complete submission to his parents. Native education is also characterized by this lack of authoritarianism; little effort is made to specifically direct the child's assimilation of cultural routines and in a great deal of learning children are left to work out their own answers to problems. In general, the child grows up easily and independently and with a large amount of freedom from supervision and authority. What are the consequences of these patterns for Kaska personality?

In the first place, we note that sphincter training is not severe and therefore is not a situation in which parental disciplines can frustrate the child's capacities. Integrated as it is with other parental attitudes, toilet training is conducive to developing a sense of independence and personal responsibility. The absence of severe discipline or authoritarian attitudes therefore lends to the oedipal situation a flavor of permissiveness. The child's individuality is respected and no sense of blind obedience is ever imposed. Among the most important results of these patterns are the development of deference, egocentricity, and flexibility.

Deference is directly learned from the injunctions of parents warning children against aggression but is also indirectly assimilated in the absence of a frustrating and authoritarian oedipal situation. Following the child's emotional rejection, no new blocks or frustrations are set in the path of the developing ego, although it cannot be denied that the personality continues to carry the memory of this trauma whose anxieties continue to interfere with the richest development of ego functions. Kaska parents, therefore, do not demand sub-mission and self-abnegation which in an authoritarian climate may undermine self-esteem and engender hostility.[92] In the absence of such instigations to hostility, the positive lessons of parents against aggression can take a firm hold. This learning, it must be pointed out, further takes place in a personality whose emotional expressiveness, because of the emotion-ally isolating tendencies of the parents, is not being strongly stimulated. Positive injunctions to deference are therefore uncontested by alien forces or labile emotionality. The picture may be characterized as one of introversive isolation, and it is in such a restrictive setting that the tendencies of egocentricity, emotional isolation, and deference become intensified. The nonauthoritarian parents influence the adoption of a religious view lacking a stern, authoritarian, nondeferent deity such as might be traced back to a harsh parental image.

The previously achieved degree of ego tonicity is maintained by the fact that shame and ridicule are not used as disciplinary measure. In the absence of a strongly inculcated sense of duty and obedience, the child, to a considerable extent, decides his own course of behavior against the introjected standards of his group. This does not imply failure to teach the child what is expected of him. The emphasis in such teaching, however, is to preserve the child's initiative, an effect that is further aided by the absence of constant adult watch-fulness, supervision, or overprotection. The Kaska child finds this freedom to develop res-ponsibility and independence congenial, perceiving the value of these attitudes as defenses against the traumatic effects of emotional rejection and regressive dependence. He gradually drops the overt forms of a compulsive search for love and is better off than he would be in a society that not only patterned a withdrawal of affection but also prevented the develop-ment of egocentric attitudes. The expressed fear lest a child be "pleased" too much (that is, lest the child be spoiled) may be understood as a desire to avoid inordinate permissiveness. Apparently it is not rare for permissiveness to be carried to extremes. On the other hand, it must be recognized that some parents exercise closer supervision and stricter discipline than is generally approved of.

The lack of strong parental direction and the fact that the child is left to learn many cultural routines for himself have consequences not only in further preventing the formation of a strong superego (based on the parental image) but in encouraging resourcefulness and self-sufficiency. They also make any idea of submission distasteful in later life. Such encour-agement would be of little avail without the good infantile care which originally prepared the ego to exercise forms of active mastery. Early necessity for resourcefulness, in providing the emotional readiness to invent problem solutions, plays a large role in developing the

[92] See Fromm, *Selfishness and Self-love* (1939), 514; Schilder, *Goals and Desires of Man* (1942), 49-50; Levy, *Hate as a Disease* (1943), 357-358.

practicality of the Kaska adult. From this we also learn more about how the empirical reality system gets its start in childhood. Among the Kaska, empiricism is related to good infant care, an oedipal pattern which stresses independent learning, discouragement from playing with impractical toys, encouragement of independence and self-sufficiency as defenses against emotional isolation, and the impossibility of overtly indulging passive dependent attitudes in parents.

The oedipal pattern we have described can certainly not lead to the projection of a strong authoritarian deity, and indeed the Kaska have refurbished the creation myth partially taken over from the Bible. Jesus (or God) is several times puzzled by his problems and there is no idea of God as omnipotent. The lasting idea of people as fallible and limited in their resources is another effect of the oedipal pattern and goes to reinforce the egocentric dictum: "I must do this by myself."

The influences of early parental attitudes, in association with moderate ego tonicity, on other aspects of flexibility are not hard to discern. With few rewards for the fulfillment of obligations, children are not required to learn the meaning of futurity. Compulsive qualities like duty and perfectionism are not demanded of the child nor are they available in his social environment for imitation. Similarly such compulsive ways of behaving are not acquired by the child while undergoing toilet training, where the stress on the child's preparedness and conformity are relatively mild. Few rules or formalized methods of procedure are given the child to follow. He sees no emphasis on planning and his moderate ego strength does not lead him to attempt to develop such notions. As a result, the adult is marked by a flexible approach to life which is largely used for passive purposes, to remove him from critical situations which threaten his ego resources.[93]

Identifications. Important stimulation is given to the dominant motivations by the identifications which the child creates in the oedipal situation. One expression of the effects of these identifications occurs in the conscious and unconscious attitudes characterizing adult interpersonal relations. There is no doubt that in the very early oedipal situation, before the institution of maternal emotional rejection, the mother is the most important figure in the child's life. Largely this importance is due to the mother's gratificatory role, but it also follows from the fact that the father's economic routines frequently separate him from his family. In later childhood the mother remains a powerful and significant figure but the father now becomes an equally important personage and one who suggests himself as a target for identification by children of both sexes. It must be pointed out, however, that identification with a father, or adequate father substitute, is often difficult when families are broken and children are raised by the mother or a mother surrogate like the mother's sister or the child's grandmother. Such broken families are quite common among the Kaska. The structure of the family too has an important bearing on what identifications can be

---

[93] Among the South African Lobvedu, the absence of stern parental authority also appears to be correlated with a lack of compulsiveness and tolerance for personal variation. In this society, too, we find that sphincter control is not expected before three years of age. Nevertheless there is evidence that Lobvedu spontaneity is something different from Kaska flexibility, being related to a feeling for moderation and a distaste for striving. Among the Kaska flexibility is essentially a passive reaction *from* striving. See Krige and Krige, *The Realm of a Rain-Queen* (1943), 290–292.

cathected. The Kaska do not pattern the diffusion of parental roles among many parent extensions. The family tends to be centered in its own dwelling and parents, very much as in western society, originate most action to children. Other adults with whom the child comes into contact cannot be regarded as important for early identifications.

Following withdrawal of the mother's affectional stimulation we find in both the boy and girl a tendency to identify with the father. Undoubtedly this is due to the experience of the mother as a frustrating object, whose emotional rejection continues to live in the child's personality. In the boy identification with the father is indulged; in the girl, unless the family lacks an older son, identificatory aims are often difficult to realize. We will discuss the boy's identification first.

Following his emotional rejection, the boy sees the father as generally more assertive than the mother. The father, however, is not a warmly demonstrative person in whom the boy can realize his denied affective needs. A son may, however, associate with his father, offering the latter simple assistance. In so doing he strengthens his own egocentric and utilitarian motives as further defenses against isolation and passive tendencies. Idealization of fathers by sons is also possible because of the latters' socially important role as the chief providers of the family. As a result of the precarious emotional balance of the isolated boy, identification with the father assumes an ingratiatory quality, not because of the male parent's tyrannical family role but because the boy is afraid of losing what remains as a sole, if insufficient, source of gratification. Ingratiation to the father is demonstrated in adult relationships between men, especially between Indians and white men—police, traders, the missionaries—and was also manifested toward the ethnographer. The relationship is, however, a deferent one; the father is rarely authoritarian and his behavior toward the boy expresses respect. These attitudes are also expressed between adult men and are partly responsible for the deferent individualism that is maintained in interpersonal relations. Yet the boy, for all the permissiveness extended to him, is not a tyrant in the family. He cannot deliberately offend or refuse to obey, although he can remain absent from camp for long periods. Tact, therefore, becomes essential in interpersonal relations lest hostility be aroused. This attitude also persists through life in the organization of deference.

Like her brother, the girl cannot successfully identify with the mother who emotionally isolates her. She too forms an early emotional attachment to the father and, particularly in the absence of an older son, often earns considerable satisfaction from this identification, accompanying her father on short hunting and trapping trips and, as she matures, striving to emulate the father's role as a food provider. Fathers may even offer daughters a certain amount of encouragement in this behavior. The girl's identification with the father encourages her ego development by developing the same goals, egocentricity and utilitarianism, which are patterned in the boy. We can now understand the masculine striving of women as a phenomenon partly following from identification with the father and generalization from maternal rejection to the feminine maternal role. Because of her cross-sexed identification, the girl probably becomes better able to manage intersexual relations than is the boy. Her warm attitudes toward men and her readiness to offer men emotional comforts are partially derived from this relationship.

One important class of identifications may be briefly stated, that occurring between like-sexed siblings. Between brothers this relationship often has an ambivalent quality, the functions of which are not clear, but between sisters the ties are very warm and probably give the girl a greater measure of emotional security than the boy has any opportunity of achieving. Yet sibling relationships are also influenced by the emotional isolation which never permits the child to relax completely affectional detachment.

Childhood activities. From six or seven years of age the Kaska girl is introduced to house-hold duties, often in spite of her reluctance, while the boy's economically productive role does not begin for many more years. From this age, however, both sexes are usually thrown increasingly in the company of like-sexed parents or siblings from whom they begin to per-ceive the nature of their economic roles. Meanwhile play continues until with adolescence there begins the first stirring of the sexual impulse signalling adulthood.

The early domestic role of the girl has important effects in modifying, to some extent, the egocentric component of her personality and preparing her for the relatively passive female role. She is given an opportunity to develop capacities around the camp and uncon-sciously utilizes her serving role to remove some of the pain of isolation. The cooperation of the family's female relatives further provides some affectional gratification and is accom-panied by a slight diminution of egocentricity. In general, however, the girl executes her role in autonomous terms and with a degree of individual responsibility which prevents any great development of passivity.

Egocentricity is less hindered in the boy. In the absence of early tasks, his career is freer and less subject to control and demands. On the other hand his development is more discontinuous than the girl's for, following childhood's period of freedom, he is confronted with the responsibilities of a man sized role. The situation is one which invites confusion. The fact that the boy is not trained for active serving is an important factor in this confusion and one which, in a setting of moderate ego tonicity, is responsible for the conflicts over responsibility in the adult male. On the other hand the boy comes to appreciate the values of work and general self-assertion as defenses against emotional isolation,[94] but the fact that with adolescence these gratifications entail more of a sense of duty and become less a matter of choice adds to confusion and increases readiness for dependence.

With puberty the personalities of both sexes are quite fully formed. Two behaviors appear in puberty which, perhaps, have not been clearly accounted for in the earlier de-velopment of the personality—homosexuality and promiscuity.

Three factors seem responsible for male homosexuality. The first of these is affectional neglect by the mother. This leads to the second factor, the boy's ambivalence to women, or his greater confidence in relations with youths who respect egocentric demands and do not immediately threaten emotional isolation. In other words, the passivity of homosexuality is not as threatening as dependence on women. Ambivalent feelings toward girls are also expressed in childhood, in the boy's teasing of girls, for example, a behavior which cul-minates in sexual teasing. The third factor in male homosexuality is identification with the father and the consequent development of positive attitudes toward all men; homosexuality, therefore, is unconsciously directed toward securing stronger emotional satisfactions from

[94] See Fromm, *Escape From Freedom* (1941), 30.

men than could originally be obtained from the father and than dare be sought from women who, unconsciously, are mother equivalents.

The development of homosexuality in girls is not so clear. Important factors seem to include the strong positive ties between sisters, the girl's greater ability, conditioned by early cooperation among female members of the family, and fear of the aggressive components of intersexual sexual interaction. As a result of her egocentricity, the girl is not attracted to being a masochistic sexual object. Among members of her own sex she has greater opportunity to receive affectional gratification without threat to egocentricity.

The developmental significance of promiscuity has already been mentioned as signalling a woman's rebellion against the serving role which was never wholly congenial to her egocentric orientations. In the boy varied sexual intercourse complements his economic self-assertive roles and is also a means of overcoming the potency anxieties which appear with his awakening genitality.[95]

Conclusion. Our survey of the development of Kaska ethos in childhood has stressed the patterning of the dominant motivations, to a lesser extent illustrating their early expression. We have remained conscious of the need to avoid such simplification as would lead to correlating a dominant motive with any one specific childhood pattern. The situation is far more complex. At each moment in development, impacts on the child operate on what is already present and this cumulative process continues throughout childhood.

With this picture of the development of the ethos we have also finished the description of Kaska ethos. From a sample of the society's population we have sought to relate personality and culture to meet the definition of ethos. The result of this attempt is a theory subject to all the logical and empirical tests of coherency, reliability, and validity demanded of any scientific statement. How well the theory will sustain these tests remains to be determined.

[95] Fromm, *Sex and Character* (1943).

APPENDIX A: PERSONALITY MATERIALS

OUR purpose in this appendix is to throw into relief five Kaska individuals, three men and two women. For most of these we have some autobiographical material to illustrate how their personalities developed. The P-data sheets for four of these persons also reveal their personalities in action. While we also have abundant personality data for Nitla, sufficient interpretations of his behavior have already been given to make any further analysis repetitious.

We shall see that although all of these Indians possess relatively similar world and self-views, in each idiosyncratic factors cause different expressions of the dominant motivations. Just as every individual in a society is conditioned by the social group in which he is born, so every person is also influenced by personal experiences. We do not assume that any of these subjects are typical of Kaska society, although one or another may be closer to some aspects of the ideal norm than others. Nor can it be said that they have all been selected from the more atypical, extraversive, or articulate members of the group, although the absence of a proportionate number of women certainly indicates some degree of unavoidable selection. Nitla, however, is certainly not a cultural deviant. Apart from the fact that the culture facilitated work with men, selection operated in the choice of subjects to the extent that potential collaborators had to belong to the Upper Liard tribe or camp on the north bank of the river where the ethnographer's residence was maintained. Practical difficulties made this limitation essential, but does not necessarily produce biased results. In the future it would certainly be desirable to repeat observations with members of other tribes.

The order for each subject will be to present first an autobiographical sketch which, for convenient reading, has been edited and arranged in proper sequence. No autobiography was obtained from Louisa Man. Little attempt has been made to transform life history material into literary narratives. Following this sketch, the Rorschach scores of all but one subject (no record was obtained from Harry Lang) will be given and interpreted. Finally, we will describe how each of these subjects, Nitla excepted, behaved during the term of field work, drawing upon the P-data sources for dreams, conversational remarks, and illustrative incidents. An analysis will seek to relate this behavior to the dominant motivations already described.

OLD MAN

Autobiographical Sketch

My father's father, Whiskers, was a Tagish Indian. He was born in Tagish country— maybe west of Whitehorse near the salt water. He often talked about salt water to his children. One year he put up nearly ten thousand salmon for the winter, he told us. Whiskers lived to be about eighty-four and then died at Ross River. My father's mother was also a Tagish Indian. She was one of Whiskers' four wives and her name was Šandma—Old Dog Mother.

My mother's father, Tsistsaza—Long Hair Man, belonged to the Liard River country and told me many stories about his people. He died about the time the Yukon gold rush

passed through this country (1898). He was very old before he died but still traveled around
in a dugout. For many years he had been known as a good trapper and traded at McDame
Creek, where there were many miners. He used to wear his hair long and still had the scars
in his ears and nose where earplugs and septum plugs had been worn. His brother-in-law,
Enainta—Big Speaker (Chief), was headman. I don't remember anything about my mother's
mother. She died before I was born.

My father, Kendekas, or Walks in a Rough Place, was born at Ross River where he
helped his father fish. Upon growing up he met a girl from the Liard River country, River
Joe's sister, who had come to the Pelly country to fish for salmon. He stayed with her and
came down here to live. Later he went to Dease Lake where he worked, packing things by
horse to the miners up McDame Creek. One of these miners was Dan McDames, who had
been the first man to find gold at McDame Creek.

I was born at the head of the Liard River about two years after my mother and father
had returned from Dease Lake. They returned to the Upper Liard with my older brother,
Sam. My folks died when I was three years old. When I was just a little bit of a kid, I
couldn't walk yet, I started to run someplace. I fell and hit my head on a stump. You can see
the hole yet. Maybe that's why I grew so small. Another time my brother called me to
come but I couldn't walk, I just crawled to him. My father died first. He was head sick.
Then my mother died of stomach trouble. I can still remember my mother coughing but
I never thought about sickness. They took my mother out to the brush. My father's brother
helped carry her body and then he helped raise me. I had nobody to cry to when I was
small; I tried to make toboggan for myself, a small one, but I burned it by putting it too
close to the fire. When I was a small child I was shy. I had no true mother and there was
nobody to make anything for me. Once, when I was a little boy, we came down to Lower
Post and some white people gave me chewing tobacco and yeast bread. Those things smelled
so strong that I left them lying alongside the trail. Pretty soon my uncle came behind me.
He saw this stuff and brought into it camp. When he asked me why I had left tobacco and
bread lying by the trail, I told him they smelled so strong that I figured they weren't good.
That time people didn't care much for white grub anyway. That time they were killing
kids down here in Lower Post, calling them witches. They didn't want me to get killed, so
they took me to Pelly River.

Once, when I was small, there were many people sleeping in the camp. A little hunt
dog that came from the Tahltan was sleeping next to the fire. Suddenly my mother called
everyone and said: "Look, wolf!" Sure enough, a wolf was sneaking up to the camp. Nobody had a gun. The wolf sneaked up to the fire and grabbed the half-starved dog. He bit
him in a good place, so that the dog could let out only one squeal. Then the wolf packed the
dog away. As he began to eat, a Selkirk Indian in the next camp shot and killed the wolf.
He covered the animal with a mountain of snow—like a coffin—and said: "Don't let anybody come around that place. That's danger there." My mother [mother's sister] wouldn't
let us go there. The next day we moved the camp. That's what the Selkirk Indian told us to
do. Another time, when I was a little bit of a boy, I was packing meat. I had only a little
pack but I became played out. Still I kept on going. It was moonlight and my brother was
walking ahead of me. Suddenly I heard a noise. Wolves coming! I thought there must be

fifty. I became frightened and yelled to my brother as loud as I could. My brother came back with a gun. He fired and a wolf dropped right behind me. Every one of them fell as my brother fired. That stopped the pack. My mother used to warn us children not to go out at night. She told us if we went out after dark, the last thing people would hear would be our yells when an eagle carried us up in the air.

After a while I went to Ross River to live with my mother's sister and her husband. This was the first year that the trader had started a post on an island in the river. Four years later they moved the post a half-mile to the Pelly River. I remember it was winter and we went there with toboggan, the people dragging it because there were few dogs then. There were many Indians camping at the post. The storeman, Dan, had bunks in the house for the Indians. When we got there we saw many things. That year we stayed at the post for two nights. The storeman promised to raise me when I was ready to live with him.

At this time my mother told me many stories. She told me about a woman who could never snare any gopher but would come home empty-handed and eat lice. She grew weaker and weaker. Finally, the lice started coming out of her nose. The people thought that she must have swallowed them without chewing and the lice continued to live inside her body. Finally the woman died. When I was small my mother had many lice. People that time could never get rid of them; they didn't even try, but just picked and chewed them. My brother always used to eat marrow with a scissors. He was only five years old. One cold day, the scissors froze against his lower lip. He cried for his mother and they put boiling water on the metal to free it. Later water came out of his lip.

Soon I started trapping for the first time. I had about twelve traps, including ten iron traps that Dan gave me. We went to Pelly River and I caught ten marten. We came to Pelly Banks, where there was a small post run by Mr. Mail. Here I bought a .22. I was going to buy a big gun, but my brother told me it would be too heavy. Towards spring my uncle died from a hole in the side of his body through which rotten stuff poured. He thought that, because he had taken away a man's gun, somebody was making bad medicine for him. The man had owed him some money. It was April when he died and we were living in an open camp. They took him to Pelly Banks, where the white people insisted on building a coffin for the body.

In the summer my aunt went to Ross River, remembering Dan's promise to bring me up. Dan took me away from my folks and brought me to his home across the slough. He was going to raise me because he had no son. I was wearing ragged clothes. Dan and another man threw away my clothes. They bathed me and gave me nice things to wear. My aunt cried but I didn't. I was satisfied and figured I was going to live good. The next morning I began to help Dan plant spuds. My mother missed me and I could hear her crying every evening on the island across the slough where many Ross River Indians were living. She was really my aunt, but just the same as my mother. The Indians were living on store grub and in open camps—just a tarp covering bedding and other stuff. Although my mother had nine sons, two of them married, she still missed me because I had done a lot of work around the camp. She didn't want me to live with the white man because she wanted me to be an Indian, like an old timer. She thought that after she died I would look after my sister [cousin]. She knew I was good hearted and kind.

In August my mother still had quite a few marten that her husband had trapped. She came to see Dan with the skins and said: "I'll give you three hundred dollars to buy my kid back. He's my sister's son." A half-breed was the interpreter. Dan said: "I don't want your money. We'll give you back your son in two days." Then they gave me back to her. They also gave her a pile of blankets and plenty of grub. They gave me back because my mother cried so much. I went with her toward Pelly River and we stayed there for two years. I trapped marten and some lynx.

I never thought about girls and marriage. I just looked to my traps. I never got into any fights. Then my mother died of indigestion. Her daughter's husband, my brother-in-law took her down to Pelly Banks and buried her near where my uncle was buried. We stayed at Ross River a while, trapping the country, and then came down close to Frances Lake where we found the tracks of many people. We followed the tracks and found Enainta's son. This was the first time they had come to Frances Lake. Usually they lived in the Hyland River country. We stayed with them till spring came on and then the old chief called a meeting. He talked a long time about how wise people had been in the old days and how good the old people had been in caring for widows. The chief took me and said I was going to help him till he got old. I worked with him for about a year. Then my cousin, Little Willy, saw me and I went down to Lower Post with him. We went to the Hyland River to trap; Skipper came along too. We came back to hunt beaver on the Liard around Albert [Cormier] Creek, where the bridge is now.

When my brother [cousin], Willy, was full grown, he suggested we go down to Fort Liard. So we walked through Hell's Gate Canyon and then made a scow. I was about twenty-five years old then. Fort Liard was a nice place. We bought an outfit and I decided to come back again in two or three years. Then we went to Fort Nelson. The post was on the east bank near the mouth of the Muskwa River. Here we met people who were very much like the Fort Liard people, but nicer. I figured I'd get married here, having my eyes on a nice girl, Marie. Her father was white and her mother came from Fort Norman on the Mackenzie. She left the key to the house for me and I went there about twelve o'clock at night. I climbed up the ladder to her room. Downstairs her folks were drunk. I stayed with her that night. I went home in daylight and came back the next night. We did this until one time her mother came upstairs and found me. She asked me if we were going to be married and I said we were. Her mother said that was all right. But Marie's father didn't want it. He wanted Marie to marry a white man.

I came back to Lower Post and found Oscar Anderson running the store here. I worked for Anderson a long time, helping around the store, hauling wood and water, cleaning, and working in the garden. He treated me fine and always gave me a drink. One time Old Anderson met me when I was so drunk that I couldn't walk but crawled. He asked: "Can I carry you home?" "No," I said, "I can make it." The next day he asked me: "What were you drinking?" I told him, two bottles of rum. He said that was all right but warned me not to drink home brew. "You'll kill yourself that way," he promised. In the winter time I trapped for fur.

Then, one summer, I went to work tracking boats up Dease River for the Hudson's Bay Company. Since then I haven't been off the river for a single year until this summer.

Any strangers coming from Telegraph Creek knew me as a good river man and they'd hire me to take them down to Lower Post.

A few years later I went back fo Fort Liard to sell some skins. Before I went I bought a little outfit. Oscar helped me. He gave me good advice. "Don't trade for credit," he said, "They cheat you every time. If the storeman doesn't use the scale make him use it. Tell him we're going to report him if he doesn't use it." At that time the storeman in Fort Liard never used money. He just wrote and said: "You've got so much." Old Anderson warned me: "If he does that, you can ask for cash." I took about twenty skins to Fort Liard. Old Kean came too. He had about thirty beaver. I sold my fur and the storeman started to write it down. "You've got one hundred dollars in skins." he said. "What do you mean?" I asked. "You'd better give me cash." "This is just as good as cash," the storeman replied. "We want our money," I told him. When he went to the till he said. "I have only two hundred dollars here." I told him: "You're not going to use that for yourself, that's for the Indians." The Fort Liard Indians looked at us. He gave us all that money but said: "You'll spoil the Fort Liard Indians." "Should be all over the country like that," I told him.

In Telegraph Creek I had met Pallgrave, the Protestant churchman, who baptized me. When I got to Fort Liard I met Father Grouard. He warned me not to believe what the Protestant missionaries said about the Catholics and said the Protestants were wrong in what they preached. He asked me if I wanted to be baptized and I agreed. Later I told Pallgrave that Father Grouard had baptized me. He became angry and said I had already been baptized a Protestant.

One time I ran eighty miles across the portage from Telegraph Creek to Dease Lake. I started at seven o'clock in the morning and got there about half-past seven at night. only stopped for a little lunch. Gosh, when I got there, how my feet swelled up!

Four years after I started to work on the river, in 1914, I married Nelly. Her mother was a Nelson Indian and part Cree. Her father used to be in this country but went to Fort Nelson to work on a boat. Her parents had moved back to Lower Post about two or three years before. We were engaged for two years and when I wasn't in Telegraph Creek or working on the river I slept with her. In the winter I trapped with Nelly's father thirty miles down the Liard, near the Muddy River. My brother said: "You stay here too long just playing. You better marry her." Then we stayed together in front of everybody. She was a good wife and a good worker. In 1915 we had our first kid, a boy.

When I was first married and had only one child, I was like all young fellows. I didn't try to rustle but lay around most of the time. I hunted all right but gave all the meat away. My brother warned: "You're going to wake up yet." My wife then gave birth to a girl. I asked my brother for a hundred dollars to buy an outfit. He said: "You won't get it." He let me have fifty dollars to buy some stuff. We didn't carry much grub, a hundred pounds of flour was enough for me. I bought a case of milk and other stuff. That kid liked to eat all the time. My brother said: "You'd better rush." One time I made seventy lynx. That was during the first war and prices were way down. I got about four dollars for a lynx and two dollars for a good black marten. Nelly gave birth to three children. We were trapping near Teslin Lake when she died of flu in 1919.

My mother-in-law took care of the children and sometimes I lived there too. I used to talk fun to my father-in-law, but he was always kind of shy and old fashioned in his ways. My wife's youngest sister, Agnes, who was only sixteen, helped me. She used to cook for me but was too shy to sleep with me. When I tried to talk fun with her, she became angry and ran away. In 1921 Agnes agreed to marry me. A few years later Father Allard came to this country. He was always after me and the other people to get married in church. Finally I asked: "Why not get married yourself? Why do you want to stay single all the time?" The priest looked at me a long time. Then he said: "You must be crazy." I got married in the church at McDame after I started to hunt for Father Allard. He used to pay me for the meat I brought.

One day, while we were camping at River Joe's place, Agnes came to the tent. She was nearly crying because River Joe had accused her of being stingy. She always watched the grub carefully and had refused to give him some coffee.

Winter time we trapped up the Dease River. One summer I got a job in a mine around McDame Creek. My job was to roll gold-bearing ore out of the tunnel—an easy job. They paid me eight dollars for an eight hour day. River Joe found me working there and also wanted to get a job. I told him to see the boss. He worked in the mine two days. Then he said: "I'm a damn fool to work here. I got lots of money down at McDame." I warned him not to talk like that; the boss might hear him. Joe answered: "I just talk fun." But I saw the boss watching us. That night Joe was fired. "You got enough money," the boss told him. "What's the matter, you crazy?" Joe blustered. But the boss wouldn't have him back. We quit work on the tenth of October.

Sometimes, Saturdays, they took out a bottle. "No good for Indian," they explained. "That's right, no good for Indian," I answered. They would take some drinks. Then they would give me a couple. "That's enough," they'd say. Good old fellow, that boss. Sundays he always sent me out for goats. "You take salt," he told me. "Salt good, goats come around." He just talked fun. I got goats every time I went up the mountain. There were many goats up there.

One day River Joe's brother, Old Wiley, came to the mine. He saw me tip the ore cart over and thought I had been killed. He went home and told my wife—his sister-in-law—that I was dead. A couple of days later, Agnes came down to the mine. She saw me and started to laugh. "I came to see your body, "she said. "We had twelve moose drying. My mother said: 'Go to see his body.'" My wife stayed at the mine for two nights. When she left, the boss gave her lots of extra grub to take home—enough for four dog packs.

A year or so later, I took a party of Americans up to Frances Lake. They carried a big outfit. "You fellows can't eat all those fourteen tons," I told them. "We're twelve men," one of them said. Gosh, they had a big load. Then I started working for Bill Strong, freighting on the Dease. Once we went down the Stikine to Wrangell. I had a good time there. All the young fellows treated me. They took me into the bar and lined up many glasses of beer in front of me. They told me to drink them. "Too much," I said, "I can't drink all that!" But they insisted, and I drank it all down like water. We drank all night till I was broke. Then we went out. We came to a place where they had been laying cement. There was a fence around the wet stuff, but one young fellow jumped into the wet cement and sank down to his knees. His friends pulled him out but his shoes remained stuck in the cement.

When I was in Wrangell, a Tlingit Indian asked me to come to his house to eat. They served seal meat. I didn't like the smell of the hind quarter they put on my plate. It smelled terribly strong. Anyway I ate it. The next time I saw this man, he asked me to eat with him, but I couldn't touch the meat. Later Bill Strong went to Juneau. There they put me on the radio and I talked with somebody in Seattle. One day I saw a one legged beggar sitting on the ground in Juneau. Everybody who passed threw him some money. So I sat down at a corner too and collected nearly a dollar until Bill Strong came along and found me.

Winter time we began to trap up the Liard River. That was my grandfather's country and I wanted my children to grow up here. For a long time I used to trap in British Columbia but too many kicks started coming. They talked about registering. Billy Barre got fined. He was trapping on the other side of the river and the policeman caught him. I told Billy "If I stay here, I'll get fined too. I'd better go away." Indians are not supposed to have to register. Its Billy's fault. He went after the policeman and signed that registration book. Up on the Liard I never had any trouble, except that my family died off.

In 1930 I lost my wife from heart trouble. She died in her sleep. She had borne about six children and my mother-in-law again looked after them. Gosh, I felt bad. I got drunk and stayed drunk, and even tried to kill myself. Little Louisa cried all night. My old boss, Oscar Anderson, told me: "You're going to be just the same. You're not going to live forever." Then my daughter died. A priest came up the river and he ordered me to open the girl's coffin. "Why do you want me to do that?" I asked him. The priest said he wanted to be certain that the girl had not been put to death as a witch. That made me angry. "Do you think I would kill my own daughter?" I told the priest that I didn't follow such old fashioned thinking. Just before the girl died she had said to me: "Don't try to save me. I'm no good to you. I can't break trail. I can't hunt. I'm only a girl." All together I had nine daughters but just one boy. He died when he was small, perhaps from T. B. A great deal of froth came out of his mouth.

Old Wiley, my wife's sister's husband, came up to the Liard country after me, maybe ten years ago. He liked to move around all the time. When he stayed here I let him use my line across the river. He took it. I let my son-in-law use that line now.

One summer a Slave woman from Fort Liard met me in Lower Post. She had lost her husband in 1934 and now asked me to marry her. At first I just helped her with clothing and food. That time my children were nearly all getting married. Anna married John Kean after her sister died. But Anna left John because he didn't treat her well. One time I came back to camp and found my cache nearly empty. I knew that John had taken my stuff and I told the police. The policeman investigated but said he couldn't do anything because John had been hungry. John still has it in for me. He told me: "You reported me many times." That's not true. I reported him only once. Later Anna married Harry Lang. Harry didn't want to trap. He still never has enough grub. One time I told his uncle, Nick Lang, that Harry doesn't want to work. Nick said that I should leave the boy alone and not help him out. He told me I'm spoiling the boy. But I can't let my grandchild starve. Once I told Harry I wouldn't help him anymore. Harry went away and stayed with his uncle, but he came back again inside of a year. His uncle is too hard to get along with. After a couple of years Harry started to bother another woman—Stella Wiley. Stella didn't want him. I told Anna not to say anything. "Just wait," I said. There were other men she could marry. Anna cried a little. I told Harry if he quit me, maybe I could get another son-in-law and this time one whom I wouldn't have to feed. That time a fire broke out in Stella's tent. Everybody rushed out of my cabin. John Kean rushed into the tent and threw out the three kids. Harry didn't want to help. Two years ago Harry became very ill and we had to send him to Watson Lake. He's not really well yet.

Then Paulette married Hans Donnelly. Hans doesn't trap far. Winter time he goes to Simpson Lake and meets the Frances Lake Indians. He plays cards with them instead of working his trap line. With a child to take care of, he needs money. A single man can take it easy but a married man has to rustle. Last winter Hans didn't begin to trap till February. As long as the boys have some grub left they don't worry. Since three years ago, when we finished a bottle of rum and keg of fresh homebrew at Old Kean's place, Hans' stomach has been sick.

Another girl of mine was married in church to River Joe's boy, Bud. But he quit her and ran after Richard Day's sister. It's Bud's fault that he quit my daughter, but River Joe lays all the blame on the girl. The policeman gave Bud good advice when he quit his wife. He told Bud: "If you want to stop trouble, go back to your wife. You've got two children. I'll come back tomorrow. If you're sleeping alone, you'll be free." The policeman came back the next night but found Bud and the Day girl sleeping together. He arrested Bud and the girl. The girl's father reported it. The policeman asked me: "What are we going to do now?" I told him: "Do what you like, I have nothing to say. I know nothing about law."

Six years went past before I asked this Slave woman from Fort Liard to marry me. Now she didn't want to. I promised her that if we were married by the church, I would never leave her. But she was afraid of my mother-in-law. Then one day she heard my mother-in-law tell me to get another wife as she had no more daughters to give me. My mother-in-law warned me that I might lose my life. "I don't like to see you cook too long for yourself and wash your own clothes. Get yourself a woman." Nick Lang told me: "Marry that old woman. I'll help you make a living." Nick's brother, Peter, had married two of the old woman's daughters and both girls had died. Now Nick wanted someone to care for her. So this Slave woman changed her mind and we were married by Father Poullet in 1941. When we started living together I had trouble. She wanted to wear sweaters at night. She wouldn't eat from the table and she couldn't cook well. She told me I could leave her if I didn't like her ways. I said: "You should learn. Don't cook straight meat all the time." Sometimes she would start to cry. Now she is getting better. The first years after we were married she was strong, but now she is getting weaker. About five years ago she said: "Looks like you're going to have a baby." I went out and killed three moose. When I came back, she said: "Looks like I lost your baby." She had been cutting wood. I felt bad.

When they started to build Watson Lake Airport I got a job there for the spring. In the summer I went on the river again. They were handling a lot of freight on the river that year and altogether I earned about fifteen hundred dollars. Then I dislocated my hip. I couldn't walk. I suffered all winter and didn't trap much. The next spring I went to the hospital in Whitehorse—flew up on a plane. The doctor took my leg and gave it a twist. "Its going to hurt," he said. I couldn't see anything just stars. Then I heard the bone snap. It went back into place. I stayed in the hospital ten days and before I left the doctor told me not to lift anything for about a year and not to walk too much. He also told me not to drink. Right after I left the hospital I met an old friend who told me to come with him for a drink. I drank and drank and then could hardly walk home. While I was walking through the streets I met this doctor. "What's the matter with you?" he said. I told him I had had a few drinks and he laughed. That winter I didn't trap at all.

RORSCHACH RECORD AND ANALYSIS

The quantitative results of the test given to Old Man follow:

Total Responses = 12

W	1	8.3%	M	3	25.0%	H	4	33.3%	P	7	58.3%
D	8	66.6%	FM	1	8.3%	A	3	25.0%	O	5	41.6%
Dd	1	8.3%	F+	4	33.3%	Ad	1	8.3%			
S	2	16.6%	F−	3	25.0%	AObj	3	25.0%			
			CF	1	8.3%	N	1	8.3%			

M:sum C = 3:1

(FM+m):(Fc+c+C') = 1:0

VIII, IX, X/R = 27.2%

Ap. = ((W)), D!!, Dd S!!!!

Suc. ?

Old Man's record departs in several aspects from the mean picture obtained from an analysis of the adult protocols. Most of these departures represent the influence exerted on his personality by close relationships with white men. The outstanding feature of the performance is a drive for achievement incommensurate with the subject's capacities. In Old Man's daily behavior this drive is completely verified in his greater foresightedness, his readiness to assume work for wages with white men, his predilection to form close attachments with white men, and using these friendships to secure favors. Furthermore, the record reveals greater enthusiasm, imagination, and vision than the majority of the protocols. All these self-expansive attributes, however, are integrated in a setting of only moderate ego feeling.

The complete record indicates that the attitudes that characterize Old Man's departure from his cultural norm are only superficially related to his basic personality. The drive to achievement is stifled by emotional inhibitions quite typical of other Kaska Indians. Basically Old Man is a compliant, resigned, and passive person preoccupied with concern for himself. He possesses a readiness for meeting a fairly wide range of adaptive and social problems but is not given to critical thinking. Introversion makes him rely predominantly upon inner direction rather than on environmental stimulation. The burden of a basic or primary anxiety is also present, pointing to childhood trauma, but seems to have been in some measure overcome by the assertive trends, which were probably adopted for defense and to reward the subject with a feeling of self-confidence. When the primary anxiety is aroused, as by the black-gray cards, its unsettling results show in a disorganization of performance and inner control, revealing how little capacity for struggle the man really possesses.

Intellectually, Old Man is practical minded. He has little capacity for the degree of organization to which he aspires. The interest in other people, revealed by the test, is also reflected in his readiness to gossip and probably contributed to making him an excellent informant.

THE PERSONALITY UNDER OBSERVATION

In 1944 the ethnographer compiled a personality picture of Old Man which corresponds in many respects to the favorable picture which a number of white men in Lower Post hold of this popular Indian. The vignette follows:

> Old Man is affable and cooperative, presenting a consistently nonaggressive disposition. He manifests an alert sense of responsibility toward his family, which often serves to remind him of his growing inability to fulfill the expectations of his social role because of advancing years and illness. When his wife was ill, he showed marked depression and worry, likewise exhibiting such signs during his daughter's illness, although in the latter case he was less depressed. In his dealings with white men he often shows signs of servility, or at least extreme *politesse*. Ethically he is unimpeachable and in the ethnographer's absence was once reluctant to help himself to some carrots that we told him he could have. In discussing this incident, Old Man explained that he was afraid somebody seeing him take the vegetables would misconstrue his actions. Toward promiscuous girls he once or twice directed advice that met with little success. Yet he is reluctant to manifest himself on people who might not want his presence. If his advice is rejected, he retires without any evidence of resentment or disappointment. While this *laissez faire* attitude makes him seem rather ineffectual, it at least spares him the bitter resentment directed against someone like Nick Lang. It is doubtful if Old Man feels ineffectual. He tends to deplore the lack of initiative in the mission and church chiefs and seems to possess courage that he does not express for fear of being criticized by the community. He wants to be liked; when intoxicated he never shows hostility. At such times his ever present tendency to tease and joke becomes more pronounced. To friends he preaches a doctrine of slow drinking—"like white people." His contacts with white men have been close but he does not exploit his favorable position in this segment of the community.

Such was our impression of Old Man in 1944, after about three months of close but not intimate contact. In many respects it is a superficial picture, and one largely predicated on the notion that personality denotes the stimulus value of an individual. The true importance of many of the behavior manifestations accepted at their face value was apparent the following year, after analysis became more intense. Thus we know that Old Man does feel ineffectual and lacks the courage we generously ascribed to him. We also had no inkling of the undercurrent of hostility which the personality contained. The observation, that Old Man never sought to exploit his relations with whites, while accurate, is now known to be incomplete. What was not realized at the time was that any too manifest dependence on whites was antithetical to his basic personality. Old Man is remarkably successful in indulging dependence without making himself unduly submissive. Even his servility is not self-debasing and succeeds in making him popular with white trappers, for example, permitting him to buy liquor when it is withheld from other Indians.

During the field work period of 1945, Old Man's dreams, verbalization, and other behaviors were studied with the aim of ascertaining the dominant motivations of his personality. Besides revealing a tendency to passivity in the face of his growing physical debilities, the data show Old Man's unconscious hostility and his subjective relationship to the ethnographer.

Early in June, before rapport was firmly reestablished, Old Man showed a tendency to deny anxiety by passive dependent attitudes. "I had good rest last winter. My leg bother me and Harry Lang never let me go out." Harry, he said, did most of the trapping. Despite this assistance, Old Man admitted being "broke" except for what money his wife had earned and on which the family would live during the summer. He denied worrying.

Five weeks later there was a dream in which Old Man assisted a girl to give birth by pressing down on her abdomen. He pressed lightly for fear of injuring the girl. Soon he heard a wailing and somebody said "Baby born!" In the morning Old Man told his wife:"Maybe you're going to have baby." She denied this, saying she was too old. Asked what the dream meant, Old Man replied that a baby would be born sometime (but not soon) and that it would be difficult to deliver. Such a dream can be interpreted as a desire to have a child. Children, as we have pointed out, are regarded as of economic value. The dream reminds Old Man that if he had a boy old enough to hunt, he might be able to retire with less anxiety. The dream also suggests a realization of failing sexual powers. The subject's own interpreta-tion indicates his awareness that all of the dream's wishes are far-fetched.

As the summer went on, Old Man began to drink compulsively, using three hundred dollars of his wife's money to pay for liquor. Such behavior can be regarded as a manifesta-tion of passive trends. On August 3 he complained of his eyesight and spoke of the big money he had earned while working on Watson Lake Airport. The next day he stated that, although he used to be a good moose hunter, his eyes now hindered such activities. The previous fall he had been lucky to get a moose by shooting without being able to see the sights of his gun. Another time he had gone hunting with his wife and shot into a herd of caribou, managing to bring down ten. He said he wanted to buy glasses and wondered if the ethnographer could lend him some money. On August 12 there was an anxiety dream characterized by hostile trends such as Old Man never directly reveals.

"Fellow—I don't know his name, I forget—got shot, wounded. A tall fellow, white man. Hardly he live. He got shot in here [points to chest]. My partner [mentions the name of Marie Nolan's white husband] say: 'Here, Old Man, this is white man way. We don't want to see anything suffer. How about we finish his life?' I say: 'We got no gun.' He say: 'I gonna put eight inch nails on a pole. When the boy suffer I gonna turn it in here [points to back].' He hit the man here [points to back]. Nail go in his body. White man just fall down like that and he says: 'Good bye. . . . '"

The dream occurred while Old Man was away from home. There were no clear associa-tions, but Old Man characterized the dream as "bad," explaining that he had been thinking about people drinking in Lower Post. Aggressive impulses, fulfilled by another person, and anxiety are the principal features of the dream in which the dreamer takes the passive role, reflecting the weakening of the ego capacities. The dream also reflects aggression toward the ethnographer, the tall white man whose name could not be recalled. The suggestion of active pederasty, represented by the nail boring into the victim's back, should also not be overlooked and probably points to the beginning of Old Man's homosexual transference to the ethnographer.

The next day, while drunk, Old Man pointed out the fact that he never becomes aggressive when intoxicated and criticized Louis Maza for drunken hostility. "What's the matter Injun? Why can't he drink?" This remark is interpretable as identification with the ethnographer. When the liquor was depleted he said: "If I was girl I get something easy. Just knock on any door. Should be I dress like old woman and go around." Further passivity is revealed in this manifestation of homosexual tendencies. On August 14, while drunk, there was an overt homosexual approach to Edward Prince. As Old Man bent over the latter he said: "I'm gonna take his worm," and gestured toward the young man's genitals. On August 22, while en route to the winter settlement with the ethnographer, drinking commenced at the Bridge, and Old Man said he preferred to drink with white people who never became aggressive. "I'm shamed of my own people." He also wanted to be assured that his own behavior under the influence of alcohol was perfect. These tendencies show the growing intensity of a passive homosexual transference to the ethnographer.

In the next few days Old Man several times told, with evident pleasure, how he had shot willow grouse pointed out to him by Elsie Lang. There followed a series of dreams expressing hostility and anxiety, all characterized by the speaker receiving support from a stronger person. While these dreams resolved immediate problems arising from Old Man's quarrel with John Kean, they also reflect the general weakening of egocentricity. Independent goals were giving place to dependence. On September 9, when the ethnographer suggested that Louis Maza looked worried, Old Man interrupted with a plea for sympathy, saying: "I worry all the time."

On September 14 (at Old Kean's place) Old Man remarked that perhaps Peter Tom would soon join the people going upriver. Then he said:

> "I dream Peter give me revolver . . . I dream one Carcross Injun wants to fight us. So we scared. No use somebody kill us. Maybe I just worry about gun. So this Peter Tom give me revolver to kill this man. 'No use have trouble till I die.' I say. 'What you want to give me gun for?'"

The reference, "worry about gun," is an immediate association to the previous evening, when Adele Kean, drunk, had threatened to shoot her husband's brother, with whom she had been living. A day or so previously, Old Man had referred to Adele as a Selkirk Indian stranger and had declared that all the women of her tribe were adulterous. Asked for associations to the dream, Old Man identified Peter Tom as a hard working youth on whom Louis Maza is very dependent for meat, wood, and general assistance. To interpret the dream, Old Man is again letting somebody handle his aggressive impulses for him, but he is also revealing anxiety at his growing incapacity. He needs somebody like Peter Tom to lean on and to hunt for him, somebody with strength and resourcefulness (revolver).

On the same day Old Man repeated a folktale which he had already related to the ethnographer the previous year. In the tale a man's wife cheats her blind husband out of food. The old man is befriended by his medicine animal, a loon. The man climbs on the bird's back and is flown across a lake. The bird then dips the old man into the water. When he emerges, the man can see a little better. Once more the bird dives, and this time, upon emerging, the man discovers he can see perfectly. The loon now directs the man to his wife, but warns him to avoid trouble. Upon reaching home the man in anger kills his wife. The tale was told after a conversation in which Old Man had explained that his eyes sometimes improve for brief periods. At this point Mrs. Man left the camp, and almost immediately her husband reminded himself of the story. Analysis of the tale suggests Old Man's identification with the passivity of the leading character. The story expresses the anxiety and hostility engendered by the growing dependence of old age in which egocentricity has largely ceased to function. It also reveals that Old Man resents his growing dependence on his relatively dominant and older wife.

When Old Man's winter settlement was reached he began to complain of chronic sore throat and cough. Complaints about his sons-in-law also became frequent, although they were occasionally replaced by ostentatious flattery of Harry Lang. Old Man began to talk incessantly about his wife, criticizing her cooking and lack of progressiveness but also praising the good care she took of him. On September 27 he said: "I figger I gonna hunt every day. Can't get away." This was followed by two dreams in one night.

"I dream I eat sardine with bone. Louis Maza he feeding me that. We have brew. He say: 'Uncle, I know you been sick for long time. That's why I feeding you this.' I start to eat sardine with home brew.

"Lots more I dream. I dream on Harry. He say: 'You drink all my home brew up.' He cut me all over with a knife. I'm scared . . . After, Harry start to cry. 'I don't like to do that, make you suffer.' 'Oh,' I say, 'maybe heal up anyway.'"

No associations were forthcoming, other than the expressed fear that Harry (who was away hunting) would resent the fact that his father-in-law had taken some home brew. The second dream points directly to anxiety and dependence, with unconscious hostility toward a son-in-law, who will not fulfill his socially expected role. Old Man has nobody on whom to support his failing egocentricity. In the first dream he envies Louis Maza and indulges in regressive passive receptive oral behavior reminiscent of infancy, while in the second he steals a drink, another piece of regressive dependent behavior.

An unusual note of lack of customary optimism was struck on October 25, when Old Man left to set a fish net and to scout for moose. The ethnographer called out: "Good luck!" Old Man replied: "I don't know if I have good luck or not." On November 22 he dreamed that his wife "Have baby. She's sick. Maybe I think she's sick too long. Old woman [Metša] spirit comes back in baby [reincarnation]. Maybe she [his wife] get better in few days. I dream poor baby cry around. She want mama pretty bad. I tell her she too old for him. That baby come right to bed . . . " Several wishes are interrelated in this dream. Here is again a wish for a child and an expression of sexual inadequacy, followed by a desire for rebirth or rejuvenation. Old Metša had died a week or so previously but for Old Man the threat of death is now denied. The dream also expresses anxiety over the illness of his wife, on whose emotional comforts Old Man is ambivalently dependent. Three days later Old Man spoke of how he had attempted suicide following the death of his earlier wife.

From the end of November dreams reflect Old Man's anxiety concerning the ethnographer's forthcoming return to Lower Post and his trip out of the Cassiar. On November 27 Old Man reported: "I get scared last night. I hear dog team coming, lot of noise. Great big bell, too. I wake up. I say: 'Mama, dog team coming. Half past one too!' She hold me.

'What's the matter with you?' she say." Asked the meaning of the dream, he replied: "Means anytime some stranger coming." Did he remember such a visit by dog team late at night? "I was thinking about Nick Lang coming about eleven o'clock at night last winter." Then too he had dreamed that someone would come. "I'm dreaming about Nick before he's coming. We was drunk." Who else might be coming? "Maybe Peter Tom coming anytime this time." The dream is difficult to interpret beyond pointing to its obvious significance in relation to the forthcoming departure of the ethnographer which had been delayed by Peter Tom's failure to come upriver and guide us down. There is apparently also anxiety related to the lack of visitors; Old Man fears the loss of his popularity. The association to Nick Lang is not clear.

But why should Old Man be anxious about the ethnographer's departure? Two explanations can be given. In the first place, the unconscious transference to the ethnographer must be recalled. This unconscious, passive, homosexual relationship is threatened by the ethnographer's plans to leave. In the second place, the ethnographer's departure is being held up by the fact that there is no one to guide him and his family back to Lower Post. Harry Lang is not ready to depart. Food is running short, and the guests are becoming impatient. Old Man fears that these attitudes threaten deference; they may lead to dislike on the ethnographer's part if the latter's imputed egocentricity continues to be frustrated. Hence the anxiety.

The following night Old Man dreamed that a well known white man from Lower Post had come up the river to the winter settlement. He reported this dream ruefully, explaining that the man had wanted twenty dollars which Old Man owed him for the boat trip up the river. In the dream Old Man refused to pay, explaining that he had practically walked half the distance. The white man, however, insisted on collection. The dream seems related to financial anxiety. Old Man at the time wanted to visit his traps but was unable to leave because of his wife's illness. The situation also reveals threatened deference; by not paying his debt, as by not successfully helping the ethnographer, Old Man is imperiling his reputation and inviting loss of love. On November 30 Old Man said:

"Well, I dream Stella Wiley. That much high bed [indicates]. She tied up on leg. Her body down on the floor. I say: 'What's the matter with you, Stella?' 'I been suffer like that all winter.' 'You better take that rope off,' I say. 'I can't uncle.' Here it is lock. Somebody lose that key." Asked what this dream might mean, Old Man replied: "I don't know. Maybe she's sick." What kind of bed was Stella associated with? "Like your bed [pointing], but high." Where did he ever see a bed like this? "I never see bed like that. I know bed is larger, maybe four feet high. Stella's got long leg. I try to find key, I want to take it out. She say: 'I been like that for a whole year.' They got chain right across both legs. Maybe she's suffer, sick." Where did he ever see a chain like this? "You see chain anyplace. When you lock a house. You see chain in front of Harry Lang's home. They had little chain like that. They file it now." Old Man explained that Harry had lost or forgotten the key that was a part of the chain. Where did he ever see a leg raised like that? "I hear white people, when they got no place in jail, just hang little while. Used to be, when they got no place to put it." At this point Old Man was reminded that on the previous evening he had been talking about the custom of tying up witches by the legs. Was this perhaps connected with the dream? "Must be," he answered. "Maybe that's why I dream."

The associations are to the ethnographer's bed, the chain and lock for which Harry

Lang had lost the key, and the chaining of prisoners. The manifest content of the dream also refers to Old Man's conversations regarding witch torture and to a previous conversation in which he had told the ethnographer about his son-in-law, Harry, making sexual advances to Stella, whereupon she had repulsed him. This in turn had made Harry extremely hostile toward the girl. Interpretation reveals this to be an anxiety dream in which Old Man is once more concerned with the ethnographer's enforced stay upriver. The ethnographer is in Stella's position, being locked in a situation for which Harry has a key—i.e., we are dependent upon this man's decision to go to Lower Post. This leads directly to another aspect of interpretation. Old Man is anxious regarding Harry Lang. He cannot get rid of Harry, who often domineers him. In the dream Old Man identifies with Stella Wiley, whom Harry once sought to attack, and remembers the period of witch-fear during which some of Harry's relatives were prominent witch-hunters. Old Man's hands are tied in relation to his hostile son-in-law. He defers to the youth and would like to escape the condition, but in the dream there seems to be little likelihood that he will be able to manage. Finally the dream reflects Old Man's frustration at being kept by his wife's illness from visiting the trap line.

In the evening of the same day Old Man again referred to this dream. "I look for Stella on ice all day today—I mean animal." He explained that sometimes a dream may indicate that a hunter is going to get some game. "If you dream you play with girl," and then go hunting, a female animal is promised. In this association Old Man reveals that the dream contains a sexual component. It involves him in sadistic sexual relations with Stella. Therefore it is an expression of his ideas concerning both sexual and hunting ability, or potency in general. The nature of these ideas is probably not congenial to the dreamer; they frustrate him. To compensate for the frustration of declining potency, the dream creates a sadistic situation in which the dreamer may inordinately gratify his desire for power. The dream regarding Mrs. Louis Maza's loss of speech followed two days later. This has already been analyzed.[1]

The most significant trend to be noted in Old Man's personality is the anxiety concomitant with his approaching old age. In the face of his diminishing physical resources, specifically, failing eyesight, increasing ill health, and general debility, the egocentric motivation is seen to reluctantly yield to increasing passivity and dependence. The rise of these motives, incompatible with the self-assertive goals of egocentricity, produces anxiety and frustration from which are derived his unconscious aggressive impulses. The latter in turn dare not be directly released because of their conflict with the value of deference.

HARRY LANG

Autobiographical Sketch

My earliest memory is of a trading post sitting on a very high cutbank somewhere in Nelson River country where I was born. I could see the post from the other side of the river, but I don't know where it was. The cutbank was much higher than here at Lower Post. My mother told me there was a store on the other side of the river but she never took me across. That was the first time I ever ate a stick of candy, only then I didn't know what I was eating. I remember it was very sweet.

[1] See above, pp. 267–268.

Ever since I was about three years old my grandmother raised me. My dad quit mama and then mama quit me. She didn't like me, so it was up to grandmother to keep me. At the place where I saw that cutbank with the trading post on top, I also for the first time saw people hauling moose up the river. The storeman on the other side yelled to our people. "Moose swimming down the river." I think that's what he said but I was too young to understand. Old Charlie MacDonald and his people got in a big boat and followed the moose down the stream. I heard Charlie's father holler to the moose: "Take my bullet, that's the best bullet." In about three or four hours they brought back the meat.

My grandmother and her sister both followed one husband. My grandmother followed him around all the time. Sometimes, when she left me in camp to go out with a bunch of people, I became lonely. Once she did that and I began to cry and started out after her. Edward Cross' father, Kitsila, frightened me. He had an old muzzle loader that he filled with powder. He fired the powder at my feet. I ran home. When my grandmother came back I told her that I was going to stay with my aunt, Mildred. She told me: "Go ahead." But Mildred didn't want me. She said: "You cry too much." So I had to go back to my grand-mother.

Soon my mother took me back with her again. We crossed the river to cut wood and one of our boys caught a squirrel with a sinew snare. I wanted to steal that squirrel. I wanted it for a pet to drag around and play with. We moved to some other part of the country, I don't remember where. The next thing I remember we were staying at Lower Post. My grandmother used to come here to live every summer. That time a great flu epidemic was raging. This was during the first World War. When the flu passed, a new kind of sickness hit us. People used to jump out of their homes and sit in the snow. Nobody knew when he did that. It was during this time that Madaline died. Then when spring came, in May or June, Old Cayuse's grandchild died. The boy had already killed his first moose. He used to show me how to hunt. One day he shot a duck way out on the lake. The bird drifted down and he sent me to get it. I cried because I was afraid, but he made me go. I got the duck for him and he gave me a bite of chewing tobacco for my work. That was the first time I tasted tobacco.

This was when they tortured my uncle. They called him a witch. I saw my poor uncle tied up but I didn't know why they did that. Once I tried to untie him, but the people nearly killed me for doing it. Then my grandfather, Old Lang, came to Lower Post. We camped downriver from the stores, near where the Highway runs now. The Hudson's Bay boat came in while we were at the post, and Albert Dease found out about my uncle being tied up in the woods. Albert went in there and untied him and took the boy outside. That time mama went to Telegraph Creek and Mildred went with her. Mildred came back again in August on the boat. I stayed in Lower Post with my grandmother and Mrs. Dickson. When my aunt came back we all went down the river again. I don't know where we stopped traveling, maybe at Coal River.[2] We caught up with Old Natucka and the Stone family and stayed with them to about Christmas. After that my grandfather sent word for us to come to his place. Old Stone didn't like us to go but grandma started out. Once we got lost because we followed the wrong trail, a trail that people had used to hunt and fetch meat. The next day

[2] See Figure 1.

we turned back and took the right trail. When night came we camped. The next day we reached Old Lang's camp around noon. Old Lang had gone to Lower Post and his wife gave us meat to eat. Grandma didn't feel like eating. She told her sister: "If I eat that meat I'm going to die." Mrs. Lang asked her why. She said: "I know the flying squirrel ate that meat." Mrs. Lang said: "No, you're lying." Finally grandma ate the meat. The next day grandma became sick and Uncle Tom took me over to his camp. He kept me for about three days. Meantime my grandmother died. When he took me home I saw grandma way back in the brush on a tree. I wondered when she was going to get up again and fix the bed for me. Aunt Mildred was crying but I didn't know why. Finally my aunt fixed the bed and we went to sleep. Two days later Old Lang came home. When he heard what had happened he became angry with his wife. "Tell me why you played that dirty trick on her?" he demanded. Then the old man went to cut lumber to build a coffin for the old lady. I don't know where they buried her, but they took her down the river a way. When they came back home we all pulled out. From that time on Aunt Mildred kept me. She kept me well.

I remember one time when my aunt and I were setting marten deadfalls. I asked her why she was setting up all those funny looking sticks and logs. I didn't know about traps. My aunt told me: "I'm going to catch marten and buy some candy and clothes for you." It made me happy when she said that. After about a week we went out to look at the traps. There were no marten; the animals had taken the bait from the rear end of the traps. Aunt Mildred never set those traps again. We just traveled, going anyplace. That was a hard winter. Sometimes we had nothing to eat. It was hard to get moose. Once we camped with Piel who had killed a small beaver. It was the first time I tasted that kind of meat. At the next camp we made, I saw people chop the ice in order to set a beaver trap. I wondered what they were chopping the ice for. I didn't know what the trap was for either and wondered what they were going to do with that thing. While waiting for them to set the trap I got cold feet and so went home. When the people came back to look at the trap they didn't find any beaver.

We went down to the hot spring, where Old Tom Smith and Fred Allen were living. Tom Lang and Peter Lang started down to visit those white men with my aunt's dog. Old Tom Smith had put poison on the trail and our dog ate it. Now we had no dog. Madeline's brother had her two dogs, so they hauled our clothes, blankets, and grub. When spring came we went to Tobally Lakes. It was my first trip to that place. The people shot many swan there. The women cut the feet off and made little bags out of the skin. Leaving Tobally Lakes we went toward Lower Post and came to Lake Atsaste. Madeline's brother came to that place. When the people found him he was crazy. His old grandmother hollered at him and he began to cry. When he cried he took a piece of flint and gashed himself on the leg— all the way up. He cut his fingers too. He did these things because he wanted to die. Leaving that lake we came to Coal River. After we crossed, we went twenty miles or so up the river where we met some Mackenzie Indians—Tsatena. They lived on fish and moose up there. Uncle Tom took me with him to show me how to fish. One Tsatena gave me a big bunch of suckers. First I thought he wanted me to take them home for him, so when we got close to camp I gave them back. He told me: "You eat them." When I came home Aunt Mildred told me: "You stole those fish." I told her: "No, somebody gave them to me."

She asked me who, and I told her. "Yatse," I said. "He's going to be your uncle," Aunt Mildred told me. "I'm going to marry him." I picked up the fish. "I'm going to give them back," I said. "He talked to me but I didn't understand why he gave them to me." My aunt told me: "He will teach you."

One day I got into a fish trap and while watching it I caught many grayling. I took them home and cooked them, guts and all. When Aunt Mildred came back I told her that I had cooked fish. She tried to eat them but gave up and threw the fish to the dogs. I cried for them, but she told me: "They would kill you." The next day we pulled out, leaving the Tsatena. We went down the river and then up the Liard to Lower Post. While we were at the post, mama came back on the Hudson's Bay boat. She took me back with her. In August we started down the river again, Old Natucka, Old Stone, and Old Lang. We went forty miles down the Liard, and then Old Lang started up Iron Creek. My baby brother was born up there. I was happy when that baby was born.

Aunt Mildred went back to Watson Lake with my daddy.[3] Whenever I thought of my aunt I started to cry. Mama told me: "She's not your mother." That winter we stayed up at Baldhead Mountain and nearly starved to death. We went down again and met up with Alec, a Slave Indian from Fort Liard, and a whole bunch of people We ate moosemeat with those people until after Christmas, when Aunt Mildred came back with my daddy and my daddy's wife. We went down the river past Thirty-Mile. Old Natucka wanted us to go back to stay with him, so Aunt Mildred told mama and we went back. Old Lang didn't want me to go back but they went and took me with them. By this time they were keeping me well.

We came to Old Natucka's place and stayed with him. When spring came, my little brother took sick and they called me a witch. I didn't understand what they meant. Mrs. Piel called me that. Mama believed her and called me that too. They tied me up and hung me by the foot. Oh boy, I wish they tried that on me now! For two nights I hung there and nearly died. I heard an owl tell me: "You'll pull through!" They untied me and tied me up again. I didn't know why they were doing this to me. They asked me many questions, but I didn't understand what they wanted to find out. Once they made me go back almost thirty miles to the old camp. There they asked me: "Did you play that trick here?" "I don't know," I said. Old Madeline was up there and she told me to say: Yes." She warned me: "If you don't tell them that they're going to kill you." I believed her and told them: "Yes." Now we went back to the real camp. My hands were tied and my back was tired from traveling on the trail. They guarded me and I didn't understand why that was necessary. When we came home my little brother died. Later, while I was lying down, my hands tied and a blanket over my head, Mrs. Piel came around. The first thing I saw was my ear being cut. She was going to cut my throat—she tried but gave up. Then we started traveling. Every time we made camp my hands were tied behind my back and a blanket thrown over my face. Finally we came to a small creek, I don't remember the place, where they buried my brother. Mama pulled her scissors out. First Mrs. Piel half cut my ear and then mama finished it. She threw the piece into the fire. I could see it burning. I wished I was big! We got to Lower

---

[3] Here Harry is referring to his mother's brother. He was conceived from this couple's incestuous relationship.

Post. Mama was still watching me all the time. At the post Mrs. Piel wanted to kill me again, but I got a chance to escape. Then these kids, Little Charlie and Sylvester, suggested we play boats. They asked me how I bewitched people. I didn't know what they meant. Later I saw Mrs. Piel coming with the rope. I hid in the woods then. The whole bunch started looking for me but they never found me. Sometimes they passed close by to me, but as soon as I got a chance I beat it to another place. Finally the old man became angry. "Say," he said, "If you kill that boy I'll kill the whole works!" After being in the woods for six days I came back. Then the people started down the river but mama stayed in Lower Post. I think Frank Best, the storeman, found out about me and told the Mounties. At that time Barre, a white man, came into the country and mama went to live with him. We stayed up at Dease Lake for about a year and then went to Albert [now Cormier] Creek. Barre quit mama and she went back to the post again.

That was the first time I saw Fred Burke, a white man. Mama sent me to Albert Creek to Mildred's cabin with a dog to get a mooseskin. I saw a trail branching off and followed it to see who was there. I came across a sleigh with a big load on it but without a dog harness. Then I saw Fred Burke and Charlie Carlson. They fed me well and asked me where I came from. I told them and they gave me tobacco which I took home to mama. After I reached home mama sent me back to them again. I gave them a chicken but they fed it to the dogs. I told them: "Mama wants help." Old Burke came with me; I think he packed my sister, Papoose. We came down to the river and the next day Charlie Carlson took us down to the head of the canyon [above Lower Post.] Charlie went back from there and we fellows went down to Lower Post. I killed a moose that I caught with a dog and mama killed another moose. When the ice started to go out, a white trapper, Bob, told me to go with him. He bought clothes and blankets for me and we went down to Coal River to hunt beaver. My job was to guide him. I showed him some things but I didn't work much. He wanted me to work but I couldn't do the things he wanted. Down at Forty-Mile we met Max Croon, who went to Coal River with us. Those two men hated each other. Bob was all right, but the German hated him. We split out one day and left Max behind. Then we came across a little creek with a beaver house. Bob jumped on the house and a big beaver came out. I told him: "Beaver come out." He grabbed his rifle and killed it. The next day we went up the creek but found no beaver. We found another creek but still no beaver. Then we came to Caribou River, where we killed many beaver. On the way back we almost starved to death. We headed for the cache at Coal River and, after reaching that place, built a raft and went down to Bob's main cabin. We waited there for Angus Hall and then built two rafts. I got onto Bob's raft but the thing swamped. Then I got on Angus' raft and it was all right. Down the river we saw a moose. Bob shot a whole box of cartridges, but couldn't get the animal. Finally we caught up the with moose and Angus Hall fired two lucky shots. There was a calf too, but when we shot it the little thing sank. Angus was sorry about the calf. "Nice soft meat," he said. After loading up the meat we went downriver again. Bob had bought the policemen's dogs—this was when the police first came into the country. The dogs smelled moose and went off into the woods. We waited two days but no dogs showed up. Now we had only one dog, Angus Hall's. We started for Forty-Mile and reached there about three days after leaving Coal River. That was the time that a plane came in, the first plane. At

Forty-Mile we met two white men, Frank Perry and somebody they called Plasterer. From them we learned of the plane landing at Lower Post. I thought they were talking about a carpenter's plane. We headed for the post and built a raft to cross the Hyland River. I was their guide. In the evening we got to Lower Post. Two days later Bob left me to go outside.

Afterwards I saw a plane come in. There was a big noise. I didn't know where the noise came from. Then the Hudson's Bay boat arrived with Father Allard. He baptized us all. I couldn't understand why he poured water on our heads. That was when he took me outside to school. I don't remember how old I was—maybe about fourteen.

On the way to school we reached McDame Creek. I wasn't worried. My sister and two other girls were going to school with me. They were crying, but I laughed and told them that we would be back again. When we left McDame, Father Allard went ahead. Once the small boat in which we were traveling almost upset. Father Allard put us on the Hudson's Bay boat. After we left McDame, the boat with Father Allard and Nelson Charlie upset. It was night and we were camping when we heard somebody yelling down the river. Big George was captain. He told his boys: "Go up and see what happened." Nelson Charlie told them that everything had been lost; they had no blankets and no matches. They walked down to meet us and the men gave Father Allard a tent and blankets. I started to cry then.

After starting out the following morning we found half of the priest's outfit. We pulled up the boat and took the Elco along. At Porter's Landing, the boat left us and Marion from Telegraph Creek, took us to the head of Dease Lake. We were there a long time. Father Allard told us: "Caterpillar coming." I didn't know what he meant. Then I saw it coming out of the brush. I thought it was a big worm. We got on that worm and it made me seasick. My sister was all right and so were the other girls. When we got to Telegraph Creek, it looked good to me. They bathed me there and I put on new clothes. After waiting for the boat, we finally started down the Stikine River. This was the Barrington boat and, right close to Wrangell, Barrington said: "You tell Father Allard that you smell salt water." I didn't know what he was talking about.

In Wrangell we stayed with Mrs. Amos to wait for the big boat. Father took us to a farmer's camp for a meal. Here we got a good supper. After eating, I went outside to walk around. Then I saw the chickens. As far as I knew, they were wild chickens. I started to throw stones, trying to kill them, but I couldn't hit one. Father came out at last and explained that these people raised chickens. That frightened me, but the farmer had a good heart and said: "He doesn't know anything, anyway."

Soon I saw a big boat coming in. They told me: "That's the boat you're going to get on." First I thought a big island was coming. Father took us down to the boat at night. I hardly knew I was on a boat when it started to move. We came to Prince Rupert and saw many things. Here we stayed for three or four days and then the train came to take us to school.

It was morning when we reached the school. Father just put us to bed in a small room. The next morning they told us they would give us breakfast. They asked me my sister's name and I told them it was Marie. The other two girls were called Isabeth and Honey. I kept wondering why those women kept that white thing around their faces. The next spring my sister died, and the following winter little Isabeth died. Now only Honey and I were left, but the next summer they brought Felix Kean, Jimmy Liard, Joe Charlie, and Jennie

Charlie. I had lots of friends then, but still I didn't like the nuns. I couldn't understand them. One word I understood: "Hurry up!" That's all. Later they brought River Joe's daughter, Jenny, to school and the next summer I started back home.

When I got back to Lower Post I was sorry to see Father Allard leave me. That summer I went to a hot spring and took sick in my tonsils. Barre took me back to Lower Post to stay with my mother, only Barre was married to my aunt, Mildred, this time. For a while I lived with anybody, trying to make my living. I didn't care much about trapping. Whenever I made a little money, I spent it right away. Every summer, when he came to Lower Post, Father Allard would see me. He was going to take me out again, but he drowned the very summer that I was supposed to go. We lived across the Liard River for a while and I trapped there until Barre kicked me out. Then I trapped with Edward Prince. After that I went with Casey Jones for a while, but he got married and that left me alone again. In 1938 I got married too and went up the river. In 1939 I went down to Nine-Mile but I came back again in 1940 and I've been here ever since.

Sometimes in the winter I cook for them all. I make pie and fancy cake. I like to do that. I used to be lucky for moose. Every time I went out I got my game. Now I'm not so lucky anymore. I don't worry for myself when the grub runs out but it bothers the children. I can't let them starve. I don't think I want my boy to go to school. It's too far away. I'll teach Roger myself.

THE PERSONALITY UNDER OBSERVATION

Harry delayed a long time before giving his life story and finally did so only the day before the ethnographer's departure. Throughout our stay in his father-in-law's settlement, Harry made exaggerated gestures of generosity, giving the ethnographer game, fish, skins, and Indian manufactures for most of which he refused payment. He said, frankly, that he wanted the ethnographer to report "good word" about him when we went outside. When intoxicated, he quickly became hostile and abusive but never mistreated his wife. Two years ago he sought to leave Anna and marry Stella Wiley, but the latter refused to have him whereupon he began to abuse her verbally. He is also reported to have made sexual advances to his wife's fifteen year old sister.

Harry is extremely proud of his relations with American soldiers and corresponds with several. Beneath his flattery of the ethnographer and of all things American, there often runs a current of hostility. Usually this is directed toward Harry himself. On one occasion, when intoxicated, he spoke of "murdering" himself, asked the ethnographer if he knew about "Murder Incorporated," and rambled on about a woman with a revolver. Harry gains this sophistication from reading picture magazines and comic books. As intoxication increased on that occasion, his aggressiveness toward the ethnographer became more direct but always remained under a cloak of ingratiation. He wanted to "please" us by offering us his brew. Then he said he would murder himself if we refused to drink. Finally he threatened to strike the ethnographer if the brew was rejected. He seized the ethnographer but wavered in carrying out his threat when Old Man started to reproach him and pull him away. In a few minutes the hostility was dropped, and Harry began to apologize profusely for having lost his head. He continued to apologize for several hours and then began to alternate between self-depreciation and a new attitude that emphasized his Indian status. "To hell with whites," he said, "We don't need them . . . we're better than the whites." For several weeks after this, he seemed reluctant to meet the ethnographer but continued to send gifts through his wife and her sister.

Several times Harry is reported to have threatened self-destruction. He is quite assertive to his father-in-law, whose food he readily consumes without asking, and resents any sign of Old Man's refusal to share. He also receives help from his mother's sister, Mildred Lang, but largely ignores relations with his mother. He is as indifferent about trapping as he is enthusiastic about reading. One of his favorite pieces of reading matter is *Superman*, a comic book series.

There is no question but that Harry shows stronger overt aggressive tendencies than the average Kaska male. His domineering tendency is exceeded only by the similar behavior of his uncle, Nick Lang. This atypical labile aggressiveness seems related to his particularly severe childhood frustrations and probably also to identification with his grandfather, Old Lang, who, from all accounts, was also a very assertive person. The compulsive generosity which Harry manifests is a reaction formation initiated by fundamental selfishness. Thus when the ethnographer would not accept his generosity, the refusal was interpreted as a rejection of himself and left him without means of winning the ethnographer's approval and affection. Old Man's refusals to share had similar frustrating effects. Harry's warmest relationships have been with people who offered him protection and gave him gifts. The generosity of American soldiers, the gifts of white trappers, the care of his aunt, Mildred, all symbolize the affection of which he was deprived in infancy and childhood. The best way he knows of invoking such responses is to give gifts. When this circular process of giving (to insure love) and receiving breaks down, he is once more left as utterly alone and defenseless as in childhood. Consequently such frustrations promote rage. As a child he could devise no techniques of winning his mother's approval and therefore found it possible to hate her without risking additional punishment. In adulthood he carries on the same pattern of interpersonal relations. Harry's sexual strivings also represent a search for love. His association to a woman with a revolver and the incident of homosexual behavior reported in the cultural background reveal the strongly passive trends that underlie his conscious aggressiveness. Also noteworthy is the degree to which childhood traumas have crippled his self-assertion, making him a poor trapper and leaving him dependent on interpersonal hostility for reaffirming his self-esteem.

The following folktale was begun by Harry at a drinking party shortly after we reached Old Man's place but not concluded until several months later. Although the personae identify the story as belonging to a more eastern Athapaskan culture, the tale is apparently of strong emotional significance to Harry. We will analyze that significance following the narrative.[4]

[4] Upon inquiry Harry identified the hero of this narrative as a Caribou Indian. Although he could not explain to which tribe he referred, a small band of Caribou Hide Indians are reported to trap in the area east of the head of the Stikine River, near Thutade Lake, the source of the Finlay River. This information was sketched on a map received with an accompanying letter signed by James Coleman, Inspector of Indian Agencies, Vancouver, B. C., and dated May 19, 1943. In a letter dated February 16, 1943, Harold McGill, then Director of the

MONITŠA

Monitša was a boy whose mother was killed by the Cree while he was still a very small child. The boy escaped from his captors and for six years lived in the brush, growing up with game. Then one day he came to the Cree camp and asked for a suit of caribou clothing. When he had received this, he invited the assembled Cree hunters to shoot at him with their shotguns as he ran. He invited them to kill him. The bullets rained down on him as Monitša began to run, but they all stuck in his clothes without penetrating to his flesh.

The Cree perceived that here was a strong man. They tied him up with other men of his nation and planned how to kill these prisoners. Before they could act, the Cree hunters heard of a buffalo nearby. They planned first to hunt this animal and then to kill the prisoners. While the Cree were gone, Monitša slipped out of his bonds. He released his friends and told them to line up on each side of the trail along which the Cree would return. He told them that when he shot the rear man in the returning expedition, the latter would shout and all the other Cree would turn around. At that moment the prisoners could easily massacre their captors. The allies hid themselves in the brush along the trail and waited for the Cree to come back. Soon Monitša saw the hunters. Aiming his arrow at the last man in the party, he released the bow-string. The man who was hit cried out, calling his fellows to wait. As the rest of the party turned around, Monitša's men leapt foreward and killed all of the Cree. Now Monitša's people were free.[5]

Monitša called the animals his brothers. He said: "The caribou is my head boss. I lived with him." He talked to the caribou and one of these animals took him down into Cree country. The Cree never discovered him. After about six years he came back to his own people; the caribou brought him back. He met his brother-in-law and told the latter to give him a caribou hide "uniform." By that time the people had secured muzzle loaders from the white traders. When Monitša had donned the uniform he told his brother-in-law: "Go ahead, try and shoot me. Kill me." But the latter said: "We might kill you." Monitša answered: "I'm going to try to make war with the Cree. See what I'm going to do with them." So his brother-in-law and some friends lined up with muzzle loaders. Monitša started to run. Then they let him have the bullets. Three rounds they fired. Then Monitša came back and took off his uniform. The bullets had stuck in the skin and now dropped out.

The next day they all lined up. "We're going to fight the Cree," Monitša said. They started off and traveled a long distance until they came to a barren place where no trees grew. It was raining. Before this they had met a porcupine who invited the warriors to kill him. The porcupine told them to burn the skin and then rub themselves with the fat. They must then eat every bit of the meat and not throw any of it away. So they ate the porcupine and kept on traveling In this open country they found one big tree under which the Cree usually camped. All the warriors fell asleep. Suddenly Monitša awoke to find somebody holding him down. "Who are you?" he asked. And they asked: "Who are you?" Monitša told them and the Cree said: "I

Indian Affairs Branch, Ottawa, refers to the Caribou Hide Band as Nahane Indians who trade into Telegraph Creek. According to Jenness, however, the area in question is in Sekani country and occupied by the Sasuchan band (Jenness, *The Sekani Indians of British Columbia* [1937], frontispiece). This band corresponds to the Bear Lake Indians who, in 1944–1945, traded at both Fort Ware and Lower Post, with some of its more southerly dwelling members visiting Telegraph Creek. It is probable that we are here dealing with a Sekani folk tale, perhaps derived from one of Harry's maternal grandmothers, who were both Tsekana (Jenness: Tsekani) Indians.

[5] At this point Harry concluded the narrative on September 22, 1945. He resumed the story on December eighth.

have been looking for you to kill you." Monitša replied: "And I have come to do the same thing to you." The Cree asked which way Monitša preferred to die. "Do what you please," Monitša said. Then he heard the Cree captain say: "I'm going back to kill those three buffalo back there. I'm going to cook all the fat and boil it and then send it burning down your throat." "That will be fine," Monitša answered. The Cree tied up the warriors and gave them "smoke" to make them go to sleep. Monitša refused to smoke.

The Cree went off leaving two guards. Monitša got tired of being bound. He said to his brother-in-law: "I'm tired of these cords. I wish those two guards would go to sleep. His brother in-law said: "I know a little three year old bull moose. On a hot day he goes into a lake, feeds about twenty-five minutes, and then goes out to sleep for about five minutes. Those two guards will do the same." The two Cree dropped off asleep. Monitša stretched and the cords broke. Then he untied all his soldiers. They killed the two guards and left the two bodies sitting erect —just like live men.

Meanwhile the Cree used up all their powder and shot to kill the buffalo. Then Monitša lined his soldiers up along the trail on which the Cree would return. Soon he heard the hunters coming. They were singing in their own language. Monitša gave his boys an order. "I'm going to send my arrow across the leg of the last man in the line. When he hollers, the other soldiers will turn around. Then you let them have it." That is how it happened. Monitša's men killed all the Cree and Monitša won his first war.

When Monitša made his second war, he was stuck across a river. The Cree and Monitša came out of the brush at the same time. Shouting across the river, Monitša talked to the Cree captain on the other side. The former said: "Too bad we can't have a fight. But we have no boat, no raft, no canoe." The Cree captain asked: "Who is the best fighter?" "Say, you're captain for your side and I'm a captain too," Monitša said. "Let's dive. We will kill each other under the water." So they each jumped into the river and all the soldiers watched to see which leader would be victorious. They saw Monitša come out with the Cree captain's head. All the Cree began to cry and went home to look for another captain. Monitša promised them he would be there waiting whenever they chose to come back.

A third time Monitša went to war, but just when he came to the place on the river he saw the Cree pull out; two canoes were heading downstream. When Monitša waved, the Cree came back. They waited till morning and then began to fight. Monitša had killed all the Cree when he heard the captain singing across the river. Monitša said: "He's the man. We killed all his people and now he'll kill our people. We got nothing to say about it." But the Cree sang a little too much. Monitša became angry. He took an arrow and shot across the river to where the man was singing. Monitša got him in the back and killed him right away. Then they went home.

Now I'll tell you how they finished Monitša's life. He was an old man when the Cree came back. These were new Cree who had been born in the meantime. Monitša had married seven times and had a large family. He was so old his eyelid fell over his eye. His family cried: "The Cree will kill you." Monitša said: "I will kill seven." Taking a little stick, he supported his eye-lid with it. He stretched his nose and his mouth. Then he took seven arrows and went to meet the Cree.

Hiding behind a tree Monitša watched the Cree captain. The captain saw him and all his army began to laugh. While they were laughing, Monitša sent his seven arrows and seven Cree died. Then he ran out in the lake. All day the rest of the Cree tried to kill him. They cut him into little pieces but still he lived. So at last they asked Monitša why he didn't die. "If you will cut my finger here," he said, pointing to his palm, "and my feet, then I will die. They did that and Monitša died.

Then the Cree saw a big bumble bee flying around them. They tried to escape from it, but two Cree couldn't make it and fell down dead with blood pouring out of their mouths.

Before dying Monitša told the captain to take his wife home and not to kill his children. The captain obeyed the order. When the Cree came to Monitša's camp, they heard the bee again. Two more Cree fell into the fire. They took the woman back to Cree country. When they made the first camp, they again heard the bumble bee. Two more Cree died. Then the captain waved the woman to go home and she went. That's the end of Monitša's life.

Apart from the fact that Harry apparently identifies with the hero of this story, the tale is revealing for the manner in which it reflects the divergent passive and aggressive trends of Harry's personality. The alternate passivity and activity of the leading character may be considered an acting out of Harry's own conflict, assuring him that in back of his passivity lies a true capacity for mastery. The aggression featured in the tale is a vehicle for releasing the narrator's strong hostility component. Of particular significance is the reference to the hero having been raised by animals, which points to a seeking for more solicitous parents and a wishful projection of their discovery and beneficial care. There can be little doubt that Harry's compulsion to complete, and repeat part of, this narrative arose from its deep significance to his basic personality. Monitša, as he becomes in Harry's telling, assumes something of the glamor of Superman, another of this young man's heroes. In these superhuman figures Harry finds a wishful release from the inhibitions on his aggressiveness and self-assertion, while at the same time denying the debilitating passive trends of his personality.

DOROTHY PLOVER

Autobiographical Sketch

I remember the first time a plane came to Dease Lake. I was about three years old. We were two miles away from the post, daddy having taken us for a walk. I could see the plane land in the water. Everybody was frightened, even mama. Daddy told us it was an airplane. I guess he must have seen a plane before. There was a white man on that plane, Lou Monroe. Later he became my husband.

This wasn't my real daddy. My real daddy is here in Lower Post; he is a Kaska, like mama. Those other kids have a Tahltan daddy. I'm the oldest child. All mamma's children are still living, she never lost one. I came first, then Dell, and next Billy. Beatrice was fourth and then came Thomas Jack, Rose, Marie, June, Steve, and, last year, a little boy. That makes five girls and five boys. I can remember when Beatrice was born. Grandma told us they had found her under a tree. Grandma was always fooling us. My mother's brother, Dick Mountain, lived with us too; my daddy raised him.

Mama says I was sick when I was five years old. I had whooping cough and measles. Mama nearly lost me. Aunt Minny lost her first baby that time from measles. After that, mama went to Prince Rupert. My sister, Beatrice, was only a baby. Mama's sister, Aunt Minny, took care of the family, but she went to dances nearly every night. There used to be many dances in Dease Lake. Daddy was captain on a river boat, but he didn't want to leave us. When he had to go to work he sometimes left us with Aunt Frances, Minny's sister.

When I was a little girl I never ate much. I was always afraid to eat. I was afraid of choking. I'm still like that and so is my little sister, Marie. Once, when she was two years old, Marie choked on bread. When I was small we ate moose meat, fish, dry meat, and bone grease. I never cooked till I was ten years old. When we played, I made a little house with brush and put a dolly in it. We made dollies out of sticks or anything. Dell played shooting moose. The boys killed squirrels with rocks and cooked them, and then we all ate the meat. It was good.

I don't know how old I was when they left me at grandma's. They say they made me help set rabbit snares. I can just faintly remember grandma's cat getting snared. We went to visit the snares one day and there was grandma's cat hanging on the springboard. Grandma often told that story when we were grown up. I don't know why daddy and mama left me with grandma. Maybe it was because I was like grandma in some ways. She had a husband, a Tahltan. She herself was Kaska and used to be married to a Kaska man. When she lost him she kept this Tahltan. Grandma lived in Dease Lake too, so I saw mama many times.

Once daddy was working on a pack train and mama decided to go along with him. She took me and my little brother, Dell. Mama was on a horse holding me, and I was playing with a stick. The stick went into my mouth. Its just luck that it didn't kill me. When my brother and I were small we went on daddy's trap line. A moose calf had gotten up a tree [?] and we thought it was a grizzly bear. We started to run. My brother ran so hard he lost one snowshoe. I picked up the shoe and followed him. We came to mama, who asked what had frightened us. We told her that there was a grizzly bear up in a tree. Mama and my brother went back there and she laughed. She said it was a calf up in the tree. That same winter we went to set traps on a slough. My little pup went around with me everywhere. He got caught in a trap. Dell and I tried to take him out, but we couldn't make it. We began to cry and then ran to mama. When mama saw us she thought something was chasing us. I told her that my little dog was going to die. Mama went over and took the pup out of the trap. Dell and I stayed around camp and we set a big trap. Then I pulled the bitch to the trap and put her foot in. Then we ran away. We kept mama busy all the time.

Whenever daddy went away, we all cried. We cried for a long time. We missed him because we loved him so much. We didn't want him to leave us. Once when daddy was away, mama burned down a tree. We didn't know why she did that and wondered if she was afraid of the coyote. We thought the coyote was a killer. Mama said she burned the tree so that any grizzly bear would smell smoke and stay away from the camp. Daddy was trapping beaver that time. The first time I saw a beaver, I thought it was a lynx. When I got big I found out the difference.

When Dell and I were small, mama and daddy both got sick with sore throat. We cut and packed wood. Then we saw a caribou. Daddy was weak, but he shot it. We packed the meat to the house and cooked it. When we started to eat, a piece of meat stuck in my tonsils. Daddy made pincers and took it out. I had always been afraid of choking, even before that happened.

One fall, when the moose were running, daddy went hunting and didn't return till day-light. He climbed up a hill and looked for moose. He killed a cow, but then a bull moose came around and daddy climbed up a tree. The bull wouldn't go away. Daddy hollered at him and even told him: "I'm going to shoot you!" But the bull wouldn't move.

Later Daddy told us where to set traps and we caught a wolverine. We were afraid and threw sticks at the animal. At last we threw the ax but even that didn't finish him. I got one big stick and tried to reach the wolverine with it. The wolverine started to go for me. Quickly my brother grabbed the ax and killed the animal. We went up the mountain and then found a marten caught in a trap. Dell got a stick and put it on the animal's back for me to stand on. The marten lifted me up. My brother picked up a pole and killed the animal. When we brought the wolverine home, daddy dried out the stomach for us to drink water from. In that way we could never get diarrhea.

Another time, when daddy sent us to the mountains with four dogs, we were frightened by some tracks. People were always talking about the mountain lion. We found a mountain lion's tracks and turned back. My little brother lay in the sleigh and I held the handlebars. When mama saw us, she wanted to know why we were back so soon. I told her we had seen the tracks of a mountain lion. I guess it was only a wolf track. Mama saw a mountain lion track once, when she was setting traps with my brother. She said the lion went right through the snow crust. They picked up all the traps and came home.

Pretty soon daddy started sending me trapping with my sister Beatrice. We had three dogs hitched to a sleigh. I don't remember what frightened me, but all of a sudden the dogs started to run and we turned back. When Beatrice started to work, she made many mistakes. She thought it was all right to use any kind of a rag to wash dishes. She used a little baby moccasin and, when it was wet, she wrung it out and put it on the stove to dry. Soon it was all burned up.

When I got older I went hunting with my brother, Dell. I didn't know how to hunt, but still I tried to teach him. He was afraid of moose, and when we shot one, he would send me to see if the animal was dead. He had the gun; I had nothing. He told me to kick the moose and see if he was still living. I had to butcher the animal too, because he was afraid. He was too scared to let me have the gun. I guess I was about fourteen years old that time— the first time we killed moose. The next spring Dell climbed a tree and saw a moose. We killed and skinned the animal and then wounded another. We were scared of that wounded moose and ran until we came to the truck road crossing the portage. We could hear the wounded moose right in front of us. It was dark.

Sometimes we kids used to fight. Once Dell hit me in the head with a rock. I took a willow and chased my brother. When I caught him, I spanked him. If I had no whip, I bit his finger till grandma got after me. Daddy and mama never licked me; they hit my sister Beatrice, though. They didn't want her to be so crazy.

When my Aunt Fanny started to get month sick, she lived in a small tent alone. Mine came during the winter, so I stayed in the house with grandma. When grandpa came back I went with my aunt. When a man came into the house, I couldn't look at him, though I could talk to him. My grandma always watched me. I wanted to go to a dance that time and I started to sneak away. But I heard grandma coming so I went back. Gee, did I get mad! Mama and daddy went to the dance too, but grandma watched me just like a policeman. I stayed in the house one month and never saw my brother. Mama had to cook two bannocks, one for the men. I could only eat dry meat and I had to pick the needles of spruce brush one by one, so that I would become a good sewer. If I ate fresh meat my uncle or my daddy would have to chew it for me. And I wasn't allowed to laugh. When my aunt Dolly got month sick she would let the boys sneak into her tent while grandma slept. That's why Dolly lost many children. Aunt Frances never told grandma when she first started to get month sick.

One spring we were on our way to Dease Lake for grub. All of a sudden the dogs started to bark and we saw a bear in a tree. Uncle Alfred and I climbed up a tree and started to shoot everyplace. My aunts climbed up a tree too; we had frightened them with our hollering and shooting. We thought we had shot the bear, but everybody was afraid to go look for him, because we weren't sure he was dead. We made a long detour trying to find daddy's camp but couldn't reach it. So we had to make our own camp. Nobody slept all night. The next day we went on to Dease Lake. Coming back, Uncle Alfred and I traveled alone. We were afraid that my little sister, May, would cry and bring on the grizzly bear, so we left her. When we reached the beaver dam, the dogs started to bark. We thought sure there was a grizzly coming and hid under a willow bush, but the dogs came back and we went on.

Another time Uncle Peter, my brother, Dell, and I went to a mountain and saw a moose through a glass. Dell shot and wounded him. Then Uncle Peter and Dell climbed up a fallen tree and sent me to the moose. I asked them to give me a gun, but they wouldn't. When I got to the moose, it jumped up. My brother hollered and I ran back quickly. After climbing into the tree with them, they shot again. That moose had big horns. After he fell down, they told me to go back and make sure he was dead. I went and hit him with a stick. Then I told them that he was dead. Peter must have been about ten years old then; Dell was about fifteen and I was seventeen.

Once daddy killed a moose and built a scarecrow by the meat to keep the grizzly bear away. When we came back the next day we found that a grizzly had bothered the cache. We took all the fat and almost all the meat, because we were afraid the grizzly would come back. We had to make another trip for more meat. When we came close to the cache, Peter and Dell shot the grizzly. Gee, he was big! Dell was excited and could hardly shoot. We all went over, but daddy warned us that he might still be alive. I wasn't afraid. I ran right over to the bear and daddy hollered. I skinned the grizzly too.

Sometimes kids tried to scare us girls. Once Dell and Jimmy Barre told us a grizzly bear was coming. My little sister and I hid, but the boys were only fooling. The same time my little sister, Anne, Dell, Jimmy, and I were hunting porcupine. We sat down and the boys went up the mountain. They knocked down a rock and Anne and I hid under a thick balsam. We thought a grizzly bear was coming down to us.

There were many gopher in those mountains. Daddy and mama set snares for them, getting thirty or forty each day. When a grizzly bear digs gopher out of the ground, he stands up every once in the while to listen. He does that when he digs up groundhog too. This mountain where we hunted is on the other side of Tsasel River; we call it Tzanłode— Sharp Mountain.

I spent two winters in Telegraph Creek. Then I married Lou Monroe. When I married

Lou, we were living up McDame Creek, twelve miles from the post. Before I married him, I had a baby. He was born in November and his father was a white man, the policeman. Daddy used to work for the police. The baby died. I lived with Lou until April and then went up the river to see mama. Lou sent a letter up for me and I came down to him on a plane. It was the first time I had been in a plane, but I wasn't afraid. Everybody missed me when I left papa and mama. I was about eighteen years old. All the kids missed me, because I used to work for them. I helped mama look after the babies. Sometimes I cut wood, when daddy was out hunting with my brothers.

RORSCHACH RECORD AND ANALYSIS

The quantitative results of Dorothy's Rorschach record, one of the longest collected, is summarized below.

Total Responses = 90

W	3	3.3%	M	10	11.1%	H	9	10.0%	P	44	48.8%
D	46	51.1%	FM	8	8.8%	Hd	10	11.1%	O	46	51.1%
Dd	37	41.1%	K	1	1.1%	A	45	50.0%			
S	4	4.4%	F+	41	45.5%	Ad	20	22.2%			
			F−	27	30.0%	AObj	1	1.1%			
			C	3	3.3%	Obj	2	2.2%			
						N	2	2.2%			
						Abst	1	1.1%			

M:sum C = 9:4.5
(FM+m):(Fc+c+C') = 8:1
VIII, IX, X/R = 30%

Ap. = ((W)), D, Dd S!!!!
Suc. = Confused

In her approach to the test Dorothy reveals certain attitudes typical of her society but which have additional personal significance for understanding her personality. Although overtly more relaxed and cooperative than most Kaska subjects—in fact, she seemed to enjoy the Rorschach situation—her performance reveals the tendency to avoid any forth-right grip with the problems presented by an unfamiliar situation. Rather she pretends to cooperate. This pretension reveals Dorothy's ambition to impress people. She attempted to impress the tester with the volume of her responses, which for her had the value of quality. Old Man and Dorothy Plover are the only two subjects whose W:M ratios show the greatest weight on the M side—indicating aspiration levels beyond the subjects' capacities.

Dorothy is self-consciously very concerned with the facade that identifies her in society, but underneath this pretentious role she is beset by feelings of inferiority and insecurity. This is revealed in a number of responses involving animals and people that are "looking" and "looking back." Many of her answers also mention seated humans; apparently there is safety for this relatively short girl in seated figures, while standing persons are productive of anxiety.

Intellectually Dorothy makes no effort to generalize or conceptualize from experience, is moderately critical in her perception, and shows an adequate command of the practical aspects of living. Her thinking is often careless of reality. In her interests she ventures be-yond her capacity. All these intellectually limited factors, however, spring from emotional inhibitions rather than from mental dullness.

Emotionally she is guarded, tense, and reserved, except for momentary episodes when an emotional experience carries her away. In general she protects herself against threatening or devastating external emotional stimuli, which suggests that instances of disorganized con-trol arise when she finds herself in situations that hold deep personal significance. Dorothy's emotional contacts with people cannot be close and warm, because she is too restricted in her affectional expression and too self-occupied. Despite her emotional withdrawal from the world, and her moderately developed ego strength, the personality shown in the Rorschach record is characterized by a tendency toward assertive self-expression toward the environ-ment. Much of this self-assertion, however, represents energy expended in meeting the opposition of conflicting attitudes. The struggle between introversive apathy and extra-tensive assertion suggests that we may here be dealing, at least in part, with the struggle of masculine self-assertion versus feminine dependence. In this connection, it is of interest to note that in her initial response to the first card Dorothy saw a male breast. This suggests an identification with a man at the expense of her mother; the man may well be her foster father as personality data to be presented will indicate. It is also likely that her ambitious self-assertion may have been developed as a compensation for the threatening effects of basic anxiety. Although this anxiety is present in her record, it is not manifested as severely as it is in some Kaska subjects. In other words, through volume-productivity she has avoided being overcome by the menace of the shading cards.

To sum up, the record reveals an emotionally constricted girl, who is striving to act out a role of which she is not wholly certain and in which she is unable to release much creativity. She is uncertain of her potential command over this role (in fact, the role exceeds her capac-ities) and also doubts the society's judgment of her performance. Because of this uncer-tainty, Dorothy is often frustrated. When such provocation becomes too intense, she is liable to react with blind and uncontrolled hostility.

The Personality under Observation

The following characterization of Dorothy Plover was prepared at the end of the 1944 season of field work by Irma Honigmann. It was done prior to, as well as independent of, the Rorschach interpretation.

> Dorothy Plover may be briefly described as vain, opportunistic, intelligent (or clever), cautious, lying, and possessed of high self-esteem.
>
> During our period of friendship, she tried constantly to convince us that she was something which she manifestly was not. Thus she explained her riding with American soldiers saying: "I go for long ride with soldiers, that's all." She denied that they ever became "fresh," but ac-cused other girls of promiscuity. In her own case, we knew that she was lying because soldiers frankly admitted having slept with her. She even told her husband of her dates, in that way avoiding the threats made by some members of the community to tell Lou about her behavior.
>
> Dorothy is a young, attractive woman married to an elderly white man of slight Cree an-cestry. The impression is that she dominates the household. Certainly she gets what she wants.

She is never disrespectful about her husband, receiving his consent before buying clothes, and always receiving it. When she goes on dates, Lou watches their little boy. He also does the cooking and often washes the dishes.

For a time we referred to Dorothy as the Grand Duchess surrounded by ladies-in-waiting. The latter consisted of young female relatives and friends, whose cooperation she succeeded in enlisting. First there was Annette, seven year old daughter of her maternal uncle, Dick Mountain. This girl tagged along with Dorothy, minding the latter's son, David; going to the stores, and doing odd jobs. Once Dorothy utilized a seven year old orphan boy to pack David for her. Following Annette's departure from Lower Post came Skipper's two granddaughters. They were Dorothy's constant companions toward the end of the summer, escorting her on rides with unfamiliar soldiers and helping with housework. These girls also packed David for her and carried home packages from the stores. They were welcome company for Dorothy, who did not hesitate to make what use she could of them. When we left Lower Post in September, Skipper and his granddaughters had left for the bush, and Stella Wiley was living with Dorothy. It was Stella who sewed the moccasins that Dorothy had promised to sew for our children. Yet in undertaking this obligation, Dorothy had said: "I like to sew. As soon as mama send me caribou hide I make lots of things." When the unsmoked hide arrived, Dorothy gave it to Mrs. Man for smoking and then postponed sewing for over a month, until Stella came to live in her house.

Her lying was manifested in many things she said. Once when Dorothy was intoxicated she told us that she had to rush away for a date. The soldier, however, failed to show up. Later, when we queried Dorothy about the date, she said she had rushed away to keep Stella company. Only after much teasing did she admit that her date had disappointed her. Although Dorothy drank readily, she rarely became drunk. Even when she was once strongly intoxicated, she retained her self-control and showed no tendency to violent behavior or unrestrained sexuality.

She enjoyed leading boys on a string, even when she apparently never intended to gratify them. She would tell us how she had told a certain young man that she would meet him after a dance and how she then slipped away before he could catch her. This kind of teasing amuses her. One night she refused to go riding in a truck with Flower, Irene, and three soldiers. The soldiers caught her and insisted that she join the party. Being overpowered, Dorothy consented. As soon as they released her, however, she ran away. On several other occasions she utilized such ruses to escape unpleasant sexual attention. Laughter is another typical response by which Dorothy seeks to cover an embarrassing situation.

One day she told a white man how the girls, including Stella, carried on with soldiers. At this time she was the white man's mistress and was manifestly trying to impress him with her virtue. Stella, shyly standing behind a door, heard Dorothy's statement and became rather belligerent. Slyly Dorothy twisted her words and succeeded in mollifying the other girl by saying that it was only Irene Wiley and Flower Joe to whom she had referred. The white man could not have been fooled. He had reason to know Dorothy's behavior well from his own close friendships with soldiers.

Frequently Dorothy spoke of Irene's and Flower's promiscuity in such a way as to give the impression that this was behavior in which she never participated and strongly disapproved. She accused these girls of being venereally diseased. In general she revealed a tendency to gossip without restraint. We even learned that she had maliciously talked about our family.[6]

---

[6] Judging from Old Man and Dorothy, it seems likely that Kaska Indians with a W: M ratio in which M is greater are predisposed to ready gossip. This behavior, by emphasizing other people's failures or delicts, probably serves to cover up the subjects' inadequacy to achieve desirable ideals.

Dorothy does not reveal her emotions readily, always maintaining a placid, smiling, and rather pleasing exterior. Once, when she was very drunk and being teased about her love for a young, blonde, American soldier, who was currently associating with Flower Joe, she indirectly agreed to the truth of this allegation and even expressed some fondness for the boy. Later, when she was sober, we had occasion to observe her in the presence of this soldier and Flower. Not by a word or gesture did she reveal either love or jealousy. Apparently Dorothy has strong determination, because she refused to accompany her former lover on any rides once he began to sleep with Flower. Even though the boy sometimes paid considerable attention to her, she refused to yield. Until Flower arrived, Dorothy had been the belle of the town with the American troops. Flower quickly supplanted her. Although Dorothy never showed too strong evidence of her feelings, it was now that she began to spread rumors of Flower's sexual disease and would not be convinced that she might be wrong. The evidence suggests that Dorothy was secretly very jealous of her rival.

One evening in late summer Dorothy said that, if Lou sold his trap line she would go to Dease Lake for the winter. She claimed that she liked life on the trap line. This statement seems to have been inspired by the ideal pattern that one is supposed to like the trap line. Actually, most women do, but it is doubtful if Dorothy cares for either the isolation or the work. That evening she took her first ride with soldiers in several weeks, Lower Post having for some time been out of bounds. Later that evening she told another woman that she would stay in Lower Post all winter. The truth probably is, that Dorothy was disgusted with Lower Post because of the dearth of soldiers. The withdrawal of troops also promised to make for a dull winter. She therefore wanted to visit her family at Dease Lake. When things momentarily picked up, she became reconciled to staying. It was shortly after this that she became the white man's mistress.

Although Dorothy is strongly attached to David, she gives little evidence of being very maternal. She even said that she didn't want any more children. During the summer, a consistent practice was to put David to bed early, so that she could be free to go out for the evening. One evening we heard David crying. We went into the store, where Dorothy was sitting in the blonde soldier's arms, and told her that the boy was awake. "He'll go to sleep again," she replied. "If I go in, he'll be worse." Her husband was very ill at the time and could do little for the child. Her treatment of David was outstanding in that she gave him more "don'ts" than is usual in the community. On the whole, however, her discipline was extremely mild and she easily yielded to the child's demands. Once she told her maternal uncle, Dick, to take the scissors away from David. Her own request for the instrument failed to produce results.

When we returned to Lower Post in June 1945, we found Dorothy alternating between two men. A few weeks previously she had borne her lover's son and now both men were assisting in the housework while the mother recovered. She showed considerable affection for the new baby, insisted that it never be left alone and often imposing its care on either of the two men. Twice she went to a dance and was followed by her lover who, obviously jealous of her absence, informed her that the baby was crying. One night she was loitering with other young people, when this man angrily burst out with the news that the baby was crying. He commanded Dorothy to stop her disrespectful behavior and to get where she belonged. Without a word Dorothy followed him. Although there is evidence that this man loved her deeply, absolutely nothing indicates her feelings toward him. Her position, however, benefited her in many ways. Whereas her husband was ill and had sold his trap line, the second man was somewhat younger and held a good job. He spent money lavishly on the girl and she proudly demonstrated her large wardrobe of dresses and coats, also changing her costume two or more times a day.

The situation was not conducive to securing intimate personality data, but three dreams were collected in late July. These are given below.

She dreamed that she had left the new baby at her foster father's cabin in Lou's care. Then she heard that the baby was without food and freezing. With her brother, Dell, she ran to save the infant. She woke up relieved to discover it was summertime and that there was no frost.

She dreamed that David was drowning in the Liard River. Her mother was looking on but made no move to save him. Later, however, her mother rescued the child.

She was walking along with Lou Monroe and her lover, together with the new infant. A bearded white trapper came along and attacked the lover, trying to choke him. Dorothy gave the baby to someone—it seemed like Alice Nolan—and tried to help her lover. In her associations, Dorothy went on to explain that her father's dreams always come true and her mother's frequently. Her dreams also often materialize.

Three vectors of hostility are revealed in these dreams. In the first, Dorothy's hostility is directed primarily to her husband, Lou, who is probably an inconvenient adjunct in her new affair. She visualizes Lou's resentment of her lover's baby, at the same time deviously expressing her own aggression toward the infant. The significance of the brother is not clear, but his appearance in the dream probably represents the strong bonds between these two siblings. A similar function may be inferred from the fact that the dream takes place at her foster father's cabin; a father attachment thereby being indicated. In the second dream, the hostility is dramatically directed toward David, with the expectation that her mother will save the child. Here there is a wish for the grandmother to assume the child's care, in other words, an expression of Dorothy's emotional rejection of the boy. The third dream pictures the polyandrous ménage, complete except for David, who has apparently already been disposed of. Hostility is now indirectly released against her lover, but is ambivalent. Dorothy tries to help her lover while the baby is given to an exceedingly tender, maternal figure. The wish-fulfillment element is clearly stressed in Dorothy's association to dreams that have come true. The total sequence of dreams therefore indicates the girl's confusion in her current situation and her ambivalent desire to escape from it and assume her independence. They reflect the anxiety connected with the role she is playing, her self-consciousness, her fear of public criticism, and uncertainty.

Certainly Dorothy has cause for uncertainty. She is widely disliked by many people, and only her affected indifference to criticism and public opinion, together with her persistent lying to save face, protect her from manifesting the anxiety attached to her position. Unfortunately we have only meager data for discovering how she came to be the person that she is.

Probably one of the most important influences in her life was her identification with her foster father, a strong, self-willed Tahltan Indian, who manifests the same pride in his own status that Dorothy affects. Dorothy is intensely proud of her Tahltan heritage and fond of talking about the stimulation to be found in Telegraph Creek. This pride in status, it must be pointed out, is a familiar trait of Tahltan men and some Tahltan women, but is notably lacking in Kaska individuals. Even dominant Kaska men are not proud or pretentious. In this, therefore, Dorothy's personality reflects Tahltan influence. From her foster father the girl acquired the self-assertion which helped her, the family's eldest daughter, to assume many male roles and to fulfill them more adequately than her next youngest brother. It is also from her foster father that she derived the boastfulness which, for example, she scarcely attempted to conceal in speaking about her brother's and uncle's timidity.

The incentive to develop strong father ties came from the early emotional rejection of her mother. Such rejection is indicated in the story of being sent to live with her grandmother and aunt. The throat constriction, from which Dorothy suffered as a child, and the attendant eating difficulties may be symptoms related to this period of childhood. If the close connection between oral activities and the security associated with the mother's breast is assumed, the frustration of security seeking tendencies and the concomitant anxiety may well transfer to acts symbolic of this primary mother-child relationship. In a psychosomatic inability to swallow, the tense child may then be expressing the longing for a gratification which he has come to fear.[7] Dorothy's intense preoccupation with the grizzly bear, already identified as a parent symbol, is also significant in this respect.

Dorothy's promiscuity is of long standing. It serves as an expression of the egocentric component of her personality and is therefore a vehicle for masculine striving. The choice of very much older white men (the policeman, Lou Monroe, and the white man in Lower Post) for sex objects suggests that in these cases sexual relations provide an opportunity to act out the oedipal identification with her foster father; these men are father images, in whom Dorothy is forced to invest an unconscious dependence which is antithetical to her egocentric wishes. Whether she was really in love with the blonde soldier, or if her expression of fondness was conditioned by jealousy for the more popular Flower, is difficult to answer. From what we know of her self-centeredness, jealousy arising from being preferred to a rival could be a critical experience, because it would threaten her personal image, in which so much energy has been invested and through which she realizes her goal of resourcefulness. Her personality is not equipped to love. Her whole career demonstrates her capacity to use people for her own ends. Her marriages and liaisons with white men have been profitable, each attachment advancing her material status, contributing to her role. The fact that ideals of status progression, so well served by white men, were originally derived from her boastful and narcissistic Tahltan foster father is further evidence for the interpretation that Dorothy's compulsive sexual behavior is closely related to her oedipal situation.

Dorothy's behavior, therefore, can be understood in terms of strong egocentricity and correlated masculine striving derived from identification with her foster father. That this man happened to be Tahltan, and therefore distinguished in personality, is accidental, but served to give her personality a color different from that expected in her community. From him she learned to direct her egocentricity into very un-Kaska-like pretence and display. Narcissism became one of the defenses against emotional isolation and dependence. To realize her status ambition, however, she was compulsively forced into dependence on father images for her enduring relationships. In this way her affect hunger and dependency strivings found expression. The role she played was never wholly congenial. She constantly re-

---

[7] See Fenichel, *The Psychoanalytic Theory of Neuroses* (1945), 195–196.

mained uncertain of her facade. At the time of observation this uncertainty was particularly severe. Her dependence on Lou had been alleviated by the egocentric gratifications derived from promiscuity with soldiers. When the troops began to be withdrawn, she was faced with returning to Lou, whose financial position had worsened and who could no longer compensate her dependence with narcissistic rewards. She now formed a second attachment contemporaneously with her marriage and thereby began to earn a greater share of social disapproval, which more than ever imperiled her facade. The hostility released in the three dreams is derived from the frustration produced by her precarious situation.

NITLA KEAN

Autobiographical Sketch

I was born close to Frances Lake. A day and half after I was born, my mother died. So my father gave me to an old lady, Old Metša, who raised me. Many years ago she had come to Frances Lake from the Nelson country. She had lost her husband and only one of her children still lived, Mrs. Susa. So Metša raised me in Frances Lake country. She was an old woman when she took me and didn't have any milk. When I was put to the breast, I was always hungry and cried all the time. They tried to feed me moose milk in a cup. Then pretty soon milk came to the old lady. God helped her, I guess. I nursed for about three or four years, and after a while she gave me rabbit brains to eat and fish guts to suck on. That's good for children. When I was about four years old, Metša for the first time bought a case of milk. I never thought about anything. I didn't worry who my father was or what happened to my mother. I thought the old lady was my mother.

Metša treated me well. I played many games. With a bow and arrows I killed rabbits and chicken. Every boy does that. Sometimes I had to fight. Some kids were known to be fighters and sometimes a boy like that licked me and hurt me. Then I would fight back to even the score. I never was a good fighter though; I can box pretty well, but that's all. When other kids bothered me, I fought them. Some people's kids were worse than others. They would throw rocks, but that's a dangerous thing to do and when the older folks saw it, they would become angry and beat those kids.

Gee, I wore out many pairs of moccasins and pants when I played around as a kid. I couldn't stop playing. I ran around all day. Just the same I was too frightened to go far from camp. I was scared of everything. A rabbit in a snare used to frighten me. Once I was out with mama, when we saw a trapped rabbit. I ran home and got a stick to knock it out. When I saw a stranger coming to the camp, I got scared; I would sit in the camp and never move. Sometimes, when I played around too much, mama would try to stop me. She even beat me. I didn't like to be beaten, it made me scared of mama. A couple of times my daddy came around but I didn't like him. He was too damned cranky. I wanted to be my own boss. My brother, John, is cranky too. He used to get tough with me. I don't like cranky people. Another thing that scared me as a child was to see grown-up people fighting. Sometimes a husband told his wife to do something and she didn't do it. Then, when the man came home, he would fight her. That made me scared. I used to run away. At Frances Lake I once saw a fellow attack his daughter with a knife. Somebody tried to stop him, but they couldn't. The man swung the knife, but he missed the girl. I ran away crying.

When I got into trouble Metša would frighten me to make me sit down and stop playing. She used to tell me stories about old fashioned people going to war against each other. I heard her tell of a man who beat his wife when she made a little hole in meat that she was slicing for drying. Nowadays people aren't so mean. Metša told me about the elephant that ate men and about the man-eating snake. There was a big eagle too that used to snatch people. That's what she told me. She said the devil made those animals. There used to be a jackfish that ate men, and once upon a time the otter were people who killed Indians. In the beginning the grizzly bear walked around and spoke just like the Indians. The wolverine, fox, crow, and all the other animals were people too. Metša used to scare me when she told me those stories. Then she told me about high water coming. All the animals, including the elephant, went up to a high mountain. The people made a raft and sailed up to a big hill and stayed there until the water went down. After hearing some of those stories, we kids used to stay close to camp. We were afraid that if we walked around the bad animals would smell us, follow us, and catch us.

When I got older, I used to play on a raft and push it down a little nearby slough. I made a spruce bark canoe, too, and sewed it together. We used to play store, piling up a lot of logs for the trading post and make believe we had eggs, oranges, and rice. When somebody came along, I'd say: "You want to buy stuff?" I sold him lots and he'd give a skin. All the kids played that game. In winter I made a little toboggan and loaded it with stones. All the kids used to make candles out of moose fat and a piece of string. Now children don't do that anymore. If I found a piece of tin, I filed it down to make a knife. After tying a handle to the blade, I tried to cut meat with it. If the meat wasn't too tough, it worked; but most of the time the knife would bend. With a jam can I made a little teapot. Sometimes the kids made camp with a campfire. We boiled meat and ate it. Then somebody would decide to move camp. We'd sew up a bag and put everything in it and go someplace else.

After playing, I used to get hungry and look for something to eat. If there was any boiled meat, I'd eat it; but I was too young to know how to cook. Sometimes I'd broil a steak.

Once, when I was making an arrow, a big nail went right through my hand. Jesus! I pushed it back. It burned like fire. I could feel my heart getting weak. As a child my heart and lungs were always sore. I felt poor all the time. I looked bad, and my eyes got weak. Rotten stuff came out of my mouth. Not long ago I started to feel better. I boiled up balsam and made medicine. That helped me. Now I feel fine. When I started to use an ax, I cut the top of my foot. I wasn't smart enough yet to know how to use an ax. The blood poured out of the cut. Mama and I patched it up so that no dirt would get in. Another time I cut my hand with a knife that somebody had sharped to use in working moosehide. When I handed it to the woman, I cut my hand.

Pretty soon I heard about the otter woman. It used to be that the otter was a girl, and if a man put his penis in her vagina, she would chew it. They say there's a weasel in the vagina. When he chews the penis, the man dies. Lots of men died that way. The mink is woman too; sometimes she does the same thing to a man who tries to sleep with her.

When I had to go into the bush alone I was scared. I looked around before I moved. People told me to watch out for the grizzly bear. If the grizzly caught a man, they said, he would tear him to pieces. The first game I ever got was a caribou. I could hardly skin him; I was too weak to turn him over. It took me about six hours to finish the job. When I came home, I had blood all over me. Once I went to a moose lick to try for a moose. It was a hot day and, while I sat watching for a moose to come, I began to feel sleepy. Finally I went to sleep. I woke up and I saw a moose. That was the second game I killed. I turned him over, all right. I got goats too, but I never killed sheep. As soon as I started to bring home meat, I fed myself. Metša didn't have to feed me anymore. I brought home everything—rabbits, fish, chicken, porcupine, and moose.

Just once I tried to stay out in the brush long enough to get medicine. But nothing saw me. I wasn't lucky. Nothing wanted me.

When I was still a kid, I saw a fellow playing with a girl. "What the hell?" I said. It scared me. I thought I would kill a girl if I ever tried that. By the time I started to grow whiskers, I was playing with girls myself. At first I was scared, but when I found out what is was—by Jesus, I liked it! One girl wanted me, but I didn't want her. She liked me and kept bothering me. She made me run after her and then I caught her.

When I was about eighteen years old, I stayed with Martin's bunch. Charlie was Martin's kid. Charlie was living with that bunch and had a kid, Adele. Adele's mother had come from Fort Selkirk, but she was dead. Now Charlie was keeping another woman who had two kids in Pelly Banks. Adele ran around and a young fellow slept with her. He made her pregnant and Charlie was ashamed. Many times he asked me to marry Adele. He wanted me to help him out. It was pretty hard for me to live alone. Nobody cooked for me; I'd come home late at night, tired, and sleep alone. So I told Charlie "All right." I was ready to keep his girl. When the baby was born, Charlie took him. My father-in-law treated me well. He's just like my real daddy. When I get moose, I give him meat. He's not my boss. Nobody is boss for another man. My father-in-law talked to me and said: "Don't fool around. Stay in the post. Don't play around. Don't drink."

Every fall we went into the brush with a little grub. That soon ran out, though, and then we lived on meat. I'd go hunting, come back tired, and go to sleep. The next day, hunt again. When there was no meat and when we got tired of meat, we lived on fish. Everybody fishes at Frances Lake. Winter time is no good. Sometimes, in the fall, the snow would fly and I'd have no snowshoes. That made for hard traveling. Lots of wood would have to be cut. Everything was frozen up. Life was hard up at Frances Lake. People didn't catch much fur. They didn't have enough credit to live on, and everybody was afraid of starving. We had to hunt, hunt, hunt. Maybe, if I stayed out five days, I'd get a moose. After I brought the meat home, I'd go out again and set some traps. Soon the meat was all gone. That meant it was time to hunt again. If there was no moose, we lived on snared rabbits. All the time camp was being moved. Sometimes I'd have to work while I was hungry. Then you feel weak and sick. Your stomach is empty. A man feels strong only when he has food. Sometimes we cooked wild rhubarb. On the mountains there is a little leaf that tastes just like sugar when it is boiled up. Indians have a hard life. One time I cut my knee and pus came out. For a whole month I couldn't work. My leg was stiff. I also went to Pelly Banks to hunt caribou; there are many caribou up there. About two years ago, while I was trapping, I had to travel all night. I looked up and the moon was only half in the sky. The other half went into the sky. You could see a fire. Then the other half of the moon came back. I had never seen that happen before.

My father-in-law trapped around Simpson Lake. In October we hunted moose there. In

November we started to set traps. Then maybe there was no meat. The lake froze over and he would set a fish net under the ice. December came around and still no meat. He couldn't move the camp. Maybe in January we would all move down to the Big River—Frances River. Then we'd trap there till February. When the snow began to crust, I went to the trading post—Frances Lake or Lower Post. Pretty soon Adele had another baby, a girl. Last year a third baby was born at Simpson Lake, but it died right away. Hans' sister died around the same time. We wanted to bring the girl's body to Frances Lake Post, but no trail was broken. We loaded the big box on a sleigh and I started up for the post. I had a hell of a time getting through.

My brother, John, wanted to sleep with my wife, but I wouldn't let him. He told Adele that I had refused. She said to me: "Me, you won't give him. Your brother tell me that." I didn't want to do that. If a man wants a woman, why doesn't he get married? River Joe told John the same thing. He told him: "If you take my daughter, keep her." But John wouldn't listen. Now he tries to be boss of my wife. He keeps my wife and is mean to her. A man should be a stranger to his brother's wife. If I die, then, after two or three years, John can take my wife. Adele doesn't want to do anything for me. She kicks all the time. My wife wasn't always like that. I've got a hole in my pants, but there's nobody to patch it. Why have I kept that girl for so many years?

RORSCHACH RECORD AND ANALYSIS

The quantitative results of Nitla's Rorschach record follow:

Total Responses = 36

W	6	16.6%	FM	6	16.6%	Hd	7	19.4%	P	18	50.0%
DW	2	5.5%	F+	16	44.4%	A	15	41.6%	O	18	50.0%
D	11	30.5%	F−	12	33.3%	Ad	6	16.6%			
Dd	17	47.2%	Fc	1	2.8%	At	6	16.6%			
			FC	1	2.8%	Sex	1	2.8%			
						N	1	2.8%			

M:sum C = 0:0.5

(FM +m):(Fc +c +C') = 6:1

VIII, IX, X/R = 33.3%

Ap. = W, (D), Dd!!!!

Suc. = Loose

The most striking feature of this record is its total absence of movement responses and the almost complete lack of color stimulated responses. In other words, Nitla is completely lacking imagination or fantasy, and at the same time is distrustful of his external environment.

Generally, the record conforms to the pattern of the society, exhibiting the subject's cooperation with the tester in a passively rebellious sort of way. In this case, however, we are dealing with an intelligence more limited than the average, which tries to exceed its potentialities. There is considerable pretence in the performance, indicating that Nitla tried to meet what he thought were the expectations of the tester. His basic uncertainty, however, reveals itself in the fact that many of the generalizations are uncertainly made. Clearly the subject has no talent or ability for this kind of conceptual activity. In other words, we are dealing with intellectualized anxiety. Behaviorally this quality is reflected in

Nitla's earnest efforts to learn writing (with very slow progress), and his unreasonably intense ambition to teach the ethnographer to speak Kaska. The latter's failure to learn gave Nitla a sense of superiority that was sometimes expressed in mockery. The record also reveals the subject's inadequate attention to the practical problems of daily life.

Emotionally, Nitla is dissatisfied with the fact that he cannot adequately realize his unconscious wishes—not even in fantasy. He is lost with himself, confused toward the world, and his life lacks direction. Failure to understand his own values goes hand in hand with a tendency to seize on other people's values, but these he is also incapable of fully grasping. Illustrations from Nitla's behavior corroborating this interpretation are plentiful and include his ineffectual trapping, the indifferent care he took of his wife, and his chronic inability to make up his mind (whether to go back to the Highway crossing where his wife was or stay in Lower Post; whether to get a job in Lower Post or hope for a trader's generous extension of credit, etc.). The deep passivity and lack of self-assertion very poorly fit the subject for life. Because of the lack of inner control, Nitla has placed a strong damper on his affectivity, crippling his spontaneity, and then trying to compensate for the loss by an exhibitionistic playfulness. This too is reflected in behavior—in the peals of loud laughter that do not seem warranted by the situations in which they occur, the erratic body habits (jumping up, shifting, etc.), and, perhaps, in his ideomotor tendency (imitating the ethnographer's hand movements while the latter writes).

The record also contains signs of basic anxiety, pointing to severe childhood frustration. Here we may recall the fact that in infancy his foster mother at first lacked milk with which to feed him; prolonged nursing does not seem to have overcome the primary crisis which so strongly determined his future attitudes toward the world. Nitla's pretentiousness is one means of overcoming the effects of that profound emotional disturbance; his rejection of spontaneity in favor of constriction, another. But the anxiety is far from mastered and is pushing him in directions which he cannot fathom and where he is loath to follow. To sum up, we are dealing with an uncertain, bewildered, and immature individual, for whom life is a constant series of unmanageable hazards.

LOUISA MAN
Rorschach Record and Analysis

The tabulation of Louisa's record follows:

Total Responses = 16

W	3	18.8%	M	2	12.5%	H	2	12.5%	P	9	56.2%
DW	3	18.8%	FM	3	18.8%	Hd	1	6.5%	O	7	43.7%
D	5	31.2%	m	1	6.5%	A	11	68.7%			
Dd	5	31.2%	F +	4	25.0%	Obj	2	12.5%			
			F −	3	18.8%						
			Fc	2	12.5%						
			FC	1	6.5%						

M:sum C = 2:0.5

(FM + m):(Fc + c + C') = 5:2

VIII, IX, X/R = 25%

Ap. = W!, (D) Dd!!!!

Suc. = Loose

Intellectually this fifteen year old girl is characterized by an ability, greater than that of the average Kaska adult, to conceptualize experience. Her thinking, however, lacks critical perception, rigorousness, and sufficient attention to routine problems of existence.

Emotionally, Louisa is not a child and shows an awareness of her sensual appetites. Her behavior is determined by the same passive rebelliousness which we have already noted to be a normal feature of Kaska Rorschach performance. Characteristically Louisa inhibits almost any response to the emotional stimulation of her environment. Although she is emotionally less constricted than the average Kaska, her fantasy life is still determined in large part by rather immature ideas and wishes, with some of which she is ill at ease. It may be that it is her impulsiveness and relatively greater freedom from constriction of which she is mistrustful and against which she must be on guard, lest they get her into trouble. The black-gray cards arouse anxiety, particularly when associated with sexual stimuli (Cards VI and VII), which leads to some momentary confusion and decreased productivity. In general her tendency is to avoid novel or intense situations that threaten her resources and to remain friendly to people.

The Personality under Observation

The personality sketch of Louisa Man which follows was prepared by Irma Honigmann, who also administered the Rorschach test.

Louisa is a restless, animated adolescent, somewhat more forthright and aggressive than most Kaska girls. It is difficult to estimate her intelligence, as her restless shifting from task to task prevents her from fulfilling any efficiently. She takes poorly to household duties and is a careless worker. While living with her sister, Anna, during the winter of 1945, she appeared to settle down somewhat and helped with many domestic tasks, without, however, ever completely tanning a small hide that Anna had given her. What portion of the task she did complete (through the softening process) was not well done. Aware that the ethnographer wanted cultural specimens, she hastily prepared a large number of miniature mittens and moccasins, all of very poor workmanship (she originally forgot to put a thumb on one of the mittens). Moccasins made for our son showed equal crudity and signs of haste. In this lack of perfectionism, Louisa is more extreme than most Kaska women; she is, for example, much more careless than her eleven year old friend, Elsie Lang, who far more neatly duplicated many of Louisa's assignments.

Yet despite her inefficiency and impatience with everyday things, she gives the impression of being gay, animated, and alert. Out in the bush she generally runs ahead. She wades into streams, trying to catch fish, not for the purpose of securing food but to demonstrate a feat.

It would appear that Louisa does not easily tolerate authority. She left her father's home, according to Old Man, because she was criticized too much. She then moved in with her sister, Anna, and found little authority to contend with. She is direct and effective in rejecting unwanted sexual overtures. She kicked Hans Donnelly in the stomach for bothering her while he was drunk and once told Nitla to "get the hell out of here you son-of-a-bitch," when he teased her verbally with sexual allusions.

In her seeming inability to adjust to the expected female role, Louisa reminds one of

Irene Wiley. Once, during the summer of 1944, she accompanied the latter girl for a ride in an army truck but was reprimanded by her father. It seems likely that an element of masculine protest operates in both these assertive, independent Kaska girls. Very likely Louisa, in about a year, will take up the pattern of promiscuity for which Irene is already notorious.

APPENDIX B: SOME CONCEPTS OF ETHOS

IN the following brief outline form we have endeavored to indicate most of the concepts developed by anthropologists, sociologists, and other social scientists concerned with phenomena related or similar to that which we have defined as ethos. The term used to designate the concept is given at the left, followed by the definition, and the source with the author.

Ethos	" . . . the sum of the characteristic usages, ideas," standards, and codes differentiating and individualizing one group "in character from other groups."	Sumner, *Folkways* (1906), 36.
Ethos	"Societal character . . . those patterns of culture of a particular society which most distinguish it from other societies."	Young, *An Introductory Sociology* (1934), 26–27.
Ethos	"*Die Gesamtheit der menschlichen Einstellungen, Willens- und Bildungsrichtungen . . .*"	*Die Wandlung des Ethos* (1925), 4.
Ethos	The emotional emphases of the culture as revealed in a series of emotionally toned behaviors. " . . . the system of emotional attitudes which governs what values a community shall set upon the various satisfactions or dissatisfactions which the contexts of life may offer."	Bateson, *Naven* (1936), 32, 120, 220.
Ethos	An ethos accrues in an art style, idea, or composition not from the personal experience of the artist but from "the hopes and fears, the moods and intentions, of his people." Ethos designates, "the underlying dynamics of the common faith."	Kallen, *Art and Freedom* (1942), 863.
Ethos	For Scheler the ethos of a society stands for "the guiding values and ideas upon which the leaders of a group, and in and through them the group itself, are oriented."	Dahlke, *The Sociology of Knowledge* (1940), 75.
Ethos	"The sum of the varied behavior, ideas and aims of a social group."	Gorer, *Society as Viewed by the Anthropologist* (1940), 25.
Ethos	Ethos implies "certain colloquial connotations of temperament like 'cheerful, sullen, etc.' to which must be added the additional values developed in anthropology, particularly in the configurational approach of Benedict and the systematic work of Bateson."	Landes, *The Ethos of the Negro in the New World* (Ms.).
Ethos	The "dominant master configuration" which may be designated as "the integrating principle	Kluckhohn, *Covert Culture and Administrative*

	of the culture." It is "a pervasive and dominant single 'principle' which is . . . 'the genius' of the tribe or nation."	*Problems* (1943), 218–219.
Ethos	"National culture pattern."	Bossard and Ball, *Family Situations* (1943), 58.
Ethos	"The ethos that pervades any social system is a very private, a very unique, multiple of values. It is a summary—an unwritten summary—of all the efforts, strivings, successes and failures of all the past that makes the present what it is."	Tannenbaum, *On Certain Characteristics of American Democracy* (1945), 343.
Temper	" . . . The nature and ways of the people as a whole."	Belo, *The Balinese Temper* (1935), 120.
Feel	" . . . the observer's sense of what is congruous, probable, and fitting in the way of behavior patterned in accordance with the basic principles of the culture under consideration—especially with respect to non-verbalized, non-overt systems within the whole complex."	Hoebel, *Discussion* (1943), 228.
Genius	A single term embracing "those general attitudes, views of life, and specific manifestations of civilization that give a particular people its distinctive place in the world."	Sapir, *Culture, Genuine and Spurious* (1925), 168.
World Image	A perceptual system organized around a series of values and principles.	Erikson, *Observations on the Yurok* (1943), 273–274.
View of Life	A society's characteristic set of unstated premises and presuppositions about the world.	Kluckhohn and Kelly, *The Concept of Culture* (1945), 99–100.
Theme	" . . . a postulate or position declared or implied, and usually controlling behavior or stimulating activity, which is tacitly approved or openly promoted in a society."	Opler, *Themes as Dynamic Forces in Culture* (1945), 198.
Temperament	The values which "a culture . . . embodies . . . in its structure, in its politics and religious systems, in its art and literature . . . each new generation is shaped, firmly and definitely, to the dominant trends."	Mead, *Sex and Temperament* (1939), vi.
Sentiments	"The word 'sentiments' will be used by us in a special sense as a brief equivalent of opinions and attitudes. Sentiments are ideas or action tendencies charged with emotions and persistent like habits—they are partially cognitive, partially affective, and partially conative."	Leighton, *The Governing of Men* (1945), 383.

| Basic Personality Structure | "Environmental conditions and some aspects of social organization included under the term primary institutions create the basic problems of adaptation for the individual. To these he must develop certain methods of accommodation, because they are fixed and unchangeable conditions. Food scarcity, sexual prohibitions, disciplines of one kind or another are conditions which the individual cannot directly control; he can only take an attitude to them and accommodate himself according to an array of patterns which have some variety. The basic constellations in the individual created by these conditions are his ego structure, subjectively considered, or his basic personality structure, objectively considered." | Kardiner, *The Individual and His Society* (1939), 131. |

BIBLIOGRAPHY

ACKERKNECHT, E. H. *On the Collecting of Data Concerning Primitive Medicine* (American Anthropologist, n.s., vol. 47, pp. 427–432, Menasha, 1945).

ADLER, A. *Understanding Human Nature* (New York, 1927).

ALBEE, W. H., and R. ALBEE. *Family Afoot in the Yukon Wilds* (National Geographic Magazine, vol. 81, pp. 589–616, Washington, 1942).

ALLARD, E. *Notes on the Kaska and Upper Liard Indians* (Primitive Man, vol. 1, pp. 24–26, Washington, 1928).

APFELDORF, M. *Rorschach Theory and Psychoanalytic Theory* (Rorschach Research Exchange, vol. 8, pp. 189–191, New York, 1944).

AYAU, A. E. *The Social Psychology of Hunger and Sex* (Cambridge, 1939).

BARBEAU, M. *Mountain Cloud* (Caldwell, 1944).

BATESON, G. *Naven* (Cambridge, 1936).

BATESON, G., and M. MEAD. *Balinese Character* (Special Publications, New York Academy of Sciences, vol. 2, New York, 1942).

BEAGLEHOLE, E. *Character Structure* (Psychiatry, vol. 7, pp. 145–162, Washington, 1944).

BECK, S. J. *Rorschach's Test. I. Basic Processes* (New York, 1944).

BECK, S. J. *Rorschach's Test. II. A Variety of Personality Pictures* (New York, 1945).

BELO, J. *The Balinese Temper* (Character and Personality, vol. 4, pp. 120–146, Durham, 1935–1936).

BENEDICT, R. *Continuities and Discontinuities in Cultural Conditioning* (Psychiatry, vol. 1, pp. 161–167, Washington, 1938).

BENEDICT, R. *Patterns of Culture* (Boston, 1934).

BOAS, F. *James A. Teit* (American Anthropologist, n.s., vol. 24, pp. 490–492, Menasha, 1922).

BOAS, F. *James A. Teit* (Journal of American Folklore, vol. 36, pp. 102–103, Lancaster, 1923).

BOHNER, R., AND F. HALPERN. *The Clinical Application of the Rorschach Test* (New York, 1945).

BOSSARD, J. H. S., AND E. S. BOLL. *Family Situations* (Philadelphia, 1943).

BRITISH COLUMBIA. *Report of the Superintendent of Provincial Police for the Year Ended December 31st 1924* (Victoria, 1925).

BROWN, L. C. *Social Pathology* (New York, 1942).

BURPEE, L. J. *Campbell of the Yukon* (Canadian Geographical Journal, vol. 30, pp. 200–201, Ottawa 1945).

CAMPBELL, R. *The Discovery and Exploration of the Pelly (Yukon) River* (In: *The Royal Reader, Fifth Book of Reading Lessons*, Toronto, 1883).

CANADA. *Annual Report of the Department of Indian Affairs for the Year Ended March 31* (Ottawa, 1914 to 1934).

CANADA. *Annual Report of the Royal Canadian Mounted Police for the Year Ended September 30, 1925 and 1926* (Ottawa, 1926 and 1927).

CANADA. *Stikine Indian Agency Census as at March 31st, 1944* (typescript, Vancouver, 1944).

CARROLL, J. *The Vicariate of Prince Rupert* (Oblate Missions, Annual of the Missionary Association of Mary Immaculate, Ottawa, 1945).

CHAPMAN, J. W. *Notes on the Tinneh Tribe of Anvik, Alaska* (Comptes Rendu, Congrès Internationale des Américanistes, vol. 15, part 2, pp. 7–38, Quebec, 1907).

CZAPLIKA, M. A. *Aboriginal Siberia, A Study in Social Anthropology* (Oxford, 1914).

DAHLKE, O. *The Sociology of Knowledge* (In: Barnes, H. E., Becker, H., and Becker, E. B., eds., *Contemporary Social Theory*, New York, 1940).

DAI, B. *Divided Loyalty in War* (Psychiatry, vol. 7, pp. 327–340, Washington, 1944).

DAWSON, G. M. *Extracts from the Report on an Exploration Made in 1887 in the Yukon District, N. W. T., and Adjacent Northern Portion of British Columbia* (In: Trimmer, F. M., ed., *The Yukon Territory*, London, 1898).

DAWSON, G. M. *Report of an Exploration in the Yukon District, N. W. T., and Adjacent Northern Portion of British Columbia, 1887* (Annual Report of the Canadian Geological Survey, n.s., vol. 3, Ottawa, 1887–1888).

Dennis, A. P. *Life on a Yukon Trail* (National Geographic Magazine, vol. 10, pp. 377–390, 457–466, Washington, 1899).

Deutsch, H. *The Psychology of Women. II. Motherhood* (New York, 1945).

Du Bois, C. *The People of Alor* (Minneapolis, 1944).

Dupouy, R., and J. Picard. *Une erotomanie médicale. Considerations sur l'erotomanie feminine* (Annales Médico-Psychologiques, vol. 86, pp. 47–54, Paris, 1928).

Elwin, V. *Maria Murder and Suicide* (London, 1943).

English, O. S., and G. H. J. Pearson. *Emotional Problems of Living* (New York, 1945).

Erikson, E. H. *Observations on Sioux Education* (Journal of Psychology, vol. 7, pp. 101–156, Provincetown, 1939).

Erikson, E. H. *Observations on the Yurok: Childhood and World Image* (University of California Publications in American Archaeology and Ethnology, vol. 35, pp. 257–302, Berkeley, 1943).

Evans-Pritchard, E. E. *Heredity and Gestation, as the Azande See Them* (Sociologus, vol. 8, pp. 400–413, Leipzig, 1932).

Fenichel, O. *The Psychoanalytic Theory of Neuroses* (New York, 1945).

Fenichel, O. *The Psychopathology of Coughing* (Psychosomatic Medicine, vol. 5, pp. 181–184, Washington, 1943).

Field, P. Unpublished Manuscript (Dated Ross River, Feb. 8, 1913. Copy in Department of Anthropology, Yale Peabody Museum, New Haven).

Ford, C. S. *A Comparative Study of Human Reproduction* (Yale University Publications in Anthropology, no. 32, New Haven, 1945).

Ford, C. S. *Society, Culture, and the Human Organism* (Journal of Genetic Psychology, vol. 20, pp. 135–179, Worcester, 1939).

French, C. H., and W. Ware. *British Columbia Posts; No. 7, McDame's Creek Post* (The Beaver, vol. 4, p. 395, Winnepeg, 1923–1924).

Freud, S. *Group Psychology and the Analysis of the Ego* (International Psycho-Analytical Library, no. 6, London, 1922).

Freud, S. *The Interpretation of Dreams* (In: Brill, A. A., ed., *The Basic Writings of Sigmund Freud*, New York, 1938).

Fromm, E. *Escape from Freedom* (New York, 1941).

Fromm, E. *Selfishness and Self-Love* (Psychiatry, vol. 2, pp. 507–524, Washington, 1939).

Fromm, E. *Sex and Character* (Psychiatry, vol. 6, pp. 21–31, Washington, 1943).

Gesell, A., and F. L. Ilg. *Infant and Child in the Culture of Today* (New York, 1943).

Godsell, P. H. *Romance of the Alaska Highway* (Toronto, 1945).

Gorer, G. *Society as Viewed by the Anthropologist* (In: Ware, C., ed., *The Cultural Approach of History*, New York, 1940).

Graumont, R., and J. Hensel. *Encyclopedia of Knots* (New York, 1942).

Griffin, H. *Alaska and the Canadian Northwest* (New York, 1944).

Grouard, E. J. B., *Souvenirs de mes Soixante Ans d'Apostolat dans l'Athabaska-Mackenzie* (Winnepeg, n.d.).

Gutheil, E. A. *The Language of the Dream* (New York, 1939).

Hahn, T. *Tsuni ‖ Goam, The Supreme Being of the Khoi-Khoi* (London, 1881).

Hallowell, A. I. *Aggression in Saulteaux Society* (Psychiatry, vol. 3, pp. 395–407, Washington, 1940).

Hallowell, A. I. *The Rorschach Technique in the Study of Personality and Culture* (American Anthropologist, n.s., vol. 47, pp. 195–209, Menasha, 1945).

Hallowell, A. I. *Some Empirical Aspects of Northern Saulteaux Religion* (American Anthropologist, n.s., vol. 36, pp. 389–404, Menasha, 1934).

Hebb, D. O. *Emotion in Man and Animal: An Analysis of the Intuitive Processes of Recognition* (Psychological Review, vol. 43, pp. 88–106, Lancaster, 1946).

Henry, J. *Jungle People* (New York, 1941).

Hertz, F. *Nationality in History and Politics* (London, 1944).

Hoebel, E. A. *Discussion following presentation of Clyde Kluckhohn's Paper at the Centenary Meeting of the American Ethnological Society* (American Anthropologist, n.s., vol. 45, pp. 227–229, Menasha, 1943).

HONIGMANN, J. J. *A Cultural Theory of Obscenity* (Journal of Criminal Psychopathology, vol. 5, pp. 715–734, Monticello, 1944).

HONIGMANN, J. J. *Ethnography and Acculturation of the Fort Nelson Slave* (Yale University Publications in Anthropology, no. 33, New Haven, 1946).

HONIGMANN, J. J. *Northern and Southern Athapaskan Eschatology* (American Anthropologist, n.s., vol. 47, pp. 467–469, Menasha, 1945).

HONIGMANN, J. J. *Witch-Fear in Post-Contact Kaska Society* (American Anthropologist, n.s.,vol. 49, pp. 222–243, Menasha, 1947).

HONIGMANN, J. J. AND I. HONIGMANN. *Alcoholic Drinking in an Indian-White Community* (Quarterly Journal of Studies on Alcohol, vol. 5, pp. 576–619, New Haven, 1945).

HONIGMANN, J. J., AND I. HONIGMANN. *A Kaska Indian String Oracle* (Man, vol. 47, article 159, London, 1947).

HORNEY, K. *New Ways in Psychoanalysis* (New York, 1939).

HORNEY, K. *Our Inner Conflicts* (New York, 1945).

HORNEY, K. *The Problem of Feminine Masochism* (Psychoanalytic Review, vol. 22, pp. 241–257, Lancaster, 1935).

HUXLEY, J. S., AND A. C. HADDON. *We Europeans* (London, 1935)

ISRAELI, N. *Originality in Planning* (Psychiatry, vol. 8, pp. 139–145, Washington, 1945).

JENNESS, D. *The Indians of Canada* (Bulletin of the Canadian Department of Mines, National Museum of Canada, no. 65, Ottawa, 1932).

JENNESS, D. *The Sekani Indians of British Columbia* (Bulletin of the Canadian Department of Mines and Resources, National Museum of Canada, no. 84, Anthropological Series no. 20, Ottawa, 1937).

JOHNSTON, W. A. *Gold Placers of Dease Lake Area, Cassiar District, B. C.* (Summary Report of the Canadian Department of Mines, Geological Survey, 1925, part A, Ottawa, 1926).

KALLEN, H. M. *Art and Freedom* (New York, 1942).

KARDINER, A. *The Individual and His Society* (New York, 1939).

KARDINER, A. *The Concept of Basic Personality Structure as an Operational Tool in the Social Sciences* (In: Linton, R., ed., *The Science of Man in the World Crisis*. New York, 1945).

KARDINER, A. *The Psychological Frontiers of Society* (New York, 1945).

KLINEBERG, O. *A Science of National Character* (Journal of Social Psychology, S.P.S.S.I. Bulletin, vol. 19, pp. 147–162, Worcester, 1944).

KLOPFER, B. AND D. M. KELLEY. *The Rorschach Technique* (Yonkers, 1942).

KLUCKHOHN, C. *Covert Culture and Administrative Problems* (American Anthropologist, n.s., vol. 45, pp. 213–229, Menasha, 1943).

KLUCKHOHN, C. *Navaho Witchcraft* (Papers of the Peabody Museum of American Archaeology and Ethnology, Harvard University, vol. 22, no. 2, Cambridge, 1944).

KLUCKHOHN, C. *The Personal Document in Anthropological Science* (In: Gottschalk, L., C. Kluckhohn, and R. Angell, *The Use of Personal Documents in History, Anthropology, and Sociology*, New York, 1945).

KLUCKHOHN, C., AND W. H. KELLY. *The Concept of Culture* (In: Linton, R., ed., *The Science of Man in the World Crisis*. New York, 1945).

KRAUSE, A. *Die Tlinkit-Indianer* (Jena, 1885).

KRIGE, E. J., AND J. D. KRIGE. *The Realm of a Rain-Queen* (London, 1943).

KRIGE, J. D. *The Magical Thought-Pattern of the Bantu in Relation to Health Services* (African Studies, vol. 3, pp. 1–13, Johannesburg, 1944).

KROEBER, A. L. *Configurations of Culture Growth* (Berkeley, 1944).

KROEBER, A. L. *Cultural and Natural Areas of Native North America* (University of California Publications in American Archaeology and Ethnology, vol. 38, pp. 1–242, Berkeley, 1939).

LA BARRE, W. *Some Observations on Character Structure in the Orient. The Japanese* (Psychiatry, vol. 8, pp. 319–342, Washington, 1945).

LANDES, R. *The Ethos of the Negro in the New World* (Unpublished manuscript in the Schomburg Collection, New York Public Library, Harlem Branch).

LEES, E. J. *Geology of the Teslin-Quiet Lake Area, Yukon* (Memoirs of the Canadian Department of Mines, Bureau of Economic Geology, Geological Survey, no. 203, Ottawa, 1936).

LEIGHTON, A. *The Governing of Men* (Princeton, 1945).

LEVY, D. M. *Hate as a Disease* (Journal of Educational Sociology, vol. 16, pp. 354–358, New York, 1942–1943).

LEVY, D. M. *Primary Affect Hunger* (American Journal of Psychiatry, vol. 94, pp. 643–652, Toronto, 1937).

LEVY, D. M. *Psychopathic Personality and Crime* (Journal of Educational Sociology, vol. 16, pp. 99–114, New York, 1942–1943).

LINTON, R. *The Cultural Background of Personality* (New York, 1945).

LOWY, S. *Psychological and Biological Foundations of Dream-Interpretation* (London, 1942).

MALINOWSKI, B. *Sex and Repression in Savage Society* (New York, 1927).

MARCHAND, J. F. *Tribal Epidemics in the Yukon* (Journal of the American Medical Association, vol. 143, pp. 1019–1020, Chicago, 1943).

MASLOW, A. H. *Dynamics of Personality Organization* (Psychological Review, vol. 50, pp. 514–558, Princeton, 1943.)

MASLOW, A. H. *Self-Esteem (Dominance-Feeling) and Sexuality in Women* (Journal of Social Psychology, vol. 16, pp. 259–294. Worcester, 1942).

MASLOW, A. H. *A Theory of Human Motivation* (In: Harriman, P. L., ed., *Twentieth Century Psychology*, New York, 1946).

MASLOW, A. H., AND B. MITTELMANN. *Principles of Abnormal Psychology* (New York, 1941).

MASLOW, P. *Rorschach Psychology* (Brooklyn, 1945).

MASLOW, P. *Rorschach Theory* (Brooklyn, 1944).

McCONNELL, R. G. *Report on an Exploration in the Yukon and Mackenzie Basins* (Annual Report of the Geological and Natural History Survey of Canada, n.s., vol. 4, pt. D, Montreal, 1890).

MEAD, M. *And Keep Your Powder Dry* (New York, 1942).

MEAD, M. *Cultural Approach to Personality. Anthropological Comment on the Frame of Reference of Andras Angyal* (Transactions of the New York Academy of Sciences, ser. 2, vol. 6, pp. 93–101, New York, 1943).

MEAD, M. *Educative Effects of Social Environments as Disclosed by Studies of Primitive Societies* (Environment and Education, Supplementary Monographs, no. 54, Chicago, 1942).

MEAD, M. *The Family in the Future* (In: Anshen, R. N., ed., *Beyond Victory*, New York, 1942).

MEAD, M. *The Mountain Arapesh. II. Supernaturalism* (Anthropological Papers of the American Museum of Natural History, vol. 37, pp. 317–452, New York, 1940).

MEAD, M. *Researches in Bali, 1936–1939* (Transactions of the New York Academy of Sciences, ser. 2, vol. 2, pp. 24–31, New York, 1939).

MEAD, M. *Sex and Temperament* (In: Mead, M., *From the South Seas*, New York, 1939).

MILLER, N. E., AND J. DOLLARD. *Social Learning and Imitation* (New Haven, 1941).

MIURA, K. *Ueber japanische Traumdeuterei* (Mitteilungen der deutschen Gesselschaft fuer Natur- und Voelkerkunde Ostasiens,vol. 10, pp. 291–305, Tokyo, 1905).

MONTAGU, M. F. A. *Climate and Reproduction* (Science, vol. 89, pp. 290–292, Cambridge, 1939).

MORICE, A. G. *The Fur Trader in Anthropology: and a Few Related Questions* (American Anthropologist, n.s., vol. 30, pp. 60–84, Menasha, 1928).

MORICE, A. G. *The Nah-ane and Their Language* (Transactions of the Canadian Institute, vol. 7, pp. 517–534, Ottawa, 1900–1903).

MUMFORD, L. *The Culture of Cities* (New York, 1938).

MURDOCK, G. P. *The Common Denominator of Cultures* (In: Linton, R., ed., *The Science of Man in the World Crisis*, New York, 1945).

MURDOCK, G. P., C. S. FORD, A. E. HUDSON, R. KENNEDY, L. W. SIMMONS, AND J. W. M. WHITING. *Outline of Cultural Materials* (Yale Anthropological Studies, vol. 2, New Haven, 1945).

NADEL, S. F. *Review of "Naven"* (Man, vol. 38, pp. 44–46, London, 1938).

NADEL, S. F. *The Typological Approach to Culture* (Character and Personality, vol. 5, pp. 267–284, Durham, 1936–1937).

OLSON, R. L. *Some Trading Customs of the Chilkat Tlingit* (In: *Essays Presented to A. L. Kroeber*, Berkeley, 1936).

OPLER, M. E. *An Interpretation of Ambivalence of Two American Indian Tribes* (Journal of Social Psychology, vol. 7, pp. 82–116, Worcester, 1936).

OPLER, M. E. *Further Comparative Anthropological Data Bearing on the Solution of a Psychological Problem* (Journal of Social Psychology, vol. 9, pp. 477–483, Worcester, 1938).

OPLER, M. E. *Themes as Dynamic Forces in Culture* (American Journal of Sociology, vol. 51, pp. 198–206, Chicago, 1945).

OSGOOD, C. *The Distribution of the Northern Athapaskan Indians* (Yale University Publications in Anthropology, no. 7, New Haven, 1936).

OSGOOD, C. *Ingalik Material Culture* (Yale University Publications in Anthropology, no. 22, New Haven, 1940).

PARSONS, E. C. *Holding Back in Crisis Ceremonialism* (American Anthropologist, n.s., vol. 18, pp. 41–52, Menasha, 1916).

PHILLIPS, L. Unpublished Manuscript dated 1944 (in possession of Irma Honigmann).

PIKE, W. *Through the Subarctic Forest* (London and New York, 1896).

PINART, A. *Notes sur les Koloches* (Bulletin de la Société d'Anthropologie, ser. 2, vol. 7, pp. 788–811, Paris, 1872).

PLAUT, P. *Zur Psychologie der Notzucht und ihre forensische Begutachtung* (Kriminalistische Monatshefte, vol. 4, pp. 106–110, Berlin, 1930).

RATTRAY, R. S. *Religion and Art in Ashanti* (Oxford, 1927).

RIBBLE, M. A. *The Rights of Infants* (New York, 1943).

RICHARDS, A. I. *The Political System of the Bemba Tribe—North-Eastern Rhodesia* (In: Fortes, M., and Evans-Pritchard, E. E., eds., *African Political Systems*, London, 1940).

RITCHIE, J. F. *African as Suckling and Child* (Papers of the Rhodes Livingstone Institute, no. 9, Livingstone, N. R., 1945).

SAPIR, E. *Cultural Anthropology and Psychiatry* (Journal of Abnormal and Social Psychology, vol. 27, pp. 234–235, Boston, 1932).

SAPIR, E. *Culture, Genuine and Spurious* (American Journal of Sociology, vol. 29, pp. 401–430, Chicago, 1925).

SAPIR, E. *The Na-Dene Languages, A Preliminary Report* (American Anthropologist, n.s., vol. 17, pp. 534–558, Menasha, 1915).

SCHACHTEL, E. G. *On Color and Affect* (Psychiatry, vol. 6, pp. 393–409, Washington, 1943).

SCHACHTEL, E. G. *Subjective Definitions of the Rorschach Test Situation and Their Effect on Test Performance* (Psychiatry, vol. 8, pp. 419–448, Washington, 1945).

SCHILDER, P. *Goals and Desires of Man* (New York, 1942).

SETON, E. T. *Lives of Game Animals* (4 vols., Garden City, 1929).

SEWARD, G. H. *Sex and the Social Order* (New York, 1946).

SHARPE, E. F. *Dream Analysis* (New York, 1937).

SIMMONS, L. W. *A Prospectus for Field-Research in the Position and Treatment of the Aged in Primitive and Other Societies* (American Anthropologist, n.s., vol. 47, pp. 433–438, Menasha, 1945).

SKINNER, A., AND J. V. SATTERLEE. *Folklore of the Menomini Indians* (Anthropological Papers of the American Museum of Natural History, vol. 13, pp. 217–546, New York, 1915).

SPIER, L. *The Prophet Dance of the Northwest and its Derivatives* (General Series in Anthropology, vol. 1, Menasha, 1935).

SPENGLER, O. *Decline of the West* (2 vols., New York, 1926).

STAGNER, R. *Psychology of Personality* (New York, 1937).

STEKEL, W. *The Interpretation of Dreams* (2 vols., New York, 1943).

SUMNER, W. G. *Folkways* (Boston, 1906).

SWANTON, J. R. *Social Condition, Beliefs, and Linguistic Relationship of the Tlingit Indians* (Annual Report of the Bureau of American Ethnology, no. 26, Washington, 1908).

TANNENBAUM, F. *On Certain Characteristics of American Democracy* (Political Science Quarterly, vol. 60, pp. 343–350, Boston, 1945).

TEIT, J. A. *Kaska Tales* (Journal of American Folklore, vol. 30, pp. 427–473, Lancaster, 1917).

TEIT, J. A. *On Tahltan (Athabaskan) Work, 1912* (Summary Report of the Canadian Geological Survey, Ottawa, 1912).

TEN KATE, H. *Beitraege zur Kenntnis des japanischen Volksglauben* (Anthropos, vol. 7, pp. 389–406, St. Gabriel-Moedling, 1912).

TOLLEMACHE, S. H. R. L. *Reminiscences of the Yukon* (London, 1912).

VAN LOON, F. H. C., AND R. THURNWALD. *Un questionnaire psycho-physio-morphologique pour l'étude de la psychologie des races* (Revue Anthropologique, vol. 40, pp. 262–277, Paris, 1930).

VOORHIS, E. *Historic Forts and Trading Posts of the French Regime and of the English Fur Trading Companies* (Canadian Department of the Interior, mimeographed, Ottawa, 1930).

Wandlung des Ethos, Die. (Ethos, vol. 1, pp. 1–5, Karlsruhe, i.B., 1925–1926).

WATTS, G. O., AND R. A. WILSON. *A Study of Personality Factors Among Venereal Disease Patients* (Journal of the Canadian Medical Association, vol. 53, pp. 119–122, Toronto, 1945).

WEXBERG, E. *The Psychology of Sex* (New York, 1931).

WHITING, J. W. M. *Becoming a Kwoma* (New Haven, 1941).

WILLIAMS, M. Y. *Geological Investigations Along the Alaska Highway from Fort Nelson, British Columbia, to Watson Lake, Yukon* (Paper of the Canadian Geological Survey, no. 44–28, mimeographed, with map, Ottawa, 1944).

WILSON, G., AND M. WILSON. *The Analysis of Social Change* (Cambridge, 1945).

WILSON, J. A. *Northwest Passage by Air* (Canadian Geographical Journal, vol. 26, pp. 107–129, Ottawa, 1943).

WITTKOWER, E. D., AND J. COWAN. *Some Psychological Aspects of Sexual Promiscuity* (Psychosomatic Medicine, vol. 6, pp. 287–294, Washington, 1944).

YANG, M. C. *A Chinese Village* (New York, 1945).

YOUNG, K. *An Introductory Sociology* (New York, 1934).

EXPLANATION OF PLATES

PLATE 1. *Lower Post, Alaska Highway, and Dease River.*

A, Lower Post as seen from the Liard River. The three buildings to the left belong to the Taku Trading Co. The large white house at the right is the residence of the Hudson's Bay's manager. B, The Taku Trading Company's residence, store, and warehouse along the road that skirts the cutbank. C, The Hudson's Bay Company's store and warehouse fronting the Alaska Highway; built in 1944. D, The confluence of the Dease and Liard Rivers from the high cutbank on the north bank of the Liard.

PLATE 2. *Kaska Indian Men.*

PLATE 3. *Kaska Indian Women.*

PLATE 4. *Parents and Children.*

A, A *métis* with a baby that is three quarters white. B, Shawl packing is a common means of carrying young children. C, A two weeks old infant, securely wrapped. D, Bashful girl. E, The little boy is being toilet trained and wears no pants. F, Young boy.

PLATE 5. *Early to Late Adolescence.*

PLATE 6. *Construction.*

A, The bending frame, used for bending lumber, lying on a piece of semi-tanned hide. B, Bending lumber for a toboggan. The tent in the foreground was used by a very old and partly senile old woman who died in November 1945. C, Building the foundation of a tent frame. D, Constructing a large log cabin with a roof of mill sawed lumber.

PLATE 7. *Transportation and Travel.*

A, Women pack the dogs. B, Wood being hauled upriver on a toboggan. C and D, Making camp and preparing dog food after a winter journey with toboggan and sled. The temperature is about twenty below zero Fahrenheit.

PLATE 8. *Processing Hide.*

A. Fleshing; the women support themselves on a pole stretched across the hide and anchored in the lashing. B, Scraping hair from the hide. C, Smoking a small caribou hide. D, Two girls softening a caribou hide.

PLATE 9. *Enroute to the Bush and Camp Scene.*

A, A demolished camp in Lower Post, showing goods packed and ready for transportation. B, Additional winter supplies are picked up at the store. The truck, hired from a whiteman, will take the outfit to the Highway crossing where boat transportation begins upriver. C, The Liard Indians traveling upriver in a hired boat. D, An autumn camp in the bush. Meat is drying across the extension of the ridge pole.

PLATE 10. *Work, Play, and Snowshoe Bending.*

A, Washing clothes. B, A five year old boy making a rolling toy with the cover of a vacuum tin. C, The violin is a popular musical instrument. D, Snowshoe frames drying in a bending apparatus.

PLATE 11. *Summer Idling.*

A, Purchasing soft drinks. B, Old men sitting in the evening. C and D, Waiting for the boat from Dease Lake to arrive.

PLATE 12. *Death.*

A, The dogs require assistance up the steep ascent to the graveyard. B, Covering the coffin with dress material. C, Preparing the coffin. D, A grave in a winter settlement with a scarf flying as a flag. The temperature when these pictures were taken was about thirty degrees below zero Fahrenheit.

LOWER POST, ALASKA HIGHWAY, AND DEASE RIVER

KASKA INDIAN MEN

KASKA INDIAN WOMEN

PARENTS AND CHILDREN

A

B

C

D

EARLY TO LATE ADOLESCENCE

CONSTRUCTION

TRANSPORTATION AND TRAVEL

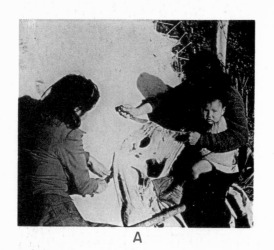

A

B

C

D

PROCESSING HIDE

A

B

C

D

Enroute to the Bush and Camp Scene

WORK, PLAY, AND SNOWSHOE BENDING

B

D

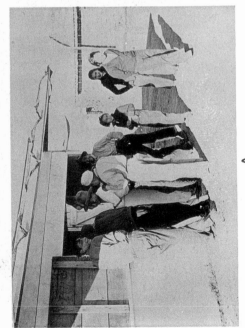

A

C

SUMMER IDLING

A

B

C

D

DEATH

Rosa Lee Walter — end